MW00786980

Dialogues with Davidson

Dialogues with Davidson

Acting, Interpreting, Understanding

edited by Jeff Malpas

The MIT Press
Cambridge, Massachusetts
London, England

For information about special quantity discounts, please email special_sales@mitpress.mit.edu

This book was set in Stone Sans and Stone Serif by Graphic Composition, Inc. Printed and bound in the United States of America.

Library of Congress Cataloging-in-Publication Data

Dialogues with Davidson : acting, interpreting, understanding / edited by Jeff Malpas.
p. cm.
Includes bibliographical references and index.
ISBN 978-0-262-01556-1 (hardcover : alk. paper)
1. Davidson, Donald, 1917–2003. I. Malpas, Jeff.
B945.D384D53 2011
191—dc22
2010049674

10 9 8 7 6 5 4 3 2 1

The analytic method in philosophy . . . provokes argument and when practiced with an open mind it engenders dialogue. At its best, dialogue creates mutual understanding, fresh insights, sympathy with past thinkers, and, occasionally, genuinely new ideas.

—Donald Davidson, "Foreword," in *Two Roads to Wisdom: Chinese and Analytic Philosophical Traditions*, edited by Bo Mou

Contents

Foreword

Dagfinn Føllesdal

What struck me the most about Davidson when we became colleagues at Stanford in 1966 was the wide scope of his interests and abilities. He taught courses ranging from logic and decision theory to ethics, epistemology, philosophy of science, philosophy of language, history of philosophy (ancient, medieval, and modern), philosophy of music, and philosophy and literature. And he enjoyed it. Anything he became interested in he wanted to master, not just in philosophy but in very diverse fields, among them music, where he experimented with various instruments and did well enough on piano to play four-handed with Leonard Bernstein; sports, where he enjoyed skiing, climbing, surfing, flying, and gliding; and practical matters, where he quickly saw how mechanical or electronic devices functioned and could repair them.

It took him long to discover the point of publishing. His first noteworthy article, "Actions, Reasons, and Causes," came in 1963, when he was 46. It has been reprinted in close to thirty anthologies in nine languages and continues to be reprinted and translated. In the following years it was followed by an impressive sequence of highly influential articles. They were collected into volumes, but not until he was 86 did he finish his first little book, *Truth and Predication*, which was published posthumously. (His 1949 dissertation on Plato's *Philebus* was published in 1990.) There is probably no other philosopher who has been comparably influential just on the basis of articles.

Davidson told me that a seminar he took with Quine as a first year graduate student changed his attitude to philosophy. Since then his general outlook to philosophy was very close to Quine's, but there are important differences. I will mention the three I consider the most important.

First, Davidson made use of Tarski's theory of truth to account for how sentences are interconnected in our web of belief. Quine, in *Word and Object*, especially in section 3, talks about our cutting sentences into words that can be combined in new ways to make sentences we have never heard before. However, he does not take up the semantic nature of these interconnections between sentences. Davidson made use of Tarski's theory of truth for this purpose. Very many linguistic constructions, for example adverbs, were not covered by Tarski's theory, and Davidson initiated a program to show how Tarski's theory could be extended to these further constructions.

Second, Davidson developed what he called "a unified theory of thought and action." In his early work on decision making he noticed that a person's behavior can be explained by different combinations of beliefs and values and that the behavior does not enable us to pin down one of these combinations as the correct one. Quine's "indeterminacy of translation" similarly reflects the fact that a person's assent to or dissent from sentences can be accounted for through different combinations of beliefs and meaning. Both indeterminacies can be reduced by noticing that the two pairs, beliefs/values and beliefs/meaning, have one component in common, namely belief. Thereby observation of action can help us to narrow down indeterminacy of translation, and observation of assent and dissent can help constrain our explanations of action.

Third, Davidson objected to the role that perception plays in Quine's theory of translation. There are two stages here in Davidson's opposition to Quine.

The first stage ran until 1973. Until then, Davidson argued that translation should aim solely at "maximizing agreement." Quine had put forth two kinds of constraints on translation, one based on stimulations of our sensory receptors and one that he called "the principle of charity," roughly: never attribute to the other views that are obviously absurd. The first of these constraints leads to great difficulties, and Davidson proposed to drop it in favor of a strengthened principle of charity: translate the other in such a way that you come out agreeing on as many points as possible. (Davidson preferred focusing on interpretation, rather than translation, but that difference does not matter as far as these issues are concerned.)

In 1973, faced with the example of "the rabbit behind the tree," Davidson admitted that perception has to play a role in translation and interpretation. (Briefly: if you have formed the hypothesis that 'Gavagai' should be translated as 'Rabbit' and your native friend dissents when you utter 'Gavagai' in the neighborhood of a rabbit, you will not regard this as going against your hypothesis if the rabbit is hidden to the native behind a big tree.) Davidson never talked about maximizing agreement after 1973. After some years of reflection he came up with the idea of "triangulation," which he discussed in several of his later articles. This idea was a major topic of discussion between Davidson, Quine, Dreben, and myself in a five-day closed session at Stanford in 1986.

The first two of these three differences between Quine and Davidson are in my opinion valuable improvements of Quine's view. The third difference, however, is more complicated. Clearly, the "maximize agreement" thesis had to be given up. In view of the "rabbit behind the tree" example, we should say "maximize agreement where you should expect agreement." That is, we have to ask: What beliefs would it be likely that the other person has, given her present and past experiences, upbringing, and culture? This means that meaning and communication presuppose epistemology. The converse also holds; we have holism all the way down.

The difference between Davidson and Quine after Davidson turned to triangulation is often labeled the "distal/proximal disagreement." It is often said that Quine focused on the proximal, stimulations of our nerve endings, whereas Davidson focused on the distal, the objects perceived. However, things are not that simple. Already in the very opening sentences of *Word and Object* Quine stated the distal view. He stressed how language learning builds on distal objects, the objects that we perceive and talk about:

> Each of us learns his language from other people, through the observable mouthing of words under conspicuously intersubjective circumstances. Linguistically, and hence conceptually, the things in sharpest focus are the things that are public enough to be talked of publicly, common and conspicuous enough to be talked of often, and near enough to sense to be quickly identified and learned by name; it is to these that words apply first and foremost.[1]

Why, then, did Quine turn to stimuli? He saw, I think, clearer than it had ever been seen before, how intricate the notion of an object is. We cannot determine through observation which objects other people perceive; what others perceive is dependent upon how they conceive of the world and structure it, and that is just what we are trying to find out. When we study communication and understanding, we should not uncritically assume that the other shares our conception of the world and our ontology. If we do, we will not discover how we understand other people, and we will not notice the important phenomena of indeterminacy of translation and of reference. Already in chapter 3 of *Word and Object*, the chapter following the one where he introduces stimuli, Quine discusses the ontogenesis of reference, and the discussion of this topic takes up several of the following chapters.

Introducing epistemology is also needed in order to get beyond the simple perceptual triangular situations; we may interpret sentences that relate to situations and objects that we have not perceived and cannot perceive, and sentences produced by people who are not around to triangulate with us. As pointed out by Lee Braver in his contribution to this volume, this enables us to bring in perspectives that are very alien to us, historically and/or culturally very distant. It also helps us to see why Quine in his discussions with Davidson emphasized the possibility of radically different perspectives.

What is needed for an adequate view on communication and understanding is therefore a satisfactory theory of perception, which takes properly into account the theory-ladenness of perception, including a theory of reification and the "constitution" of objects, to use a word from Husserl. Quine saw this and devoted many of his later years to this topic.

This intricate nexus of issues is now receiving much attention following Quine and Davidson's work. Davidson, who as a student had concentrated on literature and classics, applied these ideas to issues in the interpretation of literature. He wrote on metaphors, on the role of speaker's intention and on "locating literary language," and also on James Joyce and on the minimalist artist Robert Morris. Also, where Quine discussed translation, Davidson focused on interpretation. This made it easy to connect him with the hermeneutic tradition, particularly the new hermeneutics, Heidegger and Gadamer and their followers. Gadamer, in particular, was a natural point of contact. His *Truth and Method* takes up many of the same issues as are discussed by Davidson, and Davidson read Gadamer's habilitation thesis on Plato's *Philebus* while he was writing his own dissertation on the same topic. Davidson tells that when he wrote his dissertation, "the only commentary that seemed to me to have any philosophical merit was Hans-Georg Gadamer's dissertation, written very much under the influence of Heidegger."[2] However, he also states that he "unfortunately learned very little from Gadamer."[3]

Gadamer's comments on Davidson made it clear that he had not read him. The same holds for most of the other figures discussed in this volume, such as Heidegger and Derrida. The similarities and differences that are discussed are therefore not due to influence, but rather result from the topics that are discussed and the way they are interconnected: meaning, interpretation, action, the mind, self-knowledge, subjectivity, intersubjectivity, objectivity, relativism, representation, realism, externalism, certainty, and truth. These are all interconnected in Davidson, and many of these interconnections are also found in some of these other philosophers.

These interconnections are especially prominent in Husserl. His studies of subjectivity inspired much of what has been called "continental" philosophy. However, many of his followers were extreme relativists and did not note that Husserl went on to give one of the most careful and detailed studies of intersubjectivity and objectivity that has ever been given. For him, as for Davidson, subjectivity, intersubjectivity, and objectivity were intimately intertwined. Also, Davidson's holism and his nonfoundationalism have their parallels in Husserl. Many readers get misled by Husserl's seemingly foundationalist statements. However, he had a very carefully developed nonfoundationalist view, and he also saw an intimate connection between scientific theory and what he called the lifeworld:

> everything which contemporary natural science has furnished as determinations of what exists also belong to us, to the world, as this world is pregiven to the adults of our time. And even if we are not personally interested in natural science, and even if we know nothing of its results, still, what exists is pregiven to us in advance as determined in such a way that we at least grasp it as being in principle scientifically determinable.[4]

A detailed study of similarities and differences between Davidson and Husserl would be interesting, especially since Husserl inspired so much of what has been going on in continental philosophy. Thus, for example, many of Gadamer's points about interpretation, for which Gadamer gives credit to Heidegger, are found with more richness and more precision in Husserl, where they are set into a broader philosophical context that has many striking similarities with what we find in Davidson—but also many differences, which are well worth reflection.

Notes

1. Quine, *Word and Object* (Cambridge, MA: MIT Press, 1960), p. 1.

2. Davidson, "Intellectual Autobiography," in *The Philosophy of Donald Davidson*, ed. Lewis Edwin Hahn, Library of Living Philosophers, vol. 27 (Chicago: Open Court, 1999), p. 27.

3. See Robert Dostal's essay in this volume for more on this issue.

4. Edmund Husserl, *Erfahrung und Urteil*, ed. Ludwig Landgrebe (Prag: Academia/ Verlagsbuchhandlung, 1939), section 10, p. 39; *Experience and Judgment*, trans. J. Churchill and K. Ameriks (Evanston: Northwestern University Press, 1973), p. 42. For more on Husserl's nonfoundationalism, see my "Husserl on Evidence and Justification," in *Edmund Husserl and the Phenomenological Tradition: Essays in*

Phenomenology, ed. Robert Sokolowski (proceedings of a lecture series in the fall of 1985), *Studies in Philosophy and the History of Philosophy*, vol. 18 (Washington: The Catholic University of America Press, 1988), pp. 107–129; see also my "Husserl and Wittgenstein on Ultimate Justification," in *Experience and Analysis. Erfahrung und Analyze*, ed. Johann Christian Marek and Maria Elisabeth Reicher, Proceedings of the 27th International Wittgenstein Symposium, August 8–14, 2004 (Wien: hpt et öbv, 2005), pp. 127–142.

Acknowledgments

This volume took much longer in preparation that I could ever have anticipated, while its final publication was also further delayed by some unexpected developments. I am grateful to all of the contributors for having been so cooperative in working with me over the time it took to get this volume from its initial inception to the final printing. I would especially like to thank Dagfinn Føllesdal for agreeing to provide the foreword for the volume, and also to express my gratitude to Richard Rorty for sending me his short piece on Davidson at a time when he was already too sick even to revise or expand it. Rorty, like Davidson himself, is greatly missed. I am grateful to Nicholas Malpas for his assistance with translation and other matters, and especially to my wife Margaret for her continuing support in this work as in much else. Thanks are also due to the School of Philosophy at the University of Tasmania, and my colleagues there, especially Ingo Farin and Lucy Tatman; to the Department of Philosophy at LaTrobe University, particularly Andrew Brennan and Norva Lo; to Philip Laughlin at MIT Press for his assistance in finally getting the volume into print; and to many other colleagues, some of whom are included here, most notably, Fred Stoutland, Gordan Brittan, and Louise Röska-Hardy. I would also like to thank the Australian Research Council for providing funding for the Fellowship of which this volume is one result. Finally, this volume constitutes some small repayment of the enormous debt I owe to both Marcia Cavell, and, of course, to Donald Davidson himself. Not only was Don an inspiring philosopher, he was unfailingly generous and supportive, and always ready to listen to new and interesting ideas—even if they might sometimes have seemed to come from an unexpected quarter.

Introduction: Davidson and Contemporary Thought

Jeff Malpas

The second half of the twentieth century may well be viewed by subsequent historians of philosophy as something of a golden age for English-speaking philosophy, especially in the United States. The influx of European philosophers into the United States from the 1930s onward gave an enormous boost to philosophical thinking in a number of schools and traditions (and not only the "analytic"), while the influence of American pragmatism also developed in a more expansive way, permeating the work of many thinkers who would not have taken the label for themselves. Two figures stand out as especially important in this "golden age": Willard van Orman Quine and Donald Herbert Davidson. The work of these two thinkers is inextricably linked, and yet in spite of the enormous commonality between them, Davidson's work is also quite distinct from, and sometimes opposed to, that of Quine.

Whereas Quine remained within a much more readily recognizable philosophical framework, Davidson's thought has always been harder to pin down, and the formative influences upon him, apart from that of Quine himself, sometimes difficult to discern. Quine's own thinking was essentially defined by the problems and approaches set down by the new empiricist philosophies of science and language that had their origin in the first half of the century, most notably, of course, in the work of thinkers such as Carnap, Schlick, and Neurath; Davidson, on the other hand, was more a product of his early work in psychology and decision theory, and of the Oxbridge philosophers with whom he was in contact from the late 1950s onward (perhaps there was also some residual effect from his undergraduate training in literature and the history of ideas, although, if so, it remained very much in the background[1]). Moreover, whereas Davidson's work from the 1960s and 1970s has the appearance of a certain sort of technical philosophical analysis based in a relatively formal approach to issues of language, action, and mind, the way that work develops in the

1980s, 1990s, and into the new millennium, while undoubtedly continuous with the earlier work, also exhibits a much broader perspective, a more idiosyncratic style, and an engagement with a wider range of problems and approaches. In this respect, it is notable that the contemporary philosopher with whom Davidson saw himself as having most in common in his later years was Richard Rorty.[2]

There is, however, a clear tendency in the reading of Davidson that has arisen since his sudden and unexpected death in 2003 to advance a much narrower interpretation of his work that gives priority to the earlier essays over any of the later writings and the broader style of thinking that they develop. Such a reading seems characteristic of the extensive treatment of Davidson that has been developed by Ernest Lepore and Kirk Ludwig. Critical of many of the more encompassing claims that characterize Davidson's thinking, they advance a picture of what is valuable in Davidson's work that focuses on his earlier work in philosophy of action and philosophy of language, and especially on his work in truth-theoretic semantics.[3] Their somewhat restricted approach (an approach that, not surprisingly, runs counter to Davidson's own sense of the structure of his thought) has led one reviewer of their 2005 volume, *Donald Davidson: Meaning, Truth, Language, and Reality*,[4] to write that "Readers should be warned that one is likely to finish this book feeling depressed about Davidson's achievement,"[5] since, on the account offered by Lepore and Ludwig, a good deal of Davidson's thinking appears mistaken or even confused. One need not agree with a philosopher, of course, to recognize his or her significance, but readings that do not, at the very least, try to engage with the overall framework of a philosopher's thinking, and that attribute too much in the way of misunderstanding and fundamental error to that thinking, are also likely to lead to a diminished sense of its philosophical worth—a somewhat paradoxical outcome, given the amount of attention that writers such as Lepore and Ludwig seem willing to give to Davidson's work. Such readings are also, as the underlying conception of hermeneutic engagement that is expressed in the principle of charity would suggest, likely to create significant difficulties in understanding. Indeed, in Davidson's case, the account offered by Lepore and Ludwig essentially seems to forgo any attempt to make overall sense of Davidson's thought—at least in a way that encompasses the later thinking as much as the earlier.

The response to Davidson that is exemplified in the work of Lepore and Ludwig is itself partly driven by Lepore and Ludwig's own more particular philosophical interests—interests that already incline them toward the earlier and more technical essays. In its general form, however, it also seems to constitute a reaction to the various attempts to read Davidson, along with contemporaries such as Putnam and Rorty, as part of a "postanalytic" development in late-twentieth-century American philosophy, and explicitly to connect his thought with that of philosophers from outside the usual analytic canon. This is a phenomenon that Davidson himself acknowledged, if with a certain puzzlement, in the early 1990s, although his puzzlement was perhaps more at the association of his thinking with the idea of some form of "postphilosophical" development, than at the connection with other thinkers as such. In the catalog essay for Robert Morris's *Blind Time* drawings, Davidson writes:

> This is not the first time I have found my writing in unexpected surroundings: nothing has surprised me more than to discover myself anthologized in books with titles such as *Post-Analytic Philosophy* or *After Philosophy*. That *after* haunts me again in an about-to-be-published book with the title *Literary Theory After Davidson*. Is there something sinister, or at least fin de siècle, in my views that I have failed to recognize, something that portends the dissolution not only of the sort of philosophy I do but of philosophy itself? Why else would I find my name linked with Heidegger and Derrida?[6]

In this respect, the more restrictive reading of Davidson's work can itself be seen as part of an attempt, not only to rescue his own thinking from such "fin de siècle" associations, and but also as operating against certain forms of philosophical pluralism or ecumenicalism that would seek to find points of contact between the so-called analytic and continental modes of contemporary philosophy.

The idea that underpins this volume runs directly counter to this reactive tendency—whether expressed in terms of a narrowing in the reading of Davidson's own work or in a narrowing of philosophical perspectives in general. While it should not be viewed as necessarily endorsing the fin de siècle or postphilosophical reading that puzzles Davidson in the passage quoted above, the volume is oriented toward an appreciation of the significance of Davidson's work as it extends beyond the narrowly analytic, thereby also bringing it into an engagement with other aspects of contemporary thought—and not only the "continental." In the case of some of the essays here, that involves showing the way in which Davidson's work can be understood as convergent with other approaches and styles of thinking; in other cases, the argument is made for significant differences between Davidson and, for instance, thinkers such as Gadamer and Heidegger. Nevertheless, the very fact that such convergence and divergence can appear as an issue is itself indicative of the way in which Davidson's philosophy participates in a much wider philosophical conversation than just that of, for instance, semantic theory alone. It also indicates the real philosophical significance and fruitfulness of Davidson's wide-ranging and sometimes idiosyncratic mode of thought.

Although Davidson stands as one of the central figures in twentieth-century Anglo-American analytic philosophy, and his early work in philosophy of language was once seen to constitute a well-defined research program, Davidson always occupied a position that was independent of the philosophical orthodoxy around him, and often he stood directly counter to that orthodoxy. It is almost always a mistake to read Davidson, a truly individual thinker, in ways that assume too much or that take the vocabulary and conceptual framework that he employs as already given and understood—one has to approach his work on its own terms, in a way that is attentive to the particular character of his arguments as well as to the overall tenor of his thinking and is always prepared for the possibility that things are not what they may, at first, have seemed.

Although Davidson promised book-length treatments of various topics (at different times a book was presaged on ethics, on objectivity, and finally on predication, only the last of which was realized), the vast majority of his work is in essay form—essays that were almost always written as the result of specific requests and invitations. Moreover, many readers remain familiar with Davidson largely through the essays contained in the first two volumes of his work, *Essays on Actions and Events* and *Inquiries into Truth and Interpretation*, published now over twenty years ago, in 1982 and 1984, respectively. Of the other three volumes of collected essays, only one was published before his death, with the remaining two, together with the short monograph, *Truth and Predication*, published posthumously.[7] The result is that there is often a tendency toward a rather piecemeal appreciation of Davidson's writing—something that Davidson himself recognized as a problem—with many readers knowing his ideas only as set out in an individual essay or group of essays, and with particular aspects of Davidson's thinking often being treated in separation from his thought in general, and without regard to any broader overarching horizon. Although one might argue that some of the essays contained here also continue this tendency, for the most part they treat of Davidson's thinking in a way that does attempt to understand it from a broader perspective, and in a way that takes up the overall patterns of thinking that run across his work as a whole.

One of the difficulties in approaching Davidson's work, increasingly so in later years, is that it resists simple compartmentalization. His essays on one topic will typically draw on ideas developed in relation to another, and his thinking, even if developed in separate essays, actually exhibits a high degree of interconnection and integration. The lack of easy thematic separation in Davidson's work is itself evident in the overlapping character of the essays contained here. The volume is loosely organized into three broad sections: "On Language, Mind, and World"; "On Interpretation and Understanding"; and "On Action, Reason, and Knowledge." Under these three headings are included essays that deal with issues in philosophy of language and mind, philosophy of action, metaphysics, epistemology, and ethics, and the approaches adopted range from the hermeneutic and phenomenological to the feminist and the sociotheoretic. Davidson's thinking is also brought into explicit connection with that of a number of other thinkers, including Collingwood, Kant, Derrida (and, although not directly thematized, Wittgenstein), as well as Heidegger and Gadamer.

The latter conjunction is the main focus for at least five of the essays contained here, and this reflects not only the interpretive focus on Davidson's own work, which naturally suggests comparisons with Gadamer's own philosophical hermeneutics, but also a level of personal engagement between them. It was Gadamer who nominated Davidson for the Hegel Prize awarded in Stuttgart in 1991, and the two corresponded during the 1990s. Gadamer also invited Davidson to contribute to his Library of Living Philosophers volume,[8] but the result was not especially productive[9]—an outcome that was probably not surprising given the differences in background that separated them (and in this regard, the lack of fruitfulness in the engagement between Davidson and Gadamer—an engagement in which each seems to pass the other by—was not peculiar to their encounter alone, but seems characteristic of many such attempts to speak across cultural and philosophical divides[10]). The question as to how Davidson's thought may relate to that of Gadamer is one that is variously answered by the different contributions here—where some of the essays, my own included, argue for important points of convergence in the approaches of the two thinkers, others argue for a deeper level of disagreement, in some cases suggesting that there are certain intrinsic limitations in Davidson's approach as opposed to that of Gadamer. This volume does not, of course, aim at a resolution of such apparently divergent judgments—the aim, as I indicated above, is simply to open up a more encompassing philosophical space in which Davidson's work can be approached. Certainly, the issue of Davidson's relation to Gadamer, and to hermeneutic thinking more generally, has yet to be properly explored, and though the essays contained here provide important steps in the direction of such an exploration, they by no means constitute a definitive survey of the territory.

Although Davidson expressed bemusement at the unexpected circumstances in which his work was sometimes taken up, he also offered a possible explanation for the juxtaposition of his name with that of philosophers such as Heidegger and Derrida. The answer, he said, "may turn on my rejection of subjectivist theories of epistemology and meaning, and my conviction that thought is essentially social."[11] Both of these themes are taken up by Richard Rorty in the short essay that opens the volume,[12] and they connect not only to the naturalistic form of anti-Cartesianism that is Rorty's focus, but also to the externalism and holism that characterize much of Davidson's thinking, especially his later work. These themes run through many of the essays included here, and they connect discussions of Davidson's views on language, mind, and world with his approach to action, understanding, and knowledge. Indeed, rather than making up merely one strand in Davidson's thinking, these themes appear to constitute its very heart. Part of the underlying argument of this volume is the need to situate Davidson within a wider philosophical framework, but also that it is only by looking to his antisubjectivism, to his social conception of thought and meaning, and to the holist and externalist elements with which these are combined, that the broader philosophical significance of Davidson's thought properly becomes evident. These, of course, are also the very aspects of Davidson's work that have generated the greatest, and certainly the most wide-ranging, interest, both positive and negative, within contemporary philosophy and beyond (Davidson himself was particular pleased by the way his work was taken up in literary theory[13]), but it is significant that these are also the aspects of his work that increasingly preoccupied Davidson himself—as his own comments make clear. This is not to say that the interest in more specific issues in, for instance, the philosophy of language disappears from Davidson's work, but rather that he came to see those issues as inevitably connected up with, and as leading toward, a much larger set of issues involving the relation between meaning, thought, and world—a connection and direction made particularly evident in *Truth and Predication*.

There are few philosophers who have made so many important and influential interventions in such a range of philosophical debates as has Donald Davidson. Not only was his work at the center of new developments in truth-theoretic semantics, but he also made groundbreaking and often provocative contributions to almost every other area in which he engaged. This breadth of contribution and of influence is clearly shown by the range of topics discussed in the essays here, but they also demonstrate that the continuing relevance of Davidson's thought, and perhaps also its lasting significance, is not merely to be found in the power or persuasiveness that may attach to particular ideas, but also in the multiplicity of connections those ideas engender, in the stimulation that they offer, and in the conversations that they provoke.

Notes

1. Davidson was, for a time in the 1930s, a student of Alfred North Whitehead, but it is only in his later essays that something of the historical orientation associated with a Whiteheadian approach reemerged in Davidson's thinking—although it was far removed from Whitehead's own. Moreover, as Gordon Brittan comments in chapter 4 of this volume, when Davidson did reread Whitehead later in his career, there was little that he found useful for his own thinking.

2. Rorty himself acknowledged an enormous debt to Davidson, writing in the introduction to the first volume of his *Philosophical Papers* that "I have come to think of Davidson's work as deepening and extending the lines of thought traced by Sellars and Quine. So I have been writing more and more about Davidson—trying to clarify his views to myself, to defend them against possible and actual objection, and to extend them into areas which Davidson himself has not yet explored." Rorty, *Objectivity, Relativism, and Truth: Philosophical Papers*, vol. 1 (Cambridge: Cambridge University Press, 1991), p. 1. Davidson also acknowledged the proximity of Rorty's thinking to his own—in conversation, if not explicitly in print—noting that Rorty one of the very few people who had a good understanding of his work.

3. For an outline of their approach see the introduction to Lepore and Ludwig, *Donald Davidson: Meaning, Truth, Language, and Reality* (Oxford: Clarendon Press, 2005), pp. 1–18.

4. This volume is one of a number of works that Lepore and Ludwig have produced since Davidson's death, including a second jointly authored monograph, *Donald Davidson's Truth-Theoretic Semantics* (New York: Oxford University Press, 2007), as well as two edited volumes, one by Ludwig (but with contributions by Lepore), *Donald Davidson* (New York: Cambridge University Press, 2003), and one edited jointly by Lepore and Ludwig, *The Essential Davidson* (New York: Oxford University Press, 2006), the latter comprising a selection of Davidson's essays from the period up until the mid-1980s (a selection that seems to reflect Lepore and Ludwig's own assessment of the essence of Davidson's thought). In many respects, Lepore's collaboration with Ludwig, and the critical perspective on Davidson's work that it sets forth, can be seen to be a continuation of Lepore's earlier collaboration with Jerry Fodor in *Holism: A Shopper's Guide* (New York: Blackwell, 1992), in which Davidson was a major target (Davidson himself conducted a graduate seminar in Berkeley in the summer of 1993 in which he made very clear his deep unhappiness with the way his work had been treated in the book). Significantly, however, Lepore was also responsible for the two

crucial volumes from the 1980s that did much to cement Davidson's philosophical reputation—*Actions and Events: Perspectives of the Philosophy of Donald Davidson*, ed. Ernest Lepore and Brian McLaughlin (Oxford: Blackwell, 1988), and *Truth and Interpretation: Perspectives on the Philosophy of Donald Davidson*, ed. Ernest Lepore (Oxford: Blackwell, 1986)—while Lepore also played a significant role in the posthumous publication of Davidson's work.

5. James W. Garson, "Review of Ernest Lepore and Kirk Ludwig, *Donald Davidson: Meaning, Truth, Language, and Reality*," *Notre Dame Philosophical Reviews*, <http://ndpr.nd.edu/review.cfm?id=5681> (accessed March 2009). See also Frederick Stoutland's review essay on Lepore and Ludwig's 2005 volume, "A Mistaken View of Davidson's Legacy: A Critical Notice of Earnest Lepore and Kirk Ludwig, *Donald Davidson: Meaning, Truth, Language, and Reality*," *International Journal of Philosophical Studies* 14 (2006): 579–596, as well as the ensuring exchange, Ernest Lepore and Kirk Ludwig, "Radical Misinterpretation: A Reply to Stoutland," *International Journal of Philosophical Studies* 15 (2007): 557–585, and Frederick Stoutland, "Radical Misinterpretation Indeed: Response to Lepore and Ludwig," *International Journal of Philosophical Studies* 15 (2007): 587–597.

6. Donald Davidson, "The Third Man," in *Truth, Language, and History* (Oxford: Clarendon Press, 2005), p. 159.

7. The publications are as follows: *Essays on Actions and Events* (Oxford: Clarendon Press, 1980; 2nd ed., 2001); *Inquiries into Truth and interpretation* (Oxford: Clarendon Press, 1984; 2nd ed., 2001); *Subjective, Intersubjective, Objective* (Oxford: Clarendon Press, 2001); *Problems of Rationality* (Oxford: Clarendon Press, 2004); *Truth, Language, and History* (Oxford: Clarendon Press, 2005); *Truth and Predication* (Cambridge, MA: Harvard University Press, 2005).

8. See Davidson, "Gadamer and Plato's *Philebus*," in *Truth, Language, and History*, pp. 261–276. Although Davidson was unsure as to how he might engage with Gadamer's work, I suspect he felt a certain sense of obligation that meant he could not refuse the request. He took the task up with some seriousness, however, attempting, with difficulty, to read *Truth and Method*.

9. See Davidson's essay ("Gadamer and Plato's *Philebus*"), and Gadamer's reply, in *The Philosophy of Hans-Georg Gadamer*, ed. Lewis Edwin Hahn, The Library of Living Philosophers, vol. 24 (Chicago: Open Court, 1997), pp. 421–432 and 433–436.

10. Indeed, it is perhaps worth noting that Gadamer's other efforts at philosophical conversation—with figures such as Derrida and Habermas—have, for the most part, been no more successful than his engagement with Davidson (and sometimes have been even less so). Moreover, it seems to me that this is not due to any philosophical failure on Gadamer's part, but simply a function of the inevitable difficulties of interpersonal engagement—difficulties that are as much to do with contingent features of personality and behavior than with any necessary philosophical predisposition.

11. "The Third Man," p. 159.

12. The only essay that has appeared previously, the piece was originally written by Rorty as a philosophical obituary for Davidson, appearing in the *Boston Globe* on October 5, 2003, under the title "Out of the Matrix: How the Late Philosopher Donald Davidson Showed That Reality Can't Be an Illusion."

13. See *Literary Theory After Davidson*, ed. Reed Way Dasenbrook (University Park: Pennsylvania State University Press, 1989).

I On Language, Mind, and World

1 Davidson versus Descartes

Richard Rorty

Maybe life is a dream. Maybe reality is utterly different from what it appears to human beings to be. Maybe human language is inadequate to represent it. Maybe our minds simply cannot grasp what is going on. Maybe we are brains in vats, being fed electrical impulses by computers—impulses that alter our brain states and thereby create pseudo-experiences, and beliefs about a world that does not exist.

This string of skeptical "maybes" is our heritage from René Descartes, the seventeenth-century philosopher who first saddled us with the idea that what goes on in our minds might have nothing to do what was going on outside them. Donald Davidson did his best to dissipate this Cartesian fantasy, providing us with an account of language and mind that provides no foothold for Cartesian skepticism.

One of Davidson's central doctrines was that most beliefs—anybody's beliefs—must be true. Consider beliefs about beavers. If you don't believe that beavers are good swimmers, that they are smaller than tigers but larger than moles, that they have flat tails and gnaw down trees, then you do not have beliefs *about beavers* at all. You have to know a lot about something, Davidson pointed out, before you can have any false beliefs about it. Descartes could doubt that he was really sitting at a desk, but he could only do so because he knew that desks were things human beings could sit at and write on, that they were usually made of wood, and so on and on. If he managed to doubt all these commonplaces at once, he would not have been having doubts *about desks*.

The same goes for the possibility that life is a dream. Before you can ponder this suggestion, you have to know that people have dreams when asleep, that the dreams do not cohere very well with what happens when you are awake, and so on. A great deal of such knowledge is contained in your ability to use the word "dream." Analogously, before you can begin to worry about whether you are a brain in a vat, you have to know a lot about brains, vats, computers, electricity, neurology, evil scientists, and the like.

Davidson, however, had a more striking and more original objection to the suggestion that we might be brains in vats—one that cuts deeper. To see his point, consider the case of a brain that has been raised from infancy in a vat, continuously fed with electrical impulses from a computer in whose data banks repose the results of telemetered scans of the brain of some unvatted person—you, for example. The result is to copy your brain states into the neural works of the vatted brain. When stimulated in certain ways, a loudspeaker attached to the vatted brain's language center makes noises like "I'm strolling down the beach" and "I'm eating tofu." The evil scientist chuckles with glee at the thought that the hopelessly deluded brain thinks it is living your life.

Davidson thought such glee unjustified. Why, he asked, think that if you duplicate brain states you duplicate thoughts? To assume that you do is like assuming that you can read off the program state of a computer from its hardware state. But to know what program a computer is running you need to do more than keep track of the ones and zeros that are flicking about inside it. You have to know about the computer's environment—in particular, who has programmed it to do what.

The evil scientist is mistaken, Davidson claimed, to think that the noises on the loudspeaker tell her what the vatted brain is thinking. Why interpret noises made by something that has had no dealings with beaches and tofu as sentences referring to beaches and tofu? Consider, he suggested, how an anthropologist goes about learning the language of a hitherto unknown tribe. She correlates noise with features of the environment: if members of the tribe go "grok" only when a beaver surfaces, for example, it is likely that "grok" means "beaver" in their language. You should, Davidson suggested, treat the brain in the vat as the anthropologist treats members of the new tribe.

That brain too is reacting to features of its environment. But its environment is the computer's data bank. The only way you can translate the noises it makes is to correlate them with the bits of data that the computer is feeding in. So the noises that sounds like "It's Tuesday the 7th of October, 2003, and I am eating tofu" must mean something like "Now I am hooked up to sector 43762 of the hard drive." For most of the envatted brain's beliefs, like most of ours, must be true. It is not as easy to delude a brain as the evil scientist thinks.

This is because the point of attributing a particular belief or thought to a person, or to a computer, is to predict what it will do in response to various environmental situations. If the beliefs you ascribe to something have no relevance to such predictions, then you are attributing the wrong beliefs. Attribution of thoughts to others is not a matter of guessing what is currently going on inside them—what is visible to the eye of their introspecting mind in those private places that Daniel Dennett (another distinguished contemporary anti-Cartesian) mockingly calls "Cartesian theaters." Instead, it is a matter of figuring what the other person is likely to do under what circumstances—of correlating its behavior with ours and with that of non-human things (a process Davidson called "triangulation").

This means that people only start having minds, and begin thinking, when they learn languages. If an organism doesn't start triangulating, and thereby start picking up a language, it will remain incapable of thought. Analogously, a piece of hardware that hasn't been programmed will just sit there, never doing any computation. Language and thought are interpersonal phenomena. Descartes, unfortunately, did not realize that being rational is not something any organism could possibly do on its own. It takes a community. As Davidson put it, "only social exchange can explain the fact that our thoughts and utterances can be true or false."

For followers of Descartes, who include most philosophers of the past three hundred years (and, alas, many contemporary philosophers as well), mentality precedes language: you start off thinking, and then you get in touch with other people, with whose assistance you learn to think better. You are always watching the screen in your inner theater, but what is displayed there gets more interesting after you engage in social interaction. Davidson argued that if you start off with that unfortunate Cartesian picture in mind, all those skeptical "maybes" will seem inevitable and irresolvable. But if instead you think of human beings as animals whose extra neurons provide the hardware necessary to install rather complicated programs you will be unable to make sense of Cartesian skepticism.

If you see things from Davidson's angle, mentality will look like a set of capacities for dealing with other people and with the non-human environment, rather than like the ability to enter a private realm, one that may have nothing to do with the real world. You will think of "the real world" simply as a name for a highly miscellaneous collection—all the familiar things that we have true and false beliefs about: for example, beavers, atoms, desks, numbers, virtues, people, stars, and governments. You will cease to think of it as something remote and mysterious—something from which we might be cut off by the weakness of our minds, or the limitations of our language.

Davidson's views are still highly controversial, but few philosophers would contest that his ideas are brilliantly original and that his arguments need to be pondered. Inspired by the work of Ludwig Wittgenstein and Willard van Orman Quine, Davidson went far beyond his teachers. Their writings and his, taken together with those of Wilfrid Sellars and Robert Brandom, have helped make possible what Davidson called "a sea-change" in the way we think about what it is to be a human being.

Davidson was a philosopher's philosopher. He never wrote for the general public. His marvelously concise and carefully chiseled arguments are not easily grasped even by specialists. But his ideas are gradually being appropriated in larger and larger intellectual circles. Histories of twentieth-century philosophy will have to include a sizable chapter on Davidson.

2 What Subjectivity Isn't

David Couzens Hoy and Christoph Durt

Donald Davidson is not studied quite as much for his account of subjectivity as he is for his philosophy of language or his theory of action. Yet the latter aspects of his thought are not completely understood without understanding the conception of subjectivity that goes along with them. The implications of Davidson's account of the mental are far-reaching and radical. In particular, his revision of the Cartesian conception of subjectivity changes much of what philosophers can say about the mind.

Of course, Davidson is not alone in his interest in subjectivity and his critique of Cartesianism. Subjectivity has also been a central concern in the continental tradition of philosophy. Edmund Husserl, for instance, made subjectivity the main topic of his phenomenology. In the 1920s his student Martin Heidegger took a more radical stance and completely avoided the notion of subjectivity and the mentalistic vocabulary of consciousness. In spite of their differences, both represent prominent ways of undermining what Davidson calls the "myth of the subjective." In recent Anglo-American philosophy the very idea of subjectivity has been attacked by Daniel Dennett and Richard Rorty—Dennett in his book, *Consciousness Explained,*[1] published in 1991, and Rorty even in such early papers as "Strawson's Objectivity Argument," published in 1970.[2] Calling subjectivity a myth is reminiscent of Wilfrid Sellars's attack on the "myth of the given." John McDowell's *Mind and World* is one among several contemporary efforts to find middle ground between the two poles of the given and the subjective. McDowell claims to be influenced by Hans-Georg Gadamer's hermeneutical philosophy, and McDowell's philosophy demonstrates how the two traditions can benefit each other when brought into dialogue.[3] Davidson does not similarly call on the continental tradition, but that does not mean that he would deny that his philosophy and contemporary hermeneutical philosophy have any points of contact.[4]

In this essay we read Davidson from within this hermeneutical tradition, showing that hermeneutics involves an analysis of subjectivity that is similar to Davidson's. We do not intend to equate the continental philosophers with Davidson. Nevertheless, we think that comparing them can be illuminating in reciprocal ways. In particular, we investigate some aspects of Davidson's critique of the view of the mind as akin to an internal theater whereby the mind watches representations of outer objects moving by. After first presenting the views of both Davidson and hermeneutics on subjectivity, we will turn to the phenomenological account. In addition to the writings of Husserl, we will also be considering Dan Zahavi's account of self-awareness. A philosopher of consciousness as well as a major Husserl scholar, Zahavi draws on Husserl's phenomenology in his recent book, *Subjectivity and Selfhood: Investigating the First-Person Perspective*.[5] Our thesis is that despite drastic differences in philosophical style, Heidegger, Gadamer, and by implication, Davidson can all be read as rejecting an interpretation of phenomenology that posits uninterpreted subjective experience as a foundational "bottom line." The need of hermeneutical reflection even in the investigation of subjectivity is confirmed by the fact that Husserl himself incorporated hermeneutical ideas in his later work. Beyond Husserl, we will argue for the more radical stance that the pervasiveness of hermeneutics entails that subjectivity is not the foundation of meaning and understanding.

In addition to the issue of the nature of the subjective, a metaphilosophical issue is also at stake. This issue concerns whether philosophy aims, by bracketing the issue of factual existence, to be pure, presuppositionless description that supplies the foundation for the rest of philosophy. In *Philosophy as Rigorous Science* (1911), Husserl wrote that his method of seeing essences (*Wesensschau*) would allow for "rigorous and in its kind objective and absolutely valid statements."[6] This foundationalist phenomenology is to be distinguished from hermeneutical phenomenology. The latter sees philosophy as invariably interpretive and therefore does not accept the notion of a presuppositionless starting point or a foundational bottom line. Hermeneutic phenomenology does not aspire to Husserl's ideal of rigorous science. The attempt of foundationalist phenomenology to discover a theory-free basic experience is resisted by the hermeneutical Heidegger, who sees *Dasein* not as a private subject, but as a being who is always situated in the world.

This conflict then evolves into one between the philosophy of consciousness and the philosophy of language. The subjectivistic philosophy of consciousness assumes that because anything to which we have access comes to us through consciousness, a theory of consciousness would therefore be the basis of a theory of everything else. The hermeneutical philosophy of language, in contrast, maintains that everything that can be known must be expressible in language. This thesis is the kernel of the "linguistic turn" in philosophy. Insofar as philosophical hermeneutics takes this turn, however, it does not then assert that the theory of language takes priority over theories of anything else. Instead, hermeneutical philosophy as we understand it maintains that if language is invariably interpretive, then the philosophy of language should also see itself as only ever an interpretation and not as the necessary starting point for a philosophy of everything.

Prima facie, therefore, we see two conflicting paradigms of philosophy, one that depends on starting philosophy from a phenomenological emphasis on consciousness and another that instead starts from the hermeneutical theory of language and interpretation. The standard reading of Husserl takes him to be demanding that philosophy must be grounded in uninterpreted phenomenological description. On our reading, however, Husserl came more and more to integrate interpretation into phenomenology. We believe that he did not go as far as Heidegger in the direction of a fully historical hermeneutics. Nevertheless, we follow the direction shown by the more hermeneutical Husserl and further pursued by Heidegger in believing that the phenomenological is never pure or presuppositionless, but that philosophy is, so to speak, interpretive "all the way down." We identify this antifoundationalist conception as "hermeneutical" and we argue for a reading of Davidson that sees him as allied with the hermeneutical tradition.

1 The Hermeneutic Davidson

Davidson, in his 1987 essay "Knowing One's Own Mind," gives the following account of the traditional view of the mental as an internal theater, a view that he rejects:

> There is a picture of the mind which has become so ingrained in our philosophical tradition that it is almost impossible to escape its influence even when its faults are recognized and repudiated. In one crude, but familiar, version it goes like this: the mind is a theater in which the conscious self watches a passing show (the shadows on the wall). The show consists of "appearances," sense data, qualia, what is "given" in experience. What appear on the stage are not the ordinary objects in the world that the outer eye registers and the heart loves, but their purported representatives. Whatever we know about the world outside depends on what we can glean from the inner clues.[7]

In 1991 Dennett dubbed this view the "Cartesian Theater," and he also attacked it.[8] Davidson and Dennett both caught the wave of rapid developments in cognitive psychology, neuroscience, and computer science.

The similar criticisms of Cartesianism by Husserl and Heidegger were raised in a markedly different philosophical climate. Husserl rejected the neo-Kantian categorical distinction between a thing-in-itself and its appearance. He maintained that some people are tricked into this error by the thought that phenomenal qualities are pictures or signs of the real objects.[9] Heidegger and Gadamer take a further step by claiming that language is always part of experience and thus there are no uninterpreted phenomena.

Naturally there are differences between Davidson and Husserl because of the different contexts from which they start. Thus, whereas Davidson grounds this critique in his Tarskian account of truth and language, Husserl reacts on the one hand to reductionism and particularly psychologism, and on the other to neo-Kantianism. In turn, Heidegger and Gadamer are reacting to the phenomenology of Husserl. Both Heidegger and Gadamer see hermeneutics, with its emphasis on the interpretive character of all understanding, as taking priority over phenomenology, with its program of bracketing the world and analyzing the resultant phenomenon of consciousness. Evidently, Heidegger's own label of "hermeneutic phenomenology" for his method in *Being and Time* suggests that both perspectives can be combined so as to enrich each other.

Davidson does not reject subjectivity entirely, of course. Clearly we do have thoughts that other people cannot access in the same way we can. Davidson allows for ordinary understandings of the mental. The particular conception of subjectivity that he opposes is the one that posits objects of the mind. For Davidson the doctrine causing the philosophical problems is that "to have a thought is to have an object before the mind."[10] The "myth of the subjective" is quintessentially, as Davidson defines it, "the idea that thoughts require mental objects."[11]

Heidegger would agree that the normal understanding of subjectivity unnecessarily multiplies entities in the theoretical explanation of cognitive activity. Although he would not express the point this way, the mind experiences not representations of objects but objects directly.[12] In *Being and Time* Heidegger maintains, for instance, that one does not first hear a noise and then infer that one is hearing a motorcycle. Instead, one hears the motorcycle directly: "What we 'first' hear is never noises or complexes of sounds, but the creaking wagon, the motor-cycle. We hear the column on the march, the north wind, the woodpecker tapping, the fire crackling."[13] In fact, we would add, some people can hear particular kinds of motorcycles, or even particular motorcycles. Sometimes, of course, one can hear a sound and wonder what the sound is (e.g., whether a certain burbling noise is a running faucet or a broken hose). Heidegger thus grants that "it requires a very artificial and complicated frame of mind to 'hear' a 'pure noise.'"[14] Nevertheless, the sound is heard as occurring in the world, and the question is only about what in the world is its cause. Even tinnitus is heard as being in the world, even if it is only in one's body and one's ears.

Whereas Cartesians assume that mental activity is not in the world but in the mind, Heideggerians maintain that thoughts are objective events that require explanation, just as physical events do. We read both Heidegger and Davidson as seeing the subjective not as opposed to the objective, but as a subspecies of it. In his 1991 essay, "Three Varieties of Knowledge," Davidson explains that he rejects

> this popular conception [that] holds that the subjective is prior to the objective, that there is a subjective world prior to knowledge of external reality. It is evident that the picture of thought and meaning I have sketched here leaves no room for such priority since it predicates self-knowledge on knowledge of other minds and of the world. The objective and the intersubjective are thus essential to anything we can call subjectivity, and constitute the context in which it takes form.[15]

This passage shows Davidson joining Heidegger in rethinking the meaning of the subjective and the objective by detaching that distinction from its Cartesian association with the inner–outer distinction. States of mind are just as real as physical objects. To label mental states as "inner" as opposed to "outer," where the outer is the paradigm of the "real," has been the source of philosophical error.

Realism is not the issue that we wish to address, however. Rather, we are interested in what Davidson thinks the subjective comes to. What he says is that once philosophical theories of subjectivity are discarded, the subjective comes down to two features: privacy and first-person authority. Privacy indicates that thoughts belong to one person only. First-person authority is the claim that one has access to one's thoughts that no one else can have. In Davidson's hands, these two points are not identical insofar as the first feature is a descriptive claim, whereas the second is an epistemic point. Heidegger appears to us to have combined these two features into the single phenomenon that he calls *Jemeinigkeit*, or "mine-ness." This mine-ness is the first feature that Heidegger attributes to *Dasein* in *Being and Time.* A corollary of this phenomenon is, to speak in the philosophical first person, that I cannot be mistaken about whose experiences I am having. I know that they are mine without needing any criteria or evidence for that knowledge.

An objection to Heidegger that comes up at this point is whether the idea of *Jemeinigkeit* or mine-ness does not merely reintroduce the Cartesian *cogito* that Heidegger is concerned to avoid. One might think that the thought that my experiences are my own presupposes the *cogito* insofar as without the "I think" there would be no basis to self-identify with the experiences. Heidegger could rebut this objection, however, by pointing out that the Cartesian *cogito* is not simply the locus of subjectivity, but that positing it involves at least two mistaken assumptions. The first assumption is that the *cogito* is transparent to itself. The second is that the *cogito* is not simply thinking, but that it is a thinking thing. Kant famously rejected both of these assumptions as committing the fallacy of paralogism. For Kant, the *I think* that can accompany any and every experience has no content and cannot be equated with the empirical ego of introspective inner sense. Furthermore, on Kant's reading, Descartes moves fallaciously from "there is some thinking" to "there must be something that is doing the thinking."

This brief reference to Kant is offered simply as a reminder of an earlier chapter in the history of consciousness, one that provides background for the comparison of Heidegger and Davidson on the issue of mine-ness. The point here is just that when philosophers such as Jean-Paul Sartre or Jacques Lacan (as interpreted by Slavoj Žižek) maintain that philosophy must start from the Cartesian *cogito*,[16] they realize that they are taking on complex philosophical issues that commit them to problematic assumptions. A central example of such an assumption is that we know our own minds better than we know the minds of others. Although Davidson argues for first-person authority, he also thinks that one can be mistaken about what one is thinking. This is not to say that one can be completely mistaken in all of one's beliefs about one's mental states. His principles of charity and correspondence lead to the inference that the world must be largely as we take it to be, and the world includes our mental states.

Of course, in addition to knowing what one thinks, one knows that one is having the thought. Is this latter belief incorrigible? Davidson distinguishes the content of the thought from the holding of it. He grants that we know our own thoughts in a way no one else can. In contrast to the *holding* of the thought, however, the *content* of the thought is not a private matter. In fact, Davidson insists that the content is as public as anything is. "The thoughts we form and entertain," he writes, "are located conceptually in the world we inhabit, and know we inhabit, with others. Even our thoughts about our own mental states occupy the same conceptual space and are located on the same public map."[17]

For Davidson, intersubjectivity is essential to subjectivity. His argument is, in a quick gloss, that there is no I without a We. He writes, "If I did not know what others think, I would have no thoughts of my own and so would not know what I think."[18] But just as there is no subjectivity without intersubjectivity, there could also be no intersubjectivity without subjectivity, and thus, without the first-person authority of mine-ness: "If I did not know what I think, I would lack the ability to gauge the thoughts of others."[19] The third leg of this epistemological tripod is the objectivity of the world: "Gauging the thoughts of others requires that I live in the same world with them, sharing many reactions to its major features, including its values."[20]

For Davidson, objectivity follows from the public, social nature of language. What we think can generally be expressed in sentences, and others can comprehend these sentences. There is no "private" language, if by that one means language that in principle only I can understand and use to communicate with myself. Even if thoughts and especially feelings often appear to be richer than the sentences that express them, anything that counts as a thought must be expressible in a sentence. Davidson in his later work uses the example of "triangulation" to make this point. This notion is the keystone of Davidson's theoretical model of "radical interpretation." Radical interpretation is unlike ordinary interpretation whereby the interpreter already knows the language.[21] Radical interpretation is closer to Quine's idea of radical translation, except that Davidson's theory goes even deeper and does not presuppose that the interpreter already knows a language (although radical interpretation could also involve someone who has a language but knows nothing about the other person's language). Instead, Davidson is arguing for an idealized model whereby the understanding of particular utterances is not given in advance. He is trying to explain how, even in the most primordial case where one does not yet master one's own language, understanding *could* result. Triangulation is an abstract model whereby each of two conspecific speakers determines the meaning of their terms by determining how the two speakers triangulate on each other and a common object. On this model the three-way relation is the minimal structure of understanding and intelligibility. It also shows that interpretive understanding is paradigmatically a social practice that requires language. If language can be explained through this idealization of how we come to understand each other even if initially we do not understand the other's language, then the concrete social emergence of a shared world is more readily understandable.

2 Davidsonian Hermeneutics

Now that we have shown some hermeneutic points in Davidson, we can turn to some Davidsonian points in hermeneutics. In particular, the hermeneutical philosophy of Heidegger and Gadamer recognizes the linguisticality (*Sprachlichkeit*) of our being-in-the-world. In *Truth and Method*, for instance, Gadamer makes it clear that understanding and interpretation are invariably linguistic. He sums up his theory with the famous sentence: "Being that can be understood is language" ("Sein, das verstanden werden kann, ist Sprache").[22] This sentence has its own "effective history."[23] In 1967 Gadamer interpreted this sentence as meaning that "We should try to understand everything that can be understood" ("Alles verstehen wollen, was sich verstehen läßt").[24] In 1984 he glossed it less strongly as "that which is, can never be completely understood" ("daß das, was ist, nie ganz verstanden werden kann").[25] The second formulation strikes us as preferable and more Davidsonian because it does not posit an apparent *telos* or closure to interpretation. In Davidsonian parlance, we would say that on either reading, the holism in Gadamer's position is clear. He can also be read as agreeing with Davidson that there is no mental content where there is no language.

The effective history of the sentence that "Being that can be understood is language" goes beyond Gadamer himself. In a piece written for Gadamer's hundredth birthday, Richard Rorty interprets this sentence as expressing the bit that was correct in the metaphysical positions of nominalism and idealism, even if these are no longer tenable today. Rorty defines nominalism as "the claim that all essences are nominal and all necessities *de dicto*."[26] He then translates the thesis that "we never understand anything except under a description, and there are no privileged descriptions" into the semantic claim that "only a sentence can be relevant to the truth of another sentence."[27] For Rorty, then, Gadamer's statement is not a latter-day version of linguistic idealism, because it can be read without taking on any metaphysical baggage.[28]

We hope to have shown that there is indeed a philosophical alliance between Davidson and the hermeneutical thinkers, despite the wide gap that separates their methods of analysis and argument. A question that poses a potential problem for our reading of Davidson as a hermeneutic philosopher, however, is the following. Is it the case that just when hermeneutics appears to be taking a linguistic turn and emphasizing *Sprachlichkeit* as foundational to understanding and interpretation, Davidson takes a different turn when he announces that "there is no such thing as a language"?[29]

Does this bold assertion undermine the connection that this essay sees between Davidson and Gadamer?

Exactly what Davidson means when he makes this seemingly paradoxical assertion raises complex issues in the philosophy of language that go beyond what this essay can deal with in the present context. We read this statement, however, not as a move away from Gadamer, but toward him. Some philosophers dispute the hermeneutical insistence on the circularity of understanding on the grounds that the hermeneutic circle leaves out the fact that the interpreter has to start somewhere. In particular, these critics of hermeneutics would argue that the interpreter has to know a language before the interpreter can start interpreting.

This criticism makes several assumptions about language that Davidson's theory corrects. First, a language is not a fixed set of words and rules, but is particular to determinate speakers. Second, if Davidson is right, the process of radical interpretation is itself a circular process whereby the cospeakers determine the referents of their words by using other words. Third, what Davidson means by his provocative statement that there is no such thing as a language is that language is not a thing-in-itself with fixed and rigid ways of constraining what can be said and understood. Knowing a language is not prior to interpretation and does not make linguistic communication possible. Davidson wants to reverse the assumption that knowing a language is logically prior to interpretation. We think that Bjørn Ramberg sums up Davidson's argument correctly when he says that this reversal results in the conclusion that "the concept of a language derives its content from our theory of interpretation, not vice versa."[30] In other words, radical interpretation is an explanation of how the social practice of engaging in language communicatively is even possible. In saying that there is no such *thing* as a language, Davidson is insisting that as a social practice language undergoes the constant makings and remakings of conversational negotiation. So the relation of language and interpretation itself turns out to be a variant of the hermeneutic circle. Presumably this circle is not a logically vicious circle, but an interpretation that helps us to understand how understanding, linguistic or otherwise, is even possible.

3 Self-Awareness and the Social Nature of Thought

Connecting Davidson to the phenomenological tradition of Husserl is more difficult and controversial than connecting him to the hermeneutical tradition. Like hermeneutics and unlike phenomenology, Davidson is concerned with the linguistic rather than the experiential. Whereas phenomenology is usually expressed as if it were talking about prelinguistic experience, Davidson's critique of the Cartesian account of subjectivity might well be inferred as being a critique of this conception of pure experience. In fact, this inference would not be completely incorrect. Nevertheless, phenomenology is rich and there are many significant intersections between Husserl and Davidson that can contribute to a better understanding of the underlying problems. In particular, Husserl in his many studies of intersubjectivity has anticipated Davidson's work on the social nature of thought.

Already in *Ideas I* Husserl writes: "I continually find as my counterpart the one spatiotemporal reality to which I belong like all other human beings who are to be found in it and who are related to it as I am."[31] The experienced reality should not merely be thought of as physical, but as involving everything with which we are concerned practically. Husserl maintains, for instance, that values are perceived just as immediately as other characteristics of the things around us.[32] The intersubjective world of things, values, interests, and other practical aspects of human life Husserl later calls the "life-world" (*Lebenswelt*). Before we go more deeply into the implications of this account of the social life-world and its contributions to our discussion, however, we must consider the idea that subjectivity has to be defined by being a certain qualitative experience peculiar to each self and that it is therefore inevitably private. In spite of the explicit rejection by Husserl of Cartesianism, this conception of subjectivity is often ascribed uncritically to phenomenology. Our encounter with Davidson leads us to want to rethink this conception.

Dan Zahavi interprets Husserl as distinguishing "between (1) what the object is like for the subject and (2) what the experience of the object is like for the subject."[33] We think this distinction is mistaken about Husserl because we think that it mischaracterizes Husserl's basic notion of intentionality. If we take Husserl's idea of intentionality as something like "awareness is always awareness of . . . ," then it seems obvious that for Husserl there is no such thing as "an awareness of awareness itself." That experience is always about something else would seem to preclude the idea of an experience of experience itself.

Zahavi draws his distinction in opposition to contemporary analytic philosophers who deny that there is anything it is like to have an experience in addition to the object experienced. Zahavi sees both Fred Dretske and Michael Tye as examples of philosophers of perception who refuse to make this distinction. What Zahavi thinks Dretske and Tye are missing is the difference between an awareness of the object and an awareness of the experience of the object. The latter includes awareness of how the object is given to me, that is, whether I am directly perceiving it, or imagining it, or remembering it, or anticipating it.

We hypothesize that skeptics about the experience of qualia will deny the validity of this distinction between properties of the object and properties of the subjective experience. Such qualia-skeptics include philosophers as diverse as Hume and Nietzsche. Hume famously makes the following remark in his *Treatise of Human Nature*:

> For my part, when I enter most intimately into what I call *myself*, I always stumble on some particular perception or other, of heat or cold, light or shade, love or hatred, pain or pleasure. I never catch *myself* at any time without a perception, and *never can observe any thing but the perception.*[34]

This last statement, which we have emphasized, shows that Hume is a skeptic not only about the self, but also about the claim that there is anything that an experience is like in addition to the content that is experienced. Nietzsche can be added to this list of skeptics about the primacy of the subject for unpublished statements like the following: "The 'subject' is not something given, it is something added and invented and projected behind what there is."[35]

Zahavi tries to block such attacks by admitting that the distinction between the object and the experience of the object is only a conceptual one, and not one that can be drawn in experience itself. He does think, however, that there is a difference between what the object seems like and what the perceiving feels like. If one accepts this distinction, then there would in fact seem to be an experiential difference, and not merely a conceptual one, involved in attending to the object as opposed to attending to how I am accessing the object.

In defending the need for a subjectivistic account of experience, Zahavi thus insists that this "first-personal givenness" is what makes experience *subjective*. The first-personal givenness of experience, he claims, "entails a built-in self-reference, a primitive experiential self-referentiality."[36] This claim strikes us as very similar to the notion of subjectivity that Davidson rejects as mythical. The first-personal givenness, on Zahavi's account, is manifested in the fact that all my experiences are my own. Like Heidegger (see above), Zahavi also refers to this feature of experience as *mine-ness*.[37] The crucial question then becomes whether *mine-ness* entails *selfhood*.

To make this question manageable, Zahavi points out that we have to know what we mean by "self." Instead of dealing with the twenty-one different conceptions of the term "self" identified by Galen Strawson, Zahavi sensibly limits the discussion to three: the Kantian view of the self as an identity-pole; the hermeneutical conception of the self as a narrative construction; and the phenomenological description of the self as an experiential dimension. He follows the French philosopher Michel Henry in thinking of this self minimally as "having first-personal access to one's own experiential life."[38] The phenomenological account is the one that he thinks gets it right because the narratival personhood of the hermeneutical conception presupposes the phenomenologist's experiential selfhood, but not vice versa. "In short," he concludes, "the self is conceived neither as an ineffable transcendental precondition, nor as a mere social construct that evolves through time; it is taken to be an integral part of our conscious life with an immediate experiential reality."[39]

The hope is to have such a minimal notion of the self that anyone could accept it. In that regard, Zahavi and Davidson would appear to share a similar goal. Zahavi rightly points out that the Husserlian conception of the self is not Cartesian: it is not a "self-enclosed and self-sufficient interiority" but rather a "world-immersed self."[40] Zahavi tries to capture this by saying that he is describing the "subjectivity of experience," not some substantial "subject of experience."[41] He thus does not want to commit the fallacy that Kant called paralogism. He also does not want to make the mistake of reifying the subject into an object, a mistake that Heidegger often pointed out.

Does Zahavi indeed prove, however, that there is a "what it is like" in addition to the experience? This almost seems like asking whether the experiencing itself has qualia, or whether qualia have qualia. Furthermore, one must also ask whether his idea of a "minimal self" is convincing from a Davidsonian perspective.

To deal with these questions, we will first discuss whether Zahavi's conception of the self is really as minimalist as he says it is. Zahavi's case for his concept of the self draws indirectly on Thomas Nagel's characterization of subjectivity as "what it is like" to be a certain sort of creature. For Nagel there is something that it is like to be a bat that we humans will never experience. But notice again that much depends on the word "experience," and in particular, that "what it is like" is internal rather than external. Zahavi changes the "what it is like" and makes it apply to every conscious state, not simply to the creature as such. "Every conscious state," he writes, "be it a perception, an emotion, a recollection, or an abstract belief, has a certain subjective character, a certain phenomenal quality of 'what it is like' to live through or undergo that state."[42] Indeed, he believes that this phenomenal quality is what makes a mental state *conscious*. So once again he insists on the difference between the experience of the object and the experience of the experience of the object. This "experience of experience," however, sounds like "qualia of qualia" and in any case is exactly what skeptics about qualia deny. Although Davidson mainly discusses propositional attitudes and not sensations, the quotation from "Knowing One's Own Mind" with which we began clearly rejects qualia as a lingering vestige of Cartesianism. Part of the picture that he is opposed to there is that the content of the passing show "consists of 'appearances,' sense data, qualia, what is 'given' in experience." We take Husserl to be similarly rejecting such an idea when he writes in the *Phenomenology of the Consciousness of Internal Time* that "an impression . . . is to be grasped as a primary consciousness that has no further consciousness behind it in which we are aware of it."[43] Husserl wants to avoid the infinite regress that would result by positing a consciousness of consciousness.

Furthermore, Zahavi's insistence on first-personal *givenness* is problematic. If pragmatists like Sellars and Rorty think that the givenness of physical objects is a myth, they are not going to understand the value of this insistence on the givenness of subjectivity either. As a holist Davidson would also reject this turn of phrase. Holism is the view that sentences get their sense from their relation to other sentences, not from some experiential givenness. In Davidson's words, "Beliefs are identified and described only within a dense pattern of belief."[44] This insistence on the "pattern" of belief is much like the hermeneutical emphasis on the importance of "context" in determining the sense of an utterance.

Finally, Zahavi runs the risk of reifying the subject after all by turning it into something that is experienced. "When we investigate appearing objects," he affirms, "we also disclose ourselves as datives of manifestation, as those to whom objects appear."[45] Although the phrase "datives of manifestation" seems to refer to a merely grammatical structure, we suspect that it hides the paralogism of moving from thinking to a thing that thinks. Positing a locus of experience comes to much the same thing as positing a *res cogitans*. That Hume and others do not find the self in their introspections is not due to the fact that Hume was looking for it in the wrong place, as Zahavi claims. Instead, as Davidson's critique of the Cartesian theater makes clear, there is no "place" in which to look.

4 The Hermeneutic Husserl

Although Zahavi is a subtle interpreter of Husserl, we have been arguing that his exposition of subjectivity in Husserl is not fully informed by Davidson's thesis of the myth of subjectivity. Husserl did want to ground phenomenology in subjective experience, but he also wished to distance phenomenology from the Cartesian *cogito*. A reading of Husserl that is better informed by Davidson is, we believe, philosophically more viable. We acknowledge, however, that there is room for more than one interpretation. Although the sheer quantity of Husserl's writings, many of which still are not yet published, makes following through his every thought very difficult, it is nevertheless crucial for any interpretation of Husserl to take into account the further development of his work. Considering only one phase of his ongoing investigations can be seriously misleading. In what follows we therefore sketch an interpretation of the later Husserl that is more compatible with Davidson's account of subjectivity and that we find historically more accurate and philosophically more digestible than Zahavi's.

The work in which Husserl's investigations come closest to hypostatizing a foundation of phenomenology in subjectivity is his book, *Cartesian Meditations*. The material here goes back to two two-hour lectures delivered at the Sorbonne in 1929 and then published in French in 1931. In these lectures Husserl uses the admittedly Cartesian method to bracket the existence of the external world and to suspend theoretical categorizations. He also rejects, however, many of the claims derived from the Cartesian method, including some of Descartes's own thoughts. For instance, for Husserl there is no gap between clear and distinct perceptions of the mind and an "external world." Husserl calls the problem of their relation an absurdity (*Widersinn*). He writes that Descartes succumbed to it because he missed the "genuine sense of his transcendental epoché."[46] According to Husserl, Descartes failed to take the abstract self as a vantage point and instead started from the self as a natural human being. The latter, however, already presupposes an "Outside Me" because it implies perceiving myself as being in a space.[47] Questioning the existence of the "external" world as a counterpart of the natural self therefore already presupposes the existence of the external world. For Husserl, the "genuine" sense of the epoché lies in the systematic clarification of the transcendental ego as a precondition of knowledge. The role of epistemology thus sheds light on how subjectivity is part of, and not independent of, our worldly experience.

The reference to "transcendental" here does not imply *psychological* idealism. Husserl is not making a Cartesian inference from the inner to the outer, that is, from our subjective experience to the objective world. His position is also not a Kantianism that "leaves open at least as a limit-concept the possibility of a world of things-in-themselves."[48] Although Husserl does identify his position as a version of transcendental idealism based on the "self-interpretation of my Ego as a subject of all possible cognition, namely with respect to all meaning of being,"[49] this transcendental idealism is not antinaturalistic, but simply antireductionist. Zahavi is thus correct that for Husserl the ego is experienced. For Husserl, however, the ego is not a further component in personal experience. Rather, the ego is the structure *of* experience that makes experience intentional, "about" something. Husserl's phenomenology is transcendental in that it investigates the intentional structure of experience. Husserl's position thus shares at least one conclusion with Davidson's "anomalous monism," namely, its antireductionism. Davidson posits the identity of mental events and physical events, but the identity is a token–token, not a type–type identity. With his notion of weak supervenience, Davidson avoids reductionism in the strong causal sense that antimaterialistic phenomenologists deplore.

Husserl maintains that to learn more about subjectivity we have to start from where we are: from the world we know through our everyday activities, the world we live in. It is thus not surprising that the emphasis of Husserl's investigation shifted more and more from the ego to the life-world. In fact, he was not satisfied with the *Cartesian Meditations*, and he never authorized their publication. Instead, from 1932 until his death in 1938 he worked on writings that have in large parts been published posthumously in 1954 as *The Crisis of the European Sciences and Transcendental Philosophy* (*Husserliana VI*),[50] a supplementary volume published in 1993 (*Husserliana XXIX*), and *The Lifeworld* in 2008 (*Husserliana XXXIX*).

In these works he explicitly speaks against his earlier "Cartesian way" and contrasts it with the "way from the life-world" as well as with the "way from psychology."[51] In addition, Husserl further elaborates the concept of the life-world and introduces the notion of history. Husserl traces not only subjectivity, but also all kinds of meaning back to the life-world. We cannot find a direct correlate in Davidson for the notion of the life-world. On our reading, however, it corresponds to the social and historical situation in which radical interpretation takes place, but about which Davidson does not have much to say. For Husserl, in contrast, the life-world is the basis of experience. On the one hand, the life-world is said to be a *Sinnesfundament* (foundation of sense), because it is connected to our sense experiences. The life-world is the world as experienced, the "world of sense-intuition, a sensible world of appearances."[52] On the other hand, the life-world is also the basis for both descriptive and normative meaning. All human actions occur in it and all our theories ultimately have to prove their claims to truth with regard to it. Not the sciences but the "immediately intuited world" is the "original meaning-giving achievement."[53]

One objection to our attempt to connect the later Husserl with hermeneutics concerns the fact that hermeneutics is broadly historical and historicist. In contrast, Husserl's rejection of historicism suggests to some that he is an unhistorical philosopher. The later Husserl, however, surprises us with his insistence on the historical dimension of experience. For instance, he provides detailed historical accounts of how the sciences developed from the life-world. These investigations represent Husserl's first efforts to show the dependence of our "objective" way of thinking on historical development. The aim of these historical investigations is not to reveal empirical facts about our ways of thinking, but to identify their preconditions. This project brings him much closer than is commonly supposed to the broadly hermeneutical insistence on the historicity of thought. He recognizes that our understanding of history itself is dependent on the course of this very history.

In the *Crisis* Husserl does not use the expression "hermeneutical circle," but he does speak of a "kind of circle" between understanding the origins of scientific ways of thinking and those ways of thinking today.[54] To understand the scientific ways of thinking since the Enlightenment, we have to understand their origins and subsequent development. That is, we have to think historically. But we also have to understand this historical way of thinking itself in order to understand *its* origin and subsequent development. Husserl writes that we have to go forward and backward in zigzag movements (*im Zickzack*) and thereby reciprocally reach a clearer understanding of our way of thinking today as well as its origin and development.[55]

In sum, the methodological problem with the life-world is analogous to Husserl's search for a historical origin. Our ways of thinking go back to the life-world, which in turn has to be investigated using these very ways of thinking. So on the one hand, we have to use ordinary life with its "naive manner of speaking."[56] We have to go back to the naiveté of the everyday life-world to understand the extent to which our scientific and philosophical thinking might be equally naive. On the other hand, we have to use scientific and philosophical thinking to understand the life-world. Husserl in his later philosophy thus recognizes the circular as opposed to the foundational character of philosophical investigation into the preconditions of our thinking, be it the historical origin or the life-world: To understand the preconditions we have to understand our way of thinking and vice versa. This back and forth motion is essentially the hermeneutic circle.

5 Conclusion: Linguistic Turns and Hermeneutic Circles

In our view, although Husserl anticipates the hermeneutical and holistic approaches of Heidegger, Gadamer, and Davidson, he does not take the crucial next step and give up foundationalism entirely. Although he recognizes the circularity of his method, he still takes history to develop teleologically from an "entelechy."[57] He believes that the life-world is a "foundation" that is "pregiven to us . . . always and necessarily as the universal field of all actual and possible praxis, as horizon."[58] As a universal structure, the life-world is static and unhistorical. Husserl insists, for instance, that it will not be changed by the theories that develop from it: "This actually intuited, actually experienced and experienceable world, in which practically our whole life takes place, remains unchanged as what it is, in its own essential structure and its own concrete causal style, whatever we may do with or without techniques."[59] We could agree that changes in theories (for instance, in the sciences) do not always necessitate changes in how the world is perceived. Acknowledging this point does not entail, however, that our life-worldly perception is immune to changes in theory, which can lead to changes in what even counts as a phenomenon. In contrast to Husserl, then, we do not think that the concretely experienced life-world is fixed and pregiven, but that it both influences and is influenced by changes in belief and theory.

Despite the later Husserl's implicit recognition of the hermeneutic circle, his inclinations toward foundationalism influenced his progeny. For instance, Maurice Merleau-Ponty claims in *The Primacy of Perception* that "the perceived world is the always presupposed foundation of all rationality, all value and all existence."[60] At least at one point, then, Merleau-Ponty uses the metaphor for phenomenology of an archeological dig down through the sedimented layers of experience before reaching "the structure of the perceived world [that] is buried under the sedimentations of later knowledge," the "universal style shared in by all perceptual beings."[61] This image suggests that there is a bottom line for philosophy, and that it consists of the universals of perception.

The work on history and life-world as preconditions of thinking by the later Husserl, Merleau-Ponty, and other phenomenologists is indeed valuable, and it deserves to be considered in current philosophical discussions. We question, however, whether the "foundation" they hypothesize is prior to interpretation. Is the alleged bottom stratum presuppositionless or is it given only through interpretation? The underlying presupposition of foundational phenomenology seems to be that the foundation has to be universal and free of interpretation to allow for rigorous science. In contrast, we follow the hermeneutical approach in claiming that there is no need for a sharp distinction between universal and relative preconditions of theory. The life-world as construed by the later Husserl implies language as much as forms of perception and is therefore interpretive all the way down. This is not to say there is no difference between experience and theory. But even our most basic experiences are structured by language and therefore open to interpretation.

Applying Davidson's critique of subjectivity to the classic standoff between phenomenology and hermeneutics has led us to the conclusion that phenomenology presupposes hermeneutics. Understanding Davidson helps to see why Husserl had good reason to move from a phenomenology anchored in a supposedly uninterpreted experience toward a more hermeneutical life-world in which the social, historical, and interpretive nature of thought is recognized and validated. In our opinion, this is the most viable direction in which not only phenomenology and hermeneutics, but also continental and analytic philosophy more generally, ought to be heading today.

Acknowledgments

Our thanks to Jonathan Ellis and Colin Koopman for their careful readings and insightful suggestions concerning early drafts.

Notes

1. Daniel C. Dennett, *Consciousness Explained* (Boston: Little, Brown, 1991).

2. Richard Rorty, "Strawson's Objectivity Argument," *Review of Metaphysics* 24 (1970): 207–244. This critique of Cartesian consciousness and the deconstruction of the subject–object opposition has deep roots in American pragmatism. An anonymous reviewer reminds us that as early as 1904 William James in his article "Does 'Consciousness' Exist?" attacks the kind of subjectivism that makes consciousness into a thing. See the *Journal of Philosophy, Psychology, and Scientific Method* 1: 477–491.

3. John McDowell, *Mind and World* (Cambridge, MA: Harvard University Press, 1994), pp. 115ff.

4. One occasion at which Davidson heard and responded to many discussions of the connections between his views and the continental tradition was the six-week long NEH Summer Institute on the topic, "Heidegger and Davidson: Critics of Cartesianism," organized in 1990 by Hubert Dreyfus and David Hoy at the University of California, Santa Cruz.

5. Dan Zahavi, *Subjectivity and Selfhood: Investigating the First-Person Perspective* (Cambridge, MA: MIT Press, 2005).

6. Edmund Husserl, *Philosophie als Strenge Wissenschaft*, ed. W. Szilasi (Frankfurt: Klostermann, 1965), p. 33. All translations from Husserl's texts are by Christoph Durt unless otherwise noted.

7. Donald Davidson, *Subjective, Intersubjective, Objective* (Oxford: Clarendon Press, 2001), p. 34.

8. Dennett, *Consciousness Explained*, p. 101.

9. See Edmund Husserl, *Ideen zu einer reinen Phänomenologie und phänomenologischen Philosophie*, ed. K. Schuhmann (The Hague: Martinus Nijhoff, 1967), pp. 89ff. (sec. 43).

10. Davidson, *Subjective, Intersubjective, Objective*, p. 37.

11. Ibid., p. 38.

12. In the continental tradition, the doctrine that we experience not the objects but representations of the objects is frequently referred to as representationalism. In the analytic tradition, however, representationalism is often the doctrine that objects are experienced directly. To avoid misleading labels, we prefer not to use the term "representationalism." We will also avoid standard epistemological terms such as "internalism" and "externalism" because these commit one to the inside–outside distinction that is being challenged in this essay. Insofar as Davidson is standardly classified as an externalist, however, then so are we.

13. Martin Heidegger, *Being and Time*, trans. J. Macquarrie and E. Robinson (New York: Harper & Row, 1962), p. 207.

14. Ibid.

15. Davidson, *Subjective, Intersubjective, Objective*, p. 219.

16. In *Being and Nothingness* (New York: Washington Square Press, 1956), Sartre insists that for philosophers, given Hegel's failure, "the only point of departure possible is the Cartesian *cogito*" (p. 338). Citing Lacan's claim that the *cogito* is the subject of the unconscious, Žižek says approvingly of Lacan and critically of the poststructuralist attempt to eliminate the metaphysical concern with subjectivity, "The specter of the 'Cartesian paradigm' roams around, simultaneously proclaimed dead and feared as the ultimate threat to our survival. In clear contrast to this proclaimed *doxa*, Lacan pleads for a psychoanalytic *return to cogito*," in *Cogito and the Unconscious*, ed. Slavoj Žižek (Durham: Duke University Press, 1998), p. 6—albeit for Žižek the *cogito* in question is "a subject bereft of subjectivity" (ibid., p. 7).

17. Davidson, *Subjective, Intersubjective, Objective*, p. 218.

18. Ibid., pp. 219–220.

19. Ibid., p. 220.

20. Ibid.

21. See David Couzens Hoy, "Post-Cartesian Interpretation: Hans-Georg Gadamer and Donald Davidson," in *The Philosophy of Hans-Georg Gadamer,* ed. L. E. Hahn (Chicago: Open Court, 1997), pp. 111–130. Further, see Jonathan Ellis, "The Relevance of Radical Interpretation for the Understanding of Mind," this volume.

22. Hans-Georg Gadamer, *Wahrheit und Methode,* 2nd ed. (Tübingen: J. C. B. Mohr, 1965), p. xxi.

23. See David Couzens Hoy and Thomas McCarthy, *Critical Theory* (Oxford: Blackwell, 1994), p. 191.

24. Hans-Georg Gadamer, *Kleine Schriften I* (Tübingen: J. C. B. Mohr, 1967), p. 123. See Brice Wachterhauser, *Hermeneutics and Modern Philosophy* (New York: SUNY Press, 1986), pp. 288–289.

25. Hans-Georg Gadamer, "Text und Interpretation," in *Text und Interpretation,* ed. Philippe Forget (Munich: Wilhelm Fink Verlag, 1984), p. 29. See Wachterhauser, *Hermeneutics and Modern Philosophy,* p. 382.

26. Richard Rorty, "Being That Can Be Understood Is Language," in *Gadamer's Repercussions: Reconsidering Philosophical Hermeneutics,* ed. B. Krajewski (Berkeley: University of California Press, 2004), p. 22.

27. Ibid., pp. 23, 25.

28. According to Durt's notes, in an oral reply to an early version of Rorty's paper as well as to two other presentations, Gadamer was generally pleased with Rorty's talk, but he criticized all three presentations for giving insufficient consideration to the "life-world" ("[die Vorträge sind] zu wenig von der Lebenswelt her gedacht"). See also Christoph Durt, "Gadamer's 100. Geburtstag," *Information Philosophie* 2 (2000): 118–119.

29. Donald Davidson, "A Nice Derangement of Epitaphs," in *Truth and Interpretation: Perspectives on the Philosophy of Donald Davidson,* ed. E. Lepore (Oxford: Blackwell, 1986), p. 446.

30. Bjørn Ramberg, *Donald Davidson's Philosophy of Language: An Introduction* (Oxford: Blackwell, 1989), p. 110.

31. Edmund Husserl, *Ideen zu einer reinen Phänomenologie und phänomenologischen Philosophie,* p. 61 (sec. 30).

32. Ibid., p. 58 (sec. 27).

33. Zahavi, *Subjectivity and Selfhood,* p. 121.

34. David Hume, *A Treatise of Human Nature* (Oxford: Clarendon Press, 1888), p. 252. Cited by Zahavi, *Subjectivity and Selfhood*, p. 101; emphasis added.

35. Friedrich Nietzsche, *Werke III* (Munich: Carl Hanser Verlag, 1960), p. 903. Cited by Zahavi, *Subjectivity and Selfhood*, p. 101.

36. Zahavi, *Subjectivity and Selfhood*, p. 122.

37. Ibid., p. 124.

38. Ibid., p. 106.

39. Ibid.

40. Ibid., p. 126.

41. Ibid.

42. Ibid., p. 119.

43. Cited by Paul Ricoeur, *Time and Narrative*, vol. 3, trans. K. Blamey and D. Pellauer (Chicago: University of Chicago Press, 1988), p. 44.

44. Donald Davidson, *Inquiries into Truth and Interpretation* (Oxford: Clarendon Press, 1984), p. 200.

45. Zahavi, *Subjectivity and Selfhood*, p. 123.

46. Edmund Husserl, *Cartesianische Meditationen*, ed. E. Ströker (Hamburg: Felix Meiner, 1987), p. 85.

47. Ibid., p. 86.

48. Ibid., p. 88.

49. Ibid.

50. Edmund Husserl, *Die Krisis der Europäischen Wissenschaften und die Transzendentale Phänomenologie* (The Hague: Martinus Nijhoff, 1962).

51. Ibid., pp. 157, 105, and 194.

52. Ibid., p. 108.

53. Ibid., p. 49.

54. Ibid., p. 59.

55. Ibid.

56. Ibid., p. 60.

57. Ibid., p. 14.

58. Edmund Husserl, *The Crisis of European Sciences and Transcendental Phenomenology: An Introduction to Phenomenological Philosophy*, trans. David Carr (Evanston: Northwestern University Press, 1970), p. 142.

59. Ibid., pp. 50–51.

60. Maurice Merleau-Ponty, *The Primacy of Perception and Other Essays* (Evanston: Northwestern University Press, 1964), p. 13.

61. Ibid., pp. 5–6.

3 Davidson, Derrida, and *Differance*

Samuel C. Wheeler III

1 Introduction

Several philosophers[1] have argued for a genuine affinity between Derrida and Davidson. That alleged affinity demands detailed support, in light of some apparent central differences in their views. So, here is some of that detailed argument. This essay argues that Davidson is implicitly committed to free play and *differance*.

Let me first outline how one important strand of analytic philosophy, the strand roughly characterized as "logical empiricism," led to the anti-logo-centrism of Quine and Davidson: Philosophers such as Carnap had always been antimetaphysical, regarding metaphysical questions as concealed questions about language. Their critique of metaphysics interpreted metaphysical questions as questions about "conventions about what meanings to assign to one's words." Quine, in one of the most famous (analytic) essays of the twentieth century, "Two Dogmas of Empiricism,"[2] argued that logical empiricists were committed to one group of metaphysical entities, meanings. Quine showed that meanings themselves could not be given an empirical account that accorded with logo-centric tradition. Synonymy and analyticity, for instance, could not be empirically founded concepts. In effect, Quine deconstructs the empiricist account of metaphysics as misunderstood proposals about meaning—he shows that, on empiricist principles themselves, there cannot be language-transcendent meanings about which to make proposals.

Now, once Quine rejects transcendent meanings as nonempirical, a very radical linguisticism is in place. Language is, as it were, as good as it gets. Quine still was an empiricist, however, because he considered that stimulations could be used to ground a connection between the world and the sentences we use. A sentence for a person at a time is associated with the stimulations that induce assent to it. Since these associations are mediated and modified by what other sentences the person assents to, "stimulus meaning" is radically holistic and revisable.

Davidson recognized that Quine's appeal to kinds of stimulations as the same or different independently of predicate scheme committed Quine to taking some entities to have a criterion of sameness independent of a predicate scheme. That is, Quine remained committed to essentialism about the domain of stimulations that was divided up in various ways. When a pair of stimuli were the same or different was intrinsic to those stimuli.

Davidson rejects stimulus meaning as yet another version of the "dualism of scheme and content,"[3] the idea of a given domain of objects available to be sorted into extensions of predicates. The metaphor of dividing up or organizing the world with a predicate-scheme is, Davidson argues, incoherent. If one does not believe in essential natures, sameness is relative to a predicate scheme, not a given. Any "given" domain of objects would have an intrinsic, privileged sameness relation, in effect the essences of the entities out there. Davidson is then left with neither transcendent meanings nor samenesses given in nature to yield a "ground" for meaning. How, then, according to Davidson, can language get a purchase on the world at all without some domain for a predicate scheme to butcher, whether at the joints or by means of a grinder?

Davidson's answer depends on his notion of truth. Davidson follows Quine, who follows Frege, in taking the basic unit of contact with the world to be the sentence. Given that sentences, as Frege indicated, do not refer to anything other than their truth-values, this means that reference, what the singular terms refer to and what predicates apply to, is basically an organizational system for sentences assented to, that is, taken to be true. Without stimulus meanings grounding sentences' truth-values, truth itself is the primitive semantic notion. For Davidson, nothing makes sentences true; rather, what there is supervenes on truths.[4]

Language itself, concrete speech behavior, is fundamental. Language is not to be understood as an expression or manifestation of language-transcendent *logoi* such as Platonic Forms, Fregean senses, or some construction out of possible worlds. Thus, an account of meaning or truth conditions can only be given by connecting mentioned sentences with words used to say what the world has to be like for the sentence to be true. There is no better explication of the truth conditions of "Joe is a frog" than "'Joe is a frog' is true if and only if Joe is a frog." For a person's language as a whole, a systematic way of generating all such sentences is a semantics for a language.

An important consequence of taking language as primary is that the only account of metaphor and other figuration available is a rhetorical account. Since there are no language-transcendent meanings, there are no metaphorical meanings. Davidson in "What Metaphors Mean"[5] proposes such an account. An expression used metaphorically has its usual truth conditions, but is presented for some other reason than saying what is the case. That is, Davidson distinguishes between what the words mean (their truth conditions) and what the person means by using the words. So, figuration is treated in the way hyperbole or sarcasm is treated. A person says something sarcastic not in order to communicate a belief that the sentence uttered is true, but for another purpose entirely.

The consequences of Davidson's account of metaphor for the Davidsonian account of predicate extension match in important detail some of the consequences of "difference,"[6] as I will show below. These consequences of "*differance*" are thus features of both philosophers' thought. These consequences are in effect already implicit in the joint denial of transcendent meanings and a given, common to both philosophers' thought.

2 Truth

Let me first dispel one apparent disagreement between Derrida and Davidson. Derrida apparently takes a dim view of "truth,"[7] whereas that is the central concept in Davidson's account of language and mind.

Derrida's target is the classical conception of truth as the matching of a *logos* present to the mind with its natural referent, roughly speaking. The "presence" of the *logos* is in effect the phenomenological version of the meanings to which analytic philosophers have had recourse. Those meanings require a magic language of thought in which terms by their very nature (i.e., by their senses or by the Platonic Form they reveal) have the referents they do. According to the classical conception, a true sentence is true in virtue of these meanings fitting natural referents. Truth is the accord between tokens of thought and being. Derrida argues[8] that there are no such tokens, that there is no "magic language" of terms that by nature refer to particular beings.[9] Thus, truth is a notion that must be overcome by showing the incoherence of its founding notions, largely by examination of important texts—that is, by deconstruction.

Davidson, while he explicitly makes "truth" the central concept in his theory, abandons correspondence in any but the disquotational sense. Truth for Davidson is the central connecting notion linking belief, desire, action, and other elements of the "intentional" family of concepts. Truth conditions give meaning, truth is undefinable, truth connects belief, desire, and action.[10]

Briefly, then, Derrida's view is that, since "truth" is correspondence of *logos* to entity, there is no truth.[11] Davidson's view is that, since there is no sense to be made of a correspondence of *logos* to entity, truth is not correspondence of *logos* to entity.[12] Thus there is no fundamental disagreement.

3 Slippery Figures

Metaphors, according to Davidson,[13] are utterances or inscriptions that are produced for some other purpose than to indicate that the sentence is true. A metaphor illuminates something, but is not in general true. So, I say "Celeste is an eggplant," teasing my guinea pig; what I say is obviously not true and is not intended to be true. Metaphors and many other figures, that is, are treated in the way that sarcasm, hyperbole, and understatement are treated—as rhetorical rather than semantic phenomena. That is, the intention with which the utterance is produced determines whether an utterance is a metaphor or other figure of speech rather than an assertion, command, or question. The utterance has truth conditions, which are just the literal truth conditions,[14] and those truth conditions are crucial to the speech act accomplishing what is intended.

Once we examine cases beyond the central, clear cases in which the intention is clear and the truth-value is clear, though, the rhetorical forces, truth conditions, and intentions become more opaque. There are two ways to see this, the first rather superficial and obvious, the second more startling:

1. First, we can note that, within a culture, metaphors die. We can reflect on the implications of this gradual demise for issues of truth and falsity. The vocabulary of the Indo-European languages, at least, reflects a history of metaphors becoming literal meanings, those new literal meanings being used metaphorically, and then those new metaphorical extensions becoming literal.[15] Those mundane metaphors can become additional senses of words of the language.[16] Metaphors and other figures sometimes become independent words, when the words of which they are figural extensions pass away or are unfamiliar to most speakers.[17] This kind of borderline indeterminacy could be accommodated as just a process of meaning change, without supposing any indeterminacy or "undecidability," but rather just the familiar vagueness of macro-phenomena. For a Davidsonian, the idiolect is primary,[18] and so the vagueness of whether the arbitrary construction

we call "English" has one word or two words spelled and pronounced "crush" is not philosophically interesting.

2. The second way to see the unsettling effect[19] of metaphor focuses on the individual speaker/thinker. Since the phenomenon of metaphor is rhetorical, it is distinguished by intentions. If intention is the distinguishing feature of a figure, whether an occurrence of a predicate is metaphorical must be a matter of whether the appropriate *individual* intention was present. A metaphor can be a metaphor only relative to an idiolect at a time.

This second consideration is the fundamental one. For Davidson, each person's language is slightly different from anyone else's, so there is no useful precise concept of "language" that nonarbitrarily groups dialects as "one language." For semantic purposes, then, the idiolect is the primary phenomenon.[20] Loss of metaphoricity is then a matter of the intention with which a particular person's speech act is produced. So, the death of a metaphor in an individual idiolect must be a matter of that individual coming to use a predicate that could be a metaphor[21] with the intention of saying something true.

But the intentions that define different rhetorical forces are very often hard to detect. Can you tell whether you are using "crush" literally or figuratively?[22] That is, can you tell "from the inside" whether you have two words or one? Certainly the existence of the appropriate intention is phenomenologically obscure. On Davidsonian grounds, one would argue that there is nothing in the brain that decides such matters, either.[23] When what is perhaps a metaphor is familiar and routine, it can be indeterminate whether a metaphorical communicative intention exists. This is as we should expect, given the Davidsonian approach to interpretation and mental predicates.

On a Davidsonian account of the mental, intention is one of the family of concepts that are applied holistically and nonreductively in interpretation. Intention is part of the network of concepts that we apply in interpreting physical events of other agents as actions. "Intends" is, after all, a propositional attitude verb like "believes" and "desires." Intentions are assigned as part of interpretation; they are not independently given bases for interpretation. Intentions are not independently identifiable psychological states or events inhabiting the mind, but are rather ascribed as part of a theory of action interpretation, interpreting actions both of ourselves and of others.[24]

A Davidsonian should expect that whether "crush" is one predicate or two would be indeterminate for exactly the reasons that we find indeterminacy in exchanging belief and meaning. In the case of indeterminate intentions, however, the phenomenon is very widespread. In the previous sentence, for instance, one could ask whether "case" is the same or a different word from the "case" that applies to bookcases, whether the component "how" of "however" is the same "how" as in "how do you do?," and whether the wideness of "wide" in "widespread" is the same or different from the "wide" in "wide expanse," at least.

A deceptive feature of Davidson's account of metaphor in "What Metaphors Mean" is that, by concentrating on great poetic metaphors, where intention is clear, he misleadingly presumes intention to be transparent to the speaker in the general case of metaphorical speech acts. For the clear examples of metaphoricity Davidson discusses, the intention is clear, and the metaphors are clearly metaphors. In the more normal sort of cases we are discussing, however, both the intention and the truth conditions of the utterance are indeterminate. The truth conditions can be ascribed differently by reinterpreting the predicate, with a corresponding reinterpretation of the intention.[25]

Indeterminacy of rhetorical force, though, is much more common and widespread than the Quinean cases of mismatch in seeking agreement with another by adjusting meanings and beliefs. Such indeterminacy arises with every sentence using a dead or maybe dead metaphor, and for sentences using any word with a variety of uses where it is not determinate whether there is homonymy, such as "how" in "however." Furthermore, the indeterminacy of intention arises within a single speaker. That is, even in interpreting oneself, the question arises of whether what you said was true according to your own lights.

The indeterminacy can be represented as alternative distinct predicate-rosters in the semantics of the idiolect of the speaker or writer. On the one account, there are two predicates; on the other account, when the attributed intention is not to say something true, there is one predicate.

4 Back to *Differance* via Truth

What does a Davidsonian say about truth and truth conditions over the period when what was originally a metaphor ceases to be clearly either metaphorical or literal? More generally, what does a Davidsonian say about utterances such that the speaker has no opinion about whether the utterance is true or not? In Davidsonian terms, we know the truth conditions of the sentence. "The Celtics crushed the Knicks" is true if and only if the Celtics crushed the Knicks. We know what the satisfaction conditions of our predicates are, as well. An ordered pair of entities satisfies "crushed" if and only if the first entity crushed the second. So we are always aware of the meanings of terms, and should be alert to any shifts. There's nothing but language here.

However, an utterance that would have been false before is now true, and the difference has nothing to do with indexicals. Intuitively, the facts haven't changed, except for this one, that something that was false is now true. By our disquotational account treating meaning as truth conditions, the meaning hasn't changed. (One way of putting this: All the other truths relevant to whether the Celtics crushed the Knicks may stay true, while this one shifts from true to false.) Since meaning is truth conditions, we cannot simply describe the change as a change of meaning. On the other hand, it is difficult to call the change a change in view about whether crushing really took place. Without something like "stimulus situations" or facts, that is, the "given" that Davidson denies, there is nothing that helpfully expands on the "mere disquotational" account of what it takes for an utterance to be true.

What does it take for the utterance to be true? Just the following: (1) that "The Celtics crushed the Knicks" is true if and only if the Celtics crushed the Knicks; and (2) the Celtics crushed the Knicks.

The lack of something beyond a merely disquotational "fit" of what is said to what is the case is a consequence of taking truth to be primary, that is, denying meanings except as contributions to truth conditions, and denying a given. Without meanings or a given, there is no outside control to restrict the shifting truth-values of sentences. Correctness of application of predicates floats free of any absolute constraints.

Just as a Davidsonian account of interpretation does not appeal to meanings as constraints on interpretation, so a Davidsonian account of truth of application of predicates does not appeal to facts. Constraints on correctness of application are holistic. The lack of "outside" constraints (meanings, facts) does not mean that what is true is fixed by what people in a society believe, any more than what people mean is fixed by beliefs. Extensions are not determined by use, even though, necessarily, most of what most people believe is true. Patterns of use are evidence for assigning truth conditions, and so truth-values, but they are neither meanings nor truth-values.

Davidson's view thus does not disconnect language from the world. A Davidsonian (and a Derridian) is an externalist about reference and content. "Is a dog" is true of an object if and only if that object is a dog. That is, reference is fixed by how things are.

Is this puzzling shift that cannot be quite accommodated as change of view or change of meaning an effect of *differance*? "*Differance*" is both (1) the deferral (so to speak[26]) of words from their meanings, and (2) a kind of differing that Derrida portrays as somehow pre- or nonconceptual. Here is how to interpret *differance* in Davidsonian terms at least in these two respects:

1. *Deferral*: For Davidson, there is no notation more direct than language. Thought and anything else that has truth-value is language-like in that component tokens could have meant something different. That is, their tokens are marks. Everything a series of marks expresses has a contingent or arbitrary relation to a meaning. Derrida uses the metaphor of "deferral" as a constant feature of all meaningful marks in order to deny a distinction that is only possible if there is a magic language of transcendent meanings. For instance, writing stands for speech, and speech stands for thought. Thoughts, it is supposed by the "presence"-theory, by their very nature have the meanings they have. The "deferral" component of *differance* is a way of denying a magic language of tokens that have meanings by their very nature. Davidson, on the other hand, assumes acceptance of Quine's arguments against transcendent, magic-language meanings, and does not directly argue against magic-language hypotheses. So, although Davidson is committed to the theses about *differance,* he does not put them in Derrida's way. This is the "deferral" component.
2. *Differing*: A new "case" can be a case of anything. Nothing naturally forces any application of any predicate. "Sameness" is relative to a predicate, and no predicates come naturally attached to objects. So, new cases are "naturally" just different but not in virtue of some features distinguishing them. If nothing in nature forces a predication, then the distinctness of a new case is, in its nature, primitive.

Without a given, there are no metaphysical "natural kinds" that require to be called by the same predicate. Thus, the application of a predicate to a new case is always underdetermined. Every new case is different from every previous case, and nothing forces the application of any general term.[27] But if nothing forces the application of any term, the difference between the new case and anything else is not to be explicated by some predicate being true of one that is not true of the other. If meaning is truth conditions, and correct predication is "true of" conditions, each new case, though different, is not in its nature different relative to anything. Of course, depending on what is true, the new case is such that, for every predicate, that predicate either applies to it or not. That application is determined by truth, though, not by the given nature of the case.

Nothing, neither our dispositions to apply terms nor given natures, that is, natural joints in the world, *makes* it correct to call some new animal a dog. If truth is primitive, there is no deeper *analysis* than that "is a dog" is true of the object just in case it is a dog. As Davidson says, nothing *makes* a sentence true.[28]

Our dispositions to apply terms do indeed determine what we *call* dogs, but we can mistakenly call something a dog.[29] One feature of the truth predicate is precisely this difference between all the things that lead us to call something a dog and the thing's being a dog.

5 Why not *Differance* for Davidson?

So, why doesn't Davidson invoke *differance* or some notion like it to describe the above situation? One way to see why Davidson would abstain from talking about *differance* is to focus on the use of "case" in "new case" above. Davidson does not believe that any sense is to be made of a preconceptual array, of cases or whatever. If there is no given, there is no sequence of cases, either. So, the very picture this essay used to state the idea that the world does not come cut along the joints or otherwise presumes that it does. Davidson does think there is a way the world is in itself. Our true sentences describe the world as it is. The world, for instance, has contained dogs and buildings in itself, not "relative to English."

The way to describe anything is in one's language. The truths one utters characterize the world. To try to say how the world is "in itself" apart from a description in language is not a reasonable project. If it can't be said, it can't be whistled. If we spoke differently, different things would be true, but that does not mean that the truths we utter are not true.

Notes

1. Most prominently, Richard Rorty, in numerous works. See also Samuel Wheeler, *Deconstruction as Analytic Philosophy* (Stanford: Stanford University Press, 2000). No one could reasonably claim that Davidson is a "poststructuralist," any more than one could say that Derrida is a "post-Carnapian" or "post–logical positivist." Such characterizations, I take it, are tradition-specific.

2. In W. V. O. Quine, *From a Logical Point of View* (New York: Harper & Row, 1963).

3. Donald Davidson, "On the Very Idea of a Conceptual Scheme," in *Inquiries into Truth and Interpretation* (New York: Oxford University Press, 1984), p. 189.

4. This slogan, "Being supervenes on truth," has to be used with caution. It doesn't mean that if people had never existed, there would be no entities in that situation

for truths to be about. There are truths about that situation which we can formulate, including that there would not be truths. So, what sentences are true and what there is do not depend on the existence of minds or things like that. What it means is that reference and "is a thing" primarily organize truths, rather than there being a given domain of entities with essences (= *de re* necessities) that true sentences characterize.

5. Donald Davidson, "What Metaphors Mean," in *Inquiries into Truth and Interpretation*, pp. 245–264.

6. There are some aspects of the notion of *differance* that do not show up in Davidson. For instance, *differance*'s connection with Saussure's idea that systems of meaning are systems of differences is not mirrored in Davidson; see Ferdinand Saussure, *Course in General Linguistics* (New York: McGraw-Hill, 1966). There are some passages in "Differance," in Jacques Derrida, *Margins of Philosophy*, (Chicago: University of Chicago Press, 1982), pp. 1–27, where Derrida tries to characterize *differance* as some kind of non-thing or non-phenomenon. He is in effect recognizing that while there is no pre-conceptual given, "the world" is not homogeneous and exists whether or not we exist to conceptualize about it. Davidson engages in none of this, and would regard the mysterious nature of *differance* as a pseudo-question.

7. See for instance Derrida's "White Mythology," in *Margins of Philosophy*, p. 270: "Henceforth the entire teleology of meaning, which constructs the philosophical concept of metaphor, coordinates metaphor with the manifestation of truth, with the production of truth as presence without veil." See also Derrida's *Of Grammatology* (Baltimore: Johns Hopkins University Press, 1976), pp. 10–11: "Further, it [writing, correctly construed] inaugurates the destruction, not the demolition but the de-sedimentation, the de-construction, of all the significations that have their source in that of the logos. Particularly the signification of *truth*."

8. The arguments Derrida deploys come from a tradition different from the tradition of Quine and Davidson. Those arguments have a different philosophical style. Part of the interest of Derrida to an analytic philosopher of the Davidsonian brand is seeing how such continental arguments supplement and provide a different take on the considerations that move Davidson.

9. Derrida doesn't think nothing is true—rather nothing is "true" "in the classical sense." That is, Derrida is not committed to denying that there are better and worse objective results on true–false exams. Exactly what Derrida would want to say about the commonsense uses of "true" is hard to determine. He does seem to hold that somehow the philosophical theory of presence and being has thoroughly infected the culture and the language of that culture.

10. Truth, while central, is not reducible to anything else. Truth is definitely not the opening of presence. Rather, truths are what we start with, and from the truths, we posit beings. Davidson, following Quine, accepts the primacy of truth over being. Beings are posited to organize truths—being supervenes on truth, rather than

vice versa. So, this is very different from meanings fitting being as presence, giving truth. Davidson's truth is not truth as "presence." Far be it from Davidson to say such things.

11. Derrida also is addressing the truth-with-the-genitive, "the truth of" understood as "the true nature of," that we find in Hegel.

12. Does Derrida then think that a sentence like "It is true that there have been dogs" is true? He can say something like this: An atheist deals with religious people who preface many of their remarks with "By the grace of God." When one of them says, "By the grace of God, it's sunny outside," when indeed it is sunny outside, is what is said true or false, according to the atheist? Now, suppose that "by the grace of God" is always meant, but is a silent particle, sort of like PRO or TRACE.

Derrida, following Heidegger, takes metaphysics to have invaded the content of "ordinary language." Davidson, following Wittgenstein, and taking the idiolect as primary, does not suppose that metaphysical theories are part of the content of terms.

13. One marker of the huge difference between Davidson's and Derrida's styles and approach is the great difference between Davidson's "What Metaphors Mean" and Derrida's "White Mythology." Davidson does not discuss metaphor in the history of philosophy and doesn't discuss the conception of meaning embedded in the metaphor of metaphor. Derrida, on the other hand, doesn't feel called on to give an account of the difference between metaphorical and literal use, for reasons very like the ones that led Davidson to abandon the term "literal." Derrida would hesitate to say that the difference is between the literal and the rhetorical for some of the reasons that we will bring out below. Davidson, with his Wittgensteinian leanings, can be comfortable with distinctions that are unprincipled; Derrida seems not to accept such.

14. This is another manifestation of the "semantic innocence" that is the keystone of Davidson's "On Saying That," in *Inquiries into Truth and Interpretation*, pp. 93–108.

15. "Fornicate" was originally a metonymy, an indirect way of alluding to activities in fornice, the arches. Examples could be multiplied at dictionary length. "Sobriquet," now meaning "nickname," originally was a chuck under the chin. "Futile" comes from flowing, by the flowing of words from the foolish, then, by another turn, "hopeless."

16. Other times, metaphors become catch-phrases or idioms that survive the extinction of the original word. For example, in the English idiom "hoist on his own petard," probably fewer than one in a hundred English speakers know what a petard is. For another example, very few speakers of English know that the "shrift" in the common phrase, "given short shrift" has anything to do with making a confession. The etymologies of English words show that their history is often that of metaphorical applications of terms becoming routine, and then becoming the literal meanings

of terms. Figures can become literal, sometimes passing beyond the "dead" stage, where the "literal" meaning is still present to speakers, to the stage where the figuration is available only to the scholar. Other metaphors become distinct senses of words. "Berth" was originally a space for a ship to pass at sea. This sense is still present in English, at least in the metaphorical extension "giving *X* wide berth." "Berth" now means a place for a ship to dock, and most frequently, now a place on a train, boat, or other transport in which a person can sleep. The English speaker plausibly has three distinct words, about which he might speculate that they have something to do with one another historically.

Speculations by speakers about the connections among their words are often quite erroneous. A speaker of English might conjecture that since "halter" is a device one can seize to halt animals, it is derived from the verb "to halt."

17. The Rev. A. Smythe Palmer's nineteenth-century compilation *Folk Etymology* (New York: Henry Holt, 1883) has numerous such examples, many of which historically affected pronunciation and even spelling. A familiar example is the Jerusalem artichoke, misunderstood from the Italian "girasol," or sunflower. Another example of how such speculations can be very wide of the mark. Most English speakers would think that "swim" in the phrase "makes your head swim" has some figural or historical connection with "swim" as a mode of motion through the water. "Swim" meaning "dizzy" goes back to an Indo-European root, whereas "swim" meaning motion through water (cognate with "sound" as in Long Island Sound) has another root.

18. See Davidson's "A Nice Derangement of Epitaphs," in *Truth and Interpretation: Perspectives on the Philosophy of Donald Davidson*, ed. Ernest Lepore (New York: Blackwell, 1986), pp. 433–446. There Davidson famously says that there is "no such thing as a language, not if a language is anything like what many linguists and philosophers have supposed" (p. 446). The idiolect at a time is what matters in interpretation and understanding.

19. See Derrida's term "solicit" in "Differance," in *Margins of Philosophy*, p. 21.

20. One of the important differences between Davidson and Derrida is what features of language they focus on. Davidson does not concern himself with how the history of language affects what it is really possible to think or say. He shows no interest in the idea that philosophical ideas pervade "ordinary" thought and speech. He is interested primarily in a priori conditions of communication. He is also impressed with the creativity of language, and so disregards some of the "social" aspects of language that concern Derrida. Although he would acknowledge those aspects, he holds that creative people can break free of them.

Some other differences arise from his concentration on speech as opposed to texts, as Derrida would argue. In spite of taking speech as basic, however, he ends up committed to an account on which there is no difference in principle between speech and text.

21. "Could be a metaphor" is a question of whether the interpreter could treat the expression as a metaphor, i.e., whether there is a plausible interpretation of the utterance as metaphorical.

22. Since we do often agree and disagree with routine metaphorical utterances, these agreements and disagreements could be taken to indicate the truth and falsity of the utterances. When someone says, "The Lions crushed the Bengals," an interlocutor may say "They sure did." Thus, speaker and hearer might be understood as treating the utterances as true or false, and so an indication that those utterances really are true or false, and so, on the rhetorical account, literal. But consider the miniature conversation, "I believe it's raining," "Yes, indeed." The first utterance has the truth conditions of a report on the speaker's cognitive state, but the agreement is with the message that the speaker was communicating. Something similar can happen with, for instance, hyperbole, in the example above, where the interlocutor agrees with the utterance "Bush is an idiot," even though neither speaker nor hearer believe Bush meets the clinical criteria. Agreement, on reflection, turns out not to be a very good guide to whether either the speaker or the interlocutor holds that the truth conditions of an utterance obtain.

23. The main reason people might think that there is an objective difference between a word having two senses and having routine metaphorical application is that it is plausible that some objective difference obtains in neurological correlates of homonyms such as "bank" in its various meanings. Presumably these words are stored differently and interpretation of a sound as one or the other of them activates different brain areas. That this is plausible for very clear cases of distinct words does not make it plausible that there are neural correlates indicating differences in these borderline cases. If the difference between a dying metaphor and a dead metaphor is rhetorical, then there should be a neurological marker only if other rhetorical phenomena, such as hyperbole and sarcasm, were also so marked. This would mean that a marker for the intention to say something true on the given occasion would be either present or absent. The picture such a view implies is of a very strong isomorphism between the predicates of the "mental" description scheme and the physiological. For a Davidsonian, this is quite implausible. Davidson's views on the relation between the mental and the physical are laid out in "Mental Events," in *Essays on Actions and Events* (New York: Oxford University Press, 1980), pp. 207–224. Davidson's argument that there will not be detailed neurophysiological correlates of mental states, including intentions involving speech acts, is part of his anomalous monism. This is the thesis that, although every mental event is identical with some physical event, there is no systematic relation of mental, i.e., intentional, predicates to physical predicates. Given anomalous monism, and given that the difference between metaphorical and literal use depends on the intentional content of a particular intention, the possibility that such differences would be physically definable and so determinate disappears. Davidson's anomalous monism gets independent

support from philosophers like Paul Churchland, who argue from results in brain physiology that intentional concepts, the categories and kinds of the "intentional stance" (to use Dennett's term from *Content and Consciousness*), correlate with nothing in the brain. Churchland takes this to be an argument that intentional concepts, which collectively constitute "folk psychology," do not designate anything real. See Paul Churchland, *Scientific Realism and the Plasticity of Mind* (New York: Cambridge University Press, 1979). This conception of the consequences of the lack of fit between the physiological and the psychological is shared with thinkers like Quine and Dennett. Churchland's proposal is to reform the language of psychology and to abandon "folk psychology." Davidson's view on the reality of the mental follows from his conception of interpretation. There is no possibility of adopting a language that gives up the idea that we and others are agents, since the very idea of a language as something interpretable presupposes that speech acts are acts, i.e., things done by agents with beliefs and desires. Churchland's arguments on the lack of fit between the brain and the "linguaformal" account of reasons, beliefs, and desires is thus, for Davidson, an empirical argument that supplements the a priori arguments about rational constraints on application of predicates.

24. In many cases, we have "privileged access" to our intentions and can know the intentions of others. It is usually no mystery what a person intends when that person puts a key in a lock. But this does not mean that we can tell the difference between intending to say a truth or not when we use "crush" in "The Bengals crushed the Rams."

25. This indeterminacy of intention is an everyday occurrence. It causes no practical problems, because there is complete practical agreement between the speaker and hearer. So, there is no difficulty in determining what the speaker intends to communicate, but the truth-value of the utterance is indeterminate. If interpreted metaphorically, then the utterance is false. If interpreted as using a term in a different sense, then the utterance is true, and there are two distinct predicate clauses in the appropriate truth definition.

26. We need the "so to speak" because there are no magic language tokens, and so no meanings that are *not* deferred.

27. I discuss the idea of difference as a kind of metaphysically prior notion in "Derrida's *Differance* and Plato's Different," *Philosophy and Phenomenological Research* 59 (December 1999): 999–1013.

28. Davidson, "True to the Facts," in *Inquiries into Truth and Interpretation*, pp. 37–54 and elsewhere.

29. If we specify our dispositions so as to make them definitionally accurate, we get something like "We are disposed to call dogs 'dogs'"; that is, "disposed to" takes on a probabilistic sense.

4 Davidson, Kant, and Double-Aspect Ontologies

Gordon G. Brittan, Jr.

The history of philosophy has a variety of uses. One of them is to illuminate contemporary positions by placing them in a larger context, not so much to trace influences or impose taxonomies as to force their deeper understanding. This is what I propose to do here by way of focusing on certain of the "Kantian" dimensions of Donald Davidson's thought. Davidson was very much influenced by Kant, although, so far as I know, the only text on which he comments directly is the *Foundations of the Metaphysics of Morals*. As he put it in the autobiographical introduction to the Library of Living Philosophers volume devoted to his work, of all the great philosophers, "Kant's influence has been the most pervasive, but it runs so deep that I have seldom acknowledged it in print."[1] At the same time, it would be a mistake to think that Davidson simply rethought or reworked, even more so that he simply appropriated, anything of Kant's that he had read.[2] The influence was, I believe, indirect and came by way of C. I. Lewis, to whose epistemological views an entire generation of American philosophers—Quine, Chisholm, and Goodman included—were indebted, in part by way of their criticism of him. Rather, or so I suggest, Davidson found in Kant confirmation of positions that he had arrived at independently, although the revival of interest in Kant in the 1950s and 1960s was linked to the decline of logical positivism and was very much part of a widely shared background.[3]

Still, there are deep and important similarities between the two of them. For one thing, Davidson's project is in a way very much like Kant's, with this adjustment: that it has to do not with the conditions of possible experience in general, but with the possibility of what might be called linguistic experience (although our own time sees no sharp difference between them). In both cases, some fact is taken as basic, that we do have (objective) experience, and that we do communicate (successfully). The task is to provide something like an explanation of this fact, a list of its a priori presuppositions, causality, for example, in the case of Kant, charity and rationality in the case of Davidson, although in neither case is it a question of reconstructing the actual procedures followed by a working physicist or field linguist.[4]

The major difference between the two in this respect is that Kant had a theory, Newton's, whose application serves to distinguish what is objective in our experience from what is not, and in the process, not surprisingly, fits his conditions (with some significant tinkering) to a tee. Davidson did not yet have such a theory, only fragments of it, a general program (adapted from Frege's and taking first-order quantification theory as canonical), and a standard like Newton's of empirical success (Tarski's "Convention T") that it would have to meet. Put another way, Kant could proceed analytically, working backward so to speak, from a fully articulated theory to the conditions of its possibility, whereas Davidson had to proceed synthetically, toward a theory whose requirements he had made clear, but which remained, despite his efforts to add to and make the fragments cohere, in important respects unfinished. Among the most appealing aspects of his work is the frank admission of this fact.[5]

For another thing, both Kant and Davidson break rather sharply with the (first-half) eighteenth- and twentieth-century mainstreams in their rejection of foundationalism and reductionism. As regards the first, neither conceives of philosophy as a justificatory enterprise; it suffices to show that skepticism is itself deeply incoherent. As regards the second, Kant rejects the attempts by Leibniz, on the one hand, to reduce space and time to sets of relations on objects and events, and arithmetic to definitions and the principle of contradiction, and by Hume, on the other hand, to reduce objects and causes to bundles and sequences of sense-impressions. Davidson adds ethical naturalism, instrumentalism, the causal theory of meaning, and behaviorism to the list.[6] Indeed, in their defense of the irreducible character of truth and their insistence on our common humanity, both are Enlightenment philosophers. At the same time, of course, Davidson breaks sharply with Kant in rejecting any sort of sharp distinction between form and content,[7] on which the success of the latter's project ostensibly depends, and which will be the subject of my concluding remarks.

For a third thing, Davidson and Kant share a common method. They begin with antinomies that defy easy resolution, proceed to draw fundamental distinctions, and reach a kind of synthesis or resolution at the end. Kantian examples are too familiar to cite. One among many Davidsonian examples is in "How Is Weakness of the Will Possible?" which opens with an inconsistent triad of propositions and closes with a distinction between conditional and unconditional judgments. If not an explicit contradiction, each tends to start off with a question,[8] "is metaphysics possible?" (in the case of Kant), and "what is the relation between a reason and an action when the reason explains the action by giving the agent's reason for doing what he did?" (in the case of Davidson), to which two answers, both initially intuitive, can be given. "Two intuitions seem to be at war," Davidson writes in "Actions, Reasons, and Causes," "and the territory that is threatened with destruction is occupied by the causal theory." Or again in "Truth and Meaning": "Logicians have often reacted by downgrading natural language and trying to show how to get along without demonstratives; their critics react by downgrading logic and formal semantics. None of this can make me happy." Happily, the antinomy is eventually, although with difficulty, resolved—at great length in the case of Kant, sometimes too briefly in the case of Davidson. In "On Saying That," Davidson writes that

> The paradox that sentences (utterances) in *oratio obliqua* do not have the logical consequences they should have if truth is to be defined, is resolved. What follows the verb "said" has only the structure of a singular term, usually the demonstrative "that." Assuming the "that" refers, we can infer that Galileo said something from "Galileo said that"; but this is welcome.[9]

I could go on in this vein, noting resemblances (and occasional differences) between them along the way. But I want instead to focus on the one place where, so far as I know, Davidson makes more than passing mention of Kant. It comes in his essay "Mental Events," which may be taken as his gloss on the Third Antinomy. Davidson starts "from the assumption that both the causal dependence, and the anomalousness, of mental events are undeniable facts." He goes on:

> My aim is therefore to explain, in the face of apparent difficulties, how this can be. I am in sympathy with Kant when he says, "it is as impossible for the subtlest philosophy as for the commonest reasoning to argue freedom away. Philosophy must therefore assume that no true contradiction will be found between freedom and natural necessity in the same human actions, for it cannot give up the idea of nature any more than that of freedom. Hence even if we should never be able to conceive how freedom is possible, at least this apparent contradiction must be convincingly eradicated. For if the thought of freedom contradicts itself or nature . . . it would have to be surrendered in competition with natural necessity." Generalize human actions to mental events, substitute anomaly for freedom, and this is a description of my problem. And of course the connection is closer, since Kant believed freedom entails anomaly.[10]

Three principles generate the apparent paradox. The first is that mental events at least on occasion cause physical events, as when my having a particular desire, say, to provide an introductory philosophy class with an example of a voluntary action, and my having a particular belief, that walking over to the classroom door and opening it would be the simplest way to provide an example, causes me to walk over to the door and open it. The second principle is that where there are causes and effects there must be laws linking them, where by a "law" we understand, at a first approximation, any universal generalization of the form "All *A* are *B*" capable of entailing a subjunctive conditional of the form "if anything were to have property *A* it would have property *B*." The third principle is that there are no such laws linking mental causes to physical effects.[11]

The problem is not simply that the three principles are, as they stand, jointly inconsistent, but also that each is deeply intuitive. In order better to understand the eventual contrast with Kant's position, it is necessary to sketch the case that Davidson makes for them, however briefly. He defends the first along three different lines. One, we typically explain human actions by indicating the reasons for which they are done, what, from the agent's point of view and in particular circumstances, makes them rational to perform. There are a variety of ways in which any action can be thus "rationalized," a variety of reasons that serve to make it intelligible. First, a particular reason, most often a desire paired with a belief in the way already indicated, explains why an agent acted as he did only if "the agent performed the action *because* he had the reason."[12] Second, unless we can say that the action was *caused* by a desire or belief (or in some *mens rea* equivalent way), then we cannot attribute *responsibility* for it to the agent, for the attribution of responsibility presupposes that the agent herself, and not some other factor external to the agent, brought the action about, and "bringing about" can only be analyzed in causal terms. Third, as they are ordinarily understood, mental concepts have a causal-functional character; desires and beliefs, for example, are defined by the roles they play, given certain environmental inputs, in producing certain kinds of behavior.

The second principle, that causality can only be understood in terms of lawlike connections between events, is so generally accepted that it is not necessary to argue for it here, nor does Davidson anywhere. Its classic defense is in the Second Analogy. The occasional objection to it is that the word "cause" is used so broadly as to include cases where no laws are involved. The point can be granted. Both Kant and Davidson would insist in reply, however, that all actions involve *changes*, that all changes are *events*, and that the only way in which we can distinguish between events that come after one another, mere succession, and those that are causally connected, is to say that in the second case there is a law that, taken together with a description of the first event, licenses the prediction of the second. When the laws in question are deterministic, then, given the cause, the effect is necessary.

The third principle, that there are no laws, properly so called, linking mental causes to physical effects, is more difficult, in part because Davidson invokes rather sweeping claims made in his theory of language to defend it. But the basic idea involved is straightforward. It may be spelled out in two rather closely related ways.[13] Both begin with the form of putative "laws" linking the mental to the physical. In the simplest case, they would take some such form as "if any agent *x* desires that *p* and believes that performing *a* in circumstances *C* will bring it about that *p*, then, other things being equal (e.g., *x* does not believe that there is an alternative or better way than *a* to bring it about that *p*), *x* does *a*." But, first, such a law is not empirical. For if *x* did not do *a* in the circumstances described, it would not follow that the "law" was false so much as it would that our original attributions of a particular belief and a desire to *x* were mistaken. We could not, in fact, begin to understand why *x* acted as she did if her beliefs and desires did not in fact fit together in some way that was intelligible to us. A failure of the "law" would be tantamount to admitting that we had not really understood why she was acting as she did, had not grasped the relevant pattern in her behavior. Still another way to make approximately the same point is to underline the fact that we could determine on the basis of her behavior that *x* had a desire that *p* only if we also *assumed* at the same time that she believed that *a* was a means to bringing about that *p*. Or, the other way around, we could determine the belief on the basis of the behavior only if we held the desire constant, either way assuming as well that the agent is rational. But if so, then the "law" is not testable, since we could (indeed, always would) question the assumption rather than reject the "law." And, second, the only way to establish or recover *x*'s desires and beliefs is after the fact, on the basis of the way in which she behaved,[14] in which case the "law" could not be used, as genuine laws are used in the physical sciences, to *predict* the behavior. Davidson dubs the principle that "*there are no laws linking mental causes to physical effects*" the anomalousness of the mental.

At this point, the three principles are reconciled in a beguilingly simple way. The very same events described in a physical vocabulary can also be described in a mental vocabulary. Under their mental descriptions, for the reasons just stated, there are no laws on the basis of which subsequent events, described in either a mental or a physical vocabulary, can be predicted. If we add that a necessary condition on determined or "unfree" action is that it can be predicted, then it follows that all intentional behavior, described and understood in intentional terms, is not determined. Such an account of intentional behavior, Davidson concludes, operates "in a conceptual framework removed from the direct reach of physical law by describing both cause and effect, reason and action, as aspects of a portrait of a human agent."[15] Yet the mental events invoked in an intentional account of behavior are rightly labeled *causes* insofar as they are identical with neural events that are connected, in a lawlike way, with other events such as bodily movements, in which case prediction of these latter is possible. One event, two descriptions, with respect to one kind of which we are rational agents, our actions unpredictable, and with respect to the other kind of which we are physical objects like any others, whose movements are determined by antecedent conditions. Since kinds of mental events cannot be correlated with kinds of physical events, still less the descriptions of the former be translated without loss of meaning into descriptions of the latter, the implicit causality of the intentional account of behavior does not depend on any sort of "reduction" of the mental to the physical.

There are at least three things to be said in favor of anomalous monism as a gloss on what Kant calls "negative freedom."[16] First, anomalous monism, as just noted, does not involve any sort of "reduction," as the term is usually employed. As in the case of Kant, there is no commitment to "materialism," the view that the mind is nothing more than the body or the brain. Second, anomalousness is for Kant as well a necessary condition on free action; to the extent that an event can be predicted, via causal laws, it cannot be free. Third, anomalousness is, in turn, a function of taking one but not the other of two ways of describing, and hence of explaining or rendering intelligible, human behavior. It is with respect to the latter two points especially that Davidson quotes Kant in support and clarification of his own position:

> It is an indispensable problem of speculative philosophy to show that its illusion respecting the contradiction rests on this, that we think of man in a different sense and relation when we call him free, and when we regard him as subject to the laws of nature. . . . It must therefore show that not only can both of these very well co-exist, but that both must be thought of as *necessarily united* in the same subject.[17]

In other respects, however, and whatever its considerable philosophical merits, Davidson's account does not provide us with an adequate reading of Kant, not because it does not also capture what he says about "positive" freedom, but because Kant does not think that the mental is anomalous in the desired ways.[18] This is not the time or the place for a detailed consideration of Kant's views. My use of him in this essay is merely tactical. But there are at least two clear reasons for not attributing Davidson's position to him. First, despite his nuanced and somewhat equivocal discussion of the possibility of "psychological laws,"[19] Kant (following Hume) thinks that mental events described as such are causes in the intended sense of the term, that is, they are connected in a lawlike way with behavioral effects. How else are we to read this passage from the *Critique of Practical Reason*?

> In the question of freedom which lies at the foundation of all moral laws and accountability to them, it is really not at all a question of whether the causality determined by a natural law is necessary through determining grounds lying within or without the subject, or whether, if they lie within him, they are in instinct or in grounds of determination thought by reason . . . ; and if they do not have mechanical causality but a psychological causality through conceptions instead of through bodily movements: they are nonetheless determining grounds of the causality of a being so far as its existence is determinable in time.[20]

Second, Kant does not identify the standpoint from which it is possible to construe human beings as free and moral as "mental," but as "noumenal." To put it as simply as possible, the "mental" is knowable, the "noumenal" is not. One aspect of its knowability is that what passes for "mental" takes place in time; talking about mental *events* characterizes them as such. The "noumenal," on the other hand, by definition has to do with that which cannot be given in time or space.

Moreover, Davidson's account of the anomalousness of the mental has its own problems, quite apart from taking it as an adequate reading of Kant.[21] Perhaps chief among these problems concerns the apparent vacuousness of "mental causation" on this account. If mental events are causally efficacious only because they are identical with causally efficacious physical events, then there is nothing about mental events, even in their character as desires that have traditionally been held to "move" us in a way in which beliefs by themselves do not, that bears in the slightest on the way in which they *cause* our behavior. A mental event's "causal relations are fixed, wholly and exclusively, by the totality of its physical properties, and there is in this picture no causal work that [mental properties] can, or need to, contribute."[22] If this is so, however, then mental events are "causes" only *de grace*, and Davidson's first principle, that "mental events on some occasions cause physical events," needs to be kept in quotation marks. The causal-functional character of mental concepts mentioned earlier in connection with our attempts to make human behavior intelligible, and the role of rationality in their success, simply drops out of our description of the causal structure of the world.[23]

Originally in passing,[24] more systematically as his position came to be criticized,[25] Davidson appealed to the idea of supervenience to establish some sort of connection between the properties of mental and physical events. Put in its usual formulaic way, this is the idea that there is no mental difference without a physical difference. But this is no more than to say that mental properties vary as a function of the physical properties on which they ostensibly depend; it does not make precise the nature of this dependence or, as a result, the specific character of mental properties that make a difference, so to speak, in the causation of particular behavioral routines.

David Chalmers, among others, picks up on both of these difficulties and in the process moves the idea of supervenience to the forefront of the discussion.[26] In his view, it is a mistake to identify the mental with the intentional. Intentional states (beliefs, desires, and all the rest) are, Davidson correctly indicated, to be identified with their causal-functional roles, but these roles can, in turn, be played or "realized" by particular physical structures.

This sort of criticism of Davidson's account has more to do with its anomalousness than with its monism, although there is evidently a close connection between the two. But its deeper difficulties concern the monism. However inaccurate his account is as a reading of Kant, however inadequate as an explanation of mental causation, the fundamental problem involves the identity between mental and physical events that is at its heart.[27] Importantly, it shares this difficulty with every other double-aspect ontology—Spinoza's, Kant's, and Strawson's included.[28]

Davidson contends that we can give mental and physical descriptions of the *same* event. Beliefs, desires, and neural states are not events, of course, so we should instead talk of having or acquiring beliefs and desires and coming into a neural state. Largely because he thinks that an adequate semantics for action sentences requires them, Davidson admits events as such into his ontology. On the very plausible dictum that there is no entity without identity, he had to supply a criterion of identity for them. This demand is all the more pressing when we speak, as he does, of the "same" event under two or more descriptions.

What are appropriate identity conditions for events?[29] Davidson initially proposed that "events are identical if and only if they have exactly the same causes and effects."[30] The problem with this criterion is that "causes" and "effects" are themselves events, linked in a lawlike way, in which case the identity conditions are, if not exactly circular, then question-begging, a fact that Davidson himself was quick to acknowledge.[31] He then adopted Quine's criterion that events are identical if and only if they occur in the same space at the same time. But this second criterion in turn is problematic. For one thing, as Davidson had noted prior to adopting it,[32] "If a metal ball becomes warmer during a certain minute, and during the same minute rotates through 35 degrees, must we say that these are the same event?" On Quine's account, the answer is clearly "yes," but this seems at the very least counterintuitive. For another thing, since two physical events are identical if and only if they occur in the same space at the same time, it follows that objects and events are identical, when it is one of Davidson's main ends to distinguish them.

What is more problematic still is that on *both* criteria events must be *physical*. This accords quite naturally with Davidson's monism. But it leaves it completely mysterious not only *what* the expression "mental event" might mean (or whether it is an oxymoron), but also how one might determine (or even begin to determine) whether a particular mental description applied to "the same event" as a particular physical description. It would help, of course, if one could parse the mental description in terms of a corresponding physical description, or associate types of mental events with types of physical events (nomologically or in some other way), but this is just what Davidson's anomalousness of the mental, and with it at least part of his case for human freedom, the irreducibility and indispensability of rationality, and all of the rest, precludes.

In what seems to me a rather plaintive way, Davidson admits the problem, but attempts to defuse it: "I do not think the lack of a perfectly general and useful criterion of event identity is any more serious for events than for objects; one only gets fairly solid criteria when one considers sorts: sorts of objects or events."[33] However imprecise the notion of a "sort" might be, this seems to be right. Identity conditions are tied to the sort of object under consideration, and, in a roughly equivalent way, only sorts—*green apple* is the usual paradigm—lend themselves to counting procedures. The problem, of course, is that it is radically unclear whether mental and physical events belong to the same or different sorts. If they belong to the same sort, it would seem to follow that, as in the case of green apples, there is some group of characteristics that they share, in virtue of which they can be identified in a type–type way. But Davidson rules out the possibility of a type–type identity, in part because he wants to safeguard the realm of the characteristically human from the encroachment of physical law. If mental and physical events belong to different sorts, as is often maintained,[34] then it would seem to follow that we cannot identify them in a token–token way either, since the very conditions of their identity as individuals would differ. We have already noted how difficult it is to count physical events on Davidson's proffered criteria, even when we can locate them in particular space-time regions. The difficulty is compounded in the case of mental events if they are to be construed, as Davidson does, in terms of the causal-functional roles they play. So many different objects could, at least in principle, play these roles that we would not know how to begin to count them. I will return to this point later. For the moment it is enough to conclude that it is at the very least problematic to assert that mental and physical descriptions can be given of the *same* event. If so, then, regrettably, anomalous monism must be given up.

I indicated a moment ago that the loss is not local. The virus infects every double-aspect ontology with which I am familiar. In the passage quoted by Davidson at the very end of "Mental Events," Kant says that the perspectives from which we can think of man as both free and subject to the laws of nature "must be thought as *necessarily united* in the same subject." But what are the criteria for the "sameness of the subject" of the free/determined judgments? Insofar as our judgments concern beings subject to causal laws, these "beings" must be in space and time, and their identity construed accordingly. Insofar, on the other hand, as our judgments concern beings whose actions are self-initiated or free, the "same" beings must not be in space and time, with it left completely open how such "noumenal" objects are to be identified with their "phenomenal" counterparts, still less to be individuated among themselves. There are many different ways to interpret Kant's resolution of the freedom–determinism antinomy, and of the phenomenal–noumenal distinction on which that resolution depends, but if one interprets him as a one-world two-descriptions theorist, as is conventionally the case, then Davidson's problems are his as well.[35]

What to do? There are, so far as I can see, three main ways out. The first is to modify or deny one of the three principles that led, naturally if not also logically, to anomalous monism: that mental events at least on occasion cause physical events, that where there are causes and effects there must be laws linking them, or that there are no laws linking mental causes to physical effects. Any number of attempts have been made to do so, some of them undoubtedly in this collection of essays. It is not possible to examine them here. Suffice it to say that the idea that beliefs and desires cause at least some of our actions is so deeply rooted that our ascriptions of responsibility seem to depend upon it, that analyses of causality other than in terms of law-linked events run up against major obstacles, and that to construe ourselves in biological or similarly reductive terms would be to reconstrue ourselves, changing the subjects of our self-narratives.

The second way out of the difficulties that double-aspect monism encounters is made explicit by Spinoza, endorsed, at least indirectly, by Kant, and institutionalized by Bradley. It is that there is only one object (and no independent category of events); hence questions concerning identity and individuation do not arise.[36] At least, I can find something like this view in Kant. At A720/B748 of the *Critique of Pure Reason*, he says that there is *one* instance of an object that is not independent of our concept of it, and that is of a "thing in general."[37] This is tantamount, I would offer tentatively, to saying that the concept of a "thing in general" is a genuine singular term, the only one that picks out a unique referent (without the aid of what Kant calls "intuitions," which here we might style "demonstratives"). If we add that what is (phenomenally) real is that to which genuine singular terms refer, it follows that there is but one (phenomenally) real thing. I cannot see that Kant makes much of the point; it occurs only very late in the *Critique*. But Hegel and his successors did. For Bradley, for instance, the properly predicative form of judgment is "Reality is such that. . . ." That is to say, there is only one (genuine) subject of predication, hence only one object. Ontology as we know it, the attempt to say what *kinds* of things there are, simply disappears; monism is possible, as Parmenides taught us long ago, only insofar as there is no individuation. That this view has always seemed paradoxical, nowhere more so than in Parmenides' own case, does not by itself provide reason to reject it. Indeed, I cannot think of any decisive objections, other than to point to the fact that its various elaborations, including Bradley's own, are extremely difficult to understand. Perhaps it is enough to say that the solution to the problem seems ad hoc, designed to salvage "the two-descriptions one-world view" from the attack I have made on it here, but having little else to be said in its favor.

The third and final way out is suggested by another of Davidson's most celebrated and characteristic views, that no sharp distinction is to be made between form or scheme and content.[38] It would clearly be misleading, if not also false, to say that the "two descriptions of one object" puzzle presupposes a sharp distinction between form and content, the descriptions on one side, the object on the other, and that as soon as we abandon the form–content distinction the puzzle is solved. As Jeff Malpas has reminded me in a personal communication, "the very notion of description implies a distinction between the description and the object of description in much the same way, for instance, that the notion of belief involves a distinction between belief and the object of belief." Davidson is, again like Kant, a realist, who very much resists the contemporary attempt to assimilate objects to descriptions or reduce what there is to our interpretations of "it," in the same way that his great predecessor resisted the attempt to reduce objects and causes to sets and sequences of sense-impressions.

Yet there is a plausible and, I think, important connection. The form–content distinction presupposes that "content" can be identified independent of "form." What this amounts to, I suggest, is that identity conditions can be given for the objects and events that constitute "content" across the board, so to speak, without any further reference to their "form," which might here be taken to include the ways in which the objects are described, the properties that are attributed to them. I have argued that identity conditions are difficult to come by in the case of mental and physical events, and have added in passing that ostensibly weaker, "supervenient" conditions fare no better, even if one renders these "global" in character. Whether one identifies "the mental" with the intentional (or sapient) or phenomenal (or sentient) there is no obvious and non-question-begging way in which it can be identified with "the physical." To say this is to imply that identity (even supervenience) conditions are contextual in character, attaching, as Davidson indicated, to "sorts" of objects, and, more narrowly, to particular vocabularies and the purposes to which these are put. To say this is further to imply that "objects" and "events" do not exist, but that green apples and tropical thunderstorms do. The notion of "sameness" has application in connection with the latter only, not the former, and in neither case does it follow that particular objects and events cannot be distinguished sharply from their descriptions.

Mental objects and events cannot be identified with their ostensible physical counterparts, not because they are *something else,* as the dualist would have it, but because it makes as little sense to identify as to distinguish them. Traditional monists are as mistaken about this point as dualists. From this point of view, at least, what has come to pass for "ontology," monism versus dualism, is, as Daniel Dennett remarked to me recently, "a mug's game." Or rather, what emerges is a different kind of "anomalous monism," one that eschews distinctions between kinds of objects, where by "kinds" is understood not particular "sorts" but the most general categories of things. It is at this level that the scheme–content distinction disappears, or when it does not, it leads to intractable problems. The early Davidson insisted on a more austere, but ultimately untenable, version of the monistic position, that what there is is physical. The later Davidson revised it, at least implicitly, and in the process reconstrued and relaxed Quine's dictum that there is no entity without identity. One happy, albeit somewhat paradoxical, result is that we no longer need to be concerned after all is said and done about the "encroachment of physical law" on the distinctively human dimensions of our lives. In the very nature of the case, the events they comprise cannot be identified with, still less "reduced" to, something else.

Acknowledgments

Recent exchanges with James Allard, Kevin Lande, and Jeff Malpas have very much helped me clarify the argument of the final paragraphs, although they are not to be held responsible for the inevitably somewhat compressed result. The three anonymous referees for MIT Press have made useful suggestions, several of which have been incorporated into the text.

Notes

1. *The Philosophy of Donald Davidson*, ed. Lewis Edwin Hahn (Chicago: Open Court, 1999), p. 64.

2. Future historians of ideas will no doubt note that Whitehead was Davidson's teacher at Harvard, and that he, like Davidson, introduced events as a fundamental category (indeed, *the* fundamental category, to which all others were reducible) into his ontology, and infer that he somehow influenced Davidson in this respect. But Davidson himself told me that he made the connection only after the publication of "The Logic of Action Sentences," when friends reminded him of Whitehead's view. "Of course, Whitehead!" he said to himself, and ran off to read what the latter had written on the subject. Disappointment set in quickly when all he could recover from Whitehead's text were such otherwise unhelpful items as that enduring perceptual and physical objects, as well as scientific objects and minds, or souls, are repetitions of patterns inherited through a series of events or occasions, and that the union of any two events is an event.

3. If Quine had anything to say about Kant, it was only very indirectly and by way of criticism, of the analytic–synthetic distinction, for example.

4. Interestingly, Kant also and often avails himself of the expression "logical form" (*logische Form*), as at A262/B318 of the first *Critique*, and likens his enterprise to collecting the elements of a "grammar" in a way reminiscent of Davidson, importantly in the "Appendix to Pure Natural Science: On the System of Categories" in the *Prolegomena to Any Future Metaphysics*.

5. "Since I think there is no alternative, I have taken an optimistic and programmatic view of the possibilities for a formal characterization of the truth predicate for a natural language. But it must be allowed that a staggering list of difficulties and conundrums remains." From "Truth and Meaning," *Synthese* 17 (1967), p. 123. Kant thought, at least at the time of publication of the three *Critiques*, that his system was "complete."

6. In his words, "the catalogue of philosophy's defeats." See *Essays on Action and Events* (Oxford: Clarendon Press, 1980), pp. 216–217.

7. Or for that matter between the descriptive and the normative.

8. Roughly half of the essays in *Essays on Actions and Events* begin with questions.

9. Davidson, "On Saying That," in *Inquiries into Truth and Interpretation* (Oxford: Oxford University Press, 1984), p. 108.

10. Davidson, "Mental Events," in *Essays on Actions and Events*, p. 207.

11. Or, for that matter, linking mental causes to mental effects or physical causes to mental effects.

12. For criticism of this view, and some second thoughts for attributing it to Davidson without reservation, see Frederick Stoutland, "The Real Reasons," in *Human Action, Deliberation, and Causation*, ed. Jan Bransen and Stefaan E. Cuypers (Dordrecht: Kluwer, 1998), pp. 43–66.

13. I follow Peter Lanz's admirable discussion in "The Explanatory Force of Action Explanations," in *Reflecting Davidson: Donald Davidson Responding to an International Forum of Philosophers*, ed. Ralf Stoecker (Berlin: Walter de Gruyter, 1993), pp. 394ff., although the idea had already been developed by Melden and von Wright, among others.

14. We often recover our own (real) desires and beliefs after the fact: "I thought I loved her, but that couldn't possibly have been the case given the fact that I treated her so badly."

15. Davidson, *Essays on Actions and Events*, p. 225.

16. The most developed and careful attempt to interpret Kant's position in anomalous monistic terms is by Ralf Meerbote, "Kant on the Nondeterminate Character of Human Actions," in *Kant on Causality, Freedom, and Objectivity*, ed. William A. Harper and Ralf Meerbote (Minneapolis: University of Minnesota Press, 1984), pp. 138–163.

17. *Essays on Actions and Events*, p. 25; original (with italics) in the *Fundamental Principles of the Metaphysics of Morals* (1785), trans. Thomas K. Abbott (Prentice-Hall, 1949), p. 76.

18. Henry Allison criticizes Meerbote's reconstruction in some detail, although the full force of these criticisms is a function of the extent to which Allison's own, somewhat idiosyncratic, account is plausible. See his *Kant's Theory of Freedom* (Cambridge: Cambridge University Press, 1990), pp. 76–82.

19. For example in the *Metaphysical Foundations of Natural Science*, trans. James W. Ellington (Indianapolis: Bobbs-Merrill, 1970), p. 8.

20. From the Beck translation (Indianapolis: Bobbs-Merrill, 1956), p. 100. See also the *Critique of Pure Reason*, A549–550/B777–578.

21. See Jaegwon Kim, *Mind in a Physical World: An Essay on the Mind–Body Problem and Mental Causation* (Cambridge, MA: MIT Press, 1998), especially pp. 32–35 and the references in note 5 to chapter 2.

22. Ibid., p. 34.

23. It is revealing that Meerbote requires as part of his analysis that the agent tells himself an "appropriate internal story" with regard to the desires and beliefs with respect to which he first deliberates and then acts as if the action is to be construed as nondeterminate, the word "story" suggesting strongly that the agent must engage in a piece of self-deception regarding the *real* causes of his action.

24. In Davidson, "Mental Events," *Essays on Action and Events*, p. 214. It is worth noting that the word "supervenience" does not even make the book's index.

25. See Davidson, "Thinking Causes," in *Mental Causation*, ed. John Heil and Alfred Mele (Oxford: Clarendon Press, 1993).

26. David Chalmers, *The Conscious Mind: In Search of a Fundamental Theory* (New York: Oxford University Press, 1996). Of course, Davidson did no more than deny that mental events were "naturally" supervenient on physical events, in the sense that there are no "laws" connecting the former with the latter. Chalmers makes explicit a notion of "logical" supervenience, which Davidson's monism might seem to require; there is no logically possible world in which a particular mental property or event is instantiated or occurs in which a particular physical property or event is not also instantiated or occurs.

27. Chalmers asserts that his own argument for a double-aspect ontology (on which the two "aspects," or in his case *properties*, are not the intentional and the physical, as in the case of Davidson, but the phenomenal and the physical) "does not turn on questions of *identity* but of *supervenience*. . . . This is an entirely different sort of argument. In general, modal arguments for dualism that are cast in terms of identity are less conclusive than modal arguments cast in terms of supervenience." Chalmers, *The Conscious Mind*, pp. 130–131. The apparent advantage is merely temporary. Arguments from supervenience, too, eventually come up against questions of identity: In every possible world in which the property shape is instantiated the property size is as well, yet neither of these properties is reducible to the other.

28. Spinoza and Strawson are self-admittedly "double-aspect" theorists (and Davidson sometimes emphasizes the parallels between Spinoza's position and his own, as on pages 63–64 of *The Philosophy of Donald Davidson*). Kant is so on the now-dominant interpretation of his position: "phenomenal" and "noumenal" pick out two kinds of descriptions of one and the same basic thing. This interpretation is

suggested by many passages, among them the footnote at Bxvii in the preface to the first *Critique*: "the same object can be considered from two different sides, *on the one side* as objects of the senses and the understanding for experience, and *on the other side* as objects that are merely thought at most for isolated reason striving beyond the bounds of experience"; from the Guyer and Wood translation.

29. There is a helpful discussion of these issues in Simon Evnine, *Donald Davidson* (Stanford: Stanford University Press, 1991), especially pp. 28–31.

30. Davidson, *Essays on Actions and Events*, p. 179.

31. Donald Davidson, "Reply to Quine on Events," in *Actions and Events: Perspectives on the Philosophy of Donald Davidson*, ed. E. Lepore and Brian McLaughlin (Oxford: Blackwell, 1985), p. 175.

32. Donald Davidson, "The Individuation of Events" (1969). See *Essays on Actions and Events*, pp. 178–179.

33. Donald Davidson, "Reply to Ralf Stoecker," in *Reflecting Davidson*, p. 288. Thus two physical objects are identical (or the terms referring to them coextensive) if and only if they occupy the same place at the same time, two sets are identical if and only if they have the same members, and so on. Indeed, one could maintain that "sorts" are distinguished by the various identity conditions for them, in which case even the token–token identification of the mental with the physical that Davidson proposes would make little sense. Furthermore, the recourse to "sorts" is of little help in the case at hand. First, as already noted, the identity conditions for *physical* events he suggests are either circular or counterintuitive, and there seem to be no others readily available. Second, it is very difficult to know where we might even begin with respect to identity conditions for *mental* events, a difficulty as much for Hume's and Kant's nomalousness of the mental as it is for Davidson's anomalous position.

34. Physical but not mental events have a spatial dimension, and so on.

35. As Meerbote says, this interpretation of Kant "would require very loose connections between the two types of descriptions, to the point where it becomes totally unclear on the basis of what sorts of considerations nondetermining descriptions are ever applied," in "Kant on the Nondeterminate Character of Human Actions," p. 157.

36. Bradley's view is more radical still, since identity is a relation and there are no relations. The very notion of "identity conditions" can make little sense. Kant's position is complicated by the fact that identity would seem to be a "logical" rather than a "real" (two-place) predicate.

37. "The matter of appearances, however, through which things in space and time are given to us, can be represented only in perception and thus *a posteriori*. The only concept that represents this empirical content of appearances *a priori* is the concept of a thing in general." Of course, this concept applies only to the phenomenal and

thus does not solve the problem of identifying what it is that the phenomenal and the noumenal in their separate ways describe. As I go on to argue, there is no way in which this "problem" can be solved, for it is misconceived. It assumes what is not the case, that at very general levels of description one can isolate "content." Kant himself sometimes suggests the same thing, that "the noumenal" does not *describe* anything at all. Rather, it's a way of talking about ways of talking.

38. See Donald Davidson, "On the Very Idea of a Conceptual Scheme," given as the Presidential Address to the American Philosophical Association in 1974, and collected in his *Inquiries into Truth and Interpretation.* As noted above, the Davidson of "Mental Events" is not in the least hesitant about speaking of "conceptual frameworks."

5 Interpretive Semantics and Ontological Commitment

Richard N. Manning

We may distinguish as clearly and profoundly as we please between particulars and universals.

—Donald Davidson, *Truth and Predication*

Entities are entities, whatever we call them.

—Donald Davidson, *Truth and Predication*[1]

1 Introduction: Generally, Where Does Davidson Fit?

Recent practitioners of Anglo-American analytic metaphysics and epistemology can be usefully, if coarsely, divided into two motley camps: the deflationists and the traditional theorizers. The first, deflationist camp contains technically inclined postpositivists like Quine and his followers as well as neo-late-Wittgensteinian and Austinian "ordinary language" types like Cavell and the recent Putnam. The postpositivists tend toward scientism and naturalism, whereas the ordinary language philosophers focus on the facts of mundane praxis, and champion literature and the arts as at least the equal of science as disclosive of truth. The deflationist camp also contains cross-over figures, unsurprisingly those heavily influenced by both Quine and the later Wittgenstein, including, for example Rorty (when he showed enough interest in metaphysics and epistemology to bother to declare them dead) and Michael Williams, who pursues something like a prolonged postmortem of the tradition whose demise Rorty pronounced. The deflationist camp partly contains another squad of antitheorists, most profoundly influenced by Kuhn, who share with the first group a fascination with natural science, and with the second an attention to concrete details of socially embedded practice.

The theorists are if anything more varied than the antitheorists. They include neo-Thomistic metaphysicians like Plantinga and van Inwagen, with both catholic and Catholic tastes in issues; philosophers of language as different as Lewis and Dummett, pursuing robust semantic theories either extensional or intensional, often with a deep concern for the metaphysics of modality; right-wing Sellarsians like Churchland and Kim, who give positive philosophical theories designed to underwrite reductive scientific materialism; and left-wing Sellarsians resisting reductionism either by respecting the *sui generis* bona fides of both the manifest and scientific images, like McDowell,[2] or by urging, like Brandom, that the idea of an objective world itself arises from our conceptual articulation of the space of reasons. This camp also includes more or less unreconstructed analysts like P. F. Strawson, who seek to trace the limits of knowledge and the general and necessary structure of reality by an elaboration of our basic concepts.

The members of the theorist camp, varied though they are, share the view that philosophical reflection is a means of coming to learn something general and indeed necessary about the structure of the world as well as our place in and grasp of it. Their means of pursuing this vision vary widely: transcendental reflection on the nature of language and thought, reflective equilibration between theoretical principles and ground-level intuitions, even the dogged pursuit of an *idée fixe* or the elaboration of a single cherished intuition concerning a bizarre thought experiment. But they all seek to provide by philosophical reflection a general and necessary picture of the world. The idea that any world we can know has a necessary structure carries implicitly with it the distinction between those objects or kinds of objects whose existence is required by such a structure and those whose existence is not. This in turn carries with it the idea of a fundamental ontology, which elaborates and studies the former sort of objects and kinds, and distinguishes such objects and kinds from those that merely happen to populate the world. The theorists tend also to share the idea that such reflection can take you only so far, in each of two directions. Above and beyond the reaches of speculation lies either nonsense or the ineffable real, below it lies the domain of properly empirical enquiry.

This characterization of the second camp has, and is intended to have, a Kantian air. For this was Kant's critical project: to delimit the bounds of metaphysical and empirical knowledge, and to glean the general and necessary structure of a world open to such knowledge. But if the theorists can be characterized as continuing the Kantian tradition this far, the first camp can even more acutely be characterized by its direct and pointed opposition to Kantian thinking. The positivism against which the first group of antitheorists moved was, and understood itself to be, deeply Kantian. The main differences are that the positivists sought to free themselves from the notion of the synthetic a priori, and claimed that what was beyond possible experience was not, as Kant had claimed, thinkable beyond empirical comprehension, but beyond thinking altogether—fully nonsense. Their efforts to reject the synthetic a priori fail, of course, since the principle of verification itself, as well as various set-theoretic postulates required to underwrite their reductionist vision, have or might have that status: No amount of finesse can render them either tautological or verifiable. But the postpositivism Quine inaugurated rejects not just the synthetic a priori, but the distinction between analytic and synthetic truth as well, and, in so doing, at least takes itself to have done away with not only analytic necessity, but necessity *tout court*. And without necessity, there can be no Kantian philosophy. There can be no distinction between truths discoverable philosophically and those beholden to experience. Thus, philosophical reflection itself could not hope to limn the general and necessary structure of the world, or itself delimit the bounds of knowledge.

The neo-late-Wittgensteinian members of the antitheory camp are alike anti-Kantian, and in a quite parallel way: Just as postpositivism rejects a deeply Kantian positivism, so too late-Wittgensteinianism rejects a deeply Kantian early Wittgensteinianism. As Kant sought the limits of the world and our knowledge by reflection on the necessary conditions for discursive judgment, the early Wittgenstein sought the limits of the world and of our possible knowledge in those imposed by the transcendentally necessary structure of any representational language. The late Wittgenstein's reaction against this quest centers on an idea of language as having a single necessary structure, and of its necessarily functioning as a means of representing. Absent the view of language as a unified logical structure of representation, there is no way to argue from that structure to the claim that the world must necessarily conform to it, and no way to argue that nothing not possessed of that structure can be known. What opens up is rather a multiplicity of structures implicitly defined by linguistic practices, each of which constitutes some piecemeal domain of knowledge, and reveals (though not necessarily by picturing) some aspect of the world. But nothing about the nature of language or logic per se can place limits on the practices, hence on the configurations of the world and the domains of knowledge they open up.

The Kuhnians partially contained in the antitheorist camp are directly anti-Kantian in their rejection of the idea of a transhistorical conceptual framework. Kant's categories marked just such a framework, necessitated, he thought, by the very forms of judgment. Moreover, passage from one historical framework to another is not on their view rationally determined, and so, even as historical eras, there can be no necessity to them (Hegel, at least as he glances back with the owl, is historistic, but no antitheorist). Kuhn himself in later years tried to develop a positive theory of the structures of conceptual taxonomy that constrain and determine vocabulary revision and hence theory choice, but his followers largely do not pick up this thread of his work.[3] Rather, they seem content to debunk the philosophical picture that insists that method and the logic of theory change can or should be given any characterization that transcends historical context and the practice of actual science, and to study actual episodes in the history of science to expose the immanent "logics" that serve those of Kuhn's points they most admire. While some Kuhnians do attempt to draw strong metaphysical and epistemological lessons from his historical studies—relativism, antirealism, irrationalism—these tend to be sociologists who fall outside the tent of analytic philosophy. Antitheoretical philosophers influenced by Kuhn tend rather to attempt to debunk as just more ill-motivated metaphysics any claims that Kuhn's observations threaten such potent consequences.

Western philosophy is, of course, made up of footnotes to Plato. But on the coarse and crude typology of recent analytic philosophy just given, the last sixty years and more of the analytic tradition (well, its whole history) are reactions to Kant: some negative, repudiating the vision of philosophical reflection as aimed at a general and necessary description of the world and the limits of our knowledge of it; others positive, pursuing in one modified form or another just that vision. Three central elements of that vision can be identified: the idea that philosophical reflection itself can reveal substantive truths about the world; the idea that such truths are necessary; and the idea of a fundamental or deep ontology—of a fundamental distinction between the kinds of beings whose existence is entailed in the very idea of a knowable world, and those whose existence is mere happenstance.

The point of my introducing this typology is to permit me to ask the following question: Where in this typology is Donald Davidson best placed? There seems an obvious answer: he is postpositivist Quinean. In at least most things, Davidson presented himself as a devoted student and follower of Quine. He strictly abjured the notion of analytic truth, plumped for thoroughgoing extensionalism in the theory of meaning, advocated a holistic epistemological coherentism that makes it hard to see either how any claims can carry necessity or how any philosophical theses have inviolable epistemic privilege, accepted (with modifications) the thesis of the indeterminacy of translation, and saw the relation between mind and the world as purely causal. His theory of radical interpretation, in particular, can seem a simple modification of Quine's own account of radical translation. There are differences, of course. Davidson was not scientistic. Unlike Quine, he saw the vocabulary of physics as but one way, not uniquely correct, of describing what there is. For related reasons, he did not reject the existence of kinds of things that could not be described in purely physical terms (though their tokens must be, if they are to be the subjects of true causal statements), and he did reject the idea that epistemology could be a chapter in physical science, patterns of surface irritations replacing sense data as the evidential interface between our beliefs and the world. But all this can be seen as friendly disagreement within Quinean holistic inquiry, a disagreement over what parts of the web are worth hanging on to, and what parts should be revised. Still, the basic philosophical outlook, with its rejection of meanings, necessity, and the idea of an unrevisable framework that provides the essential structure empirical knowledge must take, is shared. Indeed, Davidson's rejection of the very idea of a conceptual scheme—the idea that experience and knowledge of the world is mediated by a scheme of concepts that organizes the raw materials provided by the world, or to which those aspects of the world must fit for us to know them—seems just to be the logical extension of Quine's rejection of the idea that our knowledge can be separated into that part owing to our concepts or meanings, and that owing to the world independent of those concepts or meanings. If coming to know our meanings just is coming to know the world, as Davidson argues, then coming to know the world is coming to know our concepts, and it seems there is no a priori conceptual knowledge independent of empirical knowledge, so no purely philosophical knowledge that can determine even in outline the structure of the world and the limits of our knowledge of it. From this perspective, Davidson seems to be, and has been seen as (e.g., by Rorty) pounding the final nail in the coffin of traditional philosophical theorizing in the Kantian mode.

However, this tempting reading is hard to square with Davidson's thought as a whole, since many aspects of that thought seem to fit the paradigm of Kantian, theoretical philosophy I have described. For example, his arguments for richly substantive philosophical claims are generally *aprioristic*, and never scientistic. Where Quine seeks to reconfigure epistemology as a branch of natural science by replacing the traditional mentalistic conception of evidence with the behavioristically respectable notion of sensory stimulations, Davidson, on general philosophical and not scientific grounds, entirely rejects the epistemological significance of any such intermediaries between thinking and the world; in his view, the impacts of the world on our sensory apparatus are merely causally related to our beliefs. Where materialists like the Churchlands seek to eliminate the mental on grounds that a mature and properly scientific psychology has no use for mentalistic concepts, Davidson, on the basis of a priori speculation concerning the necessary structure of the domains of both psychological and physical concepts, claims that both sorts of concept are essential to our thought, that there can be no reduction of the former to the latter, and that a genuine science of psychology is impossible. And again, on the basis of an examination of our concepts of action and causation—certainly not on the basis of anything we have empirically *discovered* about action and causation—Davidson advances an ontological monism, arguing that though mental and physical vocabularies are mutually irreducible, entities described in mental vocabulary must be identical with entities described physically. Invoking arguments that make no use of empirical data as premises, Davidson also and infamously argues against the very intelligibility of the idea of alternative conceptual schemes—an idea that itself appeared, thanks to prominent sociolinguistic studies, to enjoy considerable empirical support. Moreover, despite concluding from this that there can be no such thing as even a single conceptual scheme, Davidson, on the basis of reflection about the conditions under which meaningful language is possible, makes the very substantive philosophical claim of a considerable cluster of concepts that any linguistic being must necessarily possess them. (The infamous argument is against conceptual schemes that fit or organize an unschematized reality, not against a battery of concepts essential to understanding or knowing anything.) How like this is to the Kantian claim that reflection on the nature of judgment itself reveals a set of categories to which the contents of all empirical experience must conform, hence that anyone possessed of empirical knowledge must possess and apply![4]

If there is any aspect of Davidson's thinking that seems to incline him more toward the antitheory camp, it is his semantic theory proper, especially as it pertains to ontology. Davidson's philosophy of language is squarely within the logico-semantic tradition that originates with Frege and Russell and continues through Carnap and Quine. According to this tradition, the route to ontology is through semantics: We uncover our ontological commitments—learn what there is—by figuring out what entities are countenanced in a semantic theory adequate to capture the significance of the sentences of which our best theories are comprised. Davidson promoted a distinctive and highly influential interpretivist version of this semantic approach to ontology.[5] His approach to meaning led him to insist, with

Quine, on an extensional semantics, and to reject senses, meanings, propositions, facts, properties, and reified relations as both useless for semantics and disastrous to sound philosophy in general. His insistence on extensional semantics also signals a Quinean distrust of the strong modalities that accompany traditional philosophical theorizing. But, despite the apparently sparse ontology revealed through such semantic theory, and despite the a priori tension between a resolutely extensional semantics and the idea that reflection on our concepts can reveal necessary truths, it is my purpose in the present essay to urge that Davidson's approach to semantics in fact makes room for just the sort of philosophical delimitation of the necessary basic structure of the world about which we think, and the deep ontology that characterizes the traditional philosophy that Davidson seems simultaneously to dismiss and to practice.

2 Interpretive Truth-Theoretic Semantics

The primary idea guiding Davidson's program in semantics is that interpretive, Tarski-style truth theories—what I shall refer to as "T-theories"—can serve as theories of *meaning* for natural languages. The formal task of a T-theory is to permit the derivation of theorems specifying truth conditions of every sentence of the language for which it is given. Such theorems have the form of T-sentences: "*S* is true-in-*L* if and only if *p*." Here, "*S*" describes a sentence of the language for which the theory is given, and *p* states the truth conditions of that sentence. For an instance of such a theorem to give the meaning of the object-language sentence described by "*S*," the "*p*" must constitute a translation of that sentence into the language of the theory. A T-theory whose theorems do this is materially adequate, or interpretive. Since there can in principle be many formally adequate T-theories for a given language that are not materially adequate, interpretive T-theories must be empirical, in the sense of being subject to verification. That is, there must be empirical means by which formally adequate T-theories can be tested for material adequacy.

A T-theory specifies the meaning of simple singular referring terms by giving axioms that pair them off with the objects they name. Here the semantic counterparts of such referring expressions are entities. But on Davidson's view, it would be neither necessary nor helpful to assign meaning entities to every syntactically significant piece of the language. It is enough if subsentential expressions are given axioms that display their semantic contribution to the whole sentences of which they are a part. For example, the axioms must show that "le père de *N*" refers to the father of the object referred to by "N," but there need be no entity corresponding to "le père de." In particular, the analysis of predicates (including relation terms) does not require appeal to semantic entities as their meanings. The axioms must simply make clear, for example, that "Paris est belle" is true-in-French if and only if the object designated by the referring expression "Paris" is beautiful. To handle quantifier expressions, the theory must exploit a first-order quantificational apparatus and the notion of satisfaction, a generalized form of reference. A satisfier is an infinite sequence of objects. So the semantics of quantifier expressions, like that of singular referring expressions, is given by appeal to entities.

Two points about all of this technical apparatus bear special emphasis for my purposes. First, on the canonical Davidsonian treatment, the only entities posited by the theory are the elements of satisfiers. Second, the satisfaction/reference relation itself need be given no analysis within the theory: The theory must state which unanalyzed singular referring expressions refer to which objects, and which variables designate which particular objects, relative to a sequence and axiomatization; but it need not state how or in virtue of what they do so. Indeed, reference, the sole semantic relation revealing objects, is a theoretical notion, forced on the theorist by the formal demands of a T-theory. If it were not for the need to generate T-theorems for quantifier expressions, semantic theory would reveal no ontology—no objects—at all.

3 Ontology Revealed and Constrained: Properties, Facts, and the Official Approach

To explore further the question of how, on the official Davidsonian line, ontology is revealed in the construction of T-theories for natural languages, it will be instructive to focus on the ontological status of two types of entities whose ontological bona fides Davidson has resisted: properties and facts.

Properties

Consider the following example, due to Stephen Neale:

(1) α is the same color as β.[6]

The claim in (1) cannot be analyzed as a simple predication of "is the same color as β" to α, since that will not reveal legitimate entailments of (1), such as "α is colored." Likewise with treating "is the same color as" as a primitive relation. And since (1) mentions no particular color, and moreover does not merely entail but explicitly states the sameness of the colors of the two objects, it cannot be analyzed as a conjunction whose conjuncts predicate the same color to α and β, respectively. (1) seems to involve quantifying over colors construed as properties.[7] So properties, in addition to particulars, would have to appear in the ontology of the theory.

Faced with this problem, Davidson distinguishes two issues. One, he says, "is whether there is any advantage in introducing predicates [*sic*—presumably he meant to say 'properties'] as the sole semantic item used to explain the function of predicates."[8] Another "is whether there is in general any objection to including properties in our ontology."[9] This is an extremely interesting distinction.

Introducing properties into a theory of meaning in the first manner would, according to Davidson, be disastrous for his program. He remarks, "it is essential to my idea of how a theory of truth is verified that the right side of T-sentences not employ conceptual resources not employed by the sentence for which the truth conditions are being given." This constraint, he continues, would be violated "in a basic way . . . if the work of every predicate were explained by appeal to a property (relation, etc.)."[10] Just exactly what considerations motivate this constraint, whether they are sound, and what the costs of rejecting them would be, are interesting and deep questions. For present purposes, I will accept Davidson's word that this constraint must be respected by any adequate interpretive semantics.

But evidently, the fact that properties must not be treated as semantic entities does not mean that they cannot be included in the ontology of a T-theory. Given that Davidson draws the distinction between these two issues in response to the challenge presented by sentences like (1), he is contemplating the possibility that the logical form of such sentences, as revealed by an interpretative T-theory for the language in which they appear, involves quantification over properties. Davidson's attitude toward this possibility is a blithe "so be it, as long as properties are regarded as abstracta."[11] Properties would then function as the referents-*cum*-satisfiers of quantificational variables, relative to sequences, in accord with an axiomatization; that is, they would simply appear *among* the satisfiers, and not as distinct ontologically from them in virtue of their semantic function.

Recall that being a satisfier in this (relative) way is all there is to reference, and there is no need for Davidsonian semantic theory proper "to provide an analysis of the reference relation."[12] For this reason, there is nothing the theory itself either says or needs to say positively about this relation that would indicate that referring to properties is any less or more problematic than referring to other abstracta, or even to concrete particulars. From a standpoint within a theory that incorporates properties in this way, any supposed ontological "queerness" of properties so incorporated—queerness that might make it look mysterious how they could be referred to—would remain invisible. Indeed, any ontological distinctness from other satisfiers they would have in virtue of being properties rather than particulars would be invisible as well. Of course, the truth conditions of sentences referring to or quantifying over properties would be different from sentences referring to or quantifying over other entities; but there is no reason to suppose that these differences will not reveal properties to be of a categorically different sort than other entities.

Facts

Davidson's hostility to the idea that facts form a distinctive category of entity, or that there is any philosophical utility to recognizing such a category, is well known. In particular, Davidson has often defended his semantic program by citing the so-called Slingshot argument as a reason why competing programs that treat facts as semantic counterparts of true sentences (and along with these, the correspondence theory of truth) are doomed to failure. Yet, as Davidson was well aware, the slingshot argument has received heavy, indeed devastating, criticism. Stephen Neale, whose *Facing Facts* provides the definitive treatment of the various species of this collapsing argumentation, has shown exactly how theories of facts can escape slingshot reasoning. But while one might have expected him to have taken Neale's result as a threat to his own semantic program, Davidson was not just unshaken, but encouraged. He says: "Neale's splendid discussion has encouraged me to stick to the conclusion that *facts cannot be incorporated into a satisfactory theory of truth*. Neale speaks of Russell's view of facts as 'acceptable,' but he does not show that it can be *incorporated into a Tarski-style T-theory*."[13]

But just as with properties, it is not clear that one can avoid the need to incorporate facts into a T-theory, in at least some sense of "incorporate." Consider this example from Neale:

(2) The fact that Mary left Bill's party did not worry him, but the fact that she left suddenly did.[14]

On the face of it, this sentence seems to involve quantification over facts, asserting the existence of two distinct facts, and claiming of one but not the other that it worried Bill. Given my dialectical purposes here, I need not stress the (interesting and complicated) question of whether (2) in the end must be analyzed as involving quantification over facts. The point is rather about what we should expect Davidson's attitude toward this possibility to be. He was insouciant about the prospect that properties would be required, in light of the fact that they could be treated in the (allegedly) innocent way discussed above, as the satisfiers of quantificational sentences. If facts could be treated similarly, as satisfiers, then there would be no threat to Davidsonian semantics, and Davidson's attitude should be the same as it was in the case of properties: So be it. Moreover, as with the case of properties, from a standpoint within the theory, whatever ontological queerness facts might possess would be invisible.[15]

Our discussion of properties and facts has revealed a general Davidsonian strategy. An ontological category is bona fide only if its members must be *incorporated into* a semantic theory. But there are two kinds of incorporation. One is the incorporation of entities as the semantic counterparts of given forms of expression; this kind of incorporation threatens the interpretivist semantic program, and is to be avoided. The second kind of incorporation is the inclusion of entities as referents of singular terms and in the sequences of objects that constitute satisfiers, where this is required by the analysis of particular sentences of the language for which a T-theory is given. I shall occasionally speak of this sort of incorporation, a bit loosely, in terms of entities being incorporated into the "sequence range" of a formal T-theory. From the standpoint of the formal T-theory, any distinctive ontological character such entities may have is invisible; they are objects like any other, referred to by singular terms and variables in an unanalyzed way. They would have no special ontological status solely in virtue of any distinctive semantic function they play, for they would have no such distinctive function. Distinctions among them and between them and other entities will be revealed only in terms of the sentences speakers of the language in fact hold to be true of them.

4 Questioning the Official Approach

Though the matter is far from clear, I want to concede, for purposes of argument, that it is both possible to give a complete T-theory for a given natural language without the need for the first, troubling kind of incorporation of categories of entities, and that the second, supposedly innocent kind indeed deserves acquittal. I want to pass to the question of whether, if we accept that ontology follows from the construction of interpretive T-theories, we must also accept that our ontological commitments must be determined by and limited to those revealed by what must be *incorporated*, in either of the two senses above, into the theories themselves.

Let me begin with an obviously crude and superficial analogy designed to pump a contrary intuition. There are no eggshells, chickens, pigs, or cows, and no cheese grater, bowl, or pan in the ham and Gruyere omelet I made this morning, but a consideration of the construction of that omelet does force us to recognize the reality of these things. A thorough understanding of an omelet as a culinary artifact will involve much more of the world than would a mere consideration of the chemical composition of the dish itself. Why, then, should what is revealed by the construction of interpretive T-theories be limited to what is actually incorporated as an element in the constructed theory? Why can't the construction of such theories reveal commitments, not just to what must be included explicitly in the sequence range of a theory, but also to what is required to make sense of the generation and construction of such a theory?

To explain why our ontological commitments cannot outstrip those required to serve as referents and satisfiers in the formalism of a T-theory for a language, Stephen Neale offers a creative reconstruction of what he takes to be a basic implication of Davidson's semantic program for the pursuit of ontology. This argument, schematized for convenience, is as follows:

(3) An acceptable T-theory for L delivers a true theorem of the requisite form for *every sentence* of L.

Therefore,

(4) There is nothing one can say in L that outstrips the ontology revealed by the theory.

Therefore,

(5) There is no sense to be made of ontological categories not forced upon us by the construction of a variablesemantics.[16]

Let us call this the "comprehensive coverage argument," or CCA for short.

There is much to say about the reasoning embodied in CCA. First, note that, if CCA is to show what Neale intends it to show, then we must read the phrases "revealed by" in (4) and "forced on us by the construction of" in (5) as "required to serve as referents for the singular referring terms of, and values of variables of," that is, required to serve as elements of the sequence range. Second, there are good reasons for respecting CCA insofar as it limits our ontological commitments to what in fact appears in the sequence range of an interpretive T-theory for our language. For otherwise we would be contemplating the idea that our ontology includes items that we neither refer to nor quantify over. That is a path that neither the semantic tradition nor I wish to follow. Here, the analogy with the omelet breaks down. Although the construction of the omelet may implicate the existence of a pan, there is no pan in it. Thus I will stick with CCA's conclusion that the ontology revealed by the construction of an interpretive T-theory is restricted to those entities that must be included in its sequence range.

However, this leaves entirely open what sorts of consideration can be taken to evince such a requirement. For there is more than one sense in which we can understand what it is for an ontological category to be "forced upon us by the construction of a variable semantics," or "required to provide the values of variables." It seems to me that (5) is ambiguous between:

(5a) There is no sense to be made of the idea of ontological categories not forced upon us by the formal demand to supply entities to stand as referents of singular referring expressions and as values of variables of a given T-theory;

and

(5b) There is no sense to be made of the idea of ontological categories not forced upon us by considering what is involved in constructing an interpretive T-theory.

According to (5a), only the most parsimonious possible set of entities formally needed to provide values for variables and referents for singular referring expressions of a given theory can be forced upon us. (5b), however, is more permissive. According to it, the mere possibility that we can produce a T-theory the interpretation of whose *formalism* (i.e., whose axioms permitting the derivation of T-theorems for every sentence of the language expressed in its canonical logical form) does not on its own demand that objects of a given putative ontological category be incorporated into its sequence range does not entail that we have no reason to acknowledge that category. More specifically, it does not mean that we are compelled to adopt that sequence range in preference to one that does include members of that category. Other considerations may recommend the choice of a less parsimonious range. These considerations would be extrinsic to those imposed by the formalism of the theory itself: "extra-" as opposed to "intratheoretic," as I shall say. But why choose (5a) over (5b)? Why, that is, suppose that only intratheoretic considerations have any force in determining what we should incorporate into the theory as elements of its sequence range, and thus as determining its ontology? As we saw, so long as the additional entities are not exploited in the theory as semantic counterparts for expressions other than quantificational variables, nothing in the idea of an interpretive T-theory prohibits such incorporation. Granted compelling extratheoretic considerations reasons for including entities of some kind in our ontology this way, why balk?

5 Truth Its Own Self

Davidson's own treatment of the concept of truth provides a nice analogy to the kinds of extratheoretic grounds for ontological commitment I am suggesting. Davidson famously denies that there can be any such thing as a theory of truth, and claims that it is a folly to try to define it.[17] Indeed, his specific use of Tarski-style truth theories turns Tarski's original idea on its head: Tarski defines truth in terms of a generalized, technical reference relation and takes translation for granted; Davidson, in contrast, takes truth for granted, defines meaning and translation in terms of it, and lets reference fall out where it may. In defense of this, he says that truth itself is "beautifully transparent,"[18] our simplest and most basic concept.

Moreover, Davidson claims that for a being to possess thought, and for its utterances to constitute meaningful linguistic acts, that being must have the concept of objective truth.[19] For one being, then, to interpret another as a thinker expressing thought linguistically, she must attribute to that being the concept of truth; and of course to do this, she must herself have that concept. In particular, verification of a candidate T-theory as interpretive requires a commitment to objective truth on the part of interpreters, since it must be possible for them to determine when its theorems are true, which requires that they be able to tell when conditions specified on the right-hand side of T-theorems in fact hold, that is, that they believe the right-hand side of the T-sentence is true. It is thus a condition on the intelligibility of interpretive semantics that interpreters take truth seriously.

On the other hand, as Grover, Camp, and Belnap, among others, have shown, the truth *predicate* is eliminable from English (and any other natural language) with no loss of expressive power.[20] So far as I know, Davidson does not deny this claim. But if the predicate "is true" does not need to figure in a given language, then a T-theory for that language would not, it would seem, require axioms enabling the deduction of T-sentences for *expressions explicitly concerning truth*. Since, by hypothesis, such a language has the full expressive power of a natural language like English, there is no English sentence whose canonical logical form must involve any expressions mentioning truth or containing a truth predicate. But then nothing in what must for intratheoretic reasons be incorporated into a T-theory for

English would reveal a commitment on the part of English speakers to the notion of objective truth. If intratheoretic reasons exhaust our grounds for recognizing commitments, this should betray the emptiness or misleading character of truth talk, revealing it to be merely an eliminable verbal convenience rather than a means of expressing any genuine concept. But Davidson does not draw this lesson; he takes a commitment to truth to be implicit in the very project of interpretive semantics, and to be revealed in its practice. This suggests that incorporation into a T-theory for intratheoretic reasons is not the sole criterion by which we measure the commitments revealed via the pursuit of semantic theory.

It would be a mistake to conclude straight away that (5a) is false, or that Davidson is inconsistent in holding it. (5), whether construed as (5a) or as (5b), is a thesis about how *ontology* is limited by semantics, and commitment to the concept of objective truth is not, or at least not obviously, an ontological commitment. But the example of truth is still instructive. It shows that the construction of T-theories can provide grounds for acknowledging substantial commitments that go beyond those revealed by consideration that are strictly intratheoretic. But if this is so, then why should grounds for specifically *ontological* commitment be limited to the strictly intratheoretic?

6 Interpretive T-Theories: Knowledge Of and Knowledge That

Up to this point I have argued that there is no compelling basis not to prefer (5b) to (5a), and thus acknowledge the force of extratheoretic grounds for incorporating categories of entities in the ontology of a T-theory. But I have not provided any such grounds. It is time to do so. In this section, I argue that the very idea that an interpreter's grasp of an interpretive truth theory can suffice as a theory of meaning provides extratheoretic grounds for recognizing the existence of persons, mental states, and actions.

For an interpreter to understand a language, it does not suffice for her to know an interpretive T-theory for it. She must in addition know *that* the theory is interpretive. This knowledge cannot consist of knowing that the claim that the theory is interpretive is true, for one could know that the claim is true without comprehending what it is for the theory to be interpretive.[21] What does such comprehension involve? A T-theory's being interpretive is its being such that one who used it to interpret a speaker of the language for which it is a theory could understand any sentence uttered by that speaker. Understanding a speaker, in turn, essentially involves finding him to hold sentences true when and only when either the truth conditions the interpreter assigns to those sentences obtain, or when there is some explanation available for why the speaker does not realize that they do. This is just what is involved in empirically verifying a T-theory, that is, confirming the truth of the theorems that comprise its T-sentences. So an interpreter who knows that a theory is interpretive must know what it is for such a theory to be empirically verifiable.

I already pointed out that this knowledge implies, on the part of an interpreter, a commitment to the concept of objective truth. Given that the interpreter, in verifying the theory, may not exploit any antecedent guesses about or knowledge of the meanings of the sentences of L or the psychological attitudes of L speakers, the only way to tell whether the sentence of L is true when and only when the truth conditions are satisfied is to determine whether L speakers in fact *hold* such sentences true when and only when the truth conditions obtain. Holding true is a psychological state. Recognizing it requires that the interpreter properly identify certain sorts of behaviors as manifesting this state. This, in turn, requires that she interpret the speaker not merely as believing the sentence to be true, but also as intending, by his behavior, to indicate that he so believes. That is, she must interpret the behavior as the action of expressing a belief. She can do so only if the behavior so interpreted makes sense, is rational, in light of the speaker's other beliefs and intentions. Moreover, without the additional assumptions that the speaker understands the sentence (i.e., that she is an L-speaker) and moreover manifests *true* belief by her assents, there is no reason to take the assenting behavior as evidence that the sentence is in fact true, hence no reason to take the behavior to confirm the T-theorem for that sentence. Finally, empirical verifiability is an ongoing matter. It would count against the verification of a T-theory if speakers interpreted in accord with it did not turn out to be by and large consistent with respect to the conditions under which they did and did not assent to given sentences. To comprehend the claim that a T-theory is interpretive, then, one must have the concept of a diachronically consistent, rational subject of linguistic action and psychological attitudes—in short, the concept of a person.

Possessing this battery of concepts and understanding their interrelations is required for knowing what it is for a T-theory to be interpretive. But this general conceptual knowledge does not suffice for knowing of a given T-theory that it is in fact interpretive. In addition, one must know that the theory would be verified if tested. Knowing this entails knowing that the putative speakers for whom it is interpretive are largely self-consistent, thinking, acting beings whose beliefs are largely true of the world, and expressed in linguistic acts. This is knowledge that persons, and with them mental entities or states like beliefs and intentions, as well as actions that express them, are among the entities in the world. To adopt a useful phrase from Jeffrey Malpas's Heideggerian reading of Davidson, persons, actions, and thoughts form part of the horizon of interpretive semantics, constituting it as an intelligible practice; a full grasp of that project requires a commitment to that horizon.[22] Commitment to the idea that an interpretive T-theory can in fact serve as a theory of linguistic meaning carries with itself, then, commitment to an ontology including persons, thoughts, and actions. And note, these commitments arise quite independently of, and prior to, any questions concerning whether the object language for which a given truth theory is interpretive contains expressions whose logical forms might require quantification over persons, mental entities or states, or actions. These commitments arise from considerations that are extratheoretic, in the sense I have explained.

7 Differences of Kind and Kinds of Difference

I have been speaking of (5a) and of Davidson's methodology considered as committed to (5a) as unduly restrictive, in a way that threatens to bar our recognizing the ontological bona fides of categories of entities implicated in the very idea of interpretive T theories. But one might object that this has been unfair. After all, as I mentioned in my introduction, Davidson has himself elaborated some of the ontological elements required for thought and language. He writes:

> If I am right that language and thought require the structure provided by a logic of quantification, what further conceptual resources is it reasonable to consider basic? I have no definite list in mind, but if the ontology includes macroscopic physical objects, including animals, as I think it must, then there will be sortal concepts for classifying the items in the ontology. There must be concepts for marking spatial and temporal position. There must be concepts for some of the evident properties of objects, and for expressing the various changes and activities of objects. If such changes can be characterized in turn, then the ontology must also include events, and among the concepts must be that of the relation between cause and effect. I am inclined to make some major additions to this list.[23]

While Davidson makes explicit here only that an ontology must include macrophysical objects, animals, and events, it is clear that among the major additions he would add to the list are whatever is needed to make sense of the idea of a shared reaction to a common cause, as well as of the idea of a creature that is able to recognize error. Among the animals Davidson claims must be part of any ontology, then, are thinkers, that is, persons.

Davidson agrees with my claim, then, that persons and thoughts are essential elements of any ontology.

This might seem to militate against my claims that Davidson's methodology is restrictive and his ontology sparse. It might also suggest that the considerations I advanced for incorporating persons, thoughts, causes, and effects into the ontology revealed by a T-theory pose no threat at all to the interpretivist who prefers the restrictive methodology expressed in (5a). All these considerations show, one might claim, is that one who knows that a T-theory is interpretive knows how to use language in such a way as to express what such English terms as "person," "thought," "belief," and "action" express, and holds to be true some (many) sentences whose truth conditions refer to or quantify over such things. That is to say, it reveals only that language speakers characterize some of the things to whose existence they are committed in the same ways in which we characterize persons. The differences among the many things to which their holdings true of various sentences reveal a commitment show up in a T-theory entirely in terms of the different predicates they hold to be true of them, that is, in terms of the different ways they characterize them.

That Davidson held that differences in the predicates by means of which we characterize things are fully adequate to capture whatever ontological differences there may be between them is suggested by a passage in his last work, *Truth and Predication*. In the context of discussing and criticizing yet again the idea that semantics can be usefully pursued by the postulation of different categories of meaning entities to which various classes of expression refer, Davidson writes,

> [I]f we try to explain the role of predicates by introducing entities to which they refer, it does not matter what we call the entities, or how we describe them. We may distinguish as clearly and profoundly as we please between particulars and universals, between the job that singular terms do in identifying or individuating objects and the job that predicates do in introducing generality; we will still have to describe the semantic role of predicates. . . . *[E]ntities are entities, whatever we call them.* Frege's syntax and metaphors emphasize that there is a fundamental difference between singular terms and predicates, but this difference cannot usefully be thought to consist in a difference in the entities to which they refer.[24]

Here Davidson suggests that neither what we call, nor how we characterize, a putative entity can make a difference to the sorts of work it can do in explaining the semantic roles played by different kinds of expressions. Introducing, naming, and describing entities to serve as semantic counterparts for predicates (or relations, or sentences, one may assume) is of no avail in the project of explaining the distinct role played by predicates (relation terms, sentences) in contributing to the truth conditions of the sentences in which they appear. The summary reason Davidson offers for this, at least in this passage, seems to express just the flattened ontology I have been criticizing: "entities are entities, whatever we call them." Yet almost paradoxically, Davidson also writes that "we may distinguish as clearly and profoundly as we please between particulars and universals," which certainly does not sound like the sentiment of a flattener. Such clear and profound distinctions as can be made, then, on Davidson's view, can only be reflected in something that does not matter semantically: how we characterize the entities. Universals would indeed be different than particulars, for example, but only because we hold different things to be true of them.

But this way of capturing profound ontological distinctions is unsatisfying. For it fails to take sufficiently seriously the differences between kinds of difference. What we say about things reveals clear and striking differences between, say, persons and events, but also between clams and panthers, and between piles of sand and clouds of water vapor (and omelets and pans). According to Davidson, as I have read him, entities of each of these kinds are all the same in semantic role ("entities are entities, no matter what we call them"): elements of the sequence range of a T-theory. But it seems to me that the difference between persons and events is profound in a way that those between clams and panthers, and between piles of sand and clouds of water vapor, are not. One need not, of course, have that intuition. My point is that if, as in Davidson's official line, we draw ontological differences between various objects entirely in terms of the predicates we hold true of them, then there is no satisfactory way of distinguishing between profound and ordinary differences, should we want to.

What we would need is some criterion according to which we could discriminate, or, if the terminology of "criteria" suggests more precision than is really required, some means of assessing the comparative ontological profundity of differences. Given our context of pursuing ontology through semantics, any such criterion or means should be applicable to entities or categories thereof as they are revealed in the construction of semantic theory. Surely, a distinction of semantic role would mark a profound rather than shallow difference. But on Davidson's view a difference in kind of entity is never a difference in semantic role; there is only one semantic role for objects to play. But if the way semantics reveals ontology is conceived narrowly, in accord with (5a), then I do not see what the criterion of profundity grounded in that pursuit might be. All differences between entities amount to differences in the predicates we hold true of them; all we can do is distinguish between entities in terms of the predicates held true of them.

Comparing numbers of relative differences will not help distinguish more from less profound differences. For each difference we can point to between the members of any one of a set of pairs, we will be able to find some difference between members of the others. Nor will it do to base judgments of comparative profundity of difference on the distinction between necessary and contingent existents, as revealed in the contrast between existentially quantified sentences always held to be true and those held to be true at most sometimes. Not every profound category is always instantiated (person, action).

Nor will it help to appeal to some general taxonomic structure of our concepts, saying, for example, that the farther down the taxonomic tree you have to go to find a characteristic shared by two entities, the more profound the difference between them. Such an appeal presumes a clear and ordered taxonomy of concepts that can be arrived at independently of judgments as to which categories are more fundamental than which. But it may seem easy enough to say that the distinction between a person and an event is more profound than that between a clam and a panther because one has to go farther down our taxonomic tree to find what is common to a person and an event than to find what is common to a clam and a panther. But the matter is not that simple. A particular person and a particular event may share, for example, a locational feature (being on a bridge at a particular time), as may a clam and a panther. But how does one eliminate this sort of feature as irrelevant to the question of which pair is more profoundly different? Shall we say that locational properties are not intrinsic or essential, and that properly taxonomic features are intrinsic and essential? Such metaphysical considerations are, of course, themselves judgments of comparative profundity. Conceptual taxonomy reflects such judgments, rather than providing a criterion for them.

As I said, I don't see any really promising way of drawing distinctions of comparative ontological profundity from the materials available in the interior of an interpretive T-theory. But if we permit ourselves to consider extratheoretic grounds for incorporating members of an ontological category into interpretive T-theories, then the difference between differences is indeed revealed in semantics, not by assignment of different semantic roles, nor by the particular predicates held to be true of different kinds of things, but by the fact that the existence of members of some categories of entities, and the categorical differences between them, are presumed in the very project of interpretation. These categories of entities are such that there can be no interpretation, hence no *ontology* (not to say no entities) without them. They are necessary features of any world open to us through language, what Davidson has called "the organ of propositional perception."[25] Reflection in the very idea of an interpretive T-theory reveals that no one who did not understand that there are both persons and events and that they are very different sorts of things could either pursue or be the object of an interpretive semantic theory. But no one needs to know of the existence of or difference between clams and panthers, or of piles of sand and clouds of water vapor. Just as such reflection reveals the concept of truth to be fundamental, so too does it reveal persons, thoughts, actions—and more besides—to be fundamental. The differences among these are profound. So too are the differences between these and the kinds of things commitment to which is revealed merely and entirely by the fact that we think different things are true of them. Comparatively, the differences among these are not.

8 Conclusion

To discern ontological commitments, I have reflected on the conditions that must be met if a T-theory is to serve as a theory of meaning, conditions that force us to attend to the concepts and kinds of objects necessarily implicated in the very idea of such a theory's being verifiably materially adequate, hence interpretive. The official approach, in contrast, reveals such commitments by reading them off of a completed T-theory that incorporates those entities as objects in its sequence range. It thereby seems to domesticate entities, treating their status as derivative on the legitimacy of the T-theory, rather than the other way around. On this domesticating approach, categories of things are marked out entirely in terms of the different ways in which things get characterized; hence to say of two things that they fall into different kinds is, in every case, merely to say that different things are true of them. We do, of course, hold different things to be true of members of profoundly different categories, but this is true of any two objects, however blandly empirical the differences between them may be. Hence the ontological flattening.

But this flattening is actually a result of a kind of amnesia, whether feigned or due to inattention—a forgetting of the fundamental categories and profound differences that must be in place and grasped, even if prereflectively, if the very idea of interpretive T-theories is to be intelligible. That we can, after the fact, give an interpretive T-theory for a language whose sequence range fails, from inside the theory, to reflect these categories and differences as being of a fundamentally semantic in kind does not mean that our semantic theorizing does not commit us to them as fundamental categories and profound differences. Making sense of the idea that an interpretive T-theory can suffice as a semantic theory is part of our theorizing about the semantic, if not part of the semantic theory proper. And making sense of this idea both reveals such commitments and gives us a basis for distinguishing profound differences from mundane. If you have the intuition that the difference between persons and events really is more profound than that between panthers and clams, worries about the possibility of making good sense of the difference between such differences may have led you to repudiate or suppress it. But reflection on the idea of an interpretive T-theory can validate and revitalize that intuition. If you didn't have that intuition, then perhaps such reflection suggests that you should.

Reading Davidson's philosophy of language in light of the comparatively permissive account I have recommended of how ontological commitment is revealed in the pursuit of semantic theory enables us also to see how, despite the extensional character of the theory, its dismissal of the idea that entities fall into fundamentally different semantic types, and the consequently flat ontology that appears from a perspective within a T-theory itself, Davidson's thinking as a whole is continuous with, indeed is a contribution to, the traditional Kantian vision of philosophy.[26] I earlier identified three central elements of that vision: the idea that philosophical reflection itself can reveal substantive truths about the world; the idea that such truths are necessary; and the idea of a fundamental or deep ontology. Reflection in this way on what is required for understanding reveals that the very idea of linguistic understanding involves a world populated with thoughtful persons, actions, and events in causal relation. That a world open to us linguistically must be so constituted is a substantive and a priori truth entailing a fundamental ontology. Fuller elaboration of the idea of an empirically verifiable interpretive T-theory may reveal much more in the way of necessary kinds and differences besides, kinds answering to the "major additions to the list" of essential concepts Davidson mentions. So illuminated, Davidson's thinking is disclosed as squarely within the tradition of philosophical theorizing.

9 Diagnostic Epilogue

I suspect that Davidson's restrictive approach to the way pursuit of semantic theory can reveal ontological commitments is not, in the end, motivated by any general principle of parsimony, a taste for desert landscapes. It is motivated instead by a worry that, once acknowledged, entities of various kinds will inevitably be pressed into service in putative explanatory projects that promise to engender more dead-end confusion than enlightenment. Facts, for prominent example, are to be feared because of the threat that someone will convert them to meanings, try to treat them as distinctive semantic entities, try to explain truth as correspondence to them, try to resuscitate scheme–content dualism and relativism with them, or try to deploy them as representational intermediaries between us and the world. Davidson more than anyone else has tried to liberate us from the skeptical muddles and puzzlements to which such projects lead. The restrictive approach presents a general defensive posture from which these threats can be resisted. If the price we pay for adopting this strategy is to disable ourselves from recognizing deep ontological differences, then so be it.

I have argued here that interpretivist semantics must acknowledge persons, thoughts, and actions as fundamental ontological categories. Elsewhere I have argued that the same can be said for facts. So obviously I think the costs of the general strategy are too high. But there is a better strategy. The right way to defend against the unproductive and mystifying exploitation of categories of entities in theoretical explanatory projects is to refuse the exploitation rather than to deny the existence and distinctive character of the kinds of entities abused. It cannot be assumed that because we recognize them for one reason, they must be must found useful elsewhere. Only careful critical attention can tell us whether, and in what contexts, they can be put to good purpose. And only a lack of such attention can lead us to mistake perplexities engendered by the ill-advised exploitation of legitimate categories for real philosophical puzzles. But we must be on guard against this sort of confusion in any event.

Notes

1. Both quotations are from Davidson's *Truth and Predication* (Cambridge, MA: Harvard University Press), p. 156.

2. It may seem odd that I class McDowell as a theorist, given his late-Wittgensteinian therapeutic approach to philosophy and his, maddening to some, unwillingness to engage in the elaboration of theories. But he still counts as a theorist, as I mean the term, because he employs philosophical reflection in the aim of securing for us a general and substantive conception of reality and our place in it. The McDowellian ideas, for example, that perception is the taking in of facts, that aspects of the world are inherently normative, and that the space of concepts is coextensive with that of reasons, unboundedly extending into the world whether we think it or not, are richly

and robustly metaphysical (all of these theses can be found in McDowell, *Mind and World* [Cambridge, MA: Harvard University Press, 1992]). Whether McDowell is right to characterize these commitments as just bits of good, common sense that we can feel comfortable accepting once we are freed of ill-motivated philosophical dogmas, as well as to deny that these ideas require elaboration in a detailed theory, is beside the point. Common sense may have them, and be so far right and innocent; but philosophy *attains* them.

3. See Kuhn's "Afterwords," in *World Changes: Thomas Kuhn and the Nature of Science*, ed. P. Horwich (Cambridge, MA: MIT Press, 1993), pp. 311–341.

4. Indeed, Kant's reasoning can at times seem less a priori than Davidson's. For example, his argument in the *Prolegomena* for the necessary applicability of the categories of the understanding to the content of experience presumes the reality of scientific knowledge.

5. Manifestations of this approach are evident throughout much of Davidson's corpus, but for particularly direct presentations, see "Truth and Meaning," in *Inquiries into Truth and Interpretation* (Oxford: Clarendon Press, 1984), pp. 17–36; "The Method of Truth in Metaphysics," in *Inquiries into Truth and Interpretation*, pp. 199–214; "The Logical Form of Action Sentences," in *Essays on Actions and Events* (Oxford: Clarendon Press, 1980), pp. 105–148; and, in a less technical vein, "What Thought Requires," in *Problems of Rationality* (Oxford: Oxford University Press, 2004), pp. 135–149.

6. S. Neale, *Facing Facts* (Oxford: Clarendon Press, 2001), p. 41. I simplify matters slightly by using names here rather than demonstratives.

7. Its form might be given by something like "there is a property F and a property G such that F is a color and G is a color and $F\alpha$ and $G\beta$ and $F=G$." One could use a quantifier restricted to colors, perhaps, but that would not matter for the present point.

8. Davidson, "Reply to Neale," in *Donald Davidson: Truth, Meaning, and Knowledge*, ed. U. Zeglin (London: Routledge & Kegan Paul, 1999), p. 89. This is in response to an essay by Neale in which Neale makes many of the same points about the ontological commitments of Davidsonian Truth theory he canvasses in *Facing Facts*.

9. Ibid.

10. Ibid. Davidson's formulation here is not entirely perspicuous. For one thing, sentences do not themselves employ conceptual resources; rather, speakers employ such resources in uttering sentences, intending to mean something by them, and interpreters employ conceptual resources in understanding (or misunderstanding) them.

11. Reported in Neale, *Facing Facts*, p. 41. In just this context Davidson says, "I have no general objection to abstracta, as long as they are shown to be useful; as I always say, they take up no space." Davidson, "Reply to Neale," p. 88.

12. Neale, *Facing Facts*, p. 35.

13. Davidson, "Reply to Neale," p. 89; emphasis added. Davidson seems to me seriously to mischaracterize the situation in stating that Neale "concludes that although the postulation of facts has not been proven to be disastrous no matter what assumptions are made, the cost of the postulation is so high that it is unlikely to be deemed acceptable," in Davidson, *Truth and Predication*, p. 129.

14. Neale's original example, relegated to a footnote, is slightly different: "The fact that Mary left Bill's party did not worry him, but the fact that she left *so* suddenly did," in Neale, *Facing Facts*, p. 44, n. 29; emphasis added. For the sake of simplicity, my text's (2) omits Neale's "so"; (2) presents the same challenge to Davidson as Neale's original example.

15. It should not be forgotten that events, times, and locations are particulars for Davidson, expressly quantified over in T-theories. These are each distinct sorts of entities, and there are philosophical vantage points from which each is very hard to make sense of.

16. Neale, *Facing Facts*, p. 39.

17. See Donald Davidson, "The Structure and Content of Truth," *Journal of Philosophy* 87: 279–328, and "The Folly of Trying to Define Truth," in Donald Davidson, *Truth, Language, and History* (Oxford: Oxford University Press, 2005).

18. "A Coherence Theory of Truth and Knowledge," in Donald Davidson, *Subjective, Intersubjective, Objective* (Oxford: Oxford University Press, 2004), pp. 138–153, p. 139.

19. See Davidson, "The Problem of Objectivity," in Donald Davidson, *Problems of Rationality* (Oxford: Oxford University Press, 2004), p. 9.

20. D. Grover, J. Camp, and N. Belnap, "A Prosentential Theory of Truth," *Philosophical Studies* 27 (1975): 73–124.

21. Compare: Knowing that "'Hesperus' designates Hesperus" is true does not constitute knowing that "Hesperus" designates Hesperus, both because it does not suffice for knowing that it is Hesperus that "Hesperus" designates, and because it does not suffice for knowing what it is in general that designation involves.

22. Jeff Malpas, *Donald Davidson and the Mirror of Meaning* (Cambridge: Cambridge University Press, 1992).

23. Davidson, "What Thought Requires," in *Problems of Rationality*, pp. 135–149, at p. 140.

24. Davidson, *Truth and Predication*, p. 156; emphasis added.

25. Davidson, "Seeing through Language," in *Truth, Language, and History*, p. 135.

26. The deep and genuine divergence from Kant is, it seems to me, that Davidson does away with the notion of experience. For Kant it is basic and unquestionable

that our empirical knowledge is discursive, i.e., that it essentially involves subsuming the contents of intuition under concepts of the understanding. His categories fall out of reflection of the conditions of possibility of such thinking. For Davidson, intuition—the given in experience—plays no role at all. See, e.g., Davidson, "A Coherence Theory of Truth and Knowledge," pp. 137–153. Rather, our empirical knowledge arises from our linguistic capacities—there is no difference between coming to know a language and coming to know the world. So the categories that emerge from reflection on linguistic understanding are necessarily applicable to the world, just as are, for Kant, the categories that emerge from reflection on the discursive character of empirical judgment. But the rejection of experience is not a trivial difference. To Davidson it is central to the rejection of intermediaries between mind and world, and the host of troubles they bring. Whether and to what extent we must banish experience in order to do without intermediaries of the troubling sort is a matter of great interest, at the center of the disagreement between Davidson and McDowell.

6 Davidson, Heidegger, and Truth

Mark Okrent

1 Truth and Thinking Creatures

Could something, whether a sentence or a proposition, or whatever, be true if there were no sapient entities in the world? Unless one is a certain sort of idealist, it seems obvious that many entities would have many of the properties that they do, whether or not there were any sapient creatures around. If, for example, the Earth exerts a force of attraction on the Moon of a certain magnitude and with certain effects, then it does so whether or not there is anyone around to measure that magnitude or notice those effects. On the other hand, some properties are linked, in a variety of ways, to the existence of intelligence. Nothing could be an intelligent observation, for example, unless there were intelligent observers, and there are no intelligent observers that are not thinkers. So it is possible to ask whether truth is more like exercising a gravitational pull, or more like being an intelligent observation: Could there be things that were true even if there were no rational, intelligent beings to notice them?

There are some reasons to think that there would be. Here is one such reason. In general we use the word "true" in such a way that we say that the sentence "Okrent is currently speaking" is true just when Okrent is speaking. This sentence seems to express a proposition that can also be expressed by other sentences, and that proposition is true if and only if its referent actually has the property that the proposition says it has. So if Okrent can have the property of speaking even if there are no sentient creatures (I guess in this case there must be at least one such creature), then the sentence "Okrent is speaking" can be true even if there are no sentient creatures. And if the Earth exerts a pull on the Moon even though there are no thinkers, then the proposition expressed by the sentence "The Earth exerts a pull on the Moon" is true even when there are no thinkers.

Nevertheless, there is a long tradition that denies this possibility. In particular, both Heidegger and Davidson maintain that truth depends on sapient beings in the sense that were there no sapient beings there would be nothing in the world that was true. Davidson says this in so many words: "Nothing in the world, no object or event, would be true or false if there were not thinking creatures."[1] Heidegger comes close to saying the very same thing in the same way: "'There is' truth only in so far as *Dasein* is and so long as *Dasein* is."[2] And this assertion of the dependence of truth on thinking creatures by both Heidegger and Davidson leads to a certain interpretive puzzle.

Here is the puzzle. I can think of two arguments that might lead one to assert that there could be no truths without thinkers. One argument depends on the nature of truth bearers. The other depends on accepting a form of verificationism about truth. But at a certain point I came to believe that neither of these arguments could be correctly attributed to either Heidegger or Davidson.

Here is the first possible argument. Sentences are the primary truth bearers. There are no sentences without thinkers. Therefore, there are no entities that are true without thinkers. There is good reason to think that Davidson and Heidegger were both attracted to this argument, although in Heidegger it took a slightly different form, in which a certain definite kind of intentional comportment played the role of sentences. But there seems to be an obvious rejoinder to this argument. That rejoinder is that propositions, and not sentences (or assertions, etc.), are the primary truth bearers, and propositions can be true even in the absence of sentences and sentence users. And, it seemed to me, it was just impossible for either Heidegger or Davidson to miss this potential rejoinder, so they couldn't have used this argument.

The second possible argument to the conclusion that there are no truths without *Dasein*, or thinking creatures, turns on the suggestion that the cash value of truth is warranted assertibility. If one accepts, with Quine and Peirce, "that the meaning of a sentence turns purely on what would count as evidence for its truth,"[3] then what it means to say that a sentence (or whatever) is true is specified by whatever would count as evidence for its being true, that is, by whatever would warrant us in asserting the sentence. And, since truth would then be associated with what would count as evidence for us, truth would be epistemically relativized to ourselves and our practices of verification, and there would be no truths without such practices. At one time I attributed this line of argument to both Heidegger and Davidson.[4] And I still think that there is something to be said for both of these attributions. There is only one problem with doing so: Both Heidegger and Davidson seem to reject this line of argument. Late in his career Davidson explicitly rejected epistemic views of truth in "Epistemology and Truth" and *Truth and Predication*. And, while as far as I know Heidegger never explicitly considered this form of verificationism regarding truth, in the context of a discussion of the relation between assertion and truth in *Basic Problems*, he did go out of his way to emphasize that even though truth is not "in things," "truth . . . is a possible determination of the being of the extant."[5] And, in context, this at least suggests that for Heidegger, whatever truth is, and whatever things are true, truth has to do primarily with the way a thing is rather than with the status of our knowledge of the thing.

So, in the absence of an argument in favor of the thesis that without *Dasein*, or thinking creatures, there are no truths, we are left with the following puzzle: What do Heidegger and Davidson mean to assert with this thesis, and why would anyone believe it to be true?

The key to solving the interpretive puzzle, for both Davidson and Heidegger, is given in *Truth and Predication*, the second half of which is an argument to the effect that the primary bearers of truth cannot be propositions.[6] If this is so, then we have reason to think that Davidson did use the first line of argument, which claims that there could be no truth bearers without thinkers, to argue that there is no truth without thinkers. For we now have Davidson's rejoinder to the suggestion that it is the meanings of sentences that are true or false, and what a sentence means could be true even if there were no sentences. And, armed with this Davidsonian argument it becomes possible to go back to *Basic Problems* and see that in that work Heidegger offers a surprisingly similar argument to a surprisingly similar, though not identical, conclusion.

There is one crucial difference between these two discussions of truth, however. All of Davidson's discussions of the concept of truth aim only at solving the following problem: How is it possible to assign truth conditions to all of the utterances of any speaker? Beyond achieving this goal, Davidson thinks that all theories of truth go astray. That is, Davidson wants to know how an observer could know, for any assertoric sentence uttered by a speaker, that that sentence would be true under such-and-such conditions. And, in effect, this amounts to knowing, for some language, that some particular Tarskian truth definition actually applies to that language. Saying anything about truth beyond this, Davidson thinks, is saying too much. "All attempts to characterize truth that go beyond giving empirical content to a structure of the sort Tarski taught us how to describe are empty, false, or confused."[7] For Davidson, truth is the most basic semantic concept, and there is no point in trying to understand it in terms of something else. All one can do is attempt to understand how we can *apply* the concept in interpreting what people say and do. Heidegger emphatically disagrees with this. And, once we have gone through both Davidson's and Heidegger's versions of the argument to the conclusion that there are no truths without thinkers, we will be able to understand why Heidegger thinks there is more to understand about truth than Davidson does, what he thinks there is to understand about truth that Davidson doesn't understand, and why Heidegger is right to think this. Heidegger holds, correctly, that only the utterances of agents who satisfy the principle of charity can have truth conditions, and only agents who succeed in revealing, in what they do and how they cope with the world, the way things are, can satisfy the principle of charity. And for this reason the concept of truth can and should be understood in terms of a more basic concept, the unveiling of things that is part and parcel of being in the world.

2 Davidson's Discussion of Truth

The Basic View

Late in his career, Davidson's discussions of truth, and his assertion of the dependence of truth on us, are oriented by his responses to and rejection of three distinctive ways of understanding the nature and character of truth. One of these ways of understanding truth, the "correspondence" view, has deep roots in the philosophical tradition. A second view, which Davidson labels "epistemic," identifies truth with warranted assertibility, and, while in its current form it is a descendent of positivist verificationism, the position's origins reach well back into the modern era. The third view, "disquotationalism," is entirely a creature of the analytic tradition in the twentieth century. The correspondence theory of truth turns on the suggestion that a truth vehicle, a sentence, proposition, or whatever, is true, when it is true, in virtue of "corresponding" to, or "agreeing" with, some entity, usually thought of as a fact or state of affairs. From Davidson's perspective, the correspondence view is the only way of giving content to a realist construal of truth. "The objective view of truth, if it has any content, must be based on correspondence as applied to sentences, or beliefs, or utterances, entities that are propositional in character."[8] Since, for the correspondence theorist, truth consists entirely in the agreement between the propositional content of a truth vehicle and some aspect of the world, whether or not any sentient creature knows or can know about that status is irrelevant to truth. The epistemic view of truth, on the other hand, denies that there is any coherent sense to be made of the notion that there are truths that are completely beyond the possibility of verification or justification, and in that sense this view relates the truth of a claim to its epistemic standing. Finally, over the last seventy-five years there has been a tendency to suggest that the whole issue regarding realism concerning truth is bogus. Davidson came to emphatically reject this disquotationalist tendency. On the disquotationalist view, there is no real issue about whether or not a sentence being true involves more than warranted assertibility because when one claims that a sentence is true one is not doing any more than asserting the sentence. The predicate "is true" is merely a metalinguistic device that allows us to talk about sentences, rather than talking about what the sentences talk about.

Both the tendency toward a correspondence theory of truth and the tendency toward a disquotational view of truth arise out of the same simple observation, the observation that it is correct to say of some truth vehicle that it is true just in case the conditions asserted in the proposition that it expresses actually obtain. The sentence "Okrent is currently speaking" is true just in case Okrent is currently speaking. What the sentence "Okrent is currently speaking" *says*, of course, is that Okrent, the person, is currently speaking; and the sentence is true just on those occasions when what the sentence says is going on in the world is really going on in the world. To the realist this fact suggests a way of cashing out the intuition that the truth of a sentence is radically nonepistemic: The sentence is true *because of*, the truth of the sentence is *explained by*, the correspondence between what the sentence says, its meaning, and the way the world is. But, the realist argues, the way the world is is surely independent of what we can know about it. And, even though the fact that some actual utterance has some definite meaning depends on how we use words, *that meaning itself* either agrees with or disagrees with the way the world is independently of the fact that we use words as we do and the fact that we have the cognitive abilities that we do. So whether or not what the sentence says corresponds with the way the world is is also independent of what we say or what we can know; so the truth of the proposition must also be independent of what we know, and realism regarding truth is guaranteed.

The disquotationalist starts with the same observation, that the sentence "Okrent is speaking" is true if and only if Okrent is speaking, and comes to a quite different conclusion. This trivial observation can be expressed in a single sentence: "The sentence 'Okrent is speaking' is true if and only if Okrent is speaking." This sentence is a truth-functional biconditional of the two sentences, "'Okrent is speaking' is true" and "Okrent is speaking." But what the single sentence says is that these two component sentences are true in just the same situations, the first is true just in case the second is true. But if we assume that the meaning of a sentence is fixed by its truth conditions, this suggests that the sentence that expresses our trivial observation assures that "'Okrent is speaking' is true" and "Okrent is speaking" have exactly the same meaning. According to the disquotationalist, this shows that the predicate "is true" is a mere device that adds nothing to the semantics of the original sentence. But from this she can go on to infer that both the realist and the antirealist are wrong about truth. Since for the disquotationalist "is true" adds nothing substantive to a sentence, and both the realist and antirealist assume that when one says that some sentence is true one is adding something to the mere assertion of the sentence, the disquotationalist concludes that both the realist and the antirealist are wrong.

Davidson is also struck by the apparently trivial fact that, for example, the sentence, "Okrent is currently speaking" is true just in case Okrent is currently speaking. Davidson is interested in this kind of trivial fact because these facts provide both the explananda of and the empirical evidence for Tarski-style definitions of truth in a language. "Tarki's basic insight was to make use of the apparently trivial fact that sentences of the form '"Snow is white" is true in L if and only if snow is white' must be true if the sentence quoted is a sentence of the language used to state the platitude."[9] Tarski realized that if one could provide a definition of "true-in-L" that entailed such a "T-sentence" for every sentence in L, then one's definition would pick out, using the resources of the metalanguage, the true sentences in L. But, Davidson holds, that is all that such a definition could do; it could pick out the extension of the predicate "true in L" by giving us, for every well-formed sentence of L, the conditions in which the predicate "true in L" is applicable to that sentence. But such a definition would not tell us what "true in L" means; it would not tell us what it is that one is saying when one says of a sentence that it is true. "He [Tarski] defined the class of true sentences by giving the extension of the truth predicate, but he did not give the meaning."[10] According to Davidson, a Tarski-style definition can't tell us what is meant when one says that a sentence in a language is true, because that the definition adequately picks out the true sentences in any actual language is an empirical matter, decided by how the users of the language actually speak. That the English sentence "Okrent is speaking" is true in English if and only if Okrent is speaking, and not if and only if Rouse is flying, is a fact about how the sentence is used in English. So for a Tarski-style definition of truth in a language L actually to apply to English, the

T-sentences entailed by that theory must agree with the actual conditions under which the sentences of English *are true*. But in that case, the definition can't tell us what it is for the sentences of English to be true; there could be nothing that counts as the definition's being accurate of English if there were no prior sense in which the sentences of English were true or false independent of the definition. So there must be more to truth than is expressed by the systematization of the trivial insight that "Okrent is speaking" is true just in case Okrent is speaking, and, Davidson concludes, disquotationalism is false.

But Davidson is also committed to the rejection of the realist understanding of the way in which there is more to truth than the trivial understanding systematized in a Tarski-style definition. According to the realist, the fact that the sentence "Okrent is speaking" is true just in case Okrent is speaking is explained by the fact that what the sentence says, its meaning, corresponds with the way the world is when Okrent is speaking. The basic realist suggestion is that what it is for a sentence to be true does not depend on us, or on what we can know, but rather that the truth of the sentence is in some way an objective fact. If this suggestion is to have any "content," to use Davidson's term, the realist must specify what the predicate "is true" positively adds to the sentence, or else the realist runs the danger of falling into disquotationalism. That is, to avoid disquotationalism, the realist must tell us just which fact "is true" tracks. Her response to this demand is that "is true" tracks correspondence, thereby giving content to realism.

Throughout most of his career, Davidson's explicit objection to correspondence views was that they are unintelligible, because there *is* nothing for sentences to correspond *with*. That is, his objection is to the ontological commitments of correspondence: "the real objection is rather that such [correspondence] theories fail to provide entities to which truth vehicles (whether we take these to be statements, sentences, or utterances) can be said to correspond. As I once put it, 'Nothing, no *thing* makes our statements true.'"[11] That is, Davidson holds that since the world doesn't come divided into propositionally structured chunks, it can't be the case that what makes a sentence true is that it "agrees with," or "corresponds with," some worldly, propositionally structured chunk. And, since realism regarding truth only gets content through this suggestion of correspondence, Davidson claims that realism is "unintelligible."

It is obvious that the pivot of this argument is the assertion that there is nothing for a truth vehicle to correspond with. Throughout most of his career, Davidson's explicit support for this assertion was the "slingshot" argument that he variously attributes to Frege, Alonzo Church, and

C. I. Lewis. The slingshot argument starts from two assumptions: "if two sentences are logically equivalent, they correspond to the same thing, and what a sentence corresponds to is not changed if a singular term is replaced by a coreferring singular term."[12] Given these assumptions, and the further assumption that definite descriptions are singular terms, the slingshot argument shows that any two arbitrary sentences with the same truth-value correspond to the same thing. The argument proceeds by using two devices to transform a sentence into another while, given the assumptions, the fact that is corresponded remains the same. First, one can substitute one definite description for another, without changing what the sentence corresponds to, as long as both descriptions actually apply to the entity referred to by the subject. To use a familiar example that Davidson actually cites, "Sir Walter Scott is the author of *Waverly*" corresponds to the same fact as "Sir Walter Scott is the man who wrote 29 Waverly novels altogether." Second, one can transform a sentence so that it comes to make a statement about some aspect of the identifying character of the previous predicate, a statement that is logically equivalent with the original sentence, also without changing what the sentence corresponds to. So, "Sir Walter Scott is the man who wrote 29 Waverly novels altogether" corresponds with the same fact as "The number, such that Sir Walter Scott wrote that many Waverly novels altogether is 29." But then, using the first device to transform this last sentence, and transitivity, "Sir Walter Scott is the author of *Waverly*" corresponds with the same fact as "The number of counties in Utah is 29."[13] But, as Davidson says, "this is to trivialize the concept of correspondence completely."[14]

So Davidson rejects both correspondence forms of realism and disquotationalism. There is something more to the notion of truth than is captured by disquotationalism, but that "something more" is not captured by the realist notion of correspondence. But what, then, is this "something more"? The antirealist has a ready answer. For the antirealist, when one understands what it is for a sentence to be true, what one understands are the conditions under which a speaker would be warranted in asserting the sentence. Davidson's main objection to this antirealism is that one can't make out the requisite notion of "warrant." And, we might as well add, that one can't make out that requisite notion is a function of the content of our intuitive concept of what it is for a sentence to be true. If one simply identifies what is warranted with what we currently accept as warranted around here, then, since we believe that our methods for warranting assertions seem to develop and improve, it appears obvious that what we warrant as assertible today, might not be so warranted tomorrow, whereas our fundamental intuition is that truth is not variably dependent on our contingent practices of justification. On the other hand, if "warrant" is understood as "ideally warranted," then the ideal can be associated either with what *we* could discover ideally, given our own contingent cognitive faculties, or with what an ideal observer could discover. But if we take the first interpretation, then it seems that there is still the possibility of error, thus undercutting the identity of truth and warranted assertibility. And if we take the second interpretation, then the suggestion comes to lack content, as we no longer have any sense of what must be the case for a sentence to be true, as we lack any sense of when it would be the case that a sentence was really warranted. Although Davidson recognizes that none of these considerations amount to a conclusive refutation of antirealism, he thinks that these concerns are sufficient to give us reason to believe that it is false.[15]

So Davidson rejects all three of the conceptions of truth that were offered to him by the tradition in which he operates. But how, then, does Davidson himself supplement Tarski's account of truth? According to Davidson, the key to the correct understanding of truth is to recognize the systematic connections among the concepts of truth, meaning, and belief.

> First, I assume that there are inescapable and obvious ties among the concepts of truth, belief, and meaning. If a sentence *s* of mine means that P, and I believe that P, then I believe that *s* is true. What gives my belief its content, and my sentence its meaning, is my knowledge of what is required for the belief or the sentence to be true. Since belief and truth are related in this way, belief can serve as the human attitude that connects a theory of truth to human concerns.[16]

Let's say that I assert the sentence "Okrent is currently speaking," and I understand what I am saying. Why do I say what I do, as opposed to, say, "Rouse is flying"? Well, if in my mouth "Okrent is speaking" meant Okrent is speaking and I believed that Okrent is speaking, then that *would* explain why it is that I assert the sentence "Okrent is speaking." So alluding to these two factors provides a possible explanation of the fact that I hold the sentence "Okrent is speaking" true.

Davidson holds that of these three putative facts, that what I say when I say "Okrent is speaking" means that Okrent is speaking, that I believe that Okrent is speaking, and that I hold the sentence "Okrent is speaking" to be true, only the last is observable, because only the last is an overt, if complex, fact about what I do. But, according to the above, if I believed that Okrent is speaking and "Okrent is speaking" meant that Okrent was speaking, these two facts together could *explain* that I held "Okrent is speaking" to be true, or at least they could explain this if for "Okrent is speaking" to mean Okrent is speaking is for "Okrent is speaking" to be true if and only if Okrent is speaking. And it is this linkage that supports Davidson's strategy for showing how Tarski's view of truth must be supplemented.

The Davidsonian recipe for understanding truth involves the construction of two systematically linked holistic theories to explain the actions of speaking agents. The first theory involves treating an agent's beliefs and the truth conditions on her words as the two aspects of a two-factor theoretical explanation of what sentences she holds to be true. Here is the recipe. Assuming the principle of charity, start out by assuming that the agent holds a sentence to be true only when she should, that is, only if the sentence is true. Construct a Tarski-style truth definition that allows you to infer T-sentences for all of the sentences in the speaker's language, including both those that she actually utters and all other possible sentences, and do so in such a way that the definition is maximally compatible with all of the sentences the speaker holds being true, according to the constructed definition. At the same time, using the evidential resources of both which sentences the speaker holds true and the remainder of her behavior, construct *another* two-factor theory, in this case a teleological theory, to explain the total behavior of the agent, both verbal and nonverbal, appealing to the beliefs and desires of the agent. Again taking the principle of charity for granted, assume that an agent mostly does what she has good reason to do given the situation and the kind of creature she is. But an agent acts for good reasons only if most of her beliefs are true, most of her desires are justified, and most of her inferences are rational, given her situation and desires. So the theory that is constructed involves assigning the maximum of true beliefs, justified desires, and rational inferences to the agent, compatible with her actual behavior, and using that assignment of beliefs and desires to explain the behavior.

These two theories are interconnected by the concept of belief. The agent's beliefs, together with a Tarski-style truth definition that fits her language, explains why it is that she holds just those sentences true that she holds true. The agent's beliefs, together with her desires and her instrumental rationality, explain why the agent acts as she does. Because the theories are linked in this way, the verbal behavior of the agent can serve as evidence for constructing an explanation of the nonverbal behavior of the agent, by providing evidence for the agent's beliefs, via our theory of the truth conditions on her utterances. And the nonverbal behavior of the agent can provide evidence for our ascription of meaning to her utterances, via our theory of her beliefs and desires.

It is this same concept of belief that allows us to overcome the major weakness of both of the theories. That weakness, of course, is that no agent is fully rational and no agent holds a sentence true only if it is true. According to Davidson, the role of belief in both theories is to take up the slack between these idealizations and actuality. Again, the recipe is straightforward. Having constructed one's interlocking theories, adjust one's attribution of beliefs to the agent so as to make some of them false, in such a way as to maximally explain the agent's actual behavior and which sentences she holds true.

To accurately understand Davidson's views concerning truth, it is crucial to correctly understand the ontology that he associates with the elements in these two theories. About the beliefs, desires, and truth conditions that appear in these theories, Davidson is a scientific *realist,* not an instrumentalist or verificationist. Beliefs, truth conditions, and desires are as real as atoms and geological plates, and that is as real as it gets. But what these real things *are,* what it is to be a belief, a desire, or a truth condition, is just what the theory says they are. What it is for an agent or her utterances to have any of these features is fixed by the role of these features in the theoretical explanations in which they appear. From this, however, it immediately follows that nothing in the world, no object or event, would be true or false if there were not thinking creatures, that is, if there were no agents with beliefs and desires. For Davidson, no agent can hold any overt behavior or utterance to be true, and thus to be a sentence or assertion which might be true, unless that she holds it true can be explained by appeal to her beliefs and the meaning, that is, the truth conditions in her language, of the utterance.[17] And, because what it is for some behavior to have truth conditions is tied to the conditions under which it is held to be true, no behavior can count as having truth conditions, that is, can be a candidate for truth, unless it is held to be true by some agent. For Davidson, nothing could be true or false if there were no thinking creatures because only entities that are true under certain conditions can *be* true, only objects or events that are *held* true can have conditions under which they are true, and entities, objects, or events can only be held true by entities that have beliefs and desires, by thinking creatures.[18] So, if there are no thinking creatures, no entity, object, or event can be true or false.

Predicates, Propositions, and Sentences

Much of what Davidson has to say about truth turns on the singular fact that he is committed to the view that the primary truth vehicles are things that sentient beings do (or, in the case of sentences, types of things that they do), the utterances, assertions, or sentences of thinking creatures, rather than the meanings or propositions expressed or represented by those sentences. Because he has this commitment, his principal discussions concern the relations among an actual agent's beliefs, the sentences that she utters and hears that she holds true, and the conditions under which those sentences would be true, rather than the relations between sentences and the propositions that they mean, represent, or express. In taking this approach, Davidson is rejecting an alternative tradition that focuses on propositions as the primary vehicles of truth and explains the truth of sentences in terms of the relation between sentences and the propositions they express. It is only from the perspective established by this Davidsonian commitment to sentences, rather than Platonic entities such as propositions, as the bearers of truth, that it seems obvious that there is nothing in the world that would be true or false if there were no thinking creatures.

As we saw above, during the bulk of his career Davidson offered an argument against treating propositions as the primary truth vehicles that turned on the slingshot argument. If there are no facts or states of affairs for propositionally structured entities to correspond with, as the slingshot argument concludes, then it makes no sense to speak of propositions whose identity conditions depend on their representing such facts. "If we give up facts as entities that can make sentences true, we ought to give up representations at the same time, for the legitimacy of each depends on the legitimacy of the other."[19] But the slingshot argument itself is shaky. It depends on the assumption that definite descriptions are singular terms, which is a distinctly minority view, and on intuitions about which sentences can correspond to which facts that are hazy at best. And, perhaps unsurprisingly, the slingshot argument has not been notably successful in deflating those who believe that propositions are the primary bearers of truth.

It is striking that the last thing that Davidson was preparing for publication when he died was a book on truth and predication, which is designed to combine two sets of lectures, one on truth and the other on predication, into a single volume. This juxtaposition is explained by the way in which Davidson characterizes the traditional "problem of predication." That problem has to do with how a predicate contributes to a sentence in such a way that the sentence could ever succeed in *saying* something. But from Davidson's perspective, to ask how a sentence could say something is really the problem of "what is required of a sentence if it is to be true or false."[20] That is, the problem of predication is the problem of how predicates function so that sentences can say something, and the problem of how sentences say something is the problem of how sentences can be truth vehicles. But, as we have seen, Davidson's earlier discussions of truth are incomplete precisely insofar as they leave unanswered the question of whether sentences can be true or false in virtue of their relation with the beliefs of those who utter them, or in virtue of representing propositions. So, since the problem of predication is the problem of how predicates allow sentences to say something that is true or false, the problem of predication is another way for Davidson to approach the nature of the primary truth bearers. Do predicates contribute to the possibility of a sentence's being true or false through their representative power, which in some way allows the sentence to represent or express some proposition, or do predicates function in some other way to make sentences capable of saying something?

As Davidson sees it, the problem of predication arises when we ask what is involved in a sentence's saying something. If we assume that sentences say something in virtue of the meanings of their parts, and that their parts are meaningful in virtue of standing for entities, we are confronted with the following problem.

> The sentence "Theatetus sits" has a word that refers to, or names, Theatetus, and a word whose function is somehow explained by mentioning the property (or form or universal) of Sitting. But the sentence says that Theatetus *has* this property. If referring to the two entities Theatetus and the property of Sitting exhausted the semantics of the sentence, it would be just a string of names; we would ask where the verb was. The verb, we understand, expresses the relation of instantiation. Our policy, however, is to explain verbs by relating them to properties and relations. But this cannot be the end of the matter, since we now have three entities, a person, a property, and a relation, but no verb.[21]

That is, if we understand the role of predicates in sentences as being explained by their standing for entities, even if those entities are thought of as properties, or universals, or whatever, that are ontologically different in kind from particulars, then we can't see how a sentence differs from a string of names, a string that *says* nothing—for in that case the words just stand for a group of entities. And if we treat the role of predicates as not merely indicating some entity, but also indicating that the particular referred to in the subject stands in some relation, say, instantiation, to the entity named in the predicate, then we have still failed to understand how the words *say* anything. Now we have a list that includes, for example, Theatetus, the property Sitting, the relation Instantiation, but no verb.

What the intractability of the problem of predication shows is that what predicates refer to, or whether they refer to anything at all, is irrelevant to their ability to facilitate the ability of sentences to say anything at all. But if this is the case, then the strategy of explaining the truth of sentences by first explaining the truth of propositions and then understanding the representation relation between sentences and the propositions they express is a nonstarter. This strategy is a nonstarter because any such representational account will leave unexplained how it is that anything, sentence or proposition, can say anything of anything, and thus leave unexplained how a sentence could be true or false. The detour through propositions adds nothing, and we are left with the original problem: How can sentences be true or false?

Davidson's own solution to the problem of predication turns on treating truth as the primary semantic concept: "Truth is the prime semantic concept; we could not think or speak in the sense of entertaining or communicating propositional contents without it."[22] Instead of focusing on what the parts of a sentence represent, we should focus on how the sentence says something that might be true or false. And a sentence says something just in case it *can* be true or false. So if we could explain how a predicate contributes to the truth or falsity of the sentences in which it appears, we will have explained the functional role the predicate plays in aiding the sentence to say something. But, in a sense, this is precisely what a Tarski-style definition of a truth predicate for a language does. Such a definition explains the roles of all of the particular predicates in a language by specifying the conditions under which those predicates are *true of* objects, and thus serve as part of an explanation of the truth or falsity of sentences containing those predicates. If "'Okrent is speaking' is true if and only if Okrent is speaking" is a T-sentence of English, then what explains that "Okrent is speaking" is currently true is that this T-sentence holds and that Okrent is currently speaking. And this is a sufficient account of how the predicate "is speaking" contributes to the ability of a sentence to be true or false. "[I]f we can show that our account of the role of predicates is part of an explanation of the fact that sentences containing a given predicate are true or false, then we have incorporated our account of predicates into an explanation of the most obvious sense in which sentences are unified, and so we can understand how, by using a sentence, we can make assertions and perform other speech acts."[23]

As Davidson recognizes, this solution to the problem of predication has the air of hocus pocus. In effect, Davidson gives us an account of how *each* predicate contributes to the truth conditions of the sentences in which it appears (by inferring those conditions from a Tarski-style definition of the truth predicate), without telling us *how*, in general, predication introduces truth conditions at all. Davidson professes not to be bothered by this result. His position is that this is all we can get in the way of a solution to the problem of predication, because any more we might add would just reintroduce the classic puzzles.

> It may be objected that it [Davidson's account] gives an account of how each predicate in a language contributes to the truth conditions of the sentences in which it occurs, but that it gives no general explanation of predication. It is true that no such general explanation emerges. What does emerge is a *method* for specifying the role of each and every predicate in a specific language. . . . What more can we demand? I think the history of the subject has demonstrated that more would be less.[24]

3 Heidegger on Truth

The ways in which Heidegger's manner of approaching issues relating to truth is markedly different from Davidson's approach are immediately evident. Nevertheless, there are at least two significant ways in which the contours of Heidegger's discussion coincide with Davidson's. First, there is the doxographic agreement that I have been emphasizing regarding the dependence of truth on sapient being. Second, there is a certain methodological coincidence between the way Davidson approaches truth in *Truth and Predication* and the way Heidegger approaches truth in *Basic Problems.* In *Truth and Predication* Davidson implicitly argues that the concept of truth can be grasped only through its links with the concepts of meaning and *belief.* Because of this connection between truth and belief, Davidson thinks that only occurrences that are explicable by appeal to the beliefs of agents can count as true or false. (This isn't quite true, of course, as Davidson thinks that both beliefs themselves and types of actual and possible utterances in a language, i.e., sentences, can be true and false.) In *Truth and Predication* (as opposed to the rest of his works) Davidson argues for the centrality of the relation between truth and belief by way of excluding the only conceivable alternative, that it is propositions, or the meanings of sentences, that are true or false, and that such propositions can be true even if they are neither sentences in a believer's language or ever uttered by believers. *Truth and Predication* argues against this alternative by showing that, because of the problems involved in explaining predication representationally, the representational features of sentences, by themselves, are insufficient to account for the ability of sentences to say something that might be true or false. And for that reason, sentences become capable of saying something that might be true or false only through their being uttered by believers or by being linked in the appropriate way to actual utterances by believers. In *Basic Problems,* Heidegger uses a similar strategy to reach the conclusion that truth has *Dasein*'s kind of being.

Just as in the Davidsonian strategy, Heidegger begins with a critical discussion of the history of attempts to solve the problem of the way in which the subject and predicate are related in the assertoric sentence. Heidegger starts his history with Aristotle's definition of the *logos apophantikos,* a term that he translates into German as *Aussage,* and we will translate into English as "assertion." The *Logos apophantikos* is "an articulate sound in words that is capable of signifying something and in such a way that each part of this verbal complex, each single word, already signifies something for itself, the subject concept and the predicative concept."[25] The distinctive mark of this semantic formation, that it is *apophantikos,* is articulated by Heidegger as its *exhibiting* ability, and only discourse "in which trueness and falseness occur" is exhibitive. Grammatically, the mark of the assertion is that its two main parts, the subject concept and the predicate concept, are linked by the "is" of the copula. So "being" in the sense of the copula and being in the sense of being-true are connected in the structure of the assertion: The ability of the assertion to say something that could be true or false is somehow linked with the predicative structure in the assertion. "In the logos as assertion there is present, for one thing, in conformity with its form S is P, the 'is,' being as copula. For another, each logos as assertion is either true or false."[26]

As Davidson as well as Heidegger pointed out, Aristotle, following the late Plato, already noticed that the fact that both the subject and the predicate term of the assertion represent or stand for entities does not account for the fact that the assertion says something that could be true or false. This is the way Heidegger sums up Aristotle's point:

> All these verbs *mean something* but they do not say whether what they mean *is* or *is not.* If I say "to go," "to stand," "going," "standing," then I haven't said whether anyone is *actually* going or standing. Being, not-being, to be, not to be, do not signify a thing—we would say they do not in general signify something which itself *is.* Not even if we utter the word "being" *to on,* quite nakedly for itself, for the determination being, in the sense of to-be, in the expression "being" *is nothing;* being is not itself *a* being.[27]

That is, what the assertion asserts is the *being* so and so of some entity; this is what is indicated by the copula that is the mark of the assertion's ability to say something true or false. But the "is" doesn't function like the other parts of the assertion. It doesn't represent any thing, any entity. In that sense, *being* so and so is not *a* being.

Since the assertion only says something that might be true or false by asserting that something *is* so and so, and the entities that the various parts of the sentence represent taken together do not contain this assertoric aspect of the sentence, Aristotle concludes, as Heidegger notes, that truth is not "in things." Rather, truth must be "in thought." About this "is" Aristotle says, summarized by Heidegger: "For falsity and truth are not in things . . . but in 'thought,' what this 'is' means is not a being occurring among things, something present like them, but *en dianoia*, in thinking."[28] We will see that although there is a sense in which Heidegger accepts this Aristotelian dictum that truth is not in things, from Heidegger's perspective it must be seriously qualified and modified.

After concluding his tour of the history of logic Heidegger returns to the direct consideration of the nature of assertion, and through that consideration, his discussion of truth. One of the key implications Heidegger draws from the history of the problem of predication is that attempts to solve that problem have been warped by the tendency to treat assertion as primarily a *verbal* phenomenon. Such a way of taking the problem suggests that the ability of an assertion to say something of something that might be true or false is in some way dependent on a structural feature of the sentence in which the assertion is uttered. But from Heidegger's standpoint, no such structural feature could ever account for the assertoric character of assertion. For it to do so would require that the representational aspects of the sentence by themselves could explain why it is that it is an assertion, and this, we have seen, is impossible. So whatever it is that allows the assertion to say something true or false is not contained in the verbal string itself just as a verbal string, and thus that the assertion is actually uttered is an *inessential* aspect of the assertion as assertion. "Spoken articulation can belong to the logos, but it does not have to."[29]

This Heideggerean emphasis on the possibility that assertions need not be uttered would seem to mark a crucial difference from Davidson. In fact, however, the gap between Heidegger and Davidson on this point is not as wide as it might seem. Both Heidegger and Davidson are reacting against the traditional program that attempts to understand the ability of assertions to say something primarily in terms of the representational quality of their parts. For Davidson, as well as Heidegger, this program must fail, because the most important aspect of assertion taken strictly as a verbal unit, its predicative structure or copula, does not itself represent anything. So, for Davidson, what is uttered in the sentence actually *says* anything, that might be true or false, only through its relations to the *beliefs* of the speaker—that is, through the fact that the sentence has an intentional character through its being explained by its links with the intentional states of the speaker. And, for Heidegger, the most fundamental fact about assertion is that it itself *is* a specific kind of intentional comportment. "Asserting is *one of the Dasein's intentional comportments*."[30] That is, what makes an assertion an assertion, a *logos apophantikos* that can be true or false, is nothing about its verbal structure, but rather that it is a certain kind of intentional comportment of a certain type of agent.

To say that asserting is an intentional comportment is to say that all acts of assertion are about something. Assertion shares this in common with all types of intentional comportments. Assertion is differentiated from those other comportments, however, by the kind of comportment it is. For Heidegger the differentia of assertion has three aspects. "We can define assertion as *communicatively determinant exhibition*."[31] Notice, the differentiae of assertion are characterized in terms of what the comportment that is assertion *does*. An assertion is a kind of *exhibition*, and, as intentional, it is an exhibition of something. "The basic structure of assertion is the exhibition of that about which it asserts."[32] The two other differentiae serve to distinguish assertion from other types of exhibition. Assertion exhibits by showing the going together of different specifications of the very thing that is exhibited: "it displays the belonging-together of the manifold determinations of the being which is asserted about."[33] That is, assertion essentially exhibits what it is about by predicatively determining it *as* this or that. And assertion is essentially communicative insofar as it has the function of sharing among different agents this determining predicative way of comporting toward the entity that the assertion is about.

So, for Heidegger, assertions are a kind of intentional comportment that counts as communicatively determinant exhibition. And assertions can be true and false. But what does it mean to say that an assertion is true? What does the truth of an assertion consist in? For Heidegger, the capacity of the assertion to be true or false is tied to its function as an intentional comportment rather than to its internal structure. Assertion is an intentional comportment in the sense that it has a function and as such aims at accomplishing an end. The end it aims at is that the entity it refers to be exhibited *as it is*. When this is accomplished, Heidegger says that the entity is *unveiled*. When the assertion does its job, it exhibits or unveils what it is about; that is, the assertion itself succeeds in unveiling its referent. This successful completion of its job by an assertion, its unveiling of what it is about, is what it is for an assertion to be true. "This unveiling, which is the *basic function of assertion*, constitutes the character traditionally designated as *being-true*."[34]

But notice, on this view, what it is for an assertion to be true is fixed in terms of the assertion accomplishing a task, and that task has to do with achieving something regarding its referent, in this case that the referent be unveiled. Just as my painting a house is an intentional comportment that has *that the house is painted* as its success condition, my making an assertion in regard to Okrent (say, "Okrent is speaking") is an intentional comportment that has Okrent being unveiled *as* speaking as *its* success condition. "The *intentum* of the *intentio* of . . . assertion has the character of unveiledness."[35] *What* assertion intends is *unveiledness*, but the unveiledness that is intended by assertion is always "*the unveiledness* of that to which the assertion refers."[36] When an assertion intends the object to which it refers, it intends the "being-unveiled," the "unveiledness" of that object. That unveiledness is what it is to accomplish, and if the assertion accomplishes this task, then it is true.

This is a strange way to characterize a class of intentions. What is strange about it has to do with the way that the *intentum* of the act of asserting is characterized. Consider: When I see the color of the plant in my office, I intend the plant *as green*; I intend the plant's *being green*, or the *greenness* of the plant. Similarly, when I intend to paint my house, I intend that my house comes to have been painted. The paintedness of the house or the greenness of the plant are both possible ways in which an entity itself might be. They are potential properties of things, and in that sense "among things." But the *being-unveiled*, or the "*unveiledness*" of the plant as green, is no property of the plant, and the assertion in which I claim that the plant is green *says nothing* about the plant as unveiled. That the plant be exhibited as it is, or unveiled, is no part of the *content* of the assertion. If it were, then every assertion would need to have some content in common. But the truth of the assertion about the plant consists, according to Heidegger, in the assertion succeeding in unveiling the plant. So truth is not "present among things" as Heidegger puts it, echoing Aristotle. It is no property of things that a thing might have even if there were no assertions. Truth, at least the truth of assertions, depends on the existence of beings that can make assertions that can, at least potentially, unveil entities.

As we have seen, Aristotle jumped right from the conclusion that truth is not "in things" to the implication that truth must be "in thought." But Heidegger rejects this implication: "It thus will emerge that truth is neither present in things nor does it occur in a subject but lies—taken almost literally—in the middle 'between' things and *Dasein*."[37] To say that truth is "in thought" or "in a subject" must mean, Heidegger suggests, that "truth is in some sense a determination of the mind, something inside it, immanent in consciousness." This suggestion, which takes some sort of Cartesian or German idealist conception of subjectivity as the antagonist to be defeated, clearly leaves out a different alternative. Truth might be "in thought" in the sense that truth is defined in terms of the collective procedures of justification that offer warrants for assertions within the games of giving and asking for reasons that are played by communities of intentional agents. Nevertheless, even though Heidegger in the 1920s was blind to this possibility, I don't think it would have made much of a difference to his judgment that truth can't be "in thought" in this or any other sense. Heidegger's argument here is essentially the same as Davidson's. He thinks that the intentional structure of assertion guarantees that truth is not "in the mind" in the sense of being a feature of some intentional entity that makes no essential reference to the *intentum* of that entity, as is the case for the warrant for an assertion. As an intentional comportment, an assertion is a communicating, determining exhibition of its referent itself. It is successful only if the thing itself is displayed, exhibited, unveiled as *it* is. The assertion "The plant is green" succeeds in its job only if it succeeds in displaying the plant as it is, the plant being green. For that reason, any mere epistemic characteristic of the assertion itself, such as the assertion's being warranted assertible, must be distinct from the aim of the assertion, that the plant itself be shown as it is. Since for an assertion to be warranted has to do with the assertion and not what it is about, the plant, it is always possible that the assertion is warranted even if the assertion is not true. For truth, the assertion must successfully exhibit the plant.

So, Heidegger concludes, truth is neither present among things nor in the mind. But, then, "where" is it? As he has articulated the notion, the truth of an assertion is its unveiling character, that it succeeds in exhibiting, bringing to unveiledness, displaying, the thing it is about. And truth itself is "unveiledness" as such. But for Heidegger, things can be unveiled only if there is a being that does the unveiling, a being capable of intending entities, that is, *Dasein*. The unveiling, truth, happens only in and through *Dasein*. It immediately follows from this that there is no truth without *Dasein*. "There is truth—unveiling and unveiledness—only when and as long as *Dasein* exists."

But isn't there an enormous gap in this argument? Hasn't Heidegger neglected to exclude another possibility? Can't truth be a property of propositions, rather than an epistemic property or a property of things? In fact, in *Basic Problems* Heidegger does raise this possibility, only to reject it, apparently without argument, with ridicule and contempt. Having rejected both an objectivist and a subjectivist interpretation of truth, Heidegger mentions meanings as a third realm of being: "The consequences of this impossible predicament of inquiry appear in the theory's being driven to every possible device—for instance, it sees that truth is not in objects, but also not in subjects, and so it comes up with a third realm of meaning, an invention that is no less doubtful than medieval speculation about angels."[38] But, of course, Heidegger has already given us the argument that justifies this ridicule. It is just the argument that he shares with the Davidson of *Truth and Predication*. The meaning of the assertion, what the proposition expresses, can't be what is true and false, because the only way to cash out that proposition in a way that divorces it from actual intentional agents intending the world is through the representational aspects of the parts of the assertoric sentence, and, we have seen, those representational aspects of those parts, by themselves, are inadequate to ever *say* anything. So the conclusion stands. There is no truth without *Dasein*, even though truth cannot be identified with what is warranted for *Dasein*.

4 Conclusion

As I have been telling the story, there is a great deal in common in Heidegger's and Davidson's understanding of truth. They both reject realist notions of truth for very much the same reason. Given the problem of predication it is impossible to comprehend the ability of a sentence to say something true or false solely on the basis of the representational properties of the internal structural parts of the sentence, and, because this is so, it is impossible to make coherent sense of the notion that a sentence can have a meaning that might be true or false independently of the role of the use of the sentence in the ongoing activity of an intentional agent. And for that reason there cannot be any thing in the world that might be true or false in the absence of acting, thinking creatures. But Heidegger and Davidson also agree on the limited character of the dependence of truth on sentient being. Although there is nothing in the world that could be true or false without thinkers, *which* of these items *are* true depends exclusively on the things in the world, not on the epistemic powers of its thinking inhabitants.

Having emphasized the commonality between Heidegger and Davidson, however, it is time to acknowledge the deep disagreement between them. This truly deep difference shows itself in two Heideggerean assertions concerning truth for which there are no Davidsonian analogues. First, Heidegger holds that assertion is not the primary truth bearer; for Heidegger, assertions can be true or false only because something else already unveils entities, and in that sense, is true. "Assertion does not as such primarily unveil; instead, it is always, in its sense, already related to something antecedently given as unveiled."[39] Second, Heidegger holds that the entity that does this unveiling prior to assertion, and in that sense is true in the most basic way, is *Dasein*, or sapient being itself. Here is one of the ways Heidegger puts this familiar point in *Basic Problems*:

> Intentional comportment in the sense of assertion about something is founded in its ontological structure in the basic constitution of the Dasein which we described as being-in-the-world. Only because Dasein exists in the manner of being-in-the-world is some being unveiled along with the Dasein's existence in such a way that what is thus unveiled can become the possible object of an assertion. So far as it exists, the Dasein is always already dwelling with some being or other, which is uncovered in some way or other and in some degree or other.[40]

We can get at what Heidegger is driving at in these dark sayings by focusing on the limitations of the Davidsonian project. As we have seen, what it is for a sentence to say something must be seen in terms of its ability to say something that might be true or false. But an utterance can be true (or false) only if it has associated truth conditions. Any given utterance has truth conditions only if it is the act of an agent whose verbal and nonverbal behavior, taken as a whole, is explicable by appeal to two interlocking sorts of theory, one of which explains verbal acts by alluding to a Tarski-style theory of truth conditions for a language and the beliefs of the agent, and the other of which appeals to those same beliefs and the desires of that agent to explain her acts. Armed with these theories, an observer is in a position to understand what the agent says, in the sense that she can assign conditions under which what she says would be true, for anything she should happen to say. Now, of course, the observer must have an understanding of what is involved in a sentence being true *prior* to her construction of any such theory. She needs this prior understanding for two reasons. First, in order to construct the theory the observer must be in a position to recognize that what the agent says is mostly true when she says it, and to do that the observer must have some sense of what it is for a sentence to be true. Second, for an observer to construct her theories of the agent, the observer must be able to attribute beliefs to the agent, and to do that the observer must be able to detect the falsehoods that the agent speaks. And to tell that what an agent says is false, the observer must have some sense of what it is for a sentence to be true.[41]

Davidson holds that "all attempts to characterize truth that go beyond giving empirical content to a structure of the sort Tarski taught us how to describe are empty, false, or confused."[42] And he continues by listing a series of attempts to characterize truth that he rightly thinks are empty, false, or confused. But Davidson's own views push us in a different direction. The task of "giving empirical content to a structure of the sort Tarski taught us how to describe" is just the task of constructing an overall theory that explains the behavior, verbal and nonverbal, of an agent by treating that agent as having intentional comportments such as beliefs and desires, that put the agent into vital contact with the world. This vital contact is ensured by the necessity of the principle of charity. For Davidson himself, it is a necessary ontological condition on being an intentional agent that most of the agent's acts must be successful, most of her desires must be appropriate given the kind of being that she is, and most of her beliefs must be true. That is, the condition *sine qua non* for having an intentional life is that an agent's intentions, in general, successfully uncover the entities in the world. This successful uncovering, however, can't be primarily linguistic. As Davidson himself shows, sentences can't say anything unless they have truth conditions; sentences can't have truth conditions unless the speakers of those sentences have beliefs; and speakers can't have beliefs unless they are also agents who successfully cope with things by acting in order to get what they desire. Only agents who successfully uncover the entities in the world in and by coping with that world with their perceptual, inferential, and motor intentional capacities, can uncover the world by making assertions. That is, it is a condition on making Davidson's project fly that "assertion does not as such primarily unveil; instead, it is always, in its sense, already related to something antecedently given as unveiled," and "intentional comportment in the sense of assertion about something is founded in its ontological structure in the basic constitution of the Dasein which we described as being-in-the-world."

So there is something substantial to say about truth beyond what Davidson is willing to commit himself to, and Heidegger has gone a long way toward saying it. Truth is uncovering, and it is tied ontologically to the existence of a being whose very definition consists in the ability to unveil the world by actively and successfully coping with it perceptually in a motor-intentional way. Davidson comes close to saying something similar to this, but is prevented from doing so by the limitations of his vision and philosophical upbringing.

Notes

1. Donald Davidson, *Truth and Predication* (Cambridge, MA: Harvard University Press, 2005), p. 7.

2. Martin Heidegger, *Being and Time*, trans. John Macquarrie and Edward Robinson (New York: Harper & Row, 1962), p. 269.

3. W. V. O. Quine, "Epistemology Naturalized," in W. V. O. Quine, *Ontological Relativity and Other Essays* (New York: Columbia University Press, 1969), p. 80.

4. Mark Okrent, *Heidegger's Pragmatism* (Ithaca: Cornell University Press, 1988).

5. Martin Heidegger, *The Basic Problems of Phenomenology*, trans. Albert Hofstadter (Bloomington: Indiana University Press, 1982), p. 217.

6. I borrowed the outlines of this interpretation of *Truth and Predication* from Jeff Speaks, who suggested it in a review of that book in *Notre Dame Philosophical Reviews* (August 2006), at <http://ndpr.nd.edu/review.cfm?id=7224>.

7. Donald Davidson, "Epistemology and Truth," in his *Subjective, Intersubjective, Objective* (Oxford: Oxford University Press, 2001), pp. 177–191, 190.

8. Davidson, "Epistemology and Truth," p. 185.

9. Ibid., p. 178.

10. Davidson, *Truth and Predication*, p. 27.

11. Davidson, "Epistemology and Truth," p. 184.

12. Davidson, *Truth and Predication*, p. 128.

13. Ibid., pp. 127–128.

14. Davidson, "Epistemology and Truth," p. 184.

15. See Davidson, "Epistemology and Truth," pp. 185–188.

16. Ibid., pp. 188–189.

17. It is another implication of Davidson's commitments that no agent can have beliefs and desires who does not make assertions that can be true or false. This follows from the linkages between the two theories, via belief. For what it is worth, I think Davidson is wrong about this, and that the belief/desire system can be autonomous from the language system, as it is when we attribute propositional attitudes to non-speaking animals.

18. Strictly speaking, sentences in a language, taken as potential utterance types in that language, that are never instantiated in any actual utterances, can on this view also be true or false. On Davidson's view, however, that there are such truth-bearing uninstantiated utterance types in a language is a function of the fact that the best truth theory for that language assigns truth conditions to those types of potential utterances. And, since truth conditions pertain to any utterance type only in light of the actual utterances of actual teleological rational agents, were there no such agents nothing could have such truth conditions and nothing could be a truth vehicle.

19. Davidson, "Epistemology and Truth," p. 184.

20. Davidson, *Truth and Predication*, p. 86.

21. Ibid., pp. 84–85.

22. Ibid., p. 155.

23. Ibid.

24. Ibid., p. 161.

25. Heidegger, *Basic Problems*, p. 180.

26. Ibid.

27. Ibid., p. 181.

28. Ibid., p. 182.

29. Ibid., p. 207. This conclusion doesn't actually follow from the argument as I have presented it. All that follows is that the verbal string is insufficient to explain predication, not that it is inessential.

30. Ibid.

31. Ibid., p. 210.

32. Ibid., p. 209.

33. Ibid.

34. Ibid., p. 215.

35. Ibid., p. 217.

36. Ibid.

37. Ibid., p. 214.

38. Ibid., pp. 214–215.

39. Ibid., p. 208.

40. Ibid.

41. Davidson attempts to understand this prior sense of what it is for something to be true in terms of the agreement or disagreement between the agent and the observer. As far as I can tell, this stratagem immediately tips Davidson's views over into verificationism, and makes it the case that Rorty was right about Davidson: Truth is whatever is warranted by the justificatory rules of our club.

42. Davidson, "Epistemology and Truth," p. 190.

7 Davidson and the Demise of Representationalism

Giancarlo Marchetti

The master concept of modern and contemporary epistemology, namely, the idea that thoughts, statements, and beliefs have content in virtue of their capacity to represent reality accurately,[1] has attracted the admiration and attention of many philosophers throughout the ages. Typified historically by Descartes, Locke, Kant, Frege, Russell, Tarski, Carnap, and the early Wittgenstein, this line of thought is so profoundly rooted in the tradition that it is hard to conceive of any alternative to it. Yet one prominent countertradition common to Hegel,[2] Husserl, Dewey, the later Wittgenstein, the later Heidegger,[3] Quine, Rorty, Dennett, and Davidson has shown us how to avoid representationalism, suggesting a new way of describing knowledge and inquiry.

Davidson, in particular, has given a renewed impulse to antirepresentationalism through his critique, in "On the Very Idea of a Conceptual Scheme,"[4] of the foundations of the scheme–content dichotomy. This dualism, which Davidson reconnects to the Cartesian dualism of the objective and the subjective, is grounded in the conception of the "mind with its private states and objects," and in the idea that truth consists in the correct mirroring of facts.[5]

In the wake of Davidson's critique, and without recourse to the scheme–content dichotomy, it is difficult to conceive of knowledge in terms of representational relations between language and world. The abandonment of representationalism, namely, the demolition of what Davidson calls the "myth of subjective," brings with it a refusal of the notion of correspondence between language and world, between sentences and facts—a refusal of the idea that statements and beliefs correspond or are "*made true by facts.*"[6] Davidson's refutation of the representational model begins with both Tarski's semantic conception, and Frege's argument, called by Barwise and Perry the "slingshot argument,"[7] which gives us reason for rejecting facts as such.[8]

The best-known forms of the slingshot argument are those by Frege, which Church[9] identifies in the analyses contained in Frege's "On Sense and Meaning,"[10] and the one elaborated by Gödel in his essay, "Russell's Mathematical Logic."[11] In his *Facing Facts*, Stephen Neale, who has analyzed the philosophical importance of the arguments in detail, demonstrates how "awkward" it is to elude the slingshot.[12] He also demonstrates that Gödel's slingshot is the most cogent and particularly laden with implications.[13]

The assumption from which Davidson,[14] following Church and Quine,[15] derives the slingshot argument is Fregean,[16] and the conclusion, that all true sentences, if they name anything, name the same thing, is also Fregean.[17] In "True to the Facts," Davidson puts the arguments as follows:

> The statement that Naples is farther north than Red Bluff corresponds to the fact that Naples is farther north than Red Bluff, but also, it would seem, to the fact that Red Bluff is farther south than Naples (perhaps these are the same fact). Also to the fact that Red Bluff is farther south than the largest Italian city within thirty miles of Ischia. When we reflect that Naples is the city that satisfies the following description: it is the largest city within thirty miles of Ischia, and such that London is in England, then we begin to suspect that if a statement corresponds to one fact, it corresponds to all.[18]

Davidson takes this reasoning to its extreme consequences, concluding that the slingshot, given its assumptions, does not prove there are no facts, but proves that there is at most only one all-embracing fact, the "Great Fact."[19] Such a conclusion is, however, inadequate as support for representationalism and the correspondence theory of truth. The slingshot, as Davidson makes clear, is not just an argument against facts as entities of correspondence, but an argument "against any entities that may be proposed as correspondents, say states of affairs or situations."[20] The slingshot shows that "*any* purported truth-makers we may think of will suffer the same fate, for what it shows is that whatever sentences are thought to correspond to, all true sentences must correspond to the same thing."[21]

According to Davidson, the slingshot argument demonstrates that statements and beliefs do not need entities such as facts, objects, or states of affairs. That true sentences all correspond to the same thing (the world, reality, nature) implies, says the American philosopher, the "trivialization" of the concept of correspondence. As Davidson suggests, Frege's slingshot can be formalized as follows:

> Starting from the assumptions that a true sentence cannot be made to correspond to something different by the substitution of co-referring singular terms, or by the substitution of logically equivalent sentences, it is easy to show that, if true sentences correspond to anything, they all correspond to the same thing. But this is to

> trivialize the concept of correspondence completely; there is no interest in the relation of correspondence if there is only one thing to which to correspond, since, as in any such case, the relation may as well be collapsed into a simple property: thus, "*s* corresponds to the universe," like "*s* corresponds to (or names) the True," or "*s* corresponds to the facts" can less misleadingly be read "*s* is true."[22]

The property of being true cannot be explained by the relation of correspondence, on the grounds that, if there is only one thing to which the statements can correspond, it is simpler to say "it is true" than "it corresponds to the truth."[23] For Davidson, there is nothing that can make statements true inasmuch as the notion of conformity to experience, just as the notion of being true to the facts does not add anything "intelligible" to the notion of being true.[24]

The slingshot argument demonstrates that no correspondence theory of truth can illuminate its *explanandum*: "the postulation of facts will not explain, define, or even illuminate the concept of truth."[25] For Davidson, appealing to facts in order to explain truth is of no use, "since the predicate 'corresponds to The One Fact' might as well be considered an unstructured word," and we already have a more appropriate and less misleading predicate, namely, "is true."[26] Strawson had already maintained, Davidson points out, that saying "a statement corresponds to (fits, is borne out by, agrees with) the facts," is "a variant on saying it is true."[27]

When Davidson himself was still under the influence of the realist conception of truth, he championed the correspondence theory.[28] In a later work, however, he qualified his position, arguing that it was inappropriate to refer to his conception of truth as a correspondence theory.[29] Such terminology is unfortunate, Davidson claims, in generating an entire range of conceptual confusions, and thus he writes that: "I have myself argued in the past that theories of the sort that Tarski showed how to produce were correspondence theories of a sort . . . it was a mistake to call such theories correspondence theories."[30]

For Davidson, the Tarskian conception of truth is not a correspondence theory inasmuch as such a theory does not, "like most correspondence theories, explain truth by finding entities such as facts for true sentences to correspond to."[31] In his view, Tarski's theory does not presuppose the postulation of any entity (facts or states of affaires) to which true statements must correspond, but it does imply that a "relation between entities and expressions be characterized ("satisfaction")."[32] In fact, Tarski's truth definitions are not based on the idea that a statement depicts, represents, or "corresponds" to some entity. According to Davidson, one should not take "seriously"[33] the references that Tarski makes to "states of affairs" in remarks such as: "[S]emantical concepts express certain relations between objects (and states of affairs) referred to in the language discussed and expressions of the language referring to those objects."[34] Indeed, one of Tarski's great achievements is having taught us how we can eschew the notion of fact.

Davidson identifies the element of "correspondence" in the Tarskian theory as present in the role of "satisfaction"[35] understood as a "relation between language and something else."[36] The truth of a statement, he observes, does not derive from the existence of the fact that it describes, but depends directly on the relations of satisfaction and reference. In this way, Davidson avoids the ontological category that subtends the theory of truth as correspondence.[37]

The idea of satisfaction as the key element in a theory of truth goes back to Tadeusz Kotarbiński. In fact, it is from his teacher Kotarbiński, whom he mentions favorably in his essay "The Concept of Truth in Formalized Languages,"[38] that Tarski takes his definition of truth. In *Gnosiology: The Scientific Approach to the Theory of Knowledge*, Kotarbiński claims:

> The semantic conception of truth . . . is a modern continuation, freed from common objections, of the classical interpretation of truth as agreement with reality. By that conception, the truth of a sentence consists in the fact that it is satisfied by all objects, the concept of satisfaction being not defined by reference to truth; but introduced in a different way.[39]

As Davidson sees matters, it is a good thing to be rid of correspondence, and thus also to be rid of the fallacious explanatory power that is normally attributed to it. The notion of correspondence would be useful if we could say "in an *instructive* way, which fact or slice of reality it is that makes a particular sentence true." Unfortunately, however, as Davidson argues, "No-one has succeeded in doing this."[40] From Davidson's perspective, we must accept the conclusions of the slingshot argument:

> There are no interesting and appropriate entities available which, by being somehow related to sentences, can explain why the true ones are true and the others not. There is a good reason, then, to be skeptical about the importance of the correspondence theory of truth.[41]

Davidson's work has shown us that, in the absence of facts to which true statements correspond, it is not possible to speak about representations inasmuch as "'Nothing, no *thing*, makes our statements true.' If this is right, and I am convinced it is, we ought also to question the popular assumption that sentences, or their spoken tokens, or sentence-like entities, or configurations in our brains can properly be called 'representations,' since there is nothing for them to represent."[42]

If there is only one thing to be represented, there is nothing interesting in generating representations; neither can, according to Davidson, the notion of representation allow us to make distinctions between entities such as statements and beliefs. There are, however, entities which are commonly said to "present" or "re-present" something. Referring to geographical maps, it is possible to speak of representation, since it can legitimately be said that a map of Italy represents Italy. In fact, many writers employ "words as representing the things they name or describe." Though Davidson has no "strong objection" to this use of the term, he believes that it would be better to use the words "naming" and "describing," inasmuch as they "seem better ways to express the relation between names and descriptions and what they name or describe."[43] He does, however, bridle at the idea that "any expression represents any object or event." He also claims:

> The only direct manifestations of language are utterances and inscriptions, and it is we who imbue them with significance. So language is at best an abstraction, and cannot be a medium through which we take in the world nor an intermediary between us and reality. It is like a sense organ, an organizational feature of people which allows them to perceive things as objects with a location in a public space and time, or as events with causes and effects.[44]

Following Davidson's antirepresentational "turn," Rorty too believes that, in the case of maps, it is possible to speak of representation. He says: "one can, for example, say that a certain projection produces maps of the hemispheres that are more reminiscent of the view from a moon rocket than maps using other projections." But, Rorty wonders, "what the analogue could be to that view in the case of a choice of descriptive vocabularies ?"[45] The only analogy possible, Rorty argues, is given by what Putnam calls "the view from *God's eye*"[46] that ensures some type of correspondence between depictions, understanding, and the world. According to the antirepresentationalists, however, this is not possible.

By pointing out to us the problems arising from a choice of a representational type, it seems that Davidson's contributions have definitely undermined the representational model. This has to do with problems concerning the relation between mind and world, or language and world, understood as a "relation between a medium of representation and what is purportedly represented."[47] All the problems deriving from representationalism are connected with obsolete discourses on the facts, on the *states of affairs* and on the correspondence theories of truth, on the fact that there may or may not be a *matter of fact* regarding, for example, mathematics or ethics. All these discourses have brought about sterile arguments over skepticism, relativism, representational and computational theories of the mind, over realism and antirealism, over the objective–subjective distinction, the appearance–reality distinction, and so on.[48] Skepticism, in particular, is born from the faith placed on the empty representationalist model based on the relation between self and world.

If there are no facts or things to represent them, all the traditional philosophical problems—skepticism, realism, relativism—are bound to fail.[49]

If we opt for a choice of an antirepresentationalist type deriving, also, from the abandonment of the appearance–reality distinction and the realism–antirealism distinction, and from the consequent abandonment of a "spectator" account of knowledge,[50] then the skeptical and relativist positions arising from the premises of the representational model will dissolve.

According to Rorty, Davidson's abandonment of the language–fact distinction has shed light on the untenability of the relation between propositions and world in terms of a representational relation. In "A Nice Derangement of Epitaphs," which proposes to radicalize and extend Quine's naturalistic approach to the study of linguistic behavior, Davidson invites us to abandon "the boundary between knowing a language and knowing our way around in the world generally," and to recognize that "there is no such thing as a language, not if a language is anything like what many philosophers and linguists have supposed."[51]

Sellars's attack on the "myth of the Given," in clarifying the difference between explanation and justification, definitively undermined the premise that everything is given by the mind. Quine's repudiation of the distinction between analytic and synthetic, conceptual and empirical, and Davidson's refusal of what he calls "the third dogma"[52] of empiricism, that is, scheme–content dualism, have contributed to the realization of a profound change in contemporary philosophical thought. In particular, Davidson's work, in perfecting and broadening those lines of thought developed by Sellars and Quine, is, according to Rorty, "the best contemporary expression of the main current of pragmatist thought: the naturalizing, darwinising current."[53]

Rorty considers Sellars, Quine, and Davidson to be "edifying" philosopher-therapists inasmuch as they have warned us against the embarrassing and superfluous notions of "reciprocal relations" of representing and making true relations that are at the basis of the representational foundationalist project.[54] These philosophers are drawn together by the common conviction that it is good to free oneself of the idea that accurate representations exist that mirror nature and that the idea itself of accurate representation "is simply an automatic and empty compliment which we pay to those beliefs which help us to do what we want to do."[55] They have allowed us to get over the dualism of subject–object, scheme–content, appearance–reality, and think of the relation with the rest of the world in "purely causal" terms,[56] thereby making antirepresentationalism possible.

In "On the Very Idea of a Conceptual Scheme," Davidson had already warned us against the dangers of representationalism, that is, the idea that the essential characteristic of language is its capacity to describe how things really are. He has now again attacked representationalism, affirming that "Beliefs are true or false but they represent nothing. It is good to be rid of representations, and with them the correspondence theory of truth, for it is thinking there are representations that engenders intimations of relativism."[57] If we abandon representationalism, there will not be much interest in the relation between mind and world or between language and reality. For Davidson, in fact, it is not possible to speak of a language that adequately "represents" the world, inasmuch as only further beliefs, and not the world, can make beliefs true; only further statements, and not reality, can make statements true, inasmuch as "There are no relations of 'being made true' which hold between beliefs," sentences, and the world. We understand everything there is to know on the relation between beliefs, statements and the world "when we understand their causal relations with the world."[58] The traditional conception of language understood as a depicting representation is surpassed by another according to which statements are the result of the interaction between beliefs and meanings. From the antirepresentationalist point of view, knowledge does not flow from a relation between mind and world, between statements, beliefs, and reality, but is *continuous with* the world; it is "a (playful) creative enterprise, inventing structures for whatever it encounters, and ultimately generating a variety of 'worlds.'"[59]

Rorty describes knowledge via the metaphor of "a continual reweaving of a web of beliefs and desires." If we take on this metaphor, we will come to consider the web as one, in the sense that we won't have to use epistemological distinctions to divide it up: We will no longer think of having "sources" of knowledge at our disposal called correspondence or representations.[60] Knowledge, in fact, does not derive from a relation of a representative/correspondentist type, from a process of reproduction of the world, or from a "system" that we might use in order to gain knowledge, but from an interactive dimension of a holistic type, where language is seen as an instrument or a process, rather than as a system. A conception of knowledge and language of a representationalist type in which the meanings of statements are guaranteed by the conditions that make them true or false seems extremely limiting and coercive. Such a conception crystallizes in forms of understanding based on reference, correspondence, suitability, comparison, accurate representation, and verification. In contrast to a more interactive and holistic approach, such a conception remains focused on analyzing the forms of true statements, provided there are any, as these are constituted in terms of relations between linguistic and nonlinguistic entities.[61]

Rorty, on the other hand, maintains that "*no* linguistic items represent *any* non-linguistic items."[62] He also claims that so long as knowledge is conceived in terms of representational connections, reciprocal relations between mind and world, correspondence, and *adaequatio rei et intellectus*, it will not be possible to free ourselves of one of the most powerful and elusive metaphors of modernity, that regarding the mind as mirror of nature. This metaphor has maintained an influential and dominating role in our intellectual history—but it is a metaphor that should now be abandoned.[63]

The principal difference between representational and antirepresentational inquiries could be seen as the outcome of at least two basic human stances: The first describes cognition as a process of reproduction of the world; the second describes it, instead, as a "creative enterprise" meeting and creating a plurality of worlds. Whereas the first emphasizes the "reproductive" function,[64] that is, it outlines the way in which the "contents of consciousness mirror the world—or distort it,"[65] the second one emphasizes the "productive" function,[66] focusing its attention on "those acts of meaning that not only influence structure but also enhance experience itself." Reproductive cognition uses the "pervasive mirroring metaphor." Productive or antirepresentational cognition works, instead, through the metaphors of the "interactive generation of Knowledge."[67]

Notes

1. "The picture which holds traditional philosophy captive is that of the mind as a great mirror, containing various representations—some accurate, some not—and capable of being studied by pure, nonempirical methods. Without the notion of the mind as mirror, the notion of knowledge as accuracy of representation would not have suggested itself." Richard Rorty, *Philosophy and the Mirror of Nature* (Princeton: Princeton University Press, 1979), p. 12. See also Stephen Neale, *Facing Facts* (Oxford and New York: Oxford University Press, 2001), p. 1. In writing this essay I was influenced by the arguments of Stephen Neale's *Facing Facts* even though we come to different conclusions. Some of many suggestions I have taken over from Neale's book will be outlined and only sparsely supported by quotations.

2. Hegel criticizes "representationalism" because, despite the promises made by its supporters, not only does it not provide a solution for the problems that it was intended to solve, but often it creates new ones. See Kenneth R. Westphal, *Hegel, Hume und die Identität wahrnehmbarer Dinge: Historisch-kritische Analyze zum Kapitel "Wahrnehmung" in der Phänomenologie von 1807* (Frankfurt: Klostermann, 1998); "Hegel and Hume on Perception and Concept-Empiricism, " *Journal of the History of Philosophy* 33 (1998): 99–123.

3. For Heidegger's rejection of representationalism see J. E. Malpas, *Donald Davidson and the Mirror of Meaning* (Cambridge: Cambridge University Press, 1992), pp. 262–265.

4. First published in 1974, and reprinted in *Inquiries into Truth and Interpretation* (Oxford: Clarendon Press, rev. ed. 2001), pp. 183–198.

5. Donald Davidson (1989), "The Myth of the Subjective," reprinted in his *Subjective, Intersubjective, Objective* (Oxford: Clarendon Press, 2001), p. 43; see also Donald Davidson, *Truth and Predication* (Cambridge, MA: Harvard University Press, 2005), p. 10.

6. Neale, *Facing Facts*, p. 6.

7. As Barwise and Perry say, the term "slingshot" was suggested to them by the use Davidson makes of "this compact piece of philosophical artillery in his wars against some of the giants of our industry." Jon Barwise and John Perry (1981), "Semantic Innocence and Uncompromising Situations," reprinted in *The Philosophy of Language*, ed. Aloysius P. Martinich (Oxford and New York: Oxford University Press, 1990), p. 401. Davidson's argument, say Barwise and Perry, "is so small, seldom encompassing more than half a page, and employs such a minimum of ammunition—a theory of descriptions and a popular notion of logical equivalence—that we dub it *the* slingshot" (ibid., p. 398). For an extensive and thorough discussion of the slingshot, see Neale, *Facing Facts*; Neale, "The Philosophical Significance of Gödel's Slingshot," *Mind* 104 (1995): 761–825; Stephen Neale and Josh Dever, "Slingshots and Boomerangs," *Mind* 106 (1997): 143–168.

8. Donald Davidson (1996), "The Folly of Trying to Define Truth," reprinted in *Truth, Language, and History* (Oxford: Clarendon Press, 2005), p. 23. For Davidson's slingshot, see Donald Davidson (1967), "Truth and Meaning," in *Inquiries into Truth and Interpretation* (Oxford: Oxford University Press, 2001), pp. 17–42; Davidson (1967), "The Logical Form of Action Sentences," in *Essays on Actions and Events* (Oxford: Clarendon Press, 2001), pp. 105–122; Davidson (1969), "True to the Facts," in *Inquiries into Truth and Interpretation*, pp. 43–54. This result is not without its critics. See Neale, *Facing Facts*; Graham Oppy, "The Philosophical Insignificance of Gödel's Slingshot," *Mind* 106 (1997): 121–141; see also the monographic issue of *ProtoSociology*: "Facts, Slingshots, and Anti-Representationalism: On Stephen Neale's Facing Facts," *ProtoSociology: An International Journal of Interdisciplinary Research* 23 (2006).

9. See Alonzo Church, "Carnap's Introduction to Semantics," *Philosophical Review* 52 (1943): 298–304.

10. Gottlob Frege (1892), "On Sense and Meaning," in *Collected Papers on Mathematics, Logic, and Philosophy*, ed. Brian McGuinness (Oxford: Blackwell, 1984), pp. 157–177.

11. Kurt Gödel, "Russell's Mathematical Logic," in *The Philosophy of Bertrand Russell*, ed. Paul A. Schilpp (Evanston: Northwestern University Press, 1944), pp. 123–153.

12. Davidson, "Reply to Stephen Neale," in *The Philosophy of Donald Davidson*, The Library of Living Philosophers, vol. 27, ed. Lewis E. Hahn (Chicago: Open Court, 1999), p. 667. According to Davidson, Russell's semantics evaded the slingshot "by making properties parts of facts and so the entities that correspond to predicates. This is a course, says Davidson, against which I have argued on the grounds that it cannot be incorporated into a satisfactory theory or definition of truth, and entities that are made up in part of abstract entities can hardly be thought of as empirical truth-makers" (ibid.).

13. See Neale, *Facing Facts*, ch. 9. This upshot is not without its critics. In his "The Philosophical Insignificance of Gödel's Slingshot," Oppy spells out his reasons for rejecting such views; he is skeptical of the slingshot arguments in general and of Gödel's slingshot in particular.

14. For the argument (schema), see Ernest LePore and Kirk Ludwig, *Donald Davidson: Meaning, Truth, Language, and Reality* (New York: Oxford University Press, 2005), pp. 50–51.

15. Quine uses various forms of the slingshot. The most explicit and well-known form is to be found in the discussion of what he called the principle of extensionality. See Willard Van Orman Quine, "Three Grades of Modal Involvement," reprinted in W. V. O. Quine (1953), *The Ways of Paradox, and Other Essays* (Cambridge, MA: Harvard University Press, 1976, rev. and enl. ed.), pp. 163–164. One of the first elaborations of Quinean slingshot is in W. V. O. Quine (1937), "New Foundations for Mathematical Logic," reprinted in W. V. O. Quine, *From a Logical Point of View* (Cambridge, MA: Harvard University Press, 1980), pp. 80–101.

16. See Davidson, "Truth and Meaning," p. 19, n. 3. Davidson finds the origin of slingshot argument in some remarks by Frege in which Frege draws the following conclusion: "We have seen that the meaning of sentence may always be sought, whenever the meaning of its components is involved; and that this is the case when and only when we are inquiring after the truth-value. We are therefore driven into accepting *the truth-value* of a sentence as constituting what it means" (Frege, "On Sense and Meaning," p. 163).

17. Davidson, *Truth and Predication*, p. 132.

18. Davidson (1969), "True to the Facts," *Inquiries into Truth and Interpretation*, pp. 41–42; See also Neale, *Facing Facts*, pp. 8–13, and ch. 9.

19. Davidson, "True to the Facts," p. 42.

20. Davidson, *Truth and Predication*, p. 129; see also Jon Barwise and John Perry, *Situations and Attitudes* (Cambridge, MA: MIT Press, 1983).

21. Davidson, *Truth and Predication*, pp. 129–130.

22. Ibid., p. 40; see also Davidson (1988), "Epistemology and Truth," in *Subjective, Intersubjective, Objective*, p. 184.

23. Davidson, *Truth and Predication*, p. 130.

24. See Davidson (1974), "On the Very Idea of a Conceptual Scheme," *Inquiries into Truth and Interpretation*, pp. 193–194. Davidson's thesis is close to the Fregean thesis against the correspondence theory of truth. See Frege, "Der Gedanke: Eine logische Untersuchung," *Beiträge zur Philosophie des Deutschen Idealismus* I (1818–1819), pp. 58–77.

25. Davidson, *Truth and Predication*, p. 129. See also Neale, *Facing Facts*, pp. 3–4, 49–57.

26. Davidson, "Reply to Stephen Neale," p. 667.

27. Peter Strawson, "Truth," reprinted in *Logico-Linguistic Papers* (Aldershot: Ashgate, 2004), p. 150. In the same essay Strawson claims: "it is evident that there is nothing else in the world for the statement itself to be related to. . . . And it is evident that the demand that there should be such a relatum is logically absurd. . . . But the demand for something in the world *which makes the statement true* . . . , or *to which the statement corresponds when it is true*, is just this demand" (ibid.); see also Davidson, *Epistemology and Truth*, p. 184.

28. See "True to the Facts," pp. 37–54. In *Truth and Predication*, Davidson says: "The terms 'realism' and 'correspondence' were ill-chosen because they suggest the positive endorsement of a position, or an assumption that there is a clear positive thesis to be adopted, whereas all I was entitled to maintain, and all that my position actually entailed with respect to realism and truth, was the negative view that epistemic views are false. The realist view of truth, if it has any content, must be based on the idea of correspondence, correspondence as applied to sentences or beliefs or utterances—entities that are propositional in character; and such correspondence cannot be made intelligible. I made the mistake of assuming that realism and epistemic theories exhausted the possible positions. The only legitimate reason I had for calling my position a form of realism was to reject positions like Dummett's antirealism; I was concerned to reject the doctrine that either reality or truth depends directly on our epistemic powers. There is a point in such a rejection. But it is futile either to reject or to accept the slogan that the real and the true are 'independent of our

beliefs.' The only evident positive sense we can make of this phrase, the only use that consorts with the intentions of those who prize it, derives from the idea of correspondence, and this an idea without content" (Davidson, *Truth and Predication*, pp. 41–42).

29. See Davidson, "Afterthoughts 1987," in *Subjective, Intersubjective, Objective*, p. 154; "Epistemology and Truth," p. 183. In footnote 3 of the latter essay Davidson says: "I foolishly accepted the term [correspondence] in 'True to the Facts'" (ibid., p. 182); see also Davidson, "The Structure and the Content of Truth," *Journal of Philosophy* 87, no. 1 (1990): 279–328, p. 303.

30. Davidson, *Truth and Predication*, p. 38. Despite the fact that Tarski seems to allude to a correspondence theory in which statements correspond to facts, he "ought not to be considered as giving comfort to serious partisans of correspondence theories" (Davidson, "The Folly of Trying to Define Truth," p. 25); see also Neale, *Facing Facts*, p. 45.

31. Davidson, *Inquiries into Truth and Interpretation*, p. xvi. Davidson follows C. I. Lewis in challenging the theorists of correspondence to delimit the fact, or piece of world, or of reality, to which a true statement might perhaps correspond. Clarence I. Lewis, *An Analysis of Knowledge and Valuation* (La Salle: Open Court, 1946), pp. 50–55; Lewis (1923), "Facts, Systems, and the Unity of the World," reprinted in *Collected Papers of Clarence Irving Lewis*, ed. J. L. Mothershea (Stanford: Stanford University Press, 1970), pp. 383–393.

32. Davidson, *Inquiries into Truth and Interpretation*, p. xvii. For Tarski's notion of "satisfaction," see also Davidson, "The Folly of Trying to Define Truth," p. 25; and Davidson, *Truth and Predication*, pp. 30–31, 34–36.

33. Davidson, "The Folly of Trying to Define Truth," p. 25.

34. Alfred Tarski (1936), "The Establishment of Scientific Semantics," reprinted in his *Logic, Semantics, Metamathematics: Papers from 1923 to 1938*, ed. J. H. Woodger (Oxford: Clarendon Press, 1956), p. 403; see also Davidson, "The Folly of Trying to Define Truth," p. 23.

35. As far as the notion of "satisfaction" is concerned, Davidson maintains: "It should not be that by speaking of the relations between attitudes and the world I am embracing a correspondence theory. A theory of truth of the sort I have in mind does depend on setting up a relation between certain words and objects (Tarski's relation of 'satisfaction'), but it makes no use of objects to which sentences might correspond." Donald Davidson (1997), "Indeterminism and Antirealism," in *Subjective, Intersubjective, Objective*, p. 76, n. 5.

36. Davidson, "True to the Facts," p. 48.

37. See Paul Horwich, *Truth* (Oxford: Oxford University Press, 1998), p. 104.

38. Alfred Tarski (1933), "The Concept of Truth in Formalized Languages," in *Logic, Semantics, Metamathematics*, p. 153.

39. Tadeusz Kotarbiński (1929), *Gnosiology: The Scientific Approach to the Theory of Knowledge*, ed. G. Bidwell and C. Pinder (Oxford: Pergamon Press, 1966, p. 410). See also David Wiggins, *Needs, Values, Truth: Essays in the Philosophy of Value* (Oxford: Clarendon Press, 1998), p. 333.

40. Donald Davidson (2000), "Truth Rehabilitated," in *Truth, Language, and History*, p. 5.

41. Ibid., p. 6. Rorty, on his part, follows Davidson along these lines of thought so that he can say that no relation called "correspondence with reality" manages to explain why some statements are true and others are not: According to the neo-pragmatist philosopher, we must abandon the notion of correspondence in relation both to thoughts and statements, and instead consider the statements connected to other statements rather than to reality (nature, the world). The term "correspondence with reality" is, according to Rorty, "an automatic compliment attributed to a normal, successful discourse, rather than a relation to be studied and to which to aspire through the rest of the discourse." R. Rorty, *Philosophy and the Mirror of Nature*, p. 372. See also Michael Williams, *Unnatural Doubts: Epistemological Realism and the Basis of Scepticism* (Oxford: Blackwell, 1991), p. 364, n. 51, and pp. 230–235.

42. Davidson, "Epistemology and Truth," p. 184.

43. Davidson, "Reply to Stephen Neale," pp. 667–668.

44. Ibid., p. 668. See also Davidson (1997), "Seeing through Language," in *Truth, Language, and History*, pp. 127–142.

45. Richard Rorty, "Pragmatism as Anti-representationalism," in John P. Murphy, *Pragmatism: From Peirce to Davidson* (Boulder: Westview Press, 1990), p. 3.

46. Ibid. Putnam's conception has a markedly ancient derivation. In his treatise *On Nature*, Alcmaeon states: "The gods have certainty, whereas to us as men conjecture [only is possible]." Kathleen Freeman, *Ancilla to the Pre-Socratic Philosophers* (Cambridge, MA: Harvard University Press, 1948), p. 40.

47. Richard Rorty, "Twenty-Five Years After," in *The Linguistic Turn*, ed. R. Rorty (Chicago: University of Chicago Press, 1992), p. 371.

48. See Neale, *Facing Facts*, p. 1; Neale, "On Representing," in *The Philosophy of Donald Davidson*, p. 657; see also Rorty, "Pragmatism as Anti-representationalism," pp. 3–4.

49. Neale, *Facing Facts*, p. 1. See also Carole Rovane, "Anti-Representationalism and Relativism," *Philosophical Books* 45, no. 2 (2004): 128–139.

50. See Rorty, "Twenty-Five Years After," p. 373. On the spectator theory of knowledge, see John Dewey, *The Quest for Certainty: A Study of the Relation of Knowledge and Action* (New York: Putnam's Sons, 1960), chapters 1, 2, 4; Dewey, *Reconstruction in Philosophy* (Boston: Beacon Press, 1966), ch. 1. See also Christopher B. Kulp, *The End of Epistemology: Dewey and His Current Allies on the Spectator Theory of Knowledge* (Westport, CT: Greenwood Press, 1992).

51. Davidson (1986), "A Nice Derangement of Epitaphs," in *Truth, Language, and History*, p. 107; see also Rorty, "Twenty-Five Years After," pp. 372–373.

52. The "dualism of scheme and content, of organizing system and something waiting to be organized, cannot be made intelligible and defensible. It is itself a dogma of empiricism, the third dogma. The third, and perhaps the last, for if we give it up it is not clear that there is anything distinctive left to call empiricism." D. Davidson, *On the Very Idea of a Conceptual Scheme*, p. 189.

53. R. Rorty, "Sind Aussagen universelle Geltungsansprüche?," *Deutsche Zeitschrift für Philosophie* 42, no. 6 (1994): 975.

54. See Rorty, "Introduction: Antirepresentationalism, Ethnocentrism, and Liberalism" in *Objectivity, Relativism, and Truth* (Cambridge: Cambridge University Press, 1991), vol. 1, p. 2. See also János Boros, "Repräsentationalismus und Antirepräsentationalismus: Kant, Davidson und Rorty, " *Deutsche Zeitschrift Für Philosophie* 47, no. 1 (1999): 539–551.

55. Rorty, *Philosophy and the Mirror of Nature*, p. 10.

56. For an analysis of the causal connections between world and language, see Davidson (1990), "Epistemology Externalized," in *Subjective, Intersubjective, Objective*, p. 198.

57. Davidson, "The Myth of the Subjective," p. 46.

58. Rorty, "Pragmatism, Davidson and Truth," in Rorty, *Objectivity, Relativism, and Truth: Philosophical Papers*, vol. 1, p. 128.

59. Gemma Corradi Fiumara, *The Metaphoric Process* (London: Routledge, 1995), p. 110.

60. See Rorty, "On Ethnocentrism: A Replay to Clifford Geertz," reprinted in Rorty, *Objectivity, Relativism, and Truth*, p. 208.

61. See Corradi Fiumara, *The Metaphoric Process*, pp. 6–7.

62. Rorty, "Introduction: Antirepresentationalism, Ethnocentrism, and Liberalism," p. 2.

63. See Rorty, *Philosophy and the Mirror of Nature*, pp. 10–13, 17–22, 357–394; see also Corradi Fiumara, *The Metaphoric Process*, p. 7.

64. Jerome Bruner and Carol Fleischer Feldman, "Metaphors of Consciousness and Cognition in the History of Psychology," in *Metaphors in the History of Psychology*, ed. David E. Leary (Cambridge: Cambridge University Press, 1990), p. 231.

65. Corradi Fiumara, *The Metaphoric Process*, p. 110.

66. Bruner and Fleischer Feldman, "Metaphors of Consciousness and Cognition in the History of Psychology," p. 231.

67. Corradi Fiumara, *The Metaphoric Process*, p. 110. See also Gemma Corradi Fiumara, *Spontaneity: A Psychoanalytic Inquiry* (London: Routledge, 2009).

8 Method and Metaphysics: Pragmatist Doubts

Bjørn Ramberg

Donald Davidson fits quite neatly into the resurgence of metaphysics that has been evident in Anglophone philosophy for a generation or so. At the same time, however, Davidson has been an important source—indeed, a main source—of inspiration in the development of the increasingly and self-consciously *ametaphysical* variety of pragmatism, associated with Richard Rorty, that has come to the fore during that same time. This makes Davidson a particularly interesting philosopher to engage with if one wants to understand the nature of the pragmatist critique of metaphysics—if there is one. I begin by expanding on the first claim, that Davidson is easily absorbed by metaphysics. Next, I marshal pragmatist reservations toward metaphysics and toward the metaphysical Davidson. In the third section, I ask whether it is not possible, after all, to recover a pragmatizing reading even of this Davidson. Finally, I allow myself to wonder about the force and point of the pragmatist stance against metaphysics. Even if metaphysics remains elusive, however, there is the hope that some light will have been shed on the resources that Davidson offers pragmatists trying to affect the philosophical conversation, and also on what the metaphilosophical divergences are between a naturalistic pragmatism and contemporary analytic metaphysics.

1 Metaphysical Davidson

The challenge that Davidson poses for pragmatists who wish to co-opt his work is clearly in evidence in a paper from 1977, "The Method of Truth in Metaphysics." It opens as follows:

> In sharing a language, in whatever sense this is required for communication, we share a picture of the world that must, in its large features, be true. It follows that in making manifest the large features of our language, we make manifest the large

features of reality. One way of pursuing metaphysics is therefore to study the general structure of our language.[1]

Davidson, it seems, unequivocally affirms the idea that there is a way of viewing the world such that all language-users share it, that this common picture can be characterized in terms of its general features, and that these features are ipso facto general features of the world. Metaphysics, then, is what we do when we try to say what these features are. Paying attention to language, tracing its "general structure," we may come to know something about how the world must be. This is the characteristic modality of metaphysics; it uncovers necessary truths.

In Davidson's hands, the concept of truth is methodologically central to metaphysics for a plain reason: "What a theory of truth does for a natural language," Davidson explains, "is reveal structure."[2] Metaphysics, then, is recast as the explication of the ontological commitments we must undertake as we develop a recursive theory capable of specifying the truth conditions of any of the infinitely many assertive sentences of a language. Insofar as "such a theory makes its own unavoidable demands" on ontology, we are able to say something very general about how the world must be structured.[3] The application of the method, which Davidson offers in the final part of the paper, is a matter of considering what is needed to construct "a comprehensive theory of truth." Davidson concludes that unless we wish to deny that a very large number of our most ordinary sentences can be true, we must take it that there are objects and events.

The tight connection between ontology and logical form that Davidson's method exploits depends on his initial claim, that successful communicators share a largely true picture of the world. It is in the context of this claim that Davidson's method of truth yields constraints on what the world must be like. Moreover, this claim and the argument for it are connected to a number of philosophical theses for which Davidson is famous, claims concerning the nature of minds, of knowledge, and of the interrelations between knowing subjects and the world they occupy. These theses certainly are not derived by the method just described; rather, they make up the underpinnings of it. Yet they appear to be, and are typically treated as, metaphysical theses. Considering this metaphysical underpinning a little more closely will take us into familiar Davidsonian ground.

What is needed to understand the utterances of a speaker and figure out what is on her mind must be available to observation. The stance of the interpreter is methodologically basic. What the interpreter has to go on is what a speaker says and the circumstances of her saying it. The details of the method of radical interpretation need not concern us here. The key idea is that interpretation requires that the interpreter is able to form an idea of what a speaker acting in the world is up to. This implies two things. First, what the interpreter believes about the world must give some indication of what the speaker believes about it—this is obvious when it comes to the perceptual registration of salient facts in the communication situation, but actually pertains much more generally. Second, both the inferential connections between beliefs that the interpreter is disposed to endorse, as well as the action-guiding preferences that the interpreter possesses, must give some indication of what the speaker is likely to say or do given her beliefs. Failing these requirements, that is to say, if the interpreter cannot recognize a basic rationality in the speaker, there is no connection to be made, neither between utterances and action, nor between utterances and the world, and the interpreter will literally have no clue as to what the speaker might be saying.

In "The Method of Truth in Metaphysics," Davidson is clear that these considerations initially seem to give us only agreement between interpreters. "And certainly agreement," he observes, "no matter how wide-spread, does not guarantee truth."[4] The real point is that "objective error can occur only in a setting of largely true belief. Agreement does not make for truth, but much of what is agreed must be true if some of what is agreed is false."[5] Here we confront the core thought in Davidson's philosophy: the intimate, inalienable nature of the connection between truth and meaning. The connection is emphasized wherever Davidson argues that we can describe what it is to understand a language in terms of the structure provided by a theory of truth for the language. The very same connection shows up, also, when Davidson argues against the skeptical idea that our beliefs about the world may be generally and systematically false; wherever there is any degree of real semantic understanding (such as is presupposed in any agreement), Davidson claims, there is also common knowledge of the world. This symmetry has perhaps not always been evident in debates around these claims. Still, if one doubts the Davidsonian idea that successful communication—mutual understanding of the meaning of what speakers say to one another—entails that we are largely operating knowledgeably in the world, one ought to find at least prima facie troublesome the idea that meaning is closely tied to truth conditions. One way to respond, if one remains attracted to a truth-conditional account of meaning, is to allow that we may be massively ignorant of what we really mean when we speak. Alternatively, though still in the same general neighborhood as far as one's conception of semantics goes, one may hold that meaning is tied to verification conditions, to what it is that we count, based on evidence available to creatures like us, as justifying an assertion, so that while we well understand one another's utterances and agree about many of them, we may remain systematically ignorant of the world. Both of these strategies make much of the intuition that there is a gap between what we have reason to believe and how things really are. Indeed, a large number of philosophers have argued that Davidson, in his antiskeptical line of thought, makes far too little of exactly this gap. The objective, mind-independent nature of truth is obscured, or the human capacity to know is inflated—the corrosive power of systematic doubt is not fully appreciated.

One line of thought where this alleged tension in Davidson is often diagnosed is the argument against the idea that we can make out a philosophically interesting notion of conceptual schemes.[6] Davidson identifies conceptual schemes with "sets of intertranslatable languages," and the question now becomes, "Can we then say that two people have different conceptual schemes if they speak languages that fail of intertranslatability?"[7] This is the very idea that Davidson rejects. Given that interpretation is possible only if we assume shared norms of rationality and substantial overlap in belief, we will not be able to interpret a speaker without also recognizing a core of familiar concepts in her thoughts. This is not just a matter of intersubjective agreement; the connection between truth and meaning ensures not only that we share a significant body of concepts, but also that we largely apply them correctly to the world.

Scott Soames, in his much-discussed history of twentieth-century analytical philosophy, summarizes his response to Davidson's claims as follows:

> First, the fact that we can interpret the speech of another group does *not* guarantee as much agreement between them and us as Davidson seems to assume. So long as it is possible for us to explain why the other speakers hold beliefs different from ours, we can make sense of a great deal of disagreement. Second, we can make sense of big differences between ourselves and speakers of another culture that don't involve disagreements—e.g., differences regarding which objects are basic, and most worthy of attention. These two points suggest that, contrary to Davidson, even those whose utterances we can interpret and translate may have views different enough from ours to warrant the attribution of a different conceptual scheme. Finally, we found no reason to believe that there couldn't be speakers whose conceptual schemes were so different from ours that we couldn't translate their speech.[8]

These are telling remarks. First, does Davidson underestimate the amount of disagreement there can be between us and another group? The objection suggests that the constraints Davidson articulates on radical interpretation produce a clear quantitative sense of agreement, and that such lessons from the idealized radical interpretation situation can be projected onto relations between "us" and some other group. These are questionable assumptions, but might seem natural to make on an *epistemic* reading of Davidson, that is, a reading that construes him as engaged in the project of evaluating and legitimating our beliefs. Second, may discrepancies between cultures be so great that, while they do not necessarily confound interpretation, we should take them as indicating different conceptual schemes? How we respond to this will depend on the kind of explanatory work we hope the idea of a conceptual scheme will do for us, as we will see in the third section. For now, though, a relevant question is this: Why are "differences regarding which objects are basic, and most worthy of attention" not disagreements? Perhaps these differences do not count as disagreements because they concern evaluations, how we respond to and cope with the world, not how we picture it. It is difficult to know, but certainly such a distinction may come more easily to us if we think it an important task of epistemology to sort our subjective *response* to the world as we conceive of it from our registered *picture* of it. And finally, why could there not be conceptual schemes—sets of intertranslatable languages—that we are unable to translate? Soames's reasoning continues as follows:

> Since we know that whatever attitude we are warranted in taking toward a proposition, we are similarly warranted in taking toward the claim that it is true, we will be prepared to accept and assert a new proposition just in case we are prepared to accept and assert that it is true. . . . We regard a sentence as true if it expresses a true proposition. What now becomes of the idea that there could be a language containing true sentences that are not translatable into English? This is just the idea that there could be a language that expresses true propositions that are not expressed by any sentence of English. This is no more incoherent than the claim that there are true propositions one has not yet encountered.[9]

What, asks Soames, is so special about English? Why should we think that all the truths there are may be expressed in the particular language that we happen to speak? There is something immediately persuasive about this reaction. It seems preposterous to suggest that some particular language should be the one in which we are able to express a god's-eye view of things, to formulate sentences expressing all the true propositions there are. Surely, as Soames argues, just like we now know truths that could not have been expressed by past speakers, so it seems future communities may come to know things that we are unable to express, things that they can express in their language, but that simply cannot be translated into the English that we know. Faced with an argument that precludes this eventuality, the prudent thing to do is to be suspicious of the argument.

Two issues bear on the merits of this third point against Davidson. How are languages to be individuated in the context of Davidson's discussion? What is the relation between knowledge of some particular language and the nature of communicative success considered in Davidson's third-person perspective? We will return to these questions in the third section. At this point, let us simply note the idea against which Soames reacts, namely, that there is some language mastered by a group of speakers in which all the truths there are can be expressed, and that we belong to that group. This idea is part of the context of epistemology. It is a claim pertaining to the legitimacy of our picture of reality, specifically, the legitimacy of the tools we rely on to construct it. Soames rejects it. Making his three points, Soames insists that neither our concepts nor our beliefs are as closely tailored to those of our fellow creatures or to the nature of reality as Davidson claims. Soames, in effect, is asserting a more robust gap between how things appear to us to be and how they really are than Davidson seems willing to acknowledge.

Here is where we stand. Metaphysically speaking, Davidson advertises a way to get from mere belief, appearances, to truth, to reality: Taking ourselves to be rational, communicating agents we must also take ourselves to have knowledge—of ourselves, of others, and of the world we share. Certainly, we make errors regarding all three, but errors, no matter how deep or pervasive, are parasitical on a foundation of justified, true belief; take away that basis and errors simply dissolve into pointless noise and movement.[10] This view is the context in which efforts to tease out the logical form of expressions, the forms that implement a truth theory for a language, will also be a systematic approach to metaphysical knowledge, knowledge of the large structures of the world.

The response, however, has frequently been skeptical. For those who share a basic premise of modern epistemology, that the relation between appearance and reality is subject to general consideration, it seems that the skeptical challenge to knowledge is underestimated—Davidson is simply ducking it. Yes, you can tie meaning to belief and to observable behavior, or you can tie it to truth. Do both at the same time, however, and you are a verificationist. Yet this very context in which verificationism appears as a dodge, a failure of nerve or of philosophical seriousness, is one way to characterize the target of the pragmatist critique of metaphysics. This critique, I will suggest, provides a basis for a different view of the lessons to be extracted from Davidson. First, though, it is necessary to home in more closely on the pragmatist conception of the target.

2 Pragmatist Doubts

Metaphysics probably cannot be given a useful, coherent definition, but that fact certainly need not impugn the practice of metaphysics. This, I think, is common ground between pragmatists and most practicing metaphysicians. Those working in the philosophical tradition that traces its main roots to ancient Greece have in the course of 2,500 years developed a repertoire of questions and styles of handling them that include metaphysical questions, questions we typically recognize as such even if we cannot give an adequate general description of the kind, and even if for some questions and some inquiries it is unclear or controversial whether they should be counted as metaphysics. That it recognizes this common ground is distinctive of the skepticism toward metaphysics that is characteristic of pragmatism. It means that pragmatists will not frame this skepticism in a manner that presupposes a definitional handle on metaphysical questions. So pragmatists do not want to say that all metaphysical statements are necessarily false, or that they must be meaningless, or that metaphysical questions as such point to matters beyond the reach of human cognitive capacities. That all depends, the pragmatist will want to say—some metaphysical statements are false, some perhaps meaningless (without clear point, statement we don't know what to do with), and some metaphysical questions may in fact be forever unanswerable by creatures like us. But we will not want say that these facts, when they obtain, are somehow explained by the metaphysical character of the statement or question. Paradoxically, the pragmatist's complaint against metaphysics will not be that it is metaphysical.

The paradox is only apparent, however. The appearance depends on taking two kinds of critical response as exhaustive of the options. There are, first of all, the familiar attempts, exemplified paradigmatically in recent history by the logical positivists' struggle to articulate a criterion of verification, to criticize metaphysics that end up being co-opted by metaphysics; saying what metaphysics is, even to reject it, is to do metaphysics. Then there is the call, made by the late Heidegger and ever more imaginatively heeded by Derrida, to leave metaphysics alone. This second strategy is reminiscent also of Wittgenstein; if you can't say what it is without doing it, better shut up about it, and do something different. Both these broad strategies are what we may call *puritanical*—they attempt to free our thought from a kind of activity to which it is prone, but of which no good or truth can ever come. They are putative philosophical *cures*.

The pragmatist critique of metaphysics carves out space between these two unsatisfactory strategies. It is antiessentialist about metaphysics. It takes it that whether or not a statement is metaphysical depends entirely on the purposes for which it is deployed, and that these purposes can be understood as contingent historical artifacts of human culture. Rorty is its main exponent, and his strategy has been twofold: more or less direct attacks on key ideas in a broad but specific philosophical paradigm, and deliberations about what sort of contribution to life that philosophy should be making. Let us briefly consider each in turn.

Rorty's direct engagement with metaphysics is most systematically carried out in *Philosophy and the Mirror of Nature*, as an attack on the mirror-imagery informing the Cartesian conception of mind, purified by Kant, and setting the agenda for epistemology-based philosophy.[11] Modern epistemology, in Rorty's diagnosis, is inescapably *representationalist*. Its task is to determine what the general characteristics are of mental or linguistic representations that succeed in rendering the world as it really is. In *Philosophy and the Mirror of Nature*, Rorty gives a genealogical interpretation of the conception of the mind that gives rise to this task, culminating in a set of arguments against it that he draws principally from Sellars, Quine, and Davidson. Without the myth of the given, and without a principled distinction between questions of meaning and questions of fact, the way is cleared for giving up what he later came to call the "world-picture" picture, the visual metaphors of our epistemic situation.[12] To the extent that Rorty's account of the rise and unfolding of the vocabulary of modern epistemology is convincing, his readers will come to doubt that philosophy must continue to contend with a general gap between the world as it appears to us would-be knowers and the way it really is.

The appearance–reality gap provides a connection between the kind of philosophical argument offered in the main parts of *Philosophy and the Mirror of Nature* and what we may call the external strategy pursued in much more detail in Rorty's later writings.[13] This strategy is not designed to undermine the epistemological project of the modern age by arguments that engage the project on its own terms. Rather, the point here is to read the significance of the project through a different lens; as a phenomenon of what Rorty calls cultural politics, what is the significance of representationalism? What, in cultural and political terms, is the effect of an epistemological conception that takes the essence of knowledge to be a matter of aligning appearance with reality? This is a theme that Rorty has pursued from a great many angles, not always with consistency. One persistent idea, though, is the link that Rorty finds between thinking in terms of the "picture-world" view and the hypostatization or externalization of moral, political, and epistemic authority. On this recognizably Nietzschean line of thought, we diminish our selves—our ability both to shape and to embrace our fate—by maintaining a demand for legitimization in terms of something beyond human interest.

It is a noteworthy characteristic of Rortyan pragmatism that this second, external strategy is what motivates the first, more internally directed argumentative approach to representationalism; the common end is to affect the vocabulary of philosophy in such a way that questions of cultural politics, questions regarding the social significance of philosophical vocabularies, will no longer be perceived as extraneous matters. *Representationalism* is Rorty's name for a conception of the mandate of philosophy that obstructs this change. To call it *metaphysics* is to indicate exactly this feature. As a polemical, argumentative target for pragmatism, then, metaphysics is the idea of philosophy as separable from questions of cultural politics.

Davidson, as we have seen, may be read into the project of providing philosophical legitimization for our picture of reality—in large parts and in its most general structure. But as we have also seen, on quite natural assumptions of this "picture-world" view, the legitimization Davidson offers is questionable. Reading Davidson along Kantian lines, one may well find his arguments about the inescapability of shared norms of rationality convincing, but the scope of the conclusion is restricted to how the world will *appear to us*. We human subjects cannot identify as communicators creatures with whom we do not share a basic epistemic outlook. We cannot identify creatures as thinkers without identifying them as deploying a basic core of familiar concepts. But to think that this constrains what is possible begs the question against someone who takes the objectivity of reality to consist in its independence of mind.

To the extent that he casts his central thoughts as underpinnings for a method in metaphysics, Davidson certainly may encourage such a reading. So one antimetaphysical response might be to set out to rescue the arguments from this packaging, deploying some version of the "new wine in old bottles" metaphor to set up a distinction that would free Davidson's thought of the self-imposed, nonobligatory metaphysical casing. This would be the *purification* response, and it would likely fail, for much the same reasons that what I earlier called puritanical critiques of metaphysics always fail: These critiques do not come to grips with the idea that metaphysics, as a tradition, a practice, is not something to be defined or eliminated, but something to be *transformed*—transformed, according to the pragmatist, by being treated as a species of cultural politics.

3 Pragmatist Davidson

How, then, might pragmatists incorporate the thoughts distilled in Davidson's attack on the very idea of a conceptual scheme? As a first pass, let us return to Rorty. In *Philosophy and the Mirror of Nature*, he comments as follows on Davidson's move "in the direction of a purified and de-epistemologized conception of the philosophy of language":

> One outcome of so recasting the subject is to discard what Davidson calls "the third dogma" of empiricism, namely, "the dualism of scheme and content, of organizing system and something waiting to be organized"—a dualism which I have argued . . . is central to epistemology generally as well as to empiricism in particular.[14]

For Rorty, the real gain is Davidson's critique of the metaphors of conceptual relativism—of a scheme organizing or fitting some uninterpreted deliverance from the objective side of the subject–object gap that is the heart of representationalist epistemology. The pragmatist's point here is not at all to delineate the extent of possible divergence of views. There probably is no interesting such delineation. It seems easy enough to imagine communicating organisms or systems whose makeup (say, life span) is so different from ours that communication between them and us would be impossible—perhaps we could flesh out a thought experiment such that As and Bs, happily chatting in their separate camps, would be unable even to recognize each other as communicating creatures. Would this show that Davidson is wrong? To the pragmatist, nothing Davidson says limits the extent to which the potential for communicative success remains an empirical question. The point, rather, is that we will never *explain* failures of communication and divergences of views by appealing to the notion of a conceptual scheme. Soames may well be right that on some occasions we might want to attribute different conceptual schemes to people or to cultures. What we would mean by that, however, is that their habits of acting, thinking, and speaking are different—rooted, perhaps, in vast differences in their natural or cultural environment—and that those habits are so rigid that there seems to be no way to work past them toward mutual understanding. But it wouldn't then be as if we had discovered that there are conceptual schemes after all. In such cases, we are not relying on the idea of conceptual schemes to explain anything; we are simply applying that term as shorthand for obstacles and differences that may well be quite pervasive and systematic, but whose roots and explanations are to be found in practice, in behavior, in the environment, and in interests. Indeed, it is the *explanatory uselessness* of the idea of a conceptual scheme that is the immediate pragmatist lesson of Davidson's attack on the idea.

This lesson, moreover, steers us in the direction of a deeper point. To see explanatory value, where communication fails, in the idea of a conceptual scheme, one has to think of it as applying not primarily to would-be communicators and their practical situations, but to a relation between differing systems of thought or speech in which such noncommunicants are trapped. Crudely put: Communication fails because their representations are structured differently. Davidson deals explicitly with this idea in "On the Very Idea of a Conceptual Scheme." But there is an associated notion that may well survive the attack, in part because Davidson does not face up to it until later. This is the idea that the communicative capacities of speakers can be characterized in terms of knowledge of a shared language. That idea is explicitly challenged in "A Nice Derangement of Epitaphs."[15] In this paper, Davidson sets out to preserve the distinction between literal meaning and speaker's meaning in the face of difficulties posed by innovative, humorous, erroneous, idiosyncratic—in a word, nonstandard—use of language. A critical tool is the distinction he draws between *passing theories* and *prior theories*:

> For the hearer, the prior theory expresses how he is prepared in advance to interpret an utterance of the speaker, while the passing theory is how he *does* interpret the utterance. For the speaker, the prior theory is what he *believes* the interpreter's prior theory to be, while his passing theory is the theory he *intends* the interpreter to use.[16]

The distinction makes it possible to distinguish what Davidson calls *first meanings*, even where idiosyncratic, from *speaker's meaning*, but it spells trouble for a combination of views of how communicative ability relates to language mastery:

> The asymptote of agreement and understanding is when passing theories coincide. But the passing theory cannot in general correspond to an interpreter's linguistic competence. Not only does it have its changing list of proper names and gerrymandered vocabulary, but it includes every successful—i.e., correctly interpreted—use of any other word or phrase, no matter how far out of the ordinary.[17]

Communicative success, on this view, is a matter of transient convergence: "knowing a passing theory is only knowing how to interpret a particular utterance on a particular occasion."[18] If we spell out the nature of semantic competence with reference to knowledge of a truth theory for a language, then we cannot also think of that competence as something stable, shared, and learned. As Davidson puts it: "We must give up the idea of a clearly defined shared structure which language-users acquire and then apply to cases."[19]

There is much to attract Rortyans to this view.[20] For our purposes, the relevant point is that the paper suggests a shift in what accounts for communicative success, and so also in what may be derived from such success. As long as we think that actual communicative success attests to a substantive, shared structure, we will be tempted of think of the features of that structure as in some sense defining the limits of what we are able to say, think, or know about the world. This is the real import of the idea of a conceptual scheme, and herein lies its connection to a representationalist conception of knowledge. By contrast, Davidson's attack on conceptual schemes is important because it helps clear the way past just those assumptions that make conceptual schemes a natural and interesting thing to imagine. Instead of structures—languages, conceptual systems—Davidson moves communicators and their activity into the center of explanation. That there are no conceptual schemes means that the linguistic resources of communicating agents are by their nature plastic, transformable, and adaptable in response to the situations of communication they are deployed in; if we want to say what is special about linguistic communicators, we need to consider the skills that support this process.

The third-person perspective, as Davidson develops it into a story about agents coordinating their responses in a shared world, contributes to a shift away from representationalism; instead of asking how it is that the rational subject can come to have knowledge of an objective world, Davidson, as pragmatists read him, asks how it is that organisms like us coordinate our activities into rational, communicating agency. The immediate objection is that we are communicating agents precisely because of our knowledge. But that is precisely where pragmatists want to stretch philosophical intuition: Our hunch is that the concept of knowledge will fall nicely into place, connected to our needs, wants, and interests, once we are allowed to address the question of what it is to be a communicating agent without importing representationalist assumptions.

From this point of view, the charge of verificationism seems simply misplaced, for this is just the charge that no amount of belaboring how things appear to us can get us to how they really are. For the pragmatist, the point is to get away from the representationalist vocabulary that sustains the idea of this gap, the idea that reality may contrast with our picture of it in general, and not just in some particular respect or on some particular occasion. Consider, in this light, the line of objection discussed in section 1, that there may be truths not expressible in a particular language, and that there may be conceptual variation between speakers exceeding what can be captured in the resources of the language of one of them. These protests against Davidson presuppose an idea of communicators working within fixed schemes of concepts or stable languages—communicators with fixed repertoires that limit what they can know or say. But from the pragmatist perspective elaborated here, these worries fall away. For the dynamical, adaptive nature of interpretation that characterizes successful communication just is the ability to transcend at any moment the resources depicted in the frozen abstraction of a truth theory. This means, too, that although successful communicators believe true things about the world, there is no picture of the world such that all successful communicators share it; we have cut off the ascent (if that is what it is) from the idea of communication as a practice that puts speakers in touch with each other and the world to the idea of a general picture of the world that they all share, even if as abstract a picture as a general ontological structure. We can happily take ourselves to be in touch with the world, locally and perspectivally, but not with a general structure of all such being in touch.

Davidson's "method of truth in metaphysics" is impressive, but it is in the end not in itself very damaging to ametaphysical readers of Davidson. The real battle concerns how to understand Davidson's claims about the meaning-constituting role of reason, the social nature of thought, and the veridicality of belief. If we allow these to be cast in the mode of constructive representationalism, as purported philosophical discoveries about how things must be, a route from appearance to reality, then, sure enough, the formal semantics of the Davidsonian program is also reinflated into representationalist ontology, in spite of Davidson's own view—famously dim—of the promise of a theoretical notion of representation. However, as I have tried to make vivid in the discussion of the idea of a conceptual scheme, it is possible to resist this tendency. Instead of reading Davidson through the metaphors of representationalism, and as subject to the vocabulary that entrenches them, pragmatists will want to read Davidson's work as a contribution to the struggle to break free from those metaphors and that vocabulary. If this succeeds, then formal semantics and the "demands of a truth theory" will no longer strike us as the way, finally, to answer "perennial" philosophical questions about what there is and what we can know.

4 Concluding Doubts

Metaphysics belongs to metaphysics. That is to say, the pragmatist takes the idea of the metaphysical as a category of inquiry as part of the broad project of supporting a representational conception of knowledge, of communication, and of human agency. It belongs, in a word, to the "world-picture" view of knowledge and agents. The central characteristic of this picture is to enforce a principled distinction between what we believe or *know*, that is, our representations, and what we *do*, that is, how we act in subjective response. The general structure of the world, the ultimate nature of reality, the general categories of being: These are all notions that we deploy, typically, to prop up this picture. The pragmatist, by contrast, thinks of all knowledge as a form of active, interested engagement with the world, not as a matter of peeling away the distorting influence of interest from receptive representational capacities.

The challenge I have addressed here is that this supporting idea of metaphysics, that there is such a general picture, is one to which Davidson appears explicitly to suscribe. This is also what informs the metaphysical readings of his work. From this perspective, Davidson's contribution is twofold: He provides a view of meaning that entails bold and striking claims about the relation between our beliefs and those of others, and between our shared picture of the world and the world itself. This, in turn, supports the elaboration of a specific way, encapsulated in "The Method of Truth in Metaphysics," to determine the large features of our shared picture—where, so to speak, its joints lie. However, I have suggested, metaphysical success is at best conditional; Davidson's account gets us across the gap between subjective appearance and objective reality only by diminishing it.

From the pragmatist side, things look different. Verificationism is what antirepresentationlism looks like when viewed through metaphysical spectacles. This is not a mandatory prescription. One finds support for the "world-picture" view in Davidson principally by taking communication to depend on a system of learned regularities that delineate not just a language, but also what a speaker is capable of thinking and uttering—on the idea of the mind as a structured system of propositions forming what we might call a global outlook. This image of mind as, for philosophical purposes, a set of propositions adding up to a picture of reality tempts one to read Davidson's reflections on conceptual schemes as pertaining to the relation between how things appear to us to be and how they actually are. But there are clear indications in Davidson's writings, most strikingly present in "A Nice Derangement of Epitaphs," of a different view, one that rejects the idea of a global outlook and challenges the representationalist roots of that notion. On this alternative, pragmatist view, we place the dynamic nature of actual communicative encounters at the center of our account. We see the idiolects specified by truth theories as idealized moments, abstracted out of the dynamic process of collaborative interaction that is communication, and not as an actual picture of a temporary mind from which a global view of things may be extracted. We emphasize the capacity for adaptation and change, the historicity of meaning, the contextual and shifting nature of communication-supporting agreement, and the ubiquitous sensitivity (and resulting malleability) of concepts to practical interest. On this view, that communicators on the whole interact knowledgeably in the world does not mean that there is some general picture to be uncovered that they must all share. We are all knowledgeable about the world, but there is no particular general picture we must have in common, no master constraints to which we are all subject.

What, then, are we to say of Davidson's method of truth in metaphysics? Using the structure of a truth theory to say something about the most general categories of ontology—there are objects, there are events—Davidson purports, sure enough, to display general features of reality. He writes:

> Metaphysics has generality as an aim; the method of truth expresses that demand by requiring a theory that touches all the bases. Thus the problems of metaphysics, while neither solved nor replaced, come to be seen as the problems of all good theory building. We want a theory . . . that accounts for the facts about how our language works. What those facts are may remain somewhat in dispute, as will certainly the wisdom of various trade-offs between simplicity and clarity. These questions will be, I do not doubt, the old questions of metaphysics in new dress. But the new dress is in many ways an attractive one.[21]

The pragmatist, as we have seen, has no reason to recoil from aspirations to explanatory generality per se. The pragmatist's skepticism toward metaphysics is that the historical project of epistemology is representationalist in nature, fostering the regulative idea of a chief vocabulary, a scale, a hierarchy of forms of description, a hierarchy that may be discovered, that would be independently authoritative, and final. Pragmatists go after this ideal whenever and wherever they find it, because, we think, it sells human freedom short. We think this, though, not because we imagine, frivolously, that our freedom is fostered by our ignoring reality. We don't doubt that the world constrains us in intransigent ways. What we doubt is the fruitfulness of the pursuit of a final, independently authoritative account of the general structure of such constraint. That project, we claim, turns its back on cultural politics; it sells freedom short by diminishing our active participation in, and thus our willingness and ability to take responsibility for, any particular rendering of our relations to the world, to each other, and to ourselves. The ascent to explanatory generality by itself, however, need have no such effect—once it is decoupled from the representationalist framework, from the idea that we are specifying features of global outlooks, features that must be true of any such. There may be, as Davidson acknowledges, many lines of ascent to generality, different ways of specifying structure—what we must turn our backs on is the idea that they will take us from what merely appears to us to be so to what is really real.

It is, then, the penultimate sentence in the quotation above from which the pragmatist should dissent. The questions raised by the semantic exploitation of truth-theoretic structure are indeed different questions—when they are liberated from representationalist epistemology and no longer serve those purposes that make the pragmatist stand against metaphysics. Should we then say that Davidson's self-proclaimed pursuit of metaphysics isn't really metaphysics after all, that he misdescribes his own most useful contribution? We might be stuck with this option, as an expression of minority protest, if representationalist thinking prevails and remains the lens through which Davidson's contributions are generally assessed. For in this case, the best we can hope for is to continue taking swipes at metaphysics, using whatever resources are to hand. Then again, perhaps Davidson's own sense that a major shift is occurring in philosophical intuitions about what it is to be a communicating agent in the world will turn out to have been prescient.[22] Perhaps the "world-picture" view is fading. In that case, it won't matter very much how Davidson describes his contribution, and the hopeful thing to say will be that metaphysics did not belong to metaphysics after all.

Notes

1. Donald Davidson, "The Method of Truth in Metaphysics," in his *Inquiries into Truth and Interpretation* (Oxford: Clarendon Press, 1984), p. 199.

2. Ibid., p. 205.

3. Ibid.

4. Ibid., p. 200.

5. Ibid.

6. Donald Davidson, "On the Very Idea of a Conceptual Scheme," in *Inquiries into Truth and Interpretation*, pp. 183–198.

7. Ibid., p. 185.

8. Scott Soames, *Philosophical Analysis in the Twentieth Century*, vol. 2: *The Age of Meaning* (Princeton: Princeton University Press, 2003), p. 330.

9. Ibid., pp. 329–330.

10. These claims run through much of Davidson's work, but are most fully elaborated in Donald Davidson, "A Coherence Theory of Truth and Knowledge," in *Subjective, Intersubjective, Objective* (Oxford: Clarendon Press, 2001), pp. 137–153, and Donald Davidson, "Three Varieties of Knowledge," in *Subjective, Intersubjective, Objective*, pp. 205–220.

11. Richard Rorty, *Philosophy and the Mirror of Nature* (Princeton: Princeton University Press, 1979).

12. Richard Rorty, "Naturalism and Quietism," in *Philosophy as Cultural Politics* (Cambridge: Cambridge University Press, 2007), p. 150.

13. See, in particular, Richard Rorty, *Contingency, Irony, and Solidarity* (Cambridge: Cambridge University Press, 1989), and Richard Rorty, *Philosophy as Cultural Politics*.

14. Rorty, *Philosophy and the Mirror of Nature*, p. 259, quoting Davidson, "On the Very Idea of a Conceptual Scheme."

15. Donald Davidson, "A Nice Derangement of Epitaphs," in *Truth, Language, and History* (Oxford: Clarendon Press, 2005), pp. 89–107.

16. Ibid., p. 101.

17. Ibid., p. 102.

18. Ibid.

19. Ibid., p. 107.

20. For a discussion, see Richard Rorty, "Response to Donald Davidson," in *Rorty and His Critics*, ed. Robert B. Brandom (Oxford: Blackwell, 2000), pp. 75–76.

21. Davidson, "The Method of Truth in Metaphysics," p. 214.

22. Regarding the dualism of the subjective and the objective, mind and nature, Davidson says, "Some of . . . [the associated] ideas are now coming under critical scrutiny, and the result promises to mark a sea change in contemporary philosophical thought." Donald Davidson, "The Myth of the Subjective," in *Subjective, Intersubjective, Objective*, p. 39.

II On Interpretation and Understanding

9 Davidson's Reading of Gadamer: Triangulation, Conversation, and the Analytic–Continental Divide

Lee Braver

In his acceptance speech for the Stuttgart Hegel prize, Donald Davidson welcomes the "remarkable rapprochement"[1] he sees emerging between analytic and continental thought, to which he contributes two essays on the preeminent continental philosopher of interpretation, Hans-Georg Gadamer.[2] His respect for Gadamer's work, as well as the fact that both philosophers work on the problem of how to understand others in the absence of a common language or set of assumptions, hold out the promise of a felicitous encounter between top-notch thinkers from the two camps. This looks to be a particularly auspicious opportunity for a "free exchange of ideas drawn from philosophical cultures that until recently often seemed so disparate as to preclude productive conversation,"[3] an exchange that can replace earlier encounters such as Carnap's dismissal of Heidegger,[4] or Searle and Derrida's brawl. Although the Davidson–Gadamer affair is indeed happily lacking in acrimony, neither does it yield mutual understanding or learning.

In this essay I want to perform a kind of "autopsy" on what could have been a productive dialogue between two of the twentieth century's greatest philosophers of interpretation as well as a breakthrough in analytic–continental relations. I will show how Davidson misreads Gadamer, largely because of his incorrect assumption that they share the same understanding of dialogue. I will then demonstrate that although his early work is quite distant from Gadamer, Davidson developed a much closer view of interpretation toward the end of his career. I will conclude by reflecting on the lessons we can draw from this encounter for analytic–continental dialogue in general.

Based on a rather narrow selection of Gadamer's writings,[5] Davidson views Gadamer's inquiry into the conditions for having a world[6] as an analysis of "the foundation of the possibility of objective thought,"[7] which concludes "that it is only in interpersonal communication that there can be thought, a grasping of the fact of an objective, that is, a shared, world."[8] Davidson's own theory of triangulation addresses this problem by illuminating the way humans move from merely reacting differentially to stimuli—recoiling from fire while seeking out berries—to being able to think about them. Thought requires the metabelief that I am holding a belief, since this entails that the world might not be as I think it is, thus producing the notion of a world separate from my opinions, that is, the idea of objectivity.[9] Davidson argues that an individual left to her own devices could not achieve this awareness.[10] Only another person's disagreement with my views pierces my solipsistic-idealist shell to put me in touch with an objective world that extends beyond my view. Such disagreement forms "the entering wedge for correction and the dawning of a sense of an independent reality."[11] One cannot simply reach out and grasp external reality for Davidson;[12] the concept of objectivity only emerges from interpersonal divergence.

Gadamer's claim that dialogue is the condition of objective thought leads Davidson to conclude that Gadamer holds a very similar view,[13] and his triangulation does in fact have much in common with Gadamer's analysis of conversation, just not in the way that Davidson thinks. Drawing heavily on Heidegger's "fore-structures" of understanding,[14] themselves descendants of Kant's transcendental forms and concepts,[15] Gadamer argues that "all understanding inevitably involves some prejudice,"[16] that is, a set of orienting expectations and concepts that organize our thought. These "fundamental, enabling prejudices"[17] are necessary conditions of knowledge and experience; but, if allowed to ossify, they become a Procrustean bed, leading us to interpret everything in our own terms and assimilate anything new or surprising to what we already believe. Like other continental thinkers such as Levinas, Derrida, Foucault, and Lyotard, Gadamer warns of "the danger of 'appropriating' the other person in one's own understanding and thereby failing to recognize his or her otherness."[18] Davidson's early analysis of interpretation commits precisely this hermeneutic error, since his initial version of the principle of charity requires us to interpret others as overwhelmingly like ourselves.[19] I will discuss this further below.

These two interpretive projects are quite similar in broad outline. Both analyze the way we escape an initial state of naive self-confirmation, explaining (in Gadamer's terms) "how we can break the spell of our own fore-meanings."[20] Both find the solution in the meta-awareness of judgments as judgments rather than immediate and absolute truths: "foregrounding a prejudice clearly requires suspending its validity for us. For as long as our mind is influenced by a prejudice, we do not consider it a judgment."[21] We cannot simply shed our preconceptions by fiat; nor can we compare them with reality itself,[22] since they structure any such comparison. Like Davidson, Gadamer argues that challenges from other points of view are what make us aware that we too inhabit a perspective. "It is impossible to make ourselves aware of a prejudice while it is constantly operating unnoticed, but only when it is, so to speak, provoked."[23] Just as the dogmatic wearer of Kant's pink sunglasses thinks the world pink, so prejudices appear to be objective truth to the naive, neither questionable nor in need of questioning. It is only when they actually get questioned that they show up as judgments rather than simply the truth. Engaging someone who lacks them, in other words, shows us that we have them. Objectivity dawns—"the reality beyond every individual consciousness becomes visible"[24]—rendering prejudices susceptible to refinement or rejection. Davidson finds a version of his own notion of triangulation in Gadamer's claim that encountering the world occurs in language which, in turn, "has its true being only in dialogue."[25] Davidson lectures Gadamer that "we can never assume we mean the same thing by our words that our partners in discussion mean,"[26] but this is precisely what he does in assimilating Gadamer's work to his own without carefully examining how their notions of dialogue differ.

Following Quine, Davidson argues from the claim that all linguistic meaning must take place in overt behavior and thus be publicly available (as opposed to reposing in the privacy of one's mind)[27] to the idea that meaning must be entirely derivable from observable phenomena.[28] This means that in principle, a person radically ignorant of another's language must be able to understand her solely on the basis of her utterances and observable behavior; after all, in the absence of telepathy, this is what we are doing all the time. The features highlighted by Quine's famous thought experiment of translating a tribe's language upon first contact are actually present in all communication: "all understanding of the speech of another involves radical interpretation."[29] When Davidson turns to on the idea of triangulation in his later work, he incorporates radical interpretation into it.[30]

Radical interpretation's bracketing of all background knowledge and assumptions makes two supplementary sources of information essential. First, the interpreter needs to observe the speaker interacting with her environment in order to link her occasion sentences to events and objects,[31] for example, to see what triggers the utterance "Gavagai." Second, he must be able to test meaning hypotheses on the speaker, for example, by pointing to various objects and asking "Gavagai?" The fact that this information can only be gathered from face-to-face encounters gives direct interactions an essential primacy, placing writing at an insurmountable disadvantage.[32] Reading a text deprives the interpreter of both forms of supplemental information required by radical interpretation, rendering texts incapable of being triangulation partners: "writing deviates startlingly from the original triangle. . . . The interaction between perceiving creatures that is the foundation of communication is lost."[33] When Davidson talks about dialogue, he means spoken interactions.

For Gadamer, on the other hand, conversations serve as the model for understanding in general, applying to reading texts just as much as to talking with living participants:[34] "it is more than a metaphor . . . to describe the task of hermeneutics as entering into dialogue with the text."[35] Writing even enjoys a certain priority.[36] Because preconceptions guide an entire culture in a historical period, like Hegel's *Zeitgeist* or Heidegger's epochal understandings of Being, our contemporaries are much less likely to confront us with the genuinely challenging perspectives that expand our horizons than interlocutors from other time periods: "we are continually having to test all our prejudices. An important part of this testing occurs in encountering the past."[37] Because we need significantly divergent views in order to provoke the meta-awareness of our own judgments, past works often provide more fruitful conversations than face-to-face discussions with contemporaries. Pursuing the same goal, Davidson and Gadamer hit on diametrically opposed strategies.

Although this disagreement about the medium of conversation may appear trivial, it actually leads to a crucial difference between the two philosophers' systems. Triangulation charts the transformation of merely reacting creatures into a community of rational agents equipped with the same ontology and basic concepts.[38] This transition is tremendously important, of course, but it marks the sole substantive step of intellectual evolution for Davidson, at least in his earlier work. To be a rational agent capable of communicating with others at all, one must grasp the same fundamental structure of reality and share almost all the same beliefs.[39] This reduces all cognitive differences between cultures and times to a matter of marginally disparate distributions of truth conditions. Richard Rorty puts the point well:

> For Davidson, everybody has always talked about mostly real things, and has made mostly true statements. The only difference between primitive animists and us, or us and the Galactics, is that the latecomers can make a few extra true statements which their ancestors did not know how to make (and avoid a few falsehoods). . . . A massive amount of true belief and successful picking-out was already in place when the

first Neanderthal went metalinguistic and found words in which to explain to her mate that one of his beliefs was false.[40]

Since rational beings must identify basically the same referents in basically the same ways for communication to work at all, there can be no deep differences between people, cultures, or eras.

Such wide-ranging homogeneity means that we can only receive relatively superficial corrections from others. A wide enough divergence blows the fuse of mutual understanding, requiring me to doubt the accuracy of my translation or the rationality of my interlocutor. However, triangulation correlates objectivity with intersubjectivity.[41] The diversity of and distance between the perspectives brought to bear on the world determine the breadth of the reality revealed, as suggested by Davidson's metaphor of multiple spatial points of view "inflating" an object that had appeared two-dimensional to a single immobile observer.[42] Ruling out texts as triangulation partners limits us to conversations with contemporaries who, if Gadamer is right, share our basic perspective. This restriction dramatically limits the range of possible disagreements that can challenge interpreters, which in turn restricts the prejudices or judgments we can become aware of and so reject or refine, which thus places a severe limit on the dimensions the world can show us.

Gadamer agrees with Davidson that "a community of minds" is the "ultimate standard"[43] of knowledge instead of comparisons with reality-in-itself; allowing texts to be conversational partners, however, vastly expands this community, turning the canon into "a conversation going on through the ages."[44] In a sense, Gadamerian conversation inserts entire cultures into the position held by individuals in Davidsonian triangulation so that, in a Hegelian–Popperian spirit (to make an unorthodox joining), the "conjectures and refutations" issuing from the broader historical community provide widely divergent perspectives, which creates a much greater expanse of objectivity.[45] Bringing voices from the past into the conversation via texts exponentially increases the number and variety of corrections available to us, opening up a correspondingly richer world. Although we will almost certainly reject the vast majority of these corrections, they highlight our judgments as judgments, which imparts a proportionate sense of the world's independence. Where contemporary interlocutors illuminate the causal independence of objects from me, studying Aristotle and Newton shows the world to be conceptually independent of Einstein, that is, that even our community's best theories at present do not necessarily coincide with reality. Conversing with texts confers the status of metabelief on wide swaths of our beliefs, including the single ontology Davidson insists on.[46] Whereas Davidson concludes that "rationality is a social trait,"[47] Gadamer takes this a step further to claim that reason is historical.

Although his earlier work is quite distant from Gadamer, Davidson's later thought develops a much more compatible conception of interpretation, beginning with his "improvement"[48] of the principle of charity.[49] Whereas the principle originally required the interpreter to render as many of the speaker's beliefs true by the interpreter's own lights as possible, the new version of charity "prompts the interpreter to maximize the intelligibility of the speaker, not sameness of belief."[50] Interpreters are now allowed to attribute many false beliefs to the speaker as long as they can explain why she holds them. A speaker's dissent to the query "Gavagai?" in the presence of a rabbit undermines neither the hypothesis that "Gavagai" means rabbit nor the speaker's competence if her view of the rabbit is blocked.

The second part of this development is Davidson's conclusion that perception is theory laden, which means that what people perceive varies with what they know and believe, even when viewing the same object.

> There is no reason to think all perceptual sentences [i.e., "sentences directly tied to perception"] are simple, or that they are the same for everyone. Not necessarily simple, since some of us learn to know directly, just by looking at the glass, that stormy weather is ahead. . . . And not the same for everyone. Some people don't perceive that stormy weather ahead because they haven't learned to read a barometer.[51]

This idea weakens the radical interpreter's ability to connect a speaker's utterances with the environment, since ascertaining what exactly the speaker is seeing and responding to is no longer a simple matter; when she looks at the barometer, does she see a piece of glass or storms a-brewin'? Radical ignorance prohibits interpreters from relying on any knowledge beyond the utterances emitted by the speaker in reaction to her environment, but this only works if I know how the speaker perceives her environment. This relative transparency was enabled by my sharing her ontology; this is why Davidson finds that Quine's allowance of alternative ontologies renders radical interpretation impossible. If people can see entirely different things when looking at the same object, then "interpretation must take into account probable errors due to bad positioning, deficient sensory apparatus, and *differences in background knowledge*."[52] The factors that can influence a speaker's perceptions and beliefs, and so must be taken into account in interpreting her according to the improved principle of charity, range from her access to empirical data (can she get a good look at the rabbit?) to what she knows and believes (is she a lagomorphologist? A rabbit-worshipper?), conditions that, as David Lewis argues, eventually lead to the speaker's entire "life history of evidence and training."[53]

This is where history and culture could enter Davidson's system. The improved principle of charity, combined with the idea that perception is theory laden, requires us to investigate the speaker's views in order to understand why she believes what she does, and the range of views available and plausible to her is largely determined by her community and time period. Instead of assuming a single ontology common to both speaker and interpreter that synchronizes perceptions to the point that the mere observation of interactions suffices for understanding, these ideas make the examination of a speaker's time and culture a necessary element of interpretation. This is just the kind of research that Gadamer's interpreter resorts to when puzzled by an author's statements.

> The real problem of understanding obviously arises when, in the endeavor to understand the content of what is said, the reflective question arises: how did he come to such an opinion? For this kind of a question reveals an alienness that . . . signifies a renunciation of shared meaning. . . . The breakdown of the immediate understanding of things in their truth is the motive for the detour into history.[54]

Both thinkers could agree that, motivated by charity, we need to study the speaker or author's historical context to see how she arrives at claims that appear obviously false to us.

This also allows Davidson's later thought to accommodate greater conceptual variety and change than his earlier work. Continuing his famous early assault on multiple conceptual schemes (although his rejection of multiple conceptual schemes originally entailed the incoherence of the very idea, his later work does not shy away from the idea), Davidson generally maintains that all mature triangulated humans capture the same reality with the same concepts. His late writings, however, are peppered with discussions of fully competent language-users acquiring new concepts,[55] an ongoing development that imparts a "dynamic flow"[56] to our web of belief. He does quarantine these mutable concepts in the

> suburbs of the core. Their addition may in some cases put a strain on how the words in the central core are understood by those who lack the suburb, but generally not enough to hinder communication. It was not my idea that every new word or concept produced a new conceptual scheme. The scheme is the core we all share.[57]

All rational beings possess this core scheme of fundamental organizing concepts, while semantic drift is kept safely within the gated communities of the suburbs. The problem is that Davidson's rejection of the analytic–synthetic distinction and his holism make it impossible to construct such a rigid barrier between a language's core and periphery. Granting that most new concepts barely jostle the network,[58] history demonstrates the impossibility of predicting which changes may prove revolutionary. In a holistic network of concepts, core and periphery can merge over time or even trade places, like Wittgenstein's river and riverbed.[59]

In these later writings Davidson describes a triangulation that is not a single event which imprints the same ontology onto everyone upon waking to the world, but instead forms a continuing enterprise with varying degrees of sophistication. The low end is one's first initiation into rationality and objectivity[60] that had originally exhausted the entire process. The high end is an "ongoing process" that employs "linguistic and cultural institutions" to "[melt] down" and reshape[61] concepts. Since these institutions and the background knowledge that informs perception vary historically, concepts can change profoundly. Corrections and thus learning can progress indefinitely with no expectation of a final answer. Davidson criticizes the idea of epistemic truth—that is, that what we are warranted in asserting must be true of the world—because it would "reduce reality to so much less than we believe there is."[62] Interestingly, this is just how Gadamer objects to Hegel's positing of a final conclusion to our inquiry into reality. Gadamer prefers what Hegel maligns as "bad infinity," meaning that our understanding and discovery just keep going:

> Experience is initially always experience of negation: something is not what we supposed it to be. . . . The nature of experience is conceived in terms of something that surpasses it. . . . The truth of experience always implies an orientation toward new experience. . . . The dialectic of experience has its proper fulfillment not in definitive knowledge but in the openness to experience.[63]

Here we have the elements of Davidsonian triangulation—corrections leading to the sense of independent reality—to which Gadamer adds the idea that it is always possible to learn not just new truths but new kinds of truths.

This endless horizon of discovery results largely from the participation of texts in our conversation. The vast expansion of the corrections available to us opens up a much richer and more dynamic sense of objectivity; the "highway of despair" behind us keeps us from assuming that we have hit upon the final analysis of reality once and for all.

> We live in what has been handed down to us. . . . It is *the world itself* which is communicatively experienced and continuously entrusted to us as an always open-ended task. It is never the world as it was on its first day but as it has come down to us.[64]

Since tradition will keep going, the world will continue unfolding new dimensions; what we believe there is does not exhaust what there is. This ever-present possibility of surprise is essential to Gadamer's sense of objectivity; to believe otherwise is to commit the mistake Davidson attributes to epistemic truth: It is to reduce reality to what we know of it.[65]

Davidson intertwines his reading of Gadamer with a "renewed interest in Plato,"[66] since, like Gadamer, Davidson finds the paradigm of ongoing triangulation in

> the Socratic elenchus as a crucible in which some of our most important words, and the concepts they express, are tested, melted down, reshaped, and given a new edge. It is a microcosm of the ongoing process of language formation itself, though a sophisticated and self-conscious microcosm which takes advantage of rich and complex linguistic and cultural institutions already in existence.[67]

Ironically, although Davidson agrees with Plato that writings cannot engage in the stimulating "process of question and answer," "thus eliminating the interaction of minds in which words can be bent to new uses and ideas progressively shaped,"[68] his inspiration to modify triangulation comes from some of the oldest texts in the canon.

Davidson's reading of Gadamer is an extraordinarily reflexive moment in the history of philosophy: two thinkers who work on the problem of communicating without a shared language, concepts, or assumptions strive to understand each other in precisely such a situation. I have tried to show that, starting with his reform of the principle of charity and commitment to theory-laden perception, Davidson develops a form of triangulation different from his early thoughts on interpretation but rather close to Gadamer's. Unfortunately, his reading of Gadamer enacts the earlier form of interpretation. He quickly assumes that Gadamer is using terms such as "language," "world," and "dialogue" the same way he does, a strategy that only works if speakers are as epistemologically homogeneous as his early views on radical interpretation had it: "the radical interpreter . . . can assume he and [his informants] share most basic concepts. Thus a first guess is apt to be right, though there can be no assurance of this."[69] When he finds Gadamer disagreeing with him, he merely lists these differences along with why Gadamer is wrong instead of trying to understand why Gadamer holds these views, as demanded by the improved principle of charity. Even Davidson's willingness to write on Gadamer without a solid grasp of his work, while motivated by good intentions, reflects radical interpretation's misguided confidence. If, as Davidson claims in his later work, "the identity of a thought cannot be divorced from its place in the logical network of other thoughts,"[70] then he needed to master considerably more of Gadamer's "network" before he could grasp any specific ideas. In his response to Davidson's paper, Gadamer evinces hermeneutic modesty by limiting himself to "a few marginal comments."[71]

Hermeneutics emphasizes texts because they preserve a reservoir of alien perspectives. Reading texts from the past is paradigmatic of hermeneutics because they are prime instances of the exegetical difficulties that form the discipline's true province, which occur in any attempt to converse across cultures.[72]

> Interpretive distance does not always have to be historical distance. . . . Even in simultaneity, distance can function as an important hermeneutical element; for example, in the encounter between persons who try to find a common ground in conversation, and also in the encounter with persons who speak an alien language or live in an alien culture. Every encounter of this kind allows us to become conscious of our own preconceptions in matters which seemed so self-evident to oneself that one could not even notice one's naïve process of assuming that the other person's conception was the same as one's own, an assumption which generates misunderstanding.[73]

The benefits of confronting alien traditions suggest that philosophy's present division between two camps who share few assumptions, influences, and terms actually presents a tremendous opportunity, if we could generate the right kind of dialogue between them. The failure of the Davidson–Gadamer encounter indicates two conditions for a productive exchange.

First, bridging this gap requires an attitude of hermeneutic humility and charity. Each side must begin with the guiding assumption—always subject to disproof, of course—that the other tradition has something to teach them, that its members might have insights that have eluded their own. This not only aids understanding but justifies the endeavor in the first place; why go to such lengths just to discover false ideas or to learn what we already know? The expectation that the other has something to teach us is Gadamer's version of charity, which forms the necessary beginning point for all interpretation. Hermeneuticism's "modesty consists in the fact that for it there is no higher principle than this: holding oneself open to the conversation. This means, however, constantly recognizing in advance the possibility that your partner is right."[74]

The second necessary factor, which I suspect has been the dominant obstacle heretofore, is a significant knowledge of the other side. Narrow familiarity leads to premature dismissal or identification, which I have tried to show occurred in Davidson's reading of Gadamer. In particular, each participant must be sensitive to the subtle differences in how the other side frames issues. Bjørn Ramberg makes this point well in a paper on Davidson and Gadamer: "the commensuration of different philosophical perspectives is achieved, if at all, only slowly, by virtue of sensitive work. . . . Much of the effort consists precisely in not taking the identity of key concepts for granted."[75] There have to be sufficient commensurable topics and vocabulary for the conversation to succeed, as Davidson insists, but this must always be balanced by taking great care to preserve the interlocutor's particular way of thinking. This is both a matter of respect and the only way one can actually learn from an alien tradition. Davidson's thought was developing toward this view of interpretation but, despite good intentions, his reading of Gadamer does not live up to it; and so it takes its place as another misfired attempt at analytic–continental dialogue.[76]

Acknowledgments

I want to thank Jeff Malpas for his helpful comments on this essay.

Notes

1. Donald Davidson, *Truth, Language, and History* (Oxford: Clarendon Press, 2005), p. 251.

2. Donald Davidson, "Dialectic and Dialogue" (1994) and "Gadamer and Plato's *Philebus*" (1997), both reprinted in Davidson, *Truth, Language, and History*.

3. Davidson, *Truth, Language, and History*, p. 252.

4. Michael Friedman's *A Parting of the Ways: Carnap, Cassirer, and Heidegger* (Chicago: Open Court, 2000) presents Carnap as better informed and more engaged than most have thought.

5. Hans-Georg Gadamer, *Truth and Method*, 2nd rev. ed., trans. Joel Weinsheimer and Donald G. Marshall (New York: Continuum, 1989). Except for one quotation from p. 275 of *Truth and Method* in *Truth, Language, and History*, p. 181, Davidson only discusses about 60 pages of Gadamer's 579-page magnum opus.

6. Davidson, *Truth, Language, and History*, p. 274.

7. "Language is not just one of man's possessions in the world; rather, on it depends the fact that man has a world at all" (Gadamer, *Truth and Method*, p. 443, quoted in Davidson, *Truth, Language, and History*, p. 274).

8. Davidson, *Truth, Language, and History*, p. 261.

9. See Donald Davidson, *Subjective, Intersubjective, Objective* (Oxford: Clarendon Press, 2001), pp. 104–105, 129, 209–210; Davidson, *Problems of Rationality* (Oxford: Clarendon Press, 2004), pp. 7–9, 137–138; and Davidson, "Externalisms," in

Interpreting Davidson, ed. Petr Kotatko, Peter Pagin, and Gabriel Segal (Stanford: CSLI Publications, 2001), p. 4.

10. Davidson attributes the inspiration for this argument to Kripke's take on Wittgenstein's private language argument. See *Truth, Language, and History*, p. 119; *Subjective, Intersubjective, Objective*, pp. 121, 209, n. 1; *Problems of Rationality*, pp. 143–144; and "Externalisms," p. 2. "As Wittgenstein says, by yourself you can't tell the difference between the situations seeming the same and being the same" (*Truth, Language, and History*, p. 124). See Wittgenstein: "one would like to say: whatever is going to seem right to me is right. And that only means that here we can't talk about 'right,'" in *Philosophical Investigations*, 3rd ed., trans. G. E. M. Anscombe (Madsen: Blackwell, 2001), §258. I cannot discover my error on my own since "justification consists in appealing to something independent"; checking my own impressions or memories to see if I am following a rule correctly is like someone buying "several copies of the morning paper to assure himself that what it said was true" (ibid., §265).

11. Davidson, "Reply to Dagfinn Føllesdal," in *The Philosophy of Donald Davidson*, The Library of Living Philosophers, vol. 27, ed. Lewis E. Hahn (Chicago: Open Court, 1999), p. 731. See also pp. 164, 194; *Truth, Language, and History*, p. 124; *Subjective, Intersubjective, Objective*, p. 83; "Externalisms," p. 13; Davidson, "Comments on the Karlovy Vary Papers," in Kotatko, Pagin, and Segal (eds.), *Interpreting Davidson*, p. 293.

12. See Davidson, *Subjective, Intersubjective, Objective*, pp. 70, 137, 144; "The Structure and Content of Truth," *Journal of Philosophy* 87, no. 6 (June 1990): 279–328, p. 304.

13. A number of commentators have followed Davidson in finding significant similarity between the two: see Jeff Malpas, "Gadamer, Davidson, and Ground of Understanding," in *Gadamer's Century: Essays in Honor of Hans-Georg Gadamer*, ed. Jeff Malpas, Ulrich Arnswald, and Jens Kertscher (Cambridge, MA: MIT Press, 2002), p. 195; David Hoy, "Post-Cartesian Interpretation: Hans-Georg Gadamer and Donald Davidson," in *The Philosophy of Hans-Georg Gadamer*, The Library of Living Philosophers, vol. 24, ed. Lewis Hahn (Chicago: Open Court, 1997), pp. 111–128; Joel Weinsheimer, "Charity Militant: Gadamer, Davidson, and Post-Critical Hermeneutics," *Revue Internationale de Philosophie* 54, no. 213 (2000): 418; Karsten Stueber, "Understanding Truth and Objectivity: A Dialogue between Donald Davidson and Hans-Georg Gadamer," in *Hermeneutics and Truth*, ed. Brice R. Wachterhauser (Evanston: Northwestern University Press, 1994), p. 172; Richard J. Bernstein, *Beyond Objectivism and Relativism: Science, Hermeneutics, and Praxis* (University Park: University of Pennsylvania Press, 1988), pp. 141–142; and Bjørn T. Ramberg, *Donald Davidson's Philosophy of Language: An Introduction* (New York: Blackwell, 1989), pp. 138–141. However, Gadamer himself expresses strong reservations, in *The Philosophy of Hans-Georg Gadamer*, p. 129.

14. See Martin Heidegger, *Being and Time*, trans. John Macquarrie and Edward Robinson (San Francisco: HarperSanFrancisco, 1962), pp. 191–195/150–153, and Gadamer, *Truth and Method*, pp. 266, 293.

15. See Heidegger, *Being and Time*, pp. 54–55/31. For more on this connection, see chapter 5 of my *A Thing of This World: A History of Continental Anti-Realism* (Evanston: Northwestern University Press, 2007).

16. Gadamer, *Truth and Method*, p. 270.

17. Ibid., p. 295.

18. Ibid., p. 299, n. 230.

19. See Donald Davidson, *Inquiries into Truth and Interpretation* (Oxford: Oxford University Press, 2001), p. 101; *Problems of Rationality*, pp. 114–115, 144.

20. Gadamer, *Truth and Method*, p. 268.

21. Ibid., p. 299; see also pp. 268, 360, 443. Gadamer's analysis draws on the phenomenological *epoché*.

22. Ibid., pp. 447, 452.

23. Ibid., p. 299; see also pp. 269–270, 465, and "Text and Interpretation," in *Dialogue and Deconstruction: The Gadamer-Derrida Encounter*, ed. Diane Michelfelder and Richard Palmer (Albany: SUNY Press, 1989), p. 26. Gadamer is applying Heidegger's early analysis of inconspicuousness to prejudices here (see *Being and Time*, pp. 54–55/31, 59/35).

24. Gadamer, *Truth and Method*, p. 449; see also Hans-Georg Gadamer, *Philosophical Hermeneutics*, trans. and ed. David E. Linge (Berkeley: University of California Press, 1976), p. 38. A similar claim is made in *Truth and Method*, p. 357.

25. Gadamer, *Truth and Method*, p. 446, quoted in Davidson, *Truth, Language, and History*, p. 274; see also "Text and Interpretation," p. 23, "Letter to Dallmayr," p. 99, "*Destruktion* and Deconstruction," p. 106, in Michelfelder and Palmer (eds.), *Dialogue and Deconstruction*.

26. Davidson, *Truth, Language, and History*, p. 275; see also p. 255, and Bjørn Ramberg, "Illuminating Language: Interpretation and Understanding in Gadamer and Davidson," in *A House Divided: Comparing Analytic and Continental Philosophy*, ed. C. G. Prado (Amherst, NY: Humanity Books, 2003), pp. 214, 231.

27. "Perhaps the most important thing [Quine] taught me was that there can be no more to the communicative content of words than is conveyed by verbal behavior," "Reply to W. V. Quine," in Hahn (ed.), *The Philosophy of Donald Davidson*, p. 80; see also pp. "Reply to A. C. Genova," p. 192, "Reply to Dagfinn Føllesdal," p. 729; W. V. O. Quine, *Ontological Relativity and Other Essays* (New York: Columbia University Press, 1969), pp. 26–27, 81; Quine, "Indeterminacy of Translation Again,"

Journal of Philosophy 84, no. 1 (January 1987): 5–10, p. 8; W. V. O. Quine, *Pursuit of Truth*, rev. ed. (Cambridge, MA: Harvard University Press, 1992), p. 38.

28. See Donald Davidson, "The Structure and Content of Truth," *Journal of Philosophy* 87, no. 6 (June 1990): 279–328, *Subjective, Intersubjective, Objective*, pp. 77, 174, 182, 215; *Problems of Rationality*, pp. 65, 183; *Truth, Language, and History*, p. 245.

29. Davidson, *Inquiries into Truth and Interpretation*, p. 125; see also p. 279; *Subjective, Intersubjective, Objective*, pp. 147–148; *Truth, Language, and History*, pp. 62, 107; replies to papers in *Reflecting Davidson: Donald Davidson Responding to an International Forum of Philosophers*, ed. Ralf Stocker (Berlin: de Gruyter, 1993), pp. 82, n. 5, 84; *Problems of Rationality*, p. 143. This is what Quine means when he says that "radical translation begins at home" (Quine, *Ontological Relativity*, p. 46; see also Quine, *Pursuit of Truth*, p. 48). Davidson's later writings complicate this position by sometimes denying that his account is or ever was supposed to describe actual linguistic behavior (see *Truth, Language, and History*, pp. 111–112; "The Structure and Content of Truth," pp. 324–325; *Problems of Rationality*, pp. 127–128). Besides being inaccurate—his early discussions do attribute radical interpretation to all speech—this portrayal also requires a serious reconsideration of the conclusions drawn from his discussions. For a useful discussion of this topic, see Paisley Livingston, "Writing Action: Davidson, Rationality, and Literary Research," in *Literary Theory After Davidson*, ed. Reed Way Dasenbrock (University Park: Pennsylvania State University Press, 1993), pp. 269–270, 275.

30. "My recent [1999] emphasis on the triangle . . . connects the radical interpreter, her interpretee, and the world," "Reply to Simon Evnine," in Hahn (ed.), *The Philosophy of Donald Davidson*, p. 310 (see also p. 460); see also Davidson, *Truth, Language, and History*, pp. 176–177; *Problems of Rationality*, p. 143; *Subjective, Intersubjective, Objective*, pp. 88, 210; "Comments on the Karlovy Vary Papers," pp. 292–294.

31. See, e.g., Davidson, *Subjective, Intersubjective, Objective*, p. 211.

32. Davidson approvingly quotes Plato in the *Phaedrus* and *Seventh Letter* on this subject; see *Truth, Language, and History*, pp. 249, 254.

33. Davidson, *Truth, Language, and History*, p. 161; see also pp. 177, 255.

34. Ironically, Gadamer also finds his views in Plato, even in the same places as Davidson. Gadamer describes his work as pursuing "the hermeneutic effort to think the nature of language in terms of dialogue—inevitable for me as a lifelong student of Plato," "Question and Answer Play Back and Forth between the Text and Its Interpreter," in *Genius: In Their Own Words*, ed. Daniel Ramsay Steele (Chicago: Open Court, 2002), p. 215. See also Gadamer, *Truth and Method*, pp. 365, 369, 377, and "*Destruktion* and Deconstruction," in Michelfelder and Palmer (ed.), *Dialogue and Deconstruction*, p. 111. Gadamer's Plato does not subscribe to the primacy of writing over speech: "when [Plato] calls on dialectic to come to the aid of the weakness of speech, while declaring the condition of the written word beyond hope, this is

obviously an ironic exaggeration with which to conceal his own writing and his own art," in Gadamer, *Truth and Method*, p. 393.

35. Gadamer, *Truth and Method*, p. 368; see also p. 385; "Question and Answer Play Back and Forth," in Steele (ed.), *Genius*, p. 213; Hans-Georg Gadamer, *Philosophical Hermeneutics*, trans. and ed. David E. Linge (Berkeley: University of California Press), p. 57; Hans-Georg Gadamer, *The Beginning of Philosophy*, trans. Rod Coltman (New York: The Continuum, 1998), p. 49. Several critics have noted this difference between Davidson and Gadamer: Samuel C. Wheeler III, *Deconstruction as Analytic Philosophy* (Stanford: Stanford University Press, 2000), p. 32; Thomas Kent, "Interpretation and Triangulation: A Davidsonian Critique of Reader-Oriented Literary Theory," in Dasenbrock (ed.), *Literary Theory After Davidson*, p. 37; Pascal Engel, "Interpretation without Hermeneutics: A Plea Against Ecumenism," *Topoi* 10, no. 2 (September 1991): 137–146, p. 138; Karsten R. Stueber, "Understanding Truth and Objectivity: A Dialogue between Donald Davidson and Hans-Georg Gadamer," in *Hermeneutics and Truth*, ed. Brice R. Wachterhauser (Evanston: Northwestern University Press, 1994), p. 181; Hoy, "Post-Cartesian Interpretation," p. 117. Gadamer himself plays down the difference in "Reply to David C. Hoy" in Hahn (ed.), *The Philosophy of Hans-Georg Gadamer*, p. 129, wrongly in my opinion.

36. "Everything written is, in fact, the paradigmatic object of hermeneutics," in Gadamer, *Truth and Method*, p. 394; see also "Question and Answer Play Back and Forth," in Steele (ed.), *Genius*, p. 230.

37. Gadamer, *Truth and Method*, p. 306; see also pp. 299, 463.

38. "Reply to Simon Evnine" in Hahn (ed.), *The Philosophy of Donald Davidson*, p. 308; see also "Reply to Barry Stroud," p. 165; *Problems of Rationality*, p. 140.

39. Or explicably false beliefs by the improved principle of charity, as I will discuss below.

40. Richard Rorty, *Philosophical Papers*, vol. 1: *Objectivity, Relativism, and Truth* (New York: Cambridge University Press, 1991), pp. 159–160.

41. Davidson, *Subjective, Intersubjective, Objective*, pp. 105, 218.

42. Ibid., p. 105.

43. Ibid., p. 218; see also p. 83; "Externalisms," p. 13.

44. Gadamer, "Question and Answer Play Back and Forth," in Steele (ed.), *Genius*, p. 228.

45. "The important thing is to recognize temporal distance as a positive and productive condition enabling understanding." Gadamer, *Truth and Method*, p. 297.

46. In his "Intellectual Autobiography," Davidson states that "Kant's influence has been the most pervasive, but it runs so deep that I have seldom acknowledged it in

print" ("Intellectual Autobiography of Donald Davidson," in Hahn [ed.], *The Philosophy of Donald Davidson*, p. 64). We can certainly see a Kantian element in his insistence on a single ontology, making my projection of Gadamer's reaction something of a replay of Hegel's arguing for historical plurality against Kant's ahistorical uniqueness. Obviously, I would not want to push this parallel too far.

47. Davidson, *Subjective, Intersubjective, Objective*, p. 105.

48. Davidson singles out David Lewis's objections (reprinted in David Lewis, *Philosophical Papers*, vol. I [New York: Oxford University Press, 1983], pp. 108–118) as provoking this change. Dagfinn Føllesdal claims credit for raising the similar point in conversation with Davidson in 1973 that a speaker's view being impeded by a tree could explain her negative response to the query, "Gavagai?" in the presence of a rabbit ("Triangulation," in Hahn [ed.], *The Philosophy of Donald Davidson*, pp. 723, 727, n. 7). Davidson uses this specific example in his response to Lewis (*Inquiries into Truth and Interpretation*, p. 282), though without mentioning Føllesdal.

49. Commentators have noted that both thinkers agree on some form of charity in understanding. Cf. Stueber in *Hermeneutics and Truth*, p. 180; Hoy, "Post-Cartesian Interpretation," pp. 119–126. Gadamer himself suggests that he accepts Hoy's description of the principle in "Reply to David C. Hoy," p. 129.

50. Davidson, *Inquiries into Truth and Interpretation*, p. xix; see also *Subjective, Intersubjective, Objective*, p. 152, and "Reply to Simon Evnine," in Hahn (ed.), *The Philosophy of Donald Davidson*, p. 307.

51. Davidson, *Inquiries into Truth and Interpretation*, p. 137; see also *The Philosophy of Donald Davidson*, p. 254; "Comments on the Karlovy Vary Papers," in Kotatko, Pagin, and Segal (ed.), *Interpreting Davidson*, p. 290.

52. Davidson, *Inquiries into Truth and Interpretation*, p. xix; emphasis added.

53. Lewis, *Philosophical Papers*, p. 112.

54. Gadamer, *Truth and Method*, pp. 180–181; see also pp. 373–374.

55. This is one point on which I disagree with Ramberg's contrast of Davidson and Gadamer: "in Davidson's account, the radical interpreter fuses no horizons, suffers no experience, and attains no transforming insights" (Ramberg, "Illuminating Language," p. 231). Although this is true of much of Davidson's work, especially the earlier writings, the strain in Davidson I am trying to bring out is more amenable to such transformations.

56. Davidson, *Problems of Rationality*, p. 15.

57. Davidson, "Reply to Simon Evnine" in Hahn (ed.), *Philosophy of Donald Davidson*, pp. 308–309; see also *Truth, Language, and History*, p. 128.

58. Davidson, *Problems of Rationality*, pp. 14–15; see also W. V. O. Quine, *From a Logical Point of View: Nine Logico-Philosophical Essays*, 2nd ed. (Cambridge, MA: Harvard University Press, 1980), pp. 78–79.

59. Ludwig Wittgenstein, *On Certainty*, ed. G. E. M. Anscombe and G. H. von Wright, trans. Denis Paul and G. E. M. Anscombe (New York: Harper Torchbooks, 1969), §§96–97.

60. Even here, though, his admission that training can play a role allows culture a toehold. See *The Philosophy of Donald Davidson*, p. 731; *Problems of Rationality*, p. 137; and "Externalisms," p. 5.

61. Davidson, *Truth, Language and History*, p. 258.

62. Davidson, *Subjective, Intersubjective, Objective*, p. 178; see also "The Structure of Content and Truth," pp. 298–299.

63. Gadamer, *Truth and Method*, pp. 354–355; see also pp. 298, 302, 342, 570; "Reply to Jacques Derrida," in Michelfelder and Palmer (ed.), *Dialogue and Deconstruction*, p. 57, and "Letter to Dallmayr," in the same vol., p. 95; Gadamer, *The Beginning of Philosophy*, p. 46; Hans-Georg Gadamer, *Reason in the Age of Science*, trans. Frederick G. Lawrence (Cambridge, MA: MIT Press, 1981), p. 40.

64. Gadamer, "Question and Answer Play Back and Forth," in Steele (ed.), *Genius: In Their Own Words*, pp. 204–205; emphasis in original.

65. See Gadamer, *Truth and Method*, p. 447: "the infinite perfectibility of the human experience of the world means that, whatever language we use, we never succeed in seeing anything but an ever more extended aspect, a 'view' of the world. Those views of the world are not relative in the sense that one could oppose them to the 'world in itself.' . . . In every worldview the existence of the world-in-itself is intended. It is the whole to which linguistically schematized experience refers."

66. Davidson, *Truth, Language, and History*, pp. 263–264. One of the reasons Davidson writes about Gadamer is that he found Gadamer's early work on the *Philebus* "unique," "stunning," and "eye-opening" (*Truth, Language, and History*, p. 262) while writing his dissertation.

67. Davidson, *Truth, Language, and History*, p. 258; see also pp. 100, 254. However, he still insists that written works cannot perform this function: "writing reduces the number of active interpreters to one, the reader, thus eliminating the interaction of minds in which words can be bent to new uses and ideas progressively shaped. Writing may portray, but cannot constitute, the intersubjective exchanges in which meanings are created and firmed" (ibid., p. 255). The one exception Davidson allows is when "writers like Shakespeare, Dante, Joyce, Beckett strain our interpretive powers and thus force us into retrospective dialogue with the text" (ibid., p. 162). Sufficient textual opacity provokes the kind of interpretive energy that gives reading

the qualities of a dialogue. Since Gadamer's focus is on texts from the past that present just such interpretive puzzles, Davidson's admission here hints at a potential harmony. It could also shed interesting light on one of the most common analytic criticisms of continental philosophy, namely, its obscure writing style.

68. Davidson, *Truth, Language, and History*, p. 255; see also pp. 161, 177, 249.

69. Davidson, *Problems of Rationality*, p. 144; see also p. 49. The timing of comments like this, published in 2001, make my chronological ordering of Davidson's development only approximate.

70. Davidson, *Subjective, Intersubjective, Objective*, p. 99.

71. "Reply to Donald Davidson," in Hahn (ed.), *The Philosophy of Hans-Georg Gadamer*, p. 433. Gadamer also notes, in contrast to Davidson's confidence, "how great the distance and the differences with respect to the treatment of the same topic are on both sides. . . . It is really astonishing for me to see how difficult it is to reenact the train of thought and the basic position of the other" (ibid.).

72. In fact, Gadamer claims that any instance of understanding involves hermeneutics, making its scope universal; but we are talking about the paradigms of the philosophy that involve obstacles to communication.

73. Gadamer, "Question and Answer Play Back and Forth," in Steele (ed.), *Genius*, p. 224.

74. Ibid., p. 213; see also Gadamer, *Truth and Method*, pp. 292, 297, 299, 303, 335, 361, 394, 442.

75. Ramberg, "Illuminating Language," p. 214.

76. In *A Thing of This World*, I attempt to facilitate mutual understanding by explaining continental philosophy in terms of the analytic topic of antirealism without simplifying or distorting either.

10 In Gadamer's Neighborhood

Robert Dostal

1 Introduction and Historical Background

In 1997, in the Library of Living Philosophers volume dedicated to the work of Gadamer, Davidson contributes an essay in which he writes of his own intellectual development: "I . . . have . . . arrived in Gadamer's intellectual neighborhood."[1] In this late essay Davidson does not elaborate on what he means by this, though by way of conclusion he does mention very briefly what he takes to be some differences. In this essay I explore this neighborhood—what the neighborhood looks like and how these two neighbors agree and disagree. It would be interesting to consider how they came to find themselves in the same neighborhood, since the traditions of philosophical discourse within which they developed their respective positions are so remarkably different; but I cannot pursue the question of the development of their respective positions here. The most important thinker for Davidson is Quine; for Gadamer, Heidegger. Gadamer gives no indication of ever having read Davidson until late in life.[2] Davidson tells us that he read Gadamer's habilitation thesis on Plato's *Philebus* in the late 1930s, that he was "impressed" with the work, and that he "unfortunately learned very little from Gadamer."[3] Davidson's subsequent, but brief, work on Plato was most influenced by Gregory Vlastos. Apparently only very late in his life did Davidson read any more of Gadamer. He then discovered their proximity—a neighborhood arrived at by very different routes.

Four basic agreements stand out: (1) that all understanding is linguistic; (2) that all understanding is interpretive; (3) that the principle of charity is a necessary principle of interpretation; and (4) that we should reject the distinction of scheme–content (or worldview–world). Much is implicated in these four agreed upon commitments. For both philosophers the concept of truth is important but the concept of reference is not. Both are realists and holists (though Davidson importantly qualifies his realism in the Dewey lectures of 1990—see below). Both have critics who find that it is impossible to be both a realist and a holist and consider the holism and coherentism to trump the realism such that, in the end, Davidson and Gadamer should be considered, according to these critics, linguistic idealists and relativists, though neither considered himself to be such. The consideration of these questions leads us to consider the ontological, epistemological, and transcendental status of their arguments. This essay looks also at Davidson's statement of his disagreement with Gadamer, namely, that dialogue does not presuppose a common language, nor does it create it. This requires us to look more carefully at their respective concepts of language. The essay concludes with a suggestion of a Gadamerian critique of Davidson and a consideration of John McDowell's and Charles Taylor's advocacy of Gadamer in relation to Davidson.

2 Gadamer's and Davidson's Agreements

In his essay about Gadamer, Davidson cites Gadamer's main work, *Truth and Method*, where Gadamer states that "all understanding is interpretation," and he indicates his agreement with Gadamer.[4] There are important similarities in their respective notions of interpretation. For one, neither believes that interpretation should be considered an algorithmic or machine-like process. The very title of Gadamer's main work on interpretation, *Truth and Method*, ironically suggests a disjunction, not a conjunction. Truth is our concern in interpretation, but method does not provide it. Gadamer concludes the work with a distinction of method and discipline: "Rather, what the tool of method does not achieve must—and really can—be achieved by a discipline of questioning and inquiring, a discipline that guarantees truth."[5] Davidson writes that "any hope of a universal method of interpretation must be abandoned."[6] Elsewhere he explicitly rejects any machine-like construal of interpretation: "For we have discovered . . . no portable interpreting machine set to grind out the meaning of an arbitrary utterance"; we need "wit, luck, and wisdom . . . rules of thumb."[7]

Another important similarity with regard to interpretation is the principle of charity. Davidson argues, in his much-cited essay "On the Very Idea of a Conceptual Scheme," that for there to be meaningful disagreement, there must be "*some* foundation—in agreement."[8] If our apparent differences are due to our working within different conceptual schemes, then we are not really disagreeing with one another but simply operating according to different schemes—in other words, living in different worlds. For us to disagree, we must be in the same world, disagreeing about the same thing.

That is, there has to be background agreement that it is the same thing about which we are in disagreement. Gadamer makes a similar claim when he writes: "we do not first decide to agree but are always already in agreement, as Aristotle showed."[9] A corollary of this necessary presumption of agreement is the presumption in disagreement that the other may be right. This Davidson calls the principle of charity for any interpretation: "Charity is forced on us; whether we like it or not, if we want to understand others, we must count them right in most matters."[10] A similar principle of hermeneutics is found throughout Gadamer's writings. In "Text and Interpretation" Gadamer refers to it as the "good will" toward the other: "Both partners must have the good will to try to understand one another."[11] Elsewhere Gadamer writes that we should always enter a conversation or take up a text with the presumption that the other may be right.[12] Accordingly, I have elsewhere called Gadamer's hermeneutics a hermeneutics of trust.[13] But neither Gadamer's trust nor Davidson's charity requires that we believe that the other is simply right, only that the other *may* be right.

Not only is understanding interpretive and charitable, it is linguistic as well. Gadamer writes, "all interpretation takes place in the medium of language."[14] He writes further that "Being that can be understood is language."[15] With this, too, Davidson agrees. The hermeneutic and the linguistic turns for them are one and the same. But remarkably, the interpretive and linguistic character of understanding does not mean that one understands via a conceptual scheme (Davidson) or a worldview (Gadamer).[16] Accordingly, they both reject the relativism of schemes or worldviews. This rejection of the scheme–content distinction is closely related to the discussion of the necessary presumption of a background agreement, stated briefly above.

3 Truth and Representation: An Apparent Contradiction

Claims (1) and (2), that all understanding is linguistic and interpretive, seem for many readers of Davidson and Gadamer to contradict claim (4), that we should reject the scheme–content (worldview–world) distinction. Such readers either reject their position as incoherent or reconstrue them as holding the first claim but not the third. This fairly standard view of the matter may be simply stated as follows. If all understanding of the world is an interpretation of the world, then what we have is an interpretation of the world and not the world itself. The world is made up of physical things and, arguably, nonphysical things. Our grasp of the world in the understanding is, according to Gadamer and Davidson, in language. Language is not one of the things in the world. Language resides in the subject. It is the way we take up the things of the world. Different languages interpret the world differently. One can go on to distinguish concepts from ordinary language and to consider various conceptual frames within which we view the world; but this adds little to the essential picture. An assumption of this way of taking Davidson and/or Gadamer is that language (or a conceptual scheme) provides a kind of screen or filter that the subject sits behind and cannot thereby say what is on the other side of the screen but only what appears to him or her on the subject side of the screen.[17] This way of thinking is characteristic not only of much of modern and contemporary philosophy but has become "common sense" in the global village.

This sketch is, of course, a simplified version of Kant and his distinction between appearances and things in themselves. For Kant, we cannot know things as they are in themselves; we can only know the appearances of things. However much talk about the thing in itself or things in themselves makes post-Kantian philosophers uncomfortable, the prominence of this way of understanding language and, accordingly, understanding Davidson and Gadamer attests to how much contemporary philosophy remains neo-Kantian. Davidson and Gadamer, as we shall see, reject this view. Both see such a view as a logical outcome of the starting point of Descartes, who begins by assuming that, though the external world is dubitable, the internal world of the subject is indubitable. With the latter, we begin our ascent to truth.

Another useful way to state this concisely is to say that, for Descartes and much of modern and contemporary philosophy, what we have is a representation of the world. And that is all we have. There is no way for us to answer the question as to whether our representations are accurate or true about the world. We cannot compare our representations to the world, for all we have are representations. There is no stepping out of consciousness to compare the representations of consciousness with that which they presumably represent. In Davidson's words, "Once the Cartesian starting point has been chosen, there is no saying what the evidence is evidence for, or so it seems. Idealism, reductionist forms of empiricism, and skepticism loom."[18] Hume's recognition of this conundrum led him to academic skepticism and common sense. Kant's response to the problem is to endorse the impossibility of making claims on things in themselves and to suggest a science of appearances. The word that Kant uses for the stuff of consciousness (Locke's ideas) is *Vorstellung* (representation). Thus, one way to formulate Davidson's and Gadamer's neighborhood in a negative phrase is the rejection of representationalism.

Davidson sometimes uses this term, "representation," to present or summarize his position. In "The Myth of the Subjective"(1986) he writes: "It is good to be rid of representations . . . for it is thinking there are representations that engenders intimations of relativism."[19] Here, representations for Davidson are the content of the scheme–content duality. The implications in ridding ourselves of this way of thinking about things, Davidson says in the same essay, are enormous.[20] By this "good riddance" to representationalism, we rid ourselves at the same time of subjects and objects: "Once we take this step, no *objects* will be left."[21] This essay is entitled "The Myth of the Subject" because we will simultaneously be doing away with the subject. "Subject" and "object" are correlative terms; you can't have one without the other. The "subject" is where the representation is located. In concluding the essay Davidson acknowledges a minimal way in which the notion of subjectivity makes some sense, but importantly for Davidson, the standards for thought are public. We are, on his account, in "unmediated touch" with the things of our experience.[22]

Gadamer's position is very like the one just described, though we shall see that, at least in some respects, Gadamer more consistently upholds the position. In German philosophy the critique of representationalism goes back to Hegel. Quite independent of Hegel, Edmund Husserl makes a clean break with representationalism as he establishes his phenomenological method. Gadamer owes much to both these philosophers—perhaps more to Husserl. His debt to Husserl is both direct and indirect, through Heidegger. Gadamer does not adopt the quasi-technical language of Husserl, but he clearly accepts his concept of intentionality and his critique of representationalism. Though our relation to the world is complex and multilayered (in which there remains a place for representations of various kinds), nonetheless there is an important sense in which we are in direct contact with the world according to the phenomenology of Husserl, Heidegger, and Gadamer. The Kantian distinction of appearances and things in themselves, which Hegel challenged earlier, is similarly rejected by these twentieth-century German thinkers. Gadamer writes: "The verbal world in which we live is not a barrier that prevents knowledge of being-in-itself but fundamentally embraces everything in which our insight can be enlarged and deepened."[23] And further: "In language the reality beyond every individual consciousness becomes visible."[24]

A consequence that Heidegger and Gadamer drew from this is an explicit rejection of the language of "subject" and "object." Like Heidegger, Gadamer never talks about the "subject." Gadamer talks rather about the "self" or "consciousness."[25] Gadamer also never talks about the "object," except in the special sense in which an item of experience is objectified in a particular way—most prominently by the scientific method. We do experience things. Our talk is about something. What it is that our talk is about, Gadamer sometimes refers to with the word *Ding* (thing), but more often and quite consistently with the word *Sache*, which might most simply (but perhaps awkwardly) be translated as "the matter at hand." The philosophical paternity of *Sache* is again both Hegel and Husserl, quite independent of one another. Gadamer addresses this term most directly in a lecture from 1960, entitled "Die Natur der Sache und die Sprache der Dinge," which has been translated as "The Nature of Things and the Language of Things."[26] Note how the English neglects the distinction of *Sache* and *Ding*. Gadamer points out that *Sache* means, first of all, *causa*, in the Roman legal sense of "case." Gadamer finds this word and its range of meanings, both historical and philosophical, appropriate because he wants to convey that we, for the most part, talk about whatever enterprise (*Sache*) with which we are engaged. With this term he is at the same time cutting across the theory–practice distinction. We do not find ourselves, in the first place, in a world of scientific objects, but in a world with which we are engaged in a variety of ways. We find ourselves engaged with things and with others, not over against them.

But the translators of *Truth and Method* found it impossible to consistently translate *Sache*. They have translated it as "thing," "content," "subject," "subject matter," and, yes, "object." The first English edition was more egregious in its usage of "object." Joel Weinsheimer and Donald G. Marshall, who revised the translation, did change a number of the occurrences of "object" for "*Sache*" to "thing," or "content," or "subject matter." But they did not rid the English text of "object" entirely. If one looks at the one long and important citation from *Truth and Method* in Davidson's essay on Gadamer, one finds the word "object" twice.[27] Both times in the German, the word is "*Sache*." As noted in the footnote above, Davidson is citing the first edition. The second edition changes the first occurrence to "subject matter," but leaves the second occurrence as "object." Thus the revised text reads that "in a successful conversation they [the partners in a conversation] both come under the influence of the truth of the object."[28] This seems to return us to the paradigm of subject and object and the representational truth that the subject might have of the object. But, as I have pointed out, Gadamer consistently avoids this term. Davidson, in the essay, "The Myth of the Subjective," writes about the "demise of the subjective,"[29] and how no objects will be left, if we make the appropriate philosophical turn. Yet in his subsequent writings he continues to write about "objects." Gadamer does not, but the translation betrays this.

For Davidson, ridding ourselves of representations is closely connected with ridding ourselves of meanings, reference, and the standard version of a correspondence theory of truth. A meaning is a kind of stand-in for a representation. We can find a similar notion in Gadamer when he writes: "Hence hermeneutics has to see through the dogmatism of a 'meaning-in-itself' in exactly the same way critical philosophy has seen through the dogmatism of experience."[30] Though Davidson sometimes uses the word "reference" in a positive and ordinary commonsensical way, when he writes about dispensing with reference, he is thinking about the irresolvable and ultimately needless problem of determining whether one's representation accurately refers to an item in the external world. This, for him, is also the problem at the core of the correspondence theory of truth. The correspondence theory of truth is implicated in representationalism. Some might want to say that correspondence need not be implicated in representationalism and point to its roots in Aristotle. Davidson usually has little to say about Aristotle, but in the posthumously published work *Truth and Predication,* anticipating just such a remark, he writes: "But Aristotle was no correspondence theorist." He explains that a "serious" correspondence theory requires a reference to facts, and that Aristotle "postulates no entities like facts."[31] In this specific sense, neither does twentieth-century phenomenology, nor Gadamer's hermeneutics, subscribe to a correspondence theory of truth.

Both Davidson and Gadamer make use of the analogy of perceptual perspectivism to discuss the question of truth and conceptual relativism, though the analogy does perhaps more work for Gadamer. Both endorse a kind of perspectivism—what Davidson calls a "harmless" relativism.[32] Attention to this analogy shows at least three things: (1) that the perspectives of any two individuals are inevitably different; (2) that, in principle, we can assume the spatial position of the other (though not at the same time); and (3) that we share a common world. Davidson writes that "there is at most one world."[33] Gadamer expresses this so: "Thus the world is the common ground, trodden by none and recognized by all, uniting all who talk to one another."[34] Commitment to a common world anchors Davidson's and Gadamer's realism (such as it is) and their rejection of stronger and harmful sorts of conceptual relativism. This, of course, distinguishes them from, among others, Nelson Goodman's many worlds and ways of world-making, and from Rorty, for whom the world is "well lost."[35]

4 Holism and Realism: Triangulation

For both Gadamer and Davidson, it is important to recognize the contextuality of language. Words do their work in relation to other words in a specific language. Apart from names, words and sentences do not have a one-to-one relation to things, nor, usually, to words and sentences in another language. A consideration of the philosophical significance of this leads Davidson, at one point, to endorse a coherentist or holist view of truth. Yet, at the same time, as I suggested above, he endorses a kind of realism. Davidson concludes what is perhaps his most cited essay, "On the Very Idea of a Conceptual Scheme," with the following two sentences:

> Of course truth of sentences remains relative to language, but that is as objective as can be. In giving up the dualism of scheme and world, we do not give up the world, but re-establish unmediated touch with the familiar objects whose antics make our sentences and opinions true or false.[36]

In short, sentences are relative to language, but the things of the world make our sentences true or false. Davidson talks about these factors in considering the question of truth and our relation to the world as "triangulation." The speaker and his or her sentences are importantly related both to a language and a speech community as well as to the things or states of affairs in the world about which he or she speaks.

In the introduction to his essay "A Coherence Theory of Truth and Knowledge," he writes: "In this paper I defend what may as well be called a coherence theory of truth and knowledge. The theory I defend is not in competition with a correspondence theory, but depends for its defense on an argument that purports to show that coherence yields correspondence."[37] Coherence has to yield correspondence, according to Davidson, because truth is a "primitive." Davidson makes clear that he is not proposing coherence as a way of defining truth. He rather makes sense of coherence and belief in terms of truth. As a primitive, truth means "correspondence to the way things are."[38] A coherence theory has to do justice to this "primitive." Coherence concerns the relativity of sentences to language, that is, holism; and correspondence concerns the relation of speech to the world, that is, realism. As I indicated above, many readers and critics responded that one cannot have it both ways. The correspondence theory (or theories) of truth is an alternative to the coherence theory (or theories). On the standard view, they are not compatible. The one does not and cannot yield the other.

Gadamer too would have it both ways. And I would suggest he proposes something very like Davidson's triangulation. Gadamer places language in the larger context of history and tradition. Any speech makes sense only in the context or horizon of the other speeches of the language historically made present to us in tradition. At the same time, Gadamer writes that language, with its history and tradition, provides an opening or perspective on the world. As we saw above, he writes that "in language . . . reality . . . becomes visible."[39]

Yet Gadamer does not propose a theory of truth, and he does not address the theories of truth of others. As I have mentioned above, *Truth and Method* is notorious for its lack of any discussion of truth. Any reader with a concern for a theory of truth comes away from Gadamer's principal work frustrated. One might observe, in this regard, that Gadamer's German philosophical context was quite unlike the Anglo-American philosophical community that Davidson addresses, in which epistemology was paramount. This is so. One might also observe that Gadamer's having it both ways is a legacy of Hegel for whom coherence yields correspondence. This is also so. But, more importantly, Gadamer's approach to the question of truth is much indebted to Heidegger, who declared in *Being and Time* that both realism and idealism are mistaken notions and that the philosophical debates about realism and idealism are a waste of time.[40] This debate arises from the Cartesian and representationalist assumptions that both parties to the debate share. Realism is naive and cannot give an adequate account of the linguistic, practical, and historical context of truth claims. And idealism is subjectivistic and abandons any claim on the way things are—which Davidson refers to as "the familiar objects whose antics make our sentences and opinions true or false."[41] Heidegger does more than reject these alternatives because of their shortcomings; he also shows how the shortcomings arise in their common presuppositions of representationalism. Gadamer moves forward in this phenomenological context, considers the case settled, and does not take up the questions of realism or idealism, correspondence or coherence. For Gadamer, too, truth is a "primitive," though he does not use this term. This is one way to understand why he has so little to say about truth, though it plays a central role in his account of interpretation.

Davidson, however, continues to consider various arguments and positions concerning truth and various theories of truth. He does so in consideration of the views of Dewey, Ramsey, Strawson, Dummett, Putnam, and Rorty, among others—the figures in relation to whom he develops his own views. But late in life he comes to reject both the coherence theory and the correspondence theory of truth. It might be said that he comes to agree with the objections that one can legitimately hold both theories as he had earlier claimed to do. But this late view does not so much focus on the incompatibility of the views as on the difficulties with each view. He had always oriented his view of truth on Tarski, and he continues to do so in the late work. He writes in *Truth and Predication* that earlier he had branded his and Tarski's view as realism because of the importance of independence of the external world from our beliefs.[42] He continues to hold to this notion but finds that the correspondence theory has great difficulty in explaining that to which sentences correspond. Putnam and Dummett come to stand for him for the alternatives of realism and antirealism. He finds fault with both positions and rejects them both. By way of summary he writes:

> I rejected deflationary views of truth. . . . We should not say that truth is correspondence, coherence, warranted assertability, ideally justified assertability, what is accepted in the conversation of the right people, what science will end up maintaining, what explains the convergence on final theories of science, or the success of our ordinary beliefs.[43]

These differing views of truth, according to Davidson, have all succumbed to what he calls "the epistemological virus."[44] This is, equivalently, representationalism. And though in this late period Davidson explicitly rejects realism as a theory, he continues to maintain the notion of triangulation. In "Could There Be a Science of Rationality?" (1995), he writes: "The meanings of our sentences are indeed dependent on our relations to the world which those sentences are about, and our linguistic interactions with others."[45] By moving away from both correspondence and coherence (the two views that over the years Davidson most seriously considered as candidates for an adequate theory of truth) as well as other Anglo-American alternatives, while yet maintaining "triangulation," Davidson finds even greater proximity to Gadamer, who is not subject to the epistemological virus and who defends none of the views of truth that Davidson lists above as poor candidates for a truth theory.

5 Davidson's Disagreements with Gadamer

Davidson's expressed disagreements with Gadamer are not as substantive or significant as his agreements. He devotes his essay on Gadamer almost entirely to a discussion of Plato's *Philebus*, a dialogue to which Gadamer has also given a good amount of attention. Davidson expresses his admiration for Gadamer's reading of the *Philebus* but suggests that Gadamer does not pay sufficient attention to the extraordinary character of the *Philebus* within Plato's corpus and within the development of Plato's thought.[46] Gadamer emphasizes the continuity of Plato's thought within the Platonic corpus and with Aristotle. For Gadamer, for example, the *Parmenides* shows that Plato does not hold a theory of the ideas that commits him to two worlds.[47] Davidson, like many other Plato scholars, rather sees a development in Plato's thought such that the later Plato in the *Parmenides* comes to see the inadequacy of his own earlier two-world view. Davidson suggests that a development view might fit better with Gadamer's own hermeneutical views about coming to an understanding through a willingness to change one's own ideas.[48] In addition, Davidson wants to show that, for the most part, Plato's dialogues are not good examples of the kind of the conversation and dialogue that Gadamer presents as essential to understanding. In his brief response, Gadamer acknowledges the different roles that Socrates plays in the dialogues but argues that these differences are "dramatological," not philosophically substantive.[49]

However much Davidson and Gadamer might agree and/or disagree about Plato, Davidson ties his discussion of Plato to Gadamer's views about dialogue, language, and truth, especially as found in *Truth and Method*. Among these, the most important are that thought depends on language and that language "has its true being only in conversation." Davidson acknowledges his agreement with this and finds Gadamer's views, in this regard, consonant with his own basic view of triangulation: "Coming to an agreement about an object and coming to understand each other's speech are not independent moments but part of the same interpersonal process of triangulating the world."[50]

Davidson expresses disagreement with Gadamer's proposition that "every conversation presupposes a common language, or, it creates a common language."[51] Davidson writes:

> I would not say a conversation presupposes a common language, nor even that it requires one. Understanding, to my mind, is always a matter not only of interpretation but of translation, since we can never assume we mean the same thing by our words that our partners in discussion mean. What is created in dialogue is not a common language but understanding; each partner comes to understand the other.[52]

Gadamer's brief reply to Davidson addresses only the Plato interpretation and not this stated disagreement. In *Truth and Method* Gadamer acknowledges the distinction of translation and interpretation, but he argues that, in the end, every translation is at the same time an interpretation since the interpreter must translate what is to be understood into the "context in which the other lives."[53] Gadamer argues further that in a conversation when one uses an interpreter (*Dolmetscher*), there are really two conversations going on—those between the interpreter and each of the speakers.

Gadamer claims that the gap between the original speech and the translation "can never be completely closed."[54] Elsewhere he acknowledges that in many contexts the gap is virtually closed but that in poetry, especially lyric poetry, the gap is inevitably large.

In the end, Gadamer would not deny what Davidson asserts, namely, that through translation an understanding can be achieved—and even that sometimes we might need to translate a speech in one's own language. "What is she talking about?" one might ask oneself or others of a speaker speaking one's own language. The difference between Gadamer and Davidson about this is not great. What difference there is comes from accentuating differently one of the two sides of Davidson's triangulation. Davidson sees Gadamer insisting on working out first a common language and then coming to an agreement (or disagreement) about the topic of conversation. Davidson objects that the language does not come first, but rather that "it is only in the presence of shared objects that understanding can come about."[55] Gadamer should not accept Davidson's characterization of his view here, for Gadamer would deny that language could be worked out "first" without reference to life in a world.[56] Neither side, language or world, is first. Davidson would agree.

6 A Gadamerian Critique of Davidson

As noted above (note 2), Gadamer's single reference to Davidson in his self-edited, ten-volume edition of his collected works is a late addition (1986) to a footnote in *Truth and Method*, which acknowledges that Davidson too has addressed the question of the significance of the difference between what is said and what is meant: "These problems have meanwhile been much disputed, in my view, on too narrowly semantic a basis. See Donald Davidson, *Inquiries into Truth and Interpretation*."[57] This brief comment points to an important difference between Gadamer and Davidson. Davidson is concerned with utterances and their truth-values. For Gadamer, following Heidegger, Davidson is concerned with the "truth of assertion" as opposed to the "truth of disclosure." For Gadamer and Heidegger, the truth of assertion is a derivative kind of truth—derivative from the truth of disclosure. The latter is experiential, practical, and pre- or proto-propositional.[58] From a Gadamerian perspective Davidson's concerns are too narrowly propositional, "too narrowly semantic." Davidson recognizes that ordinary speech (utterances) is often not in propositional form and he is concerned with ordinary speech. Nonetheless, he writes, for example:

> Success in communicating propositional contents—not just accidental or sporadic success, but more or less reliable success, achieved by employing devices capable of a wide range of expression—such success is what we need to understand before we ask about the nature of meaning or of language, for the concepts of a language or of meaning, like those of a sentence or a name or of reference or of truth, are concepts we can grasp and employ only when the communication of propositional contents is established.[59]

Gadamer does not anchor his project to the task of explaining the success of communicating propositional contents. His concern is explaining the event of understanding. He attempts to do so without taking a close look at linguistic usage. He paints with broad strokes the historical and linguistic character of the understanding.[60]

Davidson would never countenance talk of "being" in the way that Gadamer does in the concluding section of *Truth and Method*: "Someone who speaks is behaving speculatively when his words do not reflect beings but express a relation to the whole of being."[61] Though they have many of the same concerns, Gadamer would see himself concerned with something more fundamental and within a larger context than Davidson's concerns—what it is that the understanding *is*.

Gadamer's concerns are expressly ontological, Davidson's epistemological. In his regard, I would agree with David Hoy, who makes this same observation, and I would disagree with Jeff Malpas, who acknowledges that Davidson "makes use of the language of epistemology," but who asserts nonetheless that Davidson "ought to be viewed as properly ontological in much the same sense that the term is used by Heidegger and Gadamer."[62] In his response to Hoy's essay in the Library of Living Philosophers' volume, Gadamer expresses his reservations about making too much of the similarity of his own hermeneutics with Davidson's concept of radical interpretation. Gadamer there suggests by implication that he understands Davidson to be primarily concerned with science and epistemology.[63] As we have just seen, Davidson is concerned with finding a theory that can explain the success of communicating propositional contents. In addition, Davidson is a naturalist for whom perception is to be understood causally. Davidson is happy to talk about perception in terms of "stimuli" and "external promptings."[64] Here we see a difference between Davidson's views and those of Gadamer. Gadamer is clear about his rejection of naturalism. He has very little to say about perception, but it is clear that he accepts or is sympathetic with the phenomenological accounts of perception by Husserl and Merleau-Ponty. Such an account does not reject causality in the account of perception but it is not "brutely causal" in the way that Davidson's account is.[65]

Acknowledging these great differences and the limits of any comparison between Davidson and Gadamer should not keep us from recognizing what might be considered the "transcendental" character of both their projects. Both are concerned with explaining the conditions of understanding one another and understanding the world; in short, both are concerned with providing an account of understanding. However much Davidson is a naturalist, he is not content to simply defer the question until physioneurology and psycholinguistics can provide an adequate scientific account. Davidson distinguishes the empirical question from the philosophical question. Both are concerned philosophically with what must obtain for understanding to happen. Though Gadamer proceeds in a descriptive way and avoids the Kantian language of "the necessary conditions of possibility," he is happy to use the language of "constitution"[66] and "must"—what we must take to be the case. For example, "hermeneutical experience *must* take everything that becomes present to it as a genuine experience."[67] Gadamer is laying out what he takes to be the constitutive aspects of, or necessary conditions for, understanding. Similarly, Davidson presents his work as taking something that we know to be the case and asking "the philosophical question . . . what makes it possible?"[68] And, though Gadamer's project is ontological in the sense that he is concerned with what understanding is, he does not address the question of being as such but rather the being of understanding. Both Gadamer and Davidson are concerned with answering the question of what makes understanding possible; the answer to the question is a sketch of the necessary conditions for understanding. In this sense, both projects are transcendental.

Among these conditions importantly and controversially for Gadamer is its historical situatedness, a condition that Gadamer, for the most part, addresses through the concept of tradition. We find ourselves in a world that is not of our own making—a world that is natural and cultural.[69] We find ourselves speaking a language that has been given us and has a history. Constitutive of our cultural world are sets of practices to which our language is closely wedded. Our world and our language, of course, also have a present and a future—a present and a future to which we contribute.

Tradition is not an important concept for Davidson, but he does consider what he calls the "social aspects of language": "verbal behavior is necessarily social."[70] He often speaks about such behavior in terms of "practices." When Davidson uses the term "practice," he usually is referring to linguistic conventions, not to "ways of life" or human institutions. In fact he makes explicit reference to "ways of life" as "non-linguistic institutions."[71] For Gadamer, it does not make sense to talk about nonlinguistic institutions. Language is interwoven into the very heart of human institutions. Thus Davidson is happy to consider language apart from its historical and social context. He talks much about "practices," but in this context by "practices" he means linguistic conventions. He acknowledges that these are historical and social, but he analyzes these as independent from "ways of life" or "non-linguistic institutions." If pressed, Davidson perhaps would acknowledge the embeddedness of language in human practices and tradition, but Davidson does not make much of it in his account. Rather, Davidson is keen on insisting on the importance of recognizing the sometimes idiosyncratic use of language by the individual. He sometimes and revealingly talks about linguistic conventions, that is, shared linguistic practices, in terms of conformity.[72] He claims that "there is no fundamental reason why practices must be shared."[73] He draws the conclusion: "The theoretical possibility of communication without shared practices remains philosophically important because it shows that such sharing cannot be an essential constituent in meaning and communication."[74]

Though Gadamer recognizes that, in a certain sense, "everyone has his own language," he would deny that "sharing" is inessential to meaning and communication.[75] This question is too large and complex a theme in Gadamer to address adequately here, but Gadamer's account of language and our conversation with one another provides for both an I-we aspect and an I-you (or "thou"). The language that *we* speak is a "we" moment. But when *I* address *you* in conversation (or, *you* address *me*), we are separate, distinct, and different—an *I-Thou* moment. It's more complicated if we speak different languages, but if there is communication, we find a way to translate—which Gadamer talks about (perhaps too loosely) as finding a common language. Though language itself places us within a language community, a *we*, this does not mean that solidarity with others is simply given. Solidarity is something that must be achieved. The contrast between Gadamer's sought-for solidarity and Davidson's feared conformity opens for us importantly different directions in their thought.

Gadamer has often been criticized for valorizing the *we* at the cost of the *you*, for talking too easily about agreement, for insufficiently appreciating the "otherness of the other."[76] Gadamer's later work is sensitive to this critique, and though he does not change his position, he strives to show how his account of the understanding—an account that makes agreement the aim—recognizes how different the other and his or her cultural context may be and how difficult it may be to come to any kind of understanding.

Gadamer continues to insist that these differences may be transcended but only with the hermeneutical virtues of patient listening, the willingness to be corrected, and an openness to the otherness of the other. The key for Gadamer, as it is for Davidson, is that in any such conversation we are not merely trying to understand the other but trying to understand what it is that the other is trying to say to us—what the conversation is about. The subject matter of the conversation brings us before the common world that we share. It is this very appreciation of the possibly deep cultural differences between speakers that leads Gadamer sometimes, not often, to use the language of the plurality of worlds in the sense of cultural worlds. For this reason, Charles Taylor praises Gadamer and explicitly contrasts Gadamer with Davidson, whose work does not pay sufficient attention to cultural difference and how understanding in such contexts might be achieved. Taylor accepts Davidson's argument against conceptual schemes, but finds it "in this real-life situation . . . less useful."[77] From a Gadamerian perspective, the narrow semantic approach of Davidson does not sufficiently appreciate the density of such sets of wedded practice and language, that is, tradition.

7 Conclusion

Following Davidson's metaphor with which this essay begins, we might say that Davidson and Gadamer live in the same neighborhood, but they are only neighbors. They do not reside at the same address. There are real limits to the fruitfulness of any comparison of their work. They come to their agreements about interpretation by very different routes. Neither thinker influenced the other. Their coming to proximity is not the result of a conversation, however construed. One might be tempted to say that their accord is not philosophically interesting. Yes, they agree about certain propositions concerning interpretation, but when one asks them for their reasons for holding the propositions, they give what appear to be different answers. It is with these answers that things begin to get philosophically interesting. Thus, their agreements, such as they are, are not philosophically very interesting. They appear to be circumstantial. But, as I have argued above, their arguments on behalf of their views about interpretation are not as different as it might appear. Most importantly, both are reacting against what might be called the modern epistemological paradigm of representationalism. Their primary arguments against representationalism are quite similar. Both would eliminate the scheme–content distinct for much the same reasons. Both would return us to our common shared world in which it is important to distinguish, with however much difficulty (especially in the context of cultural difference), what is true from what is false.

These shared philosophical concerns are not peripheral or secondary to their work. They are at the center. If we recognize this, then we do find it remarkable that these two important thinkers from such different philosophical milieus came to find themselves in the same neighborhood. It suggests that there is a kind of proximity of the philosophical problematic of the so-called continental and Anglo-American modes of doing philosophy. This proximity may be located in Kant and the neo-Kantianism that prevailed at the beginning of the twentieth century both in Germany and in Britain. This proximity is the legacy of representationalism. Davidson and Gadamer have importantly helped us see how this modern epistemological paradigm might be overcome. At the same time, these neighbors also show us how we might see through the sometimes dogmatic differences between twentieth-century "continental" thought and Anglo-American "analytical" philosophy, and how these two tendencies in contemporary philosophy might be neighborly.

Notes

1. Donald Davidson, "Gadamer and Plato's *Philebus*," in *The Philosophy of Hans-Georg Gadamer*, ed. Lewis Hahn, The Library of Living Philosophers vol. 24 (Chicago: Open Court, 1997), p. 421. Gadamer acknowledges their neighborliness in his "Reply to Donald Davidson," with the opening remark that "what characterizes both our scholarly paths is no more nor less than a mutual overtaking of each other"(p. 433).

Others have commented on parallels between Davidson and Gadamer. See David Hoy, "Post-Cartesian Interpretation: Hans-Georg Gadamer and Donald Davidson," in Hahn (ed.), *The Philosophy of Hans-Georg Gadamer*, pp. 111–128. There are three essays that comment on Gadamer and Davidson in *Gadamer's Century: Essays in Honor of Hans-Georg Gadamer*, ed. Jeff Malpas, Ulrich Arnswald, and Jens Kertscher (Cambridge, MA: MIT Press, 2002): Jeff Malpas, "Gadamer, Davidson, and the Ground of Understanding," pp. 195–216; Charles Taylor, "Understanding the Other: A Gadamerian View on Conceptual Schemes," pp. 279–298; and John McDowell, "Gadamer and Davidson on Understanding and Relativism," pp. 173–194.

2. Only once in his collected works does Gadamer cite or refer to Davidson. In 1986 in the republication of *Truth and Method* (originally published in 1960) as the first volume of his collected works (*Gesammelte Werke*, 10 vols.) Gadamer made a very few text changes and a few additions to the footnotes. The additions to the footnotes are indicated by brackets both in the German and revised English editions. In a footnote that concerns the agreement in understanding, Gadamer adds a reference to

Davidson's *Inquiries into Truth and Interpretation* with the comment that "these problems have meanwhile been much disputed, in my view, on too narrowly semantic a basis." *Truth and Method*, 2nd rev. ed., trans. revised by Joel Weinsheimer and Donald G. Marshall (New York: Continuum, 1999), p. 295; for the German see *Gesammelte Werke* 1 (Tübingen: J. C. B. Mohr, 1990), p. 300. In his "Reply" to Davidson (1997), Gadamer makes reference to a "conversation during many decades," which "should have led to a real proximity between us." But this "conversation" seems to be a reference to Davidson's "returning to my later works again and again"—that is, to Davidson reading Gadamer, not Gadamer reading Davidson. Gadamer follows this remark about the expectation of proximity with a comment about how "astonishing . . . the great distance and the differences with respect to the treatment of the same topic" (p. 433). The "same topic" here is Plato. I find it surprising that Gadamer finds their differences astonishing. Davidson tells us he learned little from Gadamer and that for his Plato interpretation Vlastos was the most important influence. There is no evidence here or elsewhere that Davidson returned "to my [Gadamer's] works again and again." On the contrary, Davidson suggests he arrived in Gadamer's neighborhood by a route quite independent of Gadamer.

3. Davidson, "Gadamer and Plato's *Philebus*," p. 422. He learned little, in part, because he was so unfamiliar with "the Heideggerian background of his ideas." Davidson wrote his dissertation at Harvard under the direction of Werner Jaeger. One of Gadamer's first publications (1927) was an essay criticizing Jaeger's treatment of the development of Aristotle's thought, "Der aristotelische 'Protreptikos' und die entwicklungsgeschichtliche Betrachtung der aristotelischen Ethik," *Gesammelte Werke* 5, pp. 164–186. David Hoy is largely, but not entirely, right, then, when he writes that "there is no historical connection between Gadamer and Davidson," in "Post-Cartesian Interpretation," p. 112.

4. "Gadamer and Plato's *Philebus*," p. 431. Davidson cites the first edition of the English translation of *Truth and Method*, p. 350. The citation can be found in the second and improved edition, p. 389. Joel Weinsheimer and Donald G. Marshall revised the translation (New York: Continuum, 1989). For the German, see Gadamer, *Gesammelte Werke* 1, p. 392.

5. Gadamer, *Truth and Method*, p. 491.

6. Donald Davidson, "Radical Interpretation," in *Inquiries into Truth and Interpretation* (Oxford: Clarendon Press, 1984), p. 128.

7. Donald Davidson, "A Nice Derangement of Epitaphs," in *Truth, Language, and History* (Oxford: Clarendon Press, 2005), pp. 89–108. In this essay Davidson argues that for interpretation we need a machine-like theoretical system of interpretation for the literal meaning. But over and above this we need what he calls a "passing theory" to account for the creative and idiosyncratic usage of language. A passing theory, he tells us, "is derived by wit, luck, and wisdom . . . rules of thumb," and so on (p. 107).

Gadamer would liken this to Aristotelian prudence (*phronesis*), a fundamental aspect of Gadamer's account of interpretation.

8. Donald Davidson, "On the Very Idea of a Conceptual Scheme," in *Inquiries into Truth and Interpretation*, p. 197.

9. Gadamer, *Truth and Method*, p. 446. This notion of a background agreement and the intent of any conversation to come to an explicit agreement or common understanding (*Einverständnis*) emerged as a central theme of contention in Gadamer's exchange with Derrida. See their exchange in *Dialogue and Deconstruction: The Gadamer-Derrida Encounter*, ed. Diane P. Michelfelder and Richard E. Palmer (Albany: SUNY Press, 1989), pp. 21–71.

10. Davidson, "On the Very Idea of a Conceptual Scheme," p. 197.

11. Gadamer, "Text and Interpretation," in Michelfelder and Palmer (ed.), *Dialogue and Deconstruction*, p. 33.

12. Gadamer, "Reflections on My Philosophical Journey," in Hahn (ed.), *The Philosophy of Hans-Georg Gadamer*, p. 36.

13. See my "The World Never Lost: The Hermeneutics of Trust," *Philosophy and Phenomenological Research* 47 (March 1987): 413–434. See also my "Philosophical Discourse and the Ethics of Hermeneutics," in *Festivals of Interpretation*, ed. Kathleen Wright (Albany: SUNY Press, 1990), pp. 63–88. Gadamer never refers to his hermeneutics in this way, though he does contrast his own hermeneutics with a hermeneutics of suspicion—a phrase he borrows from Paul Ricoeur. See Gadamer, "The Hermeneutics of Suspicion," *Man and World* 17 (1984): 313–323. This essay can also be found in *Hermeneutics: Questions and Prospects*, ed. G. Shapiro and A. Sica (Amherst: University of Massachusetts Press, 1984), pp. 54–65.

14. Gadamer, *Truth and Method*, p. 389.

15. Ibid., p. 474.

16. For Davidson, see his "On the Very Idea of a Conceptual Scheme," in *Inquiries into Truth and Interpretation*, pp. 183–198. This was first published in the *Proceedings of the American Philosophical Association* 47 (1974). For Gadamer, see his discussion of the concept of a worldview in *Truth and Method*, pp. 439–444, where he discusses Humboldt's notion of a worldview (*Weltanschauung*) or a world-picture (*Welt-Bild*). Gadamer's discussion owes much to the phenomenology of Husserl and the early Heidegger and to Heidegger's lecture from 1936, "Die Zeit des Weltbildes," in *Holzwege* (Frankfurt: Vittorio Klostermann, 1950), pp. 69–104. Davidson's discussion is largely, but not solely, a response to Quine.

17. In the introduction to the *Inquiries* volume, Davidson writes: "The argument against conceptual relativism shows rather that language is not a screen or filter through which our knowledge of the world must pass" (p. xviii). The argument that

he is referring to is presented in "On the Very Idea of a Conceptual Scheme," in which he writes: "Alternatively, there is the idea that *any* language distorts reality which implies that it is only wordlessly if at all that the mind comes to grips with things as they really are. This is to conceive language as an inert (though necessarily distorting) medium independent of the human agencies that employ it; a view of language that surely cannot be maintained" (p. 185). Similarly, for Gadamer, language is not a barrier but an opening or a bridge.

18. Davidson, "The Myth of the Subjective," in *Subjective, Intersubjective, Objective* (Oxford: Clarendon Press, 2001), p. 43. In this essay Davidson describes modern philosophy much as I have here. In the same essay Davidson writes: "To a large extent this picture of mind and its place in nature has defined the problems modern philosophy has thought it had to solve" (p. 41).

19. Davidson, "The Myth of the Subjective," in *Subjective, Intersubjective, Objective*, p. 46.

20. Ibid., p. 39: "This dualism [between subjectivity and objectivity], though in its way too obvious to question, carries with it in our tradition a large, and not necessarily appropriate, burden of associated ideas. Some of these ideas are now coming under critical scrutiny and the result promises to mark a sea change in contemporary philosophical thought—a change so profound that we may not recognize that it is occurring." Further on in the same essay (p. 47) he writes: "Familiarity with many of the points I have been making is fairly widespread among philosophers today. But only a few among these philosophers, as far as I know, have appreciated the scope of the entailed revolution in our ways of thinking about philosophy."

21. Ibid., p. 46.

22. Davidson, "On the Very Idea of a Conceptual Scheme," p. 198.

23. Gadamer, *Truth and Method*, p. 447.

24. Ibid., p. 449.

25. Heidegger was critical of Gadamer for his usage of "consciousness." He considered talk of "consciousness," like that of Husserl, to have made only a partial break with the Cartesian subject–object paradigm.

26. This lecture was first published in *Kleine Schriften* I (Tübingen: J. C. B. Mohr, 1967), pp. 69–81. It has been republished in *Gesammelte Werke* II, pp. 66–76. For the English, see *Philosophical Hermeneutics*, trans. David E. Linge (Berkeley: University of California Press, 1977), pp. 69–81.

27. Davidson, "Gadamer and Plato's *Philebus*," p. 431.

28. Gadamer, *Truth and Method*, p. 379.

29. Davidson, "The Myth of the Subjective," p. 47.

30. Gadamer, *Truth and Method*, p. 473.

31. Davidson, *Truth and Predication* (Cambridge, MA: Harvard University Press, 2005), pp. 126–127.

32. "Each of us has one's own position in the world, and hence one's own perspective on it. It is easy to slide from this truism to some confused notion of conceptual relativism. The former, harmless, relativism is just the familiar relativism of position in space and time. Because each of us preempts a volume of space-time, two of us cannot be in exactly the same place at the same time. The relations among our positions are intelligible because we can locate each person in a single, common world and shared time frame." Davidson, "The Myth of the Subjective," p. 39. Compare Gadamer, *Truth and Method*, pp. 446–448, where he refers the reader to Husserl's phenomenological account of the perspectivism of experience.

33. "On the Very Idea of a Conceptual Scheme," p. 187.

34. Gadamer, *Truth and Method*, p. 446.

35. Richard Rorty, "The World Well Lost," in his *Consequences of Pragmatism* (Minneapolis: University of Minnesota Press, 1982), p. 16. Rorty is citing Goodman, who in *The Ways of Worldmaking* (Indianapolis: Hackett Press, 1978) writes that the notion of the same world is "a world not worth fighting for or against" (p. 20); such a world "is perhaps on the whole a world well lost" (p. 4). See my "The World Never Lost."

36. Davidson, *Inquiries into Truth and Interpretation*, p. 198.

37. Davidson, "A Coherence Theory of Truth and Knowledge," in *Subjective, Intersubjective, Objective*, p. 137. This paper was first published in 1983.

38. Ibid., p. 139.

39. Gadamer, *Truth and Method*, p. 449.

40. For a discussion of Gadamer's concept of truth and his debt to Heidegger, see my "The Experience of Truth for Gadamer and Heidegger: Taking Time and Sudden Lightning," in *Hermeneutics and Truth*, ed. Brice Wachterhauser (Evanston: Northwestern University Press, 1994), pp. 47–67. For Heidegger's comments about the realism–idealism debate, see *Being and Time*, trans. John Macquarie and Edward Robinson (New York: Harper & Row, 1962), §43.

41. Davidson, *Inquiries into Truth and Interpretation*, p. 198.

42. Davidson, *Truth and Predication*, p. 41.

43. Ibid., pp. 47–48. This posthumously published book represents Davidson's recasting of the Dewey lectures of 1989 (published in 1990) and the Hermes lectures at the University of Perugia in 2001.

44. Ibid., p. 33.

45. Donald Davidson, "Could There Be a Science of Rationality?" in his *Problems of Rationality* (Oxford: Clarendon Press, 2004), p. 134. In the same volume, in "What Thought Requires," he writes explicitly about triangulation and what must be the case for it to "work" (p. 148).

46. For Gadamer's interpretation of the *Philebus* see especially his habilitation from 1931, *Plato's Dialectical Ethics*, trans. Robert Wallace (New Haven: Yale University Press, 1991), and *The Idea of the Good in Platonic-Aristotelian Philosophy*, trans. P. Christopher Smith (New Haven: Yale University Press, 1986).

47. "Reply to Nicholas P. White," in *Platonic Writings/Platonic Readings*, ed. Charles L. Griswold (London: Routledge, 1988), p. 260; in German, *Gesammelte Werke* 7, p. 331.

48. "I think a Platonic dialectic seen as more open to serious revision would cohabit more happily with Gadamer's own conception of dialogue and conversation." Davidson, "Gadamer and Plato's *Philebus*," p. 430.

49. Ibid., p. 434.

50. Ibid., p. 432.

51. Gadamer, *Truth and Method*, p. 378.

52. Davidson, "Gadamer and Plato's Philebus," pp. 431–432.

53. Gadamer, *Truth and Method*, p. 384.

54. Ibid.

55. Davidson, "Gadamer and Plato's Philebus," p. 432.

56. But, as I have pointed out, Gadamer does not address Davidson's comments about this.

57. Gadamer, *Truth and Method*, p. 295.

58. I am assuming an accord between Gadamer and Heidegger here and disagree with Hubert Dreyfus who claims that Heidegger is a practical holist and Gadamer a theoretical holist. See H. Dreyfus, "Holism and Hermeneutics," *Review of Metaphysics* 34 (September 1980): 3–23.

59. Davidson, "The Social Aspect of Language," in *The Philosophy of Michael Dummett*, ed. Brian McGuinness and Gianluigi Oliveri (Dordrecht: Kluwer, 1994), p. 11.

60. Though this difference between a close "analytical" look and broad "phenomenological" strokes often is characteristic of the difference between analytic and continental philosophy, this is not necessarily always so. Some phenomenologists have objected to the very broad strokes of Gadamer's account.

61. Gadamer, *Truth and Method*, p. 469.

62. See Hoy, "Post-Cartesian Interpretation." For Malpas's claim, see "Gadamer, Davidson, and the Ground of Understanding," in *Gadamer's Century*, p. 207.

63. "I would also say that what has been presented under the concept of the 'radical interpretation' corresponds precisely to what I . . . regard as a self-evident presupposition for every attempt at understanding. At this point, however, I have certain reservations concerning a further elaboration of the investigation of the relations between Davidson's efforts and my own. . . . But what is fundamentally at issue is not primarily science and epistemology but, to speak with Mr. Hoy, the 'ontology' of life communicating itself through language." Gadamer, response to Hoy, in Hahn (ed.), *The Philosophy of Hans-Georg Gadamer*, p. 129. It should also be added that there is little evidence that Gadamer knew Davidson's work very well.

64. See, for example, Davidson, "What Thought Requires," in *Problems of Rationality*, pp. 135–149.

65. John McDowell calls the way Davidson conceives of the impact of the world on thought "brutely causal." McDowell says that this is "out of line with Davidson's best thinking." See McDowell, "Gadamer and Davidson on Understanding and Relativism," in Malpas, Arnswald, and Kertscher (ed.), *Gadamer's Century*, p. 178.

66. For example, Gadamer, *Truth and Method*, p. 463.

67. Ibid.; emphasis added.

68. Davidson, *Truth and Predication*, p. 74.

69. To use Heideggerian language, we have an *Umwelt* (environment) and a *Mitwelt* (a world shared with others).

70. See his "The Social Aspect of Language," p. 5.

71. Ibid., p. 10.

72. Ibid.

73. Ibid., p. 16.

74. Ibid., p. 10. Davidson argues from examples of names, malapropisms, and idiolects.

75. Gadamer, "What Is Truth?" in Wachterhauser (ed.), *Hermeneutics and Truth*, pp. 45–46.

76. The critique of the "left" in Germany in the 1960s saw Gadamer as a kind of right-wing Hegelian, endorsing a traditional, conservative we, the status quo. The Levinasians would insist on the ultimately resistant otherness of the other. Some feminists present a similar critique. See, e.g., Marie Fleming, "Gadamer's Conversation: Does the Other Have a Say?" in *Feminist Interpretations of Hans-Georg Gadamer*,

ed. Lorraine Code (University Park: Pennsylvania State University Press, 2003), pp. 109–132.

77. It is less useful, he says, "because it seems to discredit the idea of 'conceptual schemes' altogether—this in spite of the fact that the argument only rules out our meeting a totally unintelligible one." Charles Taylor, "Understanding the Other: A Gadamerian View of Conceptual Schemes," in Malpas, Arnswald, and Kertscher (eds.), *Gadamer's Century*, p. 291. Taylor makes the same point in his essay, "Foundationalism and the Inner-Outer Distinction," in *Reading McDowell: On Mind and World*, ed. Nicholas H. Smith (London: Routledge, 2002), pp. 106–119.

11 The Relevance of Radical Interpretation to the Understanding of Mind

Jonathan Ellis

There is an interesting parallel to be drawn between the method of Davidson's philosophy and what Davidson's philosophy is about or purports to show. Throughout his writings, considerations of language and interpretation are what consistently and ultimately yield his varied and bold views on the mental. Perhaps the most central of those views—and here is the parallel—is that mental states, or thought in general, emerge only in the context of communication and interpretation. The mind is born of interpretation, or language, as Davidson's own philosophy of mind is born of his philosophy of language.

Drawing the parallel reveals what I think is a persistent bias in Davidson's work. Asking for the source of that parallel can lead one on a journey through Davidson's assorted writings in pursuit of the origin, and thus foundation, of those views of the mental that appear to spring so directly from his remarks on interpretation. What that inquiry reveals, what the parallel calls attention to, is a consistent confidence on Davidson's part in the primacy and possibility of interpretation of the mental. An appreciation of the dependence of Davidson's arguments on a prior view about interpretation is important. Many philosophers would not endorse such a view, which is perhaps one reason that exploring interpretation continues to be an uncommon approach for investigations into the nature of the mind. The very relevance of interpretation for understanding the nature of the mind—or at least the deep relevance Davidson sees in it—turns on a prior and controversial view.

What is that view, and is it supported by Davidson's work? That is the focus of this essay. When we look carefully at Davidson's body of work, explicit justification or explanation for the view we will identify is difficult to find. Moreover, the little justification to be found appeals itself to interpretation, an appeal that we will see depends on the very view about interpretation in question. Much of Davidson's philosophy depends on—starts with—a view of the mind that is unsupported by anything Davidson says about interpretation, or about anything else. Our investigation will not suggest that this view is incorrect (nor will it suggest that it is correct). But it will raise interesting questions about the force of Davidson's arguments and, more generally, about the starting point in Davidsonian philosophy.

1 Davidson's Theory of Belief

Many of the substantial conclusions Davidson draws about the nature of mental phenomena (for him, the propositional attitudes) emerge largely through discussions of belief in particular. And invariably, his method is to "adopt the stance of a radical interpreter when asking about the nature of belief."[1] Two such conclusions are his anomalous monism and his claim that thought is possible only for creatures in communication with others. What leads Davidson to proclaim his principle of the anomalism of the mental and, in turn, to establish anomalous monism is the purported fact that the correct attribution of beliefs requires sensitivity to normative principles of coherency and rationality, which he infers from the constraints on a successful radical interpreter.[2] His conclusion that thought is possible only for creatures in communication with others stems from other, related constraints on the radical interpreter. If a radical interpreter is to be successful, he argues, she must take her subject's beliefs often to be about those objects and events that she thinks cause those beliefs. One's beliefs, Davidson ultimately concludes, are in the most basic cases about precisely those objects and events in one's environment that cause those beliefs. For any belief, however, there are many events that play a causal role in its coming to be. What determines which of those many causes is the content of the belief, according to Davidson, is a process of triangulation involving interpreter(s) and subject.[3]

Although there is no one article in which he details all aspects of his conception of belief (a nonrepresentational and, as he calls it, "antisubjectivist" view[4]), a detailed composite can be put together from the wide variety of his articles that concern belief in one way or another.[5] According to Davidson, we are no longer to think of beliefs either as entities or as involving objects—propositions, representations, sense data—that the mind somehow contemplates or "grasps."[6] That is an old and pernicious picture of the mind, what he calls "the myth of the subjective,"[7] which we are to abandon at once. Rather, we are advised to think of beliefs as "constructs"[8] of our own theories of interpretation and action. Beliefs have "jobs"[9] to perform in the interpretation and understanding of the behavior of others (and ourselves) and are thus "built"[10] by us to fulfill such roles. Beliefs, as he says, are then "best understood in their role of rationalizing choices or preferences."[11]

Since an important condition of successful interpretation is that the subject be rendered rational (according to the interpreter), an essential feature of belief is that its attribution always be held to normative constraints of rationality and consistency with respect to the totality of one's actions and utterances. For Davidson, any set of beliefs must largely abide by such normative principles. To the extent that there exists more than one theory about a person's set of beliefs that optimize his rationality, that is, to the extent that a number of theories explain his behavior equally well, it is an indeterminate matter as to which theory is correct about his beliefs. It is not that the evidence is insufficient to tell which theory is right—it is not epistemological in that sense—but rather that each of those theories, while attributing different beliefs to the person, simply captures everything of relevance there is to capture.[12] The propositions we might use to express the objects of particular beliefs, Davidson suggests, might thus be "overdesigned"[13] for their jobs. That beliefs are always as unique and fine, as our ways of describing and attributing them might suggest, is a false thought, and one only further encouraged by the view that beliefs have propositions as their objects.[14]

According to Davidson, then, beliefs are primarily to be construed as elements or "constructs" of a third-person explanation of behavior. That is not to say that we do not really have beliefs; we do. Having been built in the context of interpretation, the created predicates, Davidson believes, are then objectively true or false of us. What have been constructed are predicates that capture aspects of the complicated structure of one's behavior and dispositions to behavior. That is why, like meaning, belief is public, open to view, and, in principle, entirely interpretable. Some philosophers thus attribute to Davidson "constitutive interpretationism," according to which a statement of what it is for *S* to believe that *p* makes essential reference to the idea of *S*'s being interpretable as believing that *p*.[15] On another formulation of constitutive interpretationism, *S*'s believing that *p* "consists in" or is "nothing more than" *S*'s being such that *S* is *interpretable* as believing that *p*. Constitutive interpretationism is stronger than the claim, also attributed to Davidson, that *S* believes that *p* if and only if *S* is interpretable as believing that *p*.

The public nature of belief can also be seen in part from the fact that what in the most basic cases determines the contents of our beliefs are, for Davidson, the objects and events that actually cause those beliefs.[16] Those are what the beliefs they effect are *about*. An interpreter who had complete knowledge of all of a subject's potential behavior and the circumstances under which it occurred would be in the position to know everything a speaker believes.[17] Belief is thus no longer "subjective" or private in the way it is sometimes thought to be; but rather "as a private attitude it is not intelligible except as an adjustment to the public norm provided by language."[18] Not only is belief public in this epistemological sense concerning the fully informed interpreter, but there is even the further conclusion, mentioned above, that belief in general is only possible for creatures already engaged in communication; thought emerges only in the context of interpretation, and it is thus essentially social.

Such a conception of belief stands in contrast to more traditional or "Cartesian" conceptions of the mind, according to which beliefs are "internal" entities or involve mental objects or representations the mind grasps. For those who view belief in this way, whether a subject has a given belief will seem quite a determinate matter of fact. And although it may turn out that often the set of one's beliefs does satisfy normative ideals of rationality and consistency, that it does is not always, on such accounts, an essential mark of the mental. Nor on such conceptions is the mental typically thought to be essentially interpretable, or entirely "public." There is rarely reason on such models to suppose that one's having a belief presupposes one's being in communication with others. Far from being essentially social, belief often seems essentially individual. And far from being essentially public, it often seems essentially private.

It is worth emphasizing that Davidson's picture of belief is not only what grounds his influential claims in the philosophy of mind (e.g., concerning anomalous monism and the social character of thought), it is also what fuels many of his most provocative and ambitious claims in epistemology. We are to avoid skepticism of the senses, we are told, once we realize that the contents of beliefs are in general what cause those beliefs.[19] Knowledge of other minds is also easily secured given that thought is essentially social. Abandoning the idea of objects of the mind is helpful for a number of reasons. Besides ridding us of a number of traditional worries concerning representation (such as how such objects represent, what it is they represent, and how the mind relates to those representations), discarding that view is what Davidson believes allows an externalist such as himself to maintain first-person authority.[20] Additionally, he claims that that picture of the mind is the source of the "deep mistake" we have long made in distinguishing scheme and content.[21]

Davidson's conception of belief is thus one reason his philosophy has such breadth. However, I am interested not in these larger conclusions but in Davidson's conception of belief itself, and in particular, in his appeal to radical interpretation in support of this conception. It is not clear precisely how this appeal is to work. The formidable consequences Davidson hopes to attain from his conception of belief only make such an inquiry all the more worthwhile.

2 Radical Interpretation

As I have said, Davidson portrays many aspects of his conception of belief as ultimately stemming from considerations about radical interpretation. It will be helpful, then, to begin with a description of the situation of radical interpretation and some of the initial conclusions Davidson draws from it. She who finds herself in the situation of radical interpretation is faced with the task of forming a theory of interpretation for a given speaker (or speakers)—a theory of what that speaker means by his utterances—without knowing anything at all to begin with about what that speaker means. Neither, though, is the interpreter able to make use of evidence involving the speaker's beliefs or intentions, for, as Davidson is apt to point out, she could not have evidence of these without already having a working theory of her speaker's meanings. This is because of the crucial connection between meaning and belief: To be justified in attributing certain meanings to a speaker we must know something about what he believes and intends, and to be justified in attributing certain beliefs and intentions to him, we must know something about what he means by his words. This insight we see put to use in a number of ways in Davidson's philosophy. Not only has the task of the interpreter expanded—now she must simultaneously find a theory of belief (and desire and intention) as well as a theory of interpretation—but her evidential base has become more stark. All she has to go on are the speaker's actual utterances and the circumstances under which they are uttered.

Davidson takes it for granted that in addition to her speaker's actual utterances and the circumstances under which they are uttered, an interpreter would also be able to detect when her speaker holds particular utterances or sentences to be true. The difficulty, however, is that one holds a sentence to be true both because of what one means by it and because of what one believes. Davidson calls the attitude of holding true a "vector" of meaning and belief, neither of which our interpreter knows at this point. Suppose, for example, that the interpreter detects that her speaker holds the utterance "Gavagai" to be true in all and only those circumstances in which the interpreter sees a rabbit passing in front of the speaker. Without reason to think that in these circumstances the speaker *himself* believes that there is a rabbit in the vicinity, there is little reason to think that "Gavagai" for him has anything at all to do with rabbits. But at this juncture a radical interpreter does not know anything about her speaker's beliefs. Disentangling the effects of meaning and belief becomes a central task of the interpreter.

From Frank Ramsey's method in decision theory, Davidson adopts the idea that in order to disentangle these effects, our interpreter must find a legitimate way to hold one of the two factors fixed while solving for the other.[22] That way is at hand, Davidson believes, once we see that an interpreter is justified in assuming that most of some central core of her speaker's beliefs are in agreement with her own. What justifies such an assumption is the fact that disagreement, and the identification of belief in general, are possible only against a background of massive agreement. Appealing to Quine, Davidson writes, "Quine's key idea is that the correct interpretation of an agent by another cannot intelligibly admit certain kinds and degrees of difference between interpreter and interpreted with respect to belief."[23] Such agreement encompasses not only the beliefs themselves but the principles of rationality and logic that connect and ground those beliefs. Without assuming that her speaker's beliefs adhere to a similar rational structure as her own, there would be nothing to guide her construction of her theory. The strategy of interpretation, then, is to assume, until proven wrong, that the speaker believes (and reasons) as the interpreter does. Although that assumption might be wrong, assuming agreement is at least always a good strategy. For if such agreement is not generally there, interpretation was doomed from the start, according to Davidson. Such agreement is thus both a finding of and a requirement for successful interpretation.

The interpreter can now justifiably begin to correlate sentences that her speaker holds true on certain occasions with that which is going on in the environment at those times. By looking at what in the environment the interpreter believes is systematically causing her speaker to hold such sentences true, the interpreter can begin to determine what her subject means by his words. For the interpreter can now assume that what she herself believes is going on in the environment at those times is just what her speaker believes is going on. Successful interpreters, according to Davidson, must thus generally take their subject's most basic utterances and beliefs to be about just those things in the world that cause those utterances and beliefs. Once the interpreter has a handle on those of her speaker's utterances that concern the more observable goings-on in the environment, she can then proceed to attempt to determine, by way of that which she has already learned, the meanings of those utterances that are not as directly tied to the observable environment.

The central role of belief, though, has not yet emerged. For belief has little role when speaker and interpreter are in agreement; the assumption of agreement is helpful precisely because it takes belief *out* of the picture. The interpreter's assumption of agreement, however, will at some point render the speaker's behavior quite irrational, as there is bound to be considerable disagreement between them. For Davidson, the central role of belief is to render this behavior rational. And to do that, the interpreter attributes error to the speaker. As Davidson says, "Error is what gives belief its point." And later:

> Since the attitude of holding true is the same, whether the sentence is true or not, it corresponds directly to belief. The concept of belief thus stands ready to take up the slack between objective truth and the held true, and we come to understand it just in this connection.[24]

It is helpful here to understand "the objective truth" as referring to what the interpreter *considers* to be the objective truth, that is, as referring to what the interpreter believes. Belief comes in when the interpreter cannot preserve full rationality simply by adjusting her speaker's meanings.

That is the method of the radical interpreter, and it is from considerations about this method that Davidson often quickly draws conclusions about the nature of belief. He says, for instance (directly after outlining the procedures of the interpreter and certain ideas from decision theory), "Broadly stated, my theme is that we should think of meanings and beliefs as interrelated *constructs* of a single theory just as we already view subjective values and probabilities as interrelated constructs of decision theory."[25] Once we are to think of belief in this way, it becomes clear why it is sometimes an indeterminate matter as to whether one has a particular belief or not, and also why we are not to think of beliefs either as entities or as involving objects—propositions, representations, sense data—that the mind somehow contemplates or grasps. Furthermore, not only are we to think of beliefs as theoretical "constructs," but the construction of such theories is the very context in which we get our idea of belief in the first place. We "come to understand it" in precisely that context. "What makes a social theory of interpretation possible is that we can construct a plurality of private belief structures: belief is built to take up the slack between sentences held true by individuals and sentences true (or false) by public standards."[26]

3 The Relevance of Conditions for Successful Interpretation

As I have noted, Davidson's method is invariably to "adopt the stance of a radical interpreter when asking about the nature of belief."[27] Why does Davidson adopt this method? Why does Davidson believe that investigating what one would do, even must do, in the unique and seemingly hypothetical situation of radical interpretation will shed light on the nature of belief in general? When we start to inquire, explicit explanation on Davidson's part is difficult to find.

In one of Davidson's early articles on the topic, "Radical Interpretation," where he says the most about its actual role in our lives, he implies that we find ourselves in this situation *every* time we understand what another person says. Radical interpretation is applicable not only to interpreters of speakers of a language entirely foreign to them; rather, *all* instances of understanding what another speaker says are supposed to be instances of, or require, radical interpretation. He says,

> The problem of interpretation is domestic as well as foreign: it surfaces for speakers of the same language in the form of the question, how can it be determined that the language is the same? Speakers of the same language can go on the assumption that for them the same expressions are to be interpreted in the same way, but this does not indicate what justifies the assumption. *All understanding of the speech of another involves radical interpretation.*[28]

However, Davidson later abandons the idea that all understanding requires radical interpretation. He writes more recently, "The approach to the problems of meaning, belief, and desire which I have outlined is not, I am sure it is clear, meant to throw any direct light on how in real life we come to understand each other."[29] The situation of radical interpretation is thus better thought of as the subject of a thought experiment.[30] The question is: If radical interpretation is not a situation we typically or ever find ourselves in, why should consideration of what we would do in that situation yield insights into the nature of belief?

In one of the few places where Davidson explicitly addresses the relevance of an appeal to radical interpretation, he writes (after what I just quoted): "I have been engaged in a conceptual exercise aimed at revealing the dependencies among our basic propositional attitudes at a level fundamental enough to avoid the assumption that we can come to grasp them—or intelligibly attribute them to others—one at a time."[31] Investigation of the situation of radical interpretation, even if it is not meant to be an investigation of anything that actually happens, is intended to shed light on the "dependencies" among the propositional attitudes that we do have, such as our particular beliefs and meanings. What we realize when we consider how one must go about radically interpreting a given speaker is how dependent one's correct attributions of a speaker's propositional attitudes are on others of one's correct attributions of the speaker's propositional attitudes. Often we do not realize these dependencies when we attribute beliefs on a daily basis, since in those cases we already know so many of the propositional attitudes of our speaker. We are hardly aware of our knowledge of those dependencies, and more importantly, of the role that our knowledge of them and that our sensitivity to principles of rationality play in our understanding of others. That is why it is sometimes easy to suppose that "we can come to grasp them—or intelligibly attribute them to others—one at a time." Consideration of the radical interpreter helps us to appreciate and acknowledge these dependencies, principles, and relations that must exist and by which we must abide.

These dependencies take center stage in the prescribed method of the radical interpreter. The reason the radical interpreter must implement such a complex method in order to discern one's meanings and beliefs is that what the interpreter observes—the holding true of sentences under certain circumstances—is the product of at least two forces: meaning and belief. The crucial point is that, as we saw, we cannot ascertain what a speaker means by a given sentence that we know he holds true without already knowing the belief that the speaker has about the world that is the basis for his assent to the sentence. No matter what circumstances *we* believe obtain when he assents to that sentence, we cannot tell what he means by that sentence unless we know what circumstances *he* believes obtain. Likewise, we cannot ascertain from his assent to a particular sentence the belief that is the basis of his assent without knowing what he means by that sentence.

Untangling the effects due to meaning and belief is the goal of the method Davidson prescribes; it is what the method is invented to solve. The method is first to assume that our speaker's beliefs are true. Holding belief fixed in that way, we can then solve for meaning. Subsequent adjusting of the theory to comport with the individual's particular idiosyncrasies only further brings out the normative principles and relations of rationality and consistency with which we inevitably endow our subject's attitudes.

However, the interdependencies of these propositional attitudes are emphasized only in consideration of what we must do to *ascertain* someone's propositional attitudes. The context in which these propositional attitudes are concluded to be interdependent is always an *epistemological* one. These aspects of the mental might not be brought out were we to consider what must be the case for someone to *have* a given belief, as opposed to considering what must be the case for one to *attribute correctly to someone* a given belief. From the fact that our correct attribution of someone's beliefs depends on our correct attribution of what he means, it does not follow that his very having of those beliefs itself depends on his very having of those meanings. For these considerations about correct attribution to yield such conclusions, something more would be needed than that which has been said thus far.

Had a thesis such as constitutive interpretationism already been secured, belief's interdependency with meaning might follow. If a correct statement of what it is for *S* to believe that *p* makes essential reference to the idea of *S*'s being interpretable as believing that *p*, and if successful belief attribution always depends on successful meaning attribution and vice versa, then perhaps it would be harmless to consider belief and meaning to be interdependent. Reasoning in this way would require that we have reason to embrace this constitutive conception of belief, yet it is the source of that and other aspects of Davidson's conception of belief that is the subject of our inquiry.

Likewise, it does not follow solely from the fact that a successful interpreter must assume and attribute normative principles of rationality and consistency to her subject that belief is essentially normative in character, that is, that it is in the nature of belief that one's set of beliefs (and other attitudes) is always founded upon, and held together by, such normative principles of rationality and consistency. There may be good reason on *other* grounds, independent of considerations of interpretation, to suppose belief is essentially normative in character. Indeed, Davidson sometimes offers such grounds. My point here is only that such a claim about the nature of belief does not follow from consideration of interpretation alone. These considerations of interpretation so far entail nothing at all about what beliefs *are* or *are like in general*. They entail merely something about their correct attribution (as well as perhaps something about what they must be like if they are to be correctly attributed).

This point can be brought out in a different way. Those who disagree with Davidson's conception of belief could agree with everything Davidson says about the difficulties a radical interpreter would face, the procedures she would have to implement, and the constraints by which she would have to abide in order successfully to interpret her speaker. For the sake of example, consider the antiquated view—what Quine calls the "myth of a museum"—according to which meanings (and, in our case, beliefs) are inner items that glide across one's internal stage. This is perhaps close to what Locke or Hume thought, and it is an extreme version of the traditional "Cartesian" picture of the mind that Davidson wants to abandon. But even this position is not incompatible with Davidson's conclusions about the methods of and constraints on a radical interpreter. It is instructive to investigate what implications Davidson's considerations about radical interpretation have for such a view.

One who held such a conception of belief (call it the "museum conception") might conclude about the plight of the radical interpreter much the same as Davidson concludes. For instance, he would most likely agree that a radical interpreter could not ascertain what a given speaker believes without assuming something about what that speaker means and vice versa. For according to our museum theorist, one's meanings and beliefs consist in the appearance of certain mental entities before one's mind, and the interpreter would not have access to these entities. The museum theorist would perhaps also thus agree that some procedure of holding one of the two fixed (e.g., by assuming largely shared belief) would have to be implemented; otherwise, an interpreter could not untangle the effect of the two. He might thus agree that successful interpretation always guarantees, and thus requires, massive agreement. The museum theorist could—and perhaps would—agree with all this, and yet still hold that what a belief *is* is the appearance in one's mind of an inner, mental entity.

The museum theorist would also likely agree that in order successfully to interpret her speaker, an interpreter would have to proceed on the assumption that her speaker's attitudes adhered to normative ideals of rationality and consistency. Otherwise, there would be nothing to guide the interpreter's construction of her theory. Successful interpretation, he would acknowledge, must always render one's beliefs and meanings as largely satisfying normative ideals. The museum theorist might even hold that one's set of beliefs actually *does*, or even must, adhere to such normative principles. That claim is also not incompatible with a museum conception of belief, though perhaps it is not entailed by it.

Our museum theorist could therefore agree with much of what Davidson argues about the epistemological limitations of and constraints on the radical interpreter and about the procedures one would have to implement to radically interpret a speaker, yet not agree with, say, the constitutive conception of belief, or with the idea that beliefs are not inner items that glide across an internal stage, or the idea that it is sometimes a wholly indeterminate matter what beliefs one has, and so on. Concluding that an interpreter must construct a theory of belief in such a way does not commit one to very much at all about the nature of belief. What the constructed theory could do, for someone such as our museum theorist, is attribute determinate entities or objects that do appear in the speaker's mind.

The museum conception of belief is a confused one. But that only illuminates the explanatory status of radical interpretation all the more.

4 The Possibility of Interpretation

I have claimed that radical interpretation as considered so far entails nothing at all about what beliefs are, or are in general like, just something about their correct attribution, as well as something about what they must be like in the case in which they are to be successfully interpreted. Perhaps radical interpretation would show more about the general nature of belief were there reason to think that a creature's set of beliefs is always of a nature such that successful interpretation of it is possible. Davidson does emphasize the importance of the very possibility of interpretation. This passage from "The Structure and Content of Truth" from which I have already quoted addresses the issue more directly than any other. The bulk of the passage reads as follows:

> I have been engaged in a conceptual exercise aimed at revealing the dependencies among our basic propositional attitudes. . . . Performing the exercise has required showing how it is in principle possible to arrive at all of them at once. Showing this amounts to presenting an informal proof that we have endowed thought, desire, and speech with a structure that makes interpretation possible. Of course, we knew it was possible in advance. The philosophical question was, *what* makes it possible?
>
> What makes the task practicable at all is the structure the normative character of thought, desire, speech, and action imposes on correct attributions of attitudes to others, and hence on interpretations of their speech and explanations of their actions.[32]

Here the emphasis has been placed on the very possibility of interpretation. Perhaps that is the key to Davidson's appeal to radical interpretation.

From what Davidson has said so far about radical interpretation, it is true that we could infer certain things about the mental states of two speakers each of whom is able to interpret the other successfully and radically. If speaker A is able successfully to interpret speaker B, not only must both A's and B's sets of beliefs themselves abide by, and be founded upon, normative principles of rationality and consistency, but A's and B's principles must be very similar. They could not be too different, or else interpretation of one by the other would not be possible. There must also be massive agreement among A's and B's beliefs. And so if we had reason to believe that for any mindful being at all, any other mindful being could, in principle, successfully interpret the first being on the basis of his potential behavior (i.e., his behavior under all possible circumstances), then we would have reason to conclude that all mindful beings in large part share sets of beliefs and principles of rationality. That would be something we could infer from what Davidson has shown us are the conditions of successful interpretation, and that would be quite a conclusion to be able to draw.

Do we have reason to believe that? More importantly, do we have reason to believe the weaker claim that for any mindful being at all, there is some possible interpreter who could successfully interpret him on the basis of his potential behavior? If this weaker claim were true, we could infer from the conditions on successful interpretation—from what must be true of a subject's mental makeup for that person to be successfully interpreted—conclusions about the nature of the mental in general, conclusions about the nature of all possible thought.

Of course, Davidson himself clearly endorses this claim. He says that "[w]hat a fully informed interpreter could learn about what a speaker [believes] is all there is to learn,"[33] and that "the nature of language and thought is such as to make them interpretable."[34] And elsewhere he writes, "Thoughts, desires, and other attitudes are in their nature states we are equipped to interpret; what we could not interpret is not thought."[35] A similar idea is found in Quine, according to whom "[t]here are no meanings, nor likenesses nor distinctions of meaning, beyond what are implicit in people's dispositions to overt behavior."[36] The same is to go for all the attitudes.

Is successful interpretation of a thinker always possible? We obviously have good reason to think that interpretation of thought and belief is possible in one sense. We know it is possible, because we know it often goes on, even if it is not always—or ever—radical. In that sense of possibility, interpretation is indeed possible, and any theory of belief should account for that possibility. From that fact, we can conclude that *some* thought must satisfy those conditions that Davidson has shown must obtain for interpretation to be successful. But from the fact that interpretation is possible in this sense, we cannot conclude that all thought must fulfill those conditions that a particular thinker's mental makeup must fulfill in order for that thinker to be interpretable. We know it is possible for chairs to be comfortable, for some certainly are. And if it is a condition on a chair's being comfortable that it feels good to sit in, then we can conclude that some chairs feel good. But it would be a mistake to infer from the possibility of chairs being comfortable that it is therefore an essential mark of chairhood that they feel good.

That is why Davidson could not merely be asking about what is required to make sense of the fact that we ourselves engage in practices in which we do in fact understand each other. From what is required of our thought for us to engage in such practices, Davidson could not legitimately draw conclusions about all possible thought, that is, about the nature of thought in general. Yet the conclusions he draws—for instance, that thought is only possible for creatures in communication with others—seem to concern precisely that.

Davidson would need a stronger premise about the possibility of interpretation than simply that it is possible in the sense given above. He needs what I just referred to as the "weaker claim":

(N) For any thoughtful being, there is some possible interpreter such that, had she access to all of the being's potential behavior, she could ascertain his beliefs.

I refer to this premise as "(N)," because it holds that the possibility of interpretation (in the sense in (N)) is *necessary* for thought. If, for any being with beliefs, there is always at least *some* possible being who could in principle interpret that being, and if considerations of radical interpretation illustrate that certain things must be true about a thoughtful being for him to be able to be successfully interpreted, then radical interpretation would help guarantee that those things that must be true about a thinker for him to be able to be successfully interpreted must be true of all thinkers. Every believer would be in principle interpretable. Conclusions about belief *in general* could legitimately be drawn. But if interpretation is not always possible in this sense, that is, if it is possible for there to be a thoughtful being whom no possible interpreter could interpret, then we would not be justified in concluding that the characteristics with which we endow the mental *in order to make interpretation possible* should be essential to thought, or that all thought must exhibit such properties.

Such a conception of the mental—(N)—does not result from anything that has been said so far about the situation of radical interpretation. Our considerations of radical interpretation have primarily concerned the necessary conditions for successful interpretation, not the range of believers for whom such interpretation is possible. For radical interpretation to acquire its relevance from the possibility of interpretation, this view of the interpretability of the mental must be secured, or at least assumed, prior to the very appeal to interpretation.

The premise, (N), however, is substantial, and there are many who would deny it. Colin McGinn, for example, writes,

> It is a *condition of interpretability* that the subject by and large believes what he perceives. . . . (This is not to say [that a person who systematically and globally refuses

to let his beliefs be shaped by his experience] is *impossible;* it is just that he is not *interpretable.*)[37]

John Searle would also reject (N). Searle denies that "there is some sort of conceptual or logical connection between conscious mental phenomena and external behavior."[38] He says,

> *Ontologically speaking, behavior, functional role, and causal relations are irrelevant to the existence of conscious mental phenomena. Epistemically,* we do learn about other people's conscious mental states *in part* from their behavior. *Causally,* consciousness serves to mediate the causal relations between input stimuli and output behavior; and from an *evolutionary* point of view, the conscious mind functions causally to control behavior. But *ontologically* speaking, the phenomena in question can exist completely and have all of their essential properties independent of any behavioral output.[39]

Elsewhere, when discussing meaning, Searle claims that it is false to suppose that "what isn't conclusively testable by third-person means isn't actual."[40] Presumably, he would say the same for belief and the other attitudes. Those who support premises like (N), Searle would say, do not respect the "first-person, 'subjective' point of view."[41]

In the remainder of this essay, I want to explore whether there is good reason to endorse (N). It is important to note first, though, that even equipped with (N), Davidson's appeal to the radical interpreter would still yield only *some* of the aspects of belief he thinks can be gleaned from radical interpretation. Even if belief is in principle interpretable, in the sense given above, it would still not follow from what Davidson says about the conditions of successful interpretation that constitutive interpretationism is true, or that having a belief does not involve mental objects or representations that the mind somehow grasps. Nor would it follow from Davidson's considerations about interpretation that it is sometimes an indeterminate matter what beliefs a subject has.

One thing that *would* follow, however, is the essentially normative character of belief and thought. If for any thoughtful being there is some possible interpreter who could successfully interpret him, and if successful interpretation requires that the thoughts of the interpreted adhere to normative principles of rationality and consistency, then the thoughts of all possible thinkers must satisfy such principles. Likewise, if for interpretation to be successful an interpreter must take her subject's most basic beliefs to be about the very things in the world that cause those beliefs, and if successful interpretation is always possible, then the most basic beliefs of all possible thinkers must generally be about the very things in the world that cause those beliefs. And indeed, it is this latter conclusion concerning the connection between cause and content that provides the basis for Davidson's argument against skepticism of the senses, as well as for one of his arguments for the social character of thought.

Before looking at the explicit support Davidson himself provides for (N), it is worth addressing one plausible idea that might appear to lead to (N). One reason someone might be inclined to accept (N) is that what human beings do—how they behave—is in part explained by their mental states. I take an umbrella with me when I leave the house, because I believe it will rain (and because I desire to stay dry, etc.). Mental states and events explain what we do. Perhaps for any particular action most of my mental states will not factor into an explanation of it. My belief that Van Gogh painted in the nineteenth century does not help to explain my taking an umbrella. What may be true, though, is that for each of my mental states, there are possible circumstances under which the behavior I would engage in would be partly explained by that state. About intention, for instance, Charles Taylor writes, "This is part of what we mean by 'intending *X*,' that, in the absence of interfering factors, it is followed by doing *X*. I could not be said to intend *X* if, even with no obstacles or other countervailing factors, I still did not do it."[42] The same would go perhaps (though not as directly) for all propositional attitudes.

Someone might embrace (N), then, because she endorses some premise like the following:

(C) For every one of a subject's mental states, there are (perhaps infinite) possible circumstances under which that mental state would play a causal role in bringing about some piece of behavior.

Some readers will be less comfortable with (C), which concerns causation, than with a premise that emphasizes explanation, such as:

(C*) For every one of a subject's mental states, there are (perhaps infinite) possible circumstances under which that mental state would serve to explain some piece of behavior.

But let us grant (C) for the sake of argument. Premise (C*) cannot support (N) for the same reasons that we will see that (C) cannot support (N).

If (C) is correct, then for every one of a subject's beliefs there would be some possible circumstances in which that belief would play a causal role in bringing about some piece of behavior, and an interpreter would in principle have access to all of those circumstances and behavior. However, for any piece of behavior, there are countless ways in which it could come about, countless combinations of mental states that could cause one to behave in that way. Davidson's discussion of the connection between meaning and belief reveals the point well. One holds a particular sentence to be true (and thus assents to that sentence) both because of what one means by the sentence and because of what one believes. The attitude of holding true, we remember, is a "vector" of meaning and belief. And so for any sentence, there are many (perhaps infinite) combinations of meaning and belief that could be the cause of someone's assent to the sentence. That itself does not imply that an interpreter could not determine which of all those possible combinations was the one the subject had. Often interpreters do ascertain this. The question for our purposes is whether one always could. Indeed, I think we can imagine thinkers for whom it is plausible to claim that there is no such interpreter. They are admittedly far-fetched cases, not ones we normally confront. However, because Davidson's conclusions are to apply to all *possible* belief, it is appropriate for us to appeal to such cases. One of Davidson's conclusions, we remember, is that thought is possible only for linguistic creatures.

Consider, then, a person whose overriding goal in life is to deceive those who attempt to identify his thoughts. For whatever reason, this goal is of such high priority to him that he would sacrifice his life in order not to reveal his mental makeup. There strikes me as little *prima facie* reason to suppose either that such a person is not possible, or that there is a possible interpreter who would be able to determine this person's mental makeup from his potential behavior. It is not clear, for instance, that any interpreter would be able to discern *why* the deceitful person is so intent on deceiving, or even *that* he is intent on deceiving. The possibility of this thinker is not incompatible with (C). The subject's behavior would still be a causal effect of his mental states. His behavior is the result of his (strange) intentions (as well as of his beliefs, desires, etc.). Or consider the possibility Colin McGinn mentions in the passage I have already quoted:

> It is a *condition of interpretability* that the subject by and large believes what he perceives. . . . (This is not to say [that a person who systematically and globally refuses to let his beliefs be shaped by his experience] is *impossible*; it is just that he is not *interpretable*.)

Indeed, it seems we could concoct countless such examples.

It might be protested that these sorts of thinkers are irrational. But our countenancing irrational thought is not inappropriate at this juncture. The possibility of irrational thought or action has not yet been ruled out. Davidson may hold that there is a limit on how much irrationality an interpreter can find in her subject. But to suppose that irrationality—even a hearty dose—is not possible because an interpreter would not be able to determine which mental states her subject has (or even whether he has any) would require the presupposition that successful interpretation is always possible, or that there is no more to the mental than what a fully informed interpreter could ascertain from all of a subject's potential behavior. And that is precisely the view under consideration. The constraint of rationality we have granted so far concerns only what must be the case if successful interpretation is to be possible.

Let us turn now to the way in which Davidson himself supports theses such as (N). He introduces the situation of radical interpretation in "A Coherence Theory of Truth and Knowledge" in this way:

> A speaker who wishes his words to be understood cannot systematically deceive his would-be interpreters about when he assents to sentences—that is, holds them true. As a matter of principle, then, meaning, and by its connection with meaning, belief also, are open to public determination. *I shall take advantage of this fact in what follows and adopt the stance of a radical interpreter when asking about the nature of belief.* What a fully informed interpreter could learn about what a speaker means is all there is to learn; the same goes for what the speaker believes.[43]

In the italicized sentence, Davidson appears to acknowledge that the publicity of meaning and belief is what *allows* him to appeal to the situation of the radical interpreter. Were belief not known to be public, he intimates, the relevance or justification for adopting that "stance" might not be at hand.

But the little support Davidson gives for this now prior claim about the publicity of belief is itself unclear. Davidson appeals to the fact that meaning is public and that so too must be belief, because of belief's "connection with meaning." But when briefly discussing how it is that belief depends on meaning a few paragraphs above, all Davidson says is that "[b]elief, however, depends equally on meaning, for the only access to the fine structure and individuation of beliefs is through the sentences speakers and interpreters of speakers use to express and describe beliefs."[44] This is the insight that in order successfully to attribute beliefs to a given speaker, one must know something about what that speaker means by his words. But even if that were true, that dependence, or "connection," is thus far only an epistemological one. It is a connection that must exist and that the interpreter must rely on if the project of belief or meaning attribution is to be successful. But there is nothing about that epistemological connection that reveals that beliefs cannot exist where meanings do not, or that they are essentially interpretable, even if meanings are so. Or at least there isn't without some prior view of belief already in place.

Even if we grant Davidson a conception of *meaning* as essentially interpretable, it still would not be clear that he would be justified in concluding anything general about the nature of belief.[45] As we have seen, in order to determine a speaker's meanings, one must know something about his beliefs. So if the meanings of all speakers are interpretable, then perhaps so are their beliefs.[46] But that would be to say something only about the beliefs of beings who are involved in communication; it would not be to say anything about all possible belief, or about the essential nature of belief.

Davidson might be justified in drawing a conclusion about belief in general had he already secured the conclusion that only linguistic beings, or those involved in communication, are capable of thought. If the beliefs of linguistic beings are always in principle interpretable, and if only linguistic beings are capable of thought, then the beliefs of all beings would be in principle interpretable. And indeed, Davidson does claim that only linguistic beings are capable of thought. Perhaps, then, one might suppose it is Davidson's reasoning for *this* claim that secures (N). But a close look at Davidson's reasoning for this claim, to which I now turn, reveals that it too depends on (N) (or on something even stronger) and thus cannot support (N).

There are two, perhaps related, routes by which Davidson arrives at this conclusion about the impossibility of thought without language. One emphasizes the importance and origin of the very *concept of* belief; the other emphasizes the necessity of the process of triangulation.[47] It is not clear whether Davidson considers these arguments entirely distinct, or whether the latter is something of a development of the former. I will consider each separately.

In order for a creature to have a belief at all, Davidson argues in the first of those arguments, that creature must have the *concept* of belief. Having that concept involves grasping the distinction between truth and error, understanding that there is a difference between something's being the case and something's only seeming to be the case, having the concept of objectivity. The only way in which a creature could ever attain that concept (or concepts), Davidson believes, is through interpersonal communication, through the context of interpretation. We remember that we "come to understand" the concept of belief just in this connection, and that, as he says, "We have the idea of belief only from the role of belief in the interpretation of language."[48] Therefore, any creature capable of thought must be, or must have been at some point, involved in communication with others. Those two steps inform Davidson's first argument for thought's dependence on language.

Were we to grant Davidson his contestable first premise (that for one to have a belief at all one must also have the concept of belief), Davidson's reasons for regarding the context of interpretation as being the only situation in which one could ever attain that concept are still scarce and difficult to discern. In one of the few places where he appears to give any argumentation for this claim, Davidson alludes briefly to what he takes to be Wittgenstein's private language argument.[49] However, there is little explanation of the argument, nor any discussion of how it is to be extended to his particular point about the conditions for one's having the concept of objectivity. Davidson claims that having this concept requires having "the standard provided by a shared language," but he does not explain why that is. Besides that, however, there is little else given to convince potential objectors that the concept of belief could not possibly be acquired in some other way, for example, innately, or that one's acquiring the concept is not simply a matter of acquiring a particular brain state, as some philosophers would have it. Davidson himself admits in "Rational Animals" that "[t]o complete the 'argument,' however, I need to show that the *only* way one could come to have the belief-truth contrast is through having the concept of intersubjective truth. I confess I do not know how to show this. But neither do I have any idea how else one could arrive at the concept of an objective truth."[50]

Davidson may be right that the concept of belief is necessary for successful interpretation, and thus that any successful interpreter must have it. But that does not imply that the context of interpretation is where the interpreter acquires that concept. Of course, for one who already holds that belief and thought (and therefore concepts too) arise only in contexts of interpretation, it will naturally follow that the particular concept of belief can only be had by those involved in interpretation. But that would be to presuppose the very thesis about the social character of thought for which we are seeking support.

Of course, one *might* get the concept from the situation of interpretation. Davidson provides a plausible, perhaps enticing suggestion as to where we *do* get this concept. But Davidson gives little reason to suppose, not just that the way he suggests we acquire the concept is the way that we definitely *do* get it, but that it is the way that we, or any creature at all, *must* get it. Yet that latter claim is what is required.

Similar problems afflict Davidson's second argument. That argument appeals to the way in which our beliefs and meanings acquire their content. In the most basic cases, Davidson argues, the contents of our beliefs are determined by the objects and events in the world that cause them; those causes are what those beliefs are in general about. But for any given belief, as for any event at all, there are many causal chains extending back in time. Every one of those chains consists of many events each of which might appropriately be considered a cause of that belief. (The big bang, for example, Davidson points out, is one of the many causes of any given belief.) What is necessary, then, to determine the *unique* cause that is what determines the content of a particular belief and that is what that belief is therefore about, Davidson believes, is a process of triangulation that occurs between two or more people. Triangulation is necessary for beliefs to have content, he argues, for only that process could determine, of the many causes, the unique cause that gives a particular belief its content. Belief is thus essentially social, as there could be no content at all apart from the context of triangulation.

However, Davidson supports the first premise of this argument—that the contents of beliefs are in the simplest cases determined by those things that cause those beliefs—once again only by appeal to radical interpretation, by looking at how a radical interpreter would have to go about interpreting her subject's beliefs. What an interpreter would take her speaker's words to refer to are those objects or events in the environment that the interpreter thinks systematically cause the speaker to utter those words (e.g., rabbits).[51] That is why Davidson believes that "we can't in general first identify beliefs and meanings and then ask what caused them."[52] And that seems correct. But these are still just facts about the successful attribution of belief. The purported fact that an interpreter must take her subject's beliefs to be about those things that she believes cause them, and that those beliefs must really be about such things, does not imply anything about what determines the contents of *any* mindful being's beliefs, or about what is necessary for a belief to have content at all or for a mindful being to have belief at all. The inevitability of successful interpretation is precisely what is in question; the relevance of investigating the conditions on successful interpretation for understanding the nature of belief in general is still the subject of the larger inquiry of which our discussion about the social nature of thought is merely a part.

These arguments for the social character of thought, then, cannot provide the required support for the thesis that belief is in principle interpretable. The success of those arguments still depends on one or another significant presupposition about belief that has yet to be secured. Indeed, the most likely candidate to provide the support for those arguments is the very presupposition we have been looking to Davidson's arguments for the social character of thought to *support*: the thesis that belief is in principle interpretable. Those arguments cannot support that thesis, because they depend on it. And his reasoning for that thesis, we have seen, seems to rely on the conclusion of those arguments: the social character of thought. They both involve a prior confidence in the relevance of radical interpretation for understanding the nature of the mind. Indeed, it is interesting that even those arguments for the social nature of thought require such relevance, because sometimes Davidson seems to intimate that one reason we may feel justified looking to the radical interpreter is precisely that thought is only possible for those in communication.[53]

5 Conclusion

We are therefore left with no reason from Davidson's philosophy to suppose that (N) is true. This is of importance given that Davidson's appeal to the situation of radical interpretation for the purpose of securing his substantial conclusions about mental phenomena depends precisely on some premise like (N). Indeed, once we appreciate that dependence, it becomes much less surprising that Davidson is able to draw such formidable conclusions about the mental merely from considerations about the conditions on attribution. The bulk of the work is being done by an unsupported presupposition.

That Davidson's endorsement of a substantial conception of the mind comes prior to his appeal to radical interpretation explains the parallel with which I began, between the method of Davidson's philosophy and what Davidson's philosophy is about or purports to show. The mind emerges from contexts of interpretation, just as Davidson's conclusions about the mind emerge from his inquiries into interpretation. Both strands of the parallel are grounded in a prior conviction that the situation of interpretation is relevant for understanding the nature of the mind. Such a conviction goes hand in hand with the view of the mental as in principle interpretable. Only such a view as (N) (or something stronger, such as the constitutive view) could make successful an appeal to interpretation for many of the ends Davidson asks of it. Whether Davidson's conviction that radical interpretation is relevant for understanding the mind stems from a prior subscription to (N) (or to the constitutive view), or whether his subscription to (N) stems from a prior conviction that radical interpretation is relevant, is unclear.

Of course, nothing I have said in this essay shows that any of these prior views is false. Nor does anything I have said show that any of the conclusions Davidson draws about the mental from investigating the situation of radical interpretation is false. Indeed, those who are partial to one of the required presuppositions may well find Davidson's appeal to radical interpretation to bear considerable promise. From what is learned about the conditions on successful interpretation—about what a subject's thought must be like in order for him to be successfully interpreted—we could draw conclusions about all possible thought, that is, about the nature of thought in general.

Whether those who endorse (N) would agree with the *particular* conclusions Davidson draws about the nature of the mental would depend on whether they agree with the particular conditions Davidson identifies. One still could not abstract anything like the constitutive view of the mental from a consideration of radical interpretation. That is precisely the sort of view one might embrace prior to one's appeal to radical interpretation. It entails (N). If, however, one agrees with Davidson that a condition on successful interpretation is that a subject's mental makeup abides largely by normative constraints of rationality and consistency, and one embraces (N), then one might agree that the mental must abide by normative constraints of rationality (and also, in turn, perhaps agree with Davidson's claim about the anomalism of the mental, even anomalous monism). If one agrees with what Davidson concludes about the relation in which the contents of one's beliefs must stand to their causes in order for there to be successful interpretation, and one embraces (N), then one might endorse Davidson's refutation of skepticism. And if one also agrees with the purported fact that some process of triangulation is what determines precisely which causes stand in that relation to one's beliefs, then one might also go along with Davidson's conclusion that thought is only possible for linguistic beings.

But for any of these lines of argument to be successful, one would need to provide grounds for believing (N). Those grounds are not to come from the situation of radical interpretation, as Davidson suggests, but must come from elsewhere.[54]

What are we to conclude from the fact that there may be such a circularity in Davidson's philosophy? Did Davidson simply fail to see this? Or did he see it but not consider it a handicap? Not all circularities are vicious. Indeed, some philosophers have argued that transcendental philosophy itself (of which Davidson's philosophy is often considered a form) is inherently circular, yet that the circular nature of transcendental philosophy does not constitute a problem or difficulty for it.[55] I suspect that the circularity I have identified is problematic, that it reveals that Davidson's work does not contain adequate justification for the controversial view of interpretation on which many of his arguments depend. At the very least, a great deal would certainly need to be said in order to show that the view is justified by way of this circle. I do not have the space here to investigate the prospects of showing this. What I hope to have done is to have established that such a circularity does exist in Davidson's philosophy.

Acknowledgments

I am grateful to Donald Davidson, Jason Bridges, John Heil, Sean Kelly, Jeff Malpas, John Searle, Barry Stroud, Bruce Vermazen, and Wai-hung Wong for their help on earlier drafts of this essay.

Notes

1. Donald Davidson, "A Coherence Theory of Truth and Knowledge" (1983), reprinted in his *Subjective, Intersubjective, Objective* (Oxford: Oxford University Press, 2001), p. 148. In the sentence I quote, Davidson is describing the method of the particular argument he is about to provide for his claim that belief is "in its nature veridical."

2. Donald Davidson, "Mental Events" (1970), reprinted in his *Essays on Actions and Events* (Oxford: Oxford University Press, 1980).

3. See Donald Davidson, "Three Varieties of Knowledge" (1991), reprinted in *Subjective, Intersubjective, Objective*, pp. 205–220; and Donald Davidson, "Epistemology Externalized" (1990), reprinted in *Subjective, Intersubjective, Objective*, pp. 193–204.

4. Donald Davidson, "The Myth of the Subjective" (1988), reprinted in *Subjective, Intersubjective, Objective*, p. 47.

5. Davidson's papers involving issues about belief span more than two decades. It is perhaps best to regard his many ideas over those years as constituting an evolving conception of belief, and not a position that was entirely there from the start.

6. See Donald Davidson, "Knowing One's Own Mind" (1987), reprinted in *Subjective, Intersubjective, Objective*, pp. 36–37; and also "The Myth of the Subjective," pp. 51–52.

7. Davidson, "Knowing One's Own Mind," p. 38.

8. Donald Davidson, "Belief and the Basis of Meaning" (1974), reprinted in his *Inquiries into Truth and Interpretation* (Oxford: Oxford University Press, 1984), p. 146.

9. Ibid., p. 147.

10. Ibid., p. 153.

11. Ibid., p. 147.

12. Ibid., p. 154.

13. Ibid., p. 147.

14. Ibid.

15. See W. Child, *Causality, Interpretation, and the Mind* (Oxford: Oxford University Press, 1994), pp. 48–53.

16. Davidson, "A Coherence Theory of Truth and Knowledge."

17. Ibid., p. 148.

18. Donald Davidson, "Thought and Talk" (1975), reprinted in *Inquiries into Truth and Interpretation*, p. 170.

19. Davidson, "A Coherence Theory of Truth and Knowledge," p. 151.

20. Davidson, "Knowing One's Own Mind," pp. 37–38.

21. Davidson, "The Myth of the Subjective," p. 52.

22. F. P. Ramsey, "Truth and Probability" (1926), reprinted in his *Foundations of Mathematics* (New York: Humanities Press, 1950).

23. Donald Davidson, "The Structure and Content of Truth," *Journal of Philosophy* 87 (1990): 279–328, p. 319.

24. Davidson, "Thought and Talk," p. 170.

25. Davidson, "Belief and the Basis of Meaning," p. 146; emphasis added.

26. Ibid., p. 153. Which of these claims about belief Davidson intends to infer from his considerations about radical interpretation, and which he intends simply to make along with them, is in some cases unclear. It often seems the former. Our investigation will be revealing in either case.

27. Davidson, "A Coherence Theory of Truth and Knowledge," p. 148.

28. Donald Davidson, "Radical Interpretation" (1973), reprinted in *Inquiries into Truth and Interpretation*, p. 125; emphasis added.

29. Davidson, "The Structure and Content of Truth," pp. 324–325.

30. Davidson's remarks here are in tension perhaps with his description elsewhere of the advantage of his arguments for externalism about content over those of Tyler Burge and Hilary Putnam. His own arguments, he says there, "do not rest on intuitions concerning what we would say if certain counterfactuals were true. No science fiction or thought experiments are required." Davidson, "Knowing One's Own Mind," p. 29.

31. Davidson, "The Structure and Content of Truth," p. 325.

32. Ibid.

33. Davidson, "A Coherence Theory of Truth and Knowledge," p. 148.

34. Davidson, "The Myth of the Subjective," p. 47.

35. D. Davidson, "Representation and Interpretation," in *Modeling the Mind*, ed. W. H. Newton-Smith and K. V. Wilkes (Oxford: Oxford University Press, 1990), p. 14.

36. W. V. O. Quine, "Ontological Relativity," *Journal of Philosophy* 65 (1968): 185–212, p. 187.

37. C. McGinn, "Radical Interpretation and Epistemology," in *Truth and Interpretation: Perspectives on the Philosophy of Donald Davidson*, ed. E. Lepore (Oxford: Blackwell, 1986), p. 367.

38. J. R. Searle, *Rediscovery of the Mind* (Cambridge, MA: MIT Press, 1992), p. 69.

39. Ibid.

40. J. R. Searle, "Indeterminacy, Empiricism, and the First-Person," *Journal of Philosophy* 84 (1987): 123–146, p. 146.

41. Ibid., p. 145.

42. C. Taylor, *The Explanation of Behavior* (London: Routledge & Kegan Paul, 1964), p. 33.

43. Davidson, "A Coherence Theory of Truth and Knowledge," pp. 147–148; emphasis added.

44. Ibid., p. 147.

45. Of course, one who held that meaning is essentially public might hold that belief is public for the very same reason, i.e., not because one holds that meaning is public and that belief is connected to meaning, but because the very considerations that lead one to conclude that meaning is public might equally apply to belief. But that is not how Davidson here explains his reasoning.

46. Even this may not be true. What follows from the fact that all of one's meanings are interpretable may be only that some of one's beliefs are interpretable.

47. The first is found, e.g., in Davidson, "Thought and Talk," and "Rational Animals" (1982), reprinted in *Subjective, Intersubjective, Objective*, and "Three Varieties of Knowledge." The second is found, e.g., in Davidson, "Three Varieties of Knowledge," and "Epistemology Externalized."

48. Davidson, "Thought and Talk," p. 170.

49. Davidson, "Three Varieties of Knowledge," p. 209.

50. Davidson, "Rational Animals," p. 105.

51. The sorts of interpretation Davidson considers when he argues for this premise are not always "radical." For example, see Davidson, "Epistemology Externalized," pp. 196–197.

52. Davidson, "A Coherence Theory of Truth and Knowledge," p. 150.

53. Davidson, "Three Varieties of Knowledge," p. 208.

54. William Child, who also emphasizes the importance of (N) for many of Davidson's arguments concerning the mental, finds compelling support for it in the work of Ludwig Wittgenstein (see Child, *Causality, Interpretation, and the Mind*, pp. 35–37). Whether Wittgenstein's philosophy provides good reason for believing (N) is unfortunately not something I can pursue here.

55. J. Malpas, "The Transcendental Circle," *Australasian Journal of Philosophy* 75 (1997): 1–20. The sort of circle Malpas identifies is different from the one I have identified.

12 Incommensurability in Davidson and Gadamer

Barbara Fultner

Understanding the other is the most difficult of human tasks.
—Hans-Georg Gadamer[1]

Conceptual relativism is a heady and exotic doctrine, or would be if we could make good sense of it.
—Donald Davidson[2]

The term "incommensurability" has entered a wide range of philosophical discussions from philosophy of science to moral theory and does not mean the same thing to all people.[3] Its original home is mathematics: The hypotenuse of a right-angled isosceles triangle, for instance, is incommensurable with its sides; there is no common measure for them. This has been taken to mean that incommensurability implies *incomparability*. My primary concern here is with semantic incommensurability: roughly, the idea that the meanings of one language cannot be mapped without remainder onto the meanings of another. In this context, incommensurability usually means *untranslatability*. In the wake of the linguistic turn, semantic incommensurability can be understood to imply conceptual incommensurability and hence relativism. Truth or truths are seen as relative to conceptual schemes, perspectives, or worldviews. Different schemes or perspectives presumably give rise to different truths, which, in turn, are incommensurable. In these discussions, incommensurability often also stands for *incompatibility*.

Donald Davidson has famously argued against the idea of incommensurable theories, languages, or conceptual schemes, as has Hans-Georg Gadamer. Neither Davidson nor Gadamer denies that people speak different languages and hold different—and often incompatible—beliefs. What they deny is that these languages and belief systems could be in principle mutually inaccessible or unintelligible. For them, incommensurability thus takes on the meaning of *unintelligibility*. Although there are parallels between

Davidson and Gadamer's arguments against incommensurability, there are some significant differences as well. Both reject the scheme–content distinction, as I show in section 1, albeit on somewhat different grounds, and endorse meaning–belief holism. Although both are critical of semantic conventionalism, however, I argue in section 2 that Davidson's outright rejection of conceptual schemes needs to be modulated by Gadamer's concept of horizon and the conception of understanding as a fusion of horizons in order better to account for linguistic and cultural difference in the absence of incommensurability. In section 3, I turn to the tension between convention and invention in language, which both authors acknowledge. I argue that the later Davidson's emphasis on idiolects and Gadamer's recognition of an individualizing tendency in language respectively represent limit cases of translatability and hence vestiges of incommensurability.

1 Rejecting the Scheme–Content Distinction

Davidson's Formal Argument

Davidson's argument against incommensurability is intended as an argument against "the heady and exotic doctrine" of conceptual relativism. Conceptual relativism, he argues, presupposes a distinction between a conceptual scheme and content (experience) to which the scheme is applied. But since no clear sense can be made of this distinction, the position is incoherent. For Davidson, the metaphor underlying conceptual relativism, that of differing points of view, is inherently paradoxical: Different points of view only make sense in the context of a common coordinate system, but the latter is at odds with the claim of "dramatic incomparability." Calling for an account of the "limits of conceptual contrast," he writes, "There are extreme suppositions that founder on paradox or contradiction; there are modest examples we have no trouble understanding. What determines where we cross from the merely strange or novel to the absurd?"[4] Is the difference between these merely a matter of degree for Davidson? Are the sorts of (cultural) differences that persuade others of the truth of conceptual relativism differences of the sort "we have no trouble understanding"? Are they, as Davidson seems to think, philosophically uninteresting? These are questions to which I shall return in section 2.

Davidson wants to allow for differences between languages, but he does not think such differences can be made intelligible in terms of divergent *conceptual schemes*. Having identified conceptual schemes with mutually translatable languages, he considers the possibilities of complete and partial failure of translatability. First, he argues that complete failure is incoherent. The argument rests on rejecting the "third dogma of empiricism," the scheme–content distinction. That distinction, so Davidson, underlies a Kuhnian conception of conceptual relativism, according to which different conceptual schemes give rise to multiple points of view or perspectives on a single world.[5] If, Davidson argues, we follow Quine in rejecting the first dogma of empiricism, the analytic–synthetic distinction, and accept that all sentences have empirical content, we can "retain the idea of language embodying a conceptual scheme" only at the cost of subscribing to a "new dualism between conceptual scheme and uninterpreted empirical content."[6] He considers two ways of cashing out this dualism, namely, in terms of language *organizing* or *fitting* experience. The former has to do with a language's referential system, the latter with whole sentences—that is, truth. Neither gives a robust sense to the notion of incommensurable conceptual schemes. On the one hand, if languages or conceptual schemes organize experience (or reality or the Given), this presupposes a common ontology of things being organized. If there is a common ontology, we have no radical incommensurability. On the other hand, to say that the sentences of a language "fit" experience is just to say that they are true, and Davidson holds that we cannot make sense of truth independently of translation.[7] Hence the notion of a language whose sentences are (largely) true but not translatable is meaningless. Since untranslatability is criterial for incommensurability, the idea of fitting experience is no more help in making sense of the idea of incommensurable conceptual schemes than that of organizing it. Thus, Davidson rejects the idea of the possibility of total failure of translation as a criterion for difference of conceptual schemes. He concludes:

> Neither a fixed stock of meanings, nor a theory-neutral reality, can provide, then, a ground for comparison of conceptual schemes. It would be a mistake to look further for such a ground if by that we mean something conceived as common to incommensurable schemes. In abandoning this search, we abandon the attempt to make sense of the metaphor of a single space within which each scheme has a position and provides a point of view.[8]

Otherwise, we would return to the paradox with which Davidson began. *Pace* Davidson, a committed relativist might agree that there could be no basis of comparison between incommensurable schemes. This would render different conceptual schemes radically mutually unintelligible. On this view, an alien scheme, from our perspective, would not be anything we could recognize as a human, perhaps even intelligent, form of life. Yet this kind of relativism would be far removed from cultural relativism as normally conceived.

In encounters with other cultures, our challenge seems to be not total but partial failures of translation. Davidson at first appears sympathetic to this problem. When arguing against total failure of translatability, he writes,

> We can be clear about breakdowns in translation when they are local enough, for a background of generally successful translation provides what is needed to make the failures intelligible. But we were after larger game: we wanted to make sense of a language we could not translate at all.[9]

This suggests that we may consider different conceptual schemes, as long as we do not regard them as dramatically or radically but merely partly incommensurable. Partial failure of translation "introduces the possibility of making changes and contrasts in conceptual schemes intelligible by reference to the common part."[10]

Even when discussing partial untranslatability, the conceptual relativist appeals to the scheme–content distinction. Now, however, she runs up against the problem of meaning–belief holism. Davidson argues that even if we grant partial failures of translatability between languages, we cannot get a firm hold on conceptual relativism because, once we give up the analytic–synthetic distinction, there is no principled way of distinguishing between differences in beliefs (content) and differences in concepts (scheme). "Given the underlying methodology of interpretation, we could not be in a position to judge that others had concepts or beliefs radically different from our own."[11] Whether and how we are able to judge differences in belief at all is a question to which I return below. Because of the inability to assess whether others have radically different beliefs, Davidson rejects the idea of conceptual scheme(s) wholesale; there are neither many different conceptual schemes nor a single one we all share. Instead, he opts for a direct realism according to which we have "unmediated touch with the familiar objects" that make up our world.

Gadamer's Phenomenological Argument: Toward a Fusion of Horizons

Like Davidson, Gadamer rejects the scheme–content distinction. His rejection of the distinction, however, is grounded in the phenomenology of hermeneutic experience. Gadamer, like Humboldt, takes languages to embody "particular view[s] of the world."[12] Yet he criticizes Humboldt for abstracting "the linguistic faculty down to a form that could, presumably, be applied to any content: anything that could be thought," in other words, for distinguishing between form and content. In contrast, Gadamer maintains, "*Linguistic form and the content that is passed on cannot be separated in hermeneutic experience.* If every language is a view of the world, it is so not primarily because it is a particular type of language (in the way that linguists view language) but because of what is said or handed down in this language."[13] What differentiates languages from one another, in other words, is not merely that they conceptualize the same world differently, but that they say something different about different things; these two aspects are inseparable. The point can be seen as a kind of onto-phenomenological analogue to Davidson's meaning–belief holism.

For Gadamer, there is really no difference between the notion of a worldview and a "language-view"; the world we encounter is linguistically constituted, and in that sense, we have no "unmediated contact" with reality. This may make him appear to be a kind of linguistic idealist. However, he also maintains that "The world is the common ground, trodden by none and recognized by all, uniting all who talk to one another."[14] The very fact that this common ground is linguistically constituted makes communication and indeed learning about the world (and the worlds of others) possible:

> It is true that those who are brought up in a particular linguistic and cultural tradition see the world in a different way from those who belong to other traditions. It is true that the historical "worlds" that succeed one another in the course of history are different from one another and from the world of today; but . . . [a]s verbally constituted, every such world is of itself always open to every possible insight and hence to every expansion of its own world picture, and is accordingly available to others.[15]

This position is grounded in a rejection of the distinction between a linguistic scheme and uninterpreted, nonlinguistically constituted reality ("the world in itself") and, with that, of relativism: "Those views are not relative in the sense that one could oppose them to the 'world in itself,' as if the right view from some possible position outside the human, linguistic world could discover it in its being-in-itself."[16] The idea of a linguistic scheme organizing or fitting nonlinguistic experience or reality does not make sense to Gadamer any more than it does to Davidson as a means of shoring up conceptual relativism. However, for Davidson the world is not linguistically constituted as it is for Gadamer; a view that insists on *unmediated* contact with reality allows no room for it. Simon Blackburn has suggested that Davidson sets up a false dichotomy in how he frames his argument against conceptual schemes and "ignores [a] natural third account" of the relationship between conceptual schemes and content according to which "conceptual schemes neither organize nor fit experience, but rather *shape* experience."[17] Something like this third option seems to be what Gadamer has in mind: He allows for traditions or cultures to shape our views of the world.

Gadamer contrasts the linguistic constitution of the world with perception:

> As with perception we can speak of the "linguistic shadings" that the world undergoes in different language-worlds. But there remains a characteristic difference: every "shading" of the object of perception is exclusively distinct from every other, and each helps co-constitute the "thing-in-itself" as the continuum of these nuances—whereas, in the case of the shadings of verbal worldviews, each one potentially contains every other one within it—i.e., each worldview can be extended into every other. It can understand and comprehend, from within itself, the "view" of the world presented in another language.[18]

Different perspectives or worlds are not in principle mutually "exclusive" or unintelligible. In other words, they are *not incommensurable*. This means, here, that they can enter into conversation with each other.

Because Gadamer's argument is grounded in the phenomenology of hermeneutic experience rather than being formal or conceptual in nature as is Davidson's, perhaps also because he seems to be more impressed than Davidson by difficulties of translation and cross-cultural communication as philosophically significant, he replaces the idea of conceptual schemes with that of *horizons*.[19] The fusion of horizons is Gadamer's foundational metaphor for reaching mutual understanding among two interlocutors.[20] The notion of horizon is crucial to Gadamer's contextualist conception of situated understanding:

> We define the concept of "situation" by saying that it represents a standpoint that limits the possibility of vision. Hence essential to the concept of situation is the concept of "*horizon*." The horizon is the range of vision that includes everything that can be seen from a particular vantage point.[21]

Yet a horizon is not "a rigid boundary but something that moves with one and invites one to advance further."[22] It is a "boundless space."[23] One might say that one's horizon is constantly receding from one as one seeks to reach it. A horizon is thus starkly different from a conceptual scheme or *web*, in which one is caught.

Unlike a conceptual scheme, a horizon is not a *closed* system; the metaphor conveys both the limits of what is visible and the openness of what is beyond the horizon. Invoking Robinson Crusoe, Gadamer writes,

> just as the individual is never simply an individual because he is always in understanding with others, so too *the closed horizon that is supposed to enclose a culture is an abstraction*. The historical movement of human life consists in the fact that it is never

absolutely bound to any one standpoint, and hence can never have a truly closed horizon. The horizon is, rather, something into which we move and that moves with us. Horizons change for a person who is moving. Thus the horizon of the past, out of which all human life lives and which exists in the form of tradition, is always in motion.[24]

The relativism and incommensurability theses rest precisely on this kind of abstraction—and indeed *reification*—of a culture or conceptual scheme. By contrast, the openness and fluidity of horizons make their fusion possible. Davidson holds that if we cannot make sense of multiple incommensurable conceptual schemes, we cannot make sense of a single one, either. Similarly, Gadamer maintains that even though it doesn't make sense to speak of neatly distinct horizons, we cannot not just talk about a single one. However, Gadamer holds on to a plurality of horizons precisely because he conceives understanding as a fusion thereof. There is a "manifold of horizons that we ought not to reduce by means of some kind of particular unifying mechanism," he writes in the 1980s:

> The pluralistic world in which we find ourselves is like the new Babel. But our pluralistic world presents us with tasks, and these consist not so much in rational planning and overplanning [*Verplanung*], but in the perception of the open spaces of human togetherness, even beyond what is alien or other.[25]

What unifies the manifold for Gadamer, one might say on analogy with Kant, is the universality of hermeneutic experience.

To recapitulate, whereas Davidson emphasizes the logical incoherence of the very idea of conceptual schemes, Gadamer focuses on the phenomenology of hermeneutic experience. Though their arguments differ, both subscribe to meaning–belief holism. Davidson rejects incommensurability on formal grounds because the incommensurability thesis presupposes the scheme–content distinction; Gadamer rejects incommensurability because of the open nature of horizons of intelligibility.

To deny incommensurability is not to deny that there can be significant differences between cultures and individuals. In the next section, I address the diverging ways in which Gadamer and Davidson handle such differences.

2 Toward an Understanding of Difference

Arguing against a wholesale dismissal of conceptual schemes, Charles Taylor concurs with Davidson's argument against *radical* incommensurability insofar as it shows that "total unintelligibility of another culture is not an option. To experience another group as unintelligible over some range of their practices, we have to find them quite understandable over other (very substantial) ranges."[26] If something is a language it must be in principle intelligible. This is consistent with a key component of the Davidsonian view, namely, the principle of charity. We get interpretation off the ground by holding belief constant and, indeed, maximizing agreement (in beliefs) while solving for meaning. Taylor argues, however, that the argument is in effect too powerful and doesn't help us deal with the everyday situations of "partial and (we hope) surmountable noncommunication."[27] Taylor himself is reluctant to give up the idea of conceptual schemes altogether. He maintains that

> in dealing with the real, partial barriers to understanding, we need to be able to identify what is blocking us. And for this we need some way of picking out the systematic differences in construal between two different cultures, without either reifying them or branding them as ineradicable. This is what Gadamer does with the image of the horizon. . . . It is what Davidson's position as yet lacks. Without this, Davidson's principle of charity is vulnerable to being abused to ethnocentric ends.[28]

His worry is that the interpretive maxim of the principle of charity, to maximize agreement, leads an interpreter falsely to project her own beliefs onto the other. Although Taylor appeals to the notion of horizon here, he does not acknowledge any differences between conceptual schemes and horizons. Moreover, he addresses neither Davidson's arguments regarding the scheme–content distinction nor his meaning–belief holism. As a result, he overlooks the extent to which the (Gadamerian) notion of conceptual scheme he defends in fact differs from the one Davidson rejects. "Systematic differences in construal" between cultures may be differences in conceptual scheme or differences in belief content. If we grant that we cannot draw a clear line between the two, according to Davidson's argument, we must abandon the idea of conceptual schemes.

As indicated above, Davidson does not aim to eliminate the concept or intelligibility of disagreement when differences are "local enough." For him, the systematic differences Taylor has in mind may well be local relative to the vast background of agreement our theories of interpretation postulate. "Local," in other words, may boil down to "articulable." Hence Taylor's criticism of Davidson misses its mark. That said, he is right that Davidson tends to pay insufficient attention to differences that are "real barriers to understanding." Since incommensurability appeals to conceptual relativists insisting on irreducible differences between perspectives, what happens to difference absent (radical) incommensurability?

Difference in Dialogue

"Understanding the other," Gadamer claims, "is the most difficult of human tasks."[29] The fusion of horizons—though it may go "beyond what is alien"—must both preserve the voice of the other (and of self) while at the same time transforming them. Gadamer's interpreter relies on a constellation of prejudices, preconceptions, and preunderstandings when approaching any interpretive situation. These prejudices constitute our horizon. In a passage reminiscent of Quine and anticipating Davidson, he writes, "the horizon of the present is continually in the process of being formed because we are continually having to test all our prejudices." In contrast to Quine, for Gadamer the "tribunal of experience" is not limited or reducible to sense experience, but explicitly involves engagement with one's past and one's tradition; understanding for him is always already historical. "There is no more an isolated horizon of the present in itself than there are historical horizons which have to be acquired. *Rather, understanding is always the fusion of these horizons supposedly existing by themselves.*"[30]

Gadamer argues that the goal of genuine conversation is not simply to place oneself in the other's position, but to develop a shared position with her, for in a true conversation we seek to reach agreement about something with someone. A *real* conversation "is a process of coming to an understanding" and of opening oneself to the other.[31] In this sense, dialogue incorporates the notion of difference as well as the possibility of overcoming difference: For interlocutors engage one another *as other* in order to reach a *shared* understanding. If we converse with another simply in order to find out "where she is coming from," Gadamer tells us, we may acknowledge her otherness, but in a way that effectively silences her by our "fundamental suspension of [her] claim to truth."[32] Such an articulation of difference is, as it were, impotent. Neither we nor our interlocutor is affected by it.

In hermeneutic conversation, "something is expressed that is not only mine or my author's, but common."[33] This means that for Gadamer, quite unlike for Davidson, language is inherently something shared:

> Language in which something comes to speak is not a possession at the disposal of one or the other of the interlocutors. Every conversation presupposes a common language, or better, creates a common language. . . . to reach an understanding in a dialogue is not merely a matter of putting oneself forward and successful asserting one's own point of view, but being transformed into a communion in which we do not remain what we were.[34]

Conversation, in other words, is a phenomenon whereby both speaker and interpreter are transformed and where something new is created that is shared between them. This is something that Kuhn fails to appreciate sufficiently and Davidson barely seems to take into account. This neglect is evident in the latter's account of communication in terms of prior and passing theories (see below). For Gadamer, the resulting language will rise "to a higher universality that overcomes not only our own particularity but also that of the other."[35] This can be achieved neither by mere empathy for the other nor by imposing one's own standards on her, but rather requires the application of "the true productivity of language" whereby we seek to attain "real solidarity" in the midst of a manifold of linguistic cultures and traditions .[36] For Gadamer, then, it is the very nature of language to make it possible for us to reach mutual understanding.

Difference as Anomalous Details

To what extent is Davidson able to account for difference in light of his argument against incommensurability? As we have seen, he links translatability with intelligibility: The more we can translate, the more we can understand difference. Difference is intelligible only against a background of agreement (which, for Davidson, is ultimately based on the fact that human beings share needs and interests and the fact that we live in the same objective world). The function of the principle of charity is analogous to that of Gadamer's horizon in the sense that both provide a background of intelligibility and operate quasi-transcendentally. Recall that Davidson's interpreter, faced with the problem of meaning–belief holism, holds belief constant (i.e., attributes to the interpretee beliefs that she herself holds true) and solves for meaning. Whatever differences there are, then, between the interpreter and interpretee will presumably be cashed out in terms of differences between sets of sentences they respectively hold true. We will still be able to identify these differences, even though we may not be able to determine whether these are differences between beliefs or concepts. Davidson describes the differences between interlocutors as "anomalous details" and provides the "undramatic" example of someone using the term "yawl" for what the interpreter takes to be a ketch so that the interpreter cannot tell whether the speaker has misperceived a ketch for a yawl or whether he understands the term differently.

How do we handle the "interpretation of anomalous details"? We are able to work things out "off the cuff" because the "interpretation of anomalous details" happens against a background of common beliefs and a going method of translation. Davidson claims:

> The method is not designed to eliminate disagreement, nor can it; its purpose is to make meaningful disagreement possible; and this depends entirely on a foundation—*some* foundation—in agreement. This agreement may take the form of

widespread sharing of sentences held true by speakers of "the same language," or agreement in the large mediated by a theory of truth contrived by an interpreter for speakers of another language.[37]

Such a theory is "contrived" by applying the principle of charity—which rests on the interpreter presuming agreement with the interpretee. Practically in the same breath, Davidson then weds intelligibility to agreement, yet asserts the greater intelligibility of *difference* against a greater background of agreement:

> We make maximum sense of the words and thoughts of others when we interpret in a way that optimizes agreement (this includes room, as we said, for explicable error, i.e., differences of opinion). . . . we improve the clarity and bite of declarations of difference, whether of scheme or opinion, by enlarging the basis of shared (translatable) language or of shared opinion. Indeed no clear line between the cases can be made out.[38]

It is, presumably, precisely these *details* that give rise to the heady doctrine of relativism. Davidson is at least partly correct in that the same kinds of considerations that apply to the ketch/yawl case also apply to more "exotic" cases such as Eskimo infanticide. What at first appears to be a radically incommensurable value system turns out to be a function of beliefs about one's environment.[39] Notwithstanding, what are we to understand by the improved "clarity and bite of declarations of difference" if not decreased unintelligibility or untranslatability? Davidson has created a tight conceptual circle between commensurability, translatability, and intelligibility. What room is there in this circle to distinguish between false belief, nonsense, and poetic license?

3 Malaprops, Poetry, and the Limits of Translation

The later Davidson continues to be deeply impressed by the ease with which we interpret others so as to make them intelligible. The development of Davidson's thought is foreshadowed in "On the Very Idea of a Conceptual Scheme." With reference to the ketch/yawl example, which he uses to illustrate meaning–belief holism, he says, "We do this sort of off the cuff interpretation all the time, deciding in favour of reinterpretation of words in order to preserve a reasonable theory of belief. As philosophers we are particularly tolerant of systematic *malapropism,* and practised at interpreting the result."[40] In "A Nice Derangement of Epitaphs," he uses our ability to interpret malaprops and other linguistic gaffes or jokes to argue that there is no such thing as a language in the sense of a set of linguistic conventions that we must share in order to be able to communicate.[41] This is a—perhaps the most—significant difference between him and Gadamer, who takes conventions to be an inherent part of language.

Davidson conceives communication as a constant flux of "prior" and "passing" theories. He writes: "For the hearer, the prior theory expresses how he is prepared in advance to interpret an utterance of the speaker, while the passing theory is how he *does* interpret the utterance. For the speaker, the prior theory is what he *believes* the interpreter's prior theory to be, while his passing theory is the theory he *intends* the interpreter to use."[42] Although each interlocutor approaches an interaction with her own prior theory of interpretation (for a speaker), that theory need not be shared with the other. In the course of conversation, the interpreter may adjust her theory of interpretation in order to understand the speaker, and vice versa. But, though it may be shared, such a passing theory is not something learned and is geared to the moment. The flux of prior and passing theories of interpretation can be seen as a truncated version of the Gadamerian shifting of horizons, one that lacks any *dialogical* dimension or emergence of a shared language. The fact that speakers do, as a matter of fact, speak the same language is a mere contingency, not required for communicative success.[43] Davidson famously turns against the idea that language is a system of shared rules or conventions that determine meaning and make possible mutual understanding. He denies that what makes communication possible is that interlocutors share (prior to communicating) a convention- or rule-governed language. Even if the result of communication may be that interlocutors come to share a passing theory, and even though communication may be helped if they happen to share a prior theory, this account privileges idiolects and distorts the social aspects of language.[44]

For Davidson, understanding (or agreement) is a matter of degree, perfect agreement being a regulative ideal. This is simply an empirical fact: We all have different beliefs, most of us use at least some terms idiosyncratically, and our theories of interpretation are always fallible. So perhaps the best we can hope for in successful communication is converging passing theories. Nevertheless, it is worth asking whether Davidson overestimates the ease with which we adjust to the idiolects of others. Consider, for instance, the passage about Ace Goodman that he cites from the *New Yorker*. It is chock-full of examples like this one: "he will maneuver until he selects the ideal phrase for the situation, hitting the nail right on the thumb." Do we really do it justice by taking "thumb" to mean "head"? That kind of reinterpretation—or passing theory—would surely take all the humor out of the passage. But taken literally (in our conventional sense of the term), is it fully intelligible? Or rather, is it *translatable*? (Some, maybe most, jokes cannot be paraphrased.) Is it not the element of nonsense that makes it funny? One might say at this point that nonsense is indeed untranslatable—there is, after all, no *meaning* to be rendered. Nonetheless, do we not here have a limit case of translatability or, at any rate, of the "strange and novel" having turned "absurd"? Indeed there are slips of the tongue, where easy "repair" work is possible for the interpreter. But there are instances where an idiolect geared to a particular occasion will lose at least some of its particularity of meaning when interpreted into another idiom.

While Gadamer is famous for holding that understanding is essentially an interpretive process—which, after all, is a chief reason for bringing him and Davidson into conversation—it is important to remember what he says about translation in *Truth and Method* and elsewhere. Although he claims that "every translation is at the same time an interpretation," if only because translation must preserve meaning,[45] the process of translation draws our attention to the fact that language as medium of understanding is itself created through mediation. This sounds very much like Davidson. Translation by itself, however, cannot produce understanding. It is a process going from one known language to another known language and therefore represents neither what happens in standard conversation nor how foreign languages are best learned. Moreover, perfect translation is impossible: "Where a translation is necessary, the gap between the spirit of the original words and that of their reproduction must be taken into account and cannot be completely closed."[46] By contrast, "where there is understanding there is not translation but speech. To understand a foreign language means that we do not need to translate it into our own. When we really master a language, then no translation is necessary—in fact, any translation seems impossible."[47] In short, although good translation requires interpretation, not every interpretation is a translation.[48] To understand a language, rather, is to *live* it. Someone who learns a language by immersion may well not be able to translate between her first and second languages. Are the two languages therefore incommensurable for her? As any experienced translator knows, translation is always a balancing act of compromises. Finally, literal translation taken to the extreme is either humorous (as when my bilingual son says "tooth meat" in English to refer to his gums [*Zahnfleisch*]) or intellectually frustrating (as when reading some Heidegger translations). Translation, in other words, is a skill added on to our fundamental linguistic (interpretive) competence. Hence Gadamer sunders the tight conceptual connection between translatability and intelligibility that we saw Davidson forge.

Elsewhere Gadamer aligns untranslatability with the unique and individual in language. He argues that poetry is the most individualized form of language since, by its very nature, there is but one right word or way of putting it. Yet, he asks rhetorically, is the difference in word choice between what we would describe as synonymous terms (e.g., *home* vs. *abode*) really a semantic difference (*Sinndifferenz*)? "Is it not merely an aesthetic difference with emotional or euphonic valence? . . . Indeed, it is difficult to find a better definition for the sense [*Sinn*] or reference [*Bedeutung*] or *the meaning* of an expression than its substitutability."[49] The question assumes that meaning (or reference) is a purely cognitive, rational, or denotative value, distinct from conative or connotative aspects of communication, and I take it that Gadamer rejects such an assumption. For Gadamer, a semantics that explains meaning purely in terms of substitutability and correspondence relations is limited. Whatever equivalence relations there are among expressions, they are "not unchanging mappings; rather they arise and atrophy, as the spirit of the times is reflected from one decade to the next in semantic change."[50] Language is a living thing—a thing that *we live.* To understand a language, once more, is to live it. And that is to say that language and meaning are always tied to other human practices.

Davidson appears to make a similar argument when he explicitly rejects commonly held theories of meaning (including ones to which he has himself subscribed). He asserts in "A Nice Derangement of Epitaphs" that there is no "boundary between knowing a language and knowing our way around in the world generally," and that we "must give up the idea of a clearly defined shared structure which language-users acquire and then apply to cases. And we should try again to say how convention in any important sense is involved in language; or, as I think, we should give up the attempt to illuminate how we communicate by appeal to conventions."[51] This final conclusion, however, is at odds with Gadamer's position.

Gadamer identifies a tension in language between an individualizing and a conventionalizing tendency. Echoing Wittgenstein, he writes,

> Someone speaking a private language that no one understands does not speak at all. Yet on the other hand, someone who only speaks one language the conventional nature of which in vocabulary choice, syntax, and style has become absolute, loses the power of address and of evocation which is accessible only by means of the individualization of the linguistic vocabulary and other linguistic means.[52]

He exemplifies this tension with reference to the relationship between theoretical vocabulary and ordinary language, in particular, the scientific use of the term *Kraft* in German Romanticism, which he claims to be individualized to the point of untranslatability. Parallels with Kuhn surface once again. There is a deep semantic contextualism at work in Gadamer here, comparable to that of Derrida and Davidson. Poetry is the perfect realization of this individualization:

> The untranslatability that marks the extreme case of lyric poetry so that it cannot be translated from one language into another at all without losing its entire poetic expressiveness [*Sagkraft*], clearly implies the failure of the idea of substitution, of replacing one expression by another. This seems to hold more generally, independently of the special phenomenon of highly individualized poetic language. If I'm right, substitutability runs counter to the individualizing moment in language [*Sprachvollzug*] as such.[53]

Intended meaning (*Sinnmeinung*) develops in the course of speaking, *in the course* of substituting expressions for one another. Conversation takes the form, as Gadamer puts it here, of a *fluid uniqueness*. Thinking that we can substitute one term for another with the same meaning breaks the flow and constitutes an abstraction that distorts the reality of lived language. For Gadamer, the true nature of language (the "productivity of speech") is the fact that we are able to communicate without having to rely on rigid systems of rules that govern how to make correct and incorrect distinctions.[54] To that extent, he is in agreement with Davidson's critique of semantic conventionalism. Yet whereas Davidson rejects conventionality as philosophically insignificant, Gadamer takes this tension to be emblematic of language. As a result, I believe, he is able to account philosophically for a wider range of our linguistic intuitions than Davidson. In particular, he is better able to account for the social aspects of language. For even if there is no "clearly defined shared structure" or "rigid system of rules" that accounts for how we manage to communicate, this does not mean that rules or conventions play no role at all in explaining communication.

Perhaps nowhere is Davidson's appreciation of linguistic and literary creativity more evident than in his essay on Joyce,[55] where he asks how Joyce was able to "fly by the net of language." He writes, "Flying by the net of language could not . . . imply the unconstrained invention of meaning, Humpty Dumpty style." Rather, "[i]n speaking or writing we intend to be understood. We cannot intend what we know to be impossible; people can only understand words they are somehow prepared in advance to understand. No one knew this better than Joyce."[56] One might say, *pace* Davidson, that Joyce is able to break with tradition or convention only by appealing to them. Even where he is annihilating and re-creating language, he does so by playing with semantic and literary conventions, by implicit references to history or mythology, and so on. To be sure, this transcends any alleged boundary between language and "other ways of getting around in the world." Someone who knew only the semantics and syntax of English would not "get" Joyce (or much else). Davidson argues persuasively that reading—and understanding—Joyce requires a much broader cultural knowledge. He goes so far as to acknowledge that there is a "tension between invention and tradition," but he claims that Joyce "resolves" it in favor of invention.[57] The following passage is emblematic of both the kinship between Davidson and Gadamer and their divergences:

> All reading is interpretation, and all interpretation demands some degree of invention. It is Joyce's extraordinary idea to raise the price of admission to the point where we are inclined to feel that almost as much is demanded from the reader as of the author. . . . By fragmenting familiar languages and recycling the raw material Joyce provokes the reader into involuntary collaboration, and enlists him as a member of his private linguistic community. Coopted into Joyce's world of verbal exile, we are forced to share in the annihilation of old meanings and the creation—not really *ex nihilo*, but on the basis of our stock of common lore—of a new language. All communication involves such joint effort to some degree, but Joyce is unusual in first warning us of this, and then making the effort so extreme. Joyce takes us back to the foundations and origins of communication; he puts us in the situation of the jungle linguist. . . . The center of creative energy is thus moved from the artist to a point between the writer and the audience. The engagement of the reader in the process of interpretation, forced on him by Joyce's dense, unknown idiom, bestows on the author himself a kind of invisibility, leaving the interpreter alone with the author's handiwork, absorbed in his own creative task.[58]

Davidson may come as close here as anywhere in his writings to a Gadamerian position. For Gadamer, interpretation is also a creative enterprise involving both author and reader. But whereas Gadamer regards hermeneutic engagement with a text as a dialogue, Davidson frames it as a solitary struggle: The reader is "forced" against her will, it seems, into Joyce's "private linguistic community" and is like Quine's "jungle linguist" who may assume no shared meanings. The center of creative energy may be moved to a place between author and audience, but it remains in the control of the author until, that is, in the end, the author abandons his reader—never an interlocutor—leaving her to her own devices. Davidson's essay leaves little doubt that interpreting Joyce has rich rewards indeed and can be a transformative experience. By the same token, whereas Gadamer writes that understanding another is the most difficult of human tasks, on Davidson's account it may be an impossible one.

If Gadamer is right that individualization implies untranslatability and untranslatability implies incommensurability, then we find vestiges of incommensurability in both Gadamer's and Davidson's individualized languages. To be sure, it is not the "heady and exotic" incommensurability between different conceptual schemes. It is a usually highly localized form of incommensurability. But it does present a limit case of intelligibility, on the one hand, and, on the other, challenges our notions about the parameters or limits of a philosophical account of meaning.[59]

Acknowledgments

I thank Jonathan Maskit for comments on an earlier draft of this essay, Jeff Malpas for reminding me of the importance of "James Joyce and Humpty Dumpty," and audiences at the 2007 Eastern APA and North American Society for Philosophical Hermeneutics meetings for their feedback. I am grateful for the support of a University of Connecticut Humanities Institute Faculty Research Fellowship and a Denison University R. C. Good Fellowship.

Notes

1. Hans-Georg Gadamer, "Die Vielfalt der Sprachen und das Verstehen der Welt," in *Gesammelte Werke*, vol. 8 (Tübingen: Mohr Siebeck, 1999), p. 346.

2. Donald Davidson, "On the Very Idea of a Conceptual Scheme," in *Inquiries into Truth and Interpretation* (Oxford: Oxford University Press, 1984), p. 183.

3. Thomas Kuhn reminds us that he and Paul Feyerabend adopted the term simultaneously in 1962, i.e., two years after the first edition of Gadamer's *Truth and Method* was published. Davidson flatly asserts it is their term for "not intertranslatable" (Davidson, "On the Very Idea of a Conceptual Scheme," p. 190—the essay was originally published in 1974). Kuhn further insists that this does not mean they are *incomparable*. See Thomas Kuhn, "Commensurability, Comparability, Communicability," in Thomas Kuhn, *The Road Since Structure: Philosophical Essays*, ed. James Conant and John Haugeland (Chicago: Chicago University Press, 2000). Kuhn's own view thus stands in direct opposition to that of someone like James Griffin who, writing about value incommensurability, defines it in terms of incomparability. See James Griffin, "Incommensurability: What's the Problem?" in *Incommensurability, Incomparability, and Practical Reason*, ed. Ruth Chang (Cambridge, MA: Harvard University Press, 1997), pp. 35–51.

4. Davidson, "On the Very Idea of a Conceptual Scheme," p. 184.

5. Davidson contrasts this with a Strawsonian model of conceptual relativism, according to which we describe alternative worlds from a single point of view, that is, in our language. The Strawsonian metaphor, he writes, "requires a distinction within language of concept and content: using a fixed system of concepts . . . we describe

alternative universes" ("On the Very Idea of a Conceptual Scheme," p. 187). The two models, he claims, are not inconsistent, but rejecting the Strawsonian model (on the grounds of rejecting the analytic–synthetic distinction) can push one toward the Kuhnian—and thus to a commitment to a scheme–content distinction.

6. Davidson, "On the Very Idea of a Conceptual Scheme," p. 189.

7. This claim, to be sure, rests on accepting Davidson's overall semantic framework.

8. Davidson, "On the Very Idea of a Conceptual Scheme," p. 195.

9. Ibid., p. 192.

10. Ibid., p. 195.

11. Ibid., p. 197. Davidson illustrates meaning–belief holism with the "undramatic" example of the ketch/yawl where the interpreter cannot tell whether the speaker has misperceived a ketch for a yawl (false belief) or whether he understands the terms differently (different concept). More on that below.

12. Hans-Georg Gadamer, *Truth and Method,* 2nd ed., trans. Joel Weinsheimer and Donald G. Marshall (New York: Continuum, 1994), p. 441.

13. Ibid., trans. mod.

14. Ibid., p. 446.

15. Ibid., p. 447.

16. Ibid.

17. Simon Blackburn, "Relativism and the Abolition of the Other," *International Journal of Philosophical Studies* 12, no.3 (2004): 249. Along similar lines, John McDowell speculates that the idea of a linguistically constituted self never really occurred to Davidson. See John McDowell, "Gadamer and Davidson on Understanding and Relativism," in *Gadamer's Century: Essays in Honor of Hans-Georg Gadamer,* ed. Jeff Malpas, Ulrich Arnswald, and Jens Kertscher (Cambridge, MA: MIT Press, 2002), pp. 173–193.

18. Gadamer, *Truth and Method,* p. 448. Once more anticipating Kuhn, Gadamer points out that our language has managed to reconcile our everyday view of the world with a Copernican view: The sun still sets for us, even though we know that the Earth rotates around it.

19. Perhaps this difference can be explained in part by the extent to which each lived in a multi- vs. monolingual environment. Jeff Malpas has argued that horizonality also plays an important role in Davidson. See J. E. Malpas, *Donald Davidson and the Mirror of Meaning: Holism, Truth, Interpretation* (Cambridge: Cambridge University Press, 1992), esp. part II.

20. I should note that there may be important differences between communication between interlocutors belonging to the same culture and interlocutors from different cultures.

21. Gadamer, *Truth and Method*, p. 302.

22. Ibid., p. 245.

23. Hans-Georg Gadamer, "Die Vielfalt der Sprachen," p. 345. The essay was originally published in 1988.

24. Gadamer, *Truth and Method*, p. 304; emphasis added.

25. Gadamer, "Die Vielfalt der Sprachen," p. 348.

26. Charles Taylor, "Understanding the Other: A Gadamerian View of Conceptual Schemes," in *Gadamer's Century: Essays in Honor of Hans-Georg Gadamer*, ed. Jeff Malpas, Ulrich Arnswald, and Jens Kertscher (Cambridge, MA: MIT Press, 2002), p. 291. This general point is consistent with Wittgensteinian private language arguments. Taylor also emphasizes that the resulting language "will not be the same language in which members of that culture understand themselves . . . [but] a language that bridges those of both knower and known," p. 287. In earlier writings, he referred to this as a "language of perspicuous contrast."

27. Ibid., p. 291.

28. Ibid., pp. 291–292.

29. Gadamer, "Vielfalt der Sprachen," p. 346.

30. Gadamer, *Truth and Method*, p. 306.

31. Ibid., p. 385.

32. Ibid., p. 303. For a critique of Gadamer's account of otherness that brings him in many ways much closer to Davidson, see Marie Fleming, "Gadamer's Conversation: Does the Other Have a Say?" in *Feminist Interpretations of Gadamer*, ed. Lorraine Code (University Park: Pennsylvania State University Press, 2003), pp. 109–132.

33. Gadamer, *Truth and Method*, p. 389.

34. Ibid., pp. 378–379.

35. Ibid., p. 305. Gadamer's description of the goal of conversation is clearly reminiscent of Benjamin's account of the task of the translator in relation to universal language. See Walter Benjamin, "The Task of the Translator," in *Illuminations*, trans. H. Zorn (New York: Harcourt, Brace & World, 1968), pp. 69–82.

36. Gadamer, "Vielfalt der Sprachen," p. 346.

37. Davidson, "On the Very Idea of a Conceptual Scheme," pp. 196–197.

38. Ibid., p. 197.

39. See Paul K. Moser and Thomas L. Carson (eds.), *Moral Relativism* (Oxford: Oxford University Press, 2001).

40. Davidson, "On the Very Idea of a Conceptual Scheme," p. 196.

41. Donald Davidson, "A Nice Derangement of Epitaphs," in *Truth, Language, and History* (Oxford: Oxford University Press, 2005), pp. 89–107.

42. Davidson, "A Nice Derangement," p. 101.

43. Donald Davidson, "Communication and Convention," in *Inquiries into Truth and Interpretation* (Oxford: Oxford University Press, 1984), pp. 278–279.

44. See Davidson, "The Social Aspects of Language," in his *Truth, Language, and History* (Oxford: Oxford University Press, 2005), pp. 109–125. Cf. John McDowell, "Gadamer and Davidson on Understanding and Relativism," pp. 173–193.

45. Gadamer, *Truth and Method*, p. 384. In "Semantik und Hermeneutik," he writes that the truth of hermeneutic enlightened consciousness is "the truth of translation. It superiority lies in its ability to make what is alien one's own, not simply by critically untangling it or reproducing it uncritically, but by interpreting it with its own concepts in its own horizon and thus making it relevant [*zur Geltung bringen*]. Translating allows what is alien and what is one's own to merge in a new form by maintaining the truth [*Wahrheitspunkt*] of the other relative to oneself," p. 183. Note that Gadamer takes translation here to be an interpretive process.

46. Gadamer, *Truth and Method*, p. 384.

47. Ibid., p. 385. The wording, to be sure, leaves it open that translation is possible nonetheless.

48. The way in which Gadamer here distinguishes between translation and interpretation is uncannily similar to how Thomas Kuhn defends the notion of incommensurability in 1982. For Kuhn, translation is almost a mechanical process of rendering or rather substituting sentences from one language in another based on *a translation manual*, that is, by someone who knows both languages. He reserves the term "interpretation" for the process of making a foreign language intelligible, something that historians and anthropologists do. Interpretation is thus more like *learning* a foreign language than translating from one known language into another. In fact, he refers to interpretation recently being discussed "under the rubric of hermeneutics," citing not Gadamer but Charles Taylor. It is in interpretation, according to Kuhn, that we are liable to run up against *untranslatable* and hence incommensurable terminology. See Kuhn, "Commensurability, Comparability, and Communicability," p. 38. Similarly, Gadamer says that simultaneous interpretation [*dolmetschen*] is closer to real conversation than translation, in "Vielfalt der Sprachen," p. 347.

49. Hans-Georg Gadamer, "Semantik und Hermeneutik," in *Gesammelte Werke*, vol. 2 (Tübingen: Mohr Siebeck, 1999), p. 175.

50. Ibid., pp. 176–177. The passage is followed by a discussion of metaphor, which, too, would be interesting to compare to Davidson's theory of metaphor, particularly as it relates to the conventionality of meanings.

51. Davidson, "A Nice Derangement," p. 107.

52. Gadamer, "Semantik und Hermeneutik," p. 176.

53. Ibid., p. 177.

54. Gadamer, "Vielfalt der Sprachen," p. 345.

55. Donald Davidson, "James Joyce and Humpty Dumpty," in *Midwest Studies in Philosophy* 16 (Notre Dame: University of Notre Dame Press, 1991), pp. 1–12.

56. Ibid., p. 4.

57. Ibid., p. 8.

58. Ibid., p. 11.

13 Davidson, Gadamer, Incommensurability, and the Third Dogma of Empiricism

David Vessey

Both Hans-Georg Gadamer and Donald Davidson deny the existence of some commonly claimed forms of incommensurability. In his 1972 American Philosophical Association (APA) presidential address, Davidson issued a sweeping criticism of even the "very idea" of incommensurable conceptual schemes.[1] One part of his argument was that if one held that there are diverse conceptual schemes one could not make sense of the idea that these schemes were incommensurable. Another part of his argument was against the idea that perception operates on a two-stage model where we take in raw data about the world through our senses and then organize that data according to our concepts. If one adopts this two-stage account, then people will perceive the world differently in accordance with the various concepts they get from their particular backgrounds, cultures, or languages. Incommensurability would arise when there is no way for a person to escape his or her schematizing concepts—his or her perspective on the world—in order to perceive the world from another perspective using another's concepts. Davidson calls this scheme–content theory of perception "the third dogma of empiricism."

In this chapter, I consider the case of incommensurability arising in conjunction with the third dogma of empiricism. After spelling out some of Davidson's arguments I will turn to Gadamer who, although denying incommensurability, seems to be committed to such a scheme–content theory of perception and thus would not be entitled to his denial of incommensurability. I will argue that he, in fact, does not have a scheme–content account of perception, and the mistake arises if we fail to interpret "horizon" and "world" as technical terms with their roots in the phenomenology of Edmund Husserl and Max Scheler, respectively. After outlining Gadamer's account of the role of language in perception, drawing the important differences between his view and Davidson's, I will introduce two new arguments Gadamer can make against incommensurability. My goal is to reveal some of the fundamental differences behind the apparent agreement. I will focus more on Gadamer only because his views are less well known and require more argumentative reconstruction than Davidson's.

1 Davidson, Incommensurability, and the Third Dogma

Throughout his writings Davidson makes a number of arguments that jointly attack the third dogma of empiricism and the incommensurability that follows from it—I will briefly point to five. The first and perhaps most intuitive argument targets the possibility of completely incommensurable conceptual schemes—conceptual schemes that never line up, that disagree everywhere. Davidson makes the point that in order for two schemes to disagree there must be something that they disagree about; otherwise it would not count as a disagreement. There must be something common with respect to which the differences could count as differences. There is a general insight here that should be obvious: Disagreement only occurs on the back of much wider agreement. Gadamer says much the same thing: "a prior agreement in understanding is presupposed wherever disturbances in this agreement arise."[2] So, if one holds that there are multiple conceptual schemes that disagree about how to conceptualize the world, their disagreements cannot run across the board. Their incommensurability must be local, not global.

A second argument against global incommensurability is similarly straightforward. If our understanding of the world were wholly mediated by our conceptual scheme, and there were massive, comprehensive differences across conceptual schemes, we would never be in a position to recognize these differences; to see the differences at the level of conceptual scheme would require a perspective on them independent from our own conceptual scheme—it would require us to "take up a stance outside our own ways of thought." It is one thing to recognize a difference of opinion; it is quite another to recognize a difference of scheme. Either we are trapped or we are not: If we are trapped, we have no evidence of other conceptual schemes globally incommensurable with ours; if we are not trapped, our scheme is not globally incommensurable with other schemes.

Davidson makes a brief argument, the third of five, that I think should be read in the context of the first two. He claims that recognizing behavior as linguistic is enough to know that there could be no systematic disagreement, so even if aliens were to land and try to speak to us in their language, that would be enough to know that complete disagreement could not be the case. The best way to understand this surprising claim is to realize that the mere recognition of language use presumes a number of things. For example, it presumes the others think you exist, that they think you think they exist, that they believe you can perceive them, that there are beliefs or desires that can be communicated, that both parties can distinguish truth from falsity and understanding from misunderstanding, and so on. These commonalities suffice for showing that even the most minimal recognition—the recognition that someone is using language—presents enough of a shard basis to rule out radical conceptual differences across the different languages.[3] There might be local, partial incommensurability, but not comprehensive, global incommensurability.

A fourth argument is against such cases of partial incommensurability across conceptual schemes, cases where there is enough in common to recognize disagreement. In these cases Davidson asks what could function as a criterion for determining whether a disagreement is simply a matter of different beliefs or a matter of different conceptual schemes. All we are faced with in these situations is someone who says something different from us about something. Either they are using the words like we do and have concepts like we do and simply disagree with us, or they are using words differently and are operating with a different scheme from us. But the only evidence we have for their having a different scheme from us is our disagreement, which leaves us no criterion by which we could decide whether the disagreement occurs at the level of what we believe about the world or at the level of the different ways of speaking about the world. That is, the only evidence that a different scheme is in play is that the other person has different beliefs from ours, but having different beliefs is insufficient for concluding that there is a different conceptual scheme in play. We are never justified in concluding partial incommensurability over simply partial disagreement.

All the arguments so far line up against the possible existence of partially or completely incommensurable conceptual schemes, once you accept the existence of conceptual schemes. Davidson's real target, though, is conceptual schemes as such. For the third dogma to fall he needs additional arguments; as he says, "[e]ven those thinkers who are certain there is only one conceptual scheme are in the sway of the scheme concept."[4] His final argument strikes at the heart of how the third dogma functions within empiricism, that is, within the idea that our perceptual encounters with the world provide independent and essential information for justifying perceptual beliefs. Accompanying conceptual schemes, for an empiricist, is "the idea that there is an element in experience which serves as a basis and justification of empirical knowledge, an element which is private and subjective in the sense that it owes nothing to what is outside the mind." Such epistemic intermediaries "are given in experience" and "provide the ultimate reasons for our take on the environment."[5] Empiricism requires that our experiences play an essential role as a tribunal for justifying our beliefs, which means that experiences must both be independent of our beliefs and given with the certainty required for providing justification.

The way I've set up the question should give you a sense of how the argument will go. For the sensory givens to be able to justify perceptual beliefs they need to have some conceptual content. They need to show to us that something is the case. But it is at the heart of the scheme–content picture that the content is brute, unschematized, and, as Kant might say, "blind." Davidson is convinced that such brute content cannot play that role. His mantra is: Only beliefs can justify beliefs—only something with propositional structure like a belief can stand in a justificatory relationship to something else with propositional structure, typically another belief. It is in this respect that Davidson calls himself a coherentist.

But he is also an externalist. Davidson holds that, in virtue of our senses, the world directly causes us to have beliefs. So to see a podium is to be caused to have a perceptual belief that here is a podium. The relationship between the perceiver and the world is causal, not conceptual—causal in the manner of producing beliefs about that world. It is in this sense that we should understand Davidson's closing sentence from "On the Very Idea of a Conceptual Scheme": "In giving up the dualism of scheme and world, we do not give up the world, but re-establish unmediated touch with the familiar objects whose antics make our sentences and opinions true or false."[6] Since there is no conceptual content, only causation, in our interaction with the world, the interaction itself can't play a role in justifying beliefs; yet this is what the empiricist seeks by making our beliefs answerable to the world. Davidson's argument here against the third dogma of empiricism, the scheme–content theory of perceptual belief, is a version of the arguments against the Myth of the Given. Once the third dogma falls, so does the idea that there could be incommensurable conceptual schemes, or conceptual schemes at all, as long as these are understood as schematizing raw sensory data. Davidson critiques the third dogma both from the side of the scheme and from the side of the content; criticisms from the side of the scheme are most useful for showing the impossibility of incommensurable schemes, but it is Davidson's externalism, his view that our perceptual relation to the world is causal, not conceptual, that does the brunt of the work in his argument against the third dogma itself.

2 Gadamer's Apparent Third Dogmatism

Gadamer and Davidson could be fruitfully compared on a number of points. Focusing on incommensurability makes sense; starting from quite different philosophical backgrounds, they both reject incommensurability.[7] They share quite a few views in common; they both agree that language is social, that language is required for thought, that an awareness of other minds arises along with the use of language and with the ability to think, and that were there no humans there would be no truth. Above all, both agree that questions about the nature of interpretation are at the heart of questions about meaning. Even Davidson, after reading sections of Gadamer's *Truth and Method*, said, "I definitely admire his work and I see quite evident resemblances."[8] It is not surprising there are over a dozen articles comparing the two philosophers, yet their mutual rejection of incommensurability is rarely discussed, mainly owing to a common misunderstanding of Gadamer's views.[9] The resemblances between their positions mask significant differences about the nature of language, first-person authority, the nature of conversation, and, perhaps most deeply, the place of the history of philosophy for contemporary philosophizing. What I am most concerned about and what I will be focusing on from now on is the possibility that beneath their shared rejection of incommensurability Gadamer has, in fact, just the kind of scheme–content theory of perception Davidson rejects in his arguments against the third dogma of empiricism.

Why think this? First, Gadamer belongs to the phenomenological tradition. Although phenomenology should not be considered empiricist, it does hold, like empiricism, that careful attention to experience provides the main source of justification or rejection for empirical beliefs. Such a view runs up against Davidson's claim that experience is causal, not conceptual, and as I pointed out it is Davidson's externalism that does the work against the third dogma. Second, Gadamer has a theory that what we can understand alone is limited by our historical and cultural horizons; in dialogue with others (or with texts) with their own horizons we "fuse horizons" when we come to a new understanding that sheds light on the limitations of our previous understanding. Gadamer speaks of such changes as "gestalt switches," which suggests that a kind of incommensurability persists between horizons. Finally, Gadamer claims that "language has a tendency towards schematization. As a language is learned, it creates a view of the world which conforms to the character of the speech conventions that have been established in the language."[10] Here language is set up as the medium by which the world is made intelligible. Presumably, different languages, with different conventions and different words, would create potentially incommensurable worldviews.

Frankly, the most straightforward way of reading Gadamer is that he has a scheme–content theory of perception. Different languages amount to different worldviews, and even within a language there are multiple traditions. Traditions shape our prejudgments, which in turn set the horizons, the limits on what we experience and believe at a particular time. Through dialogue with others, we can become critically reflective of our prejudgments, and, in turn, our traditions, and we "fuse" horizons when we acquire a broader understanding, one inaccessible simply from the original point of view. Since we need the encounter with others to show us the limitations of our points of view, the limitations themselves must not be seen solely from within the point of view. But that means the new point of view acquired through the fusion of horizons amounts to a new way of seeing both what we saw before and the limitations of what we saw before. Yet, if this were his position, his view that there cannot possibly be incommensurable schemes would then simply be a kind of optimism that translation and understanding are always possible, and he would have no resources for resisting relativism. The charge, by the way, that Gadamer's view is actually relativist and the only thing keeping him from seeing that is a naive faith in the power of dialogue, is one of the most common criticisms leveled against Gadamer.

But despite how it looks, Gadamer does not have a scheme–content account of perceptual belief. He is right to reject incommensurability, and yet he does this while still holding a place for experience to justify or falsify beliefs. I want to show how he makes this work. In addition, we get two new non-Davidsonian arguments against incommensurability. To tell this story properly means looking carefully at the two claims—that "a language-view is a worldview"[11] and that every point of view is limited by a horizon—and recognizing that both "world" and "horizon" are technical terms in Gadamer's philosophical hermeneutics, terms with phenomenological roots. But in the end what must be made clear is the role language plays in experience. We need to understand what Gadamer means by his claims that all experience has a "linguistic character"[12] and that "language is the medium through which consciousness is connected with beings."[13]

3 "Horizon" as a Technical Term in Gadamer's Hermeneutics

Let's start with Gadamer's claim that

> Every finite present has its limitations. We define the concept of "situation" by saying that it represents a standpoint that limits the possibility of vision. Hence essential

to the concept of a situation is the concept of a *"horizon."* The horizon is the range of vision that includes everything that can be seen from a particular standpoint.[14]

Different people, texts, cultures, and times have different horizons, and all understanding, according to Gadamer, occurs as a fusion of horizons. Some philosophers rightly object that if a horizon is a limit on what can be seen from a vantage point, then the claim that horizons fuse makes little sense. Anything that is to transform our horizon must already belong to our horizon—to the extent it is outside our horizon it would be outside our limits of comprehension. The objection is similar to the one raised by Davidson, that were everything mediated by a conceptual scheme, we could never escape our conceptual scheme to understand how other schemes might differ. Gadamer replies by claiming that horizons are "open" and constantly changing—if we riff on the metaphor, we can see how that might be. After all, it's quite easy to see beyond our present horizon. Simply walking a short distance or going to the top floor of a building changes the horizon. Moreover, most of us know quite well what lies beyond the horizon from past experience. Again, following the metaphor, horizons might function as a limit at a particular time, but they are also gateways to something accessible, and they move as we move.

Still, rather than trying to clarify Gadamer's position by simply stressing different features of the metaphor of a horizon, we should seek an explication of exactly how a horizon functions in perceptual awareness, and how the openness and variability of horizons follow. For that we need to understand the term "horizon" as a technical term in Husserl.[15]

Husserl was concerned with a common phenomenon—we experience more than is given to our senses. Husserl pointed out that although our senses only give us incomplete information about an object, we perceive the object as a whole. Even though when looking at a chair we are only presented with one side of the chair, we perceive a chair, not a chair-side. We are not surprised when we move to see the chair has other sides to it, that it is three dimensional, and so on. In fact we would be quite shocked to find out what we thought was a chair was only a chair-facade. Likewise, we can often tell who a person is based on very little sensory information. We can recognize someone from the back of his or her head; were he or she to turn around to reveal that we were mistaken, this itself is a sign that our perception of the back of the head included more than simply the back of a head. Were it otherwise we wouldn't have been surprised to find he or she was someone we didn't expect. So perception always goes beyond what is physically presented to the senses.

The horizon, according to Husserl's technical terminology, includes all those aspects of an object that are not directly accessible to our senses, but make it possible to see an object as something. It is what is "co-given" in the perception of the object, which in turn guides our expectations of future experiences of the object. When we walk around a house we are not surprised to see it has sides, that it has a back, that it doesn't elevate off the ground, that leaves do not knock it over when they brush against it, that when we look away and look back it remains the same, and that it did not just spring into existence immediately before we saw it. Being three-dimensional, persisting through time, withstanding the impact of a leaf—all these things belong to the perception of a house; they are all horizonal elements of the perception. So obviously our perceptual horizons change, both as our perceptions change and as we acquire new perceptual expectations given our changing understanding of an object. On the one hand, it makes sense to call horizons limits, since they present the range of possible ways in which the object can be present, but they are also clearly constantly changing. In dialogue with others we encounter horizons that make something present in a different way than we are used to. Horizons fuse when these perceptual possibilities become part of our perceptual repertoire and we come to understand the contingent features of our previous horizons.

It belongs to the phenomenology of perception that we are not drawing inferences from the perceptual information we receive such that, for example, we first see a field of color and then our mind organizes the color and infers that it is some object or person. We directly perceive some thing. Husserl, like all phenomenologists, is a kind of direct realist about perception. Typically having something disclosed to our consciousness as something generates the accompanying beliefs, but that is not automatically the case. Both Heidegger and Gadamer are careful to distinguish the non-propositional yet conceptual awareness of something as something, what they call the hermeneutical-"as"-structure of perception, from the propositional expression of that awareness in language, what they refer to as the apophantic-"as"-structure of assertion. The propositional content of the belief piggybacks on the conceptual content of the disclosure, but the empirical belief is separate from the empirical disclosure of the object as something or other.

With a better understanding of how Gadamer is using "horizon" in Husserl's technical sense, we can get a clearer picture of his account of perception and how he avoids the paradoxes that come with seeing horizons as limits. Nonetheless, someone might object that even in the account of horizonal intentionality there remains the distinction between that which is present to our senses and that which is added by our minds to the sensation. Certainly for Husserl there was a kind of "absolute presence" discoverable within perception that was indubitable and that, with the proper technique, could be isolated and used to descriptively capture the essential features of the object. All this sounds like a version of the third dogma of empiricism. If Gadamer is going to reject the scheme–content distinction and still allow that our experience of the world is thoroughly informed by our concepts and habits, he is going to have to deny that there is such a given core to experience. He does just that. Here is a telling quotation:

> Max Scheler, in his very living contacts with psychologists and physiologists of this epoch as with American pragmatism, and [Martin] Heidegger demonstrated with vigor that sense perception is never given. It is rather an aspect of the pragmatic approach to the world. We are always hearing, listening *to* something and extracting *from* other things. We are *interpreting* in seeing, hearing, receiving. . . . So it is obvious that there is a real primacy of interpretation. Husserl refused to accept this analysis . . . and held that all interpretation is a secondary act.[16]

Gadamer explicitly criticizes Husserl for holding that at its core perception is nonconceptual and therefore, for Gadamer, noninterpretive. Like Davidson, Gadamer rejects the Myth of the Given. Unlike Davidson his rejection is on phenomenological grounds, and Gadamer holds that perception is interpretive, and therefore conceptual, all the way down.

Gadamer goes beyond saying perception is conceptual; according to him it as also linguistic. The same criticism he levels against Husserl he also brings to bear against Scholastic nominalists (who, it should be added, are the forerunners of modern empiricists).

> The linguistic character of the experience of the world, to which metaphysical thinking had originally oriented itself, became in the last analysis something secondary and contingent that schematizes the thinking gaze at things through linguistic conventions and closes it off from the primordial experience of being. In truth however the illusion that things precede their manifestation in language conceals the fundamentally linguistic character of our experience of the world.[17]

For Gadamer, language shapes perception all the way down; it does not play a secondary role in a two-step process. Of course, all this does not help him escape relativism, or the conclusion that there may be many incommensurable worldviews corresponding to different languages. Furthermore, since for Gadamer experience is fundamentally linguistic, it is difficult to see how experience can function any longer in the legitimation of beliefs, much less as an arbiter across worldviews. If something is going to provide a criterion for our use of words it itself should not be shaped by our use of words. Gadamer does not generate confidence when he says the following:

> It is true that those who are brought up in a particular linguistic and cultural tradition see the world in a different way from those who belong to other traditions. It is true that the historical "worlds" that succeed one another in the course of history are different from one another and from the world of today.[18]

We need to turn our attention to Gadamer's claim that language generates worldviews; in the process we will come to understanding of how Gadamer can say that (1) experience is fundamentally linguistic, yet still be a phenomenologist, and (2) take seriously the idea that our experiences can serve as a tribunal for our judgments.

First, however, someone might be tempted to reply that there is an obvious biological fact here that Gadamer misses—we take in information through our senses and our brain makes sense of that information. Language is in our brain, not our eyes, and our brain needs information from our senses to interpret—light stimulates our retinas and our brain interprets these stimuli in meaningful ways; why would one object to that description? There are clearly two stages here, the objection goes, and any story of perception must fit this obvious biological fact. The reply is to focus our biological descriptions not on the level of sensory stimulus and brain response, but on the organism as a whole perceptively engaged in its environment. Visual information does not occur by happenstance. We have biological and social habits that shape how we are perceptually responsive to the world—we should keep in mind that sensation is not simply an accumulation of sense data, but a response to an environment based on past habits, ingrained as a result of biological and conceptual goals. According to Gadamer, all seeing is already "perceiving-something-as-something";[19] by this he means that by the time we are aware of something, we have an already established perceptual and conceptual relationship to the object. Considering the biological process of perception at this level of an organism in ongoing interaction with its environment shifts us away from the picture of conceptless, retinal data organized by our brains. It helps us to see how sensory input is already conceptualized in virtue of the way our bodies reflectively and unreflectively orient themselves in their environment and in virtue of our habits of perceptual expectations. Another way to put the point is that the brain's conceptual organizing activities occur not just at the level of perceptual information, but primarily and more fundamentally at the level of the organism. Yet here we are only talking about organisms with conceptual capacities, and for both Gadamer and Davidson that means organisms with language.

4 "World" as a Technical Term in Gadamer's Hermeneutics

Even if there is nothing uninterpreted, no pure given shaped by concepts, we can still inquire into the possibility that incommensurable languages might lead to incommensurable ways of interpreting the world. Gadamer suggests as much when at a key point in *Truth and Method* he sides with Wilhelm von Humboldt's claim that different languages generate different worldviews. What, then, is Gadamer's view? Language certainly functions in acquiring and shaping concepts, which in turn shape the horizonal character of perception, but Gadamer refers to something quite different when he talks about the linguisticality of experience and the way language opens up a world for us. Just as we had to treat "horizon" as a technical term that retains its meaning found in the phenomenological tradition, likewise, we need to treat "world" as a technical term rooted in the phenomenological tradition.

In *Truth and Method* Gadamer says he has inherited from Scheler a distinction between inhabiting a world and inhabiting an environment (or a habitat). Beings incapable of language lack a world; what they have is an environment of stimuli to which they respond in impressively complex ways according to their various, sometimes conflicting biological imperatives. They are "embedded in their environment."[20] Humans, since they are able to reason about their course of action, can conceptualize their situation and establish an orientation toward it that is not limited by the pressures of their immediate biological imperatives. "For man rising above the environment means rising to a world. . . . This does not mean he leaves his habitat, but that he has another posture toward it—a free, distanced orientation—that is always realized in language."[21] The ability to reflect, derived from the ability to use language, establishes a world in which they live, in explicit contrast to the environment in which nonhuman animals live.

Although there would seem to be overlap between a nonlinguistic animal's perception if its environment and a human being's perception of its world, in fact Gadamer holds that the nature of perception is fundamentally different in these cases. Language transforms perception all the way down. Take, as an example, my cat. Even though the same objects might pass through my and my cat's fields of vision—such as the empty cat-food bowl—I see the object as belonging to a world with an orientation according to which I can discriminate features and recognize new possibilities.

I can see the situation as reflecting reasons; the cat simply responds to seeing the object in its environment according to its place in its biological imperatives. A human being with full subjectivity experiences the world as available to reasoned reflection, as available to articulation in language, and therefore as suitable as evidence for empirical beliefs.

Here is a sketch of how it works. When we acquire a language, we acquire the ability to articulate our experiences in words. This ability shapes the horizon of every experience to include the possibility of expressing what we perceive in words. So to return to the earlier example, we not only see a house as having three sides, as persisting in time, and so on, we see it as something that can be expressed in words, at least in principle. Of course, at any given time we may not be articulate enough or have the words at hand in order to put what we experience into words, but the communicatability of experience in language now belongs to the experience itself. This opens up a kind of freedom to step back from the immediacy of the experience and generate a reflective, articulate response—something nonlinguistic animals lack. It would never occur to a nonlinguistic animal to try to communicate its experiences in words, as the objects are not disclosed to them as things about which to speak. They are disclosed as things to eat, to run from, to jump on, to hide under, and so on. In this respect, animals are embedded in an environment rather than being agents in a world.

Importantly, the addition of language does not just supplement the nonconceptual elements with conceptual elements, it introduces a whole new way of responding to experience, of taking up experience propositionally, in short, of making our experiences intelligible to us and others through language. Because we have opposable thumbs we directly experience objects as things to pick up; similarly, because we have language we directly experience objects as things to express in words. This is what it means to say that language shapes our perceptions all the way down, and this is what Gadamer means when he says that language "mediates" our relation to the world and that "our verbal experience of the world is prior to everything that is recognized and addressed as existing."[22] Language mediates like our eyes mediate—we can't see without them, and the wavelengths of light we can see is limited by them; but we still see things with them, not images of or representations of things. Because we can see, we experience the world with all our senses in a fundamentally different way from sightless creatures. That the world, for Gadamer, is perceptually mediated through concepts does not mean that the world is created by concepts any more than the fact the world is perceptually mediated through our having opposable thumbs, thus as containing things to pick up, means that the world is created by our being prehensile.

Unlike the view of some critical interpreters of Gadamer, he is not embracing a form of linguistic idealism. We do not experience the world with subtitles; we regularly experience things for which we have no words. But Gadamer acknowledges that

> [t]he fundamental linguisticality of understanding cannot mean that all experiencing of the world can only take place as and in language. . . . who would deny that there are real factors conditioning human life, such as hunger, love, labor, and domination, which are not themselves language or speaking, but which for their part furnish the space within which our speaking to each other and listening to each other can take place. This fact cannot be disputed.[23]

His view, then, is that several elements, including biological needs, social customs, individual habits, and previous understandings, all shape the way the world appears to us. It also always appears to us as intelligibly expressible in language. Since our experiences are not determined by language, but simply call for articulation in language, perception is both conceptual all the way down and yet provides the friction with the world needed to confirm, revise, or reject our beliefs. The claim that a language creates a worldview seemed to suggest a possibly incommensurable diversity of worldviews, but the important part of Gadamer's claim is that language transforms an *environment* into a potentially intelligible *world*. Unless we understand "world" as a technical term, we miss this point.

5 Conclusion: Returning to the Topic of Incommensurability

We now have a rough picture of how Gadamer understands perceptual belief acquisition. As conceptually informed purposeful organisms, we live in a world where all objects are experienced as something or other. The horizons of the object are the ways the object is made present to us in perception above and beyond the direct sensory presence of the object. In addition to the role played by language in shaping the concepts that guide the as-structure of the perception, we always perceive objects as potentially intelligible in language. It is the object's disclosure through language and as potentially expressible in language that leads Gadamer to say that language mediates our relation to the world, even though we are directly aware of the world. It also links thinking with choosing the right word. It is not that we have a belief that something is the case and then we look for words that will best communicate that belief to others (this is analogous to students who claim to know what they want to say in a paper, they just have not found the right words yet); instead, thinking about a subject and finding the right words to articulate a subject are one and the same process. Bringing it into language, for Gadamer, really is the only way to make something intelligible.

There are two more pieces to add to complete Gadamer's picture. First, language is public, never of our own making. As such we are never in a position of being sure that we are using language to properly articulate the matter at hand; we are never in a position to be sure we have properly made the object intelligible. Dialogue is the way we work with others to come to a shared understanding of a matter at hand: "Language is only fully what it can be when it takes place in dialogue."[24] Second, we have no special faculty for making our own thoughts intelligible to ourselves; all anyone has for making anything intelligible, including their own thoughts, is language. But that means, too, that we need to give up a kind of first-person authority about our own beliefs. We know whereof we think only to the extent we can articulate our beliefs, and, of course, others are often better at articulating these things than we are.

Finally, Gadamer's view has two consequences for the topic of incommensurability. First, recall Davidson's argument against partial incommensurability. There is no criterion by which we can tell when we come across a disagreement in conversation whether the disagreement is simply a difference in belief or a difference in conceptual scheme. This becomes even more complicated on Gadamer's view. Perhaps because of his focus on radical interpretation, Davidson always thinks of communication as a transfer of information; according to him, to engage in conversation is to try to find the best words to communicate our beliefs to another person. The shared common language is the most useful tool, but it is not a necessary one. For Gadamer, conversation is more complicated. Since we also come to understand our own beliefs better in conversation, and since whenever we enter into dialogue it is with the knowledge that our interlocutor may know what we are talking about better than we do, conversations can't be reduced to exchanges of information between fully self-aware interlocutors. Rather, dialogue is an irreducibly social action of trying to come to an articulate understanding of a topic. We have seen how this connects to his theory about the linguisticality of experience and his views about the publicity of language. Yet a condition for engaging in dialogue is the rejection of incommensurability. We cannot at the same time embrace the possibility of incommensurability and hold that our conversation partner can find the words to help us make our own beliefs more intelligible to ourselves. We are never in a position to conclude that a disagreement in dialogue is evidence of incommensurability. Second, and more significantly, it belongs to Gadamer's theory of perceptual knowledge that we experience the world as always potentially intelligible through language. Nothing we experience, according to Gadamer, transcends the limits of language. But, of course, we often hear other people talking, we often encounter writings from other cultures; and these too we must experience as potentially intelligible. Davidson claims that to encounter something as linguistic is sufficient for knowing that it is translatable; Gadamer will similarly say that to encounter something linguistic is to encounter something potentially intelligible. I quoted him as saying "It is true that those who are brought up in a particular linguistic and cultural tradition see the world in a different way from those who belong to other traditions." The quotation continues, "In whatever tradition we consider it, it is always a human—i.e., verbally constituted—world that presents itself to us. As verbally constituted, every such world is of itself always open to every possible insight and hence every expansion of its own world picture, and is accordingly available to others."[25]

The bottom line for Gadamer is that anything intelligible to anyone is potentially intelligible to everyone. So if it's the case that different languages lead to different ways of conceptualizing experience, we only need to learn those languages to discover those conceptualizations. No way of making the world intelligible is ever precluded. In an interview with a Hungarian student he states it as clearly as one might hope. The student asks, "Are we prisoners of our mother tongue? The American anthropologist Hall maintains that everything human is firmly bound in our cultural dimension. How stiff is, however, our cultural dimension? Can we escape this?" Gadamer replies, "Yes, through learning a foreign language."[26] All there is to add is that no language is unlearnable.

Although Gadamer and Davidson agree that there are no incommensurable conceptual schemes, as there are no conceptual schemes at all, the agreement masks a deeper disagreement about the relation between thought and the world. For Davidson, the relationship is causal, and this thesis is a key element in his argument against incommensurability. For Gadamer, the relationship is linguistic, and this thesis forms a key element in his argument against incommensurability. By bringing to light these fundamental differences, we may avoid too hasty assimilations of Gadamer's and Davidson's views. Bjørn Ramberg writes about Gadamer and Davidson that "the commensuration of different philosophical positions is achieved, if at all, only slowly, by virtue of sensitive work carried out where resistance is greatest."[27] My aim here has been to make explicit a key difference to allow a comparison to fruitfully go forward.

Notes

1. Donald Davidson, "On the Very Idea of A Conceptual Scheme," in *Inquiries into Truth and Interpretation* (Oxford: Oxford University Press, 2001), pp. 183–198.

2. Gadamer, "Language and Understanding," *Theory, Culture & Society* 23, no. 1 (2006): 13–27, p. 15.

3. Davidson has an additional argument that shows up only in "On the Very Idea of a Conceptual Scheme." There he considers two metaphors meant to show how a scheme relates to the unschematized content: One might say different schemes organize what's given in different ways, or one might say different schemes fit what's given in different ways. In the first case, the given must have parts to organize, and these parts would be consistent across the schemes. But that means there can't be systematic disagreement across the schemes to be organized differently. This argument is along the lines of the first two I've presented. In the second case, where both schemes fit the given, both schemes are true, but for Davidson being true suffices for being translatable, so in this case too the differences cannot be complete. This argument relies completely on Davidson's Tarskian account of truth, and that is not a likely place where Gadamer and Davidson can be brought into dialogue.

4. Davidson, "On the Very Idea of a Conceptual Scheme," p. 183.

5. Davidson, "Comments on the Karlovy Vary Papers," in *Interpreting Davidson*, ed. Petr Kotatko, Peter Pagin, and Gabriel Segal (Stanford: CSLI Publications, 2001), p. 285.

6. Davidson, "On the Very Idea of a Conceptual Scheme," p. 198.

7. In his essay "Semantics and Hermeneutics," Gadamer appears to give two examples of incommensurability. He first discusses the way "force" has become a technical term in science, so much so that it moved away from the everyday sense of the word and "was individualized to the point of becoming untranslatable." On the next page he mentions a lyric poem that "is untranslatable to the point that it can no longer be rendered in another language at all without losing its poetic expressiveness," in *Philosophical Hermeneutics* (Berkeley: University of California Press, 1976), pp. 82–94. However, neither one is a case of untranslatability proper. One is simply the idea that there is no way to translate the technical term using the everyday meaning of the term, not that translation is impossible. The second is that any translation loses the poetic force, not the meaning, of the lyric poem, and that shouldn't surprise us. We don't expect the power of a work of art to be maintained across translations.

8. Katherin Glüer, *Donald Davidson zur Einführung* (Hamburg: Junius Verlag, 1993), p. 158.

9. Here is a certainly incomplete list: Linda Martín Alcoff, "Gadamer's Feminist Epistemology," in *Feminist Interpretations of Hans-Georg Gadamer*, ed. Lorraine Code (University Park: Pennsylvania State University Press, 2003), pp. 231–258; Lee Braver, *A Thing of This World: A History of Continental Anti-Realism* (Evanston: Northwestern University Press, 2007); Rudiger Bubner, "On the Ground of Understanding," in *Hermeneutics and Truth*, ed. Brice Wachterhauser (Evanston: Northwestern University Press, 1994), pp. 68–82; Herbert Dreyfus, "Holism and Hermeneutics," *Review of Metaphysics* 34, no. 1 (September 1980): 3–23; Vittorio Hösle, "Truth and Understanding: Analytical Philosophy (Donald Davidson), Phenomenology (Hans-Georg Gadamer), and the Desideratum of an Objective Idealist Hermeneutics," in *Between Description and Interpretation: The Hermeneutic Turn in Phenomenology*, ed. Andre Wiercinski (Toronto: The Hermeneutic Press, 2005), pp. 376–394; David Hoy, "Post-Cartesian Interpretation: Hans-Georg Gadamer and Donald Davidson," in *Philosophy of Hans-Georg Gadamer*, Library of Living Philosophers vol. 24, ed. Lewis Hahn (Chicago: Open Court, 1997), pp. 111–128; Jeff Malpas, "Gadamer, Davidson and the Ground of Understanding," in *Gadamer's Century: Essays in Honor of Hans-Georg Gadamer*, ed. Jeff Malpas, Ulrich Arnswald, and Jens Kertscher (Cambridge, MA: MIT Press, 2002), pp. 195–216; John McDowell, "Gadamer and Davidson on Understanding and Relativism," in *Gadamer's Century*, pp. 173–194; Bjørn Ramberg, chapters 9 and 10 of *Donald Davidson's Philosophy of Language* (New York: Blackwell, 1989), pp. 114–141; Bjørn Ramberg, "Illuminating Language: Interpretation and Understanding in Gadamer and Davidson," in *A House Divided: Comparing Analytic and Continental Philosophy*, ed. C. G. Prado (Amherst, NY: Humanity Books), pp. 213–234; Bjørn Ramberg, "The Source of the Subjective," in *The Philosophy of Hans-Georg Gadamer*, pp. 459–471; Charles Taylor, "Gadamer on the Human Sciences," in *The Cambridge Companion to Gadamer*, ed. Robert Dostal (Cambridge: Cambridge University Press, 2002), pp. 52–78; Charles Taylor, "Understanding the Other: A Gadamerian View on Conceptual Schemes," in *Gadamer's Century*, pp. 270–297; Karsten Stueber, "Understanding Truth and Objectivity: A Dialogue between Donald Davidson and Hans-Georg Gadamer," in Wachterhauser (ed.), *Hermeneutics and Truth*, pp. 172–189; Brice Wachterhauser, "Getting It Right: Relativism, Realism, and Truth," in *The Cambridge Companion to Gadamer*, pp. 126–142; Joel Weinsheimer, "Charity Militant: Gadamer, Davidson, and Post-critical Hermeneutics," in *The Force of Tradition*, ed. Donald Marshall (Lanham: Rowman & Littlefield, 2005), pp. 39–54. See also the contributions by Dostal, Fultner, Malpas, and Braver in this volume.

10. Gadamer, "Notes on Planning for the Future," in *Hans-Georg Gadamer on Education, Poetry, and History: Applied Hermeneutics*, ed. Dieter Misgeld and Graeme Nicholson, trans. Lawrence Schmidt and Monica Reuss (Albany: SUNY Press, 1992), p. 177.

11. Hans-Georg Gadamer, *Truth and Method* (New York: Crossroad, 1989), p. 442.

12. Gadamer, "The Nature of Language and the Nature of Things," in Hans-Georg Gadamer, *Philosophical Hermeneutics*, ed. and trans. David E. Linge (Berkeley: University of California Press, 1976), p. 77.

13. Ibid., p. 76.

14. Gadamer, *Truth and Method*, p. 302.

15. For more on Gadamer's relation to Husserl, see my articles "Gadamer and the Fusion of Horizons," *International Journal of Philosophical Studies* 17, no. 4 (2009): 531–542, and "Who Was Gadamer's Husserl?," *New Yearbook of Phenomenology and Phenomenological Philosophy* 7 (2007): 1–23.

16. Gadamer, "Hermeneutics of Suspicion," *Man and World* 17 (1984): 316–319.

17. Gadamer, "The Nature of Language and the Nature of Things," pp. 77–78.

18. Gadamer, *Truth and Method*, p. 447.

19. Gadamer, "Philosophy and Literature," p. 242.

20. Gadamer, *Truth and Method*, p. 444.

21. Ibid., p. 445.

22. Ibid., p. 450.

23. Gadamer, "Reflections on my Philosophical Journey," in Hahn (ed.), *The Philosophy of Hans-Georg Gadamer*, p. 28.

24. Gadamer, "Treatment and Dialogue," in *The Enigma of Health* (Stanford: Stanford University Press, 1996), pp. 127–128.

25. Gadamer, *Truth and Method*, p. 447.

26. Hans-Georg Gadamer, "'Suchende sind wir im Grunde alle': Farkas-Zoltán Hajdú's Gespräch mit dem Heidelberger Philosophen," <http://www.gkpn.de/gadamer.html>.

27. Bjørn Ramberg, "Illuminating Language," p. 214.

14 What Is Common to All: Davidson on Agreement and Understanding

Jeff Malpas

To those who are awake, there is one ordered world [κοσμοσ] common to all.
—Heraclitus, fragment 89

1

The essentially social nature of language, and not only of language, but also of thought, is one of the most basic ideas in the philosophy of Donald Davidson. It is an idea that Davidson articulated in various ways, most notably in the idea of triangulation, and which he also acknowledged as already present in the work of other thinkers, especially G. H. Mead (in whose work he also found a version of triangulation itself),[1] as well as in the later Wittgenstein.[2] It has not always appeared clear to all readers of Davidson's work, however, just how this claim regarding the social nature of language and thought should be understood.

One of the reasons for this is that Davidson also rejected what is probably the most widely accepted account of the nature of the sociality that might be thought to be at issue here, namely, the idea that sociality is based in *convention*—in a set of preexisting, shared rules.[3] In "A Nice Derangement of Epitaphs," Davidson even goes so far as to suggest that "there is no such thing as a language"—at least not if by "language" one means a clearly defined, shared system of syntactic and semantic rules that exists prior to any particular linguistic encounter.[4] In "On the Very Idea of a Conceptual Scheme"—surely one of the most important, but also most abused and misread essays of twentieth-century philosophy—Davidson had already presented an argument to a similar if not identical conclusion, through his undermining of the idea that there could be radical discontinuities in understanding of the sort proposed by various forms of radical relativism. As Davidson comments in his conclusion to that essay:

It would be wrong to summarize by saying we have shown how communication is possible between people who have different schemes, a way that works without need of what there cannot be, namely a neutral ground, or a common coordinate system. For we have found no intelligible basis on which it can be said that schemes are different. It would be equally wrong to announce the glorious news that all mankind—all speakers of language, at least—share a common scheme and ontology. For if we cannot intelligibly say that schemes are different, neither can we intelligibly say that they are wrong.[5]

In rejecting the idea of a common conceptual scheme as the basis for communication or understanding, Davidson also rejects the particular idea of subjectivity with which that idea is associated: the idea of an inner mental realm that is set apart from the world, "a concept of the mind with its private states and objects."[6] There is no "inner" world that stands completely apart from the public world in which we speak and act, and there is no completely "external" world that already stands apart from us and to which we gain access through our ability to apply a set of private concepts, meanings, or rules.

One simple way of putting the underlying point that is at issue here is to say that what Davidson argues against in a number of his later essays is the idea that *understanding,* whether of others or of the world, cannot depend on the existence of any form of preexisting, determinate, "internalized" *agreement*. When it comes to language, this idea is expressed in the claim that linguistic understanding depends on speakers sharing a set of linguistic rules or conventions (the issue addressed in "A Nice Derangement of Epitaphs"); when it is epistemology that is at issue, it is expressed in the claim that there must be some overall correspondence between our concepts or beliefs and the world (something explored in "A Coherence Theory of Truth and Knowledge"), or that also obtains between our beliefs and concepts and those of others (one of the concerns of "On the Very idea of a Conceptual Scheme"). All of these versions of the idea are explicitly rejected by Davidson.

It is not uncommon, however, to find Davidson being read in ways that commit him to the view that, contrary to his arguments elsewhere, understanding does indeed depend on determinate, internalized, preexisting agreement, as that is given specific form in a common "human nature." In their discussion of Davidsonian philosophy of language as applied to the philosophy of social science, for instance, Graham Macdonald and Philip Pettit claim that charity, along with the principle of "humanity," which they present as continuous with it, "rests on a belief in the unity of human nature: a belief that people in different cultures are essentially similar" and according to which "any differences there are across cultures, or at least any differences central to the attitudes and actions of people, should be explicable by reference to different circumstances."[7] The same idea is picked up, though in a slightly different way, by Anita Avramides. Focusing on Davidson's own emphasis, most famously in "Thought and Talk," on the having of the concept of belief as conditional for the having of thoughts,[8] Avramides argues that the Davidsonian position leads inevitably to the conclusion that "we have the concept of belief that we have because we are creatures who 'act in the world, and act on each other, and act in accordance with a common human nature.'"[9]

It is certainly the case that Davidson has repeatedly emphasized the dependence of the possibility of interpretation on a background of overall agreement. Thus he writes in a well-known passage from "Belief and the Basis of Meaning" that:

> Widespread agreement is the background against which disputes and mistakes can be interpreted. Making sense of the utterances and behavior of others, even their most aberrant behavior, requires us to find a great deal of reason and truth in them. . . . If the vast amount of agreement on plain matters that is assumed in communication escapes notice, it's because the shared truths are too many or too dull to bear mentioning.[10]

The question here is not whether agreement is necessary for understanding, but rather the particular sort of agreement that is so required. In his "Introduction" to *Inquiries into Truth and Interpretation*, Davidson makes this point explicit:

> The aim of interpretation is not agreement but understanding. My point has always been that understanding can be secured only by interpreting in a way that makes for the right sort of agreement. The "right sort," however, is no easier to specify than to say what constitutes a good reason for holding a particular belief.[11]

What is at issue in much of Davidson's discussion of these matters is actually the clarification of the nature of agreement as it plays a role in understanding. What Davidson rejects in essays like "A Nice Derangement of Epitaphs" or "On the Very Idea of a Conceptual Scheme" is a way of thinking about agreement that sees it as based in an essentially subjective, even if shared, structure that is prior to any encounter, and that is also capable of determinate characterization. This way of thinking recurs again and again across many different domains and in many different forms, and is so commonplace that it is seldom questioned or even made explicit. In contrast, Davidson argues for a form of agreement that is not and cannot be specified in terms of any shared set of propositions, rules, concepts, behavioral dispositions, practices, or "forms of life."[12] I shall have more to say about this in the discussion below, but the short answer to the question as to the sort of agreement that makes for understanding, and that also underpins the social nature of language and thought, is that it is an agreement consisting in our dynamic, active engagement with a set of worldly events and entities.[13]

2

Although it is commonplace to find many readers of Davidson treating the principle of charity as simply imposing an already determined set of beliefs onto those we interpret—so every one of our interlocutors believes just as we do (thus leading to the objection that charity embodies an ethnocentric approach to interpretation that erases difference)—charity as it appears in Davidson's work always refers to a dynamic process rather than a static formula.[14] The charitable advice that we should assume overall agreement in beliefs (which on the Davidsonian account means the same as assuming the overall truth of beliefs), thus provides an initial specification of beliefs that is intended to enable the interpretive process rather than complete it. Attributions of beliefs are played off against determinations of meaning, within a larger framework that also encompasses other attitudes and behavior, so as to enable us to make sense of our interlocutors in a way that is itself always subject to further articulation and revision. In this respect, we may say, using the language of "A Nice Derangement of Epitaphs," that the overall interpretive "theories" that result from the process of radical interpretation are always *passing* theories, never prior.[15]

The dynamism that characterizes the operation of charity as it is presented in Davidson's early essays on radical interpretation carries over into Davidson's later accounts of triangulation. Indeed, one might argue that the very use of the term "triangulation," which in its original sense involves the determination of location through the taking of lines of sight from each of two fixed but distinct points and on to the object that lies at their intersection, already indicates a dynamic, active process that depends on difference as the means to arrive at commonality. Moreover, the lines of connection between speaker and interpreter, and between each of these and the object that lies between them, are not constituted merely through the speaker or interpreter's passive reception of subjectively present sensory information or through the activation of a set of internalized responses. Instead, the connection of speaker to interpreter, of interpreter to speaker, and of both to the object, arises through the actions of the speaker and interpreter in relation to the entities and events around them, as well as through their being causally affected by those same entities and events. Speaker and interpreter are implicated with one another, and with the world, through their mutual entanglement in the same complex structure of causation and action.

While Davidson's own emphasis in his accounts of triangulation tends to be on the way in which the objects of belief are to be identified, in the first instance at least, with the common causes of belief, the objects of belief also appear as the focus of action. Indeed, this is why the proper objects of belief are not to be identified with the proximal causes of belief—with the privately felt stimulation of our sensory surfaces that give rise to events in our nervous systems—but rather with their distal causes—with the publicly accessible entities and events that are the causes of such stimulation. The objects about which we have beliefs are also the objects with respect to which our actions are variously oriented and directed. Through looking at the way in which action, perhaps grasped initially as mere behavior, is organized in relation to the entities and events that make up an agent's environment, we can identify the objects toward which the agent acts and so begin also to identify the objects of the agent's beliefs.[16] What we may not be able to do initially is identify the correct descriptions under which the agent's beliefs are held of those objects or under which those objects are the objects toward which action is directed. However, so long as we do not rely only on single observations, and instead triangulate between observations while also attending to the intersections between our own actions and the actions of those we seek to understand, then we will not only be able to arrive at an identification of the common causes of belief, but also be able to refine the descriptions of those causes as they are relevant to the beliefs and actions at issue.

The process here is almost exactly the same as the process that Davidson himself describes under the heading of "radical interpretation." It is a process that is predicated on the assumption that what determines the descriptions that are relevant to an agent's self-understanding is also what determines the understanding of the agent by another. This is not an assumption that Davidson has always made explicit,[17] but it does underlie much of Davidson's approach. The point that is at issue here, a point that Davidson employs specifically in relation to interpretation, connects with what initially appears to be a somewhat different point made by Strawson. In *Individuals*, Strawson argues that the notion of objectivity requires the reidentification of particulars, and that this requires a notion of an objective space in which particulars can be located, a space that is largely independent of the one making the identification and reidentification.[18] The identification of some entity as an object of belief also requires a capacity for reidentification of that entity as the same object about which beliefs are held, and such identification and reidentification must be possible both for any single individual who has beliefs, and for any individual who attempts to attribute beliefs to others. The possibility of belief, and of any contentful state, thus requires an objective but intersubjectively accessible world to which our own subjective attitudes can be related, in which the objects of our attitudes can be located, and within which our own actions can be situated. This is why intentional objects are always public objects (the point also applies as much to abstract objects, although analogously, as to the concrete).[19]

The space within which the determination of the objects, and so also the contents, of belief arises is thus not the internal space of subjectivity, but rather the externalized, public space wherein the agent acts, and wherein the encounter with others also takes place. In discussing the idea of triangulation, and comparing the Davidsonian emphasis on the distal with Quine's early emphasis on the proximal, Dagfinn Føllesdal writes:

> Why, then, did Quine turn to stimuli? He saw, I think, clearer than it had ever been seen before, how intricate the notion of an object is. We cannot determine through observation which objects other people perceive; what others perceive is dependent upon how they conceive of the world and structure it, and that is just what we are trying to find out. When we study communication and understanding, we should not uncritically assume that the other shares our conception of the world and our ontology.[20]

Yet although we may not be able to determine which objects other people perceive through observation alone (or, more precisely perhaps, we cannot determine the *descriptions* under which objects are perceived), we can determine the objects they perceive through recognizing the objects around which their actions are organized, not only as this is evident in regard to those actions taken on their own, but also as they overlap or interfere with our own actions, and our actions with theirs, and so are organized in relation to the *same* objects (even if given under different descriptions). In this respect, although we may not share the same descriptive vocabulary (the same "ontology") as our interlocutors, that does not mean that we do not stand in relation to the same objects, nor that we cannot use our own descriptive vocabulary in the process of coming to understand what may well be a different descriptive vocabulary on the part of our interlocutors.[21]

In his own discussion, Føllesdal acknowledges the importance of social considerations in coming to understand another. Yet he takes this to be a matter of attending to the intersubjective propositional structures within which perception is embedded.[22] The lesson that follows from study of the structure of triangulation is that the social is first given not in terms of shared linguistic structures, but rather through the commonality established in action. Normativity, on this account, is a process of mutual adjustment to one another that arises in the engagement between speakers, rather than a matter of conformity to any preexisting rule or principle. This means, however, that normativity arises through our orientation toward, and active engagement with, the world in which both we and our interlocutors find ourselves. Not only normativity, but also meaning and thought arise in this fashion. Thus Davidson writes that "Our thoughts neither create the world nor simply picture it; they are tied to their external sources from the beginning; those sources being the community and the environment we know we jointly occupy."[23]

3

The way Davidson views the relation between agreement and understanding, and especially his underlying rejection of understanding as based in any form of preexisting, determinate, internalized agreement, turns out to be closer to that of certain key figures within twentieth-century continental philosophy than to that of many of his analytic colleagues.[24] One of the key shifts in hermeneutic theory, for instance, especially as developed by Hans-Georg Gadamer, and as adumbrated in the work of Heidegger, is that understanding cannot be based in any attempt to rethink or reexperience that which is to be understood. This is, indeed, one of the central arguments of Gadamer's magnum opus, *Truth and Method*. In that work Gadamer sets a Hegelian conception of the nature and possibility of understanding against that of Schleiermacher. Directed at the interpretation of texts, Schleiermacher argued that understanding the meaning of a text was a matter of rethinking the thoughts of its authors (it is this idea that to a large extent was taken up and developed within nineteenth-century hermeneutics through the idea of *Verstehen*—an idea that is still present within areas of sociological thinking through the influence of Weber). Hegel, on the other hand, took understanding to be inevitably oriented to the present situation of the one who aims to understand—in historiography, for instance, this means that understanding always comes after the events it seeks to understand, and consequently it cannot be based in any recapturing of the past, but instead derives from our present situation.[25]

As Gadamer presents matters, following Hegel, and drawing on ideas to be found in Heidegger and Husserl, understanding is always based in our current situatedness, which allows us to encounter things from a particular perspective and with a particular set of interests—this is why Gadamer and Heidegger both insist on the essential historicality of understanding and the role of tradition.[26] Yet inasmuch as understanding always involves an awareness of the existence of such alternative views, so it is always directed, in spite of its partiality, to the "object" or "matter" (*Sache*) at issue. In this respect, historical situatedness and tradition function, not as a base of determinate and prior agreement from which understanding proceeds, but rather as opening up a commonality that consists simply in a commonality of engagement between different interlocutors with respect to the same objects of concern.[27] In the work of Hannah Arendt, itself directly influenced by the phenomenological-hermeneutic thinking also found in Gadamer, this idea reappears as a key element in the constitution of the realm of common engagement that Arendt calls the "public realm" and also characterizes as the realm "of the real." In what could be taken almost as a summary of the Davidsonian position itself, Arendt writes that: "Under the conditions of a common world, reality is not guaranteed primarily by the 'common nature' of all men who constitute it, but rather by the fact that, differences of position and the resulting variety of perspectives notwithstanding, everybody is always concerned with the same object."[28] In this way, our "perspectives" on the world turn out to be not a barrier to our access to the world or to others, but the very means by which such access is effected.[29]

There is nevertheless a tendency to read Gadamer (as well as Heidegger and Arendt), in a way we have also seen arise in the reading of Davidson, as holding to the view that understanding does indeed depend on some form of agreement that must obtain prior to any particular encounter and takes the form of some determinate, often internalized content or structure. Indeed, Davidson himself misreads Gadamer in just such a fashion, taking issue with what he takes to be the Gadamerian claim that "agreement concerning an object demands that a common language first be worked out," and arguing instead that "it is only in the presence of shared objects that understanding can come about."[30] The apparent disagreement is particularly significant in this context, since it focuses on just the question that is here at issue, and it is notable that Davidson makes exactly the argument that accords with his own commitment to the idea that it is our common engagement in the world that founds understanding and the determination of agreement: "Coming to an agreement about an object," he writes, "and coming to understand each other's speech are not independent moments but part of the interpersonal process of triangulating the world."[31] Davidson is correct in the general claim he makes here, but he is mistaken in assuming that Gadamer's own conception of language stands opposed to such a claim. Although differently expressed, the Gadamerian position is indeed committed to much the same dynamic, dialogic conception as that which Davidson identifies as at the heart of communication and understanding. As Gadamer so evocatively puts it, language is itself "conversation" (*Gespräch*)—a conversation that is always oriented toward its object, toward some subject matter, and in which the very being of language is constantly articulated and rearticulated.[32]

One of the points that the Gadamerian approach may be taken to draw particularly to our attention, however, and that Davidson may be thought to neglect, is the way in which the ongoing process that is understanding, which is also a process of constant determination of agreement, can also solidify into distinctive and apparently determinate forms—into what we often refer to in our ordinary usage, for instance, as "languages." Thus a group of speakers engaged in constant linguistic interaction may recognize themselves as speaking the "same" language precisely in virtue of the ongoing interaction in which they are engaged—in virtue, as it were, of their capacity for ready and regular convergence in linguistic behavior. This convergence is itself facilitated by, even though it is not founded in, the recognition, on the part of members of the community, of certain regularities that are evident in their behavior (regularities that may be misconstrued as enabling their interaction, rather than developing in that interaction). A process of self-identification may then occur around the idea of a language, perhaps a set of practices, and also a history, taken to be common to that community.

Recognition of such community and commonality may well serve to reinforce the capacity for mutual understanding and engagement, even though it does not found it; but what is perhaps more significant in the present context is precisely the way in which such recognized commonality, based always in modes of mutual action and interaction, functions to underpin notions of *identity* and *self-identity*. The commonality at issue here is not only expressed in terms of the idea of language, but also in the idea of community as such, and in the idea of the world as itself constituted always in terms of a certain mode of appearings of things. Thus different communities, which understand themselves as communities, and so in terms of a certain identity that belongs to them, will also view the world as ordered in a certain fashion, and the things that appear within the world as appearing in a certain way, and in a certain light. In summary, what we take to be important about the world, what aspects of things are taken to be significant, is itself a result of the constant formation of agreement that occurs in and through the complex and ongoing interaction that is the process of understanding, and that involves, in the terms Davidson employs, the subjective, the intersubjective, and the objective.[33]

In Gadamer, the importance of this level of commonality is evident in the emphasis given to language (an emphasis that appears to mislead Davidson) and the role of tradition. It is an emphasis that can be seen to have its origins in Heidegger's focus on what he refers to as "the happening of truth," particularly as that is developed in the essay that Gadamer cites as playing a key role in the formation of his own thinking, "The Origin of the Work of Art."[34] In the latter work, Heidegger looks to the way in which the self-identity of a community, and the appearing of the world within which the community orients itself, occurs through the ordering of things around certain common practices or things—in Heidegger's essay it is the ordering of things around the Greek temple. It is noteworthy that for Heidegger especially, the commonality that is at issue here is always articulated, not through any internalized structure, but rather through modes of action and interaction that are oriented and organized in relation to the things around us. The commonality that is given in a certain form of the world, and a certain mode of self-identity that belongs to a community, is itself shaped and determined through the broader commonality that is our mutual action and interaction as it occurs within the world as such—the world as it transcends any particular identity or mode of description within which it may be framed.[35] Although the matter is not one that can adequately be pursued as part of the present inquiry, what starts to become evident here is the complex connection, as developed in a number of Heidegger's core works, between the concepts of truth and of world, and notions of community, commonality, and action.[36] Moreover, although Davidson approaches these issues in a very different way, it should already be clear, as I have also argued at greater length elsewhere,[37] that something like a similar, if not identical, set of connections also appears in Davidson's work. On the one hand, Davidson presents a view of truth that is metaphysical modest, if not quite deflationary; on the other hand, he also embeds truth within a network of other concepts in a way that makes truth a central concept in the possibility of language, meaning, and understanding—truth turns out to be a concept inseparable from the world as that common realm of action and encounter.

What emerges here, then, are two forms of agreement or commonality that each play different roles in relation to the possibility of understanding and the formation of self-identity. There is the commonality that resides in the possibility of common engagement and obtains independently of any agreement as it might exist in the form of a shared language, or shared attitudes, dispositions, or practices; and there is also the commonality that depends on such common engagement but is articulated in those modes of determinate agreement that take the form of a shared language, or shared attitudes, dispositions, or practices, and through which our notions of identity and self-identity are articulated. These two modes of commonality—two different modes of "agreement"—also interact with one another. Our engagement with the world always occurs in the light of the particular formations of commonality that determine our identity, and so constitutes our particular situatedness in the world (our particular relation to the entities and events around us), and yet is not restricted to those formations alone. Indeed, not only is our engagement in the world such that we can come to recognize perspectives different from our own precisely through our sense of self-identity coupled with the ability to identify others through our common engagement with the same objects, but we may also be led to reinterpret, perhaps to enlarge, our own sense of commonality through just such engagement.

Put topographically (which is to say, within the context of Davidsonian triangulation), we might say that whereas our involvement with a landscape, and our ability to engage with others within that landscape, always requires that we are located somewhere within it, the fact that we are so located does not prevent us from recognizing other possible locations, nor does it prevent us from relocating ourselves, so long as we can determine the relation between locations, so long as we can establish a "mapping" from one to another. The location in which we currently find ourselves is that by means of which we are enabled to enter into the landscape in which we are located, but our engagement is not restricted to that location alone. In similar fashion, the determinate agreement that is formed in the process of sustained interaction with others and is the result of our understanding of them, though it may form the basis for our sense of identity with those others while also providing the framework within which our understanding of the world is articulated, is not itself what makes possible understanding in the first instance, nor is it that which underpins the ongoing process of understanding in any fundamental sense.[38] The commonality that is given in the self-identity of a community, and in a particular formation of the world, is a commonality that depends on our active involvement with the "same" entities and events, on our being immersed in a single, if infinitely complex, web of worldly interconnection. The latter form of commonality turns out to be a commonality that, while it remains always indeterminate, constituted as it is through activity rather than content, is actually that which enables the determination of both agreement and difference.

4

Davidson's insistence on the idea that the agreement that grounds understanding must be an agreement based in our common engagement in the world, and not in shared propositions, rules, concepts, behavioral dispositions, practices, or whatever, is something repeated across many different essays and contexts. Nevertheless, in some of his later essays, Davidson has also made certain remarks that appear to run counter to this insistence. There is, of course, no reason to suppose that Davidson should be immune to inconsistency on this or any other matter; nor is it crucial to the objectives of the present inquiry that Davidson's position remain the same across all his works—whatever reading we give to any contrary remarks in Davidson's later writings, it should be clear that the overriding argument that is sustained throughout a large number of Davidson's essays, as well as being a central theme in many of them, is that understanding does not depend on any preexisting, determinate, internalized agreement. Still, it is worth looking more closely at the comments in question here, since how those comments should be read turns out to be a little more complicated than may at first sight appear to be the case. Moreover, the issues that emerge in relation to such a closer examination turn out themselves to be particularly instructive in the consideration of the issues at stake.

In "The Second Person," Davidson provides an illustration of the structure of triangulation by reference to a simple learning situation—the example he uses is taken directly from Kripke's discussion of Wittgenstein on rule-following and concerns a situation in which a child learns to use the word "table."[39] Davidson argues that it is our ability to identify similarities between our responses and those of the child that enables us to identify the table as the common cause of both our and the child's responses, and so as being that toward which those responses are directed. As Davidson explains matters:

> The child finds tables similar; we find tables similar; and we find the child's responses in the presence of tables similar. It now makes sense for us to call the responses of the child responses to tables. Given these three patterns of response we can assign a location to the stimuli that elicit the child's responses. The relevant stimuli are the objects or events we naturally find similar (tables) which are correlated with responses of the child we find similar. It is a form of triangulation: one line goes from the child in the direction of the table, one line goes from us in the direction of the table, and the third line goes between us and the child. Where the lines from child to table converge "the" stimulus is located. Given our view of the child and world, we can pick out "the" cause of the child's response. It is the common cause of our response and the child's response. . . . if someone is the speaker of a language, there must be another sentient being whose innate similarity responses are sufficiently like his own to provide an answer to the question, what is the stimulus to which the speaker is responding?[40]

Given the considerations we have explored in the preceding pages, this passage, or more particularly, the last sentence in this passage, is somewhat puzzling. Davidson seems to claim that the basis for being able to recognize someone as speaking a language, and so also for being able to assign specific meanings to that person's utterances, is that they have the same "innate similarity responses." This is surely very close to the idea that what underpins understanding is some form of prior and internalized agreement—inasmuch as it would seem to be "innate," some form of "common nature." Davidson makes similar remarks about the importance of shared "similarity responses" elsewhere. Thus, in replying to an essay by Kirk Ludwig, Davidson writes that: "Thought and language are features and functions of rationality. . . . But interpretation requires more similarity than this: we could only understand another creature that was tuned to some of the main features of the world we are tuned to";[41] and in replying to Dagfinn Føllesdal, Davidson tells us that "Quine came to think that it was because evolution had shaped our discriminative abilities to be much alike (rather than the details of our personal neural wirings) that linguistic communication was possible, and I am sure he was right."[42]

These sorts of comments, which appear only in some of Davidson's later essays and replies, and always in connection with discussions of triangulation, might well seem, on the face of it, to provide confirmation of a Davidsonian version of the claim that understanding requires prior, internalized agreement. Yet read in such a way, these comments also seem clearly to be at odds with those long-standing elements in the Davidsonian position that have been the focus for my discussion here. Indeed, if understanding were a matter of shared "similarity responses," then we could surely imagine cases in which responses were not shared, and so could make sense of precisely what Davidson denies, namely, the idea of speakers whose language we could not understand—and just such an argument is sometimes advanced by those who see it as providing an obvious counter to the Davidsonian position.[43] What is going on here? Does Davidson encounter a set of considerations that lead him to change his mind about the sort of agreement that makes for understanding and that need to be taken account of here? Or does consideration of the role of shared similarity responses and common discriminatory capacities indicate something else about the issues at stake and the manner in which they might be approached?

The example of triangulation that Davidson considers in "The Second Person" concerns our understanding of a child who may well be in the process of acquiring a first language. If we consider the role of shared similarity responses in such cases, then it should be clear that they play a quite decisive role. Without a set of shared, innate responses it is hard to see how language would ever be able to develop in the first place. Certainly no isolated individual could ever acquire a first language, and so the very possibility of language and communication must rest, in a certain sense, in some shared cognitive and behavioral heritage. What holds for first-language acquisition, however, need not hold for the ongoing operation of understanding or for the acquisition of a second language. In particular, understanding in these cases does not depend on our having an already fixed body of discriminatory capacities that are both innate and shared.

Certainly it is the case that in order to understand another, whether or not the situation is one of first-language acquisition, one must be able to match up one's own responses with those of one's interlocutor in ways that pick out the same object. We can do this in only if there is a high degree of convergence in the way we and our interlocutor are, as Davidson puts it, "tuned into" the world, and so the possibility of understanding can indeed be said to depend on agreement in the form of such shared "tuning." Yet there is no necessity to conclude, from the mere fact that ongoing communication and understanding requires the ability for shared discrimination, that the capacity for discrimination is therefore based in, and restricted by, some biologically determined "nature." Undoubtedly, if we cannot correlate our behavior with the features of the world in a way that correlates with the behavior of some other creature, then that other creature will not be able to be understood by us. For the most part, of course, evolutionary history means that we will share, with many other creatures around us, and certainly with creatures of our own species, similar capacities that enable us to identify and track similar features of the world. But we need not rely only on our evolutionary heritage in this regard. We can augment and extend our capacities to identify and track, and we can modify what we are tuned toward. Moreover, it is precisely our encounter with creatures that have different discriminative capacities that can lead us to augment our capacities in this way[44]—in much the same way that a difficult interpretative encounter may lead us to revise, and perhaps expand, our ideas about the world; in much the same way that the linguistic encounter with another may lead us to revise our "prior" theories of interpretation to arrive at a "passing" theory suitable to that encounter.

The fact that we do not currently share certain specific capacities, or indeed certain specific dispositions to respond, with another creature does not, then, rule out our interpretation or understanding of that creature, but it does mean there is an additional challenge to be overcome. Indeed, we first need to satisfy ourselves of the likelihood that there is some feature of the world in relation to which a creature is responding, but to which we do not normally react in the same way, and then we need to be able to find a way of correlating our responses with that same feature. Moreover, that this is something we are capable of doing is exemplified by the wide range of cases in which we have been able to come to understand the behavior of creatures in spite of the fact that aspects of their behavior involve responses to quite different features of the world those to which we respond—bees, for instance, respond to features of the world, specifically the polarization of light, of which we normally have no awareness, while dogs and cats have olfactory and auditory sensitivities that go far beyond the human. What this shows is that what is crucial for understanding is not so much the particular responsive dispositions we have to start with, but the fact that we have some such capacities.

In this respect it is not the exact character of our access to the world that determines our capacity to understand, but, once again, the fact that we have some such access—and the nature of that access is that it is indeed access *to the world*, and not restricted to some part or aspect of it. What does unite our responses—those of bees, cats, and dogs, and even human beings, is the fact that such responsiveness is shaped, through evolution in the case of the species and through learning in the case of the individual, *by environmental circumstance*—it is shaped, in the broadest sense, *by the world*. Perhaps this is actually what lies behind Davidson's thinking here. Thus in "Epistemology Naturalized," he writes that "It may be that not even plants could survive in our world if they did not to some extent react in ways we find similar to events and objects that we find similar."[45] In that case, what is crucial is not so much the mere fact of a similarity of response, but of a responsiveness that is similarly shaped—a similarity that is grounded in the world.

Read against this sort of background, it is not at all clear that Davidson's remarks on the importance of shared similarity responses for the possibility of communication unequivocally represent a revision of his more general views on the nature of the agreement that is necessary for understanding as expressed elsewhere. Moreover, a closer examination of the role played by shared similarity responses or shared discriminatory abilities in first-language acquisition compared to the process of ongoing communication and understanding, suggests that there are important differences here that need to be taken into account, and that although they legitimate some respects in which such responses and abilities are necessary for the possibility of language and communication, there is another sense in which they do not. All too often, the failure to distinguish between the various cases at issue here leads to confusion as to the exact role and nature of agreement in making possible understanding. Perhaps Davidson can be accused of failing to prevent such confusion even if he does not fall prey to it himself.

5

Davidson's work has always been demanding on the reader, and so there should be no surprise in discovering some complications in Davidson's thinking about the role and nature of the agreement that makes for understanding. Yet the conception of understanding as a dynamic process that is essentially based in the interconnected engagement of speaker and interlocutor within the same worldly environment, and with respect to the same events and entities, is one that runs through much of Davidson's writing from his early essays on radical interpretation to his later writings on triangulation. Although there is a sense of agreement that does indeed found the possibility of understanding—the agreement that consists in our common engagement in the world—the determination of agreement is something that occurs in the process of coming to understand, rather than being that on which it is based. Similarly, the formation of a determinate form of commonality of the sort that is expressed in the idea of a shared language, shared practices, or shared ideals and beliefs, notwithstanding the fact that it may feed into and reinforce the capacity for arriving at a shared understanding, is not itself that which enables such understanding. Even our shared biological heritage, though essential to language *acquisition,* is not obviously essential to *understanding* as such.

Davidson's emphasis on the way understanding arises out of our active involvement in the world can be viewed as a reversal of the usual direction of explanation: Typically, philosophers have aimed to explain our engagement with others or with the world on the basis of our subjectivity, but Davidson's strategy has been to treat subjectivity as explicable only, if at all, on the basis of our engagement—subjectivity itself is thereby understood as part of a larger structure that also encompasses intersubjectivity and objectivity, and is nothing apart from this structure.[46] This is why both relativism and skepticism cannot, on the Davidsonian account, find an initial footing—both positions assume that content can be given to a notion of an internalized structure or content, subjectivity, that is understood as potentially disengaged from others and from the world. Yet if this means that relativism and skepticism cannot achieve any proper formulation, then neither can traditional epistemology, and neither can traditional accounts of the basis of knowledge or of understanding.

Davidson cannot, in this respect, be read simply as operating within the usual technical framework that governs so much contemporary analytic thinking (thereby giving some license to my own attempts to move the discussion in the direction of the hermeneutic and phenomenological). His approach is simple, in that it aims to keep to a certain everyday conception of the world and our relation to it and to eschew certain standard "philosophical" presuppositions, but it is also radical, in that it implicitly presents a completely reenvisioned conception of the core issues concerning self, meaning, knowledge, and world—a vision that may be viewed as expressing a thoroughgoing "externalism" (although of an idiosyncratic form). It is precisely because of its simplicity and radicality that Davidson's work has most often been underestimated and misunderstood by readers from both analytic and continental perspectives alike.[47]

The idea that understanding can only proceed on the basis of some preexisting, determinate, internalized agreement, and that sociality and normativity must themselves be understood as based in agreement of this sort, is one of the most commonplace of philosophical assumptions, as well as being one of the most debilitating. Part of the radicality of Davidson's position is its rejection of this idea, and part of its simplicity is the turn back toward our own active engagement in the world as primary. It is thus that, at the conclusion to the "On the Very Idea of a Conceptual Scheme," Davidson can talk, in his famous phrase, of reestablishing "unmediated touch with the familiar objects whose antics make our sentences true and false."[48] It is through being in touch with those objects that we also come to be in touch with ourselves and with others. What is common to all, then, is simply the shared connectedness that comes from our shared involvement in the world. As Heidegger writes, emphasizing the way in which even language depends on this prior connectedness and involvement:

> Words emerge from that *essential agreement* of human beings with one another, *in accordance with which they are open in their being with one another for the beings around them,* which they can then individually agree about—and this also means fail to agree about. Only on the grounds of this originary, essential agreement is discourse possible in its essential function.[49]

The agreement that enables understanding is precisely the agreement that consists in this *openness toward* the world, an agreement that can never be uniquely determined, since it is that on the basis of which any determination is possible.

Notes

1. Davidson regarded G. H. Mead's *Mind, Self, and Society* (Chicago: University of Chicago Press, 1934) as particularly relevant, although lacking in argument.

2. See especially Donald Davidson, "The Social Aspect of Language," in his *Truth, Language, and History* (Oxford: Clarendon Press, 2005), pp. 109–126; Davidson once responded to a seminar question as to how much Wittgenstein was an influence on his thinking by saying that "I try to read the *Investigations* once every couple of years to remind me of what is important."

3. See Donald Davidson, "Communication and Convention," in his *Inquiries into Truth and Interpretation* (Oxford: Clarendon Press, rev. ed., 2001), pp. 265–280; "A Nice Derangement of Epitaphs," in *Truth, Language, and History,* pp. 89–108; and "The Social Aspect of Language."

4. Davidson, "A Nice Derangement of Epitaphs," p. 107.

5. Donald Davidson, "On the Very Idea of a Conceptual Scheme," in *Inquiries into Truth and Interpretation,* p. 198.

6. Donald Davidson, "The Myth of the Subjective," in his *Subjective, Intersubjective, Objective* (Oxford: Clarendon Press, 2001), p. 43.

7. Graham Macdonald and Philip Pettit, *Semantics and Social Science* (London: Routledge & Kegan Paul, 1981), pp. 31–32. See also my *Donald Davidson and the Mirror of Meaning* (Cambridge: Cambridge University Press, 1992), pp. 154–156.

8. See Donald Davidson, "Thought and Talk," in his *Inquiries into Actions and Events* (Oxford: Oxford University Press, 1980), pp. 155–170.

9. Anita Avramides, "Davidson and the New Sceptical Problem," in *Donald Davidson: Truth, Meaning and Knowledge,* ed. Ursula M Żegleń (London: Routledge, 1999), p. 153;

Avramides refers, in the embedded quotation, to P. F. Strawson, *Individuals: An Essay in Descriptive Metaphysics* (London: Methuen, 1974), p. 112.

10. Donald Davidson, "Belief and the Basis of Meaning," in *Inquiries into Truth and Interpretation*, p. 153.

11. Donald Davidson, "Introduction," in *Inquiries into Truth and Interpretation*, p. xix.

12. The latter idea derives, of course, from Wittgenstein, and is often taken to be given particularly striking expression in Wittgenstein's famous remark that "If a lion could talk, we could not understand him" (*Philosophical Investigations*, trans. G. E. M. Anscombe, Oxford: Blackwell, rev. ed. 2001, p. 223)—the reason being, so it is usually assumed, that understanding is only possible on the basis of similar forms of life (or from within the *same* form of life), and the radical difference between human and leonine "forms of life" would therefore also preclude any understanding between them. Saul Kripke quotes this very remark, seemingly with approval, in his essay on the rule-following problem: Kripke, *Wittgenstein on Rules and Private Language* (Oxford: Blackwell, 1982), p. 96.

13. The engagement at issue here is not, it should be noted, some form of purely "pragmatic" engagement of the sort at issue, for instance, in Hubert Dreyfus's notion of "absorbed coping," nor should it be taken to involve any prioritization of the "nonconceptual" over the "conceptual." It is an engagement that takes many different forms, including both the linguistic and nonlinguistic, the "practical" and the "theoretical"—the key point is that it is an engagement that already implicates things and world.

14. As Bjørn Ramberg writes, "the radical-interpretation model must be understood as a model of a *process*, not as a model of a static state of linguistic competence," *Donald Davidson's Philosophy of Language: An Introduction* (Oxford: Blackwell, 1989), p. 78.

15. See Davidson, "A Nice Derangement of Epitaphs," p. 101.

16. It is important to recognize here that one can determine something as an object of belief or as the focus of action even though one may be unable to determine the correct description under which beliefs are held of the object or action directed toward it. This could be viewed as the correlate of the original Davidsonian claim that we can identify the attitude of holding true on the part of a speaker independently of being able to attribute meanings to her utterances.

17. Although see Davidson, "Reply to Burge," *Journal of Philosophy* 85 (1988): 664.

18. See Strawson, *Individuals*, pp. 31–38.

19. See my discussion in *Place and Experience: A Philosophical Topography* (Cambridge: Cambridge University Press, 1999), chapter 6.

20. Dagfinn Føllesdal, "Triangulation," in *The Philosophy of Donald Davidson*, Library of Living Philosophers vol. 27, ed. Lewis Edwin Hahn (Chicago: Open Court, 1999), p. 721.

21. One can see here the way in which Føllesdal's account seems essentially to consist in a restatement of the original problem set by Quine under the heading of radical translation, but without regard to Davidson's own reformulation of that problem within the framework of radical interpretation. In this respect, see Davidson's comments in "Belief and the Basis of Meaning," in *Inquiries into Truth and Interpretation*, pp. 141–154, and his claim that the indeterminacy that arises under the Quinean approach is diminished under his, at least insofar as concerns the identification of the objects of action and of belief.

22. Ibid., pp. 725–726.

23. Donald Davidson, "Reply to Dagfinn Føllesdal," in Hahn (ed.), *The Philosophy of Donald Davidson*, p. 732.

24. This is so notwithstanding the failed engagement between Davidson and Gadamer that takes place in the volume of the Library of Living Philosophers devoted to Gadamer's thought—see Davidson, "Gadamer and Plato's *Philebus*," and Gadamer, "Reply to Donald Davidson," in Hahn (ed.), *The Philosophy of Hans-Georg Gadamer*, pp. 421–436; reprinted in Davidson, *Truth, Language, and History*, pp. 261–276 (all references are to the Library of Living Philosophers edition). What is notable about that exchange—both Davidson's contribution and Gadamer's reply—is how little the two understand of one another's positions. It seems to me foolish to take this as having any real significance for the viability of their respective philosophical projects (Gadamer's problematic dialogues with other thinkers are similarly of little help in the assessment of Gadamer's own philosophical position). The failure of understanding does not derive from any inadequacy on the part of their own interpretive theories, but from contingent features of the personal and professional situation of the two thinkers—from aspects of personality, the circumstances of the engagement, and their philosophical background.

25. See Gadamer, *Truth and Method*, rev. trans. Joel Weinsheimer and Donald G. Marshall (New York: Continuum, 2nd rev. ed., 1992), esp. pp. 164–169 in which Gadamer contrasts the "restorative" conception of hermeneutics espoused by Schleiermacher with the "integrative" conception to be found in Hegel.

26. See my comments on this issue in "Sprache ist Gespräch: On Gadamer, Language and Philosophy," *Between Description and Interpretation: The Hermeneutic Turn in Phenomenology*, ed. Andrzej Wiercinski (Toronto: The Hermeneutic Press, 2005), pp. 408–417.

27. This is a summary of the arguments set out in *Truth and Method*, esp. part II, sec. II, pp. 265–380.

28. Hannah Arendt, *The Human Condition* (Chicago: Chicago University Press, 1958), pp. 57–58; see also Arendt's important discussion of the connection between speech and action in *The Human Condition*, chapter 5 (and especially her comments on

what she calls "the space of appearance," pp. 199–200). In *The Thracian Maid and the Professional Thinker: Arendt and Heidegger* (Albany: SUNY Press, 1997), pp. 92–93, Jacques Taminiuax points to the centrality of the idea of the common world in Arendt's thinking, as well as its origin in Aristotle's comment in the *Nicomachean Ethics*, 1176b36ff, that "what appears to all, this we call being."

29. This is, of course, why Gadamer can say of our prejudices (understood in the positive sense in which that term is deployed in *Truth and Method*) that they are "biases of our openness to the world." Gadamer, *Philosophical Hermeneutics*, ed. and trans. David E. Linge (Berkeley: University of California Press, 1977), p. 115.

30. Davidson, "Gadamer and Plato's *Philebus*," p. 432. It should be noted that Davidson acknowledges that his disagreement with Gadamer on this point may simply show that he has not fully understood the Gadamerian position; see "Gadamer and Plato's *Philebus*," p. 431.

31. Ibid., p. 431.

32. See my discussion in "Gadamer, Davidson, and the Ground of Understanding," in *Gadamer's Century: Essays in Honor of Hans-Georg Gadamer*, ed. Jeff Malpas, Ulrich Arnswald, and Jens Kertscher (Cambridge, MA: MIT Press, 2002), pp. 209–210; and also "*Sprache ist Gespräch*: On Gadamer, Language, and Philosophy."

33. See also my discussion in *Place and Experience*, chapters 3–6.

34. Heidegger, "The Origin of the Work of Art," in his *Off the Beaten Track* (a translation of *Holzwege*), trans. Kenneth Baynes and Julian Young (Cambridge: Cambridge University Press, 2002), pp. 1–56. See Gadamer's comments on the importance of this essay to his thinking in "Reflections on my Philosophical Journey," in Hahn (ed.), *The Philosophy of Hans-Georg Gadamer*, p. 47.

35. On the importance, within Heidegger's thought, of this idea of the thing, or as I have put it here, the world, as transcending any particular appearance, see my *Heidegger's Topology: Being, Place, World* (Cambridge, MA: MIT Press, 2006), p. 249.

36. See *Heidegger's Topology*.

37. See my *Donald Davidson and the Mirror of Meaning* (Cambridge: Cambridge University Press, 1992), but also "Locating Interpretation: The Topography of Understanding in Heidegger and Davidson," *Philosophical Topics* 27 (1999): 129–148.

38. This is a point that is often overlooked in many discussions that draw on Gadamerian and Heideggerian approaches. Hubert Dreyfus, for instance, sometimes presents the determinate commonality that appears here in a way that makes it look as if it were that which enables understanding, rather than as arising on the basis of such understanding. See, e.g., Dreyfus's discussion in "Nihilism, Art, Technology, and Politics," in *The Cambridge Companion to Heidegger*, ed. Charles Guignon (Cambridge: Cambridge University Press, 1993), pp. 290–301.

39. See Saul A. Kripke, *Wittgenstein on Rules and Private Language* (Cambridge, MA: Harvard University Press, 1982), p. 105.

40. Davidson, "The Second Person," in *Subjective, Intersubjective, Objective* (Oxford: Clarendon Press, 2001), pp. 119–120.

41. Donald Davidson, "Reply to Kirk Ludwig," in *Donald Davidson: Truth, Meaning, and Knowledge*, ed. Urszula M. Żegleń (London: Routledge, 1999), p. 47; see also Davidson's similar comments in his "Reply to Barry Stroud," in Hahn (ed.), *The Philosophy of Donald Davidson*, p. 165, and, perhaps even more strongly, in his "Reply to Dagfinn Føllesdal," in Hahn (ed.), *The Philosophy of Donald Davidson*, pp. 731–732.

42. Davidson, "Reply to Dagfinn Føllesdal," in Hahn (ed.), *The Philosophy of Donald Davidson*, p. 732.

43. See, e.g. Nicholas Rescher, "Conceptual Schemes," in *Midwest Studies in Philosophy* 5: *Studies in Epistemology*, ed. P. A. French, T. Uehling, Jr., and H. K. Wettstein (Minneapolis: University of Minnesota Press, 1980), p. 323.

44. See my discussion of this issue in Davidson's work (as developed even prior to the appearance of Davidson's explicit deployment of triangulation) in "The Intertranslatability of Natural Languages," *Synthese* 78 (1989): 233–264.

45. Davidson, "Epistemology Naturalized," in *Subjective, Intersubjective, Objective*, p. 202.

46. See Donald Davidson, "Three Varieties of Knowledge," in *Subjective, Intersubjective, Objective*, pp. 205–220, as well as "The Myth of the Subjective."

47. Leading Davidson to comment, as he did, for instance, at the end of a panel discussion on externalism in Aix-en-Provence in 1999, that it seemed to him that no one had really appreciated just how radical or idiosyncratic was his own externalism.

48. Davidson, "On the Very Idea of a Conceptual Scheme," p. 198.

49. Martin Heidegger, *The Fundamental Concepts of Metaphysics*, trans. William McNeill and Nicholas Walker (Bloomington: Indiana University Press, 1995), p. 309.

III On Action, Reason, and Knowledge

15 Davidson and the Autonomy of the Human Sciences

Giuseppina D'Oro

1 The Ontological Backlash and the Reasons–Causes Debate

The mid-twentieth century was dominated by a particular view of the role and character of philosophical analysis. According to this view, philosophy is a high-level form of conceptual analysis, and the primary task of the philosopher is to reflect on the ways in which we speak and think about the world. This metaphilosophical view was encapsulated in the work of Ryle and the later Wittgenstein. Since then the philosophical climate has altered beyond recognition. The received view in the latter half of the twentieth century is poignantly captured in John Heil's claim that "Honest philosophy requires what the Australians call ontological seriousness."[1] On the wave of a renaissance of heavy-duty metaphysics, the key philosophical treatises that captured the metaphilosophical views dominant in mid-century have been dismissed as exercises in ordinary language that fail to engage with the substantive philosophical issues, and their authors have been accused of pursuing ontologically "free lunch" solutions to philosophical problems.[2]

This return of "real" metaphysics has had a significant impact on the way in which the question of the autonomy of the *Geisteswissenschaften* (human sciences) has been formulated. In the heyday of linguistic philosophy, the autonomy of action explanation was thought to pose an exclusively conceptual question about the methodologies at work in different explanatory practices. At the same time, the role of the philosopher was seen as that of disentangling the different meanings that the term "cause" or "because" possesses in different explanatory contexts. From this metaphilosophical perspective, once conceptual clarity had been achieved, the philosopher's job was done. Indeed, it was the attempt to go beyond conceptual analysis to address issues of ontology, whether, for example, "mind matters," that was held to generate insoluble philosophical problems.[3] The ontological backlash against the linguistic turn spelled the demise of a conception of philosophy as high-level conceptual analysis and of the concomitant understanding of the challenges facing anyone intent on defending the autonomy of the *Geisteswissenschaften*. Such a defense could no longer confine itself to a reflection on methodological practices; it also had to address the ontological implications of drawing a significant distinction between the *Naturwissenschaften* and *Geisteswissenschaften*. In the philosophy of action it was Davidson who was primarily responsible for changing the question of the relationship between reasons and causes from a purely conceptual question about the methodologies at work in different explanatory contexts to an ontological question about the possibility of mental causation. Davidson brought about a paradigm shift in the reasons–causes debate by arguing that no defense of the methodological autonomy of action explanation could ignore the metaphysical question of mental causation. For Davidson rational explanations are, methodologically speaking, distinct from causal explanations, because the former have a normative dimension that the latter lack. But reasons must, ontologically speaking, be causes, or else it would be hard to see how mind could "matter." While agreeing with the previous generation of nonreductivists that identifying reasons with causes (conceptually speaking) would be tantamount to committing a naturalistic fallacy, Davidson argued that reasons and causes must be (ontologically) identical if the threat of epiphenomenalism is to be avoided. As a result, Davidson's nonreductivism differed substantially from that which prevailed in mid-century, for it diverted the debate away from the purely conceptual plane on which it had been previously conducted. For Davidson, to leave the discussion on a purely conceptual plane would be precisely to seek for what Kim calls an ontologically "free lunch" solution to the problem of mental causation.

In the following, I explore the kind of nonreductivism defended by Davidson and compare it with that which predominated in mid-century. In particular I contrast Davidson's argument for the autonomy of the human sciences with the one developed by R. G. Collingwood[4] as presented through the interpretative efforts of W. H. Dray.[5] I suggest that Davidson's arguments against the anticausalist consensus that dominated the first half of the twentieth century were not conclusive and that the success of causalism in the latter half of the century is largely to be explained by a return of heavy-duty metaphysics and an ontological backlash against the linguistic turn. Yet, although Davidson's arguments against the previous generation of nonreductivists may not be conclusive, Davidson's undeniable merit was to keep alive a kind of nonreductivism that is grounded in a distinction in kind between normative and descriptive sciences, rather than in a distinction in degree between sciences with greater or lower predictive power, a form of nonreductivism that has its historical roots in a Kantian rather than empiricist tradition.

2 The Changing Face of Nonreductivism

For the generation of nonreductivists that preceded Davidson, to be a nonreductivist was tantamount to being a noncausalist. This, at least, was the perceived implication of endorsing the view that the explanation of action is a form of rationalization that involves establishing a logical or conceptual link between the *explanans* and the *explanandum* rather than an empirical connection derived from observation and inductive generalization. Thinkers such as Dray, as an interpreter of Collingwood, Melden,[6] and von Wright,[7] were united by the view that whereas the explanations at work in natural science are causal, those at work in the sciences of mind are rational, and, crucially, that to acknowledge this difference is to accept the claim that "reasons are not causes." There was no such thing as a nonreductivist who was also a causalist, because to deny the slogan "reasons are not causes" meant *ipso facto* to deny the autonomy of the *Geisteswissenschaften*. Thus, for example, Hempel, whose 1942 essay "The Function of General Laws in History"[8] had reignited the debate for and against unity in the sciences, argued in favor of reductivism by arguing in favor of causalism. He claimed that the kind of explanations that historians provide only appear to have a different logical form from causal explanations. They appear to have a different logical form because they are mere "explanation sketches." The full explanation (if historians ever bothered to give it) would have the same logical structure as explanation in natural science. For Hempel, once the apparent methodological differences between explanations in history and the natural sciences are explained away, we can see that explanations in terms of reasons have in fact the same logical structure as causal explanations and thus that so-called rational explanations are merely incomplete causal explanations. Nonreductivists such as Dray, by contrast, defended the autonomy of the sciences of mind by rejecting causalism. They argued that Hempel had missed the point; rational explanations are not incomplete explanations of the same (causal) kind, but different kinds of explanations. Whereas rational explanations are normative, causal explanations are descriptive. History is a hermeneutic, not an empirical science: Historians are concerned with making sense of actions (and they do so by establishing a logical or conceptual connection between an action and the reason that explains it), not with predicting or retrodicting behavior on the basis of observations of how agents normally react to certain antecedent conditions. Whatever the disagreement, both those who denied the slogan "reasons are not causes" and those who endorsed it agreed that the issues at stake were logical or methodological, not ontological. The philosophical problem was whether the structure of explanation in the sciences of mind is ultimately the same as that of the nomological explanations employed in the sciences of nature, *not* whether rational and causal explanations compete for ontological space. In sum, prior to Davidson, nonreductivism was more or less synonymous with noncausalism.

The general perception of the reasons–causes debate changed with Davidson, who provided two arguments intended to sever the link between nonreductivism and anticausalism. The first appeared in "Actions, Reasons, and Causes,"[9] the second in "Mental Events."[10] In "Actions, Reasons, and Causes" Davidson attacked the noncausalist position endorsed by his predecessors by arguing that if reasons were not causes they would remain mere rationalizations, and if they remained mere rationalizations we would be unable to capture which among the various possible rational explanations that could be adduced to make sense of an action properly capture the internal monologue that moved the agent to act. Davidson's demand that the practical syllogism should capture the internal monologue of the agent substantively differs from the claims made by previous nonreductivists, for a number of reasons. First, the notion of descriptive adequacy had played no role for the previous generation of nonreductivists. Dray, for one, had rejected the view that making sense of an action requires knowing what goes on in somebody else's head, on the grounds that such a requirement ascribes to historians telepathic powers that they neither have nor need because understanding actions involves asking oneself how one would have acted against the background of certain beliefs and desires rather than accessing the agent's psyche. Further, the previous generation of nonreductivists would have argued that one cannot mix and match descriptive and normative explanations, because if an explanation is an explanation of action it must be normative. An agent may perform deeds for which there correspond no valid practical syllogisms (he or she may act in a certain way because he or she is tired, angry, etc.). In this case, the explanation will be a descriptive psychological explanation, not a normative rational explanation, or, in other words, not an explanation of action in the sense of *res gestae*. These, as Collingwood put it, "are not the actions, in the widest sense of that word, which are done by animals of the species called human; they are actions in another sense of the same word, equally familiar but narrower, actions done by reasonable agents in pursuit of ends determined by their reason."[11] Introducing the requirement for descriptive adequacy (truthfulness to the agent's psychological processes) over and beyond that of rational coherence blurs the boundaries between logic and psychology and leads to a kind of classification across categories.[12] For reasons of space I will say no more about this first argument, an argument that is usually regarded as providing independent support for Davidson's anomalous monism. I will focus instead on a second argument that he develops in "Mental Events."

Here the main motivation for advocating a shift from the anticausalist position captured by the slogan "reasons are not causes" to a causalist position is directly related to the problem of epiphenomenalism. If reasons were not causes, so Davidson argues, they would be rationally necessary but lack existential import and therefore, in the last analysis, be epiphenomenal, thus failing to explain how mind could make a causal difference. In other words, if reason explanations were pure rationalizations, they would express no more than what Hume called "relations of ideas," and as such they would have no ontological relevance. Anomalous monism is developed in response to the problem of epiphenomenalism that allegedly plagues Davidson's anticausalist predecessors.

Anomalous monism, Davidson claims, addresses the problem raised by the Kantian antinomy of freedom and determinism and seeks to solve it by reconciling three apparently incompatible premises: (1) the commonsense premise that mind matters (that mental events are causally related to physical events); (2) the methodological premise that explanation proper requires strict laws (that singular causal relations are backed by strict laws); and (3) the antinaturalist premise that there is an is–ought divide and thus the impossibility of reducing the normative/rational explanations of actions to the descriptive/causal explanations at work in the natural sciences (no psychophysical laws).

If there were strict psychophysical laws, it would be easy to see how mind could matter: Mind would matter because mental events would be nomologically reducible to physical events. Once mental events are reduced to physical events, they are subject to the same form of (causal/descriptive) explanation employed to investigate nature. This reductivist solution to the problem of mental causation, however, would also fail to safeguard the anomalous (normative) character of the mental. Anomalous monism seeks to provide a solution that (a) preserves the anomalous/normative character of the mental by denying the existence of bridge laws, (b) vindicates the commonsense premise that mind matters, thus rebutting epiphenomenalism, and crucially (c) does not relinquish the methodological premise that causal explanations require strict laws, and with it the aspiration of natural science to provide complete explanations of reality.

Anomalous monism seeks to reconcile these three premises in the context of a dual-aspect monistic ontology. Thus, while addressing the problem raised by the Kantian antinomy of freedom and determinism, Davidson offers a very different solution from Kant. Where Kant ontologically divided the noumenal from the sensible world, even if only by way of a thought experiment (to consider oneself as an agent is to view oneself as a member of an intelligible world),[13] Davidson ontologically unites what he separates methodologically and seeks to defend the autonomy of action explanation within the context of an ontological reunification. In doing so, Davidson introduces an ontological dimension in the argument for the autonomy of the human sciences, a dimension that, as I have argued, was absent in the previous generation of nonreductivism, where the discussion had been conducted on a purely conceptual plane and the debate between causalists and noncausalists was strictly methodological. With the introduction of this ontological dimension into what used to be a purely conceptual debate, a number of questions that would not have previously arisen now require an answer, questions such as: "what kind of monism is anomalous monism?"; "is it neutral or is there a level of description that is ontologically more basic than the other?"; "if there is a level of description that is ontologically more basic than the other, is it not the case that the ontologically less basic level will ultimately remain epiphenomenal?" Questions such as these lie at the basis of what has been dubbed the "standard interpretation"[14] of Davidson's anomalous monism. According to this interpretation, anomalous monism is a kind of nonreductive physicalism that maintains that although mental events are different in kind from physical events, they are token-identical with them. Type difference preserves methodological nonreductivism by denying the existence of psychophysical laws; token identity ensures ontological reduction and in so doing enables anomalous monism to escape the threat of epiphenomenalism. On the standard interpretation, the distinctive advantage of anomalous monism vis-à-vis the previous kind of purely conceptual nonreductivism would be that the token-identification of mental events with physical events entails that mental events are not "causal danglers" and thus that mind does indeed matter. Insofar as all mental events are token-identical with physical events, they are causally efficacious, because the latter are the kind of things that paradigmatically enter into causal relations. Yet, as many have been quick to point out, if Davidson's anomalous monism is a form of nonreductive or token physicalism, it merely shows that mental events are causally efficacious as physical events, not that they are causally efficacious *qua* mental. Anomalous monism is thus a form of type-epiphenomenalism.[15]

3 Epiphenomenalism and the Metaphysical Status of the Causal Relation

When an interpretation is called "standard," it is usually meant that it is unrefined, crude, or simplistic. And this is what has indeed been said of the interpretation of Davidson as a nonreductive physicalist. Davidson, so it has been argued, is no physicalist, not even of a nonreductive kind, for he holds "physical" and "mental" to be predicates or types that apply to the *explanandum* of the natural and human sciences, respectively, not to particulars *simpliciter*. Davidson is simply not interested in providing a characterization of reality as being ultimately mental or physical. His monism is thus genuinely ontologically neutral between the mental and the physical. Davidson's argument against the epiphenomenality of the mental rests not on prioritizing a physicalist over a spiritual ontology, as proponents of the standard interpretation have assumed, but on the claim that causal relations hold between particulars irrespectively of how they are described (as mental or as physical). On this more nuanced reading of anomalous monism, there is an important distinction to be made between causal relations and causal explanations, a distinction that is not adequately acknowledged by reading Davidson as a nonreductivist with an ontological commitment to physicalism. Causal explanations apply to particulars insofar as they form the *explanandum* of the sciences of nature and are described as physical. But *causal relations*, as opposed to *causal explanations*, apply to particulars independently of how they are described. Whereas causal explanations and rational explanations are intensional relations that hold between the *explanans* and the *explanandum* of the human and natural sciences, respectively, the causal relation is an extensional relation that holds between particulars *simpliciter*. This is indeed how Davidson responds to those critics who, on the basis of the standard interpretation, accuse him of being an epiphenomenalist *malgré lui*.[16]

It is unclear, however, that even this more nuanced interpretation of Davidson can save anomalous monism from the charge of epiphenomenalism, for, if Davidson's nonreductivism rests on a dual-aspect ontological monism it cannot ultimately be exempt from providing an answer to the question: "which intensional explanation (rational or causal) is true of particulars *simpliciter*" or, in other words, "do causal relations resemble rational or causal explanations?" Given that rational and causal explanations cannot both be true of the same bare particulars, the problem of explanatory exclusion raises its head once again, and with it the threat of epiphenomenalism. Anomalous monism may thus be unable to avoid the problem of explanatory exclusion even if Davidson's monism does not declare a preference for either the view that reality is ultimately physical or that it is ultimately mental. If these considerations are correct, then Davidson's nonreductivism is subject to the very drawbacks he ascribed to his predecessors and fails to provide a strong dialectical motivation for abandoning the anticausalist consensus that characterized the previous generation of nonreductivists. In fact, one might go so far as to argue that, contrary to what Davidson claims, pre-Davidsonian nonreductivism was not vulnerable to the problem of explanatory exclusion and the concomitant threat of epiphenomenalism precisely because, being of a purely conceptual nature, it claimed that rational and causal explanations explain different categories of things, that is, they have a different *explanandum* and as such they are not in competition with each other. The ghost of epiphenomenalism, which Davidson invoked in order to advocate a shift from an anticausalist to a causalist position, arises only if one takes the argument for the autonomy of the human sciences beyond considerations concerning explanatory practices and introduces the notions of "bare particulars" and of "real relations." It is precisely because Davidson's anomalous monism allows for the distinction between merely intensional/explanatory and extensional/real relations that the question of correspondence becomes a legitimate philosophical question and explanatory exclusion a problem to be reckoned with. These considerations would suggest not only that the epiphenomenalist threat fails to apply to first-generation nonreductivism, but that the problem of epiphenomenalism is generated by the very kind of nonreductivism Davidson advocates.

Yet, although this more nuanced interpretation, with its appeal to a distinction between causal relations and causal explanations, may be ultimately unable save anomalous monism from the charge of epiphenomenalism, Davidson's extensionalist reply does enable us to identify more accurately the issue at stake between Davidson and his anticausalist predecessors. The antiepiphenomenalist move that Davidson makes in response to his critics relies on a realist claim about the nature of the causal relation, as it takes causal relations to be "transcendentally real." As we have seen, for Davidson's predecessors, the debate concerned explanation, not causation, and to articulate a defense of the autonomy of the human sciences it was sufficient to show that such sciences, being normative rather than descriptive, enjoy a distinctive methodology. To believe that one could say anything of particulars independently of the investigative goals of a science was presumptuous insofar as it required one to jump outside one's own philosophical skin. Collingwood, for example, claimed that there are different senses of causation at work in different explanatory contexts and that these different senses of causation correspond to the investigative goals of different sciences.[17] In history, which for Collingwood is a hermeneutic science concerned with meaning, the term "cause" is used in sense I to indicate a motive that makes sense, rationally speaking, of an action. In the practical sciences of nature, such as medicine and engineering, which are concerned with the manipulation and control of the environment for the sake of human well-being, the term "cause" is employed in sense II, to indicate an "event or state of things by producing or preventing which we can produce or prevent that whose cause it is said to be."[18] Finally, in the theoretical sciences of nature, such as physics, which abstract from human interests, the term "cause" is employed in sense III, and "that which is caused is an event or state of things and its cause is another event or state of things such that (a) if the cause happens or exists, the effect must happen or exist even if no further conditions are fulfilled, (b) the effect cannot happen or exist unless the cause happens or exists."[19] So far, Davidson might have agreed. But, and this is a crucial caveat, for Collingwood, as indeed for the generation of nonreductivists united by the slogan "reasons are not causes," there is in fact no such thing as a science that studies particulars independently of how they are described in a given investigative context and thus no meaningful sense that could be attached to the distinction between causal explanations and causal relations.

Davidson's extensionalist reply to the charge of epiphenomenalism makes clear that the bone of contention between him and his anticausalist predecessors concerns the metaphysical status of the causal relation. Davidson's predecessors claimed that the debate is about explanation, not causation, because they were antirealists about the nature of the causal relation. Davidson, by contrast, claims that the debate cannot merely concern explanation, because he is a realist about causal relations. It is Davidson's realism about causal relations that resonated with many contemporary critics of the slogan that "reasons may not be causes." Thus, for example, Crane condemns an emphasis on explanatory practices that neglects to engage with the ontological dimension of the action–event distinction by claiming that

> The issue is one about causation, not explanation. There are many ways of explaining events and processes in the physical world; but if the completeness of physics is true, then there is one special kind of *cause*. To state the problem, then, requires us to distinguish between causation and explanation, since the completeness of physics is a claim about causation.[20]

Even more aggressively, E. Lepore and B. Lower have dismissed Collingwood-style anticausalism as exemplifying the then-fashionable but no longer seriously tenable views that belonged to the era of "little red books":

> During the heyday of neo-Wittgensteinian and Rylean philosophy of mind, the era of little red books, it was said that propositional attitude explanations are not causal explanations and that beliefs, intendings, imaginings, and the like are not even candidates to be causes. Indeed, to treat mentalistic language as describing causes or causal processes is, it was said, a logical error. We have come a long way since then. The work of Davidson, Armstrong, Putnam, and Fodor (among others) has reversed what was once the orthodoxy and it is now widely agreed that propositional attitude attributions describe states and episodes which enter into causal relations.[21]

In sum, Davidson's extensionalist reply to the charge of epiphenomenalism draws attention to the fact that the issue at stake between Davidson and his anticausalist predecessors concerns the metaphysical status of the causal relation. The causalist consensus that has come to dominate the philosophy of action in the aftermath of Davidson is premised precisely on the view that causal relations are ontologically real relations, not merely intensional relations holding between particulars insofar as they are brought under some description or other.

4 Method and Metaphysics

Pre-Davidsonian nonreductivists would simply not have allowed for the notion of a bare particular and of extensional relations holding between particulars *simpliciter*. For Davidson's predecessors, method determined metaphysics in the sense that if a particular is explained rationally, it falls under the category of "action" (*res gestae*). If a particular is explained inductively, it falls under the category of "event." In other words, the concepts of "event" and of "causal explanation" are reciprocal concepts, because to explain something as an event is to explain it causally. And the same applies *mutatis mutandi* to the concepts of "action" and of "rational explanation," because to explain something as an action is to explain it rationally. Thus, Davidson's predecessors would never have claimed that the class of actions is a subset of the class of events or, to paraphrase Davidson slightly, that "whilst all events are physical, not all events are mental."[22] In Collingwood's view, for example, "actions" and "events" are categorial descriptions of reality that apply universally to all actions and to all events. For historians, "all actions are expressions of thought" precisely because by "action" one means particulars that are explained rationally and which have already been identified as falling under the domain of enquiry of the *Geisteswissenschaften*. For natural scientists, by contrast, "all events are governed by general laws" precisely because that is what one means by an "event," that is, a particular that has been identified as falling under the domain of inquiry of the *Naturwissenschaften*. Unlike Davidson, Collingwood developed his nonreductivism in the context of a descriptive metaphysics, which he referred to interchangeably as a metaphysics without ontology or a metaphysics of absolute presuppositions. Within the context of this metaphysics, questions of truth and falsity can only be settled within the investigative parameters of a science. In claiming that truth and falsity are relative to the kind of questions one asks and the presuppositions one makes, Collingwood placed meaning in the driving seat of philosophical analysis and ruled out the possibility that questions of truth and falsity could be raised independently of the investigative goals of a science. Nor is this all. Collingwood also dismissed the traditional conception of metaphysics on the grounds that the identification of metaphysics with the study of what is real independently of the set of questions and presuppositions that characterize a form of investigation is premised on the erroneous assumption that in the order of logical priority truth comes before meaning and thus that it is possible to refer to a particular independently of the categorial descriptions of reality that determine what kind of thing one is discussing in the first place. Collingwood identified metaphysics understood traditionally as an attempt to grasp reality in itself and dismissed the possibility of knowing real relations on the grounds that there can be no such thing as a science of "pure being." A science of pure being, he claimed, would be a science without a subject matter, for the subject matter of a science is determined by the kind of questions it asks and the kind of presuppositions it makes. Metaphysics is thus possible only as a science of absolute presuppositions whose task is to make explicit the categorial descriptions of reality that are at work in different explanatory contexts.[23] Crucially, rather than abandoning metaphysics in favor of linguistic analysis, Collingwood sought to correct a misunderstanding about what metaphysics truly is, a misunderstanding that is ultimately traceable to the question concerning the proper relationship between truth and meaning. It is a divergence on these key issues, and whether one's metaphysics should be "real" or descriptive, that underpins the debate between Davidson's nonreductivism and that of his anticausalist predecessors. Davidson's anticausalist predecessors developed their nonreductivism within the context of a descriptive metaphysics whose goal was to render explicit the presuppositions we make when we employ the term "cause" or "because" in different explanatory contexts. And they denied that there is any sense that can be attached to the distinction between causation and explanation on the grounds that particulars can only be identified and reidentified in virtue of how they are described. Their denial that reasons are causes is part and parcel of a descriptive conception of metaphysics in which questions of meaning are logically prior to questions of truth. Davidson by contrast developed his nonreductivism in the context of a different conception of metaphysics, one in which truth is ultimately independent of meaning. Thus, while he agreed with his anticausalist predecessors that the explanation of action is a hermeneutic enterprise, he did not believe such methodological considerations to be of metaphysical significance, since within Davidson's metaphysics questions of truth are independent of questions of meaning.

5 Concluding Remarks

Whether or not one thinks the reasons–causes debate to have been conclusively settled either in favor of causalism or anticausalism, it is clearly to Davidson's merit to have kept alive a kind of nonreductivism that is grounded in the view that the distinction between the human and the natural sciences is a distinction in kind, between normative and descriptive sciences, rather than a distinction in degree, between sciences with different levels of predictive power. As we have seen, for Davidson the anomalous character of the mental has to do with its normative nature and has very little in common with the claim that the laws of the special sciences, unlike those of physics, are hedged by *ceteris paribus* clauses and are consequently unable to deliver precise predictions. Thus, although Davidson's anomalous monism may have slung the door open for causalism, his causalism is fundamentally different in character from the one endorsed by functionalists such a Fodor[24] who believe the relevant distinction to be not so much between normative and descriptive sciences as between sciences such as physics whose laws are strict, on the one hand, and sciences whose laws are hedged by *ceteris paribus* clauses, sciences such as chemistry, biology, geology, and psychology, on the other.[25] Later attempts to defend the autonomy of the human sciences by arguing in support of the causal efficacy of psychological explanations have much more in common with a tradition that springs from Mill and views the philosophically relevant distinction to be between the exact and inexact sciences rather than the sciences of mind and nature.[26] Davidson's nonreductivism, unlike that of later causalists, arose in response to the Kantian antinomy of freedom and determinism and located the philosophically relevant distinction at the crossroads between theoretical and practical reasoning. To this extent Davidson agreed with the previous generation of nonreductivists that there is a genuinely methodological divide between the sciences of nature and mind, and his argument for the causal efficacy of the mental was formulated against the background assumption of the disunity rather than the unity of science.

Notes

1. John Heil, *From an Ontological Point of View* (Oxford: Clarendon Press, 2003), pp. 1–2.

2. Jaegwon Kim, *Mind in a Physical World* (Cambridge, MA: MIT Press, 1998), p. 59.

3. As Collingwood puts it, the relationship between the mind and the body "is the relation between the sciences of the body, or natural sciences, and the sciences of the mind; that is the relation inquiry into which ought to be substituted for the make-believe inquiry into the make-believe problem of 'the relation between body and mind.'" R. G. Collingwood, *The New Leviathan: Or Man, Society, Civilization and Barbarism*, revised edition with an introduction by David Boucher (Oxford: Clarendon Press, 1992 [1942]), 2.49, p. 11.

4. R. G. Collingwood, *The Idea of History* (Oxford: Clarendon Press, 1946); R. G. Collingwood, *The Principles of History*, ed. W. H. Dray and J. Van der Dussen (Oxford: Oxford University Press, 1999).

5. See William H. Dray, *Laws and Explanations in History* (London: Oxford University Press, 1957), and William H. Dray, "The Historical Explanation of Actions Reconsidered," in *Philosophy and History*, ed. S. Hook (New York: New York University Press, 1963).

6. Abraham Melden, *Free Action* (London: Routledge & Kegan Paul, 1961).

7. G. H. von Wright, *Explanation and Understanding* (London: Routledge & Kegan Paul, 1971).

8. C. Hempel, "The Function of General Laws in History," *Journal of Philosophy* 39 (1942): 35–48.

9. Donald Davidson, "Actions, Reasons, and Causes," in *Essays on Actions and Events* (Oxford: Clarendon Press, 1980), pp. 3–19; first published in *Journal of Philosophy* 60 (1963): 685–700.

10. Donald Davidson, "Mental Events," in *Essays on Actions and Events*, pp. 207–225.

11. Collingwood, *The Principles of History*, p. 46.

12. For a recent argument against the Davidsonian view that reasons must be identified with causes in order to be able to distinguish the agent's reasons for acting from mere rationalizations, see G. H. von Wright, "Explanation and the Understanding of Actions," in *Contemporary Action Theory*, vol. 1, ed. G. Holstrom-Hintikka and R. Tuomela (Dordrecht: Kluwer Academic, 1997).

13. Immanuel Kant, *Groundwork of the Metaphysic of Morals*, trans. H. J. Paton (New York: Harper Torchbooks, 1964).

14. See F. Stoutland, "Interpreting Davidson on Intentional Action," in this anthology.

15. On this see B. McLaughlin, "Type Epiphenomenalism, Type Dualism, and the Causal Priority of the Physical," *Philosophical Perspectives* 3 (1989): 109–135.

16. Donald Davidson, "Thinking Causes," in *Truth, Language, and History* (Oxford: Clarendon Press, 2005), pp. 188–189.

17. R. G. Collingwood, *An Essay on Metaphysics*, revised edition with an introduction by Rex Martin (Oxford: Oxford University Press, 1998 [1940]).

18. Ibid., pp. 296–297.

19. Ibid., pp. 285–286.

20. T. Crane, *Elements of Mind* (Oxford: Oxford University Press, 2001), p. 60.

21. E. Lepore and B. Lower, "More on Making Mind Matter," *Philosophical Topics* 17, no. 1 (1989): 175–191.

22. Davidson, *Essays on Actions and Events*, p. 207.

23. For an account of Collingwood's descriptive metaphysics, see my *Collingwood and the Metaphysics of Experience* (New York and London: Routledge & Kegan Paul, 2002).

24. J. A. Fodor, "Making Mind Matter More," *Philosophical Topics* 17, no. 1 (1989): 59–79.

25. On the differences between functionalism and anomalous monism, see J. McDowell, "Functionalism and Anomalous Monism," in *Actions and Events: Perspectives on the Philosophy of Donald Davidson*, ed. Ernest Lepore and Brian McLaughlin (Oxford: Blackwell, 1985), pp. 387–398.

26. For Mill, the reason the human sciences are unable to provide precise predictions is of no deep methodological significance; it merely reflects the complexity of initial conditions with which they have to deal. The distinction between explanations employed in the natural and human sciences is thus not a distinction in kind between normative and descriptive sciences, but a distinction in degree between sciences that have and sciences that lack strict laws. See J. S. Mill, *System of Logic: Ratiocinative and Inductive*, in *Collected Works of John Stuart Mill*, ed. J. M. Robson (Toronto: University of Toronto Press, 1963–1991 [1843]).

16 Interpreting Davidson on Intentional Action

Frederick Stoutland

Davidson's early papers on philosophy of action were immensely influential and no doubt largely responsible for there being a "standard story": Actions are those bodily movements caused and rationalized by beliefs and desires. It is not false to say that Davidson asserted that claim, but proponents of the standard story understand it somewhat differently than he did. His writings, I shall argue, spawned a widely accepted view that differs from his own in a number of respects.[1]

Wittgensteinian critics of the standard story generally assume that Davidson accepted it, as do its defenders, who invariably cite him as their inspiration and often credit him for rooting the story in physicalism. Jaegwon Kim, for instance, writes that Davidson's "main task has been that of finding for mind a place in an essentially physical world . . . [in which] we find nothing but bits of matter and increasingly complex aggregates made up of bits of matter."[2]

But both critics and defenders overlook the substantial influence of Elizabeth Anscombe's work on Davidson, who took her *Intention* to be "the most important treatment of action since Aristotle."[3] Although usually viewed as having replaced an account like Anscombe's with the standard story, Davidson rather thought that such an account was consistent with a causal account of action. He also thought that the latter was consistent with significant claims of other philosophers influenced by Wittgenstein—von Wright, for example, or Kenny, Melden, and Hampshire—whom he read and learned from, as he did from Wittgenstein himself, noting "those long hours I spent years ago admiring and puzzling over the *Investigations*."[4] He was critical of their work, and in the last analysis his view was quite distinct from theirs; but an adequate interpretation of his philosophy of action must nevertheless see it against the background of all these philosophers.

1

The most consequential misunderstanding of Davidson's account of action rests on missing the import of his distinction between causal *relations* and causal *explanations*. His well-known claim, that to differentiate an agent's acting *because* of a reason from her merely *having* a reason requires a causal "because," is often misunderstood since merely asserting that reasons cause actions blurs that distinction. Causal relations hold *only* between *events* (hence Davidson called this "event causation"), and they obtain no matter how the events are described, so that sentences ascribing them are *extensional*. Ascriptions of causal relations need not, therefore, *explain* phenomena: Saying truly that what Karl referred to last night was the event-cause of what happened to Linda a year ago does not explain what happened to Linda a year ago.

Although event causation holds only between particulars, Davidson thought it involves generality, hence his thesis of the "nomological character of causality": If events are causally related, there must be a *strict law* instantiated by true descriptions of the events.[5] We need not know those descriptions, but since laws are strict only if the events described belong to a *closed system* (one such that whatever can affect the system is part of the system being described), and since, Davidson held, only physics describes a closed system, all strict laws belong to (a completed) physics.[6] Because Davidson held that events are physical if they have a physical description, he also held that all causally related events are physical.

It does not follow that event causation does not involve mental events: Since events are mental if they have a mental description, and since events are causally related no matter how described, mental events can be causally related to either physical or mental events.[7] What does follow is that *reasons* are not causally related to actions, since the beliefs and desires Davidson took to be reasons are not events. "'Primary reasons'. . . are certainly not events. . . . Beliefs and desires are not changes. They are states, and since I don't think that states are *entities* of any sort, and so are not events, I do not think beliefs and desires are events."[8]

When Davidson asserted that reasons cause actions, he meant they causally *explain* actions: His view was that *rational explanation is a kind of causal explanation*. An explanation relates not to events but to sentences (propositions, facts), since to explain phenomena is always to explain them *as* such and such, that is, under a description (so that explanation sentences are *intensional*).[9] The point of an explanation is to render phenomena intelligible, and what does so under one description of the phenomena may not do so under another. Moreover, the same phenomenon may have different kinds of explanation, each explaining it under a different description.[10]

Not all explanation is causal; to be *causal* an explanation should, according to Davidson, meet three conditions.[11] First, its *explanandum* should describe either an event or a state whose existence entails an event. If the *explanandum* is that the bridge is slippery (a state), it follows that it became slippery, which is an event.

Second, its *explanans* should either describe an event *causally related* to the *explanandum* or entail that there is an *associated* event[12] so causally related. That is, if A causally explains B, "A" describes either an event causally related to B or an event associated with it that is so causally related. What "associated with" denotes will vary. The description of A may entail a description of the associated event: For example, if the car skids because the road is icy (a state), the associated event is the car's contacting the ice. Or there may be a generalization connecting A with the associated event: If the slippery road explains the car accident, the associated event is the car's skidding. Or the associated event may occur without anyone knowing what it is.

Third, the explanation depends on an empirical generalization that connects a description of the cause with a description of the effect but which is a rough generalization and not a strict law. Davidson held that causal explanations must involve generality but do not cite strict laws since their point is to explain phenomena when we do not know, or because there cannot be, strict laws covering the phenomena. Since Davidson often called these strict laws "causal laws," he said that the causal *concepts* involved in a causal explanation do not figure in causal *laws*. "It is causal *relations*, not [causal] concepts that imply the existence of [strict] laws. . . . Causal *concepts* don't sit well with strict causal laws because they enable us to evade providing strict laws."[13] While physics has lots of causal *laws*, "it is a sign of progress in a science that it rids itself of causal concepts."[14]

Davidson held that *rational* explanations meet these conditions. They meet the first because their *explananda* describe actions, which are events. They meet the second because, although an agent's reasons for action are states and not events, the *explanans* of a rational explanation (like that of causal explanations generally) entails that there is an event *associated with* the reason that is causally *related* to the action. Sometimes the reason *entails* the associated event: If Mark bought a book because he believed it important for his work, the associated event is his coming to believe that. Sometimes the context determines the event: If I wave to you because you are my neighbor, the event is my recognizing you across the street. Or we may not know what the event is, but there is, nevertheless, an event that causes the action at a particular time and place.

They meet the third condition because desires are dispositional states, and hence ascribing a desire to an agent entails a rough generalization connecting the desire with a description of her action. "A want is, or entails, a certain disposition to act to obtain what one wants. That someone has a certain disposition may be expressed as a generalization or law governing the behavior of that person. . . . [It means] we can say of someone who has a desire or end that he will tend to behave in certain ways under specified circumstances."[15] These generalizations are lawlike because they support claims about what someone *would* do *were* he to have those desires, but they are not strict laws since they require *ceteris paribus* conditions.

They are empirical but in the special sense of being implicit in the concept of desire: To know someone's desire is *thereby* to know a rough generalization about what she would tend to do given certain conditions. What is empirical is whether someone has a certain desire; if she does, her action will necessarily (*ceteris paribus*) exemplify a rough generalization.[16] The latter is very low level, however, since what someone with a given desire would tend to do depends on her belief about how to fulfill it, and the generalization applies only to someone who has the relevant belief. "The laws implicit in reason explanations are simply the generalizations implied by attributions of dispositions. But then the 'laws' are peculiar to individuals at particular moments."[17]

Although such low-grade generalizations yield little explanatory force, Davidson insisted that "the main *empirical* thrust of . . . a reason explanation [comes from] the attributions of desires, preferences, or beliefs,"[18] and he refused to give these generalizations a more significant role by extending their scope to what *all* agents would do under certain conditions. Any list of such conditions that made a generalization about what all agents would do plausible, would also make the generalization nonempirical. It cannot be empirical, for example, that *anyone* who has a desire for fresh air and believes opening the window will provide it, opens the window, provided he meets a list of conditions. If someone appeared to have the desire and belief and to meet the conditions but had no tendency to open the window, we would conclude, not that the generalization was false, but that we were mistaken about his attitudes, about our list, or about whether he met the conditions. We must not look to empirical generalizations to understand the force of rational explanations.

2

If we take seriously the distinction between causal relations and causal explanations, Davidson's claim that reasons cause actions looks different than often supposed. It does not mean that reasons are event-causes, but that they are states whose contents causally *explain* actions, a claim Davidson defended against two criticisms. The first appealed to Hume's thesis that causal explanations require general laws, the criticism being that since there are no general laws covering reasons and actions (no laws connecting content descriptions of reasons with descriptions of actions as intentional), reasons cannot causally explain actions. Von Wright accepted that criticism because he accepted Hume's thesis, but since Davidson rejected the thesis, he could claim that rational explanations are causal (in a non-Humean sense) even if there are no general laws connecting reasons and actions. Davidson and von Wright agreed, therefore, that rational explanations required no covering laws, but disagreed on what it is for an explanation to be causal.[19]

The second criticism (also credited to Hume, who asserted that cause and effect are distinct existences) was that conceptual connections exclude causal connections, and hence the conceptual connections between reasons and actions entail that reasons do not causally explain actions. Davidson recognized such connections, but rejected the criticism by appealing to the distinction between causal relations and causal explanations. The claim that cause and effect are distinct existences applies only to *events* and hence only to causal *relations* between events. *Conceptual* connections hold, not between events, but between sentences (propositions) or descriptions and hence are relevant only to causal *explanations*. The claim that causes and effects cannot be conceptually connected is, therefore, either nonsense or false. It is nonsense to speak of *events* as conceptually connected, while it is false to claim that *descriptions* of events (even if causes and effects) cannot be conceptually connected. It is a conceptual truth, for instance, that the cause of E causes E, but the connection between the *descriptions* "the cause of E" and "E" is distinct from the causal relation between the *events* described. Whether descriptions are conceptually connected is independent of whether the events described are causally related.

Davidson saw conceptual connections between reasons and actions as crucial to rational explanation. He wrote, for instance, that "There is a conceptual connection between pro attitudes and actions. . . . When we explain an action, by giving the reason, we do redescribe the action;

redescribing the action gives the action a place in a pattern, and in this way the action is explained."[20] Indeed, he held that there is no principled distinction between what *constitutes* action and what *explains* it. "Explanation is built into the concepts of action, belief, and desire. . . . We already know, from the description of the action, that it must have been caused by such a belief-desire pair, and we know that such an action is just what such a belief-desire pair is suited to cause. . . . Beliefs and desires explain actions only when they are described in such a way as to reveal their suitability for causing the action. . . . [They] explain an action only if [their] contents . . . entail that there is something desirable about the action, given the description under which the action is being explained."[21]

Why did Davidson hold that such explanation is *causal*? After all, explanation always aims at understanding phenomena—at rendering them intelligible—which can be achieved in different ways. One might redescribe the phenomena, specify their parts, spell out their function in a system, articulate the role they play in a narrative—or construct a causal explanation of them. Why count explanations that meet Davidson's three conditions as *causal*?

John McDowell claims that an explanation is causal "if the understanding it supplies is causal understanding," which rational explanations provide because they involve "responsiveness to reason [which] makes a difference to what happens—a causal difference."[22] An explanation yields causal understanding if it describes the *explanans* in a way that makes it intelligible why the *explanandum*—as described—*came, ceased,* or *continued* to be. This allows for different kinds of causal explanation. On Davidson's view, rational explanations provide causal understanding in that they describe, redescribe, or interpret an agent's acting, not instead of, but as a way of explaining *why* she acted intentionally as she did. They specify the reasons that made a difference in what she did and as a result in what happened. They are, therefore, *causal* even though they cite no exceptionless general laws or identify a reason with the event that causes the action.

3

Davidson's account of rational explanation includes a condition central to the standard story that Wittgensteinian accounts omit, namely, that as causal it involves a causal *relation.* Although reasons are states and not events, Davidson thinks they explain actions only if there are associated events that cause the actions.

Most defenders of the standard story find no difficulty in this condition. They think the distinction between causal relations and explanations is irrelevant since beliefs and desires are easily construed as events, either by turning the nouns—"beliefs" and "desires"—into verbs—"believing" and "desiring"—or by speaking of *coming* to believe or desire, which are changes and hence events. In my view, both moves are objectionable.

The former changes labels but does not alter the status of beliefs and desires, which Davidson insisted are states and not events. It is, in any case, the *contents* of the attitudes that play the crucial role as reasons for action, and they are not event-causes.

Davidson himself suggested the latter move, but it is problematic. Whether a reason explains an action is independent of its coming to be. Furthermore, even if my coming to have a belief or desire is an event associated with my reason, it is seldom the reason for which I act. If I buy a book because it is important for my work, my reason for buying it is not my coming to believe that but the content of the belief I have come to have. In any case, Davidson did not require that the associated event be conceptually connected with the reason. For instance, the event-cause of an agent's waving at someone may be his recognizing her across the street, but his reason for waving is his desire to be friendly to his neighbor. Besides, since the event-cause of an action may, Davidson held, be unknown to the agent, it is evident that such an event does not increase the force of an explanatory reason.

Davidson insisted, nevertheless, that although reasons are not event-causes of actions,[23] there must be event-causes associated with explanatory reasons. He had, apparently, three reasons for this, which, however, I do not find persuasive.

The first is that a rational explanation should account for an agent's acting at a time and place, and hence there must be an event causing the action to occur at that time and place. This strikes me as weak: Even if there is such an event, it is irrelevant to the many explanations that do not account for an agent acting at a particular time and place. Buying a book because I needed it for my work does not explain why I bought it when or where I did (for which there may be no *rational* explanation). If time and place *are* significant, they will be integral to the reason for the action: If I bought the book at Border's before 10:00 because of their short-term sale, then the time and place of my action are explained by my wanting to save money, not by an event that caused the action then and there.

The second is that Davidson thought the difference between an agent merely *having* a reason and her acting *because* of it is not in the content of the reason but is additional. My reason to buy a book is that I need it for my work. If I do not buy the book, I merely have that reason, but if I buy it because of it, then there is an associated event that causes my buying the book. The reason is the same in both cases, but in the second there is an event-cause in addition to the content.

Davidson, unlike defenders of the standard story, did not think this account *explains why* an agent acted because of some reason. Any explanation of that is not part of a rational explanation, since the latter "provides no reason for saying that one suitable belief-desire pair rather than another (which may also have been present in the agent) did the causing,"[24] that is, was associated with an event that caused the action. Davidson elucidated what we *mean* by the assertion, "She acted because of reason R," but he gave no account of why she acted because of reason R rather than another reason.[25]

Davidson did not hold that *verifying* that an agent acted because of a certain reason requires verifying that an associated event caused the action (or that the associated event and the action have descriptions instantiated by a strict law). His view that what an agent did and her reason for doing it are conceptually connected means that they cannot be verified independently. This sets up an interpretive circle, and there is no appeal except to interpretation in order to verify whether an agent acted *because* of a reason.[26] Having established a plausible interpretation of an agent's reasons and actions, we do not establish *in addition* that there was an associated event that caused her action, since (Davidson claimed) the interpretive conclusion that she acted because of a certain reason *entails* that there was an event associated with that reason that caused the action.

This meets one objection to Davidson's account but strengthens another, since it implies that knowing there is an associated event comes *after* having established an explanation of the agent's action, which means the associated event is irrelevant to the force of the explanation. To claim that such an event is entailed is unobjectionable, simply because "associated event" is so broad there can hardly fail to be one. If we are more specific, however, the idea looks implausible. Consider actions like driving to Chicago or writing a paper, each of which is *an* action done for a reason. We can speak here of *an* action only if we count a complex and disorderly cluster of events as *an* event that is an action, whose event-cause must also consist of such a cluster. We could get the appropriate cause and effect only by implausibly cutting and stretching the notion of event. To respond that this is a mere consequence of the requirement that there be such causes and effects simply undermines the requirement.

4

Davidson's third reason for his claim about associated events is that it yields a plausible account of the relation between rational and nomological explanation. Given that if an agent acts for a reason, there is an event that causes her action, and given Davidson's view of the nomological character of causality, it follows that there are physical descriptions of the event and of her action that instantiate a law of physics. This shows that rational explanations not only do not conflict with the laws of physics but are linked with them.

This is often construed as physicalism because it is thought that Davidson took events to be causes *in virtue of* having physical descriptions and hence concluded that all events that are causes or effects are physical rather than mental. Kim, for instance, argued that Davidson held that mental events as such are causally impotent since they have causal force only because they have physical descriptions, which "renders mental properties and kinds causally irrelevant. . . . [They are] causal idlers with no work to do,"[27] which is epiphenomenalism about the mental. This assumes, however, that events are causes *because* they have physical descriptions that instantiate the laws of physics, a claim that Davidson rejected along with all its variants—that events are causes *in virtue of* their physical properties, *because* they fall under physical kinds, or *qua* being physical—as inconsistent with events being causes no matter how described, the latter entailing that "it makes no literal sense" to speak of events as causing things because of, or in virtue of, anything.[28]

By the nomological character of causality, Davidson meant that A's causing B *entails* that there are physical descriptions of A and B that instantiate a law of physics. His defense of this was that events require *real* changes, which are not relative to how a situation is described, a point he illustrated by Goodman's discussion of predicates like green, grue, blue, and bleen. An object, Davidson wrote, may "change" from being grue to being bleen, but that is not a real change, for the real color of the object stays the same. Descriptions of real changes involve projectible, lawlike predicates, and since causal relations obtain only between real changes, there are causal relations only where there are laws, which shows that "singular causal statements . . . entail the existence of strict laws [of physics]."[29]

That summary does not do justice to Davidson's paper,[30] which defended a subtle Kantian view, but I'm not persuaded that a causal relation between events entails a law of *physics* covering the events. He wrote that "The ground floor connection of causality with regularity is not made by experience, but is built into the idea of objects whose changes are causally tied to other changes. . . . Events are as much caught up in this highly general net of concepts as objects."[31] Accepting that obscure claim does not imply that whatever regularity causality involves entails laws of *physics* and hence physicalistic (not merely physical) predicates.[32]

In any case, arguing that there are causal relations only where there are strict laws is quite different from *grounding* rational explanations in the laws of physics, and Davidson rejected the latter in denying that events are causes *because of* physical laws. His account of the role of event causation in rational explanation was not intended to develop or defend physicalism. It is, moreover, different from the standard story because the latter makes event causation central to explanation of action, whereas in Davidson's account it is, as I have argued, peripheral to causal explanation. I would disregard it,[33] which brings his account closer to Wittgensteinian ones, but even if it is kept, Davidson's view lends no support to claims like Hartry Field's "that there is an important sense in which all facts depend on physical facts and all good causal explanations depend on good physical explanations."[34]

5

Unlike most defenders of the standard story, Davidson held that "there is an irreducible difference between psychological explanations that involve the propositional attitudes and explanations in sciences like physics and physiology."[35] He accepted Collingwood's view that "the methodology of history (or, for that matter, any of the social sciences that treat individual human behavior) differs markedly from the methodology of the natural sciences."[36] The former belongs, as Sellers put it, to the logical space of reasons, the latter to the logical space of laws. Davidson noted three significant differences between these two kinds of explanation.

The fundamental one is the *normativity* of rational explanations, which has two dimensions.[37] One is that ascriptions to an agent of beliefs, desires, intentions, intentional actions, and the like must preserve the rationality (or intelligibility) of the agent and hence meet standards of consistency and correctness: There cannot *be* attitudes or intentional actions that do not meet such norms. The other is that rational explanations appeal to reasons for action, which are considerations that bear normatively on an agent's acting by showing it to be good in some sense. Both are lacking in the physical sciences, which "treat the world as mindless,"[38] making it irrelevant whether the subject matter investigated meets normative standards.

Phenomena treated as mindless do not occur because it would be good (or apparently good) if they did.

The second is that rational explanations can be verified only by *interpretive* inquiry that resembles interpreting a text. We want to understand a text in its own terms but we do not know what those terms are unless we already understand the text (the "hermeneutical circle"). So with action: We want to explain an agent's actions in terms of her own standards of rationality or intelligibility—in terms of what she takes to be sufficient reasons to act—but we do not know what those standards are unless we already know what she is doing intentionally and hence her reasons for so acting. Assuming we *share* standards of rationality would be idle, for that simply assumes we already know what her standards are. Nor can we appeal to the standards of others to show that our standards are correct, because we must assume that our own are correct in order to determine the standards of others. "The interpreter has . . . no other standards of rationality to fall back on than his own. . . . There is no going outside this standard to check whether we have things right, any more than we can check whether the platinum-iridium standard kept at the International Bureau of Weights and Standards in Sevres, France weighs a kilogram."[39]

The physical sciences are different, for "when we try to understand the world as physicists . . . we do not aim to discover rationality in the phenomena,"[40] and hence we use standards that we share with other investigators and that must be agreed on before using them.

> The physical world and the numbers we use to calibrate it are common property, the material and abstract objects and events that we can agree on and share. But it makes no sense to speak of comparing, or coming to agree on, ultimate common standards of rationality, since it is our own standards to which we must turn in interpreting others. This should not be thought of as a failure of objectivity but as the point at which questions come to an end. Understanding the mental states of others and understanding nature are cases where the questions come to an end at different stages. How we measure physical quantities is decided intersubjectively. We cannot in the same way go behind our own ultimate norms of rationality in interpreting others.[41]

The third difference is that rational explanations are *first-person* explanations: they appeal to, and hence require that we identify, what the agent took herself to have done and to be her reason for doing it. They are first person because the normative significance of states of affairs—their practical significance as reasons for an agent's action—is manifest only when viewed from that agent's point of view. Understanding why someone takes a Stockhausen concert to be a reason to go to Chicago requires understanding what it is about that concert that appeals to him—requires grasping, without necessarily accepting, that person's point of view. The physical sciences, by contrast, aim at a kind of understanding and explanation that does not depend on understanding the agent's own point of view. Neuroscientific explanations, for instance, cite brain states, cellular structures, computational mechanisms, and the like that experts in the field understand but that may be unintelligible to the agents whose behavior is being explained.

That rational explanations are first person is consistent with their being interpretive, because the aim of the interpreter in using his own standards is to interpret other agents' understanding of their own actions. It is also consistent with *radical* interpretation, which is a third-person point of view but a feature not of rational explanation but of Davidson's approach to mental phenomena. Its purpose is to show that meaning, thought, and action are socially grounded and hence publicly accessible: "What a fully informed interpreter could learn about what a speaker means is all there is to learn; the same goes for what the speaker believes."[42] What a fully informed interpreter could learn is precisely the features of meaning, thought, and action that are first person, and hence Davidson denied that first-person phenomena are private, internal, or known only to introspection. The third-person point of view does not exclude the first but is a philosophically perspicuous way of understanding it: "The point of the study of radical interpretation is to grasp how it is possible for one person to come to understand the speech and thoughts of another, for this ability is basic to our sense of a world independent of ourselves, and hence to the possibility of thought itself."[43]

6

These considerations show that Davidson rejected physicalistic reductions of rational explanations and did not attempt to ground them in the laws of physics. But it is widely thought that he embraced nonreductive physicalism as a consequence of his commitment to supervenience, and he has undoubtedly motivated many philosophers to accept such a view. I think, nevertheless, that the monism entailed by Davidson's conception of supervenience is not physicalism even of the nonreductive kind.

Davidson characterized physicalism as an antirealism that "tries to trim reality down to fit within its epistemology,"[44] writing that "I have resisted calling my position either materialism or physicalism because, unlike most materialists or physicalists, I do not think mental properties (or predicates) are reducible to physical properties (or predicates), nor that we could, conceptually or otherwise, get along without mental concepts. . . .

Being mental is not an eliminable or derivative property."[45] He rejected both physicalism and dualism—physicalism because entities can have both mental and physical predicates, dualism because there is but one kind of entity. Showing how to reject both was one of his most significant achievements.

He first formulated supervenience as follows: "Mental characteristics are in some sense dependent, or supervenient, on physical characteristics. Such supervenience might be taken to mean that there cannot be two events alike in all physical respects but differing in some mental respect, or that an object cannot alter in some mental respect without altering in some physical respect."[46] This implies that "a change in mental properties is always accompanied by a change in physical properties, but it does not imply that the same physical properties change with the same mental properties."[47] He later wrote[48] that his first formulation is "easily misunderstood" in using "dependent on" as equivalent to "supervenient on," which suggests that an object's physical predicates *explain* its mental predicates. But he denied that supervenience is explanatory, agreeing with Kim that "Supervenience itself is not an explanatory relation. . . . It is a 'surface' relation that reports a pattern of property covariation."[49]

But Davidson did not agree with Kim's further claim that supervenience suggests "the presence of an interesting dependency relation that might explain it." He gave as a "noncontroversial example of an interesting case" the supervenience of semantic on syntactical predicates:

> A truth predicate for a language cannot distinguish any sentences not distinguishable in purely syntactical terms, but for most languages truth is not definable in such terms. . . . [This] gives one possible meaning to the idea that truths expressible by the subvenient predicates "determine" the extension of the supervenient predicate, or that the extension of the supervenient predicate "depends" on the extensions of the subvenient predicates.[50]

The scare quotes are Davidson's, for he did not mean "depend" or "determine" to be explanatory: The supervenience of semantic on syntactic predicates suggests no underlying explanation, nor does the supervenience of the mental on the physical. The latter holds simply because a change in mental predicates *accompanies* some change in physical predicates, but not vice versa, which, as Davidson noted, is a very weak relation.

Davidson did hold that "supervenience in any form implies monism"[51] because, if entities having distinct mental predicates also have distinct physical predicates sufficient to distinguish the former, then all entities have physical predicates. Davidson said this meant the *identity* of mental events with physical events, but this is identity of tokens, not of types; his conception of supervenience rules out the latter because the same mental predicates may be accompanied by different physical predicates. Moreover, if a mental event is identical with a physical event, the latter is also identical with the former (identity being symmetrical). The only physical events not identical with mental events are events without mental descriptions,[52] but the latter are not mental and hence are not events physical events *could* be identical with.

Davidson's monism would be a version of physicalism only if physical predicates were more *basic* overall than mental ones. They are more basic in that every entity has a physical predicate but may not have a mental one, which implies that if you destroy everything physical, you thereby destroy everything mental but not vice versa. They are also more basic in that physical predicates are supervenient on mental predicates but not vice versa, but that has no consequences for explanation: Explanations (and causal relations) can run from the physical to the mental and from the mental to the physical, and whether a physical or mental explanation (or cause) is more basic depends on the context. In an overall sense, physical predicates are not more basic than mental ones, which means that Davidson's conception of supervenience allows for monism without commitment to physicalism of any kind.[53]

7

Davidson understood the assertion that "Actions are those bodily movements caused and rationalized by beliefs and desires" differently from the way most proponents of the standard story do. Having considered how he understood "caused and rationalized by," I want now to consider his understanding of "actions are bodily movements."

He wrote in a well-known passage that "Our primitive actions, the ones we do not by doing something else, mere movements of the body—these are all the actions there are. We never do more than move our bodies: the rest it up to nature."[54] Proponents of the standard story often see this as central to Davidson's supposed project of finding for mind a place in a physicalistic world with (in Kim's words) "nothing but bits of matter and increasingly complex aggregates made up of bits of matter." They think Davidson claimed that actions *consist of* the bodily movements of neurophysiology and hence are nothing but complex aggregates of bits of matter. While actions are *described* in other ways, *what* are described are mere bodily movements. In Quine's terms, the *ontology* of action is physicalistic, while everything else is *ideology*.

On this reading, mere bodily movements count as actions only if they are also caused (in the right way) by an agent's (coming to have) beliefs, desires, or intentions. Thus Mele: "A necessary condition of an overt action's being intentional is that (the acquisition of) a pertinent intention 'proximately causes the physiological chain' that begins concurrently with, and partially constitutes, the action. . . . The causal route from intention acquisition to overt bodily movements in beings like us involves a causal chain initiated in the brain."[55] This involves "mental causation"—neural events cause beliefs, desires, or intentions that cause the physiological chain that causes bodily movements—and hence raises the classical problem of how mental–physical causation is possible, which many defenders of the standard story would resolve by appeal to nonreductive physicalism. Thus Mele, again: "Causalism is typically embedded as part of a naturalistic stand on agency according to which mental items that play causal/explanatory roles in action are in some way dependent upon or realized in physical states and events."[56]

In brief, defenders of the standard story typically attribute to Davidson the view that action consists of mere (physicalistic) bodily movements caused (in the right way) by mental events. Although they may not regard his ontology of mental events as physicalistic, they think his ontology of *action* surely is.

There are numerous reasons for rejecting this as Davidson's view. As I have argued, he was not a nonreductive physicalist and he did not think that action explanation is dependent on physical explanation or that causal relations are fixed by anything. He denied that mental causation is a problem, writing that "the mental is not an ontological but a conceptual category,"[57] that is, a matter of how events are described. Since event causation is not dependent on how events are described, whether an event is mental or physical does not affect its causal relations to other events.

Moreover, he regarded beliefs, desires, and intentions not only as states rather than events but as states of persons not of brains (or minds): "Beliefs, desires and intentions belong to no ontology. . . . When we ascribe attitudes we are using the mental vocabulary to describe people. Beliefs and intentions are not . . . little entities lodged in the brain."[58] Since changes in attitudes are events, they can figure in event causality, but

> Since beliefs, desires, and intentions are not entities, it is a metaphor to speak of them as changing, and hence an extension of the metaphor to speak of them as causes and effects. What happens is that the descriptions of the agent changes over time. The relevant entity that changes is the person. . . . The only thing that changes when our attitudes change is us.[59]

Such changes no doubt have causes and effects, but to think that the former are neural events in the brain, or that the latter are physiological changes that produce bodily movements, is vastly oversimplified, if not far-fetched.

For Davidson, the role of beliefs, desires, and intentions is to rationally *explain* actions and hence also the bodily movements essentially involved in them (as *bodily* actions). This is fundamentally not a matter of event causation, but of causal *explanation* in the logical space of reasons,[60] and it is in the light of this that we should consider Davidson's claim that "our primitive actions . . . mere movements of the body . . . are all the actions there are."

A primitive act is one *not* done by doing some other act, hence one we must do whenever we act, on pain of a vicious regress of being unable to act until we have already acted. This formulation is misleading, however, because Davidson's view (which he ascribed to Anscombe) was that an agent whose act has many results acts only once, although her acting has as many descriptions as it has results. A primitive act is, therefore, not numerically distinct from the acts done by performing it: Whether an act is primitive depends on how it is described, so the notion is *intensional*. If I illuminate the room by pulling on the light cord by moving my arm, I act only once, but my acting has three descriptions: The first two describe what I did *by* (because caused by) moving my arm, but the first does not describe anything I did by which I moved my arm—does not describe my arm's moving as the result of anything I did—and hence, unlike the other descriptions, it is primitive.[61]

Described as primitive, my act may have a rational explanation (I moved my arm because of my desire to illuminate the room), but while it has many results, it is (as primitive) not described in terms of any of them. Nor is it (as primitive) described in terms of its cause, although as intentional it had a cause: "If my arm going up is an action, then there must also be an intention. But in my view, the intention is not part of the action, but a cause of it."[62] By "cause" here, Davidson surely meant "causally explain," since intentions are states and not events and since, if the intention were only an event-cause of the movements, it would cause them no matter how they were described, in which case it would not account for their being intentional under some descriptions but unintentional under others.

Actions described as primitive, therefore, are intentional under *some* description, and if primitive actions *are* bodily movements, the latter are also intentional under some description. Davidson held that whether we use "bodily movement" transitively—"S moved his body"—or intransitively—"S's body moved"—we describe the same event,[63] and hence if moving my body at t is intentional, so is my body's moving at t: It is an intentional bodily movement.

When Davidson wrote that "our primitive actions . . . mere movements of the body . . . are all the actions there are [and] the rest is up to nature," he did not, therefore, mean by "*mere* movements of the body" the nonintentional bodily movements of neurophysiology. He meant that actions are primitive if *merely* described as movements of the body, which must, since they are the movements of an agent who moves her body intentionally, be intentional under some description. And when he said that such bodily movements are all the actions there are, the rest being up to nature, he did not mean that we only move our bodies. He meant that we illuminate rooms, destroy buildings, start wars, make revolutions, and so on *by* moving our bodies, but that whether we succeed is up to nature because it is not up to us whether moving our bodies will actually result in rooms being illuminated, wars beginning, and so on. It is when such things do result from intentionally moving *our* bodies that they are actions *we* perform, and it is because intentionally moving our bodies is not the result of any act of ours that "moving our bodies" is a primitive description.[64]

This, then, is my reading of Davidson's claim that all actions are primitive and hence *merely* movements of the body. We can put that as the claim that actions *consist of* bodily movements only if we recognize that he meant "bodily movements *intentional* under a description." Bodily movements are, of course, nonintentional under many descriptions, but since, in his view, all actions are intentional under some description, the bodily movements of which they consist are also intentional under a description. They are movements of our limbs—our arms, legs, fingers, and so on—which, if we are not disabled, we move intentionally, something we cannot do with our fingernails, kidneys, or hearts, which are not limbs since it is not their nature to move or be moved intentionally.

It follows that Davidson is not committed to a physicalist ontology of action, because on his view whatever is intentional under a description has a mental predicate. Physicalists may think that is *ideology* and not *ontology*, the latter concerning *what* is described, namely, the bodily movements of neurophysiology. But this ignores Davidson's view that although events occur under any description, whether they are mental or physical depends on how they are described. Bodily movements described as intentional are mental; described as neurophysiological they are physical. It may be responded that nothing has yet been said about *what* is described, to which Davidson might respond with Anscombe: "The proper answer to 'What is the action, which has all these descriptions?' is to give one of the descriptions, any one, it does not matter which; or perhaps it would be better to offer a choice, saying 'Take which ever you prefer.'"[65] The claim that *what* has all these descriptions is just the movements of neurophysiology can only mean that descriptions in those terms are *basic*—that they yield the essential nature of bodily movements—whereas descriptions under which bodily movements are intentional are not basic. But Davidson did not take the logical space of laws to be more basic overall than the logical space of reasons; indeed, the latter is the basic level for understanding action, since there is no action where there is no intention. It is essential to having limbs that one can move them intentionally: They are limbs only in name if one cannot do that.

Davidson's ontology of action (like Aristotle's and Spinoza's) is "ontological monism accompanied by an uneliminable dualism of conceptual apparatus. . . . There is only one [kind of] substance [but] the mental and the physical are irreducibly different modes of apprehending, describing, and explaining what happens in nature."[66] There are no nonphysical entities—none that cannot be described as physical—but this is not physicalism, because all actions are intentional under some description and hence are (also) mental.

8

There are two objections to Davidson's account of action I want to discuss, one by defenders of the standard story, one by its critics. The first concerns the problem of *deviant causal chains*, which is taken to arise because an agent's beliefs and desires can cause his bodily movements without their being actions. An example is Davidson's climber, who "might want to rid himself of the weight and danger of holding another man on a rope, and he might know that by loosening his hold on the rope he could rid himself of the weight and danger. This belief and want might so unnerve him as to cause him to loosen his hold, and yet it might be that he . . . [did not do] it intentionally."[67] The problem is that the climber's movements are not caused in "the right way," which calls for a specification of conditions necessary and sufficient for a causal chain to constitute the agent's bodily movements as action, hence intentional under a description. Davidson contended that we cannot give conditions "that are not only necessary, but also sufficient, for an action to be intentional, using only such concepts as those of belief, desire, and cause."[68] Many have attempted, nevertheless, to specify these conditions, sometimes by appeal to scientific investigation.

His position on this issue is complex.[69] Were we to take him to mean by "cause" *event causation*, then we surely could not give the conditions necessary and sufficient for a bodily movement to be intentional using only concepts of belief, desire, and cause. Since event causation obtains between events no matter how described, an event-cause, however complex, cannot constitute an event as an intentional action, because an action is not intentional no matter how described, but intentional under some descriptions and unintentional under others. No event-cause can account for the latter, regardless of what conditions are put on it.

Davidson takes "cause" here to mean *causally explain*, and hence the problem arises because of his contention that in order for an agent's belief and desire to causally explain his action, not only must their contents be his reasons for acting, they must be associated with an event that causes the bodily movements that are intentional under a description yielded by his belief and desire. Thus, if the climber's belief and desire causally explain his intentionally letting go of the rope, their contents must not only be his reason for letting go but must be associated with an event that causes the bodily movements intentional as "letting go." In the deviant case, the agent's bodily movement are caused by his becoming nervous (associated with his belief and desire), and they are not, therefore, intentional under the description "letting go." The difficulty is that the bodily movements for which his belief and desire are a reason are not the same bodily movements caused by the event associated with his belief and desire. That requires that the bodily movements are caused in the right way, that is, that their cause is *appropriately associated* with his reason for acting. Davidson despaired of specifying the conditions for such an appropriate association and, indeed, given his overall view, he could not specify them, because that would require the kind of lawful connections his view ruled out. It was not a problem that could be solved and hence not worth pursuing.[70]

There is another way of viewing Davidson's discussion of the climber that I find more interesting. The climber has a belief and desire whose content he takes to be sufficient reason for him to act and that causes his body to move, but it is not a reason *because of* which he acts. The problem is whether we can fill in the gap between taking the content of a belief and desire to be sufficient reason to act and really acting because of that reason. If we do act because of it, then we may rightly claim that the reason causally explained our action, but we have adequate grounds for that only *after* we have acted. Before we act there is no assurance that what we take to be the strongest reason to act will actually explain our action, whereas after we act we can make that claim, at least about ourselves, and normally be right.

Davidson considered filling the gap with additional factors that would link reasons to act with acting for those reasons but concluded that "it is largely because we cannot see how to complete the statement of the causal conditions of intentional action that we cannot tell whether, if we got them right, the result would be a piece of analysis or an empirical law for predicting behavior." An *empirical* law would require stating "the antecedent conditions in physical, or at least behavioristic terms," which presumes psychophysical laws of the kind Davidson rejected and would rule out explanation in mental terms. An *analysis* would let "the terms of the antecedent conditions . . . remain mentalistic, . . . [but] the law would continue to seem analytic or constitutive" and hence not explanatory. If we were able to fill in this gap, we would eliminate the "need to depend on the open appeal to causal relations. We would simply say, given these (specified) conditions, there always is an intentional action of a specified type."[71]

The scientist in us may regret that gap, but as autonomous agents we should, in my view, prize it. It enables an explanation to be both causal and normative, since the open-ended nature of causal claims permits the adjustments in our ascriptions of attitudes and actions that may be necessary to preserve an agent's rationality. Moreover, it rules out causal laws connecting an agent's beliefs and desires with his action, thereby meeting one condition for agent autonomy.

The other objection comes from critics of the standard story, who think Davidson's view cannot accommodate the knowledge of an agent's own actions that Anscombe called "practical" in contrast with "theoretical" or "speculative" knowledge. I contend that this criticism misses the mark (though I agree with critics that practical knowledge should play a more central role in an account of action than it does in Davidson's account).

Anscombe's "certain sense of the question 'why?' [that] is given application" to events that are intentional actions is "refused application by the answer: 'I was not aware I was doing that.'"[72] Although we act in many ways of which we are not aware, we act *intentionally* only if we are aware of our acting in that way. Anscombe claimed such knowledge is not based on observation—either perceptual or introspective—for then it would be theoretical, which would make it mysterious since it is not confined to knowing our own beliefs, desires, or intentions, but includes some knowledge of what we are doing in the world, hence what happens (under a description). Knowledge by observation of what happens is theoretical, but what is essential to intentional action is *practical* knowledge—knowledge of what happens because we *do* what happens.

Rosalind Hursthouse nicely put Anscombe's account this way:

> Practical knowledge is "the cause of what it understands." . . . The intentional action must match the knowledge in order to be that action. Suppose I am intentionally painting the wall yellow. Then my knowledge of what I am doing makes it to be the case that it is so. I am so doing because (in virtue of the fact that) I know it. . . . When I am in error, the mistake lies in the performance, not in a judgment about what I am doing. . . . [The agent's knowledge] is conceptually guaranteed by the nature of intentional action itself. An intentional action essentially is that which is determined by the agent's knowledge.[73]

That is to say, what makes it the case that I am intentionally painting the wall yellow is that I know I am doing it under that description: It would not *be* that intentional act if I did not know (without observation), in doing it, what I am doing.

Hursthouse thinks no causal account of action (one that *defines* an intentional act as one with the right kind of cause) can allow for practical knowledge making it the case that the agent is acting intentionally: "Since agent's knowledge could not make it the case that the action had certain causes, the intentional action could not essentially be an action with this further feature." Nor can it allow for expressions of intention, for example, my expressing my intention to paint the wall yellow next week, which is not a prediction because if I fail to paint the wall yellow, I make an error not in judgment but in performance (or I may change my mind). But "on the causalist view, an agent's knowledge-of-his-present-or-future-intentional-action *must* be speculative knowledge of action-caused-by-certain-mental-items."[74]

This objection applies to the standard story but not to Davidson's account, for two reasons. First, Hursthouse thinks of causal accounts in terms of causal relations, not causal explanations. Her objection that an agent's knowledge "could not make it the case that the action had certain causes" is surely true if it means that prior causes of the action could not be determined by the agent's knowledge in acting. That, however, misses Davidson's view that causal *explanation* is basic to action, since reasons explain actions only under descriptions, whereas causal relations are indifferent to descriptions. Although Davidson thought that there must be an event associated with an explanatory reason, the agent need not know that event, which, therefore, plays no role in his knowledge of what he is doing or in determining the description under which his acting is intentional.

Second, Davidson held, as noted above, that there is a conceptual connection between the reason that explains an agent's acting and the description under which he acts intentionally, and hence the reason determines what the action it explains *is* (*qua* intentional) just *because* the action is causally explained by the reason. Hence to know the reason for which one is acting *is* (except in unusual cases) to know what one is doing intentionally.

This is not theoretical knowledge, because agents know the reasons for which they are acting not by observation but simply by taking considerations to be reasons for acting (on Davidson's view, by having beliefs and desires). This is a matter not of agents noticing the reasons for which they act, but of their acting for those reasons. Nor is knowledge of the intention with which one acts theoretical: If what one does is not what one intends to be doing, then the error is in what does; one is wrong about what one is accomplishing, not because one has an erroneous belief, but because what one did was not what one intended.

Conclusion

My aim has been to pry Davidson's account of action apart from the standard story and shield it from criticisms aimed at it that too often do not apply to his account but to the standard story. I do not think his account in unflawed; indeed, I think that in the end both the deep assumptions that underlie it and the belief-desire model of reasons for action that it incorporates should be rejected. But it is much better than most of its critics think—an extraordinary philosophical achievement that escapes facile objections, is philosophically penetrating and instructive, and one that no adequate account of action can ignore. He should be recognized, even by philosophers in a broadly Wittgensteinian tradition, as a collaborator in resisting physicalism and other extravagant metaphysical theories while insisting on careful distinctions, argumentative precision, and a larger vision of the aim of philosophy.

Notes

1. For the "standard story," see Michael Smith, "The Structure of Orthonomy," in *Agency and Action*, ed. John Hyman and Helen Steward (Cambridge: Cambridge University Press, 2004), p. 165. I long regarded Davidson as holding a version of the standard story, a mistake I want to correct here.

2. Jaegwon Kim, "Philosophy of Mind and Psychology," in *Donald Davidson*, ed. Kirk Ludwig (Cambridge: Cambridge University Press, 2003), p. 113.

3. From the cover of the 2000 Harvard edition of her *Intention*. My citations refer to the original edition: G. E. M. Anscombe, *Intention* (Oxford: Blackwell, 1957).

4. Donald Davidson, "Replies," in *The Philosophy of Donald Davidson*, The Library of Living Philosophers, vol. 27, ed. Lewis E. Hahn (Chicago: Open Court, 1999), p. 268.

5. "Where there is causality, there must be a law: events related as cause and effect fall under strict deterministic laws." Donald Davidson, *Essays on Actions and Events* (Oxford: Oxford University Press, 2nd ed. 2001), p. 208.

6. A strict law is "something one [can] at best hope to find in a developed physics: a generalization that [is] not only 'law-like' and true, but [is] as deterministic as nature can be found to be, [is] free from caveats and *ceteris paribus* clauses; that [can], therefore, be viewed as treating the universe as a closed system." Donald Davidson, *Truth, Language, and History* (Oxford: Clarendon Press, 2005), p. 190.

7. Cf. Davidson, *Truth, Language, and History*, p. 191: "The efficacy of an event cannot depend on how the event is described, while whether an event can be called mental, or can be said to fall under a law, depends entirely on how the event can be described." The main source for this is Davidson's "Mental Events," in Davidson, *Essays on Actions and Events* pp. 207–224. An extremely helpful supplement is the piece he wrote about his own work: Donald Davidson, "Donald Davidson," in *A Companion to the Philosophy of Mind*, ed. Samuel Guttenplan (Oxford: Blackwell, 1994).

8. Donald Davidson, "Reply to Stoecker," in *Reflecting Davidson*, ed. R. Stoecker (Berlin: Walter de Gruyter, 1994), p. 287.

9. "Explanation, like giving reasons, is geared to sentences or propositions rather than directly to what sentences are about." Davidson, *Essays on Actions and Events*, p. 171.

10. Strawson has an excellent discussion of this point, writing, for instance: "Causality is a natural relation that holds in the world between particular events or circumstances, just as the relation of temporal succession does or that of spatial proximity. . . . But if causality is a relation which holds in the natural world, explanation is a different matter. . . . It is an intellectual or rational or intensional relation and does not hold between things in the natural world . . . [but] between facts or truths." P. F. Strawson, "Causation and Explanation," in *Essays on Davidson: Actions and Events*, ed. Bruce Vermazen and Merril B. Hintikka (Oxford: Clarendon Press, 1985), p. 115.

11. Although Davidson does not put it in this way, what follows is an accurate summary of his view. I discuss this matter in more detail in my "Intentionalists and Davidson on 'Rational Explanations,'" in *Actions, Norms, and Values*, ed. G. Meggle (Berlin: Walter de Gruyter, 1999).

12. The term is Davidson's; see Davidson, *Essays on Actions and Events*, p. 12.

13. Donald Davidson, "Reply to Biere," in R. Stoecker (ed.), *Reflecting Davidson*, p. 312.

14. Davidson, "Representation and Interpretation," in his *Problems of Rationality* (Oxford: Clarendon Press, 2004), p. 96.

15. Davidson, "An Interview with Donald Davidson," in *Essays on Actions and Events*, p. 263. See also Davidson, "Problems in the Explanation of Action," in *Problems of Rationality*, p. 108: "If a person is constituted in such a way that, if he believes that by acting in a certain way he will crush a snail then he has a tendency to act in that way, then in this respect he differs from most other people, and this difference will help explain why he acts as he does. The special fact about how he is constituted is one of his causal powers, a disposition to act under specified conditions in specific ways. Such a disposition is what I mean by a pro-attitude."

16. This is like Anscombe's point that "The primitive sign of wanting [rather than wishing or hoping] is trying to get." Anscombe, *Intention*, p. 68.

17. Davidson, "Hempel on Explaining Action," in *Essays on Actions and Events*, p. 265; see also p.274: "The laws that are implicit in reason explanation seem to me to concern only individuals—they are the generalizations embedded in attributions of attitudes, beliefs and traits."

18. Ibid., p. 265.

19. Von Wright also thought that rational explanations were causal in some non-Humean sense: "Those who think that actions have causes often use 'cause' in a much broader sense than I do when I deny this. Or they may understand 'action' differently. It may very well be, then, that 'actions' in their sense have 'causes' in theirs." Georg Henrik von Wright, *Explanation and Understanding* (London: Routledge & Kegan Paul, 1971), p. viii.

20. Davidson, "Actions, Reasons, and Causes," in *Essays on Actions and Events*, p. 10.

21. Davidson, "Problems in the Explanation of Action," in *Problems of Rationality*, pp. 108, 115. This view is superficially similar to Anscombe's claim that "What distinguishes actions which are intentional from those which are not . . . is that they are actions to which a certain sense of the question 'why?' is given application; the sense is of course that in which the answer, if positive gives a reason for action." Anscombe, *Intention*, p. 9. The difference is that whereas Davidson defined an intentional action as one explained in terms of the agent's reason for acting, Anscombe did not require that the action be explained but only that the question "why?" applies—i.e., is appropriate.

22. John McDowell, "Response," in *McDowell and His Critics*, ed. Cynthia Macdonald and Graham Macdonald (Oxford: Blackwell, 2006), pp. 139, 67.

23. Cf. Davidson's "Reply to Stoecker," in R. Stoecker (ed.), *Reflecting Davidson*, p. 288: "Beliefs and desires are not changes. They are states, and since I don't think that states are *entities* of any sort, and so are not *events*, I do not think that beliefs and desires are events. . . . [There is] a broad popular use and a rather more limited use of

the notion of cause. . . . The more limited use allows only events to be causes [and in this sense] *reasons are not causes.*"

24. Davidson, "Problems in the Explanation of Action," in *Problems of Rationality*, p. 109.

25. This is contrary to Mele, who offers this as the causal theory's view: "In virtue of what is it true that he mowed his lawn for this reason and not the other, if not that the reason (or his having it) and not the other, played a suitable causal role in his mowing they lawn." Alfred Mele, "Philosophy of Action," in *Donald Davidson*, ed. Kirk Ludwig (Cambridge: Cambridge University Press, 2003), p. 70.

26. Davidson did not hold that in order to know an agent's reasons and actions we must interpret or verify them. We may, for instance, know such things simply by observing an agent.

27. Jaegwon Kim, *The Philosophy of Mind* (Boulder, CO: Westview Press, 1996), p. 138.

28. Davidson, "Thinking Causes," *Truth, Language, and History*, p. 196. The misunderstanding is partly due to some ways Davidson formulated his principle, for example, that "all causally related events instantiate the laws of physics" (ibid., p. 194) or "If a singular causal claim is true, there is a law that backs it . . ." (ibid., p. 202). But he states his view clearly in this passage: "The efficacy of an event cannot depend on how the event is described, while whether an event can be called mental, or can be said to fall under a law, depends entirely on how the event can be described. . . . It is irrelevant to the causal efficacy of physical events that they can be described in the physical vocabulary. It is *events* that have the power to change things, not our various ways of describing them" (ibid., pp. 190, 195). Kim's response to this is to insist that if the causal relation obtains between pairs of events, it *must* be "because they are events of certain kinds, or have certain properties" (Jaegwon Kim, "Can Supervenience Save Anomalous Monism?" in *Mental Causation*, ed. John Heil and Alfred Mele [Oxford: Oxford University Press, 1933, p. 22]). But that makes Davidson an epiphenomenalist only if he first accepts Kim's (metaphysical) principle that causal relations must be explained by reference to properties of the events, which Davidson rejects.

29. Davidson, "Laws and Cause," in *Truth, Language, and History*, p. 219.

30. For an excellent discussion of Davidson's paper and wider issues, see Björn Ramberg, "The Significance of Charity," in Hahn (ed.), *The Philosophy of Donald Davidson*, pp. 601–618.

31. Davidson, "Replies to Essays I–IX" in Vermazen (ed.), *Essays on Davidson*, p. 227.

32. Davidson wrote (quoted by Ramberg in "The Significance of Charity," p. 610) that "Our concept of a *physical* object is the concept of an object whose changes are governed by law" (emphasis added).

33. John McDowell makes a similar criticism of Davidson, urging that we "drop the idea that for intentional items to belong to any causal nexus at all is for them to

belong to 'the causal nexus that natural science investigates,' in a way that would need to be spelled out be redescribing them in non-intentional terms." McDowell also thinks that dropping this idea would undercut Davidson's monism because what underlies it is "the naturalistic picture of *the* causal nexus" ("Response," in *McDowell and His Critics*, p. 69). My view is that while it does undercut physicalism, it does not undercut Davidson's weak monism, which is based on supervenience. I discuss this below.

34. Hartry Field, "Physicalism," in *Inference, Explanation, and Other Frustrations*, ed. John Earman (Berkeley: University of California Press, 1992), p. 271. Field simply assumes this as "beyond serious doubt."

35. Davidson, "Problems in the Explanation of Action," in *Problems of Rationality*, p. 101.

36. Davidson, "Aristotle's Action," in *Truth, Language, and History*, p. 282.

37. I use "norms" and "normative" to refer not only to normative *requirements* but to evaluative standards generally. The notion of a reason showing an action to be good is in this sense a normative notion.

38. Davidson, "Indeterminism and Antirealism," in *Subjective, Intersubjective, Objective*, p. 71.

39. Ibid., pp. 215, 217.

40. Ibid., p. 215.

41. Davidson, "Donald Davidson," in Guttenplan (ed.), *A Companion to the Philosophy of Mind*, p. 232.

42. Davidson, "A Coherence Theory of Truth and Knowledge," in *Subjective, Intersubjective, Objective*, p. 148.

43. Ibid., p. 143.

44. Ibid., p. 69.

45. Davidson, "Replies to Essays X–XII," in Vermazen (ed.), *Essays on Davidson*, p. 244.

46. Davidson, "Mental Events," in *Actions and Events*, p. 214.

47. Davidson, "Thinking Causes," in *Truth, Language, and History*, p. 189.

48. Ibid., p. 187n.

49. Jaegwon Kim, *Supervenience and Mind* (Cambridge: Cambridge University Press, 1993), p. 167. Cf. Terry Horgan, "From Supervenience to Superdupervenience: Meeting the Demands of a Material World," in *Philosophy of Mind*, ed. David J. Chalmers (New York: Oxford University Press, 2002), p. 151.

50. Davidson, "Thinking Causes," in *Truth, Language, and History*, p. 187.

51. Ibid.

52. Davidson once noted ("Mental Events," in *Actions and Events*, p. 212) that mental descriptions can easily be constructed that apply to *every* entity so that every entity would be both physical and mental. He also noted that since this "failed to capture the intuitive concept of the mental," perhaps not all entities have mental descriptions. Even if they did, it would not make him a dualist. My own view, it should be said, is that *token* identity should also be rejected because physical and mental events (including intentional actions) are *individuated* differently.

53. In his later work, Davidson seems to have endorsed Spinoza's view that explanation in physical terms cannot *explain* the mental and vice versa, but that would only reinforce my claim that Davidson did not make physical explanations more basic overall than mental ones—see Davidson, "Spinoza's Causal Theory of the Affects," in *Truth, Language, and History*, p. 308. For further discussion of this point, see my "The Problem of Congruence" in *Philosophical Essays in Memoriam: Georg Henrik von Wright* (*Acta Philosophical Fennica*, vol. 77, 1955).

54. Davidson, "Agency," in *Actions and Events*, p. 59.

55. Alfred Mele, *Springs of Action: Understanding Intentional Behavior* (Oxford: Oxford University Press, 1992), p. 201; see Fodor, who says that "Commonsense belief/desire psychology . . . takes for granted that overt behavior comes at the end of a causal chain whose links are mental events—hence unobservable—and which may be arbitrarily long." Jerry Fodor, *Psychosemantics* (Cambridge, MA: MIT Press, 1987), p. 16.

56. Mele, "Introduction," in *The Philosophy of Action*, ed. Alfred Mele (Oxford: Oxford University Press, 1997), p. 3.

57. Davidson, "Problems in the Explanation of Action," in *Problems of Rationality*, p. 114.

58. Nor are they neural processes in the brain that either are or realize functionally defined beliefs, desires, and intentions (or our acquiring them).

59. Davidson, "Reply to Bruce Vermazen," in Hahn (ed.), *The Philosophy of Donald Davidson*, pp. 654–655.

60. Davidson would reject Fodor's claim (for example, in *Psychosemantics*, pp. 16–17) that causation is physicalistic (syntactic) and hence that content (semantic) is causally impotent. Davidson's view is that event causation is independent of ontological categories, whereas rational explanation is a matter of contents that are themselves *causally* explanatory.

61. Defenders of the standard story often think this view of the individuation of action is something one may take or leave. But Davidson (and Anscombe) thought it absurd to say that when I illuminate the room by pulling the cord by moving my

arm, I am acting three times. What is optional is a metaphysical theory about how many actions there really are somehow underneath my one acting. But that is metaphysical speculation of the kind Davidson thought pointless and not explanatory.

62. Davidson, "Problems in the Explanation of Action," in *Problems of Rationality*, p. 105.

63. Ibid.; see also pp. 102–103.

64. I think there are consequential confusions in Davidson's account of primitive actions, but I do not have the space here to discuss them.

65. G. E. M. Anscombe, "Under a Description," in *Metaphysics and Philosophy of Mind*, p. 209.

66. Davidson, "Aristotle's Action," in *Truth, Language, and History*, p. 290.

67. Davidson, "Freedom to Act," in *Actions and Events*, p. 79.

68. Ibid., p. 232.

69. Thanks to John Bishop for pushing me on this issue; I doubt that he is satisfied.

70. This problem would not even arise if we rejected Davidson's claim that causal explanation requires an event causally related to the action.

71. These quotations are from Davidson, "Freedom to Act," in *Actions and Events*, p. 80.

72. Anscombe, *Intentions*, p. 11.

73. Rosalind Hursthouse, "Intention," in *Logic, Cause, and Action: Essays in Honor of Elizabeth Anscombe*, ed. Roger Teichman (Cambridge: Cambridge University Press, 2000), p. 103.

74. Ibid., p. 104.

17 Evaluative Attitudes

Gerhard Preyer

Translated by Nicholas Malpas

The question of the objectivity of moral judgments, or the nature of moral disputes is, then, as much a question about how the content of moral judgments is determined as it is a question about the nature and source of moral values.
—Donald Davidson, "The Objectivity of Values"[1]

1 The Problem of Value in the Social Sciences

It is commonplace to observe that the so-called *problem of value*, which essentially concerns the apparent conflict between such value-ladenness and the claim to objectivity and truth, affects the social and not the natural sciences. Nevertheless, there is much disagreement about how this problem should be understood. Both the problem of the value-ladenness of social science and the associated distinction between the social and natural sciences have a long tradition that goes back to ideas within German philosophy of the nineteenth century. Wilhelm Windelband first introduced the idea of a purely *methodological* classification between the social and natural sciences, in his "History of the Natural Sciences" of 1894.[2] Arising within a neo-Kantian framework, Windelband's position was a development of Wilhelm Dilthey's distinction between *Verstehen* (understanding), which is associated with *Erleben* (experience) and *Geist* (mind), and *Erklären* (explanation), which is associated with nature. The *Geisteswissenschaften* aim at *Verstehen,* whereas the *Naturwissenscaften* aim at *Erklären.* From the perspective of this distinction, nature is viewed as merely an aspect of the external world, whereas *Erleben is* the original unity of consciousness and world. While the focus of the natural sciences is the world as presented in its externality, the object of the *Geisteswissenschaften* is human behavior (*Verhalten*), which is itself the nexus that connects life, *expression*, and *understanding*. *Verstehen*, in the *Geisteswissenschaften,* does not refer to some form of direct insight into an unchanging essence, but is instead an *Ausdrucksverstehen*, an understanding essentially oriented toward *expressions*, as these arise out of the context of life in a way that also enables an articulation of their meaning (*Bedeutung*)[3]—although not in the sense of "meaning" (*Bedeutung*=reference) employed by Frege.

The problem of value within the realm of the social, as expressed in the idea of value-ladenness, is especially important in the line of thinking inaugurated by Windelband and continued by Heinrich Rickert and most notably Max Weber, who famously set forth the ideal of value-free social science. Yet how exactly is the idea of value-ladenness to be understood? How is the issue of value-ladenness, and the supposed compromise of objectivity, to be addressed? Donald Davidson's "unified theory of meaning and action" has a particular relevance to these questions. Davidson provides the means to explain the necessary implication of value—in the form of evaluative attitudes—in the domain of social inquiry. Furthermore, through the interconnection of the evaluative with the cognitive, the Davidsonian approach also suggests a way to understand how the intrusion of the evaluative need not be taken to compromise the possibility of objectivity, although, on a modified reading of that approach, it also suggests limits to the extent of social scientific understanding

Among philosophers and social scientists, the arguments for value-ladenness in the domain of social inquiry are well known. They can be summarized as follows: (1) social scientists are themselves social agents, and as such, they have individual interests and commitments; (2) social scientists are also members of social groups, and so share in, and are oriented by, the collective dispositions and attitudes of those groups; and (3) the cognitive and evaluative attitudes whether of social scientists, or of social agents in general, are always interdependent. It is this last point, and the feature of attitudes that it highlights, that leads most directly to the conclusion that the scientific inquiry into the social is inherently value laden.

To ascribe attitudes of any sort to a speaker we need to bring into play fulfillment conditions for the semantic interpretation of utterances—in its simplest form, this means we need to connect the utterances (and actions) of the speaker with the conditions under which those utterances would be true.[4] Interpretation begins with the principle that the speaker and interpreter can each refer to the same entities and events, and that the interpreter can connect their interpretations to the utterances and actions of the speaker by means of such commonality of reference. The entities and events at issue here must include, of course, the utterances and actions of the speaker, since it is the behavior, linguistic and nonlinguistic, of the speaker that is the focus for interpretation and by means of which the speaker's attitudes are expressed. The identification of attitudes is inseparable from the interpretation of behavior, and knowing the attitudes of a speaker therefore requires associating instances of behavior with those attitudes. Where behavior changes, the attitudes ascribed to an agent may also require modification. The ascription of attitudes, which is a commonplace element of social life, is something we learn as a part of normal socialization. The social frames of reference within which we learn to ascribe attitudes provide the basis for our grasp of the intelligibility of behavior and for the identification of attitudes. This is true both for epistemic attitudes such as belief and also for evaluative attitudes such as desire. Since the context for attitude ascription is first and foremost a social and, therefore, also a communicative context, we can conclude that there is an essential sociality and communicability that pertains to attitudes as such. The necessary interconnection of attitudes with behavior can itself be seen as a expression or consequence of the social or communicative context in which attitudinal ascription arises.

In what follows, I first explore the extent of a unified approach to attitudes and behavior. I then move on to analyze how it is that we develop the ability to use propositional attitudes to explain action, and to explore the interconnection of cognitive with evaluative attitudes. My response to the problem of the value-ladenness of the social sciences is derived from the claim that much of our talk about value-ladenness mislocates and misidentifies the relevant properties of the social world, and that this can be seen to be evident on the basis of the Davidsonian account of the character of attitudes and their relation to behavior. Finally, in opposition to both standard Humean and realist construals of the nature of moral judgments, I will argue that evaluative utterances are not to be construed as expressing purely subjective preferences, and that they nevertheless also differ from cognitive beliefs in terms of their conditions of justification. Although the attribution of both evaluative and cognitive beliefs is always dependent on the social-behavioral context, I will contend that the nature of this dependence in the case of evaluative attitudes is different from that which obtains in the case of cognitive attitudes. In conjunction with this, I will argue that the Davidsonian principle of charity must be constrained by a principle of tolerance that takes into account the possibility of significant divergence in evaluative attitudes.

In the final analysis, the participation of people in common forms of behavior—shared ways of life—is an important and necessary condition for the interpretation of attitudes in general, whether evaluative or cognitive. Interpretation only arises as an issue within such shared ways of life, and such involvement provides both the impetus and the ground for interpretation as such. In this respect, my position (and so also, aspects of my reading of Davidson's position) will connect with aspects of the original neo-Kantian position I discussed briefly at the outset, since it will be my contention that inasmuch as interpretation is a matter of the identification of attitudes as these arise and are articulated within certain socio-behavioral frameworks, so interpretation can indeed be understood as a matter of gaining access to forms of *Ausdrucksverstehen*, "expressive understandings," that connect attitudes, behavior and social context. However, what matters is not simply that they interconnect, but also the manner of their interconnection—and when we look to evaluative as against cognitive attitudes, the manner of their interconnection is significantly different.

2 The Extent of the Unified Theory

According to Davidson, the relations that obtain between beliefs cannot be understood independently of the relations that obtain between beliefs and desires, that is, between cognitive and evaluative attitudes.[5] The *unified theory* of thought, meaning, and action can thus be extended to include evaluation.[6] Only creatures that have desires can also have beliefs. Desires take as their object a state of affairs that can be expressed propositionally. The propositional content of a desire in turn requires that the agent be committed to a network of beliefs, beliefs about the nature of certain states of affairs, their realizability, and so on. Moreover, to have beliefs is, in fact, to have a full panoply of evaluative attitudes including desires, intentions, moral convictions, obligations, and so on, all of which are propositional, and which are both affected by and affect behavior. Taken together, propositional attitudes cause, rationalize, and explain intentional actions. Speakers express evaluative attitudes in utterances (such as prescriptions, praise, condemnation) about what is desirable, correct, right, and so on. Referring to evaluative attitudes is also one way of explaining actions.

Does the concept of a necessary degree of consistency and coherence in the system of one's cognitive attitudes also apply to evaluative attitudes? Is it methodologically possible to show a parallel between the attribution of cognitive and evaluative attitudes? Moreover, how are the theory of interpretation and the partially external individuation of the content of attitudes connected with the objectivity of value judgments? How is it possible to claim that values are just as objective as beliefs without attributing to them a positive ontological status, or, to put it another way, without taking values as pseudo-entities?

For Davidson, the interpretation of evaluative attitudes is coupled with the interpretation of cognitive attitudes:

> The connection between cognitive and evaluative attitudes is made evident from the perspective of radical interpretation as a result of the fact that the same *sentences* are objects of beliefs and desires. It is attitudes toward the *same* sentences that is the key here. The same sentences are the objects of both belief and desire: this reinforces the claim that the interpretation of the evaluative attitudes proceeds along the same general lines as the interpretation of the cognitive attitudes.[7]

Davidson unifies the semantics of evaluative sentences and the semantics of sentences with cognitive content (a truth-value). The propositional content of attitudes is identified by an interpreter in the form of sentences. Understanding sentences means being able to specify their propositional content in terms of beliefs and desires. Davidson asks:

> But what about explicitly evaluative sentences about what is good, desirable, useful, obligatory, or our duty? The simplest view would be, as mentioned before, to identify desiring a sentence to be true with judging that it would be desirable it were true—in other words, to identify desiring that "Poverty is eradicated" be true with embracing the sentence "it is desirable that poverty be eradicated." And it is in fact hard to see how these two attitudes can be allowed to take entirely independent directions.[8]

Davidson also draws into his considerations the following distinction between evaluative attitudes and reasons for action: "judging that an act is good is not the same as judging that it ought to be performed, and certainly judging that there is an obligation to make some sentence true is not the same as judging that it is desirable to make it true."[9] This leads him to identify the *common ground* necessary for evaluative judgments and attitudes. Differences between the beliefs, desires, and evaluations of different individuals can only occur within a shared frame of reference. The circumstances of the arrangement of values in this framework are relative to particular places, times, and social contexts. The attribution and identification of values is relative to the social situation within which intelligible redescription takes place, since this situation comprises the background assumptions that inform interpretation. The situation and background assumptions may change, but having some such context is necessary for the ascription and interpretation of evaluative attitudes. Yet these assumptions should not be seen as either foundational or transcendental.

Davidson's holism of belief and meaning goes hand in hand with the holism of cognitive and evaluative attitudes. The externalist view found in Davidson encompasses the theory of evaluative and cognitive judgment because both are similarly determined by the objects to which they refer. The objects of belief and of desire are thus the causes of belief and, in a sense, of desire. Since these objects are common to both the speaker and the interpreter, values are, on the Davidsonian account, tied to things.[10] To be able to attribute evaluative attitudes to a speaker, one must, therefore, be able to recognize objects common to oneself and the speaker. The commonality of the objects to which a speaker and interpreter refer constitutes the basic condition for interpretation (be it of evaluative or cognitive attitudes) and exemplifies the connection between the interpretation of utterances (meaning) and the identification of evaluative attitudes (desire).

3 How Do We Learn Propositional Attitudes?

We generally learn to ascribe attitudes at the same time as we develop the ability to plan actions, take responsibility, and distinguish between causes and effects. Thoughts and actions work together; for example, desires combine with beliefs to bring about action. By learning our first language from others we acquire a linguistic frame of reference that enables us to explain and make sense of mental states (thoughts) and actions. But this process is *not* "theoretical" in character, since the ascription of attitudes to an agent is not based on any axioms or laws regarding the antecedents of action that is grasped abstractly. We learn to ascribe attitudes by learning the semantic features of words like "intention," "decision," "will," "desire," and "belief" at the same time and in the same circumstances in which we also learn how to explain actions. Learning to explain actions amounts, to a large extent, to being able to ascribe attitudes (such as beliefs and desires) to an agent. Explaining action involves the identification of the appropriate attitudes that accompany an action. For example, I cannot be said to know the meaning of "grief" if I do not know how grief connects to certain patterns of behavior.

On what basis is one able to grasp the conditions for the correct use of attitudinal terms? This can be elucidated by examining prototypical situations in which the meaning of mental expressions and the explanation of action is given at one and the same time. The ascription of belief and desire requires the interpretation of utterances and actions. Based on prototypical situations we ascribe evaluative and nonevaluative attitudes to the agent. We ascribe nonevaluative attitudes (beliefs) by applying epistemological principles, for example, that agents have their own sets of beliefs about how they are situated within the environment. We ascribe evaluative attitudes based on similarities to our *own* system of values and how such attitudes are understood and perceived by others. Evaluative beliefs effect desires because desire implies *something that is desirable*, that is, the object or event to which we ascribe value. A particular behavior does not necessarily justify inferring any particular attitude; for example, someone's wearing black clothing is not sufficient for us to infer that the wearer is grieving. Instead, we come to recognize the act of grieving as instantiated *in* the wearing of certain clothing. There is, therefore, a certain complementarity that obtains between the *identification* and the *verification* conditions of the ascription of attitudes. Moreover, in order to interpret actions one must be able to identify actions under the appropriate descriptions. Understanding actions is, to a large extent, a matter of assigning actions to their appropriate categories. These categories are, of course, socially determined—they are learned in particular social contexts.[11]

As we learn how to make conceptual distinctions such as that between *reflexes* (which are nonintentional) and *actions* (which are intentional), we gain confidence in the ascription and interpretation of attitudes. An understanding of intention is therefore crucial to the interpretation of action. We identify an action by saying what *the agent was intending to do*. Grasping how to make such distinctions is complicated by the fact that the ascription of intentions depends on the ascription of beliefs and other propositional attitudes. Intention consequently presupposes beliefs about the possibility of action (and alternative actions) in the given circumstances. We can only make sense of the concept of intention inasmuch as we are ourselves acquainted with the concept of successful action. Being generally successful in action, however, requires having mostly true beliefs. Intentional actions may be projected by our attitudes, but they must be brought about by *decision*. A mere desire is not yet a decision, and even the combination of desires and descriptive beliefs may be insufficient to trigger action. People may even frustrate their own desires for more or less conscious reasons.

Often a failed attempt can serve as an opportunity to modify our attitudes and thereby increase the likelihood of future success. In this sense, actions are a result of *trying*. The following characterization is helpful to understand the situation of acting:

If an agent intends to perform the action A in the situation S, it is possible to assume that the agent holds the following beliefs:

1. that is the agent is in S (the situation as given under certain descriptions);
2. that the agent does not have any attitudes opposed to A sufficient for the agent to want to refrain from doing A;
3. that the agent has the ability to do A;
4. that the agent is not prevented from performing A;

5. that the agent will perform A if and only if the agent tries to perform A (actions are the result of *trying*); and
6. that the agent's attempt to do A could succeed.

The agent and interpreter have to understand the distinction between the attempted action and the achieved action, and this also needs to be understood in relation to the action as it might be redescribed and reinterpreted in typical situations. One must distinguish, then, between *intending* and *succeeding,* while recognizing that *succeeding is* to be contrasted, at least in the case of action, with mere *attempting*. Furthermore, one must distinguish between *successful* and *unsuccessful attempts* for each class of action and its ascription. This is relevant to both interpreter and agent. The agent must, in his or her own case, be able to distinguish between what is intended and what is accomplished. The cognitive distinction between *trying* and *intending* is one of the crucial conceptual components of a theory of agency, and this is why first-person authority (which presupposes that speakers and actors know what they mean and intend) plays such an important role as an epistemic condition for the possibility of the understanding of others.[12]

But do we have privileged knowledge of our own actions? For Elizabeth Anscombe, the assumption of such knowledge is erroneous. She calls such knowledge "knowledge without observation."[13] But to characterize first-person authority in terms of such knowledge leads to misunderstandings. An agent's knowledge of the performance of a certain action (where the performance is a performance of the agent and so is known in the first person with the authority that bestows) must be distinguished from the knowledge that the performance has a certain effect. The latter is empirical knowledge. An action has a meaning (trying) that is given in answer to the question "What is the relevant description of the agent's action?" For Davidson, trying is of no importance, because

> it may seem a difficulty that primitive actions do not accommodate the concept of trying, for primitive actions are ones we just do—nothing can stand in the way, so to speak. But surely, the critic will say, there are some things we must strive to do (like hit the bull's eye). Once more the same sort of answer serves. Trying to do one thing may be simply doing another. I try to turn on the light by flicking the switch, but I simply flick the switch. Or perhaps even that is, on occasion, an attempt. Still, the attempt consists of something I can do without trying; just move my hand, perhaps.[14]

Davidson's argument results from a point of view in which one ascribes actions *directly* to an agent.[15] If one raises one's arm, then normally one knows that this is what one does. But there is no other evidential basis for the knowledge that one raises one's arm other than the fact that one raises one's arm—the only evidence is, one might say, the experiential knowledge of one's own arm raising which is also a trying. In such cases, the agent has knowledge without observation, because the agent's trying is distinct from the observable action that is performed. The description "trying" refers to mental states as well as bodily movements. In this situation, an agent has knowledge without observation because the *attempt*—itself an item of behavior—is distinct from the action that can be observed objectively. Thus the knowledge of "trying" must be understood as distinct from knowledge of "having done." On the level of belief, the distinction between what counts as trying and acting is the epistemic basis of first-person authority and so underpins the relationship between the agent and their thoughts. Different reference relations are not impossible a priori—we individuate mental states and their referents by means of *explanatory* (intelligible) *redescription* in particular cases.[16] Explanatory redescription of actions assumes that the agent functions as an agent and has some grasp of his or her own capacity for agency. Self-knowledge and an understanding of one's similarity to others are crucial for distinguishing between intentional and nonintentional behavior. This requires propositional attitudes containing mental and social predicates. Mental concepts must be understood as social, and social concepts must be understood as mental. Furthermore, in Davidson's naturalized epistemology, explanatory redescription unifies the theory of interpretation, decision, and evaluation with the externalism of common causes.

Beliefs and evaluative attitudes are situated within a social frame of reference that provides the means by which our actions and utterances as well as those of others are understood. Self-consciousness and self-reference involve reference to others since the constitution of my own consciousness involves understanding the manner in which I am similar to others as well as the manner in which I am distinct from them.[17] Acquiring knowledge of the nature of beliefs and intentions cannot be dissociated from the acquisition of conceptual distinctions and moral terms. We are not at the mercy of our dispositions, however, but can contemplate our actions from various angles, and thereby redescribe and reinterpret them. We typically individuate actions by specifying intentions within particular contexts. In order to act intentionally, an agent must possess propositional attitudes (beliefs, desires), conceptual distinctions such as truth–falsity and success–failure, and the ability to determine whether the conditions necessary for the performance of particular actions obtain (awareness of circumstances). The ability to interpret an agent's action similarly depends on grasping this cognitive framework of agency. The interpretation of behavior, linguistic and otherwise, thus requires the ability to identify (by both the agent/speaker and the interpreter) the *types* of situation (and so the types of action) in which particular actions belong.[18]

Davidson's investigation of the communicability of evaluative attitudes and how they relate to cognitive attitudes leads him to emphasize the importance of one's *own* value standards, and of the norms of *coherence* and *consistency*, in evaluative attribution. This is in line with the externalistic individuation of the content of the uttered sentences in relation to common objects. These norms are the basis of the interpersonal comparison of values and decisions, and it is impossible for us to extricate ourselves from them. Necessarily, the interpreter relies on his *own* values in interpreting and comparing the values of others.

Davidson sees something "fundamentally wrong" with the standard picture of the interpersonal comparison of values according to which "we first decide what the interests of each person are; then we compare those interests in strength; then we judge or decide what should be done."[19] For Davidson, "There is no reason we cannot judge the relative strengths of our own interests and those of others, or compare the interests of two others. My point has been that we do not have to establish, argue for, or opt for, a basis for such judgments. We already have it."[20] Therefore, within the structure of interpersonal comparison of values, we can make a distinction between *the norm of consistency (rationality) and the idea of what is valuable in itself, but the judgment we exercise in such cases is not based on anything that is freely chosen*: "What I call a "basis" for interpersonal comparison cannot be something that is freely chosen, something that may be accepted by one person or society, but not by another."[21] The basis of evaluative comparison cannot be chosen, since it is that which directs and explains our judgments and decisions.

As Davidson presents it, the basis on which interpersonal comparison rests thus appears rather like Heidegger's notion of *Seinsverständnis* (understanding of being), because this "basis" is not a medium or an entity.[22] Gadamer has developed a hermeneutic of the *Wirkungsgeschichte* of shared understanding that consists in *Horizontverschmelzung* (the fusion of horizons).[23] In this respect, Davidson can be seen as closely aligned with the hermeneutic tradition (a tradition that includes Vico, Dilthey, Heidegger, and Gadamer), which emphasizes the connection between the interpretation of texts and utterances, and the understanding of behavior in general, and also emphasizes the necessary self-reflexive character of such understanding. Moreover, this tradition is one, it should be noted, that connects directly with the neo-Kantian tradition that is exemplified by thinkers such as Windelband and Dilthey.[24]

4 Tolerance and the Relativity of Evaluation

What is the difference between evaluative and cognitive attitudes, and how are they related? People discern a wide range of disagreement between their *own* evaluative attitudes and those of other people. My evaluation of some state of affairs, object, or event need not be the same as the evaluation that others make; within limits, such differences can be tolerated, since they do not undermine the validity of my own evaluation or that of others. I call this the *principle of tolerance* in contrast to the principle of charity.[25] It is a principle that recognizes and allows for a certain degree of divergence in evaluative attitudes that reflects, among other things, the different sociobehavioral contexts in which attitudes and evaluations arise.

The disagreement that seems so readily discernible between our own evaluative attitudes and those of other people is itself suggestive of a characteristic difference between evaluative and cognitive attitudes. Whereas cognitive attitudes, especially those that relate most directly to aspects of the everyday world, have a high degree of acceptance across speakers, evaluative attitudes fare much worse in this regard. Indeed, one might argue that whereas most of our everyday cognitive beliefs, and so perhaps most of our cognitive beliefs in general, are common across different sociobehavioral contexts, most of our evaluative beliefs, even our everyday evaluative beliefs, are not shared in the same way at all. Just consider the huge variation in the evaluative beliefs that motivate behavior between the various communities that make up the primarily multi-cultural societies that are so characteristic of countries such as the United States, Great Britain or Germany (to say nothing of the difference that obtain between more geographically distant communities). Indeed, it is precisely recognition of such evaluative diversity that has led modern liberal theory to emphasis the importance of purely procedural rationality as underpinning any just system of political order. The fact of evaluative diversity and the distinction between evaluative and cognitive attitudes are not given much attention by Davidson. Instead, his tendency is to treat the degree of disagreement in respect of evaluative attitudes as on a par with that which affects cognitive attitudes. But there seems no warrant for this assumption, especially not given the prima facie evidence to the contrary. Moreover, although evaluative and cognitive attitudes are interconnected, jut as they are interconnected with other attitudes, including desires, this should not blind us to the significant differences that seem, on empirical grounds, to obtain here.

Davidson's neglect of the differences between evaluative and cognitive attitudes and his treatment of evaluative attitudes as determined in much the same way as cognitive attitudes suggest that his position is close to that of moral realism—although given his dislike of the language of realism and antirealism, as expressed elsewhere, the designation is probably one he would reject. Characterized semantically, realism takes assertions to have determinate truth-conditions, and moral realism would apply this to evaluative as much as to other statements. A realist approach to values can be stated as follows: "moral judgments are viewed as *factually cognitive*, as presenting claims about the world which can be assessed (like any then factual beliefs) as true or false, and whose truth or falsity are as much possible objects of human knowledge as any other factual claims about the world."[26] In addition, one might say that "The realist treats evaluative judgments as descriptions of the world whose literal significance (viz. truth-conditions) makes no reference, or generally makes no reference, to human desires, needs, wants or interests."[27] Moral realism thus stands opposed to the subjectivist approach exemplified by the standard Humean position, aligning evaluative with nonevaluative beliefs, and treating the intelligibility (or rationality) of evaluative beliefs in the same way as nonevaluative attitudes. On the moral realist approach, the moral properties that are the object of moral attitudes are genuine properties of things and actions.[28]

What arguments can we make against moral realism? Why shouldn't the descriptive usage and specification of evaluative words like "good," "wrong," and "bad" be analyzed in the same way as descriptive concepts used as predicates in assertions? There can be no doubt that, generally speaking, the justification of evaluative and prescriptive predications does involve the verification of certain empirical properties. Verifying whether something is "good" or "bad" depends upon using descriptive characterizations. A speaker who seeks to justify a value judgment has to show that the evaluated thing exhibits certain properties. If we suppose that a speaker could completely justify the evaluation by specifying particular properties, the justification of a value judgment would be methodologically identical with the justification of empirical assertions. Evaluative sentences would have the same cognitive status and means of verification and justification as nonevaluative or descriptive sentences—they would, in fact, be a kind of descriptive sentence.

In fact, there seems to be good reason to think that the justifications of descriptive and evaluative sentences are not equivalent, and that evaluative sentences cannot, therefore, be treated in the same way as descriptive sentences. We can see how this might be so in a way that also draws on aspects of Davidson's own position. Davidson emphasizes the interconnectedness of attitudes, and of attitudes with behavior. This might be taken to imply that evaluative and cognitive attitudes can therefore be treated as having similar justificatory and evidential grounds; but it also suggests that we should pay close attention to the way in which different attitudes connect up in different ways to one another, as well as to other attitudes and behavior, since such differences in connection may well imply differences in, among other things, the forms of justification and evidence that are relevant to those attitudes. Davidson's own emphasis on the way in which certain standards of rationality stand in the background here does not affect the possibility that the way those standards of rationality are worked out in particular cases may vary enormously—Davidson's account of rationality involves a very "thin" conception of what it is to be rational.

Davidson holds that there is no simple connection that relates preferences regarding the truth of different sentences and the values that would be realized if the sentences were true. The implication of this is that the meaning of evaluative terms such as "good" or "obligatory" need not always be the same. This seems an inevitable consequence of the fact that evaluative attitudes do not relate to social context in the same way as cognitive attitudes. There is no doubt that the social context affects the attribution of all attitudes through the way in which it is relevant to the ascription of meanings to utterances. But in the case of evaluative attitudes, the social context is also directly relevant in determining the attitudes held. Unlike cognitive attitudes, evaluative attitudes are best understood not as referring to properties that belong to things, but instead as referring to particular domains of social activity in which certain behaviors are given a positive or negative ascription. Certain variations on social context—such as one may find between, for instance, different ethnic communities—will also imply variations in the evaluative attitudes that are relevant to those social contexts, as they also imply variations in the domains of social activity.

Recognizing the difference between evaluative and cognitive beliefs and their differing relations to social context, we can understand how the lack of agreement with respect to evaluative beliefs need not affect cognitive beliefs. In other words, if evaluative and cognitive attitudes and evaluative and cognitive sentences are understood as standing in different relations to one another and to other attitudes and behavior, then the empirical fact of evaluative difference can be understood in a way that does not impugn Davidson's unified approach to attitudes and behavior. Moreover, in one important respect, evaluative and cognitive attitudes remain similar: Both are subject to *correction*, since both arise and are articulated within necessarily a broader social context. The possibility of such correction is what underpins the idea of objectivity. Evaluative attitudes can thus be objective, not because of the way they relate to objects, but because of the way they connect to practices of evaluation, action, and decision, which are constrained by particular domains of social activity, but which may also vary between social groups or practices.

Davidson's "unified theory" can thus be understood in a way that enables us to understand attitudes as interconnected with one another and with action. Yet precisely because these are complex and multiple, we cannot and should not assume that all attitudes, and especially not all evaluative attitudes, can be understood as fitting within a single overarching system. How we attribute attitudes depends on the social context in which those attitudes arise, and the particular evaluations we express depend on the way in which our actions are oriented within different domains of activity. Other writers have emphasized the way in which Davidson's "unified' approach requires that we understand attitudes as resistant to any completely consistent ordering[29]—different attitudes connect up with other attitudes and with actions in ways that are often localized and "territorial."[30] To whatever extent this may be true of cognitive attitudes (and epistemological considerations may mitigate against it), this certainly seems true of evaluative attitudes. The differences in ethnic and cultural groupings within even our own societies is itself indicative of the differences in evaluative attitudes that may obtain even alongside similarity in cognitive attitudes. It is the fact of such difference that implies that, in interpretation, charity alone is never enough—tolerance is also essential.

I began this essay with the problem of values as it arises within the social sciences. Davidson provides us with a way of seeing how values necessarily enter into social scientific inquiry, but Davidson also holds that this does not impugn the objectivity of such inquiry. What we have seen in the discussion above is that the interpersonal comparison of values is based on judgments that are certainly open to correction—by reference to the "common standards" that prevail among other members of the groups to which we belong—and so these values have a sense of "objectivity" that properly belongs to them. This is a direct consequence of the fact that evaluative attitudes, and the concept of desirability to which they are inevitably connected, are learned and are meaningful only in relation to particular contexts of behavior and social interaction—and because, unlike cognitive attitudes, evaluative attitudes are precisely attitudes that concern our orientation within such social and behavioral contexts. Yet this also has the consequence, which Davidson does not adequately acknowledge, that the standards at issue here may differ, as the social and behavioral context differs. There is thus a multiplicity of socially determined evaluative perspectives—a position that can be viewed as a version of global multiculturalism—even though there is not a multiplicity of social "worlds" in which we are somehow imprisoned. In this second case tolerance would be not possible, because difference would never even appear. The possibility of divergence in evaluative attitudes can only be made sense of within a framework in which we also recognize the interconnectedness of attitudes, evaluative and cognitive, and the complexity and diversity of the principles and standards by which they are so connected.

Acknowledgments

I would like to thank Jeff Malpas and Nicholas Malpas for their useful and illuminating comments on this essay.

Notes

1. Donald Davidson, "The Objectivity of Values," in his *Problems of Rationality* (Oxford: Clarendon Press, 2004), p. 43.

2. W. Windelband, "Geschichte der Naturwissenschaft," in *Präludien: Aufsätze und Reden zur Philosophie und ihrer Geschichte*, vol. 2 (Tübingen: Mohr, 1915), pp. 99–135. On developments in German philosophy over this period (and especially between Dilthey and Windelband), see Herbert Schnädelbach, *Philosophie in Deutschland 1831–1933* (Frankfurt, 1993), in English, *German Philosophy 1831–1933* (New York: Cambridge University Press, 1983).

3. Wilhelm Dilthey, *Einleitung in die Geisteswissenschaften*, in *Gesammelte Schriften*, vol. I (Göttingen: Vandenhoeck & Ruprecht, 1959).

4. On the use of fulfillment conditions for the semantic interpretation of utterances, see Kirk Ludwig, "The Truth about Moods," in *Concepts of Meaning. Framing an Integrated Theory of Linguistic Behavior*, ed. Gerhard Preyer, Georg Peter, and Maria Ulkan (Dordrecht: Kluwer Academic Publisher/rep. Vienna: Springer Verlag, 2003), pp. 154–159. Most philosophers take the fulfillment conditions of a belief or utterance to include both the holding true of the belief and the obtaining of the conditions under which it is true.

5. In "The Problem of Objectivity," in *Problems of Rationality*, pp. 13–17, Davidson makes a distinction between relations between attitudes of the same type, between

beliefs, for instance, or between desires (*intra*-attitudinal holism) and relations between attitudes of different types, between, for instance, beliefs and desires (*inter*-attitudinal holism). For Davidson desires depend on beliefs, and all propositional attitudes depend on language. In *Donald Davidson: Meaning, Truth, Language, and Reality* (New York: Oxford University Press, 2005), Ernest Lepore and Kirk Ludwig argue, in a way they take to run counter to many other authors, that Davidson is no "unbuttoned holist," meaning that he is not a radical meaning holist, nor is he a *rigid* or *extreme* holist (see *Donald Davidson: Meaning, Truth, Language, and Reality*, pp. 211–130), but instead accepts only a *partial* holism. For more on the issue of holism, see Herman Cappelen and Ernest Lepore, *Insensitive Semantics: A Defense of Semantic Minimalism and Speech Act Pluralism* (Malden: Blackwell, 2005); and *Context-Sensitivity and Semantic Minimalism: New Essays on Semantics and Pragmatics*, ed. Gerhard Preyer and Georg Peter (Oxford: Oxford University Press, 2007).

6. For a fuller analysis of Davidson's philosophy, see Gerhard Preyer, *Donald Davidson's Philosophy: From Radical Interpretation to Radical Contextualism* (Frankfurt: Humanities Online, 2011).

7. Davidson, "The Interpersonal Comparison of Values," in *Problems of Rationality*, p. 71.

8. Davidson, "Expressing Evaluations," in *Problems of Rationality*, p. 37.

9. Ibid.

10. Davidson, "Objectivity of Values," in *Problems of Rationality*, p. 51; see also "Expressing Evaluations," in *Problems of Rationality*, pp. 19–37, and "Appendix: Objectivity and Practical Reasoning," in *Problems of Rationality*, pp. 52–57. On the critique of Davidson's externalism as a physical and synchronic externalism, rather than social and diachronic, see Ernest Lepore and Kirk Ludwig, *Donald Davidson: Meaning, Truth, Language, and Reality*, pp. 335–340.

11. On the underlying distinction at issue here, see D. S. Shwayder, *The Stratification of Behavior: A System of Definitions Propounded and Defended*, (London: Routledge & Kegan Paul, 1965), pp. 41–51.

12. Ernest Lepore and Kirk Ludwig argue that there are serious problems with the Davidsonian explanation of first-person authority that center of a confusion between the explanans and the explanandum (see Lepore and Ludwig, *Donald Davidson: Meaning, Truth, Language, and Reality*, pp. 343–720).

13. Elizabeth Anscombe, *Intention* (Oxford: Oxford University Press, 1957), pp. 13–15.

14. Davidson, "Agency," in *Action and Events*, ed. Ernest Lepore and Brian McLaughlin (Oxford: Oxford University Press, 1980), p. 60.

15. On this problem in detail, see Preyer, *Donald Davidson's Philosophy*, pp. 168–179; on primary reasons, see pp. 212–239.

16. The difference between *explanatory* and *nonexplanatory* redescription of action is that the former supplies us with a purpose of reason on the basis of which the action was performed (Davidson, "Problems in the Explanation of Action," in *Problems of Rationality*, p. 105). Davidson also points out that all reason explanation implies the description of attitudes in terms of their semantic content in ways that also exhibit the desirability of the action from the agent's point of view ("Problems in the Explanation of Action," in *Problems of Rationality*, p.110).

17. On the reflexivity condition, see my review of D. Henrich, *Selbstbewußtsein und Selbstbestimmung. Vorlesungen zur Subjektivität* (Frankfurt: Suhrkamp Verlag, 2007), in *Philosophischer Literaturanzeiger* 2 (2009), pp. 156–165.

18. On this identification, see Preyer, *Intention and Practical Thought*, Part I; *Explaining Action* (Frankfurt: Humanities Online, 2011).

19. Davidson, "The Interpersonal Comparison of Values," pp. 73–74.

20. Ibid., p. 74.

21. Ibid., p. 63.

22. See Martin Heidegger, *Nietzsche*, 2 vols. (Pfullingen: Verlag Günther Neske, 1961).

23. For Davidson's own comments on Gadamer's continuation of Heidegger's hermeneutic ontology, see Donald Davidson, "Gadamer and Plato's *Philebus*," in his *Truth, Language, and History* (Oxford: Oxford University Press, 2005), pp. 262–275; on the hermeneutic model to be found in Davidson himself, see Davidson, "Locating Literary Language," in *Truth, Language, and History*, pp. 167–181.

24. On the relationship of Davidson to the hermeneutic tradition, see Jeff Malpas's essay in this book.

25. For an analysis of the principle of charity, see Preyer, *Donald Davidson's Philosophy*, pp. 67–133; on the epistemic restrictions of interpretation that takes effect on the application of the principle as a constraint of interpretation, see pp. 156–167; on a resystematization of charity, see Lepore and Ludwig, *Donald Davidson: Meaning, Truth, Language, and Reality*, pp. 175–208; on a critique of radical translation (interpretation) in principle, see J. Fodor, *LOT 2: The Language of Thought Revisited* (Oxford: Oxford University Press, 2008). On Fodor, see my review in *Zeitschrift für Philosophische Forschung* 1 (2010).

26. M. Platts, *Ways of Meaning*, p. 243.

27. M. Platts, "Moral Reality and the End of Desire," in Platts (ed.), *Reference, Truth, and Reality: Essays on the Philosophy of Language* (London: Routledge & Kegan Paul, 1980), p. 73.

28. See also: John McDowell, "Are Moral Requirements Hypothetical Imperatives?," in *Mind, Value, and Reality*, ed. John McDowell (Cambridge, MA: Harvard University

Press, 1998), pp. 77–95; D. McNaughton, *Moral Vision* (Oxford: Oxford University Press, 1988); D. O. Brink, "Moral Realism and the Sceptical Arguments from Disagreement and Queerness," *Australasian Journal of Philosophy* 62 (1984), pp. 111–125; Jonathan Dancy, *Moral Realism and the Foundations of Ethics* (Cambridge: Cambridge University Press, 1993); Judith Jarvis Thomson and Gilbert Harman, *Moral Relativism and Moral Objectivity* (Cambridge, MA: Blackwell, 1996). For an overview of both positions, see A. Kulenkampff and F. Siebelt, "What a Noncognitivist Might Tell a Moral Realist," in *ProtoSociology: An International Journal of Interdisciplinary Research* 14 (2000), pp. 355–377.

29. See, e.g., Jeff Malpas, *Donald Davidson and the Mirror of Meaning* (Cambridge: Cambridge University Press, 1992).

30. Davidson himself talks about the mind as "partitioned" in various ways in "Paradoxes of Irrationality," in *Problems of Irrationality*, pp. 181–185.

18 Davidson's Normativity

Stephen Turner

Introduction

Davidson's "The Very Idea of a Conceptual Scheme"[1] was a powerful and influential paper. It largely ended a prolonged discussion of the rationality of other cultures,[2] undermining particularly the claim argued at the time that there was a universal, non-culture-relative core of rationality and protocol sentence-like description that provided grounds for judging the rationality of other cultures.[3] It blunted the impact of some of the more exuberantly relativistic interpretations of the implications of Thomas Kuhn's *The Structure of Scientific Revolutions*.[4] But the paper introduced one of the least well-understood Davidsonian arguments, his attack on what he called "The Third Dogma of Empiricism," after Quine's "Two Dogmas of Empiricism."[5] The third dogma was the scheme–content distinction. The paper is basic to understanding the later Davidson. Its treatment of error pointed directly toward Davidson's most controversial claims, in "A Nice Derangement of Epitaphs,"[6] about the nonexistence of "language" as the term is usually understood: The model for the interacting language speaker correcting for error is generalized from the model of the translator in "The Very Idea."

Davidson himself thought the implications of the argument were radical, and he specifically thought that the paper was opposed to the kind of Kantianism that was present when it was written and has since, under slightly different forms, become conventional wisdom in Anglo-American philosophy, in which normative concepts constitute the world for us. Variants of this view range from the idea that normative concepts are subject to either a small or large amount of local linguistic variation to the idea that there is a large common core of reason that anyone in any culture who is properly brought up will come to recognize as binding. The essay was directly concerned with the kind of conceptual relativity supposedly warranted by the variation in concepts between languages. But as Davidson put it in the essay, the argument showed that it was also unintelligible to say "that all mankind—all speakers of language at least—share a common scheme and ontology."[7]

The way his paper has come to be interpreted in much of the subsequent discussion assimilates it to a form of conventional wisdom to which it was opposed. This occurred through two main steps. The first was to read Davidson as having established the necessity of some sort of logical or rational core to human thought that is transcultural or culturally invariant by showing that translatability was transitive, that is, that my translation from language *L* to language *P* would not be a translation if it did not include the translations into *L* from language *N*. This reading is based on a supposed dilemma: If the relation of translatability was not transitive, it would imply the possibility of incommensurable schemes, and if it was transitive, it would imply that our standards are the only standards,[8] which in turn implied that there was after all a universal scheme. If Davidson is consistent in rejecting the possibility of incommensurable schemes, it would mean that Davidson was in fact a scheme–content thinker himself, and his reservations about the scheme–content distinction were a matter of detail.

The detail was vaguely understood in terms of the idea of independence. What Davidson had shown was that there could be no understanding of schemes and content independently of one another. Accordingly, one interpretation was that he was proposing a novel "interdependence" model of the relation between the two.[9] Another interpretation deradicalized it in a different direction, by suggesting that his point had to do with "the metaphors that sustain the picture of an independent scheme and worldly content"[10] rather than the idea itself. The reinterpretation made Davidson's argument about content rather than about schemes. Davidson's explicit denial that there was "a neutral ground, or a common coordinate system" between schemes,[11] was taken to rule out an independent realm of "content," but it was not taken to rule out an independent realm consisting of a common "scheme." Indeed, it was reinterpreted in terms of the Kantian idea that, as John McDowell puts it, the world "cannot be constituted independently of the space of concepts, the space in which subjectivity has its being."[12] The distinction between denying our ability to step outside the conceptual—the Kantian thesis—and denying the scheme–content distinction, meaning denying common content, common schemes, and the independence of scheme and content alike—Davidson's thesis—was taken to be a distinction without a difference. The reinterpreters assumed that the languages of the conceptual and of normative reason are inescapable and ineliminable by any argument about schemes, because Davidson could not have possibly, or intelligibly, meant to challenge this foundation of contemporary philosophy.

The conventional accommodation or renormalization of Davidson's argument was made plausible through a feature of Davidson's argument in this same paper: the claim, as it became interpreted, that massive error about widely held beliefs is impossible. If this is the case, that is, if skepticism about significant ordinary beliefs is itself necessarily incoherent, this fact can in turn be taken to imply that various commonplace metaphysical views about ordinary beliefs are warranted. If the separate and autonomous existence of the world and the normative authority of reason are such facts, or are entailed by such facts, these facts, together with the idea that there is some sort of universal rationality, take us back to and support a basically Kantian picture of the metaphysical structure of the world, in which universal rationality interacts with a world that we can't be very wrong about. What Davidson saw as radical, in short, became, through these reinterpretations, validation for the default antinaturalist philosophy of the present. Davidson, on this account, becomes the thinker who undermined Quine's arguments in "Two Dogmas of Empiricism" from within, reestablishing the synthetic a priori in the new guise of the notion of normativity. On this view, Davidson's acknowledgment that rationality, intentionality, and belief are "normative," together with his rejection of massive error, commits him to some variant of the Kantian doctrine of normativity of Sellars,[13] Haugeland,[14] Brandom,[15] and McDowell,[16] perhaps with some idiosyncratic variations with respect to the precise location of the normative, for example, or of the nature of the interaction between the normative and the nonnormative.

Davidson's own argument that meaning, intentional ascriptions, and rationality are mutually dependent, and that they arrive together in the description of intentional action, seems congenial to this reading, because it serves to make these idiosyncratic differences less significant. Davidson might locate the normative in the universal psychological properties of the interpreting agent rather than in language, as in Brandom, or in some sort of nomic realm whose normative constraining character must be recognized, as in McDowell. But meaning, intentional ascriptions, and rationality all must be there in some fashion. The rest is detail.

The oddity of this outcome is worth reflecting on. The target of the original paper was the scheme–content distinction itself. The Kantian form of this distinction was an especially visible part of this—the term "scheme" is an echo of Kant's language. The picture of the rational ordering mind organizing the Kantian manifold was transmitted to Kuhn via the neo-Kantian historians of science, such as Alexandre Koyre, whom Kuhn admired and who played a large role in the background of Kuhn's use of the notion of paradigms. So the Kantian tradition is clearly the target of Davidson's paper. What made the paper so radical, as Richard Rorty routinely pointed out in conversation, was the way in which the argument against the scheme–content distinction could be extended throughout the history of philosophy, to undermine such variants as the concept–percept distinction, the word–world distinction, and so forth. The unradical result described above—that it is taken in support of the current "idealist" variants of the scheme–content distinction—is in open conflict with Davidson's initial point.

In what follows I will try to restore this original point. I will not be concerned with the details of this "idealist" reinterpretation of Davidson, but I will try to show why he thought the argument of his paper had radical implications, and explain what it had radical implications for. Its target, I will argue, is the whole commonplace normative conception of concepts. His approach was to show why this conception was unnecessary and deeply problematic. Explicating the argument requires more than textual analysis: The arguments to which "The Very Idea" is now being assimilated, such as those of McDowell, Brandom, and Haugeland, were not available at the time the paper was written and were in part devised to take advantage of Davidson's claims, so the original paper does not respond directly to them, and can even be construed, with effort, to support them. But the original point can, with a bit of contextualization, be reconstructed, and once reconstructed, can be seen to be the basis of the even more radical claims made in such later papers as "A Nice Derangement of Epitaphs," "The Third Man," and "The Social Aspect of Language." It is an oddity of this discussion, though not an entirely mysterious one, that some of the relevant distinctions between Davidson and the normativists map onto, and are reproduced in, social theory. Brandom, at the beginning of *Making It Explicit*, quotes Weber's phrase "the disenchantment of the world," and offers a project of reenchantment in its place. Sellars's appeal to the idea of collective intentionality, which was in turn a core of his ideas about norms, was consciously echoing Durkheim. As we will see, the differences between Davidson and the normativists follow this familiar fault line between theories of obligation: those that invoke collective facts and those which rely on individualist social theory.

1 What Is Impossible?

There is a kernel of truth to the conventional appropriation of the argument of "On the Very Idea of a Conceptual Scheme." The paper does rest on an impossibility argument, about intelligibility and the limits of intelligibility, and the argument has complex implications, far beyond the issue of conceptual relativism. But the implications are not congenial to the Kantian picture, as Davidson knew, and he contrasted it to the views of the main Kantian of the time, P. F. Strawson. The argument develops from an observation about incommensurability: that

> Whorf, wanting to demonstrate that Hopi incorporates a metaphysics so alien to ours that Hopi and English cannot—as he puts it "be calibrated," uses English to convey the contents of sample Hopi sentences. Kuhn is brilliant at saying what things were like before the revolution using—what else?—our post-revolutionary idiom.[17]

Davidson's point is that it is impossible to do otherwise. If we were faced with genuine incommensurability—speakers with a truly alien conceptual scheme—we would not even be able to understand them sufficiently to say so.

Davidson's approach to the issues goes through the problem of evidence: The evidence of "different schemes" takes the form of sentences. It is normally understood that having languages is associated with having a conceptual scheme in such a way that differences in one imply differences in the other. Benjamin Whorf, for example, uses linguistic evidence from the Hopi to make claims about their conceptual schemes, and the literature on conceptual differences in science emphasizes shifts in the meaning of terms in the context of different theories. If we restate the idea of incommensurability and intelligibility at the level of the linguistic evidence, it becomes a claim about translatability, specifically about what could count as a successful translation and what follows from failures of translation. As Davidson puts it, "it seems unlikely that we can intelligibly attribute attitudes as complex as [the ones that would allow us to recognize something as speech behavior doing something as complex as making an utterance the speaker believed in] unless we can translate his words into ours."[18] The limits of intelligibility, in short, are the limits of translation. Failure in translation makes for, and is evidence of, failure in understanding.

Davidson considers two possible kinds of failure of translatability, partial and total, and argues first "that we cannot make sense of total failure," and then examines cases of partial failure.[19] The case against total failure provides the kernel for the conventional interpretation. But the case of partial failure has the more radical implications. The impossibility argument arises in connection with purported cases of total failure of translation: The conclusion of the argument is that the only evidence in the first place that an activity is speech behavior is evidence that it can be interpreted in our language, whether directly or through translation. This turns out to have a crucial implication for the transitivity of translation: To ascribe the speech behavior "translating" to someone in translating into yet a third language requires us to translate the translation, since otherwise we would not be able to say whether we were properly translating their utterances as translation. In short, we need to know that they are not faking translation. This criterion holds for the rest of translation. This is the argument that seems to lead back to a universal core of rationality. But Davidson also makes an argument that seems to point in the opposite direction, toward the detail-oriented capacities of interpretation that are central to ordinary human interaction and understanding, as when he observes that translation requires a command of a "multitude of finely discriminated intentions and beliefs" to interpret speech as a form of human conduct. This is an important tension in his argument to which we will return. It is resolved by his normativist interpreters in the direction of normative universal rationality or the normative conceptual preconditions for language. But these options, as we have seen, seem to be ruled out by, and are indeed the target of, the argument itself.

The next step in the argument involves the contrast between mutual "contamination" of meaning and theory, that is, about what is claimed to be true—something that follows from giving up the analytic–synthetic distinction.[20] What appear to be "changes in meaning" between scientific theories, an essential element of the claim that paradigms are incommensurable, always also involves changes in what is said to be true. Failure of translation thus means failure to translate as true claims made with the same terms, so that one must say either that the meanings of the terms rather than the terms themselves must be different or that the previous claims were false. But the appeal to meanings turns out to be less than helpful, and indeed to be empty: "Meanings," in the sense of meanings in the head, are inaccessible. We don't know whether people mean the same thing as we do by the same words; we know only what they do and say. And thus the idea that truth is relative to a conceptual scheme turns out to mean nothing more than that the truth of a sentence is relative to the language in which it belongs.[21]

There is another oddity. The argument of the paper does not support the idea of a universal core of rationality common to all cultures. Indeed, it explains why the idea—promoted at the time by Martin Hollis,[22] who was concerned with the closely related question of whether we could attribute beliefs to people who did not possess modus ponens—could be given no determinate content. The reasons are Quinean. Translation operates on sets of logically and semantically linked sentences, which are open to multiple interpretations, in which the truth or falsity of any given sentence is relative to the role that sentence plays in the set as a whole, a role that can be omitted or altered depending on the roles played by the rest of the sentences and their content. Consequently, "possessing modus ponens" is a feature not of the content of the heads of the natives whose beliefs are being interpreted, but of the translations we use to make sense of them. Whether the translations ascribe modus ponens to them or not reflects choices made by the translator that could have been otherwise and still have produced intelligibility. Without such universally rational content there is nothing universal for the universalizing version of the Kantian project to work with, which gives us a reason to doubt this interpretation of Davidson.

2 The Quinean Background

As is evident from this reference to holism, Davidson's paper, and his work in this area in general, deals with a series of problems left over from Quine. In describing his position I have used Quinean language, for the most part, and done so intentionally—separating the Quinean elements from the Davidsonian ones cannot be done without an understanding of the issues that Davidson is addressing, and avoiding, in his paper. Quine left an unresolved problem: how to reconcile the fact that (a) the data for understanding human action and language were necessarily behavioral, for the language learner as well as for the interpreter and translator learning from scratch with (b) the widespread philosophical (and general) use of notions of intention and meaning, and (c) the raw fact that people do seem to be able to interpret one another, learn one another's languages, and do so in terms of intentions and meanings.

Quine himself was willing to treat this question as a matter of what would be found in a fully naturalized scientific account of these matters. This meant that notions like meaning and intention needed to be regarded as theoretical terms in an as yet uncreated predictive theory of behavior. But in their usual form they did not work very well in this role: Behavioral evidence was insufficient to produce a reasonably determinate fact of the matter of either meaning or intention. So interpretation was left hanging by Quine. Moreover, the relativistic consequences of Kuhn seemed to follow from Quine's attack on the analytic–synthetic distinction, which undercut the idea of universal a priori rational standards by relativizing considerations previously regarded as a priori to the status of part of a "theory" that faced the evidence as a whole. This, together with the underdetermination of theory by data, implied that there might be a number of theories that had different logical elements, had different true sentences, but were equally predictive, and that this was an irreducible situation. The germs of the idea of underdetermination and the relativism of logical elements and mathematical framework were already present in logical positivism. But Quine showed that these issues could not be dealt with merely by using such notions as convention to characterize the theoretical elements in question. This left a variety of puzzles about meaning: If the truth of the sentences is relative to the theory as a whole, didn't this imply that meanings changed between theories, and were thus incommensurable, making the notion of scientific progress impossible to formulate neutrally, as Paul Feyerabend pointed out?[23]

Davidson's approach to interpretation took for granted the same evidential base. But he dealt with it in a different way. He took over from G. E. M. Anscombe the notion of "under a description," and proceeded by treating intentional and meaning questions as arising under a particular description. The description, it is important to note, is in some sense a description of choice, an option (though exactly in what sense is an important consideration to which we will return). We could describe in the language of physical or neurophysiological science instead. But if we did this the problem of interpretation would be inaccessible to us. The question for Davidson involved the conditions of interpretation, that is, of getting a reasonably determinate answer to questions about intentions and meanings using the behavioral evidence we necessarily work with. "Radical interpretation" was simply interpretation under these conditions without other background knowledge, such as prior knowledge of the meanings of utterances, which is to say interpretation with the raw behavioral evidence alone. The question was what more would be needed to make any sense of this evidence in terms of meanings and intentions, or to put it differently, the implications of the choice of description in terms of intentions and meanings.

Davidson's answer was rationality, which enabled the attribution of intentions on the basis of behavioral data and knowledge of the meanings of the utterances that are part of the behavior, if there are any. The model is this: If I can take an utterance as a sincere expression of belief, and have data about behavior, I can infer meaning; if I have knowledge of meaning and behavior, I can infer intention; and if I have knowledge of meaning and intention, I can predict—to a sufficient extent at least—behavior. But none of this inferential machinery works unless the agents being interpreted are in some sense rational, and thus behave in accordance with their intentions and beliefs. One question this raises is the status of the notion of rationality here: In what sense is it optional? If it is necessary for talk about intention and meaning, is it not necessary *simpliciter*, and thus just an example of synthetic a priori truth? Isn't the argument *a reductio* of Quine's "Two Dogmas" rather than an extension consistent with it? This reasoning is the core of the idealist interpretation of "The Very Idea." Davidson's appeal to a "normative" notion of rationality seems like a straightforward capitulation to the notion of scheme.

The argument is superficially compelling. The idea is that the possible intransitivity of translation would be a refutation of the idea that there were no such things as incommensurable conceptual schemes, and that transitivity of explanation would require that we had, so to speak, all the resources for translating all languages in advance, because only this condition for the possibility would exclude the possibility of finding a language *A* that the speakers of *B* could translate from speakers of C, who could translate into *B*, but could not translate into *A*. The thought behind this is that whatever is needed to translate into *A* already has to be there in *C*. In the usual forms of this argument, this amounts to saying that "we" now must have whatever resources are necessary to translate out of any conceptual scheme. This in turn raises the question of whether speakers of some other language *D* might not have this capacity, specifically whether speakers of the language of a primitive society might be incapable of translating into and thus understanding our language. And since this does not seem to be an empirical question, and Davidson's argument is not at first blush an empirical argument, it must be a question not about what they could do but about what they possibly could do—justifying the Kantianization of the issue.

Davidson has a different and much more limited argument: If the speakers of *C* happen upon speakers of *B* translating *A*, if they could indeed translate *B*, they would, *ex hypothesis*, be able to translate these translations of *A* as well. Why would this follow but not necessarily imply the sufficiency of a single starting point for translation? The point is basic to Davidson's understanding of translation in this text: A translation is not merely a "translation manual" consisting of sentence correspondences. It is instead a combination of correspondences and explanations of the failures of correspondence that occur when something is accounted true in one language and false in another. These explanations take the form of what J. L. Mackie in a different context called "error theories." The example Davidson gives is a paradigmatic error explanation:

> If you see a ketch sailing by and your companion says "Look at that handsome yawl," you may be faced with a problem of interpretation. One natural possibility is that your friend has mistaken a ketch for a yawl, and has formed a false belief. But if his vision is good and his line of sight favourable it is even more plausible that he does

not use the word yawl quite as you do, and has made no mistake about the position of the jigger on the passing yacht.[24]

The hypothesis that he uses the word differently, in this particular behavioral context, requires us to attribute a whole set of correct beliefs (and norms of correspondence, as Davidson puts it) to our companion: that he or she has counted the masts and sails correctly, that he or she can count, that he or she is talking about the same boat, that he or she is not kidding, or testing our knowledge of nautical nomenclature, and so forth. This list could be extended. Davidson's point is that the number of correct beliefs we must attribute when we attribute error to the companion is high. And the more extensive the error, the larger the number of beliefs in the web of belief we must rely on to explain the error. This is why massive error is unintelligible: Making massive error intelligible would require an even more massive pool of correct beliefs to draw on to explain the error.

The significance of the interdependence of meaning and theory is that translations are like theories in that they already involve truth claims about the world, that they depend on the correctness of explanations and of the theories backing explanations of error, and that they are in this respect heir to all of the problems of theoretical explanation not only in the sciences, but in psychology and for that matter the social sciences, where they play a role in backing the explanations of error that translations inevitably involve. This means that they are also characterized by the usual infirmities of such theories: that they are underdetermined by the facts, so that alternative theories may be consistent with the facts; that new data, for example, new behavioral evidence, may require changes in the theories; and so forth. Davidson is explicit about this. The method forced on us of getting a first approximation by attributing to sentences of a speaker the "conditions of truth that actually obtain (in our opinion)" allows for meaningful disagreement. And the disagreements can emerge in a variety of ways: If we are in the position of the companion, we might find ourselves learning a lesson about the differences between ketches and yawls, and thus resolve the disagreement in favor of the hearer. But we might discover that we have a disagreement that present data cannot resolve.

If we cut this reasoning down to the basics, we get something like this: Interpretive charity is required by the economy of error explanations. The term means two things: We need to attribute rationality—in a sense yet to be defined—to the people we interpret, and we need to attribute a minimum of error. Attributing rationality is a precondition for any interpretation involving error, because attribution of error, at least of the kind relevant to Davidson, namely errors in utterances with truth-relevant content, requires an attribution of rationality: An error for Davidson is a rational but wrong response to something, and belief in this erroneous thing can be accounted for by reference to other wrong beliefs that are rationally connected to the wrong response. In constructing error explanations, one soon reaches a vague limit beyond which the error explanations are impossibly complex and insupportable, since each attribution of error requires a larger set of attributions of erroneous background belief—the beliefs that rationally support the error. Charity in interpretation avoids reaching this limit; attributing massive error is attributing something beyond this limit.

The upshot of this for everyday metaphysics can be illustrated by a simple example. Consider the Hindu belief that the world is an illusion. We have no trouble translating the relevant sentences, for the simple reason that the translation manages to preserve all our ordinary beliefs. Everything in an illusion appears just as the real thing would—otherwise it would not be an illusion. My belief that the coffee shop down the street serves espresso survives whether or not the espresso, the street, the shop, and the rest of it are illusions, because there is no difference between real and illusory espresso other than whether it is real. If we translate the terms they refer to the same thing, with the exception that we need to add an illusion operator to each sentence in the translation of the target language. But the addition does nothing beyond connect the sentences to the belief that the world is an illusion. And what goes for illusion goes for the rest of metaphysics—the noumenal world, empirical reality, the phenomenal world, and the rest of it. There are no interesting implications of the problem of massive error for metaphysics, since in these cases there is no massive error. There is only a very economical kind of error, or alternatively a kind of underdetermination, about metaphysical facts. There is a question of whether this holds for the "fact" of normativity itself, and here there is an ambiguity. Taken by itself, it seems that the pattern with normativity mimics the pattern for "the world is an illusion." Nothing much changes whether or not we say, for example, that normativity is a fiction or that it is real. But if normativity in the requisite sense is part of the machinery that allows us to speak in this way in the first place, namely as a condition of interpretation, matters would be different.

It might seem that we ought to get more metaphysical bang out of transitivity, especially the apparent requirement that we somehow have the resources for all possible translation, in advance, so to speak. But this is not the requirement it appears to be. Focusing merely on the problem of the truth theory for a language, and ignoring the role of error, obscures important features of translation, and also obscures the reasons translation does not require us to have all the resources for all possible translations—the resources that would define the conditions for the possibility of translating all languages, in advance. Just as theories in science grow, our theories of error and our powers of translation grow in the course of translating from one language to another. This bears on the problem of transitivity. Davidson need only argue that the augmented power of translation we possess when we adequately translate *B* from *A* enables us to translate *C* from *B*, not that we can translate *C* with the resources of *A*. What his explicit argument excludes is the following case: The speakers of *C* claim that they can understand B perfectly, but not *A* as translated into *B*. This would mean that they couldn't understand the correspondences and the explanations of error. Davidson's point is that this would be evidence that they did not understand *B*. But without the learning and error theorizing we did when we translated, translators starting with *A* might indeed be unable to understand *C*.

This suggests that truncating the discussion of rationality and translation into a discussion of the fixed (and prefixed) "conditions for the possibility" of translation is beside the point. The conditions of translation are of a piece with and depend on our ever-changing knowledge of the world. But saying this raises questions about the nature of rationality for Davidson himself, and about the larger problem of normativity that the normative concept of rationality points to. For Davidson, "the concepts we use to explain and describe thought, speech, and action, are irreducibly normative."[25] What does this mean? Even if we de-Kantianize the problem of conditions for the possibility of translation, it seems, we are forced back into another form of the scheme–content distinction by the assumption of rationality and by the normativity of word–world relations. Or is there another, better, interpretation of these two things?

Davidson's actual comments are tantalizing. He does say that interpretive charity is nonoptional and also sufficient for translation, and he does refer to norms of correspondence, meaning by this something analogous to the correspondence rules of the layer-cake model of scientific theories. He could have said, but does not, that interpretation requires an assumption of rationality and an assumption of certain common human norms of correspondence,[26] and that these are both nonoptional and universal. Instead, he says the following:

> The ineluctable normative element in interpretation has, then, two forms. First, there are the norms of pattern: the norms of deduction, induction, reasoning about how to act, and even about how to feel given other attitudes and beliefs. These are the norms of consistency and coherence. Second, there are the norms of correspondence,

which are concerned with the truth or correctness of particular beliefs and values. This second kind of norm counsels the interpreter to interpret agents he would understand as having, in important respects, beliefs that are mostly true and needs and values the interpreter shares or can imagine himself sharing if he had the history of the agent and were in comparable circumstances.[27]

The norms of correspondence are norms of interpretation, but not in the sense of rules that help decide between interpretations: They are instead a feature of making intelligible interpretations in the first place. The norms of pattern correspond to the notion of rationality. But they are not quite the same as the notion of rationality, and this is where Davidson separates himself from the Kantian interpretation. Or does he? Do they constitute a scheme, or the essential normative core of a scheme? Or do they have a different status? These are the questions on which the argument against the scheme content distinction seems to hang. And they cannot be answered directly.

Davidson might have answered them by also arguing that these two kinds of norms would be sufficient for interpretation or translation universally, that is to say, of all languages, as well as necessary, thus making them into a common scheme of a kind. He might also have said that the consideration of necessity amounts to a transcendental argument that we ourselves must be committed to these necessary elements in a metaphysical sense, that is to say, as part of our own theory of the world, and to derive from this commitment such results as a commitment to the metaphysical necessity of "normative reason" and the like. This, or some variant, is the argument that his idealist interpreters would like to read into him. But he does none of these things, and seems instead to treat the arguments about conceptual schemes as a fully sufficient alternative to these arguments. Moreover, Davidson thinks that his arguments also preclude the appeal to a universal kind of normative reason, or make it unnecessary. And because they are arguments that are assertions about necessity, about the necessity of a univocal account of normative reason construed in a certain way, showing them to be gratuitous amounts to denying them.

How does Davidson's alternative work? He says instead that interpretive charity is required to make sense of others, and that interpretive charity requires something that seems to go beyond and perhaps is different from the assumptions listed above, namely the acknowledgment that most of the beliefs of others are true, which implies that most of our beliefs are also true. But it also seems that there has to be something behind this—the things that make the beliefs true and the judgments of their intentions and utterances rational. And here is the trap that the idealist interpretation relies on.

If we acknowledge the necessary role of "rationality," it seems, we are back to the Kantian picture, with rationality having the status of "scheme." The issue of what is behind understanding turns out to be decisive, and Davidson, I will argue, has an answer to this question that differs from the usual normativist one and also precludes it. But it will take some background to get to this answer and explain its significance.

3 Getting Rid of Concepts: A Brief Excursus

Quine's example of the translation of "Gavagai" as either rabbit or undetached rabbit part, for example, points to a central feature of translation: that the same things can be translated in multiple ways, that these ways have different ontological implications, and that some divergences, at least, are ineliminable. We can correct erroneous translations on the basis of the behavioral evidence, but we cannot eliminate all translations but one. Holism, similarly, implies that adjustments in one part of a translation explanation can be made that have the effect of preserving a given translation hypothesis. Davidson assumes all of this, and it is especially relevant in the case of error, which is not a well-developed Quinean theme, in large part because of Quine's focus on ostensive definition and willingness to give up on "meanings" as ordinarily understood. But the same considerations about the web of belief hold for Davidson. As we have seen, an error explanation is an explanation that necessarily relies on the rest of the web of belief, and if too much of this web is claimed to be erroneous, we have nothing out of which a coherent error account can be constructed.

Why is this important? Why is it anything other than an exercise in hypothetical anthropology of no philosophical interest, which is how P. M. S. Hacker dismisses it?[28] To answer this question and to see the radical character of Davidson's argument, as well as the way in which this paper foreshadows and grounds the later papers, it is important again to see what Davidson and before him Quine did not say, and why they thought that what they did say precluded the kind of philosophy represented by Brandom and McDowell. The story can begin with Quine's systematic substitution of "sentences" for "propositions." Avoiding the language of Gottlob Frege was an attempt to avoid Platonism about concepts—the idea that concepts were out there in some sort of ether of thought, which the mind engaged, or acquired. This language was common in the "analytic" philosophy of the time, and in the specific context of Davidson's paper, the problem of other cultures, much discussed at the time, especially in the philosophy of social science. Peter Winch, in *The Idea of a Social Science*,[29] had operated with a notion of concepts as the mental stuff of society, and had imagined that one could have, and, because actions could only be understood under descriptions containing these concepts, had to have, a social science that began with the analysis of these concepts.

The metaphors that were common to all the standard figures of ordinary language philosophy at the time are telling. Concepts are possessed by people and are therefore shared, object-like things: possessions that one acquires. It was this autonomous existence that enabled them to be subject to a special kind of inquiry, conceptual analysis. The specific character of action was that it was done for reasons, and therefore involved concepts, the concepts possessed by the agents that supplied the relevant stock of descriptions. Behavioral descriptions were not the descriptions of the agents themselves, did not supply reasons for action, and were thus strictly speaking irrelevant to action explanation. This same picture of concepts was the source of conceptual relativism. If concepts were possessions, different people or members of different social groups or people living in different eras had different conceptual "possessions." They would say different and incommensurable things about the world, and these different things would each be true or false under the descriptions allowed by the concepts they possessed. Concepts they didn't possess would be, by definition of the term "possession," inaccessible and unintelligible to them, that is to say, incommensurable, until they came into possession of them. The only apparent solution to this problem of relativism was to insist that somehow people really possessed, at some prelinguistic Ur-level, all the same concepts, despite the surface diversity of actual usages and for that matter beliefs about the world.

Quine did not ignore these considerations of diversity: They are central to the Sapir-Whorf hypothesis, which became the Sapir-Whorf-Quine hypothesis and revealed itself in such slogans as "ontology recapitulates philology." But Quine had already stepped off the "concepts as possessions" path by being "as behaviorist as any sane person could be." And Davidson was on the same path. But Davidson realized that to deal with meaning, rational action, and the like, it was not enough to be behaviorist. So he set about constructing an alternative account that gave as little as possible away to the picture of concepts as possessions that Quine had abandoned in favor of the language of sentences, theories, and holism. This is the motivation for his attempt to restate the slogans of the "concepts as possessions" model in terms of language. When faced with the problem of conceptual incommensurability, that is to say, the condition of possession of mutually unintelligible concepts, he asks what it means in terms of sentences, and concludes that it is no more than, in terms of the evidential base, failure of translation. By moving to the behavioral level, then to sentences, then to the holistic theory-like individual webs of belief of individuals, Quine not only avoided the "concepts as possessions" model and its implications, he precluded it: The evidential base is behavioral, which is more basic than anything the concepts as possessions model operated with, and Quine could account for the diversity that was revealed in the form of this evidence without appealing to this model. The point of this argument was to make the concepts as possessions model superfluous for explanatory purposes. In Quine's exchange with Sellars, this was precisely what was at issue. Sellars wanted to show that even Quine had to accept mathematical concepts, and thus be dragged into the space of reasons, however unwillingly. Quine demurred.[30] When Davidson translates the problem of conceptual relativism into the problem of linguistic relativism, he is following Quine, with the same intent: to avoid the commitments implicit in the term "concepts" and to avoid the possessions model of concepts.

What is the significance of this? Nothing, according to the normativists: The use of "sentence" rather than "proposition" was an eccentricity that doesn't change anything. The same problem, of understanding concepts and their normative force, exists regardless of what one calls these things, because it stands behind our usages, including our usages of sentences. But something does change that is important. "Concept" in the normativists' usual sense is not only a normative concept—though it need not be, as there are plenty of naturalistic accounts of concepts as psychological facts that are not normative[31]—it is a collective one. Concepts, in the possessions model, are out there to be shared by people, to be "possessed" by multiple people. And this is the model of concepts in Brandom, and the model of reason in McDowell as well. Indeed, this is a feature of most notions of scheme—there is nothing private about them. They are jointly held, shared, whether by a group or by all intelligences.

A behaviorist account, in contrast, is not intrinsically committed to collective objects of this sort. They may prove to be explanatory necessities, which is to say that there may be something we want to explain that cannot be explained without appealing to collective objects. But then again there may not. It may be that language itself, understood as a collective object, is a fiction that is not needed to explain anything we want to explain, such as the actual linguistic interaction between two people or between two people and the world. And this is what Davidson does in fact later argue. But this gives us another puzzle. How can anything be normative without also being collective in the requisite sense? McDowell and Brandom are fond of the metaphor of binding and being bound as a way of thinking about the normative. How can we be "bound" by the norms of rationality, for example, unless they are, to use the phrase of Durkheim, "external" and also shared? What is in common between these cases is the same idea: Each involves error and correcting for error in the course of interpretation. Understanding the centrality of this idea is our next concern.

4 Intelligible Error

We often are compelled to translate, as Davidson points out, by treating the translation as a correct translation of a false belief: a case of explicable error. But error is not a behaviorist notion. It is "normative," and perhaps it is the root normative notion. So to say that considerations of error are inseparable from translation is to accept the role of the normative. And, of course, there is more normativity to be found in the conditions for translation or interpretation. Rationality is one of the conditions, and it is a normative notion. So to say that assumptions of rationality are necessary for interpretation seems not only to concede that some scheme-like element is necessary, but to refute Quine's "Two Dogmas" and concede the Kantian point by resuscitating synthetic a priori truth.

Or does it? One way of putting this issue is to separate two distinct aspects of "normativity," the sense of the normative as binding, as external and constraining (the Durkheimian sense) and a different sense, which can be labeled "intelligibility." As long as we are associating these as sociologists—an association that is neither accidental nor irrelevant, since both of them were drawing from neo-Kantianism, in different ways—we can call this second kind "Weberian." Durkheim was concerned with the binding character of obligation as it was experienced differently in different societies. Weber was concerned with subjectively meaningful behavior, and with the problem of making the behavior of other people intelligible, something he, like Davidson, thought necessarily meant "intelligible to us in our own terms." There is a normative issue here—intelligibility is a normative notion. But it is a different kind of normative notion than correctness or rationality in the "binding" sense. Understanding a subjectively intended meaning, to use the translation of Weber's phrase, is, at least on the surface, a normative as distinct from a causal matter.

Davidson's problem, like Weber's, involves the problem of intelligibility, not the problem of supposed binding norms.[32] Explicable error is intelligible error. Translation, which incorporates a hypothesis that accounts for the error and makes it intelligible, extends the limits of intelligibility—extends them as far as they go. His argument is about the limits of intelligibility: There is no language recognizable as such beyond the intelligible. But we do not reach the limits of the intelligible without charitably extending the readily intelligible to incorporate the less readily intelligible, namely that which is not intelligible without a hypothesis about error. And these hypotheses about error necessarily rely on having already made other parts of the web of belief intelligible. As we have seen, this is the basis for the claim that massive error is not intelligible: It is not intelligible because the hypothesis of massive error amounts to denying to the constructor of explicable error accounts the material needed to construct these accounts. To explain the error of a sailor's failed attempt to keep the main from backing, we need to assume that he knows what the main is, has correctly perceived the wind, knows what the tiller is supposed to do, and so on. If we deny this, we open up the explanation of his actions to such hypotheses as these: He is communicating with Martians; he doesn't experience the wind and sea as we do but in some unknown way. And these begin to hit against the limits of the intelligible, because they are explanations of error that are themselves barely intelligible, or unintelligible to us, at least at present. The use of anthropological examples is highly relevant to the problem of the limits of intelligibility. And by considering the problem of understanding other cultures, we can see the deep differences between Davidson and the concepts as possessions model more clearly.

Anthropologists face a problem which grew into the problem that in the philosophy of social science was part of the context of "The Very Idea." The problem was identification: We try a translation of the utterance of a member of a primitive society, and get something like this: "My blood is boiling." We are faced with the following kinds of alternatives: The members of the society actually believe that their blood is boiling; we just don't understand the utterance, meaning we have gotten the translation wrong in a way that can't be corrected, which would also mean that our translation of "blood" and "boiling" in other contexts, and therefore our translation project as a whole, is called into question; the utterance is false but metaphorical; the members of the society have a set of beliefs about blood and boiling that make it possible for them to erroneously believe that their blood could in fact be boiling. In the case of the last two explanations, there is also a significant amount of variation in possible hypotheses consistent with the facts. Metaphors can be interpreted in multiple ways, and the background belief structures about blood and boiling might also be constructed in various ways.

This seems like a methodological or epistemic problem—a real problem for anthropologists, perhaps, but not for anyone else, and in any case it is unilluminated by the considerations of hypothetical anthropology Davidson adduces, which don't tell us which to accept. But if we keep the contrast to the concepts as possessions picture in mind, we can see that there is more at stake here. The concepts as possessions picture had an answer to this problem: that concepts are the sorts of things we could ourselves come to possess or grasp, and then analyze. The problem of understanding a primitive society was thus one of grasping their concepts. Not only Kantianism but the problem of rule-following inherited from Wittgenstein lies behind this imagery, and both of these were assimilated in the form of an argument that possessing a concept consisted in grasping a rule. But as a solution to the identification problem, the grasp and possession model was a fiasco. Grasping was a primal act that operated on mysterious entities. There were no grounds for saying one was correctly grasping or not—correctness itself, knowing what accorded with the rule, presupposed grasping the rule. There is also a problem about evidence. For grasping, evidence is not so much irrelevant as insufficient. In particular, there is a mystery about the normative force of the concept or rule—if possession was no more than conformity with some set of behavioral patterns, what would be the source of its normative force? Is it some sort of mysterious added element?

Davidson's approach avoids these questions, by starting from a different point. The problem of identifying beliefs, of finding out what is believed and who believes it, in the famous formulation of Marcel Mauss, is a hypothesis-testing epistemic process, in which we employ what we know about ourselves and our beliefs to construct accounts of others' beliefs until our accounts begin to more or less match their behavior. Behavioral evidence is all we have, and all we want to explain, though we may employ nonbehavioral terms, such as "belief" itself, in order to do the explaining. Error is intrinsic to the process of hypothesis testing, in the sense that we can get the attribution of belief wrong, in which case we can't predict what others will do or say in a way that accords with the attribution of belief we hypothesize. But there is more to it than just predicting. We also want to make sense of the beliefs as beliefs—to make them intelligible. To put the point in a way that will help later: We want to be able to follow others, to follow their reasoning. But this is inseparable from attributing beliefs in the first place, so it is normally not an issue. The point, however, is important: If we can't reason with others, we can't attribute belief.

Where does the possession model of concepts and the problem of rules fit in with this? In terms of interpreting other cultures, these things cannot come first. We cannot first grasp others' concepts and then come to understand their utterances. Yet the possession model has a strong bias toward this kind of formulation: If we are using a concept, it is because we have grasped the rule behind it, or the concept. Our grasp is presupposed, and it is a necessary condition for "really" using it. This is the point of the celebrated arguments about the regress problem made in the first chapter of Brandom's *Making It Explicit.* Really using it, for Brandom, amounts to being able to give justificatory reasons about its use. The chain of justifications has to end somewhere. Because justification is normative, it has to end in something normative. For Brandom it ends in the normativity of language, which is in turn made normative by our "commitments" to the score-keeping system that allows for the social regulation of error.

Davidson has none of this machinery. Why? The answer is closely related to the reason he also lacks the Brandom-McDowell imagery of constraint. For Davidson, not only does the problem of intelligibility come first and get solved by the hypothesis-testing process of translation, it ends there. The claim that the rule-following, concept-possessing model deals with something more fundamental, which is common to many of these interpretations and dismissals of Davidson, depends on showing that they are "necessary" in the first place. They are not, for Davidson. To deal with the behavioral evidence is not only enough, it is all there is. The whole machinery of the concepts as possessions model is not so much beside the point in relation to this evidence, since it is after all an attempt to account for it, as it is unnecessary for accounting for it. The accounting is done once the beliefs have been identified. There is no higher form of knowledge about these beliefs that results from "grasping" the concepts or having a normative commitment to them and the like. The only knowledge we have is this hypothesis-testing knowledge.

5 Where Is the Normative?

For alien cultures, the normativist is inclined to say, this makes sense. We cannot penetrate their inner life, their normative commitments, their space of reasons. We can only make up hypotheses, provide error accounts, and the like. But for our own culture, we are in a different situation. Our statements about other cultures may be behavioral and explanatory. For ourselves, as Joseph Rouse argues, they are "expressivist." The reasons are our reasons; the normative commitments are ours; we have privileged access to them. Davidson is having none of this, either. One of the most visible consequences of the argument of "The Very Idea" is that the supposed distinction between cultures, that is, between our concepts, our rationality, and theirs, is eliminated. The difference is language, which is treated in a demystified way rather than as a mysterious order of shared presuppositions. But any other explanation of "their" beliefs is in terms—error—that equally apply to the people in our own culture using our own language. So there is no "ours" to go with the "theirs." There is no collective fact of shared concept possession behind their beliefs, because there is no fact of concept possession in the Kantian sense in Davidson in the first place.

The full implications of this reasoning are drawn out in Davidson's "A Nice Derangement of Epitaphs," which extends the use of the notion of error to ordinary linguistic interaction. When we deal with other people, we are constantly doing precisely what the anthropologist is doing: We are interpreting their behavior, revising our interpretations in light of our attempts to make sense of it, and attributing beliefs to them, attributions that often include error hypotheses. We could not function as language users or human beings without doing this. Making intelligible is a continuous process. Making inferences about what someone intends to mean, whether he or she is sincere, ironic, speaking metaphorically, or erroneously, is ubiquitous and a part of every human interaction. Moreover, this process is logically fundamental and perhaps ontogenetically fundamental: logically, because for the possession model to make sense, there is a two-stage process in which the interpreter of language learner first needs to identify something that is later fully grasped. In McDowell, for example, it is not until the traditional age of reason that the well-brought-up child grasps the normativity of reason.[33]

Learning, including language learning, is an embarrassment to the possession model. For Brandom, embracing the interdependence of inferences about rationality together with the idea of meanings as rooted in normative practices of justification underwritten by "commitment" forces him into the odd position of arguing that the prelinguistic individual does not have genuine intentions, which in turn raises the question of how he or she could have genuine commitments. Davidson avoids this problem by avoiding the possession model. Does he fall into it in another form?

For the normativist, the answer is "yes." Davidson is a fellow traveler who also acknowledges the necessary role of the normative. He simply locates the normative elsewhere. But the difference is one of emphasis only: Davidson stresses one part of the triangle, the part that involves the assessment of the rationality of the intention behind utterances, which tells us whether the speaker intended to speak truly and descriptively, which enables us to infer meaning. Meaning itself, they would say, is accounted for by the normativity of the system of linguistic practices, and rationality is accounted for by the recognition of the binding character of the universal norms of rationality, a recognition that eventually comes to every well-brought-up person, regardless of his or her culture. Other normativists, in short, are filling in gaps that Davidson, by such usages as "norms of correspondence," acknowledges.

But why should Davidson accept any of this? Consider the demands and complexity of Brandom's account in *Making It Explicit*. Meanings are not something in the interactional flux, but are rooted in a complex and massive tacit system of normative score-keeping practices that we have access to in filling in the enthymemes or missing premises of ordinary speech, especially in the context of justification. We and our peers in our linguistic community are committed to this system personally and in the collective voice, as with Sellars's notion of collective intentionality. This commitment, necessarily, is a kind of blank check written by our prelinguistic and thus preintentional selves. We commit to a system in which individuals participate in a way not dissimilar to participation in Platonic Forms, that is to say, partially, since none of us has within ourselves all the meanings or inferences that are part of the concepts that make up the system. The point of Brandom's famous regression argument is to establish this: Justification has to end someplace, but the place it ends has to be normative, and thus behind each rule is a normative end point that is a commitment to a system of this sort.

For Davidson, this whole machinery of a fixed set of normative practices revealed in the enthymemes of ordinary justificatory usage is simply unnecessary. We have no privileged access to meanings which we can then expressivistically articulate, because there is nothing like this—no massive structure of normative practices—to access. Instead, we try to follow our fellow beings and their reasoning and acting, including their speaking: We make them intelligible. And we have a tool other than the normal machinery of predictive science that makes this possible: our own rationality. Rationality is normative, but not in the sense of McDowell. It is not the rationality of constraint. Our only constraint is the limit of our capacity to make intelligible. There is no gap between what we can recognize as intentional and meaningful, and what we can make intelligible—that is to say, what we can follow, which includes intelligible error. Justification has no special status of the kind accorded it by Brandom. It is just another piece of behavior: The child learns that saying "why, Mommy, why?" gets a reaction. Eventually they come to follow the answers, to make them intelligible to themselves, and to provide them when elicited, but nothing about this activity of giving answers and asking questions gets beyond the behavioral facts, except for the matter of following or making intelligible.

For the normativists, this reply makes a fatal error: It falls back into a variant of the position they themselves hold, namely that normative rationality is "necessary." The fact that Davidson locates the relevant kind of normativity elsewhere, namely in the interpreting agent, is to fall back into the synthetic a priori, which has to be the source of these normative constraints. But it is worse than their own accounts, because it is mysterious, groundless, and arbitrary—the sort of thing that Quine correctly objected to. Moreover, they would say, Davidson leaves us with no account of the normativity of that which is generally recognized as normative, such as rule-following, 2 + 2 = 4, and so forth.

What does Davidson say about this mare's nest of issues? He says something about rationality and its normative character, but not what the normativist wants to hear. For the normativist, rationality is itself a possession, an acquisition like a concept but more fundamental, more universal. Intelligibility depends on something else: the abilities we have to follow the thinking of others. The child's game of "step on a crack, break your mother's back" is intelligible—intelligible error, perhaps, but also represents a form of reasoning that we share with primitive people and indeed all peoples. And it would be hard to construct a "theory" of this kind of inference that would make it rational.

But it is also hard to construct empirical theories of human reasoning: of what "empirical" rationality, meaning how we actually infer, rather than what normative rationality actually is. Worse, there is an odd dependence of empirical theorizing on normative theories of rationality, normative theories that are false as empirical theories. This was among the lessons he learned from the experimental study of decision making in which he participated in the 1950s. Decision theory, which is usually called a normative theory in this literature, is false as an empirical theory of rationality. People do not make decisions in the way that normative decision theory defines as rational. But "normative" decision theory is indispensable in at least this sense: To study actual decision making it is needed as a starting point. Biases, errors, and the like are biases and errors in comparison to it. And there seems to be no option here. Without notions like bias we don't have a language for describing actual decision making. There is no "empirical theory" of decision making that is an alternative to the normative account, but only one that depends on the "normative" theory in this odd way.

The normativist would argue that this is a case of a priori truth. Normativists read "indispensable" as "necessary," and "necessary" in the manner of "synthetic a priori truth." But this case doesn't fit the pattern. Empirically, it is not truth at all. But it seems to fit with other cases in which the "theory" is so deeply ingrained in our construction of empirical accounts that we can neither find an alternative to it nor dispense with it. Davidson suggests measurement theory as an example of this: It too is a case of empirical theory as classically understood, but as an empirical theory it is also literally false. The oddity has been remarked on in the literature on testing the theory of relativity: Measurements were made in accordance with the terms of the theory that relativity was to displace, rather than in relativistic terms.[34] What confirmed the theory were the errors that appeared using the old measurement theory. But this did not displace the old measurement theory, which was as Newtonian as ever.

In the case of rationality, there is an analogous problem. The fact that the theories we have of rationality are false as empirical theories of human decision making gives us no reason to discard them as normative theory, or to stop treating them as indispensable for our various theoretical and even practical purposes. But this indispensability does not confer on them any sort of metaphysical status, much less warrant any sort of claim about the metaphysical necessity of the normative as some sort of special ideal realm equivalent and coexistent with the empirically real. And indeed, rationality has properties in relation to the task of making intelligible that point in a different direction entirely.

The different direction is to acknowledge the actual diversity of the relevant kind of rationality. The rationality needed is "rudimentary"[35] and the notion of reasonable belief "flexible"[36]—very flexible. Davidson indicates how flexible in the following:

> The issue is not whether we all agree on exactly what the norms of rationality are; the point is rather that we all have such norms and we cannot recognize as thought phenomena that are too far out of line. Better say: what is too far out of line is not thought. It is only when we can see a creature (or "object") as largely rational by our own lights that we can intelligibly ascribe thoughts to it at all, or explain its behavior by reference to its ends and convictions.[37]

The contraposition of this shows how flexible the notion of rationality is for Davidson. If we can recognize something as thought, it is "rational" in the relevant sense. Recognizing something as rational is a matter of being able to follow someone's thought—to simulate their thinking well enough that what they say or do that is different from what we would say or do can be either allowed for as "normal enough" or explained as error and thus made intelligible. The normative element is not rigidly fixed, unarguable, or even free from conflict, such as conflicts which arise when there are inferences that we can follow which lead to conclusions that conflict with what we believe. This is not the kind of rationality that provides the kind of constraint and ultimate justificatory ground that is the concern of Brandom or McDowell. The only constraints are interpersonal: We are constrained in our understanding by the limits of what we can follow, constrained in communicating by the limits of what others can follow, and constrained in what counts as thought by the requirement that for something to be recognized as thought, it must be the kind of thing the recognizer can follow.

What I am calling "following" is an act of imagination.[38] This is something different from "possession of a concept." The substance is frankly psychological rather than normative in the sense of Brandom, McDowell, or the rule-following literature. It is perhaps best understood in terms of the idea of simulation in cognitive science. And it is this idea that suffices to account for our capacity to make sense of others, for intelligibility as distinct from beliefs about rightness. This is what the rule-following literature stumbles over: It cannot distinguish "possession" from "following" another person's thinking. Partly this is a matter of the diet of examples: Following the idea of "addition of two" and possession, if there is such a thing, are the same; translating and possessing seem different. Davidson could simply make the point that following is basic to, and sufficient, for both. Our capacity for learning the rule of adding two is our capacity for following the teacher, and there is no additional mystery. We do not need an additional concept of possession to account for the behavioral facts. Nor do we need some notion of the intrinsic normativity of a rule, a notion of commitment, or any reference to community. The concept is "social," but only in the interactional sense of social: We are following someone else and getting feedback from our interactions that reassure us that we are following them sufficiently to say we understand them. Simulation is also not a causal idea—so it is "normative" in a specific sense unlike the Brandom or McDowell sense, not something external and constraining, but a sense linked to the agent's own capacities. These capacities are, dare I say, naturalizable, not in the sense of the reduction of intelligibility to cause, or the elimination of intelligibility, but "disenchanted": a capacity that goes with beings with brains with particular kinds of neurons, rather than souls participating in the Forms.

Notes

1. Donald Davidson, "On the Very Idea of a Conceptual Scheme," in his *Inquiries into Truth and Interpretation* (Oxford: Clarendon, 1984 [1973–1974]), pp. 183–198.

2. Bryan Wilson (ed.), *Rationality* (Oxford: Blackwell, 1977 [1970]).

3. Martin Hollis, "The Limits of Irrationality," in Wilson (ed.), *Rationality*, pp. 214–220; Alasdair MacIntyre, "Is Understanding Religion Compatible with Believing?" in Wilson (ed.), *Rationality*, pp. 62–77; Alasdair MacIntyre, "The Idea of a Social Science," in Wilson (ed.), *Rationality*, pp. 112–130; Peter Winch, "Understanding a Primitive Society," in Wilson (ed.), *Rationality*, pp. 78–111.

4. Thomas Kuhn, *The Structure of Scientific Revolutions* (Chicago: University of Chicago Press, 1996 [1962]).

5. W. V. O. Quine, "Two Dogmas of Empiricism" ("Main Trends in Recent Philosophy: Two Dogmas of Empiricism"), *Philosophical Review* 60 (1951): 20–43.

6. Donald Davidson, "A Nice Derangement of Epitaphs," in *Truth and Interpretation: Perspectives on the Philosophy of Donald Davidson*, ed. Ernest Lepore (Cambridge: Blackwell, 1986), pp. 433–446.

7. Davidson, "On the Very Idea of a Conceptual Scheme," p. 198.

8. Susan L. Hurley, "Intelligibility, Imperialism, and Conceptual Scheme," in *Midwest Studies in Philosophy* 17, ed. P. French et al. (Notre Dame: University of Notre Dame Press, 1992), pp. 99–101; Thomas Nagel, "Thought and Reality," in his *The View from Nowhere* (New York: Oxford University Press, 1986), pp. 92–97; Hurley, "Intelligibility, Imperialism, and Conceptual Scheme," p. 108n23.

9. Hurley, "Intelligibility, Imperialism, and Conceptual Scheme," pp. 89–108.

10. Tim Thornton, *John McDowell* (Chesham, Bucks: Acumen Publishing, 2004), p. 58.

11. Davidson, "On the Very Idea of a Conceptual Scheme," in *Inquiries into Truth and Interpretation*, p. 198; cf. Ian Hacking, "Language, Truth, and Reason," in *Rationality and Relativism*, ed. Martin Hollis and Steven Lukes (Cambridge, MA: MIT Press, 1982), p. 61.

12. John McDowell, *Mind, Value, and Reality* (Cambridge, MA: Harvard University Press, 1998), p. 309.

13. Wilfrid Sellars, "Imperatives, Intentions, and the Logic of 'Ought,'" in *Morality and the Language of Content*, ed. Hector-Neri Castañeda and George Nakhnikian (Detroit: Wayne State University Press, 1963), pp. 159–218.

14. John Haugeland, *Having Thought: Essays in the Metaphysics of Mind* (Cambridge, MA: Harvard University Press, 1998).

15. Robert Brandom, *Making It Explicit: Reasoning, Representing, and Discursive Content* (Cambridge, MA: Harvard University Press, 1994).

16. John McDowell, *Mind and World* (Cambridge, MA: Harvard University Press, 1994).

17. Davidson, "On the Very Idea of a Conceptual Scheme," p. 184.

18. Ibid., p. 186.

19. Ibid., p. 185.

20. Ibid., p. 187.

21. Ibid., p. 189.

22. Martin Hollis, "The Limits of Rationality," in Wilson (ed.), *Rationality*, pp. 214–220.

23. Paul Feyerabend, "Explanation, Reduction, and Empiricism," in *Minnesota Studies in the Philosophy of Science* 3, ed. Herbert Feigl and Grover Maxwell (Minneapolis: University of Minnesota Press, 1962), pp. 28–97, especially pp. 74–95.

24. Davidson, "On the Very Idea of a Conceptual Scheme," p. 196.

25. Donald Davidson, "Reply to Pascal Engel," in *The Philosophy of Donald Davidson*, The Library of Living Philosophers vol. 27, ed. Lewis Hahn (Chicago: Open Court Press, 1999), p. 460.

26. Donald Davidson, "A New Basis for Decision Theory," *Theory and Decision* 18 (1985): 87–98.

27. Ibid., p. 92.

28. P. M. S. Hacker, "On Davidson's Idea of a Conceptual Scheme," *Philosophical Quarterly* 46 (1996): 289–307.

29. Peter Winch, *The Idea of a Social Science and Its Relation to Philosophy* (London: Routledge & Kegan Paul, 1958).

30. W. V. O. Quine, "Sellars on Behaviorism, Language, and Meaning," *Philosophical Quarterly* 61, no. 1–2 (1980): 26–30; Wilfrid Sellars, "Behaviorism, Language, and Meaning," *Philosophical Quarterly* 61, nos. 1–2 (1980): 3–25.

31. See, e.g., Vittorio Gallese and George Lakoff, "The Brain's Concepts: The Role of the Sensory-motor System in Conceptual Knowledge," *Cognitive Neuropsychology* 22, nos. 3–4 (2005): 455–479; Stephen Stich, "What Is a Theory of Mental Representation?," *Mind* 101: 402 (1992): 243–261.

32. Cf. Hurley, "Intelligibility, Imperialism, and Conceptual Scheme," pp. 89–108.

33. See McDowell, *Mind and World*.

34. Ronald Laymon, "The Michelson-Morley Experiment and the Appraisal of Theories," in *Scrutinizing Science: Empirical Studies of Scientific Change*, ed. Arthur Donovan et al. (Dordrecht:: Kluwer Academic Publishers, 1988), pp. 245–266.

35. Donald Davidson, "A New Basis for Decision Theory," *Theory and Decision*, 18 (1985): 87–98.

36. Donald Davidson, "The Social Aspect of Language," in his *Truth, Language, and History* (Oxford: Oxford University Press, 2005), p. 121.

37. Donald Davidson, "Representation and Interpretation," in his *Problems of Rationality* (Oxford: Clarendon Press, 2004), pp. 97–98.

38. Davidson, "A New Basis for Decision Theory," p. 92.

19 Davidson and the Source of Self-Knowledge

Louise Röska-Hardy

What I know about the contents of my own mind I generally know without appeal to evidence or investigation. There are exceptions, but the primacy of unmediated self-knowledge is attested by the fact that we distrust the exceptions until they can be reconciled with the unmediated.[1]

Normally, we know what we are thinking, and, if asked, we can inform others about the contents of our thoughts. Our pronouncements on our occurrent mental states are taken in the first instance to be true; usually, no supplementary evidence is expected or required. Even though error and correction by others are possible, this fact does not diminish our claim to know what we are currently thinking. With respect to pronouncements about our current thoughts we enjoy a special authority that does not accrue to our claims concerning the rest of the world or others' thoughts. In general, we take speakers' statements about their current thoughts, intentions and sensations to express a kind of knowledge, which may be termed "psychological self-knowledge." However, such knowledge seems quite unlike other kinds of knowledge. In contrast to our knowledge of the rest of the world or our knowledge of others' mental states, we usually know the contents of our current mental states without recourse to observation or inference from evidence. From an everyday standpoint, such self-knowledge appears ubiquitous and extensive. However, from a philosophical standpoint, it is quite extraordinary and its explanation poses considerable challenges, raising fundamental issues in epistemology, the philosophy of mind, and the philosophy of language.

Donald Davidson discusses the phenomenon of self-knowledge, construed as knowledge of one's particular mental states, and its puzzling features in a number of essays and accords self-knowledge of one's own thoughts an increasingly central place in his philosophy.[2] In these essays, Davidson sets out the explanatory problem posed by everyday knowledge of one's thoughts and identifies several distinctive features that any adequate philosophical account of self-knowledge of one's thoughts must explain. Davidson situates his own account of the source and special features of "psychological" self-knowledge within the larger context of his philosophical project, in which he integrates approaches in the philosophy of language, the philosophy of mind, and action theory to develop an account of objectivity and the necessary conditions of thought. The account of self-knowledge of thought he offers contrasts with more widely held special epistemic access approaches and nonepistemic explanations of self-knowledge of one's particular mental states. The Davidsonian approach to such self-knowledge and his explanation of its attendant features has occasioned perplexity, failing, as it does, to invoke a special epistemic method or mechanism on the one hand, while claiming that knowledge of the contents of one's present thought is cognitively substantial, that is, true or false, on the other.

Davidson's critics have objected that his account fails to capture the distinctive epistemological status of self-knowledge and have argued that the account cannot explain the source of the peculiar features associated with knowledge of the contents of one's particular mental states. I shall argue to the contrary that on the assumption that knowledge is propositionally structured, Davidson's account (section 1) does have the resources to account for the distinctive features of self-knowledge of certain of one's thoughts. The key lies in appreciating how Davidson's views on the linguistic self-ascription of occurrent thoughts in utterance acts (section 2), and the externalist constitution of meaning and content (section 3) combine with his account of language acquisition and use in contexts of triangulation to explain the distinctive features of self-knowledge without invoking special forms of epistemic access or construing self-knowledge as cognitively insubstantial (section 4).

The primary aim of this essay is expository. However, once we take into consideration Davidson's observations on acquiring the lexicon of one's first language in contexts of interpersonal triangulation, the Davidsonian approach to self-knowledge of one's occurrent thoughts has much to recommend it.

1 Accounting for Self-Knowledge of One's Thoughts

Traditional philosophical approaches explain self-knowledge of occurrent thoughts and its special features by means of dualist theses in ontology and epistemology. On these views, a subject enjoys a unique form of direct cognitive access to her own mental states that issues in an especially secure kind of knowledge. Positions that espouse ontological dualism trace the special access and the unusual features of self-knowledge to the nature of the mind, for example, construed as an entity or substance that differs essentially from material entities or as an autonomous realm vis à vis the material world. Although few contemporary philosophers espouse ontological dualism, many subscribe to explanations of self-knowledge that presuppose epistemological dualism. These approaches ground self-knowledge in a unique way of knowing one's own mental states. They posit a form of direct epistemic access to mental contents, for example, introspection, inner sense, higher-order perception, internal monitoring or tracking mechanisms, and contend that this mode of access yields knowledge of a greater degree of certainty. The special features of self-knowledge are attributed to the subject's epistemically privileged mode of access and to the nature of the accessed states. On the epistemological dualist view, self-knowledge is knowledge of subjective, "inner" objects or mental representations, to which subjects have unmediated access. These objects—ideas, impressions, sense data, appearances, subpersonal mental states, or objects of perception—are constituted by how things seem to the subject. Thus, the subject cannot generally err, because there is no distinction between appearance and the reality that appears; they are one and the same.

Davidson rejects all philosophical accounts of self-knowledge that rest on ontological and/or epistemological dualism. As the author of anomalous monism, he denies that minds are entities of any kind. In his view, the mental is a conceptual, not an ontological category.[3] He argues against construing the mind as a subjective realm with private states, epistemic intermediaries, or propositional objects.[4] Correlatively, he denies that self-knowledge is epistemically grounded in special methods of access to objects of thought or internal mechanisms, as many influential epistemic accounts claim. Nonetheless, Davidson maintains that we do have direct, unmediated knowledge of our own minds. He takes it as a fact that there is a basic difference in how a person usually knows what she thinks and how others know this when they do. To wit, knowledge of one's own beliefs, desires, hopes, or intentions is not generally based on evidence or observation, whereas knowledge of other's states of mind always is. In Davidson's view, explaining why our other-ascriptions of thoughts rest on evidence and inference whereas our self-ascriptions generally do not is a central task of a satisfactory account of self-knowledge of one's thoughts. However, he maintains that positing epistemically privileged ways of knowing the contents of one's own mind or a direct grasp of "objects of thought" like sense data or propositions does not provide such an account.[5]

Davidson's rejection of ontological and epistemological dualist accounts of self-knowledge might be taken to imply that he regards knowledge of one's particular mental states as "groundless." For example, he might attribute the special features of self-knowledge to a linguistic convention, as Richard Rorty suggests, or he might consider them constitutive of our language game of everyday psychological ascription, as Crispin Wright proposes.[6] However, these two proposals have the untoward consequence that self-knowledge of thoughts is knowledge only in a Pickwickean sense; it is not "cognitively substantial," to use Wright's term. Self-knowledge, thus construed, is not assessable as objectively true or false. Indeed, it stands in no relation to any facts about the individual knower. Davidson explicitly criticizes the nonepistemic, linguistic approaches of Ludwig Wittgenstein, P. F. Strawson, and Sydney Shoemaker for merely describing the distinctive features of self-knowledge of one's thoughts, rather than explaining them.[7] What explanation does he offer?

In contrast to these nonepistemic views, Davidson claims that we do have knowledge of the contents of our own minds that is based neither on inference nor evidence and he construes this knowledge as an epistemic phenomenon. He regards self-knowledge of one's thoughts as one of three varieties of empirical knowledge, along with knowledge of the world external to oneself and knowledge of other minds.[8] Although self-knowledge is distinguished from the latter two by a unique kind of authority and by its noninferential and nonobservational character, Davidson claims that it resembles them in being objective. Like these, its truth or falsity is independent of what we may believe to be true and it can for the most part be expressed by concepts that have a place in intersubjective communication.[9] In Davidson's view, self-knowledge of one's thought contents is a variety of contingent, propositional knowledge that exhibits semantic and logical continuities with knowledge about the rest of the world and with knowledge of others' minds. Thus, despite its special features, he regards it as cognitively substantial, for we can be in error and be corrected by others. At the same time, Davidson asserts that "knowledge of the contents of my own mind is special. . . . Such knowledge is basic in the sense that without it I would know nothing . . . , and special in that it is irreducibly different from other sorts of knowledge."[10] In view of Davidson's rejection of dualist epistemic approaches that posit forms of privileged epistemic access, on the one hand, and of nonepistemic approaches that offer conventional "courtesy" or "artefact of grammar" explanations, on the other, one wants to know how Davidson accounts for self-knowledge concerning the beliefs, desires, and the other states of mind that we commonly take ourselves to have. What is the source of self-knowledge—knowledge of the contents of one's thoughts—and its distinctive features, on the Davidsonian account?

Davidson locates the source of self-knowledge of one's thoughts in a necessary feature of the interpretation of speech, which he explicates in terms of radical interpretation and his externalist conception of meaning and content.[11] In his view, self-knowledge and its distinctive features are to be explained with reference to the way we understand what we and others say.[12] Crucially, he argues that understanding other speakers' utterances involves radical interpretation regardless of whether the speaker speaks one's mother tongue, an unknown language, or is learning a first language.[13] In radical interpretation, an interpreter must rely on observable linguistic and nonlinguistic behavior in contexts of use in order to simultaneously assign meaning to the speaker's sentences and content to the speaker's beliefs. The central claim is that someone who expresses what she is thinking with a contemporaneous utterance does not have to radically interpret the sentence she employs in order to know what she means or believes, whereas others must always engage in the difficult inference of radical interpretation in order to know what a speaker means or believes. They must observe the causal interaction between the speaker and the world in order to develop hypotheses about what the speaker's utterances mean and about her beliefs as part of a systematic theory of the speaker's language. Moreover, would-be interpreters must assume that the speaker's utterances are meaningful. Otherwise, there would be nothing to interpret.

In contrast, a speaker cannot confront her own sentences and beliefs with objects and events in the world in order to determine their truth conditions, that is, to radically interpret them. This is because whatever the speaker regularly applies her words to gives her words the meaning they have and her thoughts the content that they have, for it is this use that determines their truth-conditions.[14] What is more, the speaker's intentional production of an utterance act using specific linguistic means requires that she know what she means by her words. In consequence, Davidson claims that there is a presumption that, in sincere self-ascriptions concerning the contents of present states of mind, a speaker identifies her thoughts correctly when she expresses an occurrent thought by uttering a sentence of her own language. He takes this point to be a necessary condition of radical interpretation and thus a formal requirement of being able to attribute meaningful utterances to a speaker on the grounds that we must depend on accepting a speaker's actual linguistic behavior as the basis for interpreting her words.[15] Without the presumption that the speaker knows what she means in uttering her sentences, that is, is getting her own language right, there would be nothing for an interpreter to interpret. There would be no linguistic act of utterance, no proper intention in utterance, nor would there be any links to other utterances and attitudes or to objects and events in the world.[16] Thus, Davidson's explanation of self-knowledge of one's present thoughts rests on the claim that the method of radical interpretation has no application when someone contemporaneously self-ascribes an occurrent thought with her own sentence.

Davidson's account has met with numerous objections. The focus on linguistic utterances and on self-ascribing linguistic beings has been criticized.[17] It has been charged that Davidson's approach reduces the epistemic authority of self-knowledge to the semantic authority we have as speakers of our own language.[18] Some authors have objected that Davidson only develops the account for the propositional attitudes and for belief, in particular, leaving sensations and perceptions to one side.[19] Others have claimed that externalist theories of linguistic meaning and thought content cannot accommodate self-knowledge of one's thoughts, arguing that Davidson's externalist conception of meaning and content is incompatible with the claim that we have knowledge of our own thoughts.[20] Finally, several critics have argued that the third-person methodology of radical interpretation cannot capture the first-person character of self-knowledge.[21] Davidson has addressed these criticisms in numerous places. However, the Davidsonian account of knowledge of the contents of one's thoughts, depending as it does on central tenets of his integrated philosophical approach, has been insufficiently appreciated. In particular, many have failed to appreciate how Davidson's views on language and communication, the requirements for linguistic acts, and the externalist constitution of meaning and content differ from widely held conceptions of language, linguistic action, and mental content.

2 Self-Knowledge of One's Thoughts and Self-Ascriptions

In everyday circumstances, we take utterances of certain sentences to express speakers' knowledge of the contents of their own particular mental states. When someone says, 'Albert will take the job', we take the utterance of the sentence as evidence that the speaker has the particular belief. Moreover, we regard such an indicative utterance on the part of a speaker as equivalent to an utterance of 'I believe that Albert will take the job', because in uttering a token of 'Albert will take the job' the speaker endorses the sentence's content.[22] Generally, we assume that people know what they are currently thinking and that this knowledge is often expressed in what they say. Although we allow that error is possible, this possibility does not affect the presumption that linguistically competent speakers correctly express their contemporaneous thoughts whenever they intend to do so. These everyday considerations suggest that the linguistic utterances we produce in expressing and ascribing thoughts to ourselves provide a point of departure for investigating self-knowledge of one's thoughts and its special features. Davidson concurs. He claims that speakers' sincere self-ascriptions of occurrent thoughts, when they are true, express knowledge of the contents of their mental states, and he proposes to analyze this self-knowledge with respect to certain linguistic utterances.

The utterances in question are sincere, present-tense assertions in the grammatical first person, which exhibit a psychological predicate, for example, 'I believe that Albert will take the job'. Let us call the utterances that speakers employ to attribute propositional attitudes to themselves *self-ascriptions*. Self-ascriptions of thoughts are utterance acts on the part of speakers that employ what Davidson terms *psychological sentences*, that is, sentences that contain verbs of propositional attitude. As utterance acts, self-ascriptions like 'I believe that Albert will take the job' are systematically related to utterances like 'Albert will take the job', which we also take to express speakers' beliefs. Concerning the difference between saying assertively, for example, 'Albert will take the job', and saying assertively 'I believe that Albert will take the job', Davidson remarks: "The truth conditions of the assertions are not the same, but anyone who understands the first assertion knows the truth conditions of the second. . . . This is because anyone who understands speech can recognize assertions, and knows that someone who makes an assertion represents himself as believing what he says."[23]

The emphasis on utterances may appear to be a mere terminological matter. However, it is actually the decisive first step in Davidson's account of self-knowledge of one's thoughts. This move makes linguistic utterance acts and the relations between agents and utterances the focus of the analysis. Adopting this starting point has the consequence that the features of self-knowledge are to be explicated with respect to features of the linguistic actions that speakers produce in expressing and self-ascribing their thoughts.

In Davidson's opinion, those utterances we take to express self-knowledge of one's mental states pose an explanatory problem because of four distinctive features—first-person authority, a presumption of truth, an epistemic asymmetry, and a presumed univocity of everyday psychological predicates.[24] First, he notes that we treat sincere self-ascriptions of contemporaneous thoughts in the grammatical first-person singular present tense as authoritative, even though they are not generally based on observation or inference from other beliefs. Although such self-ascriptions are neither incorrigible nor infallible, he emphasizes that they are accorded an authority that our ascriptions of thoughts to others and our self-ascriptions in other tenses lack. In general, there is a presumption that when someone ascribes a present thought to herself, she has the thought she self-ascribes despite the possibility of error. Usually, the serious and sincere assertion that one has a particular thought justifies the assumption that one has that thought. Even when a self-ascription is challenged, the self-ascriber's pronouncements still carry special weight, as Davidson notes. In other words, we grant self-ascriptions of occurrent thoughts a special epistemological status. When they are true, they count as knowledge, even though they are not ascribed on the basis of evidence or inference.

Second, for Davidson first-person authority is intimately tied to the presumption that self-ascriptions of contemporaneous thoughts are true.[25] As he points out, we take self-ascriptions of occurrent thoughts to be true without demanding or expecting supplementary evidence, that is, we generally take people at their word where the contents of their current thoughts are concerned. Although mistaken self-ascriptions are possible, there is a presumption that sincere and literal self-ascriptions of present thoughts state truths about the self-ascriber. However, the presumption of truth only holds for self-ascriptions of occurrent thoughts in the present tense.

The characteristic first-person authority and the accompanying presumption of truth underscore a third feature of self-ascriptions—an epistemic asymmetry between the self-ascription of an occurrent thought and ascriptions of the same thought made by others or the speaker at other times.[26] A self-ascriber need not consult evidence in order to self-ascribe a contemporaneous thought, even if evidence is available. She simply utters a sentence in the first-person singular present tense in her language. In contrast, other speakers must always rely on observation and inference in ascribing thoughts to another. They must pay attention to what others say and do in order to identify their thoughts. In this respect, knowledge of others' minds does not differ from knowledge of the world outside oneself. Both are based on observation and reasoning from evidence. Self-knowledge of one's current thoughts seems fundamentally different, because it does not usually rest on evidence and inference; it appears to be direct and unmediated.

Finally, Davidson notes that the psychological predicates we use in first-person singular present tense ascriptions, for example, 'I *believe that Albert will take the position*', do not appear to differ in meaning when we use them to ascribe thoughts to others, for example, when you ascribe the thought to me, 'You *believe that Albert will take the position*' or when I ascribe the thought to you. The predicates appear to be univocal and we treat them so. Furthermore, we assume the predicates express uniform concepts despite the fact that they are applied on a different basis in different grammatical persons. That is to say, in self-ascriptions psychological predicates are not usually applied on the basis of observational criteria or inference, whereas in the case of other-ascriptions they must be.

Davidson argues that these four distinctive features—first-person authority, the presumption of truth, epistemic asymmetry, and assumed univocity of psychological predicates—characterize the philosophically puzzling self-ascriptions that we take to express self-knowledge of the contents of our thoughts. However, as he points out, not all psychological self-ascriptions exhibit these unusual features. In those rare cases where self-ascriptions of thought contents rest on inference or observation, for example, discoveries in psychotherapy, we do not accord the speaker any special authority nor do we presume that her self-ascription is true. In such cases, the self-ascriber is in the same position with respect to her thoughts as any other person, who has the available evidence; there is no epistemic asymmetry. Notably, the same psychological predicates are employed in cases of self-report based on evidence, in other-ascriptions of thoughts, and in those present-tense self-ascriptions of thoughts we take to exhibit the special features. This suggests that there is a semantic continuity between self-ascriptions of occurrent thoughts, on the one hand, and other-ascriptions of thoughts and self-reports that proceed on the basis of inference, evidence, and observation, on the other. This point merits closer consideration.

In self-ascribing a contemporaneous mental state, we utter a sentence of our language assertively. When I sincerely assert 'Albert will take the job', I express my belief that Albert will take the job in tokening the sentence. In Davidson's view, I identify my belief by uttering a sentence that has the same truth conditions as the belief it is used to identify.[27] The words of the sentence employed characterize an aspect of my state of mind in a systematic way, since utterances, like beliefs, are related to each other by relations of entailment and evidential support. In ascribing thoughts to others, the thought to be ascribed is also semantically identified by uttering a sentence with specific truth conditions, according to Davidson. Thus, thoughts are identified both in self-ascriptions and in other-ascriptions by the sentences speakers utter. Importantly, ascriptions of thoughts to others are routinely construed as cognitively substantial, descriptive statements, that is, as predications with truth-assessable content. Logically, self-ascriptions appear to be predications just like other-ascriptions of thoughts, for their logical behavior parallels that of other-ascriptions with regard to substitution of terms, existential generalization, and entailments.[28] This suggests that there are important semantic similarities between self-ascriptions and other-ascriptions of thoughts. These similarities provide good reason to construe self-ascriptions of thought contents as cognitively substantial, that is, as true or false.

As Ernst Tugendhat observes, first-person and other-person psychological ascriptions are symmetric with respect to truth or falsity.[29] My contemporaneous self-ascription, 'I believe that Albert will take the job', and your ascription, 'She believes that Albert will take the job', ascribed to me at the same time, are true or false in the same circumstances; they exhibit *veritative symmetry*. Moreover, it would be odd if others could make cognitively significant pronouncements about my mental states, while I am precluded from making any. These considerations suggest that self-ascriptions like other-ascriptions of thoughts are cognitively significant predications, assessable with respect to truth and falsity, and, consequently, candidates for knowledge. If this is correct, a type of knowledge is expressed in uttering a sentence of one's language to self-ascribe a present thought, when the sentence is true.

What is the source of this knowledge? This question might be construed as a request for justification in answer to the skeptic. However, in this matter Davidson follows W. V. O. Quine, who shifts the focus of epistemology from justification to describing how we arrive at knowledge.[30] Epistemology thus naturalized attempts to describe how we normally achieve knowledge. Instead of trying to answer the skeptic directly, Davidson attempts to provide a conceptual description of our normal ways of arriving at knowledge about states of mind—our own and those of others. Such a description will specify what reasons we count as justifying knowledge claims by describing our practices, rather than answering the skeptic outright. It is within this descriptive, conceptual project that Davidson's account of self-knowledge of one's contemporaneous thoughts is situated. He claims that self-ascriptions of current thought contents are characterized by a first-person authority, a presumption of truth, an epistemic asymmetry, and a presumed univocity of psychological predicates, and he contends that such self-ascriptions represent cases of empirical knowledge, knowledge of one's own mind. What explains the distinctive features and the epistemological status of self-ascriptions of present thoughts on Davidson's view?

3 Language, Meaning, and Radical Interpretation

As Davidson emphasizes, his account of self-knowledge and of the philosophically puzzling features of self-ascription rests on his view of language and his theory of meaning.[31] This crucial point is often missed. Davidson's view of language differs in important respects from those positions in the philosophy of language, which take language to be defined by linguistic norms, rules, or conventions. In these influential approaches, the meaning and the content of linguistic utterances are determined by factors that are independent of an individual's particular linguistic history and usage, for example, by the standards of her linguistic community, by the semantic rules of a language system, or by shared routines.[32] Davidson rejects these conceptions of language and communication. In his view, language is not defined by the shared practices or the conventions of a community. Instead, he takes the idiolect, the language of the individual speaker, to be primary. As he points out, the concept of language as well as the attendant concepts of sentence, word, predicate, reference, and meaning are theoretical concepts introduced to enable us to give a coherent description of speakers' speech behavior. Language is not a "thing" in the world; there are only people and their verbal activities, that is, speech behavior in concrete situations.[33] He elaborates, "We forget there is no such thing as a language apart from the sounds and marks people make, and the habits and expectations that go with them. 'Sharing a language' with someone else consists in understanding what they say, and talking pretty much the way they do. There is no additional entity we possess in common."[34] What we call "natural languages," for example, English, Japanese, or Ju/'hoansi, are ways of grouping idiolects together.

The primacy of the idiolect has important consequences for Davidson's approach to self-knowledge of one's thoughts, which are easily overlooked. First, Davidson maintains a form of individualism about language that contrasts markedly with views that take languages to rest on systems of collective practices, conventions, or semantic rules. Second, making idiolects primary entails that theories of meaning and content must take speech, the verbal behavior of individual speakers in context, as their starting point. Speech involves the production of a linguistic utterance to communicate and, as such, is a case of intentional action. As utterance acts, self-ascriptions of thoughts are intentional productions of tokens of a sentence of one's language to perform a specific action; as such, they must satisfy the requirements on intentional action. Similarly, understanding a speaker's linguistic utterances involves interpreting actions. Thus, considerations pertaining to beliefs, desires, intentions, and rationality are relevant to the production and the interpretation of all linguistic utterances. Third, taking the idiolect as basic means that an individual's actual history of language acquisition and use in communicating with other speakers in specific contexts is relevant to determining the meaning of linguistic utterance acts. This applies to the languages of both speaker and hearer. Furthermore, since each individual has a different history of language acquisition and use, no two individual's languages or idiolects are identical. Each idiolect reflects the speaker's unique first-person point of view.[35] Since idiolects differ from individual to individual, understanding another speaker's linguistic utterances requires matching the sentences of one's own language with the sentences of the other's language without being able to assume prior knowledge of what the speaker's words mean. In sum, the upshot of making idiolects conceptually primary is that understanding another speaker's linguistic utterances always involves radical interpretation.

An important corollary of making idiolects and speech behavior basic concerns the notion of linguistic communication. Davidson regards communication as the central feature of language use. However, he claims there is no algorithm or standard translation procedure based on linguistic rules, norms, or conventions that guarantees success at understanding another speaker's utterances, that is, successful communication.[36] Instead, Davidson takes linguistic communication to depend on a variety of cognitive and evaluative factors that are not specifically linguistic in nature, for example, on perceptual cues, contextual information, the intentions of the speaker, and the expectations of speaker and hearer, as well as on assumptions concerning humans' biological endowments, rationality, and the world—all this in addition to the words uttered by the speaker. The basic purpose of communication, in his view, is to convey to a hearer what one has in mind by means of words that the hearer understands as one wants him to.[37] Although speech has many other purposes, as Davidson acknowledges, he considers the intention to have one's words interpreted by a hearer as having a certain meaning to be the most basic purpose and the only purpose that is common to all linguistic acts. He claims that any speaker who produces a linguistic utterance to communicate must have this intention, which provides a norm against which speakers and others can measure the success of linguistic behavior. Communication is successful when the hearer interprets the speaker's utterance as the speaker intends in the particular context. Thus, what is shared by speaker and hearer in communication is utterance meaning—the meaning of the speaker's words on an occasion of use in a specific context.[38]

It is important to note that Davidson reverses the usual direction of explanation; he takes mutual understanding and successful verbal communication to be basic vis-à-vis the notions of meaning and of a shared language, if the latter is defined by rules or conventions. In his view, the concepts of a language or of meaning are theoretical concepts that depend on successful communication, rather than explain it. He writes, "Meaning, in the special sense . . . of what an utterance literally means, gets its life from those situations in which someone intends (or assumes or expects) that his words will be understood in a certain way, and they are."[39] Despite the role accorded the speaker's intentions, Davidson argues that linguistic meaning cannot be reductively analyzed in terms of the speaker's psychological states, for example, in the manner of H. P. Grice.[40] Rather, the speaker's intention to be understood in a certain way and the requirements for her being so understood highlight the fact that meaningful linguistic utterances are intentional actions that must satisfy certain rational and social constraints.

Davidson locates these constraints in the triadic social interchange between speaker, hearer, and the objects and events they respond to. For example, in uttering a sentence a speaker must have the intention to make herself understood and must have adequate reason to believe that she can make herself understood by employing a particular utterance, that is, reason to believe that the hearer will succeed in interpreting her as she intends. This constrains the linguistic means that she can employ and provides a norm for her linguistic behavior. As Davidson puts it, the speaker must make herself interpretable to her audience, for example, by providing the hearer with the clues needed to arrive at the correct interpretation of her utterance.[41] In his opinion, the requirement of interpretability introduces an irreducible social factor that controls what a speaker can mean by her words. It shows why a speaker cannot mean something by her words that cannot be correctly worked out by someone else.[42]

Three crucial points follow from Davidson's view of language and verbal communication. First, linguistic meaning, the meaning of all words and sentences, is dependent on language use in interpersonal communication: "[I]n the end the sole source of linguistic meaning is the intentional production of tokens of sentences. If such acts did not have meanings, nothing would. There is no harm in assigning meaning to sentences, but this must always be a meaning derived from concrete occasions on which sentences are put to work."[43] For communication to take place, it is not necessary that speakers and hearers speak the same way, that is, mean the same thing by the same words; they must only assign the same meaning to the speaker's words for communication to succeed.[44] Second, a speaker cannot mean just anything she likes by a linguistic utterance, even though the concept of language depends on a speaker's meaning something by what she says. Owing to the social constraints on communication through speech, linguistic meaning depends on having communicated with other speakers. This equally entails that there must be another person or persons who understand the speaker as she intends, if her utterances are to have a specific meaning or content. Consequently, the meaning and content of a linguistic utterance is not private or subjective; it arises in social settings. Thus, although idiolects are the languages of individuals, meaning and content are public and social. Davidson supports this claim by arguing for a form of externalism with respect to linguistic meaning and propositional content that integrates perceptual and social factors.[45]

In Davidson's version of externalism, the basic connection between words and things is established in contexts of language acquisition and communication by causal interaction between speakers, other speakers, and the world. He characterizes it as a type of triangulation.[46] Davidson claims that in language learning an essential triangle is formed between the learner, the teacher, and objects and events in the world, to which both respond as a result of their natural endowments. In this interpersonal triangle, language learners become disposed to respond differentially to objects and events. Davidson takes the dispositions that speakers acquire in such triadic interactions to be central to the meaning of their utterances and thoughts. These are facts about individual speakers and their causal histories of relations to other speakers and to the world.

Davidson maintains that the connections formed in situations of triangulation constrain what a speaker can mean by the words she uses and what they can be interpreted to mean. Importantly, he argues that a speaker's grasp of meanings is determined only by the terminal elements in the language learning process and that it is tested only by the end product, that is, the use of words geared to appropriate objects and situations.[47] A consequence of this view is that a speaker's history of language learning and of communication with other speakers grounds the meaning of her utterances. The central idea of the Davidsonian approach is that an account of the meaning of a speaker's words and sentences can be provided by relating the sentences of the speaker's idiolect to the circumstances in virtue of which her sentences acquire the truth conditions that they have.

Accordingly, Davidson's account integrates a truth-conditional thesis about meaning and content with a form of externalism, based on the interpretive triangle between the speaker, others with whom she communicates, and the nonlinguistic environment.

As is well known, Davidson endorses the claim that giving the truth conditions of a sentence is a way of giving its meaning. He contends that a theory that systematically states the truth conditions of the sentences of a speaker's language in a finite form can serve as a theory of meaning for the language.[48] This requires discerning semantic structure relevant to truth conditions, for example, the logical structure of predicates, singular terms, quantifiers, and the like. Davidson argues that one can assign structurally revealing truth conditions to a speaker's utterances by constructing a finitely specifiable theory of truth for the speaker's idiolect, *L*, modeled on a modified Tarski-style definition of truth, a T-theory$_L$. The idea is that the truth conditions of a speaker's sentences relativized to time are given by a correct systematic and comprehensive Tarskian T-theory$_L$ for the speaker's language. Strictly, the T-theory$_L$ applies to utterances and not to sentences.[49]

If meaning is given by truth conditions, as Davidson holds, in communicating through speech a speaker produces a sentence of her language that has specific truth conditions, that is, meaning, and intends that her hearer assign certain truth conditions to her utterance, that is, a certain meaning. More specifically, the hearer must ascribe those truth conditions to the speaker's utterance of a sentence that the speaker intends it to have. If the hearer is to say what a speaker's utterance means, he must find out in what conditions the speaker counts the uttered sentence true or false. Since idiolects are not shared, his T-theory$_L$ for the speaker's language cannot be based on prior knowledge of what the speaker's utterances mean. The hearer must rely on evidence and inference to discern the facts in virtue of which the speaker's sentences have specific truth conditions. This is, of course, the situation of the radical interpreter.

Starting from observed speech, the radical interpreter constructs hypotheses in the form of T-sentences about which sentences the speaker holds true in which circumstances, for example:

(T) 'Yuki ga futte iru' is true-in-*L* when spoken by *x* at time *t* if and only if it is snowing near *x* at *t*.

As interpretation progresses, the interpreter revises these in the light of additional evidence, epistemic liaisons, and relations of entailment among the T-sentences. The aim of interpretation is a recursive characterization in the interpreter's language of truth for the sentences of the speaker's language

L, of 'true-for-the-speaker', which reveals significant semantic structure in the speaker's language.[50] Since the metalanguage in which the theory is couched, the interpreter's idiolect, differs from the object language, the speaker's idiolect *L*, the interpreter's T-theory$_L$ will be a "heterophonic" truth theory. This contrasts with a "homophonic" truth theory, in which the same language serves both as metalanguage and object language. In homophonic truth theories the T-sentences are trivial, for example:

(T) 'It is snowing' is true-in-*L* when spoken by *x* at time *t* if and only if it is snowing near *x* at *t*.

No recourse to evidence or inference is necessary on the part of the speaker of *L* to check the adequacy of the T-sentences entailed by a homophonic theory, because the speaker uses her own sentences to give the truth conditions, and thus the meaning, of her words. In contrast, interpreting another speaker's utterances always requires constructing a heterophonic T-theory of the speaker's idiolect, because two idiolects are involved.

Davidson claims that the truth conditions of a speaker's sentences are given by the correct T-theory$_L$ for the speaker's language. His idea is that an account of what it is for a sentence to have specific truth conditions will also explain the facts about the speaker in virtue of which a particular T-theory$_L$ for her language is correct. He maintains that a speaker's linguistic and nonlinguistic behavior in specific contexts offers a starting point for assigning truth conditions to the sentences the speaker utters. The evidence for a heterophonic T-theory$_L$ derives from utterances of sentences that are taken by the interpreter to be held true by the speaker or cases where one sentence is taken to be preferred true to another in specific contexts.[51] The important point is that evidence and inference are always required in interpreting another speaker's utterances.

The interpreter must proceed on the basis of evidence about when the speaker is caused to hold a sentence true in order to correlate the speaker's utterances with perceptible objects and changes in the environment. Upon inferring a causal relation, he matches the speaker's verbal responses with a sentence of his own language that the perceptually accessible objects and changes would cause him to hold true or false in similar circumstances. Hence, the interpreter uses the sentences of his own language to give the truth conditions, or as Davidson puts it "to take the measure," of the speaker's utterances.[52] Meanings are shared when the same events, objects, or situations would cause acceptance or rejection of a sentence: "Communication begins where causes converge: your utterance means what mine does if belief in its truth is systematically caused by the same events and objects."[53]

In the enterprise of radical interpretation, the interpreter already has a language and possesses the concepts of truth, intention, and other states of mind like belief and desire.[54] Moreover, he assumes that the same is true of the speaker that he aims to interpret. Thus, both speaker and interpreter are presumed to be equipped with language and thought. But what confers meaning on their respective idiolects and content on their thoughts? According to Davidson, it is the pattern of sentences held true that gives one's sentences their meaning and enables the individuation of thoughts.[55] Regarding this pattern, Davidson claims that the meaning of a sentence is partly determined by its grammatical, logical, and evidential relations to other sentences the speaker holds true and partly by the situations that systematically cause the speaker to hold the sentence true or false. The first part of this claim rests on Davidson's holistic view of meaning, which construes the logical and evidential relations among the linguistic expressions of a language as central to their meaning and content. The second part reflects his version of externalism, which relates the concepts of meaning and content to perceptual abilities, to the environment, and to linguistic action in situations of triangulation. Analogous remarks apply to the contents of beliefs and other thoughts; a belief is identified by its location in a pattern of beliefs.[56] This pattern is constrained by rational considerations, for example, concerning logical and evidential relations, which play a constitutive role in the holism of the propositional mental, and by causal relations to the nonlinguistic and to the social world. Thus, the same factors confer meaning and content on one's language and one's thoughts in Davidson's view.

Davidson's version of externalism combines perceptual externalism, which maintains that there is a necessary connection between the meaning of certain words and sentences and the contents of certain thoughts and the features of the world that make them true, and social externalism, which holds that meaning and thought content depend on interaction with others. He takes externalism to be a consequence of the way the basic connection between words and things or thoughts and speech is established. Consequently, many words and sentences derive their meaning from the objects and circumstances in whose presence they were learned from other speakers.[57] Davidson concedes that not all words and sentences are learned this way, but he maintains that those that are link language to the world. This is not because such causal connections supply a special kind of evidence for speakers, but because perceptually accessible factors are often apparent to others and so form the basis for communication and language learning.

Davidson advances a similar position with respect to the content of perceptual beliefs, claiming that the events and objects that systematically cause a basic perceptual belief play a significant role in determining the content of the belief. For example, a belief that is differentially and under normal conditions caused by the presence of a tomato is the belief that a tomato is present. The idea is that the causal history of a judgment like 'This is a tomato' provides a constitutive feature of its propositional content, because the situations that normally cause such a belief determine the conditions in which it is true.[58] Davidson contends that all language and thought must have a foundation directly or indirectly in such historical, causal connections between speakers, other speakers, and the world, or in terms of the relations among words, other words, and concepts and other concepts.[59]

Crucially, Davidson situates the causal connections between individuals and the nonlinguistic environment that ground meaning and content within the interpersonal triangulation of individuals, others with whom they communicate and the objects and events to which they mutually respond. He argues that the "causes" of a speaker's verbal responses can only be identified within the social setting provided by interpersonal triangulation. This is because shared interests and shared similarity responses are required to determine what counts as the cause of a speaker's verbal response.[60] Moreover, he maintains that humans' natural endowments play an important role here. Without another creature with similar capacities, innate and learned, the triangulation that identifies the meaning- or content-determining cause, the common cause, could not take place. Until communication is established with a second person, Davidson emphasizes, an individual's thoughts or words have no specific content—that is to say, no content at all.[61] Without communication with another person, an individual has no way of pinpointing the object or event that confers content on her utterances and thoughts. A second person is needed to determine what the individual is responding to, for example, whether to proximal stimuli at her sensory surfaces, to distal stimuli, or to something else in the chain of stimulation: "It takes two to triangulate the location of the distal stimulus, two to provide an objective test of correctness and failure."[62] The similarity in response to the stimulus must be acknowledged as shared by both individuals, not just shared de facto. Thus, in order to home in on the common cause, Davidson argues that the individuals involved in an interaction must recognize the existence of a triangle between themselves and the objects and events to which they respond on the basis of their natural endowments. They must realize that each occupies an "apex of an interpretive triangle" that triangulates an object or event in a common environment. Davidson claims that this requires that they be in communication; each must speak to the other and be understood, that is, interpreted, by the other as intended.[63]

In the Davidsonian approach, the linguistic utterance acts speakers perform in communicating through speech are fundamental. The languages employed are the speakers' idiolects, and each idiolect reflects the history of the individual speaker. Nonetheless, the meaning of a speaker's sentences and the contents of her thoughts are socially and externalistically anchored in those situations of interpersonal triangulation in which the speaker acquires her language and subsequently uses linguistic utterances to communicate with others, for it is these situations of acquisition and use that largely determine truth conditions.

4 The Special Features of Self-Knowledge of One's Thoughts

With Davidson's claims about language, communication, and the constitution of meaning and content in place, we are in a position to set out his account of the special features of self-ascriptions of present thoughts. As we have seen, all thought ascriptions involve a speaker's use of a sentence of her idiolect to identify the thought ascribed. The meaning of the utterance the speaker employs is given by its truth conditions, which are partly determined by the logical and evidential relations among the sentences of the speaker's language and partly by the speaker's history of causal interactions with the world and with other speakers in triadic situations of language learning and communication. In addition, the contents of the thought the speaker ascribes are identified and individuated by the semantic features of the utterance employed, that is, its truth conditions, regardless of whether the speaker ascribes a thought to herself or to someone else. This point has important consequences.

In ascribing thoughts to others, a speaker uses a sentence of her idiolect to identify the thought she ascribes. The uttered token of the sentence employed identifies the thought by specifying its content. In the case of propositional attitude ascriptions, the speaker must characterize both the type of attitude, for example, "believing" in contradistinction to "hoping," and the content of the thought, what is believed, hoped for, and so on. On Davidson's paratactic analysis of propositional attitude ascriptions, the logical form of an ascription comprises the utterance of two sentences: 'John believes that/this: Albert will take the job'.[64] However, the important point is that the speaker utters a sentence of her idiolect to identify and to characterize the other's state of mind. In saying 'John believes that Albert will take the job', the speaker characterizes an aspect of John's state of mind by relating him to a sentence of her idiolect, which, by the speaker's lights, has the same truth conditions as John's thought. If the speaker's utterance is true, she correctly identifies the thought and specifies an objective characteristic of John.[65] As Davidson puts it, the speaker uses a sentence of her idiolect that she holds true to "gauge" or to "give the measure" of John's thoughts.

When ascribing states of minds to others, the speaker is in the position of a radical interpreter. In order to match up her own sentences and states of mind with those of another person, the speaker must observe the other's linguistic and nonlinguistic actions, attend to contextual cues, factor in information about the person, and take the relations among states of mind into account by applying her own norms of coherence and consistency. As a result, the speaker's thought ascriptions to others have the status of empirical hypotheses; they are based on observation and inductive reasoning and are revised in the light of new information. There is no general guarantee that the speaker correctly identifies another person's thought with her utterance; serious error is always possible.

This is not the case in ascribing the contents of present thoughts to oneself. In self-ascriptions of present thoughts, a speaker utters a sentence of her idiolect to identify the thought she ascribes, just as she does in ascribing a thought to some one else. However, in contrast to other-ascriptions of thoughts, the speaker self-ascribes her current thought by producing a sentence with the truth conditions of the very thought she is ascribing in her utterance act. This is the case because the meaning of the speaker's utterance and the content of the belief she expresses by uttering her sentence are conditioned by the same factors and determined in the same situations. Both are socially and externalistically grounded in triadic interactions with other speakers and the world in the course of language acquisition and in making herself understood by others. This crucial point is the key to Davidson's account of the special features of self-ascriptions of present thoughts to oneself and to his position on self-knowledge of one's occurrent thoughts. Given the way the semantic properties of a sentences and the propositional contents of thoughts are constituted, there is no room for error about the content of one's present thought of the sort that can arise with respect to the thoughts of others when one self-ascribes the thought with a sentence of one's own idiolect.[66]

In self-ascribing a current thought, the speaker simply utters a sentence of her idiolect like 'I believe that Albert will take the job' and expresses her belief by uttering a sentence with the truth conditions of the belief she is expressing. In the act of uttering, the speaker knows without observation that she herself produces the sentence, that is, that she is the agent of the utterance act. But more importantly, when the speaker is self-ascribing an occurrent thought, neither conscious reasoning nor explicit recourse to evidence is necessary in order for the speaker to identify the content of the contemporaneous thought, since the meaning of the utterance the speaker produces and the content of the thought she self-ascribes are established by the same factors. These factors determine both the contents of her thoughts and the contents of the thought she believes she has in uttering a sentence of her idiolect.

Consequently, in self-ascriptions of current thoughts, radical interpretation is neither necessary nor applicable. Unlike thought ascriptions to others, a speaker's self-ascriptions of present thoughts are not empirical hypotheses that she can test by confronting her sentences and beliefs with objects and events in the world to determine their truth conditions; they are not based on evidence the way other-ascriptions of thoughts must be.[67] Whatever she regularly applies her words to in communicating with others gives them the meaning they have and her thoughts the contents they have. As a result, the speaker is not in a position to wonder whether she is generally using her own words to apply to the right objects and events. Therefore, owing to the way meaning and content are constituted in language acquisition and in communication through interpersonal triangulation, inference and evidence do not play a role in self-ascriptions of an occurrent thought, with few exceptions. The problem of interpretation does not arise, because self-ascriptions of present thoughts involve only one language, the speaker's idiolect at the time of utterance, and the meaning of the speaker's utterances and the contents of her thoughts are determined in the same circumstances. In Davidson's terminology, an utterance act of self-ascribing a present thought by means of one's own utterance is a homophonic case, whereas radical interpretation concerns the heterophonic case of relating two languages.

In sum, the key to Davidson's explanation of the peculiar features of self-ascriptions of current thoughts lies in the way linguistic meaning and thought content are determined and the consequences of this for producing and interpreting utterance acts. The fundamental Davidsonian claim is that the situations of interpersonal triangulation that determine the truth conditions of the sentences of a speaker's idiolect, that is, their meaning, also determine the truth conditions, that is, propositional contents, of the speaker's thoughts. Since the semantic features of the sentences employed by the speaker identify the thought ascribed, Davidson's thesis entails that a speaker's self-ascription of a current thought using her own sentence has a special status, compared to her ascriptions of thoughts to others. The distinctive features that accrue to speakers' utterances of sentences in the first-person singular present tense in self-ascribing a thought derive from speakers employing a sentence of their own idiolect in an utterance act to self-ascribe a thought.

The presumption of *first-person authority* accorded self-ascriptions of present thoughts rests on the fact that what the sentences of a speaker's idiolect mean and the content of the thoughts she expresses in uttering them are fixed in the same situations of language learning and communication. Consequently, when a speaker identifies a present thought by uttering a sentence of her idiolect, there is a well-founded presumption that in a sincere self-ascription the speaker correctly identifies her current thought and consequently enjoys an authority that no one else does. Importantly, this presumption accrues only to self-ascriptions of present thoughts, that is, to contemporaneous utterances. This is because a self-ascription of a thought that is not contemporaneous with the speaker's utterance involves two languages, an idiolect 1 at t_1 and an idiolect 2 at t_2, not one. In Davidson's view, any addition or alteration in verbal resources makes one's idiolect a new language.[68] Where two languages are involved, interpretation is always necessary. In contrast, in speakers' ascriptions of occurrent thoughts only one language is involved, namely, the speaker's idiolect at the time of utterance. This why first-person authority only pertains to utterances of sentences in the first-person singular present tense to self-ascribe contemporaneous thoughts, not to self-ascriptions in other tenses or to other-ascriptions of thoughts.

The *presumption of truth* is explained by the way a speaker acquires her language and employs it in making herself understood by others. Given the way linguistic meaning and thought content are socially and externalistically established, there is a presumption that a speaker who self-ascribes a current thought is not generally mistaken about what her words mean or what the content of the thought is that she expresses with her words. Error, although rare, is possible, since what a speaker's words mean depends in part on the clues to interpretation she has given her hearer or on other evidence she justifiably believes him to have.[69] In any particular case, the speaker may be in error. Nevertheless, Davidson argues that it is impossible that the speaker should be wrong most of the time, since whatever she regularly applies her sentences to endows them with meaning. Moreover, it is this regular use that allows others to discover what the speaker means by her utterances. In Davidson's view, nothing could count as a speaker regularly misapplying her words, for unless there is a presumption that the speaker is not generally mistaken about what she means in producing a linguistic act of utterance, she would not be interpretable as a speaker at all, that is, as intending to have her words interpreted by others as having a certain meaning. Thus, the presumption of truth associated with self-ascriptions of current thoughts rests on the claim that a speaker generally correctly identifies and expresses her present thought when she utters a sentence of her idiolect in self-ascribing the thought.

In contrast, there is no presumption of authority or of truth when a speaker uses one of her sentences to identify the content of someone else's thought. This points up an asymmetry between how we know our own minds and how we know the minds of others, which Davidson explicates in terms of radical interpretation. This is an *epistemic asymmetry* in Davidson's view, for it concerns how speakers identify the contents of their own and others' thoughts. As discussed, a speaker does not have to engage in radical interpretation in order to identify the present thought she ascribes. She identifies the thought by uttering a sentence of her idiolect that has the same semantic properties as the thought she self-ascribes. This "identification" is based on the semantic properties of the uttered sentence, that is, its truth conditions, which are partly determined by the speaker's individual history of causal interactions with the world and other speakers in language acquisition and in successful communication, which cause her to hold the sentence true, and partly by the sentence's holistic logical and evidential relations to other sentences. In this view, the speaker stands in an epistemic relation to the literal truth of her uttered sentences that is distinct from that of any other speaker, for, once ontological and epistemological dualisms are rejected, the methodology of radical interpretation turns out to be an undertaking of naturalized and externalized epistemology.[70] The epistemic asymmetry between self-ascriptions of current thoughts and thought ascriptions to others is due to the way meaning and thought content are conferred and to the consequences thereof for the semantic identification of thoughts by employing a sentence of one's idiolect.

Davidson emphasizes that the presumption that sincere, literal, assertive uses of 'I believe that'-sentences are true does not rest on any sort of privileged epistemological access to one's thoughts.[71] There is no "way" a speaker knows her own mind, if this is taken to mean an epistemologically distinctive way, such as a special method or a means of access involving subjective evidence or inner objects present to the mind.[72] Thoughts are private in the sense of belonging to one person and knowledge of an occurrent thought is asymmetrical in that the person who has the thought generally knows she has it in a way others cannot. However, this is a result of the way that the meaning of sentences and the propositional contents of thoughts are established in linguistic interchange with others and of the fact that a speaker employs her own sentence in the utterance act of self-ascribing a thought.

Davidson does not explicitly discuss the univocity of psychological predicates; he takes it as a datum to be explained. However, the central role he accords language learning and communication suggests how to fill out his account. First, it is important to remember that the lexicon of one's language is learned; no one is born knowing the meaning of words like 'snow' or 'Schnee' or 'yuki'. Everyone who knows the meaning of 'snow' has heard it used in a context in which the meaning can be learned from linguistic interchange with other speakers, for example, in an English-speaking environment in contrast to a German- or Japanese-speaking environment. The phonological strings we call "words" are acquired from other speakers in situations of interpersonal triangulation through abilities that rest on humans' natural endowments—powers of sensory discrimination, perceptual capacities, and similar modes of response, as well as the ability to attend to contextual features and to generalize across instances. As Davidson observes, "[L]earning a language is not a matter of attaching the right meanings to words, but a process in which words are endowed with a use."[73] From the learner's point of view, a sound is being endowed with a meaning; it is given a meaning by the learning process itself.

Speakers serve as teachers, intentionally or inadvertently providing learners with linguistic expressions through their use of linguistic utterances in specific contexts. These contexts involve the triangular arrangement of learner, teacher, and observed and discriminated objects and events, as well as features of the environment common to the learner and the teacher. The contextually salient features not only comprise objects, properties, and events, but also perceptually accessible verbal and nonverbal behavior. The acquisition of psychological predicates like verbs of propositional attitude is plausibly scaffolded by perceptual capacities that make the expressions and reactions of others salient to us, even though states of mind like the propositional attitudes of belief, desire, or intention cannot be directly perceived or ostended.

Moreover, in numerous everyday comments on thought and action, speakers offer language learners vocabulary for talking about mental states. They ascribe beliefs, desires, intentions, and other states of mind to themselves, to others, and to preverbal children on the basis of contextual cues and assumptions. In doing so, they offer language learners psychological predicates for states of mind, keyed to features of the utterance context. What is more, speakers routinely employ these predicates in various grammatical persons, providing learners with templates for ascriptions of thoughts. Finally, speaker's ascriptions of thoughts to young children are based partly on contextual observations of behavior and on cues like facial expression, signs of affect, and focus of attention, but they are also based on the ascriber's attempt to interpret the child as an incipient rational agent.

In ascribing thoughts to others, a speaker must employ her own norms of rationality, according to Davidson. In addition, he maintains that speakers' contentful ascriptions of states of mind are also partly constituted by rational considerations concerning logical and evidential relations.[74] As a consequence, he argues that the application of psychological predicates differs from the application of predicates in the natural sciences in that the former is irreducibly normative. The normative character of their application points up the fact that acquiring linguistic expressions for states of mind is part of a process of learning to comprehend behavior as intentional action. The suggestion is that the language learner gradually masters psychological predicates by using them to describe and explain thought and intentional action in communicating with others. Over time the learner's use of psychological expressions is fine-tuned through the necessity of making himself understood to others. The univocity of psychological predicates may thus be viewed as a consequence of acquiring one's language in situations of interpersonal triangulation and of one's subsequent use of psychological predicates in making oneself understood to others with whom one communicates.

Like the features of first-person authority, presumption of truth, and epistemic asymmetry associated with self-knowledge, the univocity of psychological predicates ultimately issues from the way one's speech and thought are endowed with meaning and content in acquiring a language and are constrained by the subsequent use in making oneself understood to others with whom one communicates, that is, by the requirements of intentional action and rational agency. This explanation of the special features of those self-ascriptions we take to express self-knowledge of thoughts also reveals the source of this knowledge.

Given the way that meaning and content are conferred on an individual's speech and thoughts in interpersonal triangulation, a speaker has nonevidential knowledge of a present thought when she self-ascribes the thought in a contemporaneous utterance act using a sentence of her idiolect and the ascription is true. The first-person authority accorded the speaker derives from the fact that she self-ascribes an occurrent thought by performing an utterance act, an intentional action, by producing a sentence of her own idiolect. The self-ascriber specifies the content of her mental state on the basis of her history of language acquisition and of mutually understood utterances that fix the patterns and causes of sentences she holds true and thus determine the meaning and the content, that is, the truth conditions, of her sentences and thoughts. This is what makes her utterances meaningful and her thoughts contentful. Thus, when a speaker utters a sentence of her idiolect in self-ascribing a present thought, there is a presumption that she correctly identifies the content of her thought without recourse to evidence or inference, that is, that the self-ascription is true. The meaning of her sentences and the content of her thoughts are determined by the same factors and the same circumstances. No one else is in a similar position with respect to the speaker's idiolect or her intentions in communicating through linguistic utterance acts. Consequently, there is an epistemic asymmetry between self-ascriptions of current thoughts and thought ascriptions to others or to oneself in other tenses, despite the univocity of psychological predicates in different grammatical persons.

This account of self-knowledge of one's thoughts assumes that thought and language are mutually dependent. This tenet of the Davidsonian approach has been widely criticized for denying "thought" to languageless creatures, for example, human infants, preverbal children, and nonhuman animals. However, it is important to note that Davidson's claim concerns "propositional thought," not cognitive or affective activity generally.[75] In his opinion, the complexity required for propositional thought only comes with the ability to use language in communicating with others, because propositional thought involves classification with an awareness of the possibility of error. On Davidson's view, thoughts are defined by propositional content and propositional content is characterized by truth conditions; these are externalistically and holistically determined in the intersubjective contexts in which speakers acquire their idiolects and employ them in utterances to communicate with other speakers. Accordingly, candidates for knowledge must exhibit complex semantic structure that reflects truth conditions, for example, a structure of singular terms, predicates, and quantificational structure, if they are to be assessed as true or false. This is the kind of semantic structure and content that a T-theory$_L$ of a speaker's idiolect aims to reveal. Ultimately, Davidson's view that knowledge is propositionally structured, intersubjective, and objective rests on his contention that self-knowledge of one's own thoughts, knowledge of other's thoughts, and knowledge of the world are conceptually interdependent.[76]

The perplexity with which many authors have approached the Davidsonian account of self-knowledge is largely a result of a widespread failure to understand the way in which Davidson's treatment of self-knowledge is directly connected to his concept of knowledge as propositionally structured, and so to the necessary entanglement of knowledge and self-knowledge with linguistic practice. This is why Davidson's treatment of self-knowledge typically arises in the context of his broader discussions of radical interpretation. Indeed, not only does the examination of the nature and source of self-knowledge lead inevitably, from a Davidsonian point of view, into an examination of the nature of linguistic communication, but to understand linguistic communication correctly, one must also attend to the structure of self-knowledge—as well as to the structure of knowledge. Knowing what we are thinking turns out to be inseparable from our ability to inform others about the contents of our thoughts—that is, it turns out to be inseparable from the intersubjective linguistic context in which knowledge necessarily arises, and from the objective world that such intersubjectivity also invokes.

Notes

1. Donald Davidson, "Three Varieties of Knowledge," in his *Subjective, Intersubjective, Objective* (Oxford: Oxford University Press, 2001), p. 205.

2. Donald Davidson, "First Person Authority," in *Subjective, Intersubjective, Objective*, pp. 3–14; "Knowing One's Own Mind," in *Subjective, Intersubjective, Objective*, pp. 15–38; "What Is Present to the Mind?," in *Subjective, Intersubjective, Objective*, pp. 53–68; "The Conditions of Thought," *Grazer Philosophische Studien* 36 (1989): 193–200; "Epistemology Externalized," in *Subjective, Intersubjective, Objective*, pp. 193–204; "Three Varieties of Knowledge," in *Subjective, Intersubjective, Objective*, pp. 205–220; "The Irreducibility of the Concept of the Self," in *Subjective, Intersubjective, Objective*, pp. 85–91.

3. Donald Davidson, "Problems in the Explanation of Action," in his *Problems of Rationality* (Oxford: Oxford University Press, 2004), p. 114.

4. Donald Davidson, "The Myth of the Subjective," in *Subjective, Intersubjective, Objective*, pp. 39–52; "What Is Present to the Mind?," p. 56; see also "The Conditions of Thought."

5. Davidson, "First Person Authority," p. 5; "The Myth of the Subjective," pp. 50, 52; "What Is Present to the Mind?," pp. 54, 58–59.

6. Richard Rorty, "Incorrigibility as the Mark of the Mental," *Journal of Philosophy* 67 (1970): 399–424; Crispin Wright, "Self-Knowledge: The Wittgensteinian Legacy," in

Knowing Our Own Minds, ed. Crispin Wright, Barry C. Smith, and Cynthia Macdonald (Oxford: Oxford University Press 1998), pp. 13–45.

7. Davidson, "First Person Authority," pp. 7–10; see also "The Second Person," in *Subjective, Intersubjective, Objective*, pp. 107–122; "Reply to Bernhard Thöle," in *Reflecting Davidson*, ed. Ralf Stoecker (Berlin: Walter de Gruyter, 1993), pp. 248–250.

8. Davidson, "Three Varieties of Knowledge," pp. 205, 213, 219–220.

9. Donald Davidson, "Introduction," in *Subjective, Intersubjective, Objective*, p. xiii.

10. Donald Davidson, "The Irreducibility of the Concept of the Self," p. 87.

11. Davidson, "First Person Authority," pp. 11–14; "Knowing One's Own Mind," pp. 33, 37–38; "What Is Present to the Mind?," pp. 65–66.

12. Davidson, "Reply to Bernhard Thöle," p. 249.

13. See Donald Davidson, "Radical Interpretation," in his *Inquiries into Truth and Interpretation* (Oxford: Oxford University Press, 1984), pp. 125–129; "Belief and the Basis of Meaning," in *Inquiries into Truth and Interpretation*, pp. 141–154; "A Nice Derangement of Epitaphs," in his *Truth, Language, and History* (Oxford: Oxford University Press, 2005), pp. 89–107. Davidson calls this type of interpretation "radical," because it assumes no prior knowledge of the speaker's propositional attitudes.

14. Davidson, "Knowing One's Own Mind," p. 37.

15. Donald Davidson, "Reply to Eva Picardi," in Stoecker (ed.), *Reflecting Davidson*, p. 212.

16. I thank Jeff Malpas for this way of putting the point.

17. Barry C. Smith, "On Knowing One's Own Language," in Wright, Smith, and Macdonald (eds.), *Knowing Our Own Minds*, pp. 391–428; Ernest Lepore and Kirk Ludwig, *Donald Davidson: Meaning, Truth, Language, and Reality* (Oxford: Oxford University Press, 2005), pp. 506–507.

18. Dorit Bar-On, *Speaking My Mind: Expression and Self-Knowledge* (Oxford: Oxford University Press, 2004), pp. 174–178.

19. Lepore and Ludwig, *Donald Davidson: Meaning, Truth, Language, and Reality*, p. 506.

20. Paul Boghossian, "Content and Self-Knowledge," *Philosophical Topics* 17 (1989): 5–26; Michael McKinsey, "Anti-Individualism and Privileged Access," *Analysis* 51 (1991): 9–16; Peter Ludlow, "Social Externalism, Self-Knowledge, and Memory," *Analysis* 55 (1995): 157–159.

21. Thomas Nagel, "Subjective and Objective," in his *Mortal Questions* (New York: Cambridge University Press, 1979), pp. 196–214; Frank Jackson, "What Mary Didn't Know," *Journal of Philosophy* 83 (1986): 127–195; Lepore and Ludwig, *Donald*

Davidson: Meaning, Truth, Language, and Reality, chap. 20; John Searle, "Indeterminacy and the First Person," *Journal of Philosophy* 84 (1987): 123–146; Smith, "On Knowing One's Own Language."

22. Arguments for this equivalence are found in Röska-Hardy, "Moore's Paradox and the Expression of Belief," in *Argument und Analyze: Proceedings of GAP IV*, ed. Ansgar Beckermann and Christian Nimtz (Paderborn: Mentis, 2001), pp. 329–337.

23. Davidson, "Three Varieties of Knowledge," p. 209.

24. Davidson discusses these features in "First Person Authority," "Knowing One's Own Mind," "Epistemology Externalized," "Reply to Bernhard Thöle," "The Irreducibility of the Concept of the Self," "Three Varieties of Knowledge," and "Donald Davidson," in *A Companion to the Philosophy of Mind*, ed. Samuel Guttenplan (Oxford: Blackwell, 1994), pp. 231–236.

25. Davidson, "Reply to Eva Picardi," p. 211.

26. Davidson, "Reply to Bernhard Thöle," p. 249.

27. Davidson, "What Is Present to the Mind?," pp. 63–64.

28. The arguments for this claim are elaborated in Louise Röska-Hardy, "Idealism and the 'I' of Self-ascription," in *Indexicality and Idealism: The Self in Philosophical Perspective*, ed. Audun Øfsti, Peter Ulrich, and Truls Wyller (Paderborn: Mentis, 2000), pp. 56–57.

29. Ernst Tugendhat, *Self-Consciousness and Self-Determination* (Cambridge, MA: MIT Press, 1986), chap. 4.

30. Davidson, "Epistemology Externalized," p. 194; "The Perils and Pleasures of Interpretation," in *The Oxford Handbook of Philosophy of Language*, ed. Ernest Lepore and Barry C. Smith (Oxford: Oxford University Press, 2006), p. 1057; "Interpretation: Hard in Theory, Easy in Practice," in *Interpretations and Causes: New Perspectives on Donald Davidson's Philosophy*, ed. Mario de Caro (Dordrecht: Kluwer, 1999), p. 43; "The Problem of Objectivity," in *Problems of Rationality*, pp. 5–6.

31. Davidson writes, "[M]y article 'First Person Authority' perhaps did not sufficiently emphasize that my 'solution' to the problem about self-attributions of attitudes depended on my theory of meaning." "Reply to Bernhard Thöle," p. 250.

32. Tyler Burge, "Individualism and the Mental," *Midwest Studies in Philosophy* 4 (1979): 73–121; Michael Dummett, "What Is a Theory of Meaning?" in *Mind and Language*, ed. Samuel Guttenplan (Oxford: Clarendon Press, 1975), pp. 97–138, and "What Is a Theory of Meaning? II," in *Truth and Meaning: Essays in Semantics*, ed. Gareth Evans and John McDowell (Oxford: Clarendon Press, 1976), pp. 67–137; Saul Kripke, *Wittgenstein on Rules and Private Language* (Oxford: Oxford University Press, 1982).

33. Donald Davidson, "The Second Person," in *Subjective, Intersubjective, Objective*, p. 108; Donald Davidson, "The Social Aspect of Language," in *Truth, Language, and History*, pp. 109–125.

34. Donald Davidson, "Seeing through Language," in *Truth, Language and History*, p. 131.

35. Davidson, "The Irreducibility of the Concept of the Self," p. 89; "The Social Aspect of Language," p. 115.

36. Davidson, "Communication and Convention," pp. 271–272; "A Nice Derangement of Epitaphs," p. 101; "The Social Aspect of Language," pp. 120–121; "The Second Person," pp. 111–112, 116.

37. Davidson claims, "[W]hat matters, the point of language or speech . . . , is communication, getting across to someone else what you have in mind by means of words that they interpret (understand) as you want them to. Speech has endless other purposes, but none underlies this one." "The Social Aspect of Language," p. 120.

38. Davidson regards 'actual utterances of a speaker' and 'sentences relativized to a time and a speaker' as interchangeable ("Truth and Meaning," p. 34; "What Is Present to the Mind?," p. 63).

39. Davidson, "The Social Aspect of Language," p. 120.

40. Davidson argues in numerous places that meaning cannot be defined in terms of speakers' intentions. He clarifies that his formulation of the notion of meaning is not Gricean, for it rests on the concept of understanding, whereas Grice aimed at defining meaning generally in terms of intentions that do not involve linguistic meaning at all ("The Social Aspect of Language," p. 121, n. 13; "Locating Literary Language," in *Truth, Language, and History*, p. 173).

41. Davidson, "First Person Authority," p. 12; "Knowing One's Own Mind," p. 28.

42. Davidson, "Knowing One's Own Mind," p. 28.

43. Donald Davidson, "Locating Literary Language," p. 170.

44. Davidson, "Communication and Convention," p. 277.

45. For a discussion of Davidson's externalism, see Louise Röska-Hardy, "Internalism, Externalism, and Davidson's Conception of the Mental," in *Language, Mind and Epistemology: On Donald Davidson's Philosophy*, ed. Gerhard Preyer, Frank Siebelt, and Alexander Ulfig (Dordrecht: Kluwer, 1994), pp. 263–281.

46. Davidson introduces the notion of triangulation in "Rational Animals," in *Inquiries into Truth and Interpretation*, p. 105, and develops it in subsequent essays—see "Communication and Convention," "Epistemology Externalized," "Three Varieties of Knowledge," "The Second Person," "The Emergence of Thought," in *Subjective, Intersubjective, Objective*, pp. 123–134; Davidson, "Interpretation: Hard in Theory, Easy

in Practice," in Caro (ed.), *Interpretations and Causes*; and Davidson, "Externalisms," in *Interpreting Davidson*, ed. Petr Kotatko, Peter Pagin, and Gabriel Segal (Palo Alto: CSLI Publications, 2001), pp. 5–13.

47. Davidson, "The Myth of the Subjective," p. 44. This is of a piece with Davidson's rejection of meanings as entities and his insistence that meaning is a theoretical concept that satisfies formal and empirical constraints.

48. For details, see the essays collected in Davidson, *Inquiries into Truth and Interpretation*, and Davidson, *Truth and Predication* (Cambridge, MA: Harvard University Press, 2005), chap. 3.

49. Starting with "Truth and Meaning," Davidson has emphasized that his theory applies to utterances ("Truth and Meaning," p. 34). The Davidsonian approach is predicated on analyzing inscriptions, utterances, and speech acts, not sentence types ("On Saying that," in *Inquiries into Truth and Interpretation*, p. 106, n. 16).

50. Davidson, *Truth and Predication*, chap. 3; Davidson, "The Structure and Content of Truth," *Journal of Philosophy* 87 (1990): part III, 309–326.

51. Davidson claims that the attitudes of holding true a sentence or of preferring one sentence as true over another are neutral between meaning and belief, and he contends they can be identified in observed speech in advance of interpretation. He characterizes them as "non-individuative," because they do not presuppose specific propositional content ("The Structure and Content of Truth," p. 323). The attitude of preferring true a sentence is central for Davidson's use of decision theory in his unified theory of meaning and action (see Davidson, "A Unified Theory of Thought, Meaning, and Action," in *Problems of Rationality*, pp. 309–328). However, this evidential base presents the interpreter with a dilemma, since the attitude of holding true is the product of two factors—what the speaker takes the sentence to mean and what the speaker believes to be the case. To deal with this interdependence, Davidson suggests that the interpreter hold belief constant, in order to "solve" for meaning, e.g., by charitably assuming logical consistency and basic rationality on the speaker's part (principle of coherence), and by assuming that the speaker is cognitively similar in her responses to features of the world (principle of correspondence). This strategy endows the speaker with what the interpreter takes to be largely true beliefs about the nonlinguistic world and thus allows him to attribute meaning to utterances on the basis of inferences about beliefs. In particular, it enables the interpreter to use observations of causal interactions between the speaker and the world as a basis for assigning truth conditions and thus meaning and content to the speaker's utterances (Davidson, "Radical Interpretation," p. 136; see also see also Davidson, "Belief and the Basis of Meaning"; "Thought and Talk," in *Inquiries into Truth and Interpretation*, pp. 168–169; "Three Varieties of Knowledge," p. 211).

52. Davidson draws an analogy between a Tarski-style semantic theory and measurement theory. In the measurement analogy, the interpreter's sentences serve to

keep track of everything propositional, just as the numbers on the Celsius or the Fahrenheit scales serve to keep track of temperature. See "What Is Present to the Mind?," pp. 59–62; "The Emergence of Thought," pp. 130–133; "Indeterminism and Antirealism," in *Subjective, Intersubjective, Objective*, pp. 74–77.

53. Davidson, "A Coherence Theory of Truth and Knowledge," in *Subjective, Intersubjective, Objective*, p. 151.

54. Donald Davidson, "Radical Interpretation Interpreted," in *Philosophical Perspectives*, vol. 8: *Logic and Language*, ed. James E. Tomberlin (Atascadero, CA: Ridgeview, 1994), p. 125.

55. Davidson, "Thought and Talk," p. 162.

56. Davidson, "Thought and Talk," pp. 168–169; "The Problem of Objectivity," pp. 11–17; "The Emergence of Thought," pp. 124–126.

57. In the basic cases of perceptual or occasion sentences, Davidson argues that aspects of the situations that cause speakers to accept or reject perception sentences, i.e., to hold them true or false, endow them with meaning and content. He remarks, "A sentence which one has been conditioned by the learning process to be caused to hold true by the presence of fires will be true when there is a fire present; a word one has been conditioned to be caused to hold applicable in the presence of snakes will refer to snakes" ("The Myth of the Subjective," pp. 44–45). For Davidson's discussion of his version of externalism, see "Radical Interpretation," "Epistemology Externalized," "Meaning, Truth, and Evidence," and "Externalisms."

58. Davidson, "Conditions of Thought," p. 195; "Epistemology Externalized," pp. 196–198; "Three Varieties of Knowledge," p. 213.

59. Davidson, "The Myth of the Subjective," p. 51.

60. Davidson, "A Coherence Theory of Truth and Knowledge," p. 318; "Epistemology Externalized," pp. 201–203; "Three Varieties of Knowledge," p. 212; "The Second Person," pp. 117–121; "Interpretation: Hard in Theory, Easy in Practice," pp. 39–43; "Externalisms," pp. 5–13.

61. Davidson, "Three Varieties of Knowledge," pp. 212–213; see also "What Thought Requires," in *Problems of Rationality*, pp. 142–144, and "The Second Person."

62. Davidson, "The Irreducibility of the Concept of the Self," p. 88.

63. Davidson, "The Second Person," p. 121.

64. For Davidson's paratactic analysis of propositional attitude ascriptions, see "On Saying That," pp. 93–108; "Thought and Talk," pp. 165–166; "What Is Present to the Mind?," pp. 63–64.

65. Davidson, "Comments on Karlovy Vary Papers," in Kotatko, Pagin, and Segal (eds.), *Interpreting Davidson*, p. 299.

66. Davidson, "Epistemology Externalized," p. 198.

67. In uttering a sentence of her idiolect to self-ascribe a thought, the speaker is not in a position to step outside her language in order to judge how things are independently of how she takes them to be. See Röska-Hardy, "Moore's Paradox and the Expression of Belief," pp. 335–336.

68. Davidson, "The Irreducibility of the Concept of the Self," pp. 88–89.

69. Davidson, "First Person Authority," p. 13; "Knowing One's Own Mind," pp. 37–38.

70. Davidson, "Thought and Talk," p. 69; see also "On the Very Idea of a Conceptual Scheme" in *Inquiries into Truth and Interpretation*, pp. 183–198, and "Epistemology Externalized."

71. Davidson, "Reply to Picardi," p. 211; "Reply to Thöle," p. 248. See also Davidson, "Empirical Content," in *Inquiries into Truth and Interpretation*, p. 175.

72. Davidson, "What Is Present to the Mind?," p. 66.

73. Davidson, "Comments on Karlovy Vary Papers," p. 287; see also "Externalisms," pp. 14–15.

74. Davidson, "Comments on Karlovy Vary Papers," p. 297.

75. Davidson, "Seeing through Language," in *Truth, Language and History*, p. 135.

76. See Davidson, "Three Varieties of Knowledge," pp. 205–206, 218–220; "The Problem of Objectivity," pp. 3–4; "The Second Person," pp. 120–121.

20 Radical Interpretation, Feminism, and Science

Sharyn Clough

1 Introduction

Donald Davidson's philosophy of language provides a rich array of conceptual tools for feminist science studies. In this essay, I focus on Davidson's account of radical interpretation and the concept of triangulation as a necessary feature of communication and the formation of beliefs.

The basic features of triangulation relevant to this discussion arise out of Davidson's thought experiment, building from W. V. O. Quine, concerning the interpretational strategies of the radical interpreter—an adult who finds herself in the midst of speakers of a language completely foreign to her.[1] In the absence of a translation manual or any collateral information about the new language, how, Davidson asks, must this idealized interpreter proceed to cope with her unfamiliar world? Initially, all she has to go on, and, indeed, all she needs, says Davidson, is the development of a triangular relationship between (i) the beliefs of native speakers expressed as sentences, (ii) the features of the world to which the sentences refer, and (iii) her attention to (i) and (ii).

There are two important implications of this model of belief formation for feminists studying the effects of social location on knowledge production generally, and the production of scientific knowledge in particular.

The first is Davidson's argument that whatever there is to the meaning of any of our beliefs must in principle be available from the radical interpreter's external, third-person perspective. We can all imagine and/or have experienced successful immersion experiences in completely unfamiliar language communities. On what can this success depend? Surely not on some internal private stock of beliefs about, or expressed in, the new language that are then tested; initially in these situations, we, as radical interpreters, have no such semantic content available to us in the new language. Yet eventually we can, or at least we know people who have, learned the new language. The reason is that, in the simplest cases, at least, the content of the beliefs of the native speakers can be publicly accessed through radical interpretation. There is some debate about the role of radical interpretation in the language acquisition of children, but, in principle if not always in practice, the lesson remains.[2] Although beliefs are held by individuals and are, in some sense, idiosyncratic and/or a product of particular social forces and locations that may not be shared by everyone, still, the content of any belief must in principle be publicly accessible and communicable, for it is the public process of communication that gives rise to those beliefs in the first place. And if the content of a belief can be publicly accessed, then the relationship between the content of the belief and the features of the world to which it refers, more or less directly, can be adjudicated by anyone who cares enough to take the time to do so.

This lesson responds to those critics of feminist science studies who argue that by identifying gender, for example, as playing an important role in scientific theory formation and testing, feminists are committing themselves to an incoherent conceptual relativism. Of course, some feminist articulations of the role of gender in science *might* commit themselves in this way (see, e.g., my discussion of Sandra Harding's work, below), but there is nothing about the acknowledgment of the role of social location in knowledge that *forces* such a commitment, and no one involved in feminist science studies (certainly not Harding) would endorse the commitment. If Davidson is right, the radical conceptual relativism that results from the view that believers from different social locations, such as different genders, somehow live in different and incommensurable conceptual worlds simply cannot arise, at least not in any philosophically interesting way, and certainly not in a way that would damage the epistemic authority of feminist claims.[3]

The second important implication of triangulation for feminist science studies is that Davidson's is a holistic model that shows there is no principled, substantive difference in the triangulation process by which we form beliefs concerning basic descriptive features of the world and beliefs concerning evaluative features of the world.[4] That is, just as with descriptive judgments, feminist and other value judgments generally get their semantic content from their relationship to the world—a relationship that can in principle be objectively adjudicated. In this way, we can show that what makes feminist interpretations of particular scientific studies better than sexist interpretations is that the feminist interpretations are more empirically adequate; and the notion of empirical adequacy at work can be objectively adjudicated even by those who do not share feminist value frameworks. The key to such objective adjudication is not that the knower be neutral or value-free—that is impossible—but instead that the knower be *impartial* in her assessment of the evidence for or against a particular value judgment. The important distinctions between the impossible task of being neutral and the crucial task of being impartial, tentative, or nondogmatic are discussed by a number of philosophers who write about feminism, values, and science.[5]

2 Feminism and Relativism

I begin with the first implication of triangulation: the antirelativist point that the content of any one of our beliefs must in principle be publicly accessible and communicable; and that the truth of that belief must be available for adjudication by anyone, irrespective of his or her social location. Of course, those interpreting and adjudicating need to care enough to take the time to trace the often complex links between the content of the belief and the features of the world to which it refers, more or less directly. This is a nontrivial, practical problem to which I return below in the section entitled "Feminist Strategy."

As expressed by Helen Longino in her essay "Essential Tensions," feminists engaged in science studies have to reconcile what seem to be two conflicting claims: "that scientific inquiry is value- or ideology-laden *and* that it is productive of knowledge."[6] The values with which science is "laden" arise partly as a result of the social location of scientists. One of the stumbling blocks to reconciling the role of values in producing legitimate knowledge claims, then, is the problem of articulating a model of knowledge that shows how people from different social locations can share objective epistemic standards—that conceptual-scheme relativism is a nonstarter. Many feminists involved in science studies have shown a commitment to the claim that although the social location of knowers is relevant to the knowledge produced, this relevance does not radically foreclose the possibility of sharing objective epistemological standards between those who are working from different social locations. Feminist interpretations of particular studies are empirically better than sexist interpretations—and not better according to feminist epistemological standards, understood as subjective and relativistic, but better according to objective standards held by feminists and in principle available to any knower.

In her landmark essay "Situated Knowledges," Donna Haraway argued that "feminists have to insist on a better account of the world, it is not enough to show radical historical contingency and modes of construction for everything."[7] In the more recent book *Ecological Thinking,* Lorraine Code highlighted the ability of her ecological epistemic project to guard "against the subjectivism and/or relativism that have deterred philosophers from granting epistemic significance to place, particularity, imagination, and interpretation."[8]

However, it is not always clear how a relativism based on social location is to be avoided, as many critics of feminist work in science are quick to point out. While we feminists attend to the difficult and important task of identifying the multiple influences of "place, particularity, imagination, and interpretation," in science, we need also to be explicit in our explanations of how it is that these influences can at least in principle be identified and their strengths and weaknesses made clear to any knower who cares enough to engage in the question.

I attempted to provide such an explanation in my earliest articulation of the usefulness of Davidson's work to feminists.[9] There, I argued that an unnecessary level of relativism could be found in some of the early and classic epistemological writings of three influential feminist theorists: Longino, Harding, and Evelyn Fox Keller, and that reworking their arguments in terms of Davidson's model of radical interpretation would avoid the relativist problem.[10] Beginning with an analysis of Longino's "Can There Be a Feminist Science?" and *Science as Social Knowledge,* and proceeding to three essays from Keller's collection *Secrets of Life, Secrets of Death,* I argued that each of these writings employed, unnecessarily, a relativist claim that our theory-choices must be based not just on the empirical evidence, narrowly construed, but must also be *relative* to a political or cultural "worldview," "explanatory scheme," or "interpretive framework." I showed how this sort of relativism involves the conceptual splitting of the empirical evidence, on the one hand, from the filter of politics or culture, on the other—a split similar to that between "content" and "scheme" critically discussed by Davidson.[11]

I review here the problem of conceptual relativism that I had identified in Harding's articulation of feminist standpoint theory. Harding is appropriately critical of the claim that objective method consists in detecting a one-to-one correspondence between true representations and the world.[12] She argues that certain aspects of culture, namely the social standpoint of the theorist, filter the correspondence between any one theory and the evidence gathered in support of that theory. Harding makes the Marxist claim that one's social standpoint will "organize and set limits" on one's understanding of the world.[13] In other words, the choice of which theories of the world we take to be true will be relative, in some way, to our social standpoint. In "Rethinking Standpoint Epistemology: What Is 'Strong Objectivity'?" Harding explains her commitment to the general tenets of standpoint theory:

> The starting point of standpoint theory—and its claim that is most often misread—is that in societies stratified by race, ethnicity, class, gender, sexuality, or some other such politics shaping the very structure of a society, the activities of those at the top both organize and set limits on what persons who perform such activities can understand about themselves and the world around them. . . . In contrast, the activities of those at the bottom of such social hierarchies can provide starting points for thought—for *everyone's* research and scholarship—from which humans' relations with each other and the natural world can become visible. This is because the experience and lives of marginalized peoples, as they understand them, provide particularly significant *problems to be explained* or research agendas.[14]

In *Whose Science? Whose Knowledge?* Harding responds to worries about conceptual-scheme relativism that might seem to arise from her work, arguing that although every social standpoint filter "organizes and sets limits" on understanding, that is, every filter provides only a partial representation of reality, not all social standpoints generate *equally* partial representations or beliefs. The social standpoints of women, or feminists with "maximally liberatory social interests," for example, "have generated less partial and distorted beliefs than others."[15] She explains:

> The history of science shows that research directed by maximally liberatory social interests and values tends to be better equipped to identify partial claims and distorting assumptions, even though the credibility of the scientists who do it may not be enhanced during the short run. After all, anti-liberatory interests and values are invested in the natural inferiority of just the groups of humans who, if given real equal access (not just the formally equal access that is liberalism's goal) to public voice, would most strongly contest claims about their purported natural inferiority. Anti-liberatory interests and values silence and destroy the most likely sources of evidence against their own claims. That is what makes them rational for elites.[16]

I'm not convinced that her response to relativism works here. Harding rightly criticizes the traditional epistemological view of what she calls "objectivism." The "value-free" approach of objectivism, she argues, results in a "semi-science" that "turns away from the task of critically identifying all those broad, historical social desires, interests, and values that have shaped the agendas, contents, and results of the sciences much as they shape the rest of human affairs."[17] Harding prescribes, instead, "strong objectivity" that extends the idea of scientific research "to include systematic examination of . . . powerful background beliefs," thereby "maximizing objectivity."[18] The concern is that strong objectivity is characterized by Harding as the critical examination of linguistic or social filters, "the powerful background beliefs" that continually block our knowledge-seeking of the natural realm. Powerful background beliefs operate as filters or conceptual schemes for organizing the data from the natural world. Here a scheme–content relativism begins to reappear in Harding's work. Beliefs that we form about the natural world can never be objectively true or false on her account, only true or false relative to our subjective filters.

Indeed, because Harding acknowledges that all beliefs have a social filter, she disavows the claim that the standpoints of women or feminists will produce objectively true beliefs.[19] While she purchases some consistency by claiming that *all* knowledge is somehow distorted by conceptual frameworks, her relativist claim robs her of the foundation she then needs to argue her thesis—namely that the knowledge produced from maximally liberatory social standpoints is less distorted, generally, than that produced from others. On what can this normative comparison be based? For Harding, objective method ("strong objectivity") is simply the *least subjective* method for judging which conceptual schemes, filters, or interpretive frameworks make for the least opaque filters between us and the world. If this is the case, then, Harding (as well as critics of feminism) is right: We must concede a certain amount of relativism. When feminist scientists and science commentators choose between competing theories, our choice is made on the basis of our feminist political interpretive frameworks, understood not as evidence available for objective adjudication, but as subjective filters that *organize* the evidence.

3 A Davidsonian Prescription

Paralleling the work of many feminist critics of epistemology, Davidson argues against the claim that the objective detection of sensory data, for example, can be used to justify or stand as evidence for beliefs that represent those data. Davidson notes that for the justification process to work, we have to be aware of the detection of sense data, and this awareness is simply another belief. His argument undercuts the naive objectivist attempt to construe awareness of sensory data as an evidential entity that stands *independent from* our beliefs.

It might seem, however, that in revealing the incoherence of harnessing sensations as independent evidence, Davidson has removed any objective justificatory scheme for our empirical beliefs. This seems to leave us with the relativism encountered by Harding, a relativism that Davidson's model is supposed to avoid. All is not lost, however, as Davidson's model of the radical interpreter provides us with a good *reason* "for supposing most of our beliefs are true that is not a form of *evidence*."[20]

It is important to make clear that the term "most" in the above quotation is not meant as a quantificational claim guaranteeing, for example, that a certain *number* of our beliefs must be true. Rather, Davidson uses the concept of the radical interpreter to show that the detection of false beliefs *requires* that we have a background of true beliefs against which the error of the false beliefs can be measured. This latter claim undercuts the global skeptic who wants to make error a general concern, that is, who wants to deny or question the existence or objectivity of norms against which errors can be measured and detected.

Davidson equips the radical interpreter with the abilities of a competent adult speaker of a language. Parachuted into the midst of a foreign land, she has general expectations about how to proceed. She has a sense of basic logical structure, that is, she understands the implications of those elements of a language ("and," "if . . . then," etc.) that give the sentences that contain them their particular logical form. She also has the ability to discern when the speakers of the foreign language are making assertions, that is, expressing, in the form of sentences, beliefs held true (even though, in the beginning, she has no idea what those sentences mean).

Davidson notes that, to make any progress in her new world, the radical interpreter must watch for correlations between types of sounds uttered by the native speakers and the kinds of events in their shared world that caused the utterances. In the beginning this is all she has to go on. She does not have any preconceived notion of the particular semantic role that is played by any particular noises uttered by the native speakers. Rather, at this early stage, the radical interpreter's successful (accurate) identification of the environmental reference that prompted the native speakers' noises is what provides those noises with semantic content in the first place.

The causal triangular relationship between the interpreter, the native speakers' utterances, and the objects and events in their world requires that the interpreter assume the natives are speaking truthfully about their beliefs. Of course, while the adult language user has the ability to recognize when a native speaker is making an assertion, this recognition does not *guarantee* that the native speaker's assertion is true. But, says Davidson, at the beginning, the radical interpreter must *assume* that the native speaker's assertions are true. For interpretation to occur she must assume that the same relation between belief and truth holds for those she interprets, as for herself—what Davidson calls "the principle of charity."

Why is this agreement necessary at the beginning when the interpreter is collecting sentences in the native language and correlating them with the sorts of environmental conditions that prompted the sentences? It is necessary, says Davidson, because to identify her teachers as having *any* beliefs, she must assume the beliefs they hold are true. Once she has established an empirical base of correlations between their sentences and hers, *then* she can start to make judgments of inconsistency and falsehood. Before that point, identifying her teachers' beliefs as false would deplete the empirical base from which she needs to begin her interpretative project in the first place. As Jeff Malpas explains, assigning "too much falsity among beliefs undermines the possibility of identifying beliefs at all."[21] Identifying falsehoods and misconceptions is "parasitic" on an established coordinate of shared meaning.[22]

It might still be unclear, however, why the existence of a "shared coordinate of meaning" between the native speaker and the radical interpreter guarantees, in Davidson's words, that "it cannot happen that most of our plainest beliefs about what exists in the world are false."[23] Just because there must be *agreement* between the radical interpreter and the native speakers' about the truth of basic beliefs does not guarantee that those beliefs are, *in fact*, true. Davidson responds by examining the concept of truth itself. Where, he asks, do we come up with the concept of objective truth? The answer is in shared language. "Unless a language is shared there is no way to distinguish between using the language correctly and using it incorrectly; only communication with another can supply an objective check."[24] And communication with another can only start by assuming agreement on what makes utterances true—the principle of charity.

If the principle of charity is a precursor for successful interpretation, this means that truth must be held primitive for words and sentences to be meaningful. This takes us back to the example of the radical interpreter correlating environmental circumstances with basic native utterances. The radical interpreter has no initial preconceptions about how to link a native utterance with specific semantic content. Rather, her attention to the correct (true) reference of the native sentence is what provides her with clues to the meaning of the utterance in the first place. The meaning of an utterance is given by its truth conditions, and not the reverse.

Davidson uses these points about the radical interpreter to support his extensionalist claim that in the simplest cases of beliefs, the events and objects that cause those beliefs (the *extension* of the beliefs) also determine their contents, or meaning (the *intension* of the beliefs).[25] This means that in the simplest cases, there cannot be wholesale slippage between our understanding of the meaning of a sentence and our understanding of the conditions that would make that sentence true. Davidson describes this approach to meaning further, in the following passage:

> As long as we adhere to the basic intuition that in the simplest cases words and thoughts refer to what causes them, it is clear that it cannot happen that most of our plainest beliefs about what exists in the world are false. The reason is that we do not first form concepts and then discover what they apply to; rather, in the basic cases, the application determines the content of the concept.[26]

Davidson's extensionalist approach to meaning excludes the possibility that the speech of the radical interpreter could be in principle indistinguishable from her teachers *and* idiosyncratic with respect to meaning. In the case of simple perceptual beliefs, the meaning of her utterances is determined by their being used correctly in the presence of another speaker and the event in the world that caused the utterance. Taking a holistic approach to build from the simpler cases of beliefs to beliefs expressed in more complex value judgments, any idiosyncrasies in the radical interpreter's meaning are *in principle* available for her correction through a purely extensional examination of how she has applied her referents. Somewhere along the line, any discrepancies can in principle be revealed. There is no subjective "inside" to her beliefs that is relative to her conceptual scheme and inaccessible from the viewpoint of native speakers on the "outside."

Applying Davidson's model of language use to cases like Harding's standpoint theory, we are cautioned against the metaphysical bifurcation of inner, subjective, politically laden filters and external, objective, empirical beliefs. This advice is particularly relevant for addressing the problems that Harding encounters in her arguments about the filtering function of social standpoints. Harding argues that, because interpretive frameworks or cultural worldviews filter any evidence brought forward in support of a scientific theory or hypothesis, we cannot choose between theories or hypotheses simply on the basis of empirical evidence (where empirical evidence is narrowly construed by Harding). On her view, adjudication must ultimately be relative to our political values and worldviews. However, this construal presumes the relativist view that the "empirical evidence" and our feminist "political values" emanate from two metaphysically separate spheres—the first from the objective, external world; the second from the subjective, internal mind (or minds). The "empirical evidence" is construed as providing independent (objective) support for a theory, while political values are viewed as dependent and subjective *filters* for the evidence.

In response to this claim about the belief-independence of empirical evidence, Davidson reminds us that when we marshal empirical evidence in support of a belief or theory, we need first to be aware of the empirical evidence, and that *awareness* is itself another belief. In the project of marshaling epistemic justification for our individual beliefs, there is no independent, "nonbelief" entity to which we can appeal. The evidence for a belief must *itself* be a belief. It is also important to see that both our political values and our more straightforwardly empirical commitments are beliefs of this evidential sort. On Davidson's model, even our (feminist) political beliefs must have some weblike relation to empirical evidence, if they are to have any content. And it is this relation that can in principle be shared and evaluated objectively by anyone, regardless of political affiliations and/or worldviews.

There are a number of ways in which empirically informed feminist political values can interact with and support the more straightforwardly empirical commitments that, together, make up our growing web of beliefs (e.g., our beliefs critical of sexism and oppression in science). Consider, for example, Elizabeth Anderson's discussion of feminist social scientific research on divorce.[27] Anderson examines feminist political value judgments such as the claim that, women, just like men, cannot be adequately defined by exclusive attention to their relationships to their spouses and children.[28] Both women and men have needs, desires, and concerns that focus on aspects of their lives other than their families and homes. These sorts of political value judgments have empirical content that can be objectively evaluated, and they are relevant to the question of how to approach the scientific study of divorce. Anderson argues convincingly that the foregrounding of these feminist claims, however controversial to some, can objectively increase the empirical adequacy of research on divorce.[29] For example, by including this sort of claim, feminist researchers were encouraged to frame questions that allowed for a wider range of responses from the study participants, and hence a more empirically accurate description of the phenomenon. Feminist researchers were able to see what traditional researchers did not, namely that divorce might not always be seen as a negative life event.[30]

This brings us to the second implication of Davidson's model for feminists, namely, his fact–value holism. Recall Longino's acknowledgment that feminists engaged in science studies have to show both "that scientific inquiry is value- or ideology-laden *and* that it is productive of knowledge." On Davidson's holistic model, these two seemingly contradictory projects are shown to be of a single piece. The empirical beliefs that comprise "scientific knowledge" have no better or worse metaphysical links to the outer, independent objective world than do our beliefs about values, just as our beliefs about values are no more closely related than our more straightforwardly empirical beliefs to our inner subjective world. But this is because, on Davidson's view, there *is no* inner or outer world; there is no metaphysical bifurcation. There is only one world, an objective view of which can be made meaningful only by the language users who are part of it.

Although it is certainly possible that some of the feminist political beliefs and other value judgments that make up our belief webs might be more *geographically* remote from the simpler perceptual beliefs at the edge of our webs, the holism of Davidson's model indicates that the value judgments are still connected, by some threads, to those simpler beliefs. When we examine meaning on the model of the radical interpreter, we see that changes in those simple beliefs can, and must, in principle, affect our more complex value judgments, even if the effect is only slight. Furthermore, the links to empirical content of any given value judgments are as available to objective adjudication as are our more straightforward descriptive beliefs.

If we take Davidson's meaning holism seriously, then even our more complex political and other value judgments are importantly linked in publicly accessible ways to our more simple perceptual beliefs and, more generally, to our everyday shared experiences about, and in, the world. It is these complicated but, in principle, publicly accessible set of inferential links that give our more complex political beliefs their meaning. By tracing the inferential relationship between our value judgments and our everyday shared experiences, we can begin to adjudicate objectively the truth or falsity of the more complex evaluative judgments. As with even the most basic exchanges, the fact that we can recognize each other as holding these more complex beliefs becomes the route we take for identifying and objectively adjudicating their content.[31] Such objective adjudication is possible, though, of course, difficult.[32]

The sense of objectivity that Davidson's account reveals in the most general sense, then, is that our beliefs are objectively true or false insofar as their truth-values hold independently of "our will and our attitudes"; their truth-values are "not in general guaranteed by anything in us."[33] Wanting something to be true or false does not make it so. Of course, there are many cases of "self-fulfilling" prophecy as well as placebo effects and other social-psychological phenomena where labeling something or someone can indeed bring about a change in the world, but even these sorts of changes are dependent on the usual physical causal processes. That negative social messages about weight and body image lead some young women to develop eating disorders need not imply that this sort of illness was "willed into being" through some special metaphysical process in the arsenal of sexist advertising executives, however much one might begin to suspect just that.[34]

The innocuous notion of independence between our desires and the truth of our beliefs that underlies Davidson's claim that our beliefs can be objectively true or false applies also to the process or method by which we identify true and false beliefs and/or adjudicate between competing beliefs. That is, because the truth-values of beliefs are, in principle, objective, that means that there are features outside of our own wants and desires that we can point to in identifying those truth-values and/or in adjudicating between competing truth claims. We do not have to be neutral toward the truth of any belief in order to hold the belief up to critical scrutiny, that is, in order to give that belief or its opposite a fair hearing. Objective, rational adjudication of beliefs requires not that we be neutral, but that we be tentative and nondogmatic. The very same objective process by which we identified the truth-value of a particular belief can in principle be sensitive to new experiences that require us to change our minds.

Davidson himself does not focus on this methodological aspect of objectivity, perhaps because it tends to be addressed in venues featuring science studies rather than in the terrain of epistemology and philosophy of language. Within science studies, the question usually concerns how best to choose objectively between competing theories, where an objective process of theory-choice usually indicates, at least, a nondogmatic, fallible assessment of the relevant evidence supporting each theory. Applying Davidson's account, the process would involve tracing the public, empirically accessible route by which the content of the beliefs in question was established, and assessing the relevant evidential links between these beliefs and their causes. But again, this adjudication process can in principle be objective, insofar as the truth-values of the competing beliefs at issue are independent of the desires of the holders of the beliefs. This naturalized analysis of the objectivity of theory choice parallels the analysis offered by a number of feminist philosophers of science, such as Alison Wylie's discussion of the "security" of archaeological evidence.[35]

Of course, this Davidsonian-inspired view of beliefs about values as capable of being objectively true or false contrasts with a more popular view of values that focuses on their private or subjective nature—an inner nature that keeps value judgments from being available for objective evaluation. On some interpretations of Hume, for example, it seems that because we cannot find value judgments out in the world, in the way that we can find, say, rocks out in the world, no objective claims can be made about values. However, with Davidson, I don't think that questions of the "location" of values (out there, in here) get to the question of the *objectivity* of values. To put it another way: unless we are operating with some lingering Cartesian dualism, we shouldn't make much metaphysical noise about the difference between beliefs formed "out there" and "in here." It's not that there's *no* difference between those sorts of beliefs, just not a difference that affects our ability to objectively examine their truth.

Compare the case of making objective claims regarding other sorts of properties, such as weights or colors. There is a fact of the matter about whether something weighs five kilograms rather than ten, or is green rather than red. Insofar as we can make objective judgments about properties such as color or weight, this doesn't commit us to the view that greenness is out there in the world in the same way that rocks are out there in the world.

Note also that just because there is an objective fact about whether these predicates can be applied in any given case does not mean that we would all agree on the application criteria, or that the identification process is going to be straightforward. Compare:

1. Grass is green.
2. A person's sex-chromosomes are causally irrelevant to successful parenting.
3. Individual organisms belong to the same species just in case they can interbreed.
4. Water is the molecule H_2O.

Cases 3 and 4 might stand out as straightforwardly and objectively true descriptive judgments. However, identifying water as the molecule "H_2O" is controversial. A sample of pure H_2O does not have the properties many of us would want to associate with water; in large amounts, it is harmful to drink. Indeed the process of identifying macroproperties of the world around us by reference to their molecular properties is still debated within chemistry. Defining species categories is similarly controversial within evolutionary biology, and systematics more generally. In fact, there is probably as much if not more agreement about the application criteria and empirical evidence for the judgments involved in cases 1 and 2 than there is for cases 3 and 4. But, again, even with doubts about application criteria, there is little doubt that there is an objective fact of the matter in each of the above four cases.

So lack of agreement about how to apply a particular predicate is separate from the question of whether that predicate expresses an objective fact of the matter. And just as we would agree that there is a fact of the matter about whether something is green or red, or a member of the same species or not, there is also a fact about whether someone is a good parent and whether his or her sex chromosomes figure relevantly in this assignment. We can objectively evaluate whether these predicates are being applied correctly even if the level of agreement about application criteria varies from case to case.

Our judgments of properties such as color are similar to our judgments about properties that express values, for example, judging someone's parenting ability. Indeed, learning the correct application of the color predicate "green" or the value predicate "successful parent" requires the same sort of empirical examination that is required when we identify something as being a certain molecule, or the member of a certain species. There is a difference between each of these concepts and our own particular ability to identify and apply them. We can be right or wrong in our applications—wishing will not make it that something that is green or successful at parenting is instead blue or unsuccessful. There is an objective, though of course contingent, fact of the matter about whether something or someone can be identified as "green," or as a "successful parent," just as there is in the case of defining "species" and "water."

On Davidson's holistic account, to have meaningful beliefs at all, whether they be value judgments or descriptive judgments, is to be practically (e.g., linguistically) enmeshed in a sociophysical relationship with the world around us, including other knowers. The meaning, or cognitive content, of our judgments, both descriptive and evaluative, is produced through a triangulation between ourselves, the fellow creatures with whom we communicate and engage, and the shared bits of the world on which that communication or engagement is focused.

Insofar as value judgments *express* anything, then—that is, insofar as they are meaningful—they too are beliefs that have been acquired through the usual process of practical engagement with the world through communication with others. Learning to identify someone as a "successful" parent—learning the meaning of this value term—involves learning through experience of the world to successfully classify something as belonging to a particular category, to assign it a property. The same process is used for learning the meaning of the category terms "conducts electricity," "reflects light," and "produces heat." Insofar as values or any other kind of judgments are meaningful, they are beliefs that arise from our experience with the world—that is, they have empirical content, broadly construed.

As Anderson argues, value judgments can be shown to be amenable to reflective deliberation—they do not have to determine, inappropriately, any given interpretation of some other set of judgments. Of course, they might. Anderson argues that "we need to ensure that value judgements do not operate to drive inquiry to a predetermined conclusion."[36] I want to emphasize the holistic point that this same need holds for *any* judgment. So, while assigning some phenomenon to the category "good" might inappropriately bias our interpretations of any new evidence about that phenomenon, so too might our categorizations of it as "hot" or "reflective." Importantly, in neither case is the categorization or its effect on future interpretations immune from appropriate revision in the light of new experiences. As Anderson herself shows, any judgments can be held dogmatically, though, thankfully, they need not be. Anderson concludes that "from an epistemological point of view, value judgements function like empirical hypotheses."[37] I go further, making Davidson's holistic point that value judgments, like any other, just *are* empirical hypotheses, broadly speaking—hypotheses that can be subjected to rational processes of adjudication. They would have no meaning otherwise.[38]

4 Feminist Strategy

I have argued that there are two important implications of Davidson's work for feminist science studies. The first is the antirelativist point that whatever there is to the meaning of any of our beliefs must in principle be available from the radical interpreter's external, third-person perspective, no matter how different the social locations, worldviews, or standpoints from which the interpreter or interpreted are operating. When feminists acknowledge the importance of social location to scientific inquiry, this acknowledgment does not have to involve an incoherent scheme–content relativism. The second implication of his work is that there is no principled difference in the triangulation process by which we form beliefs concerning basic descriptive features of the world and beliefs concerning evaluative features of the world. Just as with descriptive judgments, feminist and other value judgments get their semantic content from their relationship to the world—a relationship that can, in principle, be objectively adjudicated. In this way, we can show that feminist interpretations of particular scientific studies are better than sexist interpretations—not just better from a feminist standpoint, but objectively so.

One concern that might arise for feminists at this point is that my claims about "objective adjudication" are always modified by the phrase "in principle"—in the practical, political struggles that feminists face, these sorts of idealized Davidsonian arguments might not always be relevant. The possibility of objectively detecting the truth of feminist claims about science, and of persuading the holders of false, sexist beliefs to change their minds, however objective a process, is only that—a possibility. There are structural power differences that often materially interfere with the conversations required for this process. Still, I argue that something like this approach, if not sufficient, remains at least a necessary part of the story.[39]

An opposite concern that might arise for feminist strategy is whether my claims about the possibility of the objective detection of true from false beliefs, and the objective truth of beliefs generally, serves to overemphasize the objective at the expense of the recognition of the subjective. Davidson responds to this worry in "Three Varieties of Knowledge":

> It may seem that if sharing a general view of the world is a condition of thought, the differences in intellectual and imaginative character among minds and cultures will be lost to sight. If I have given this impression, it is because I have wanted to concentrate on what seems to be primary, and so apt to go unnoticed: the necessary degree of communality essential to understanding another individual, and the extent to which such understanding provides the foundation for the concept of truth and reality upon which all thought depends.[40]

His work is completely compatible, then, with feminist interest in analyzing individual and group differences in the holding of complex beliefs, especially concerning the existence of highly stratified and isolated sets of beliefs arising out of particular social identities (in cultures such as the contemporary United States, beliefs stratified by sex/gender, racial and class divisions). Within science studies, for example, feminists have played an important role in redefining accounts of objectivity that would acknowledge and incorporate the subjective affects of social stratification on scientific theory production and justification.

Another place where feminists sometimes downplay or resist aligning themselves with certain accounts of "truth" concerns our recognition of the power that can be wielded inappropriately by those scientists who, working as part of the larger Western military industrial complex, claim access to objective Truth with a capital "T," that is, "truth" understood as some foundational and metaphysically suspect notion.

For example, in the final two chapters of her more recent book *Science and Social Inequality: Feminist and Postcolonial Issues*, Harding asks "Are Truth Claims in Science Dysfunctional?"[41] She begins with the question, "Do we need truth claims?" and continues, "The argument here is that in the case of the sciences, their costs appear to outweigh their benefits."[42] On a closer read, the question can be reasonably paraphrased as "Have the truth claims made by various scientists turned out to be as universally and transculturally true as some scientists and folks in the popular science debates believed the claims to be?" The answer to this, as most of us would now respond, is "no." This answer, of course, is itself a truth claim—indeed, it is even an *objectively true* truth claim, if anything is, and it is a truth claim with which Harding would agree.

However, Harding demurs, preferring to split the language of "objectivity" from "truth" here. Once again, though, her main point is that while she is against the notion of (capital "T") Truth, she *does not* embrace epistemological relativism. In other words, she *does* believe in the coherence of the notions of truth, accuracy, and objectivity applied in more local and metaphysically innocuous terms.

I think that feminist philosophers are right to be suspicious of the usefulness and coherence of metaphysically suspect theories of knowledge, justification, and truth that claim to rise above the empirical and fallible processes and procedures by which all of us come to know our worlds. However, I think that we should not let this suspicion rob of us of the concept of "objective truth" *tout court*. In the broadly empirical terms described by Davidson, there need be no metaphysical danger in the concept of objective truth. Feminism, by definition, involves "speaking truth to power." We have a number of objective truth claims on our side. When you've got it, use it.

To review, the two concerns about the account of objectivity provided by Davidson that might be of strategic concern to feminists are: first, that the idealized account is impractical and does not go far enough to show how claims to objectivity can aid in the practical, political struggles feminists face; and second, that the account relies *too* much on claims of objectivity and truth that downplay important subjective and social features of knowledge, with the added worry that claims to certain notions of objective truth can and have been used inappropriately as tools of oppression.

I argue that these two concerns merely reinforce the complex and contingent nature of the problems feminists working in science studies need to address. In some cases, we feminist philosophers should signal the importance of Davidson's work, highlighting the objectivity of belief, including, where relevant, the objectivity of feminist beliefs. In other cases, we should continue our project of illuminating the important, subjective, socially stratified features of belief that remain. However, this illumination itself requires that some baseline notions of objectivity be established, and that the rhetorical ground be cleared of the relativist fodder that often provokes critics of feminism.

Which aspect of the project we emphasize is going to depend on the debate we find ourselves in. The philosophical tools we need to work on these problems need to be specialized for the task at hand, and no one point of emphasis is going to cover all situations. I have argued that Davidson's work on radical interpretation, and especially his notion of triangulation, though not initially designed for use in feminist science studies, is, in fact, a particularly useful tool for us. I look forward to seeing more of his work used in these novel contexts. I am confident that he would be pleased.

Notes

1. The work of Quine, Davidson's mentor, has also proven useful to feminist science studies. See, e.g., Lynn Hankinson Nelson, *Who Knows? From Quine to a Feminist Empiricism* (Philadelphia: Temple University Press, 1990), and *Feminist Interpretations of Quine*, ed. Lynn Hankinson Nelson (State College: Pennsylvania State University Press, 2003). The characterization of radical interpretation that follows comes from Sharyn Clough, "Donald Davidson," in *The Routledge Encyclopedia of Postmodernism*, ed. Charles E. Winquist and Victor Taylor (London: Routledge, 2001), p. 82.

2. Some have argued that empirical studies regarding Chomskyan notions of deep structure show that the brain of the radical interpreter equips her with more tools than Davidson's thought experiment allows. However, it's important to note that Davidson denies only that such neurological infrastructure can provide semantic content. The claim that language acquisition requires syntactical modules in the brain does not conflict with Davidson's claim that only experience and interaction with native speakers can produce meaningful beliefs.

3. See Sharyn Clough, "A Hasty Retreat from Evidence: The Recalcitrance of Relativism in Feminist Epistemology," *Hypatia: A Journal of Feminist Philosophy* 13: 4 (1998): 88–111; Clough, *Beyond Epistemology: A Pragmatist Approach to Feminist Science Studies* (Lanham, MD: Rowman & Littlefield, 2003).

4. See Donald Davidson, "The Objectivity of Values," in his *Problems of Rationality* (Oxford: Clarendon Press, 2004); Clough, "On the Very Idea of a Feminist Epistemology of Science: Response to Commentators on *Beyond Epistemology: A Pragmatist Approach to Feminist Science Studies*," *Metascience* 15 (2006): 27–37; Clough, "Commentary on Elizabeth Anderson's 'Uses of Value Judgments in Science,'" *MIT Symposium on Gender, Race, and Philosophy*, Jan. 2006 Symposium I (2006), pp. 1–6, <http://web.mit.edu/sgrp/2006/no1/Clough0106.pdf>; Clough, "Solomon's Empirical/Non-Empirical Distinction and the Proper Place of Values in Science," *Perspectives in Science* 16, no. 3 (2008): 265–279; and Clough and Bill Loges, "Racist Value Judgments as Objectively False Beliefs: A Philosophical and Social-Psychological Analysis," *Journal of Social Philosophy* 39, no. 1 (2008): 77–95.

5. E.g., Hugh Lacey, *Is Science Value Free? Values and Scientific Understanding* (London: Routledge, 1999); Richmond Campbell, "The Virtues of Feminist Empiricism," *Hypatia: A Journal of Feminist Philosophy* 9, no. 1 (1994): 90–115; and Elizabeth Anderson,

"Uses of Value Judgments in Science," *Hypatia: A Journal of Feminist Philosophy* 19, no. 1 (2004): 1–24.

6. Helen Longino, "Essential Tensions," in *Feminist Epistemologies*, ed. Linda Alcoff and Elizabeth Potter (New York: Routledge, 1993) p. 345.

7. Donna Haraway, "Situated Knowledges," in her *Simians, Cyborgs, and Women: The Reinvention of Nature* (New York: Routledge 1991), p. 184.

8. Lorraine Code, *Ecological Thinking: The Politics of Epistemic Location* (Oxford: Oxford University Press, 2006), p. 6.

9. This next section makes use of arguments from Clough, "A Hasty Retreat"—an essay that Davidson read and about which he offered favorable and positive commentary (personal communication). He proved to be a kind and generous mentor.

10. Longino, "Can There Be a Feminist Science?," *Hypatia: A Journal of Feminist Philosophy* 2 (1987); Longino, *Science as Social Knowledge: Values and Objectivity in Scientific Inquiry* (Princeton: Princeton University Press, 1990); Evelyn Fox Keller, "Introduction," "Gender and Science: An Update," and "Critical Silences in Scientific Discourse," in her *Secrets of Life, Secrets of Death: Essays on Language, Gender, and Science* (New York: Routledge, 1992).

11. Davidson, "On the Very Idea of a Conceptual Scheme," in his *Inquiries into Truth and Interpretation* (Oxford: Clarendon Press, 1984).

12. Sandra Harding, *Whose Science? Whose Knowledge? Thinking from Women's Lives* (Ithaca: Cornell University Press, 1991); Harding, "Rethinking Standpoint Epistemology: What Is 'Strong Objectivity?'" in *Feminist Epistemologies*, ed. Linda Alcoff and Elizabeth Potter (New York: Routledge, 1993).

13. Harding, "Rethinking Standpoint Epistemology," p. 54.

14. Ibid.; italics in original.

15. Ibid., pp. 144, 148.

16. Harding, *Whose Science?* pp. 148–149.

17. Ibid., p. 143.

18. Ibid.

19. Ibid., pp. 185, 149.

20. Davidson, "A Coherence Theory of Truth and Knowledge," in his *Subjective, Intersubjective, Objective* (Oxford: Clarendon Press, 2001), p.146.

21. Jeffrey Malpas, *Donald Davidson and the Mirror of Meaning* (Cambridge: Cambridge University Press, 1992), p. 159.

22. I am grateful to Bjørn Ramberg for this interpretive point.

23. Davidson, "Epistemology Externalized," in *Subjective, Intersubjective, Objective*, p. 196.

24. Davidson, "Three Varieties of Knowledge," in *Subjective, Intersubjective, Objective*, p. 157.

25. Davidson, "The Myth of the Subjective," in *Subjective, Intersubjective, Objective*; "A Coherence Theory of Truth and Knowledge"; "Epistemology Externalized"; and "The Conditions of Thought," in *The Mind of Donald Davidson*, ed. Johannes Brands and Wolfgang Gombocz (*Grazer Philosophische Studien*, no. 36; Amsterdam: Editions Rodopi, 1989).

26. Davidson, "Epistemology Externalized," p. 195.

27. Anderson, "Uses of Value Judgments in Science."

28. Of course, to those who hold feminist values, this might sound like a straightforwardly empirical claim. To someone who does not hold feminist values, however, this "straightforward" claim is value-laden through and through (though still, I argue, empirical).

29. Anderson, "Uses of Value Judgments in Science," pp. 12–18.

30. Ibid., p. 13.

31. Portions of this argument about Davidson and the objectivity of value judgments appear in Clough, "On the Very Idea of a Feminist Epistemology," "Commentary on Elizabeth Anderson's 'Uses of Value Judgments in Science,'" "Solomon's Empirical/Nonempirical Distinction and the Proper Place of Values in Science," and Clough and Loges, "Racist Value Judgments as Objectively False Beliefs."

32. See, e.g., Davidson, "The Objectivity of Values."

33. Davidson, "The Problem of Objectivity," in his *Problems of Rationality* (Oxford: Clarendon Press, 2004), p. 7.

34. My thanks to Paul Griffiths for helping me tease apart the appropriate notions of "independent" at work here.

35. Alison Wylie, "The Constitution of Archaeological Evidence: Gender Politics and Science," in her *Thinking from Things: Essays in the Philosophy of Archaeology* (Berkeley: University of California Press, 2002). For a recent review of naturalized approaches to objectivity in feminist science studies, see Wylie and Lynn Hankinson Nelson, "Coming to Terms with the Values of Science: Insights from Feminist Science Scholarship," in *Value Free Science: Ideal or Illusion?*, ed. Harold Kincaid, John Dupré, and Alison Wylie (Oxford: Oxford University Press, 2006).

36. Anderson, "Uses of Value Judgments in Science," p. 11.

37. Ibid.

38. Sometimes, of course, meaningful empirical claims can also function more like rules or norms, where the assignment of truth-values is beside the point. See, e.g., Michael Hymers's illuminating discussion of Wittgenstein's claim regarding the dual nature of putatively descriptive propositions, like "This is my hand." This proposition can, in some contexts, function as an empirical truth, and sometimes, it can function logically as a rule around which other descriptive claims are organized and evaluated (Michael Hymers, "Putnam and the Difficulty of Renouncing All Theory," *International Studies in Philosophy* 35, no. 4 [2005]: 55–82). The capacity for a value judgment or a descriptive judgment to be true or false comes with the meaningfulness of the judgment, but the issue of whether truth-values should be assigned in any given case is relative to the context in which the judgment is being used.

39. Portions of this discussion of "feminist strategy" appear in Clough, "Drawing Battle Lines and Choosing Bedfellows: Rorty, Relativism, and Feminist Strategy," in *Feminist Interpretations of Richard Rorty*, ed. Marianne Janack (University Park: Pennsylvania State University Press, 2010), pp. 155–172.

40. Davidson, "Three Varieties of Knowledge," p. 219.

41. Harding, *Science and Social Inequality: Feminist and Postcolonial Issues* (Champaign: University of Illinois Press, 2006), reviewed by Clough, "Sandra Harding's *Science and Social Inequality*," *Hypatia: A Journal of Feminist Philosophy* 23, no. 2 (2008): 197–202.

42. Harding, *Science and Social Inequality*, p. 133.

Bibliography

Alcoff, Linda, and Elizabeth Potter, eds. *Feminist Epistemologies*. New York: Routledge & Kegan Paul, 1993.

Alcoff, Linda. Gadamer's feminist epistemology. In *Feminist Interpretations of Hans-Georg Gadamer*, ed. Lorriane Code, pp. 231–258. University Park: Pennsylvania State University Press, 2003.

Allison, Henry. *Kant's Theory of Freedom*. Cambridge: Cambridge University Press, 1990.

Anderson, Elizabeth. Uses of value judgments in science. *Hypatia: A Journal of Feminist Philosophy* 19 (2004): 1–24.

Anscombe, G. E. M. *Intention*. Oxford: Blackwell, 1957.

Anscombe, G. E. M. *Metaphysics and the Philosophy of Mind*. Minneapolis: University of Minnesota Press, 1981.

Antony, Louise M., and Charlotte E. Witt, eds. *A Mind of One's Own: Feminist Essays on Reason and Objectivity*. Boulder: Westview Press, 1993.

Arendt, Hannah. *The Human Condition*. Chicago: Chicago University Press, 1958.

Arthos, John. "The word is not reflexive": Mind and world in Aquinas and Gadamer. *American Catholic Philosophical Quarterly* 78 (2004): 587–608.

Avramides, Anita. Davidson and the new sceptical problem. In *Donald Davidson*, ed. Urszula M. Żegleń. London: Routledge & Kegan Paul, 1999, 136–156.

Ayer, A. J. *Language, Truth, and Logic*. London: Gollancz, 1936.

Bar-On, Dorit. *Speaking My Mind: Expression and Self-Knowledge*. Oxford: Oxford University Press, 2004.

Barwise, Jon, and John Perry. Semantic innocence and uncompromising situations. In *The Philosophy of Language*, ed. A. Martinich. Oxford: Oxford University Press, 1990, 401–413.

Barwise, Jon, and John Perry. *Situations and attitudes*. Cambridge, MA: MIT Press, 1983.

Beckermann, Ansgar, and Christian Nimtz, eds. *Argument und Analyse: Proceedings of GAP IV*. Paderborn: Mentis, 2001.

Bernstein, Richard J. *Beyond Objectivism and Relativism: Science, Hermeneutics, and Praxis*. University Park: University of Pennsylvania Press, 1988.

Boghossian, Paul. Content and self-knowledge. *Philosophical Topics* 17 (1989): 5–26.

Boros, J. Repräsentationalismus und Antirepräsentationalismus. Kant, Davidson und Rorty. *Deutsche Zeitschrift fur Philosophie* 47 (1999): 539–551.

Brandl, Johannes, and Wolfgang Gombocz, eds. *The Mind of Donald Davidson. Grazer Philosophische Studien* 36. Amsterdam: Editions Rodopi, 1989.

Brandom, Robert. *Making It Explicit: Reasoning, Representing, and Discursive Content*. Cambridge, MA: Harvard University Press, 1994.

Bransen, J., and Stefaan E. Cuypers, eds. *Human Action, Deliberation, and Causation*. Dordrecht: Kluwer, 1998.

Braver, Lee. *A Thing of This World: A History of Continental Anti-Realism*. Evanston: Northwestern University Press, 2007.

Brink, D. O. Moral realism and the sceptical arguments from disagreement and queerness. *Australasian Journal of Philosophy* 62 (1984): 111–125.

Bruner, Jerome, and Carol Fleischer Feldman. Metaphors of consciousness and cognition in the history of psychology. In *Metaphors in the History of Psychology*, ed. David E. Leary. Cambridge: Cambridge University Press, 1990, 230–237.

Bubner, Rudiger. On the ground of understanding. In *Hermeneutics and Truth*, ed. B. Wachterhauser. Evanston: Northwestern University Press, 1994, 68–82.

Burge, Tyler. Individualism and the mental. *Midwest Studies in Philosophy* 4 (1979): 73–121.

Campbell, Richmond. The virtues of feminist empiricism. *Hypatia: A Journal of Feminist Philosophy* 9 (1994): 90–115.

de Caro, Mario, ed. *Interpretations and Causes: New Perspectives on Donald Davidson's Philosophy*. Dordrecht: Kluwer, 1999.

Casteñada, Hector-Neri, and George Nakhnikian, eds. *Morality and the Language of Content*. Detroit: Wayne State University Press, 1963.

Chalmers, David, ed. *Philosophy of Mind: Classical and Contemporary Readings*. New York: Oxford University Press, 2002.

Chalmers, David. The conscious mind. In *In Search of a Fundamental Theory*. New York: Oxford University Press, 1996.

Chang, R., ed. *Incommensurability, Incomparability, and Practical Reason*. Cambridge, MA: Harvard University Press, 1997.

Child, W. *Causality, Interpretation, and the Mind*. Oxford: Oxford University Press, 1994.

Church, Alonso. Carnap's *Introduction to Semantics*. *Philosophical Review* 52 (1943): 298–304.

Churchland, Paul. *Scientific Realism and the Plasticity of Mind*. New York: Cambridge University Press, 1979.

Clough, Sharyn. A hasty retreat from evidence: The recalcitrance of relativism in feminist epistemology. *Hypatia: A Journal of Feminist Philosophy* 13 (1998): 88–111.

Clough, Sharyn. *Beyond Epistemology: A Pragmatist Approach to Feminist Science Studies*. Lanham, MD: Rowman & Littlefield, 2003.

Clough, Sharyn. Commentary on Elizabeth Anderson's "Uses of value judgments in science." Paper presented at MIT Symposium on Gender, Race, and Philosophy: Jan. 2006 Symposium I. <https://wikis.mit.edu/confluence/display/SGRP/Archive>.

Clough, Sharyn. Donald Davidson. In *The Routledge Encyclopedia of Postmodernism*, ed. Charles E. Winquist and Victor Taylor. London: Routledge & Kegan Paul, 2001, 82.

Clough, Sharyn. Drawing battle lines and choosing bedfellows: Rorty, relativism, and feminist strategy. In *Feminist Interpretations of Richard Rorty*, ed. Marianne Janack. University Park: Pennsylvania State University Press, 2010.

Clough, Sharyn. On the very idea of a feminist epistemology of science: Response to commentators on *Beyond Epistemology: A Pragmatist Approach to Feminist Science Studies*. *Metascience* 15 (2006): 27–37.

Clough, Sharyn. Sandra Harding's *Science and Social Inequality*. *Hypatia: A Journal of Feminist Philosophy* 23 (2008): 197–201.

Clough, Sharyn. Solomon's empirical/non-empirical distinction and the proper place of values in science. *Perspectives on Science* 16 (2008): 265–279.

Clough, Sharyn, and Bill Loges. Racist value judgments as objectively false beliefs: A philosophical and social-psychological analysis. *Journal of Social Philosophy* 39 (2008): 77–95.

Code, Lorraine. *Ecological Thinking: The Politics of Epistemic Location*. Oxford: Oxford University Press, 2006.

Code, Lorraine, ed. *Feminist Interpretations of Hans-Georg Gadamer.* University Park: Pennsylvania State University Press, 2003.

Collingwood, R. G. *An Essay on Metaphysics.* Oxford: Clarendon Press, 1940.

Collingwood, R. G. *An Essay on Metaphysics,* revised edition, with an introduction by Rex Martin. Oxford: Oxford University Press, 1998.

Collingwood, R. G. *The Idea of History.* Oxford: Clarendon Press, 1946.

Collingwood, R. G. *The New Leviathan, Or Man, Society, Civilization, and Barbarism.* Oxford: Clarendon Press, 1942.

Collingwood, R. G. *The New Leviathan, Or Man, Society, Civilization, and Barbarism,* revised edition, with an introduction by David Boucher. Oxford: Clarendon Press, 1992.

Collingwood, R. G. *The Principles of History.* Ed. W. H. Dray and J. Van der Dussen. Oxford: Oxford University Press, 1999.

Conant, James, and John Haugeland, eds. *The Road Since Structure: Philosophical Essays.* Chicago: Chicago University Press, 2000.

Corradi Fiumara, Gemma. *The Metaphoric Process.* London: Routledge & Kegan Paul, 1995.

Crane, T. *Elements of Mind.* Oxford: Oxford University Press, 2001.

Dancy, J. *Moral Realism and the Foundations of Ethics.* Cambridge: Cambridge University Press, 1993.

Dasenbrock, R. W., ed. *Literary Theory After Davidson.* University Park: Pennsylvania State University Press, 1993.

Davidson, Donald. A coherence theory of truth and knowledge. In Donald Davidson, *Subjective, Intersubjective, Objective.* Oxford: Clarendon Press, 2001, 137–153. Reprinted in *Critical Responses to Philosophy and the Mirror of Nature (and Beyond),* ed. A. Malachowski. Oxford: Blackwell, 1991, 120–134.

Davidson, Donald. Actions, reasons, and causes. *Journal of Philosophy* 60 (1963): 685–700. Reprinted in Donald Davidson, *Essays on Actions and Events.* Oxford: Clarendon Press, and New York: Oxford University Press, 1980, 3–19.

Davidson, Donald. Afterthoughts 1987. In *Reading Rorty: Critical Responses to Philosophy and the Mirror of Nature (and Beyond),* ed. A. Malachowski. Oxford: Blackwell, 1991, 134–138. Reprinted in Davidson, *Subjective, Intersubjective, Objective,* 154–157.

Davidson, Donald. A new basis for decision theory. *Theory and Decision* 18 (1985): 87–98.

Davidson, Donald. A nice derangement of epitaphs. In *Truth and Interpretation: Perspectives on the Philosophy of Donald Davidson*, ed. Ernest Lepore. New York: Blackwell, 1986, 433–446. Reprinted in Donald Davidson, *Truth, Language and History*. Oxford: Oxford University Press and Clarendon Press, 2005, 89–107.

Davidson, Donald. A unified theory of thought, meaning, and action. In Donald Davidson, *Problems of Rationality*. Oxford: Clarendon Press, 2004, 151–166.

Davidson, Donald. Belief and the basis of meaning. In Donald Davidson, *Inquiries into Truth and Interpretation*. Oxford: Clarendon Press, and New York: Oxford University Press, 1984, 141–154.

Davidson, Donald. Comments on Karlovy Vary papers. In *Interpreting Davidson*, ed. Petr Kotatko, Peter Pagin, and Gabriel Segal. Stanford: CSLI Publications, 2001, 285–309.

Davidson, Donald. Communication and convention. In Donald Davidson, *Inquiries into Truth and Interpretation*. Oxford: Clarendon Press, and New York: Oxford University Press, 1984, 265–280.

Davidson, Donald. Donald Davidson. In *A Companion to the Philosophy of Mind*, ed. Samuel Guttenplan. Oxford: Blackwell, 1994, 231–233.

Davidson, Donald. Epistemology externalized. *Dialectica* 45, nos. 2–3 (1991): 191–202. Reprinted in Donald Davidson, *Subjective, Intersubjective, Objective*. Oxford: Clarendon Press, 2001, 193–204.

Davidson, Donald. *Essays on Actions and Events*. Oxford: Clarendon Press, and New York: Oxford University Press, 1980.

Davidson, Donald. First person authority. In Donald Davidson, *Subjective, Intersubjective, Objective*. Oxford: Clarendon Press, 2001, 3–14.

Davidson, Donald. Foreword. In *Two Roads to Wisdom: Chinese and Analytic Philosophical Traditions*, ed. Bo Mou. La Salle: Open Court, 2001.

Davidson, Donald. Gadamer and Plato's *Philebus*. In *The Philosophy of Hans-Georg Gadamer*, ed. Lewis Edwin Hahn. The Library of Living Philosophers, vol. 24. Chicago: Open Court, 1997, 421–432. Reprinted in Donald Davidson, *Truth, Language, and History*. Oxford: Oxford University Press and Clarendon Press, 2005, 261–276.

Davidson, Donald. Indeterminism and Antirealism. In *Realism/Antirealism and Epistemology*, ed. Christopher B. Kulp. Lanham: Rowman & Littlefield, 1997, 109–122. Reprinted in Donald Davidson, *Subjective, Intersubjective, Objective*. Oxford: Clarendon Press, 2001, 69–84.

Davidson, Donald. *Inquiries into Truth and Interpretation*. Oxford: Clarendon Press, and New York: Oxford University Press, 1984; Oxford: Oxford University Press, 2001.

Davidson, Donald. Interpretation: Hard in theory, easy in practice. In *Interpretations and Causes: New Perspectives on Donald Davidson's Philosophy*, ed. Mario de Caro. Dordrecht: Kluwer, 1999, 39–43.

Davidson, Donald. Introduction to *Subjective, Intersubjective, Objective*. Oxford: Clarendon Press, 2001, xiii–xviii.

Davidson, Donald. Knowing one's own mind. *Proceedings and Addresses of the American Philosophical Association* 60 (1987): 453–55. Reprinted in Donald Davidson, *Subjective, Intersubjective, Objective*. Oxford: Clarendon Press, 2001, 15–38.

Davidson, Donald. Locating literary language. In Donald Davidson, *Truth, Language, and History*. Oxford: Oxford University Press and Clarendon Press, 2005, 170–171.

Davidson, Donald. Mental events. In *Experience and Theory*, ed. L. Foster and J. W. Swanson. London: Duckworth, 1970. Reprinted in Donald Davidson, *Essays on Actions and Events*. Oxford: Clarendon Press, and New York: Oxford University Press, 1980, 207–225.

Davidson, Donald. On the very idea of a conceptual scheme. In Donald Davidson, *Inquiries into Truth and Interpretation*. Oxford: Clarendon Press, and New York: Oxford University Press, 1984, 183–198.

Davidson, Donald. Problems in the explanation of action. In Donald Davidson, *Problems of Rationality*. Oxford: Clarendon Press, 2004, 101–116.

Davidson, Donald. *Problems of Rationality*. Oxford: Clarendon Press, 2004.

Davidson, Donald. Radical interpretation. In Donald Davidson, *Inquiries into Truth and Interpretation*. Oxford: Clarendon Press, and New York: Oxford University Press, 1984, 125–129.

Davidson, Donald. Radical interpretation interpreted. In *Logic and Language: Philosophical Perspectives*, vol. 8, ed. James E. Tomberlin. Atascadero, CA: Ridgeview, 1994, 121–128.

Davidson, Donald. Reply to Barry Stroud. In *The Philosophy of Donald Davidson*, ed. Lewis Edwin Hahn. The Library of Living Philosophers, vol. 27. Chicago: Open Court, 1999, 162–166.

Davidson, Donald. Reply to Bernhard Thöle. In *Reflecting Davidson: Donald Davidson Responding to an International Forum of Philosophers*, ed. R. Stoecker. Berlin: Walter de Gruyter, 1993, 248–250. Reprinted in *A Companion to the Philosophy of Mind*, ed. Samuel Guttenplan. Oxford: Blackwell, 1994, 231–236.

Davidson, Donald. Reply to Dagfinn Føllesdal. In *The Philosophy of Donald Davidson*, ed. Lewis Edwin Hahn. The Library of Living Philosophers, vol. 27. Chicago: Open Court, 1999, 729–732.

Davidson, Donald. Reply to Eva Picardi. In *Reflecting Davidson: Donald Davidson Responding to an International Forum of Philosophers*, ed. R. Stoecker. Berlin: Walter de Gruyter, 210–212.

Davidson, Donald. Reply to Kirk Ludwig. In *Donald Davidson: Truth, Meaning, and Knowledge*, ed. Urszula M. Żegleń. London: Routledge & Kegan Paul, 1999, 46–77.

Davidson, Donald. Reply to Pascal Engel. In *The Philosophy of Donald Davidson*, ed. Lewis Edwin Hahn. The Library of Living Philosophers, vol. 27. Chicago: Open Court, 1999, 460–462.

Davidson, Donald. Reply to Peter Bieri. In *Reflecting Davidson: Donald Davidson Responding to an International Forum of Philosophers*, ed. R. Stoecker. Berlin: Walter de Gruyter, 1993, 311–314.

Davidson, Donald. Reply to Ralf Stoecker. In *Reflecting Davidson: Donald Davidson Responding to an International Forum of Philosophers*, ed. R. Stoecker. Berlin: Walter de Gruyter, 1993, 287–290.

Davidson, Donald. Reply to Stephen Neale. In *Donald Davidson: Truth, Meaning, and Knowledge*, ed. Urszula M. Żegleń. London: Routledge & Kegan Paul, 1999, 87–89.

Davidson, Donald. Representation and interpretation. In *Modelling the Mind*, ed. W. H. Newton-Smith and K. V. Wilkes Oxford: Oxford University Press, 1990, 13–26. Reprinted in Donald Davidson, *Problems of Rationality*. Oxford: Clarendon Press, 2004, 87–100.

Davidson, Donald. Seeing through language. In Donald Davidson, *Truth, Language and History*. Oxford: Oxford University Press and Clarendon Press, 2005, 127–142.

Davidson, Donald. *Subjective, Intersubjective, Objective*. Oxford: Clarendon Press, 2001.

Davidson, Donald. The conditions of thought. In *The Mind of Donald Davidson*, ed. Johannes Brandl and Wolfgang Gombocz. Grazer Philosophische Studien 36. Amsterdam: Editions Rodopi, 1989, 193–200.

Davidson, Donald. The irreducibility of the concept of the self. In *A Companion to the Philosophy of Mind*, ed. Samuel Guttenplan. Oxford: Blackwell, 1994, 231–236. Reprinted in Donald Davidson, *Subjective, Intersubjective, Objective*. Oxford: Clarendon Press, 2001, 85–91.

Davidson, Donald. The logical form of action sentences. In Donald Davidson, *Essays on Actions and Events*. Oxford: Clarendon Press, and New York: Oxford University Press, 1980, 105–122.

Davidson, Donald. The myth of the subjective. In *Relativism: Interpretations and Confrontations*, ed. M. Krausz. Bloomington: Indiana University Press, 1989, 159–172. Reprinted in Donald Davidson, *Subjective, Intersubjective, Objective*. Oxford: Clarendon Press, 2001, 39–52.

Davidson, Donald. The perils and pleasures of interpretation. In *The Oxford Handbook of Philosophy of Language*, ed. Ernest Lepore and Barry C. Smith. Oxford: Oxford University Press, 2006, 1057–1068.

Davidson, Donald. The structure and content of truth. [In revised form as part of *Truth and Predication*.] *Journal of Philosophy* 87 (1990): 279–328.

Davidson, Donald. The third man. In Donald Davidson, *Truth, Language, and History*. Oxford: Clarendon Press, 2005.

Davidson, Donald. Thinking causes. In *Mental Causation*, ed. J. Heil and A. Mele. Oxford: Clarendon Press, 1993. Reprinted in Donald Davidson, *Truth, Language, and History*. Oxford: Oxford University Press and Clarendon Press, 2005, 185–200.

Davidson, Donald. Three varieties of knowledge. In Donald Davidson, *Subjective, Intersubjective, Objective*. Oxford: Clarendon Press, 2001, 205–220. Reprinted in *A Companion to the Philosophy of Mind*, ed. Samuel Guttenplan. Oxford: Blackwell, 1994, 231–236.

Davidson, Donald. True to the facts. In Donald Davidson, *Inquiries into Truth and Interpretation*. Oxford: Clarendon Press, and New York: Oxford University Press, 1984, 37–54.

Davidson, Donald. *Truth and Predication*. Cambridge, MA: Harvard University Press, 2005.

Davidson, Donald. *Truth, Language, and History*. Oxford: Oxford University Press and Clarendon Press, 2005.

Davidson, Donald. Truth rehabilitated. In Donald Davidson, *Truth, Language, and History*. Oxford: Oxford University Press and Clarendon Press, 2005, 3–18.

Davidson, Donald. What is present to the mind? In Donald Davidson, *Subjective, Intersubjective, Objective*. Oxford: Clarendon Press, 2001, 53–68.

Dennett, D. C. *Consciousness Explained*. Boston: Little, Brown, 1991.

Derrida, Jacques. *Margins of Philosophy*. Chicago: University of Chicago Press, 1982.

Derrida, Jacques. *Of Grammatology*. Baltimore: Johns Hopkins University Press, 1976.

Dewey, John. *Reconstruction in Philosophy*. Boston: Beacon Press, 1966.

Dewey, John. *The Quest for Certainty: A Study of the Relation of Knowledge and Action*. New York: Putnam's Sons, 1960.

Dilthey, W. Einleitung in die Geisteswissenschaften. In *Gesammelte Schriften*, vol. I. Stuttgart: B. G. Taubner Verlag, 1959.

Donovan, A., Larry Laudan, and Rachel Lauden, eds. *Scrutinizing Science: Empirical Studies of Scientific Change*. Dordrecht: Kluwer Academic, 1988.

D'Oro, G. *Collingwood and the Metaphysics of Experience*. New York: Routledge & Kegan Paul, 2002.

Dostal, Robert, ed. *The Cambridge Companion to Gadamer*. New York: Cambridge University Press, 2002.

Dostal, Robert. Philosophical discourse and the ethics of hermeneutics. In *Festivals of Interpretation*, ed. Kathleen Wright Wright. Albany: SUNY Press, 1990, 63–88.

Dostal, Robert. The experience of truth for Gadamer and Heidegger: Taking time and sudden lightning. In *Hermeneutics and Truth*, ed. B. Wachterhauser. Evanston: Northwestern University Press, 1994, 47–67.

Dostal, Robert. The world never lost: The hermeneutics of trust. *Philosophy and Phenomenological Research* 47 (1987): 413–434.

Dray, W. H. *Laws and Explanation in History*. London: Oxford University Press, 1957.

Dray, W. H. The historical explanation of actions reconsidered. In *Philosophy and History*, ed. S. Hook. New York: New York University Press, 1963, 105–135.

Dreyfus, H. Holism and hermeneutics. *Review of Metaphysics* 34 (1980): 3–23.

Dreyfus, H. Nihilism, art, technology, and politics. In *The Cambridge Companion to Heidegger*, ed. Charles Guignon. Cambridge: Cambridge University Press, 1993, 290–301.

Dreyfus, H. *Being-in-the-World: A Commentary on Heidegger's* Being and Time, Division I. Cambridge, MA: MIT Press, 1991.

Dummett, Michael. What is a theory of meaning? In *Mind and Language*, ed. Samuel Guttenplan. Oxford: Clarendon Press, 1975, 97–138.

Dummett, Michael. What is a theory of meaning? (II). In *Truth and Meaning: Essays in Semantics*, ed. G. Evans and John McDowell. Oxford: Clarendon Press, 1976, 67–137.

Durt, Christoph. Gadamer's 100. Geburtstag. *Information Philosophie* 2 (2000): 118–119.

Earman, J., ed. *Inference, Explanation, and Other Frustrations: Essays in the Philosophy of Science*. Los Angeles: University of California Press, 1992.

Engel, Pascal. Interpretation without hermeneutics: A plea against ecumenism. *Topoi* 10 (1991): 137–146.

Evans, G., and John McDowell, eds. *Truth and Meaning: Essays in Semantics*. Oxford: Clarendon Press, 1976.

Evnine, Simon. *Donald Davidson*. Stanford: Stanford University Press, 1991.

Feigl, Herbert, and Grover Maxwell, eds. *Minnesota Studies in the Philosophy of Science*, vol. 3. Minneapolis: University of Minnesota Press, 1962.

Feyerabend, Paul. Explanation, reduction, and empiricism. In *Minnesota Studies in the Philosophy of Science*, vol. 3, ed. Herbert Feigl and Grover Maxwell. Minneapolis: University of Minnesota Press, 1962I, 28–97.

Field, Hartry. Physicalism. In *Inference, Explanation, and Other Frustrations: Essays in the Philosophy of Science*, ed. J. Earman. Los Angeles: University of California Press, 1992.

Fleming, Marie. Gadamer's conversation: Does the other have a say? In *Feminist Interpretations of Hans-Georg Gadamer*, ed. Lorraine Code. University Park: Pennsylvania State University Press, 2003, 109–132.

Fodor, J. A. Making mind matter more. *Philosophical Topics* 17 (1989): 59–79.

Fodor, J. A. *Psychosemantics*. Cambridge, MA: MIT Press, 1987.

Føllesdal, Dagfinn. Triangulation. In *The Philosophy of Donald Davidson*, ed. Lewis Edwin Hahn. The Library of Living Philosophers, vol. 27. Chicago: Open Court, 1999, 719–728.

Forget, Philippe, ed. *Text und Interpretation*. Munich: Wilhelm Fink Verlag, 1984.

Foster, L., and J. W. Swanson, eds. *Experience and Theory*. London: Duckworth, 1970.

Frege, Gottlob. Der Gedanke: Eine logische Untersuchung. *Beiträge zur Philosophie des deutschen Idealismus* 1 (1918–1919): 58–77.

Frege, Gottlob. On sense and reference [1892]. In *Translations from the Philosophical Writings of Gottlob Frege*, ed. Peter Geach and Max Black. Oxford: Blackwell, 1952, 56–78.

French, P. A., T. Uehling, Jr., and H. K. Wettstein, eds. *The Wittgenstein Legacy: Midwest Studies in Philosophy*, vol. 17. Notre Dame: University of Notre Dame Press, 1992.

Friedman, Michael. Exorcising the philosophical tradition: Comments on John McDowell's *Mind and World*. *Philosophical Review* 105 (1996): 427–467.

Friedman, Michael. *A Parting of the Ways: Carnap, Cassirer, and Heidegger*. Chicago: Open Court, 2000.

Gadamer, Hans-Georg. *Kleine Schriften I*. Tübingen: J. C. B. Mohr, 1967.

Gadamer, Hans-Georg. Language and understanding. *Theory, Culture & Society* 23 (2006): 13–27.

Gadamer, Hans-Georg. Notes on planning for the future. In *Hans-Georg Gadamer on Education, Poetry, and History*, ed. Dieter Misgeld and Graeme Nicholson, trans. Lawrence Sclunidt and Monica Reuss. Albany: SUNY Press, 1992, 165–180.

Gadamer, Hans-Georg. *Philosophical Hermeneutics*. Ed. and trans. David E. Linge. Berkeley: University of California Press, 1976.

Gadamer, Hans-Georg. *Plato's Dialectical Ethics*. Trans. Robert Wallace. New Haven: Yale University Press, 1991.

Gadamer, Hans-Georg. Question and answer play back and forth between the text and its interpreter. In *Genius: In Their Own Words*, ed. Daniel Ramsay Steele. Chicago: Open Court, 2002, 173–238.

Gadamer, Hans-Georg. *Reason in the Age of Science*. Trans. Frederick G. Lawrence. Cambridge, MA: MIT Press, 1981.

Gadamer, Hans-Georg. Reply to Donald Davidson. In *The Philosophy of Hans-Georg Gadamer*, ed. Lewis Edwin Hahn. The Library of Living Philosophers, vol. 24. Chicago: Open Court, 1997, 433–435.

Gadamer, Hans-Georg. Text und Interpretation. In *Text und Interpretation*, ed. Philippe Forget. Munich: Wilhelm Fink Verlag, 1984, 24–55.

Gadamer, Hans-Georg. *The Beginning of Philosophy*. Trans. Rod Coltman. New York: Continuum, 1998.

Gadamer, Hans-Georg. The hermeneutics of suspicion. *Man and World* 17 (1984): 313–323. Reprinted in *Hermeneutics: Questions and Prospects*, edited by G. Shapiro and A. Sica. Amherst: University of Massachusetts Press, 1984, 54–65.

Gadamer, Hans-Georg. *The Idea of the Good in Platonic-Aristotelian Philosophy*. Trans. P. Christopher Smith. New Haven: Yale University Press, 1986.

Gadamer, Hans-Georg. Towards a phenomenology of ritual and language. In *Language and Linguisticality in Gadamer's Hermeneutics*, ed. Lawrence Schmidt. Lanham, MD: Lexington Books, 2000, 19–50.

Gadamer, Hans-Georg. Treatment and dialogue. In *The Enigma of Health,* trans. J. Gaiger and N. Walker. Stanford: Stanford University Press, 1996, 125–140.

Gadamer, Hans-Georg. *Truth and Method*, 2nd rev. ed. Trans. Joel Weinsheimer and Donald G. Marshall. New York: Continuum, 1991.

Gadamer, Hans-Georg. *Wahrheit und Methode*, 2nd ed. Tübingen: J. C. B. Mohr, 1965.

Glüer, Katherin. *Donald Davidson zur Einführung*. Hamburg: Junius Verlag, 1993.

Gödel, Kurt. Russell's Mathematical Logic. In *The Philosophy of Bertrand Russell*, ed. Paul A. Schilpp. Library of Living Philosophers, vol. 5. Evanston: Northwestern University Press, 1944, 123–153.

Goodman, Nelson. *The Ways of World-making*. Indianapolis: Hackett Press, 1978.

Griffin, James. Incommensurability: What's the Problem? In *Incommensurability, Incomparability, and Practical Reason*, ed. R. Chang. Cambridge, MA: Harvard University Press, 1997, 35–51.

Grover, D., J. Camp, and N. Belnap. A prosentential theory of truth. *Philosophical Studies* 27 (1975): 73–124.

Guignon, Charles, ed. *The Cambridge Companion to Heidegger.* Cambridge: Cambridge University Press, 1993.

Guttenplan, Samuel, ed. *Mind and Language.* Oxford: Clarendon Press, 1975.

Guttenplan, Samuel, ed. *A Companion to the Philosophy of Mind.* Oxford: Blackwell, 1994.

Hacker, P. M. S. On Davidson's idea of a conceptual scheme. *Philosophical Quarterly* 46 (1996): 289–307.

Hacking, Ian. Language, truth, and reason. In *Rationality and Relativism,* ed. Martin Hollis and Steven Lukes. Cambridge, MA: MIT Press, 1982, 48–66.

Hahn, Lewis Edwin, ed. *The Philosophy of Donald Davidson.* The Library of Living Philosophers, vol. 27. Chicago: Open Court, 1999.

Hahn, Lewis Edwin, ed. *The Philosophy of Hans-Georg Gadamer.* The Library of Living Philosophers, vol. 24. Chicago: Open Court, 1997.

Haraway, Donna. Situated knowledges: The science question in feminism and the privilege of partial perspective. In *Simians, Cyborgs and Women,* ed. Donna Haraway. New York: Routledge, 1988/1991, 183–202.

Harding, Sandra. Rethinking standpoint epistemology: What is "strong objectivity"? In *Feminist Epistemologies,* ed. Louise Alcoff and Elizabeth Potter. New York: Routledge & Kegan Paul, 1993, 49–82.

Harding, Sandra. *Science and Social Inequality: Feminist and Postcolonial Issues.* Champaign: University of Illinois Press, 2006.

Harding, Sandra. *Whose Science? Whose Knowledge? Thinking from Women's Lives.* Ithaca: Cornell University Press, 1991.

Harper, William A., and Ralf Meerbote, eds. *Kant on Causality, Freedom, and Objectivity.* Minneapolis: University of Minnesota Press, 1984.

Haugeland, John. *Having Thought: Essays in the Metaphysics of Mind.* Cambridge, MA: Harvard University Press, 1998.

Heidegger, Martin. *Being and Time.* Trans. J. Macquarrie and E. Robinson. New York: Harper & Row, 1962.

Heidegger, Martin. Die Zeit des Weltbildes. In *Holzwege.* Frankfurt: Vittorio Klostermann, 1950, 69–104.

Heidegger, Martin. *Holzwege.* Frankfurt: Vittorio Klostermann, 1950. Translated as *Off the Beaten Track.* Trans. Julian Young and Kenneth Haynes. Cambridge: Cambridge University Press, 2002.

Heidegger, Martin. *The Basic Problems of Phenomenology*. Trans. Albert Hofstadter. Bloomington: Indiana University Press, 1982.

Heidegger, Martin. *The Fundamental Concepts of Metaphysics: World, Finitude, Solitude*. Bloomington: Indiana University Press, 1995.

Heidegger, Martin. The origin of the work of art. In *Off the Beaten Track*, trans. Julian Young and Kenneth Haynes. Cambridge: Cambridge University Press, 2002, pp. 1–56.

Heil, J. *From an Ontological Point of View*. Oxford: Clarendon Press, 2003.

Heil, J., and A. Mele, eds. *Mental Causation*. Oxford: Clarendon Press, 1993.

Hempel, C. The function of general laws in history. *Journal of Philosophy* 39 (1942): 35–48.

Hollis, Martin, and Steven Lukes, eds. *Rationality and Relativism*. Cambridge, MA: MIT Press, 1982.

Hollis, Martin. The limits of irrationality. In *Rationality: Key Concepts in Social Sciences*, ed. Bryan Wilson. Oxford: Blackwell, 1970/1977, 214–220.

Holstrom-Hintikka, G., and R. Tuomela, eds. *Contemporary Action Theory*, vol. 1. Dordrecht: Kluwer Academic, 1997.

Hook, S., ed. *Philosophy and History*. New York: New York University Press, 1963.

Horgan, Terry. From supervenience to superdupervenience: Meeting the demands of a material world. In *Philosophy of Mind*, ed. D. Chalmers. Oxford: Oxford University Press, 2002.

Horwich, P., ed. *World Changes: Thomas Kuhn and the Nature of Science*. Cambridge, MA: MIT Press, 1993.

Horwich, P. *Truth*. Oxford: Oxford University Press, 1998.

Hösle, Vittorio. Truth and understanding: Analytical philosophy (Donald Davidson), phenomenology (Hans-Georg Gadamer), and the desideratum of an objective idealist hermeneutics. In *Between Description and Interpretation: The Hermeneutic Turn in Phenomenology*, ed. André Wiercinski. Toronto: The Hermeneutic Press, 2005, 376–394.

Hoy, D. C., and T. McCarthy. *Critical Theory*. Oxford: Blackwell, 1994.

Hoy, David. Post-Cartesian interpretation: Hans-Georg Gadamer and Donald Davidson. In *The Philosophy of Hans-Georg Gadamer*, ed. Lewis Edwin Hahn. The Library of Living Philosophers, vol. 24. Chicago: Open Court, 1997, 119–126.

Hume, D. *A Treatise of Human Nature*. Oxford: Clarendon Press, 1888.

Hurley, Susan L. Intelligibility, imperialism, and conceptual scheme. In *The Wittgenstein Legacy: Midwest Studies in Philosophy*, vol. 17, ed. P. French, T. Uehling, Jr., and H. K. Wettstein. Notre Dame: University of Notre Dame Press, 1992, 89–108.

Hursthouse, Rosalind. Intention. In *Logic, Cause, and Action: Essays in Honour of Elizabeth Anscombe*, ed. R. Teichmann. Royal Institute of Philosophy Supplements. Cambridge: Cambridge University Press, 2000, 83–106.

Husserl, E. In *Cartesianische Meditationen*. Ed. Elisabeth Ströker. Hamburg: Felix Meiner, 1987.

Husserl, E. *Cartesian Meditations*. Trans. Dorian Cairns. The Hague: Martinus Nijhoff, 1973.

Husserl, E. *Die Krisis der Europäischen Wissenschaften und die Transzendentale Phänomenologie*. The Hague: Northwestern University Press, 1962.

Husserl, E. *Ideas: General Introduction to Pure Phenomenology*. London: George Allen, 1969.

Husserl, E. *Ideas Pertaining to a Pure Phenomenology and to a Phenomenological Philosophy*. Dordrecht: Kluwer Academic, 1983.

Husserl, E. *Ideen zu einer reinen Phänomenologie und phänomenologischen Philosophie*. Ed. K. Schuhmann. The Hague: Martinus Nijhoff, 1967.

Husserl, E. *Philosophie als Strenge Wissenschaft*. Ed. W. Szilasi. Frankfurt: Klostermann, 1965.

Husserl, E. *The Crisis of European Sciences and Transcendental Phenomenology: An Introduction to Phenomenological Philosophy*. Trans. David Carr. Evanston: Northwestern University Press, 1970.

Hyman, J., and Helen Steward, eds. *Agency and Action*. Cambridge: Cambridge University Press, 2004.

Hymers, Michael. Putnam and the difficulty of renouncing all theory. *International Studies in Philosophy* 35 (2005): 55–82.

Jackson, Frank. What Mary didn't know. *Journal of Philosophy* 83 (1986): 127–195.

Janack, Marianne, ed. *Feminist Interpretations of Richard Rorty*. University Park: Pennsylvania State University Press, forthcoming.

Kant, I. *Groundwork of the Metaphysic of Morals*. Trans. H. J. Paton. New York: Harper Torchbooks, 1964.

Keller, Evelyn Fox. *Secrets of Life, Secrets of Death: Essays on Language, Gender, and Science*. New York: Routledge, 1992.

Kent, Thomas. Interpretation and triangulation: A Davidsonian critique of reader-oriented literary theory. In *Literary Theory After Davidson*, ed. R. W. Dasenbrock. University Park: Pennsylvania State University Press, 1993, 37–58.

Kim, Jaegwon. Can supervenience save anomalous monism? In *Mental Causation*, ed. J. Heil and A. Mele. Oxford: Clarendon Press, 1993, 19–26.

Kim, Jaewong. *Mind in a Physical World: An Essay on the Mind–Body Problem and Mental Causation*. Cambridge, MA: MIT Press, 1998.

Kim, Jaegwon. Philosophy of mind and psychology. In *Donald Davidson*, ed. K. Ludwig. Cambridge: Cambridge University Press, 2003, 113–136.

Kim, Jaegwon. *Supervenience and Mind*. Cambridge: Cambridge University Press, 1993.

Kim, Jaegwon. *The Philosophy of Mind*. Boulder, CO: Westview Press, 1996.

Kincaid, Harold, John Dupré, and Alison Wylie, eds. *Value Free Science: Ideal or Illusion?* Cambridge: Oxford University Press, 2006.

Kögler, Hans. *The Power of Dialogue: Critical Hermeneutics After Gadamer and Foucault*. Cambridge, MA: MIT Press, 1996.

Kotarbiński, Tadeusz. In *Gnosiology: The Scientific Approach to the Theory of Knowledge*, ed. G. Bidwell and C. Pinder. Oxford: Pergamon Press, 1929/1966.

Kotatko, Petr, Peter Pagin, and Gabriel Segal, eds. *Interpreting Davidson*. Stanford: CSLI Publications, 2001.

Krajewski, B., ed. *Gadamer's Repercussions: Reconsidering Philosophical Hermeneutics*. Berkeley: University of California Press, 2004.

Krausz, M., ed. *Relativism: Interpretations and Confrontations*. Bloomington: Indiana University Press, 1989.

Kripke, Saul A. *Wittgenstein on Rules and Private Language*. Oxford: Blackwell, 1982.

Kuhn, Thomas. Afterwords. In *World Changes: Thomas Kuhn and the Nature of Science*, ed. P. Horwich. Cambridge, MA: MIT Press, 1993, 311–341.

Kuhn, Thomas. *The Road Since Structure: Philosophical Essays*, ed. James Conant and John Haugeland. Chicago: University of Chicago Press, 2000.

Kuhn, Thomas. *The Structure of Scientific Revolutions*. Chicago: University of Chicago Press, 1996.

Kulenkampff, A., and F. Siebelt. What a noncognitivist might tell a moral realist. *Protosociology: An International Journal of Interdisciplinary Research* 14 (2000): 355–377.

Kulp, Christopher B., ed. *Realism/Antirealism and Epistemology*. Lanham: Rowman & Littlefield, 1997.

Kulp, Christopher B. *The End of Epistemology: Dewey and His Current Allies on the Spectator Theory of Knowledge*. Westport, CT: Greenwood Press, 1992.

Lacey, Hugh. *Is Science Value Free? Values and Scientific Understanding*. London: Routledge & Kegan Paul, 1999.

Lafont, Christina. *The Linguistic Turn in Hermeneutic Philosophy*. Cambridge, MA: MIT Press, 1999.

Lanz, Peter. The explanatory force of action explanations. In *Reflecting Davidson: Donald Davidson Responding to an International Forum of Philosophers*, ed. R. Stoecker. Berlin: Walter de Gruyter, 1993, 291–301.

Laymon, Ronald. The Michelson-Morley experiment and the appraisal of theories. In *Scrutinizing Science: Empirical Studies of Scientific Change*, ed. A. Donovan, Larry Laudan, and Rachel Lauden. Dordrecht: Kluwer Academic, 1988, 245–266.

Leary, David E., ed. *Metaphors in the History of Psychology*. Cambridge: Cambridge University Press, 1990.

Lepore, Erenest, ed. *Truth and Interpretation: Perspectives on the Philosophy of Donald Davidson*. New York: Blackwell, 1986.

Lepore, Ernest, and B. Lower. More on making mind matter. *Philosophical Topics* 17 (1989): 175–191.

Lepore, Ernest, and B. McLaughlin, eds. *Actions and Events: Perspectives on the Philosophy of Donald Davidson*. New York: Blackwell, 1985.

Lepore, Ernest, and Barry C. Smith, eds. *The Oxford Handbook of Philosophy of Language*. Oxford: Oxford University Press, 2006.

Lepore, Ernest, and K. Ludwig. *Donald Davidson: Meaning, Truth, Language, and Reality*. New York: Oxford University Press, 2005.

Lewis, Clarence. *An Analysis of Knowledge and Valuation*. La Salle: Open Court, 1946.

Lewis, Clarence. Facts, systems, and the unity of the world. In *Collected Papers of Clarence Irving Lewis*, ed. J. L. Mothershea. Stanford: Stanford University Press, 1970, 383–393.

Lewis, David. 1983. *Philosophical Papers*, vol. 1. New York: Oxford University Press, 108–118.

Livingston, Paisley. Writing Action: Davidson, Rationality, and Literary Research. In *Literary Theory After Davidson*, ed. R. W. Dasenbrock. University Park: Pennsylvania State University Press, 1993, 257–285.

Longino, Helen. Can there be a feminist science? *Hypatia: A Journal of Feminist Philosophy* 2 (1987): 51–64.

Longino, Helen. Essential tensions—phase two: Feminist, philosophical, and social studies of science. In *A Mind of One's Own: Feminist Essays on Reason and Objectivity*, ed. Louise M. Antony and Charlotte E. Witt. Boulder, CO: Westview Press, 1993, 93–109.

Longino, Helen. *Science as Social Knowledge: Values and Objectivity in Scientific Inquiry*. Princeton: Princeton University Press, 1990.

Ludwig, K., ed. *Donald Davidson*. Cambridge: Cambridge University Press, 2003.

Macdonald, C., and Graham Macdonald, eds. *McDowell and His Critics*. Oxford: Blackwell, 2006.

Macdonald, Graham, and Philip Pettit. *Semantics and Social Science*. London: Routledge & Kegan Paul, 1981.

MacIntyre, Alasdair. Is understanding religion compatible with believing? In *Rationality: Key Concepts in Social Sciences*, ed. Bryan Wilson. Oxford: Blackwell, 1970/1977, 62–77.

MacIntyre. Alasdair. The idea of a social science. In *Rationality: Key Concepts in Social Sciences*, ed. Bryan Wilson. Oxford: Blackwell, 1970/1977.

Malachowski, A., ed. *Reading Rorty: Critical Responses to Philosophy and the Mirror of Nature (and Beyond)*. Oxford: Blackwell, 1991.

Malpas, Jeff. *Donald Davidson and the Mirror of Meaning*. Cambridge: Cambridge University Press, 1992.

Malpas, Jeff. Gadamer, Davidson, and ground of understanding. In *Gadamer's Century: Essays in Honor of Hans-Georg Gadamer*, ed. Jeff Malpas, Ulrich Arnswald, and Jens Kertscher. Cambridge, MA: MIT Press, 2002, 195–216.

Malpas, Jeff. *Heidegger's Topology: Being, Place, World*. Cambridge, MA: MIT Press, 2006.

Malpas, Jeff. *Place and Experience: A Philosophical Topography*. Cambridge: Cambridge University Press, 1999.

Malpas, Jeff. *Sprache ist Gespräch*: On Gadamer, language and philosophy. In *Between Description and Interpretation: The Hermeneutic Turn in Phenomenology*, ed. André Wiercinski. Toronto: The Hermeneutic Press, 2005, 408–417.

Malpas, Jeff. The intertranslatability of natural languages. *Synthese* 78 (1989): 233–264.

Malpas, Jeff. The transcendental circle. *Australasian Journal of Philosophy* 75 (1997): 1–20.

Malpas, Jeff, Ulrich Arnswald, and Jens Kertscher, eds. *Gadamer's Century: Essays in Honor of Hans-Georg Gadamer*. Cambridge, MA: MIT Press, 2002.

Marshall, Donald, ed. *The Force of Tradition*. Lanham: Rowman & Littlefield, 2005.

Martinich, A., ed. *The Philosophy of Language*. Oxford: Oxford University Press, 1990.

McDowell, J. Are moral requirements hypothetical imperatives? In John McDowell, *Mind, Value, and Reality*. Cambridge, MA: Harvard University Press, 1998, 77–95.

McDowell, J. Functionalism and anomalous monism. In *Actions and Events: Perspectives on the Philosophy of Donald Davidson*, ed. Ernest Lepore and B. McLaughlin. New York: Blackwell, 1985, 387–398.

McDowell, J. Gadamer and Davidson on understanding and relativism. In *Gadamer's Century: Essays in Honor of Hans-Georg Gadamer*, ed. Jeff Malpas, Ulrich Arnswald and Jens Kertscher. Cambridge, MA: MIT Press, 2002, 173–194.

McDowell, J. *Mind and World*. Cambridge, MA: Harvard University Press, 1994.

McDowell, J. *Mind, Value, and Reality*. Cambridge, MA: Harvard University Press, 1998.

McDowell, J. *Reason and Nature*. Münster: LIT Verlag, 2000.

McDowell, J. Response to Bilgrami. In *McDowell and His Critics*, ed. C. Macdonald and Graham Macdonald. Oxford: Blackwell, 2006, 66–72.

McDowell, J. Response to Dancey. In *McDowell and His Critics*, ed. C. Macdonald and Graham Macdonald. Oxford: Blackwell, 2006, 134–141.

McGinn, C. Radical interpretation and epistemology. In *Truth and Interpretation: Perspectives on the Philosophy of Donald Davidson*, ed. Ernest Lepore. New York: Blackwell, 1986, 356–368.

McKinsey, Michael. Anti-individualism and privileged access. *Analysis* 51 (1991): 9–16.

McLaughlin, B. Type epiphenomenalism, type dualism, and the causal priority of the physical. *Philosophical Perspectives* 3 (1989): 109–135.

McNaughton, D. *Moral Vision*. Oxford: Oxford University Press, 1988.

Mead, G. H. *Mind, Self, and Society*. Chicago: University of Chicago Press, 1934.

Meerbote, Ralf. Kant on the nondeterminate character of human actions. In *Kant on Causality, Freedom, and Objectivity*, ed. William A. Harper and Ralf Meerbote. Minneapolis: University of Minnesota Press, 1984, 138–163.

Meggle, G. *Actions, Norms, and Values*. Berlin: Walter de Gruyter, 1999.

Melden, Abraham. *Free Action*. London: Routledge & Kegan Paul, 1961.

Mele, A. R. Philosophy of action. In *Donald Davidson*, ed. K. Ludwig. Cambridge: Cambridge University Press, 2003, 64–84.

Mele, A. R. *Springs of Action: Understanding Intentional Behavior*. Oxford: Oxford University Press, 1992.

Mele, A. R., ed. *The Philosophy of Action*. Oxford: Oxford University Press, 1997.

Merleau-Ponty, M. *The Primacy of Perception and Other Essays*. Ed. J. Edie. Evanston: Northwestern University Press, 1964.

Michelfelder, Diane P., and Richard E. Palmer, eds. *Dialogue and Deconstruction: The Gadamer-Derrida Encounter*. Albany: SUNY Press, 1989.

Mill, J. S. System of logic: Ratiocinative and inductive. In *Collected Works of John Stuart Mill*, ed. J. M. Robson. Toronto: University of Toronto Press, 1843/1974.

Moser, Paul K., and Thomas L. Carson, eds. *Moral Relativism*. Oxford: Oxford University Press, 2001.

Nagel, Thomas. Subjective and objective. In *Mortal Questions*. New York: Cambridge University Press, 1979, 196–214.

Nagel, Thomas. *The View from Nowhere*. New York: Oxford University Press, 1986.

Neale, S. *Facing Facts*. Oxford: Clarendon Press, 2001.

Neale, S. The philosophical significance of Gödel's slingshot. *Mind* 104 (1995): 761–825.

Neale, S. and Josh Dever. Slingshots and boomerangs. *Mind* 106 (1997): 143–168.

Nelson, Lynn Hankinson. *Feminist Interpretations of Quine*. University Park: Pennsylvania State University Press, 2003.

Nelson, Lynn Hankinson. *Who Knows? From Quine to a Feminist Empiricism*. Philadelphia: Temple, 1990.

Newton-Smith, W. H., and K. V. Wilkes, eds. *Modelling the Mind*. Oxford: Oxford University Press, 1990.

Nida-Rümelin, J. *Ethische Essays*. Frankfurt: Suhrkamp, 2002.

Nida-Rümelin, J. *Über menschliche Freiheit*. Stuttgart: Reclam, 2005.

Nietzsche, F. *Werke III*. Munich: Carl Hanser Verlag, 1960.

O'Callaghan, John. *Thomist Realism and the Linguistic Turn*. Notre Dame: University of Notre Dame Press, 2003.

Øfsti, Audun, Peter Ulrich, and Truls Wyller, eds. *Indexicality and Idealism: The Self in Philosophical Perspective*. Paderborn: Mentis, 2000.

Okrent, Mark. *Heidegger's Pragmatism*. Ithaca: Cornell University Press, 1988.

Palmer, Abram Smythe, Rev. *Folk Etymology*. New York: Henry Holt, 1883.

Platts, M., ed. *Truth and Reality: Essays on the Philosophy of Language*. London: Routledge & Kegan Paul, 1980.

Platts, M. Moral reality and the end of desire. In *Truth and Reality: Essays on the Philosophy of Language*, ed. M. Platts. London: Routledge & Kegan Paul, 1980, 69–82.

Platts, M. *Ways of Meaning. An Introduction to a Philosophy of Language*. London: Routledge & Kegan Paul, 1979.

Prado, C., ed. *A House Divided: Comparing Analytic and Continental Philosophers*. Amherst, NY: Humanity Books, 2003.

Preyer, G. *Donald Davidson's Philosophy: From Radical Interpretation to Radical Contextualism*. Frankfurt: Humanities Online, 2011.

Preyer, G. *Intention and Practical Thought*. Frankfurt: Humanaties Online, 2011.

Preyer, Gerhard, Frank Siebelt, and Alexander Ulfig, eds. *Language, Mind and Epistemology: On Donald Davidson's Philosophy*. Dordrecht: Kluwer, 1994.

Quine, W. V. O. *From a Logical Point of View: Nine Logico-Philosophical Essays*, 2nd rev. ed. Cambridge, MA: Harvard University Press, 1963/1980.

Quine, W. V. O. Indeterminacy of translation again. *Journal of Philosophy* 84 (1987): 5–10.

Quine, W. V. O. Main trends in recent philosophy: Two dogmas of empiricism. *Philosophical Review* 60 (1951): 20–43.

Quine, W. V. O. New foundations for mathematical logic. In W. V. O. Quine. *From a Logical Point of View: Nine Logico-Philosophical Essays*, 2nd rev. ed. Cambridge, MA: Harvard University Press, 1963/1980, 80–101.

Quine, W. V. O. *Ontological Relativity and Other Essays*. New York: Columbia University Press, 1969.

Quine, W. V. O. *Pursuit of Truth*, rev. ed. Cambridge, MA: Harvard University Press, 1992.

Quine, W. V. O. Three grades of modal involvement. In W. V. O. Quine, *The Ways of Paradox, and Other Essays*, 163–164. Cambridge, MA: Harvard University Press, 1953. Revised and enlarged edition, 1976.

Ramberg, B. T. Illuminating language: Interpretation and understanding in Gadamer and Davidson. In *A House Divided: Comparing Analytic and Continental Philosophers*, ed. C. Prado. Amherst, NY: Humanity Books, 2003, 213–234.

Ramberg, B. T. The significance of charity. In *The Philosophy of Hans-Georg Gadamer*, ed. Lewis Edwin Hahn. The Library of Living Philosophers, vol. 24. Chicago: Open Court, 1997, 601–618.

Ramberg, B. T. The source of the subjective. In *The Philosophy of Hans-Georg Gadamer*, ed. Lewis Edwin Hahn. The Library of Living Philosophers, vol. 24. Chicago: Open Court, 1997, 459–471.

Ramberg, B. T. *Donald Davidson's Philosophy of Language: An Introduction*. Oxford: Blackwell, 1989.

Ramsey, F. P. *Foundations of Mathematics*. New York: Humanities Press, 1950.

Rescher, Nicholas. Conceptual schemes. In *The Wittgenstein Legacy: Midwest Studies in Philosophy*, vol. 17, ed. P. French, T. Uehling Jr., and H. K. Wettstein. Notre Dame: University of Notre Dame Press, 1992, 323–346.

Ricoeur, P. *Time and Narrative*, vol. 3. Trans. Kathleen Blamey and David Pellauer. Chicago: University of Chicago Press, 1988.

Rogler, E., and G. Preyer. *Materialismus, anomaler Monismus und mentale Kausalität. Zur gegenwärtigen Philosophie des Mentalen bei Donald Davidson und David Lewis*. Frankfurt: Humanities Online, 2001. A shorter version is available as *Anomalous Monism and Mental Causality. On the Debate of Donald Davidson's Philosophy of the Mental*, at <https://ssl.humanities-online.de/en/neuerscheinungen.php>.

Rorty, R. Being that can be understood is language. In *Gadamer's Repercussions: Reconsidering Philosophical Hermeneutics*, ed. B. Krajewski. Berkeley: University of California Press, 2004, 21–29.

Rorty, Richard. *Consequences of Pragmatism*. Minneapolis: University of Minnesota Press, 1982.

Rorty, R. Incorrigibility as the mark of the mental. *Journal of Philosophy* 67 (1970): 399–424.

Rorty, R. Introduction: Antirepresentationalism, ethnocentrism, and liberalism. In Richard Rorty, *Objectivity, Relativism, and Truth: Philosophical Papers*, vol. 1. New York: Cambridge University Press, 1991, 1–17.

Rorty, R. *Objectivity, Relativism, and Truth: Philosophical Papers*, vol. 1. New York: Cambridge University Press, 1991.

Rorty, R. On Ethnocentrism: A Replay to Clifford Geertz. In Richard Rorty, *Objectivity, Relativism, and Truth: Philosophical Papers*. vol. 1. New York: Cambridge University Press, 1991, 203–210.

Rorty, R. *Philosophy and the Mirror of Nature*. Princeton: Princeton University Press, 1979.

Rorty, R. Pragmatism as anti-representationalism. Introduction to John P. Murphy, *Pragmatism: From Peirce to Davidson*. Boulder, CO: Westview Press, 1990, 1–6.

Rorty, R. Pragmatism, Davidson, and truth. In Richard Rorty, *Objectivity, Relativism, and Truth: Philosophical Papers*, vol. 1. New York: Cambridge University Press, 1991, 126–150.

Rorty, R. Sind Aussagen universelle Geltungsansprüche? *Deutsche Zeitschrift fur Philosophie* 42 (1994): 975–988.

Rorty, R. Strawson's objectivity argument. *Review of Metaphysics* 24 (1970): 207–244.

Rorty, R., ed. *The Linguistic Turn: Essays in Philosophical Method*. Chicago: University of Chicago Press, 1992.

Rorty, R. The world well lost. In Richard Rorty, *Consequences of Pragmatism*. Minneapolis: University of Minnesota Press, 1982, 3–17.

Rorty, R. Twenty-five years after. In *The Linguistic Turn: Essays in Philosophical Method*, ed. Richard Rorty. Chicago: University of Chicago Press, 1992, 371–374.

Röska-Hardy, Louise. Idealism and the "I" of self-ascription. In *Indexicality and Idealism: The Self in Philosophical Perspective*, ed. Audun Øfsti, Peter Ulrich, and Truls Wyller. Paderborn: Mentis, 2000, 56–57.

Röska-Hardy, Louise. Internalism, externalism, and Davidson's conception of the mental. In *Language, Mind, and Epistemology: On Donald Davidson's Philosophy*, ed. Gerhard Preyer, Frank Siebelt, and Alexander Ulfig. Dordrecht: Kluwer, 1994, 263–281.

Röska-Hardy, Louise. Moore's paradox and the expression of belief. In *Argument und Analyse: Proceedings of GAP IV*, ed. Ansgar Beckermann and Christian Nimtz. Paderborn: Mentis, 2001, 329–337.

Rovane, Carole. Anti-representationalism and relativism. *Philosophical Books* 45 (2004): 128–139.

Sartre, Jean-Paul. *Being and Nothingness*. Trans. Hazel Barnes. New York: Washington Square Press, 1956.

Saussure, Ferdinand. *Course in General Linguistics*. New York: McGraw-Hill, 1966.

Scheler, M. *Man's Place in Nature*. Trans. Hans Meyerhoff. Boston: Beacon Press, 1961.

Schilpp, Paul A., ed. *The Philosophy of Bertrand Russell*. Evanston: Northwestern University Press, 1944.

Schmidt, Lawrence, ed. *Language and Linguisticality in Gadamer's Hermeneutics*. Lanham, MD: Lexington Books, 2000.

Schnädelbach, H. *German Philosophy 1831–1933*. Trans. E. Matthews. New York: Cambridge University Press, 1983.

Schnädelbach, H. *Philosophie in Deutschland 1831–1933*. Frankfurt: Suhrkamp, 1993.

Searle, J. R. Indeterminacy, empiricism, and the first-person. *Journal of Philosophy* 84 (1987): 123–146.

Searle, J. R. *Rediscovery of the Mind*. Cambridge, MA: MIT Press, 1992.

Sellars, Wilfrid. Imperatives, intentions, and the logic of "ought." In *Morality and the Language of Content*, ed. Hector-Neri Casteñada and George Nakhnikian. Detroit: Wayne State University Press, 1963, 159–218.

Smith, Barry C. On knowing one's own language. In *Knowing Our Own Minds*, ed. Crispin Wright, Barry C. Smith, and Cynthia MacDonald. Oxford: Oxford University Press, 1998, 391–428.

Smith, Michael. The structure of orthonomy. In *Agency and Action*, ed. J. Hyman and Helen Steward. Cambridge: Cambridge University Press, 2004, 165–194.

Smith, Nicholas H., ed. *Reading McDowell: On Mind and World*. London: Routledge, 2002.

Speaks, Jeff. Review of Donald Davidson, *Truth and Predication. Notre Dame Philosophical Reviews* (August 2006), <http://ndpr.nd.edu/review.cfm?id=7224>.

Steele, Daniel Ramsay, ed. *Genius: In Their Own Words*. Chicago: Open Court, 2002.

Stevenson, C. L. *Ethic and Language*. New Haven: Yale University Press, 1944.

Stoecker, R., ed. *Reflecting Davidson: Donald Davidson Responding to an International Forum of Philosophers*. Berlin: Walter de Gruyter, 1993.

Stoutland, F. Intentionalists and Davidson on "rational explanations." In *Actions, Norms and Values: Discussions with Georg Henrik von Wright*, ed. G. Meggle. Berlin: Walter de Gruyter, 1999, 191–208.

Stoutland, Frederick. The real reasons. In *Human Action, Deliberation, and Causation*, ed. J. Bransen and Stefaan E. Cuypers. Dordrecht: Kluwer, 1998, 43–66.

Strawson, P. F. Causation and explanation. In *Essays on Davidson: Actions and Events*, ed. B. Vermazen and Merril B. Hintikka. Oxford: Clarendon Press, 1985, 115–135.

Strawson, P. F. Truth. In P. F. Strawson, *Logico-Linguistic Papers*. London: Methuen, 1971, 147–164.

Strawson, P. F. *Individuals: An Essay in Descriptive Metaphysics*. London: Methuen, 1974.

Strawson, P. F. *Logico-Linguistic Papers*. London: Methuen, 1971.

Stueber, Karsten R. Understanding truth and objectivity: A dialogue between Donald Davidson and Hans-Georg Gadamer. In *Hermeneutics and Truth*, ed. B. Wachterhauser. Evanston: Northwestern University Press, 1994, 172–189.

Taminiuax, Jacques. *The Thracian Maid and the Professional Thinker: Arendt and Heidegger*. New York: SUNY Press, 1997.

Tarski, Alfred. *Logic, Semantics, Metamathematics: Papers from 1923 to 1938*, ed. J. H. Woodger. Oxford: Clarendon Press, 1956.

Taylor, Charles. Foundationalism and the inner–outer distinction. In *Reading McDowell: On Mind and World*, ed. Nicholas H. Smith. London: Routledge, 2002, 106–119.

Taylor, Charles. Gadamer on the Human Sciences. In *The Cambridge Companion to Gadamer*, ed. Robert Dostal. New York: Cambridge University Press, 2002, 52–78.

Taylor, Charles. Understanding the other: A Gadamerian view on conceptual schemes. In *Gadamer's Century: Essays in Honor of Hans-Georg Gadamer*, ed. Jeff Malpas, Ulrich Arnswald, and Jens Kertscher. Cambridge, MA: MIT Press, 2002, 279–298.

Taylor, Charles. *The Explanation of Behaviour*. London: Routledge & Kegan Paul, 1964.

Teichmann, R., ed. *Logic, Cause, and Action: Essays in Honour of Elizabeth Anscombe*. Royal Institute of Philosophy Supplements. Cambridge: Cambridge University Press, 2000.

Thomson, J. J., and G. Harman. *Moral Relativism and Moral Objectivity*. Cambridge, MA: Blackwell, 1996.

Thornton, Tim. *John McDowell*. Chesham, Bucks: Acumen Publishing, 2004.

Tillich, Paul. *Systematic Theology*, vol. 1. Chicago: University of Chicago Press, 1951.

Tomberlin, James E., ed. *Philosophical Perspectives: Logic and Language*, vol. 8. Atascadero, CA: Ridgeview, 1994.

Tugendhat, Ernst. *Self-Consciousness and Self-Determination*. Cambridge, MA: MIT Press, 1986.

Vermazen, B., and Merril B. Hintikka, eds. *Essays on Davidson: Actions and Events*. Oxford: Clarendon Press, 1985.

von Wright, G. H. Explanation and the understanding of actions. In *Contemporary Action Theory*, vol. 1, ed. G. Holstrom-Hintikka and R. Tuomela. Dordrecht: Kluwer Academic, 1997, 1–20.

von Wright, G. H. *Explanation and Understanding*. London: Routledge & Kegan Paul, 1971.

Wachterhauser, B. Getting it right: Relativism, realism, and truth. In *The Cambridge Companion to Gadamer*, ed. Robert Dostal. New York: Cambridge University Press, 2002, 126–142.

Wachterhauser, B., ed. *Hermeneutics and Modern Philosophy*. New York: SUNY Press, 1986.

Wachterhauser, B., ed. *Hermeneutics and Truth*. Evanston: Northwestern University Press, 1994.

Weinsheimer, Joel. Charity militant: Gadamer, Davidson, and post-critical hermeneutics. *Revue Internationale de Philosophie* 54 (2000): 405–422.

Weisheimer, Joel. Charity militant: Gadamer, Davidson, and post-critical hermeneutics. In *The Force of Tradition*, ed. Donald Marshall. Lanham: Rowman & Littlefield, 2005, 39–54.

Welton, D. *The Other Husserl: The Horizons of Transcendental Phenomenology*. Bloomington: Indiana University Press, 2002.

Westphal, Kenneth R. Hegel and Hume on perception and concept-empiricism. *Journal of the History of Philosophy* 33 (1998): 99–123.

Westphal, Kenneth R. *Hegel, Hume und die Identität wahrnehmbarer Dinge. Historisch-kritische Analyse zum Kapitel "Wahrnehmung" in der Phänomenologie von 1807*. Frankfurt: Klostermann, 1998.

Wheeler, S. *Deconstruction as Analytic Philosophy*. Stanford: Stanford University Press, 2000.

Wheeler, S. Derrida's *differance* and Plato's different. *Philosophy and Phenomenological Research* 59 (1999): 999–1013.

Wiercinski, André, ed. *Between Description and Interpretation: The Hermeneutic Turn in Phenomenology*. Toronto: The Hermeneutic Press, 2005.

Wiggins, David. *Needs, Values, Truth: Essays in the Philosophy of Value*. Oxford: Clarendon Press, 1998.

Williams, Michael. *Unnatural Doubts: Epistemological Realism and the Basis of Scepticism*. Oxford: Blackwell, 1991.

Wilson, Bryan, ed. *Rationality: Key Concepts in Social Sciences*. Oxford: Blackwell, 1970/1977.

Winch, Peter. *The Idea of a Social Science: And Its Relation to Philosophy*. London: Routledge & Kegan Paul, 1958.

Winch, Peter. Understanding a primitive society. In *Rationality: Key Concepts in Social Sciences*, ed. Bryan Wilson. Oxford: Blackwell, 1970/1977, 78–111.

Windelband, W. Geschichte der Naturwissenschaft. In *Präludien II*. Tübingen: J. C. B. Mohr, 1924.

Wittgenstein, Ludwig. *On Certainty*. Ed. G. E. M. Anscombe and G. H. von Wright, trans. Denis Paul and G. E. M. Anscombe. New York: Harper Torchbooks, 1969.

Wittgenstein, Ludwig. *Philosophical Investigations*, 3rd edition. Trans. G. E. M. Anscombe. Malden: Blackwell, 2001.

Wright, Crispin. Self-knowledge: The Wittgensteinian legacy. In *Knowing Our Own Minds*, ed. Crispin Wright, Barry C. Smith, and Cynthia Macdonald. Oxford: Oxford University Press, 1998, 13–45.

Wright, Crispin, Barry C. Smith, and Cynthia MacDonald, eds. *Knowing Our Own Minds*. Oxford: Oxford University Press, 1998.

Wright, Kathleen, ed. *Festivals of Interpretation*. Albany: SUNY Press, 1990.

Wylie, Alison. The constitution of archaeological evidence: Gender politics and science. In Alison Wylie, *Thinking from Things: Essays in the Philosophy of Archaeology*. Berkeley: University of California Press, 1996, 185–199.

Wylie, Alison. *Thinking from Things: Essays in the Philosophy of Archaeology*. Berkeley: University of California Press, 1996.

Wylie, Alison, and Lynn Hankinson Nelson. Coming to terms with the values of science: Insights from feminist science scholarship. In *Value Free Science: Ideal or Illusion?*, ed. Harold Kincaid, John Dupré, and Alison Wylie. Cambridge: Oxford University Press, 2006, 58–86.

Zahavi, D. *Self-Awareness and Alterity: A Phenomenological Investigation*. Evanston: Northwestern University Press, 1999.

Zahavi, D. *Subjectivity and Selfhood: Investigating the First-Person Perspective*. Cambridge, MA: MIT Press, 2005.

Żegleń, Urszula M. *Donald Davidson: Truth, Meaning, and Knowledge*. London: Routledge & Kegan Paul, 1999.

Žižek, S., ed. *Cogito and the Unconscious*. Durham: Duke University Press, 1998.

Contributors

Lee Braver is Associate Professor in the Department of Philosophy at Hiram College, Hiram, Ohio. He is the author, among other works, of *A Thing of This World: A History of Continental Anti-Realism* (2007) and *Heidegger's Later Writings: A Reader's Guide* (2009).

Gordon G. Brittan, Jr. is Regents Professor of Philosophy at Montana State University, Montana. He is the author of, among other works, *Kant's Theory of Science* (1978) and coeditor of *Causality, Method, and Modality* (1991).

Sharyn Clough is Associate Professor in the Department of Philosophy at Oregon State University, Oregon. She is the author of *Beyond Epistemology: A Pragmatist Approach to Feminist Science Studies* (2003) and editor of *Siblings Under the Skin: Feminism, Social Justice and Analytic Philosophy* (2003).

Giuseppina D'Oro is Reader in Philosophy at Keele University, UK. She is the author of *Collingwood and the Metaphysics of Experience* (2002) and several papers addressing issues at the crossroads between meta-philosophy and the philosophy of action, and is coeditor of Collingwood's *An Essay on Philosophical Method* (2005).

Robert Dostal is Rufus Jones Professor of Philosophy and Religion at Bryn Mawr College, Bryn Mawr, Pennsylvania. He is the editor, among other works, of *The Cambridge Companion to Gadamer* (2002), and coeditor of *Phenomenology on Kant, German Idealism, Hermeneutics, and Logic (2000).*

Christoph Durt received his M.A. in Philosophy, Psychology, and Intercultural Communication from the University of Munich, Germany, and he is currently a graduate student in the Department of Philosophy at the University of California, Santa Cruz. He has published several papers on Wittgenstein, and he is completing a doctoral dissertation on Husserl entitled "'The Intersubjectivity of Consciousness."

Jonathan Ellis is Associate Professor in the Department of Philosophy at the University of California, Santa Cruz, California. He is the author of a number of papers on topics in the philosophy of mind, epistemology, and other areas, and is co-editor of *Wittgenstein and the Philosophy of Mind* (forthcoming).

Dagfinn Føllesdal is Clarence Irving Lewis Professor of Philosophy at Stanford University and Professor Emeritus at the University of Oslo. He is the author of *Referential Opacity and Modal Logic* (2004) and coeditor of *Logos and Language* (2008), as well as many other works.

Barbara Fultner is Associate Professor of Philosophy and Women's Studies at Denison University, Granville, Ohio. Among other works, she is the translator of Jürgen Habermas, *Truth and Justification* (2003) and editor of *Habermas: Key Concepts* (forthcoming).

David Couzens Hoy is Distinguished Professor of Philosophy Emeritus at the University of California, Santa Cruz. He is the author, among other works, of *The Time of Our Lives* (2009) and *Critical Resistance: From Poststructuralism to Post-Critique* (2004).

Jeff Malpas is Professor of Philosophy at the University of Tasmania, Tasmania, Australia, and Distinguished Visiting Professor at LaTrobe University, Victoria, Australia. Among recent works, he is the author of *Heidegger's Topology* (2006) and coeditor of *Perspectives on Human Dignity* (2006) and *Consequences of Hermeneutics* (2010).

Richard N. Manning is Associate Professor in the Department of Philosophy at the University of South Florida, Florida. He is the author of a number of papers, and is currently working on a volume entitled *The Ontology of Interpretation.*

Giancarlo Marchetti is Associate Professor in the Department of Philosophical Sciences at the University of Perugia. He is the author of *Ratio et superstitio* (2003), among other works.

Mark Okrent is Professor of Philosophy at Bates College, Lewiston, Maine. He is the author of *Rational Animals: The Teleological Roots of Intentionality* (2007), and *Heidegger's Pragmatism: Understanding, Being, and the Critique of Metaphysics* (1988).

Gerhard Preyer is Professor of Sociology at the Goethe-University, Frankfurt, Germany. He is the editor of *ProtoSociology: An International Journal of Interdisciplinary Research*, coeditor of *Contextualism in Philosophy* (2010), and author of *Donald Davidson's Philosophy: From Radical Interpretation to Radical Contextualism* (2011), as well as many other works.

Bjørn Ramberg is Professor of Philosophy at the University of Oslo. He is the author, among other works, of *Donald Davidson's Philosophy of Language: An Introduction* (1989), and coeditor of *Reflections and Replies: Essays on Tyler Burge* (2003).

Richard Rorty was Professor of Comparative Literature at Stanford University, Stanford, California. His many works include *Philosophy and the Mirror of Nature* (1979), *Contingency, Irony, and Solidarity* (1989), and *Philosophy and Social Hope* (2000). He died in 2007.

Louise Röska-Hardy is a researcher in the Institute for Advanced Studies in the Humanities, Essen. She is the author, among other works, of *Die Bedeutung in natürlichen Sprachen* (1988) and coeditor of *Learning from Animals* (2008).

Frederick Stoutland is Professor of Philosophy Emeritus at St. Olaf College, Minnesota, and was Permanent Visiting Professor in the Department of Philosophy at Uppsala University. He is the editor of *Philosophical Probings: Essays on von Wright's Later Work* (2009), coeditor of *Essays on Anscombe's Intention* (2010), and the author of numerous papers in the philosophy of action, language, and mind.

Stephen Turner is Graduate Research Professor in the Department of Philosophy and Director of the Center for Social and Political Thought at the University of South Florida, Florida. Among recent works, he is the author of *Brains/Practices/Relativism: Social Theory after Cognitive Science* (2002) and *Explaining the Normative* (2010), and coeditor of *Philosophy of Anthropology and Sociology* (2007) and *The Sage Handbook of Social Science Methodology* (2007).

David Vessey is an Assistant Professor at Grand Valley State University. He has been a lecturer and visiting scholar at the University of Oregon and the University of Chicago. He is the author of numerous papers on hermeneutics and philosophy of language.

Samuel C. Wheeler III is Professor of Philosophy, University of Connecticut, Storrs, Connecticut. He is the author of *Deconstruction as Analytic Philosophy* (2000), as well as numerous papers.

Index